AF126622

10th Anniversary of *Processes*: Recent Advances in Environmental and Green Processes

10th Anniversary of *Processes*: Recent Advances in Environmental and Green Processes

Guest Editor
Antoni Sánchez

Basel • Beijing • Wuhan • Barcelona • Belgrade • Novi Sad • Cluj • Manchester

Guest Editor
Antoni Sánchez
Department of Chemical,
Biological and
Environmental Engineering
Autonomous University
of Barcelona
Barcelona
Spain

Editorial Office
MDPI AG
Grosspeteranlage 5
4052 Basel, Switzerland

This is a reprint of the Special Issue, published open access by the journal *Processes* (ISSN 2227-9717), freely accessible at: https://www.mdpi.com/journal/processes/special_issues/091IVX09XU.

For citation purposes, cite each article independently as indicated on the article page online and as indicated below:

Lastname, A.A.; Lastname, B.B. Article Title. *Journal Name* **Year**, *Volume Number*, Page Range.

ISBN 978-3-7258-3661-1 (Hbk)
ISBN 978-3-7258-3662-8 (PDF)
https://doi.org/10.3390/books978-3-7258-3662-8

© 2025 by the authors. Articles in this book are Open Access and distributed under the Creative Commons Attribution (CC BY) license. The book as a whole is distributed by MDPI under the terms and conditions of the Creative Commons Attribution-NonCommercial-NoDerivs (CC BY-NC-ND) license (https://creativecommons.org/licenses/by-nc-nd/4.0/).

Contents

About the Editor ix

Antoni Sánchez
Special Issue Titled "10th Anniversary of Processes: Recent Advances in Environmental and Green Processes"
Reprinted from: *Processes* **2024**, *12*, 552, https://doi.org/10.3390/pr12030552 1

Ruimei Zhang, Xiaonan Li, Kai Zhang, Pengfei Wang, Peifeng Xue and Hailong Zhang
Research on the Application of Coal Gasification Slag in Soil Improvement
Reprinted from: *Processes* **2022**, *10*, 2690, https://doi.org/10.3390/pr10122690 5

Praveen Kumar Ghodke, Amit Kumar Sharma, Krishna Moorthy, Wei-Hsin Chen, Alok Patel and Leonidas Matsakas
Experimental Investigation on Pyrolysis of Domestic Plastic Wastes for Fuel Grade Hydrocarbons
Reprinted from: *Processes* **2023**, *11*, 71, https://doi.org/10.3390/pr11010071 21

Wenel Naudy Vásquez Salcedo, Bruno Renou and Sébastien Leveneur
Thermal Stability for the Continuous Production of γ-Valerolactone from the Hydrogenation of N-Butyl Levulinate in a CSTR
Reprinted from: *Processes* **2023**, *11*, 237, https://doi.org/10.3390/pr11010237 36

Nikolay A. Bezhin, Dmitriy A. Kremenchutskii, Evgeniy V. Slizchenko, Ol'ga N. Kozlovskaia, Iuliia G. Shibetskaia, Vitaliy V. Milyutin and Ivan G. Tananaev
Estimation of ^{137}Cs Distribution and Recovery Using Various Types of Sorbents in the Black Sea Surface Layer
Reprinted from: *Processes* **2023**, *11*, 603, https://doi.org/10.3390/pr11020603 49

Ehssan Ahmed Hassan, Maha A. Tony, Hossam A. Nabwey and Mohamed M. Awad
Management of Agricultural Water Containing Acetimidothioic Acid Pesticide through Catalytic Oxidation to Facilitate Reclaimed Water Recycling for Sustainable Food Production
Reprinted from: *Processes* **2023**, *11*, 792, https://doi.org/10.3390/pr11030792 62

Zhenhua Li, Guanghong Li and Bin Shi
Prediction of Oxygen Content in Boiler Flue Gas Based on a Convolutional Neural Network
Reprinted from: *Processes* **2023**, *11*, 990, https://doi.org/10.3390/pr11040990 81

José Luis Marín-Muñiz, Irma Zitácuaro-Contreras, Gonzalo Ortega-Pineda, Luis Manuel Álvarez-Hernández, Karina Elizabeth Martínez-Aguilar, Aarón López-Roldán and Sergio Zamora
Bibliometric Analysis of Constructed Wetlands with Ornamental Flowering Plants: The Importance of Green Technology
Reprinted from: *Processes* **2023**, *11*, 1253, https://doi.org/10.3390/pr11041253 93

Simona Cecilia Ghiga, Isabela Maria Simion, Cătălina Filote, Mihaela Roșca, Raluca Maria Hlihor and Maria Gavrilescu
Comparative Analysis of Three WEEE Management Scenarios Based on LCA Methodology: Case Study in the Municipality of Iasi, Romania
Reprinted from: *Processes* **2023**, *11*, 1305, https://doi.org/10.3390/pr11051305 114

Peng Xu, Tianyang Wu, Yang Xiang, Jimmy Yun and Lei Shao
Enhanced Treatment of Basic Red 46 by Ozonation in a Rotating Packed Bed with Liquid Detention
Reprinted from: *Processes* **2023**, *11*, 1345, https://doi.org/10.3390/pr11051345 130

Yolanda Luna-Galiano, Carlos Leiva Fernández, Rosario Villegas Sánchez and Constantino Fernández-Pereira
Development of Geopolymer Mortars Using Air-Cooled Blast Furnace Slag and Biomass Bottom Ashes as Fine Aggregates
Reprinted from: *Processes* **2023**, *11*, 1597, https://doi.org/10.3390/pr11061597 140

Roghayeh Yousef, Hazim Qiblawey and Muftah H. El-Naas
Removal of Organic Contaminants in Gas-to-Liquid (GTL) Process Water Using Adsorption on Activated Carbon Fibers (ACFs)
Reprinted from: *Processes* **2023**, *11*, 1932, https://doi.org/10.3390/pr11071932 153

Ofelia Landeta-Escamilla, Alejandro Alvarado-Lassman, Oscar Osvaldo Sandoval-González, José de Jesús Agustín Flores-Cuautle, Erik Rosas-Mendoza, Albino Martínez-Sibaja, et al.
Determination of Soil Agricultural Aptitude for Sugar Cane Production in Vertisols with Machine Learning
Reprinted from: *Processes* **2023**, *11*, 1985, https://doi.org/10.3390/pr11071985 171

Shi Yan, Li Nie, Juan Ren, Wei Wang, Jingtao Xu, Ning Wang and Qian Zhao
Complex Agent for Phosphate Sequestration from Digested Sludge Liquor: Performances and Economic Cost Analysis
Reprinted from: *Processes* **2023**, *11*, 2050, https://doi.org/10.3390/pr11072050 186

Shikai Zhu, Haoqian Hu, Haoyi Yang, Yunzhuo Qu and Yuanzhe Li
Mini-Review of Best Practices for Greenhouse Gas Reduction in Singapore's Semiconductor Industry
Reprinted from: *Processes* **2023**, *11*, 2120, https://doi.org/10.3390/pr11072120 199

Alaa Salma, Nur Maisarah Binti Faeruz, Lydia Fryda and Hayet Djelal
Harnessing Digestate Potential: Impact of Biochar and Reagent Addition on Biomethane Production in Anaerobic Digestion Systems
Reprinted from: *Processes* **2023**, *11*, 2284, https://doi.org/10.3390/pr11082284 213

Serena Simonetti and Davide Dionisi
Modelling the Effect of Water Removal by Reverse Osmosis on the Distillation of Mixtures of Short-Chain Organic Acids from Anaerobic Fermentation
Reprinted from: *Processes* **2023**, *11*, 2362, https://doi.org/10.3390/pr11082362 225

Basma G. Alhogbi, Shroog A. Al-Ansari and Mohammed S. El-Shahawi
A Comparative Study on the Bioavailability and Soil-to-Plant Transfer Factors of Potentially Toxic Element Contamination in Agricultural Soils and Their Impacts: A Case Study of Dense Farmland in the Western Region of Saudi Arabia
Reprinted from: *Processes* **2023**, *11*, 2515, https://doi.org/10.3390/pr11092515 244

Bojan Antonic, Dani Dordevic, Hana Buchtova, Bohuslava Tremlova, Simona Dordevic and Ivan Kushkevych
French Fries' Color and Frying Process in Relation to Used Plant Oils
Reprinted from: *Processes* **2023**, *11*, 2839, https://doi.org/10.3390/pr11102839 261

Li-An Kuo, Wen-Tien Tsai, Ru-Yuan Yang and Jen-Hsiung Tsai
Production of High-Porosity Biochar from Rice Husk by the Microwave Pyrolysis Process
Reprinted from: *Processes* **2023**, *11*, 3119, https://doi.org/10.3390/pr11113119 270

Ján Derco, Nikola Šoltýsová, Tomáš Kurák, Anna Vajíčeková and Jozef Dudáš
Modelling of Drinking Water Recarbonization in Fluidized Bed Reactor
Reprinted from: *Processes* **2023**, *11*, 3209, https://doi.org/10.3390/pr11113209 . . . . **282**

Jinlong Zuo, Jin Ren, Liming Jiang, Chong Tan, Junsheng Li, Zhi Xia and Wei Wang
Preparation of PVA/SA-FMB Microspheres and Their Adsorption of Cr(VI) in Aqueous Solution
Reprinted from: *Processes* **2024**, *12*, 443, https://doi.org/10.3390/pr12030443 . . . . **308**

About the Editor

Antoni Sánchez

Dr. Antoni Sánchez has led the Composting Research Group since 2000. He works as a Full Professor at the Department of Chemical, Biological and Environmental Engineering of the Autonomous University of Barcelona. His research areas cover the main aspects involved in the treatment of organic solid waste, through several strategies; composting, anaerobic digestion for biogas production, and solid-state fermentation are the main topics. He has participated and coordinated several Spanish and European projects on this topic, supervised PhD and master's theses, and is the author of more than 200 indexed papers as well as book chapters and patents.

Editorial

Special Issue Titled "10th Anniversary of Processes: Recent Advances in Environmental and Green Processes"

Antoni Sánchez

Department of Chemical, Biological and Environmental Engineering, Autonomous University of Barcelona, 08913 Barcelona, Spain; antoni.sanchez@uab.cat

Citation: Sánchez, A. Special Issue Titled "10th Anniversary of Processes: Recent Advances in Environmental and Green Processes". *Processes* **2024**, *12*, 552. https://doi.org/10.3390/pr12030552

Received: 31 January 2024
Accepted: 25 February 2024
Published: 12 March 2024

Copyright: © 2024 by the author. Licensee MDPI, Basel, Switzerland. This article is an open access article distributed under the terms and conditions of the Creative Commons Attribution (CC BY) license (https://creativecommons.org/licenses/by/4.0/).

1. Introduction

In 2019, one of the Editorial Staff of the MDPI journal *Processes*, sent me an email informing me that I was being invited to join the Editorial Board of the journal, a proposal that I accepted. At the time of that invitation, the journal was indexed by SCIE (Impact Factor: 1.963) and covered in Scopus (CiteScore: 2.05). After a brief period as a member of the Editorial Board, I was promoted to Section-in-Chief for "Environmental and Green Processes". The indexing numbers of both the journal and this specific section are now quite different, as presented in detail through this link: https://res.mdpi.com/data/2021-09-23_processes_a5-booklet-section-flyer_green-processes_web.pdf.

Moreover, in these roles, means I have spent the last five years having the gratifying experience of sharing with researchers from all over the world that we have achieved an exponential increase in the number of publications related to *Environmental and Green Processes*. From an engineering perspective, it is very important to witness how technology is allowing us to solve some of the environmental challenges that the world is facing. This topic is what this Special Issue will cover.

2. About This Collection

The "10th Anniversary of Processes: Recent Advances in Environmental and Green Processes" Special Issue is a compilation of papers written by researchers from around the world, showing that technology (*Processes*) can be a powerful tool for resolving severe environmental problems (sometimes it provides only a partial solution, but it is nonetheless welcome).

Although the list of contributions is presented at the end of this Editorial, I would like to highlight some of the topics presented in this Special Issue that, in my opinion, respond to urgent problems in environmental research. Simple ross-referencing with the Sustainable Development Goals of the United Nations (SDG, https://sdgs.un.org/goals) will show the reader that most of the studies published are in line with one or more of these goals.

2.1. Renewable Energy

The complex global political situation has increased the necessity of finding renewable and locally available sources of energy. This is coupled with the urgent need to reduce the use of non-renewable fossil fuels. Both aspects are causes of current "second youth" anaerobic digestion. Thus, the exponential increase in the use of anaerobic digesters, which are often used to treat mixtures of organic waste of different typologies, has boosted research into topics related to this area, such as the use of additives. In this paper, the role of biochar has been highlighted.

Another important and emerging area of research is the pyrolysis of organic waste, specifically forestry biomass derived from agricultural waste. Pyrolysis and its resulting products (gas, bio-oil, and biochar) are now key, new sources of energy, and research into optimizing this technology and related issues is becoming more commonplace [1,2].

2.2. Waste Management and Valorization

Circular economy plans, which are being developed in all over the world, have greatly increased the potential to conduct research related to waste management and, in particular, the valorization of previously rejected materials to change the paradigm from waste to product [3,4]. There are a number of examples of this topic in the current literature. This collection is not an exception to this fact.

2.3. Water

Once again, research and derived technologies are discussed in this collection to provide examples of processes that reuse water, vital given the situation of severe drought in large parts of the world. Therefore, the need for new sources of clean water is a consolidated research topic. In this sense, it is interesting that water-related research today more regularly focuses on recovery and reuse than treatment, although the latter topic is still very important [5].

2.4. Environmental Tools and Modeling

Finally, it is important to highlight the increasing use of both classical and new tools in environmental research. On one hand, it is evident that the Life Cycle Assessment method has consolidated its position as the predominant technique used to analyze and categorize the environmental impact of any environmental study, providing a decision tool for use by stakeholders involved in the implementation of environmental solutions. On the other hand, it is worth noting that new computational tools such as neural networks or machine learning software have created new possibilities beyond the scope of classical environmental research [6].

3. Conclusions

In summary, I think that the reader of this collection can view an number of excellent research studies that reflect some of the most urgent environmental challenges faced by society, and more importantly, the studies present potential solutions. As said in most of the studies' Conclusions sections, further research is need in all the fields that comprise this Special Issue.

Conflicts of Interest: The author declares no conflicts of interest.

List of Contributions:

1. Zhang, R.; Li, X.; Zhang, K.; Wang, P.; Xue, P.; Zhang, H. Research on the Application of Coal Gasification Slag in Soil Improvement. *Processes* **2022**, *10*, 2690. https://doi.org/10.3390/pr10122690.
2. Ghodke, P.; Sharma, A.; Moorthy, K.; Chen, W.; Patel, A.; Matsakas, L. Experimental Investigation on Pyrolysis of Domestic Plastic Wastes for Fuel Grade Hydrocarbons. *Processes* **2023**, *11*, 71. https://doi.org/10.3390/pr11010071.
3. Vásquez Salcedo, W.; Renou, B.; Leveneur, S. Thermal Stability for the Continuous Production of ϒ-Valerolactone from the Hydrogenation of N-Butyl Levulinate in a CSTR. *Processes* **2023**, *11*, 237. https://doi.org/10.3390/pr11010237.
4. Bezhin, N.; Kremenchutskii, D.; Slizchenko, E.; Kozlovskaia, O.; Shibetskaia, I.; Milyutin, V.; Tananaev, I. Estimation of ^{137}Cs Distribution and Recovery Using Various Types of Sorbents in the Black Sea Surface Layer. *Processes* **2023**, *11*, 603. https://doi.org/10.3390/pr11020603.
5. Hassan, E.; Tony, M.; Nabwey, H.; Awad, M. Management of Agricultural Water Containing Acetimidothioic Acid Pesticide through Catalytic Oxidation to Facilitate Reclaimed Water Recycling for Sustainable Food Production. *Processes* **2023**, *11*, 792. https://doi.org/10.3390/pr11030792.
6. Li, Z.; Li, G.; Shi, B. Prediction of Oxygen Content in Boiler Flue Gas Based on a Convolutional Neural Network. *Processes* **2023**, *11*, 990. https://doi.org/10.3390/pr11040990.
7. Marín-Muñiz, J.; Zitácuaro-Contreras, I.; Ortega-Pineda, G.; Álvarez-Hernández, L.; Martínez-Aguilar, K.; López-Roldán, A.; Zamora, S. Bibliometric Analysis of Constructed Wetlands with

8. Ghiga, S.; Simion, I.; Filote, C.; Roșca, M.; Hlihor, R.; Gavrilescu, M. Comparative Analysis of Three WEEE Management Scenarios Based on LCA Methodology: Case Study in the Municipality of Iasi, Romania. *Processes* **2023**, *11*, 1305. https://doi.org/10.3390/pr11051305.
9. Xu, P.; Wu, T.; Xiang, Y.; Yun, J.; Shao, L. Enhanced Treatment of Basic Red 46 by Ozonation in a Rotating Packed Bed with Liquid Detention. *Processes* **2023**, *11*, 1345. https://doi.org/10.3390/pr11051345.
10. Luna-Galiano, Y.; Leiva Fernández, C.; Villegas Sánchez, R.; Fernández-Pereira, C. Development of Geopolymer Mortars Using Air-Cooled Blast Furnace Slag and Biomass Bottom Ashes as Fine Aggregates. *Processes* **2023**, *11*, 1597. https://doi.org/10.3390/pr11061597.
11. Yousef, R.; Qiblawey, H.; El-Naas, M. Removal of Organic Contaminants in Gas-to-Liquid (GTL) Process Water Using Adsorption on Activated Carbon Fibers (ACFs). *Processes* **2023**, *11*, 1932. https://doi.org/10.3390/pr11071932
12. Landeta-Escamilla, O.; Alvarado-Lassman, A.; Sandoval-González, O.; Flores-Cuautle, J.; Rosas-Mendoza, E.; Martínez-Sibaja, A.; Vallejo Cantú, N.; Méndez Contreras, J. Determination of Soil Agricultural Aptitude for Sugar Cane Production in Vertisols with Machine Learning. *Processes* **2023**, *11*, 1985. https://doi.org/10.3390/pr11071985.
13. Yan, S.; Nie, L.; Ren, J.; Wang, W.; Xu, J.; Wang, N.; Zhao, Q. Complex Agent for Phosphate Sequestration from Digested Sludge Liquor: Performances and Economic Cost Analysis. *Processes* **2023**, *11*, 2050. https://doi.org/10.3390/pr11072050.
14. Zhu, S.; Hu, H.; Yang, H.; Qu, Y.; Li, Y. Mini-Review of Best Practices for Greenhouse Gas Reduction in Singapore's Semiconductor Industry. *Processes* **2023**, *11*, 2120. https://doi.org/10.3390/pr11072120.
15. Salma, A.; Binti Faeruz, N.; Fryda, L.; Djelal, H. Harnessing Digestate Potential: Impact of Biochar and Reagent Addition on Biomethane Production in Anaerobic Digestion Systems. *Processes* **2023**, *11*, 2284. https://doi.org/10.3390/pr11082284.
16. Simonetti, S.; Dionisi, D. Modeling the Effect of Water Removal by Reverse Osmosis on the Distillation of Mixtures of Short-Chain Organic Acids from Anaerobic Fermentation. *Processes* **2023**, *11*, 2362. https://doi.org/10.3390/pr11082362.
17. Alhogbi, B.; Al-Ansari, S.; El-Shahawi, M. A Comparative Study on the Bioavailability and Soil-to-Plant Transfer Factors of Potentially Toxic Element Contamination in Agricultural Soils and Their Impacts: A Case Study of Dense Farmland in the Western Region of Saudi Arabia. *Processes* **2023**, *11*, 2515. https://doi.org/10.3390/pr11092515.
18. Antonic, B.; Dordevic, D.; Buchtova, H.; Tremlova, B.; Dordevic, S.; Kushkevych, I. French Fries' Color and Frying Process in Relation to Used Plant Oils. *Processes* **2023**, *11*, 2839. https://doi.org/10.3390/pr11102839.
19. Kuo, L.; Tsai, W.; Yang, R.; Tsai, J. Production of High-Porosity Biochar from Rice Husk by the Microwave Pyrolysis Process. *Processes* **2023**, *11*, 3119. https://doi.org/10.3390/pr1113119.
20. Derco, J.; Šoltýsová, N.; Kurák, T.; Vajíčeková, A.; Dudáš, J. Modeling of Drinking Water Recarbonization in Fluidized Bed Reactor. *Processes* **2023**, *11*, 3209. https://doi.org/10.3390/pr11113209.
21. Zuo, J.; Ren, J.; Jiang, L.; Tan, C.; Li, J.; Xia, Z.; Wang, W. Preparation of PVA/SA-FMB Microspheres and Their Adsorption of Cr(VI) in Aqueous Solution. *Processes* **2024**, *12*, 443. https://doi.org/10.3390/pr12030443.

References

1. Manga, M.; Aragón-Briceño, C.; Boutikos, P.; Semiyaga, S.; Olabinjo, O.; Muoghalu, C.C. Biochar and Its Potential Application for the Improvement of the Anaerobic Digestion Process: A Critical Review. *Energies* **2023**, *16*, 4051. [CrossRef]
2. Afraz, M.; Muhammad, F.; Nisar, J.; Shah, A.; Munir, S.; Ali, G.; Ahmad, A. Production of value added products from biomass waste by pyrolysis: An updated review. *Waste Manag. Bull.* **2024**, *1*, 30–40. [CrossRef]
3. Cecconet, D.; Capodaglio, A.G. Sewage Sludge Biorefinery for Circular Economy. *Sustainability* **2022**, *14*, 14841. [CrossRef]
4. Kuo, L.; Tsai, W.; Yang, R.; Tsai, J. Production of High-Porosity Biochar from Rice Husk by the Microwave Pyrolysis Process. *Processes* **2023**, *11*, 3119. [CrossRef]

5. Johansson Westholm, L. Filter media for storm water treatment in sustainable cities: A review. *Front. Chem. Eng.* **2023**, *5*, 1149252. [CrossRef]
6. Luqueci Thomaz, I.P.; Mahler, C.F.; Pereira Calôba, L. Artificial Intelligence (AI) applied to waste management: A contingency measure to fill out the lack of information resulting from restrictions on field sampling. *Waste Manag. Bull.* **2023**, *1*, 11–17. [CrossRef]

Disclaimer/Publisher's Note: The statements, opinions and data contained in all publications are solely those of the individual author(s) and contributor(s) and not of MDPI and/or the editor(s). MDPI and/or the editor(s) disclaim responsibility for any injury to people or property resulting from any ideas, methods, instructions or products referred to in the content.

Article

Research on the Application of Coal Gasification Slag in Soil Improvement

Ruimei Zhang [1], Xiaonan Li [2,*], Kai Zhang [2], Pengfei Wang [3], Peifeng Xue [4] and Hailong Zhang [4]

[1] Guoneng Xinjiang Chemical Co., Ltd., Urumqi 831499, China
[2] School of Chemical and Environmental Engineering, China University of Mining and Technology (Beijing), Beijing 100083, China
[3] School of Mining Engineering, Taiyuan University of Technology, Taiyuan 030024, China
[4] Sujiagou Coal Co., Ltd., Dalat County, Ordos 014300, China
* Correspondence: lxn1110@163.com

Abstract: SEM, particle size analysis, and contaminant content of coarse coal gasification slag (CCGS) produced by Shenhua Xinjiang Chemical Co., Ltd. were measured, respectively, and the physicochemical properties of the soil after improvement using gasification slag were investigated in this paper. The results showed that the slag was porous, the particle size was small and the pollutant content was extremely low. Its pollutants were closely related to the pollutants in the raw coal. The coarse slag had a limited effect on soil particle size and texture improvement; the soil water retention performance increased with the increase of proportion of the slag, while pH and conductivity decreased; the improvement effect on soil SOM and available potassium was remarkable; the larger the proportion of the slag, the stronger the effect on maintaining soil alkali-hydrolyzed nitrogen, ammonium nitrogen, and available phosphorus. However, the effect was small, and increased the ion content, especially the cation in soil, and the sum of the eight soil ions before and after evaporation decreased. The results demonstrated that the CCGS generated by the corporation is feasible for soil improvement, and the study has important reference value for the comprehensive utilization of coal gasification slag.

Keywords: coal gasification slag; microscopic characterization; contaminant analysis

1. Introduction

The 2021 China Mineral Resources Report pointed out that China's coal consumption was 4.3 billion tons in 2020, accounting for 56.8% of the energy consumption, and will remain the main energy source in China [1].

Coal gasification slag (CGS) is a residue of molten liquid material formed after a series of complex physicochemical changes of ash and additives during the gasification of coal in a vaporizer under high temperature and pressure, which is obtained by cooling in an excitation chamber [2]. With the increase of coal production in China and the rapid development of coal chemical processing technology, the production of coal gasification slag has increased dramatically [3]. The annual output of CGS is over 33 million tons [4]. Among them, coarse slag is discharged regularly in liquid form through an air-locked slag trap, while the fine slag is discharged from the gasifier with the wastewater and settled into the slag outlet through the settling separator. The coarse slag accounts for more than 60% to 80%, and is the main object of disposal.

There is no satisfactory disposal method for CGS, which is usually disposed by backfill into the ground in China, which may cause pollution and ecological damage to the environment and occupy a large area of land resources, changing their original nature. It is of great significance to understand the nature of CGS, which can guide the recycling utilization and harmless treatment of CGS.

For this purpose, a large number of scholars at home and abroad have studied the properties of CGS. In the literature [4], the nature of CGS produced by a gasifier invented by China Academy of Launch Vehicle Technology used by Luxi Chemical Co., Ltd., a Texaco gasifier used by Weihe Chemical Co., Ltd., Xianyang Chemical Co., Ltd., Shenmu Chemical Co., Ltd., a gasifier of multi-nozzle opposed coal plasma gasification used by Hualu Hengsheng Chemical Co., Ltd., and a Shell gasifier used by Yixiang Chemical Co., Ltd. were studied. It was found that the gasification process, composition of raw coal, ash content and other factors significantly affect the CGS composition, and different gasification slags have different properties. Yang et al. [5] and Zhao et al. [6] analyzed the chemical composition and mineral composition of fine slag produced by the Texaco gasifier, GSP (Gaskombiant Schwarze pumpe) gasifier and four-nozzle CWS gasifier used by Ningxia Coal Group. Shuai et al. [2] studied the chemical composition and phase composition of CGS from various gasifiers such as Xianyang Texaco gasifier and Shenmu Texaco gasifier and concluded that the main components of both coarse and fine slags were SiO_2, Al_2O_3, Fe_2O_3, CaO, and residual carbon. Many studies demonstrate that CGS is generally a solid waste [6].

Yin et al. [7] studied the CGS of the Texaco gasifier using a scanning electron microscope (SEM) and petrographic analysis, and found that CGS is porous. Li [8] obtained similar results as Yin Acosta [9], and found that CGS had both a smooth surface and a porous matrix. The density of the coarse slag was 2.5857 g/cm^3 and the specific surface area was 1.066 m^2/g, with a predominantly smooth surface. The surface of the particles have edges and corners, which promote the melting and sintering of slag particles [5,7]; Wu et al. [10] studied the morphology of coarse and fine slags produced by the gasification of coal plasma in entrained flow beds under a microscope by oil immersion and found that CGS had both bright carbon particles and greyish-dark glassy particles, and the coarse slag samples had significantly fewer bright carbon particles than fine slags [11,12].

The residual carbon content is related to the type of coal, the gasification process conditions and operating conditions, and varied considerably between the different types of CGS. In general, the length of time that fine slag stays in the bed is shorter than that of coarse slag, resulting in the higher residual carbon content in fine slag than coarse slag and lower mechanical strength than coarse slag. In addition, the distribution of residual carbon in coarse and fine slag is not uniform [13].

It can be seen from the above studies that the characteristics of CGS vary from region to region due to the influence of raw materials and the preparation process. Xinjiang Chemical Co., Ltd. currently has a 680,000 ton/year coal-based new materials project in operation, with an annual output of 1,011,400 tons of general solid waste, of which 431,700 is coarse gasification slag, which is the main target for kackfill. In this study, the characteristics of CGS produced by Shenhua Xinjiang Chemical Co., Ltd. in Ganquanbao Industrial Zone, Urumqi, Xinjiang Uygur Autonomous Region, China were studied in terms of its microstructure, typical pollutants, and the feasibility for soil improvement. The study aimed to provide a strong scientific basis for the safe utilization of CCGS, which is of significance for green development of coal industry.

2. Overview of the Case Study Area

Shenhua Xinjiang Chemical Co., Ltd. was established in 2011. The 680,000 tons per year coal-based new material project is located on the east of No.1 Road and the south side of No.3 Road in Ganquanpu Industrial Zone, Urumqi, Xinjiang Uygur Autonomous Region. The total investment is 22 billion RMB. It is a key demonstration project of China Shenhua Coal-to-Liquid and Chemical Co., Ltd., and a key industrial project in Xinjiang. The project aims to give full play to the advantages of rich coal resources in Xinjiang, producing high value-added olefin products. The project started construction in July 2013, began commissioning a test run at the end of May 2016, produced qualified methanol on 17 June 2016, SHMTO device feeding on 23 September 2016, officially smoothed the whole process on 3 October 2016, and the production of qualified polyolefin products for the commercial operation was officially realized in 2017. The coal gasification system uses coal from Hongshaquan Coal Mine and Heishan coal mine, east of Junggar Basin, Xinjiang, and oxygen (purity vol % $\geq$ 99.6) as raw materials. Pressurized plasma gasification of coal gasification and the chilling process of General Electric Shenhua Gasification Technology Co., Ltd. was adopted to produce crude syngas with CO and H_2 as active ingredients. Gasification slag is discharged from the bottom of the furnace.

3. Sample Collection and Treatment

3.1. Sample Collection

Before collecting samples, it was necessary to first understand the generation process of coarse coal gasification slag (CCGS) in order to determine the sampling plan. The generation process of CCGS is as follows: the high temperature coarse coal and gas leaving the reaction chamber and the liquid slag enter the quench chamber together. The slag is solidified in the water bath and sinks to the bottom of the gasifier. The slag water flows into the slag trap, and relatively clean water at the upper part returns to the bottom of the quench chamber of the gasifier. Through this water circulation, the slag, and other solids at the bottom of the chilling chamber, are flushed to the slag trap. The slag trap outlet valve is opened, the water and slag in the slag trap is replaced with cleaner water, and the slag and water is sent to the slag machine in the slag tank. After the CGS is pulled out by the slag scraper, there is a temporary slag field, and the slag water containing the fine slag is sent to the first vacuum flash separator of the black water flash system. Therefore, the CCGS is collected at the slag tank and slag field. Sampling was done in strict accordance with the industrial solid waste sampling technical standard (HJ/T 20-1998).

Field sampling photos are shown in Figure 1.

Figure 1. Photos of field sampling.

3.2. Sample Treatment and Analysis

Abnormal matters were removed from the CCGS samples. Samples were kept away from the light, dried naturally and stored properly for testing. The CGS samples were made into a dispersion. After ultrasonic dispersion, samples were directly dropped on the conductive adhesive on the sample holder or on another conductive media on the sample holder for scanning electron microscope observation and analysis. According to the relevant standards, the particle size distribution of CCGS was analyzed by a laser particle size analyzer. A PHS-3E pH meter, 723 visible spectrophotometer, AFS-933 atomic fluorescence spectrometer, inductively coupled plasma emission spectrometer (ICP) ICP-5000, PXSJ-216 ion meter were used to measure the pH value and heavy metal content of the CGS.

The CCGS samples were directly dried and crushed to particle size less than 10 mm. The coal samples were divided into 100–150 g by the method of coning and quartering to prepare the analysis samples. When the coal samples were crushed, the 100–150 g analysis coal gasification crude slag samples must be crushed to less than 0.15 mm, and the particle size of 0.10–0.15 mm is required to be more than 70%. The crushed coal samples were sealed and stored in a wide mouth bottle, and the testing was completed within 30 days.

4. Testing Results of CCGS

4.1. Microscopic Characterization

The scanning electron microscope result (Figure 2) shows that the coarse slag particles of coal gasification are angular, uneven in size, amorphous carbon block distribution, and the surface is composed of irregular porous structure, showing honeycomb holes and large roughness. This morphology is related to the formation of water quenching of coarse slag in the molten state of silicon and aluminum. Porous structure can be considered as applied to adsorption, including pollution control or water and fertilizer research.

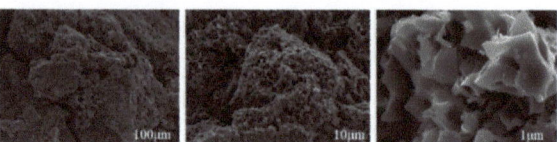

Figure 2. Scanning electron microscope image of CCGS.

It can be seen from the particle size distribution curve of CCGS in Figure 3 that the particle size distribution of CCGS is between 2.8–1022 μm, and mainly distributed between 20–500 μm.

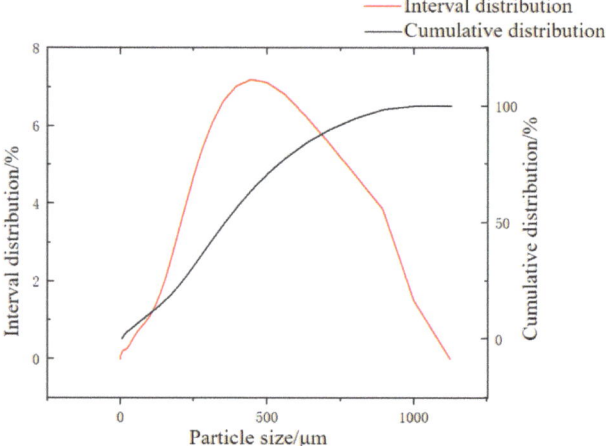

Figure 3. Particle size distribution curve of CCGS.

4.2. Pollutant Content

4.2.1. Raw Coal Analysis

Throughout the gasification process, raw coal particles will be heated and decomposed in a short time. Volatiles also volatilizes when heated, which deepens the degree of graphitization of carbon and produce char. Then, the interior of the particles is filled with the gasification agent (H_2O, O_2), and the gasification reaction proceeds accordingly. Then, the gas will be generated, discharged, and collected. At the same time, the graphitization is further deepened. The coal char particles gradually enter the critical state of crushing, and the conditions remains unchanged after reaching this state. The coal char particles naturally begin to break after exceeding the critical state. The formation of slag is closely related to this process, which is formed by homogeneous and heterogeneous reactions between coal char particles and residual minerals.

According to the company's production process of CCGS, it can be determined that the main sources of pollutants in CCGS are: (1) raw coal mainly composed of Hongshaquan coal and Heishan coal; (2) additives that play a role in regulating viscosity during gasification; and (3) water sources, such as clean water for the grinding pool, and coal to olefin (MTO) wastewater.

In the above pollutant sources, the main component of the additive is sodium lignosulfonate, without special odor, non-toxic, soluble in water and alkali. So, the presence of characteristic pollutants risk was excluded preliminarily; the clean water in the grinding tank mainly includes high-quality reclaimed water, MTO wastewater, and the reuse water used for washing pipelines. The composition of MTO wastewater is relatively complex. The water contains a variety of organic compounds (methanol, dimethyl ether, etc.), and has the characteristics of low calorific value and low COD, so the existence of characteristic pollutants in the wastewater cannot be preliminarily judged.

It can be seen from the coal gasification process that the characteristic pollutants in the CCGS are closely related to the substances in the raw coal. Therefore, it was necessary to carry out industrial analysis (moisture content, ash content, volatile, and fixed carbon) of the raw coal first, and the analysis results are shown in Figure 4.

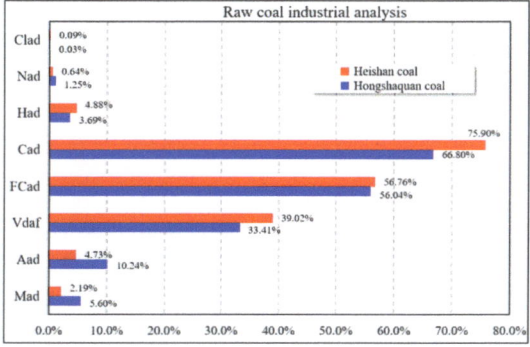

Figure 4. Raw coal industrial analysis (note: ad means air dry; Cl is chlorine; N is nitrogen; H is hydrogen; C is carbon; FC is fixed carbon; V is volatile; A is ash; M is moisture; the figure does not contain the characteristics of the two coal char residues which are both 2, the arsenic (ω(Asad)) of Hongshaquan coal sample is 1 μg/g, and that of Heishan coal sample is 3 μg/g).

According to the results of Figure 4 and the classification of Chinese coal and the ash composition table of Chinese coal, Hongshaquan coal and Heishan coal belong to bituminous coal. Hongshaquan coal has a high ash content and low volatility. A high ash content means that the coal consumption in the gasification process increases. Correspondingly, the workload of the gasifier and ash treatment system also increases. In terms of volatile matter, the content of coal with a low degree of coalification becomes higher, i.e., the 'younger' the coal, the better its reactivity in gasification, and the more efficient it will be throughout the gasification process. Compared with Hongshaquan coal, Heishan coal has the characteristics of low ash, low sulfur, and is of good quality.

Coal ash is a very complex inorganic mixture whose composition is usually represented by oxides. Coal ash is composed of SiO_2, Al_2O_3, Fe_2O_3, CaO, MgO, Na_2O, K_2O, TiO_2, etc. SiO_2, Al_2O_3 and TiO_2 are acidic oxides, while Fe_2O_3, CaO, MgO, Na_2O and K_2O are alkaline oxides.

Acid oxide has the ability to increase the ash melting temperature: the higher the acid oxide content, the higher the melting temperature. The effect of alkaline oxide is the opposite: the higher the content, the lower the melting temperature. The chemical composition of coal ash has an important influence on the formation of slag in the gasification process of raw coal through the melting temperature. The gasifier provides a high-temperature and high-pressure environment. The raw coal produces physical and chemical changes in this environment, and eventually produces solid matter, namely, the slag. The ash composition analysis of raw coal is shown in Figure 5. Compared with Heishan coal, the content of acidic oxides in Hongshaquan coal is higher and the content of alkaline oxides is lower. The above chemical composition content factors are the reason why the melting temperature of Hongshaquan coal is higher than that of Heishan coal. Overall, the chemical substances and composition in the coal sample not only affect its own melting characteristics, but also inhibit or accelerate the gasification process.

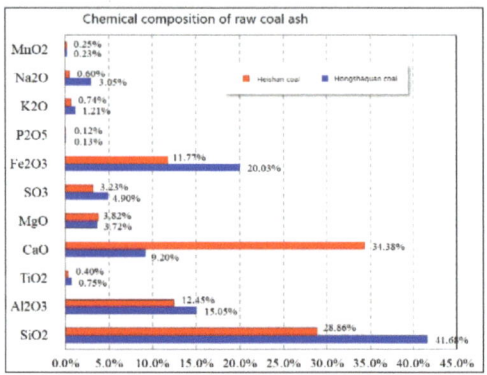

Figure 5. Chemical composition of raw coal ash.

In addition, it can also be seen that the main components of the raw coal used in coal gasification production by Xinjiang Chemical Co., Ltd. are fixed carbon and dry ash-free volatiles, do not contain radioactive substances, and contain a small amount of silicon, aluminum, iron, calcium, potassium, sodium, nickel, magnesium, manganese, titanium and other oxides, and may contain arsenic, mercury, lead and other characteristic pollutants. Therefore, it can be preliminarily estimated that characteristic pollutants can exclude the influence of radioactive pollutants.

Figure 6 shows test results of pH, fluoride, total chromium, hexavalent chromium, total cyanide, total mercury, total arsenic, total cadmium, total lead, total nickel, total zinc, total copper, total manganese, total beryllium, total silver, sulfide, alkyl mercury and other characteristic pollutants in Hongshaquan coal and Heishan coal. The samples of Hongshaquan coal were recorded as RC1, RC2, RC3 and RC4, respectively, and the samples of Heishan coal were recorded as BC1, BC2, BC3 and BC4, respectively. It is important to note that total cadmium, total chromium, total lead, total nickel, total cyanide, total copper, hexavalent chromium, total beryllium, total silver, methyl mercury and ethyl mercury were not detected.

It can be seen from the test results that only six items of total mercury, total arsenic, total zinc, total manganese, fluoride and pH were detected in the raw coal, and total zinc was only detected in the Hongshaquan coal sample, and not detected in the Heishan coal sample. It can be preliminarily estimated that if other pollutants other than these six items are detected in the CGS, it is not related to the raw coal and is deemed to be related to other materials. According to the Integrated Wastewater Discharge Standard (GB 8978-1996), the total mercury, total arsenic, total zinc, total manganese, fluoride, and pH requirements are 0.05 mg/L, 0.5 mg/L, 2.0 mg/L, 2.0 mg/L, 10 mg/L, 6-9, respectively. It can be seen that the content does not exceed the standard requirements. If these six types of pollutants are detected to exceed the standard in the test results of CCGS, it may be other materials that introduce the pollutants.

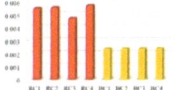
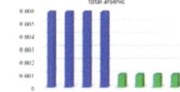
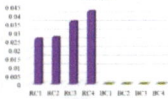
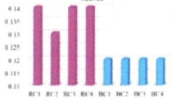
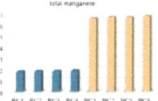

Figure 6. Analysis results of pollutants in Hongshaquan and Heishan coal samples.

4.2.2. Contents of Characteristic Pollutants in CCGS

The pH, fluoride, total chromium, hexavalent chromium, total cyanide, total mercury, total arsenic, total cadmium, total lead, total nickel, total zinc, total copper, total manganese and other characteristic pollutants of CCGS were characterized. The samples used for the detection of characteristic pollutants in CCGS were labeled as CGSP1, CGSP2, CGSP3, CGSP4, CGSP5, CGSP6, CGSP7, CGSP8, CGSP9 and CGSP10, respectively. Total cadmium, total chromium, total lead, total nickel, total cyanide, total copper, hexavalent chromium, total beryllium, total silver, methyl mercury and ethyl mercury were not detected.

The test results are shown in Figure 7. Through the data, it was found that the characteristic pollutants in the CCGS are: total mercury, total arsenic, total zinc, total manganese, fluoride, and pH. This is consistent with the characteristic pollutants detected in raw coal. Moreover, except that the pH of raw coal and CCGS is roughly the same, the remaining characteristic pollutants decreased significantly. It is speculated that the characteristic pollutants in raw coal may be distributed to other by-products or recycled materials, such as fine coal gasification slag; It is speculated that under this process condition, other materials except raw coal introduce less pollution. All the pollution did not exceed the standard GB 8978-1996. The dimensionless quantities obtained by comparing the measured values with the standard requirements were characterized, and the average values were taken. It was found that the dimensionless quantities corresponding to total mercury, total arsenic, total zinc, total manganese, and fluoride were 0.01, 0.002, 0.16, 0.26 and 0.03, respectively. Therefore, content of various pollutants was far below the standard requirements and the slag is feasible for secure application.

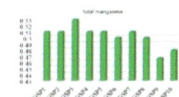

Figure 7. Test results of CCGS pollutants.

5. Feasibility Study of Gasification Slag Soil Improvement

The above research results show that the contents of the CCGS pollutants do not exceed the standard, and it was preliminarily determined that it was applicable to be used for soil improvement. The feasibility of gasification slag for soil improvement was further studied in this paper.

First, soil samples were collected at the Hongshaquan open-pit mine in June 2020, and soil samples were collected from the dump and reclaimed planted forest in the mining area as shown in Figure 8. An 'S'-shaped sampling route was used, and a soil auger was adopted to take 0~20 cm at the surface soil (because the surface 0~20 cm soil nutrient distribution and change are most obvious and most representative). The samples were placed in plastic bags, labelled, and soil samples were sent back to the laboratory, placed in a cool and ventilated area to air dry. After air drying, the large soil blocks were broken, the plant roots, deadwood, leaves, animal and plant residues and stones in the soil were picked out. After sieving with a 2 mm sieve, they were sealed and stored in plastic bags for the testing of soil basic physical and chemical properties, and soil improvement-related experiments.

Figure 8. Sampling.

In order to explore the effect of CCGS on soil water and fertilizer retention, the infiltration test of different treatments of improved materials was carried out by intermittent soil column leaching method, the characteristics of soil water content and soil fertility after leaching were analyzed, the mechanism of water and fertilizer retention of improved materials was further studied, and the water and fertilizer retention capacity of the improved materials with different ratios and pure soil was comprehensively compared and analyzed. The design of the soil column experiment is as follows: the soil column experiment was set up with four CCGS gradients (5%, 10%, 15%, 20%), and the soil column without the improved material was used as the control. Three parallel tests were performed for each ratio, as shown in Figure 9.

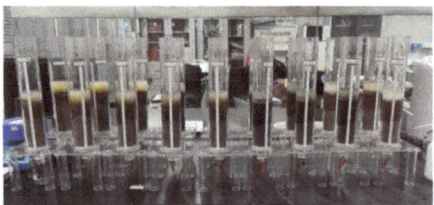

Figure 9. Soil column experiment.

(1) Soil particle size distribution with different content of CCGS

The soil particle sizes of the evenly dispersed soil samples were measured by laser particle size analyzer. According to the United States Department of Agriculture (USDA) soil texture classification system, the measured particle size distribution data were divided into three categories: sand (0.05~2 mm), silt (0.002~0.05 mm), and clay (<0.002 mm). As shown in Figure 10 and Table 1, the CCGS is mainly composed of sand, and the clay content is almost zero. The soil in the study area is mainly composed of sand, and the sand volume accounts for 75.60%. The percentage volume of silt and clay is relatively low. After adding CCGS, the soil is mainly sand. It can be seen that CCGS has a relatively poor effect on soil particle size and texture improvement.

(2) Effect of CCGS on soil water retention performance with different CCGS content

As shown in Figure 11, after adding CCGS, the soil water retention performance is better than that of the original soil from the dump of open pit mine and increases with the increase of CCGS content. In terms of the soil-water retention effect, 20% CCGS was better, but compared with planted forest, the results showed that regardless of whether CCGS is added or not, the soil moisture content is higher than that of CCGS, which may be related to the high content of fine sandy particles and coarse silty particles in the soil, less clayey particles and organic matter. The uniform and coarse single particles were rapidly settled in the water and arranged neatly and closely, appearing to have the nature of hardened pulp.

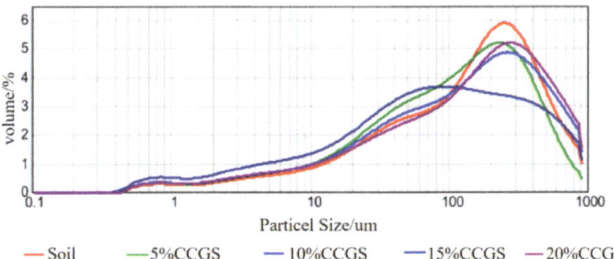

Figure 10. Effect of CCGS on soil particle size distribution with different CCGS content.

Table 1. Soil particle size distribution under different content of CCGS.

Treatment		Clayey Particles (<0.002 mm, %)	Silty Particles (0.05~0.002 mm,%)	Sandy Particles (2~0.05 mm,%)
Soil	100%	2.2	22.2	75.6
CCGS	100%	0	5.32	94.68
	5%	1.31	22.31	76.39
	10%	1.2	20.27	78.53
	15%	1.1	18.54	80.35
	20%	0.86	17.02	82.12

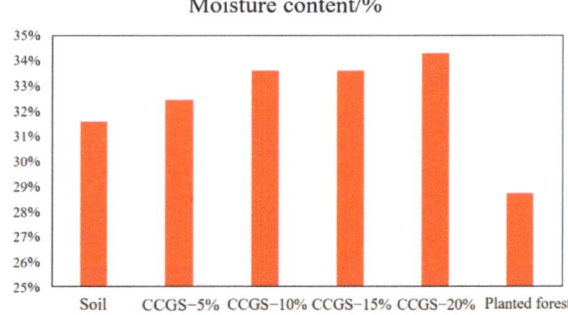

Figure 11. Effect of CCGS on soil water retention performance.

(3) Effect of CCGS on soil pH under different CCGS content before and after leaching

It can be seen from Figure 12 that pH value of soil decreased after adding CCGS before leaching, and the pH value of soil with 20% CCGS was the lowest, and there was no significant difference in pH value between different CCGS content. After leaching, the soil pH value increased. Compared with the CCGS, the soil pH was higher than that of the CCGS regardless of whether the CGS was added or not. The soil pH values of 15% and 20% CCGS were lower, and the difference was close to the CCGS. In terms of soil pH, 20% CCGS had the best effect.

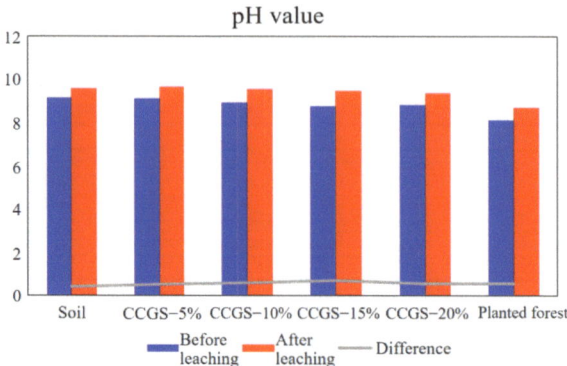

Figure 12. Effects of CCGS on soil pH.

(4) Effects of CCGS on soil electrical conductivity (EC) under different CCGS content before and after leaching

Soil electrical conductivity is an indicator of soil water-soluble salt, and soil water-soluble salt is an important attribute of soil, which is the factor to determine whether salt ions in soil influence crop growth. The analysis of water-soluble salts in soil is of great significance to understand the salt dynamics, the impact on crop growth and the formulation of improvement measures. As shown in Figure 13, the soil EC was high before leaching, and the electrical conductivity decreased with the increase of CCGS content. The soil electrical conductivity was low after leaching, and the electrical conductivity decreased with the increase of CCGS content. Compared with the planted forest sample, the conductivity value was low, and a 20% CCGS effect was best for the soil EC.

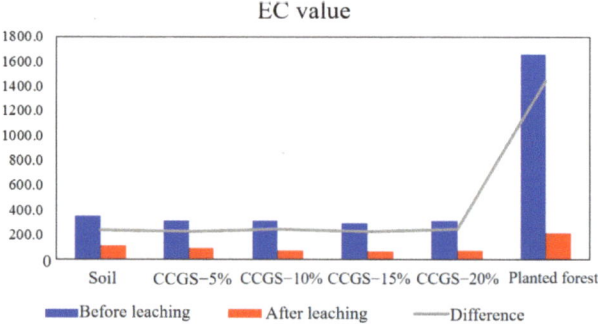

Figure 13. Effects of CCGS on soil EC.

(5) Effect of CCGS on soil fertility with different CCGS content after leaching

1) Effects of CCGS on soil organic matter with different CCGS content after leaching

The carbon content in the CCGS is very high, and these residual carbons may be derived from the volatile substances of the original coal pyrolysis, partial gasification carbon and/or unreacted pyrolysis carbon. From Figure 14, it can be seen that a 20% CCGS content has the best improvement effect on soil organic matter (SOM), and the SOM content of CCGS is higher than that of the planted forest sample.

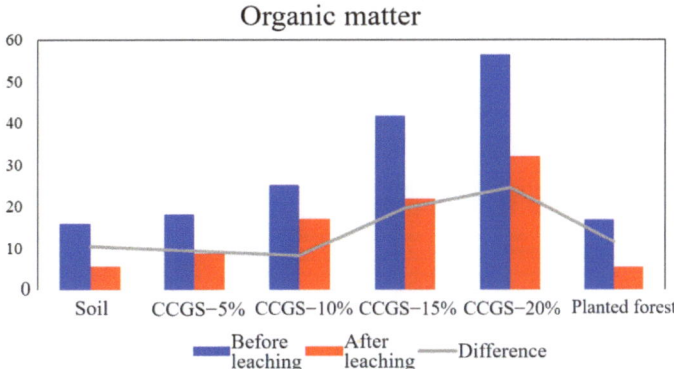

Figure 14. Effect of CCGS on SOM.

2) Effects of CCGS on soil nitrogen with different CCGS content after leaching

As shown in Figure 15, before and after leaching, with different CCGS content, the content of alkali-hydrolyzed nitrogen changed significantly, and the difference gradually decreased with the increase of CCGS content. The research showed that with the addition of CCGS, the soil alkali-hydrolyzed nitrogen could be maintained, and the higher the CCGS content, the stronger the maintenance effect. Taking the planted forest sample as the expected goal of improvement, it can be found that the addition of CCGS can improve the retention of soil alkali-hydrolyzable nitrogen after leaching, but the content of alkali-hydrolyzable nitrogen is not as high as that of the planted forest sample.

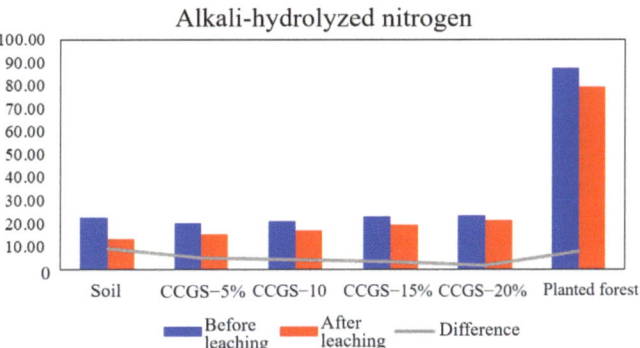

Figure 15. Effect of CCGS on alkali-hydrolyzed nitrogen.

As shown in Figure 16, before and after leaching, the content of ammonium nitrogen changed significantly with different CCGS contents, and the difference gradually decreased with the increase of CCGS content. The results showed that the addition of CGS could maintain the soil ammonium nitrogen, and the higher the content of CCGS, the stronger the retention effect. Taking the planted forest sample as the expected target of improvement, it can be found that when the CCGS is 20%, the retention effect of ammonium nitrogen is better than that of the planted forest sample, but the content is far less than that of the planted forest sample.

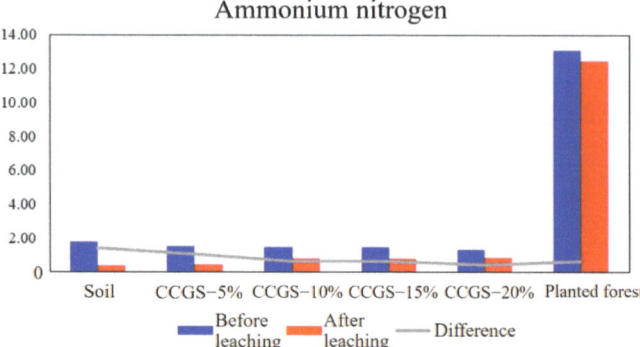

Figure 16. Effect of CCGS on ammonium nitrogen.

3) Effects of CCGS on soil phosphorus with different CCGS content after leaching

As shown in Figure 17, before and after leaching, under different mixing ratio, the relative change of available phosphorus content is not obvious, and the difference decreases with the increase of CCGS content. Studies have shown that the addition of CCGS can keep the soil-available phosphorus, and the higher the CCGS content, the stronger the retention effect. Taking the planted forest sample as the expected goal of improvement, it can be found that when the amount of CCGS is 20%, the retention effect on available phosphorus is better than that of planted forest, and the content is close to that of the planted forest sample.

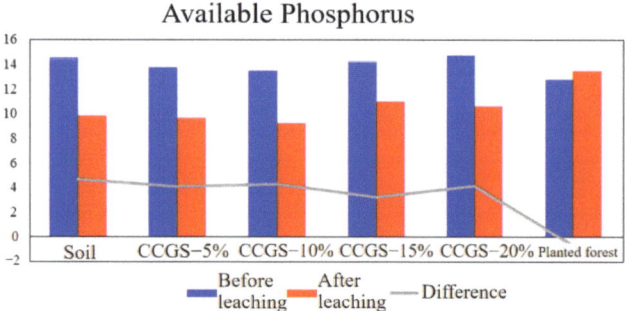

Figure 17. Effect of CCGS on Available Phosphorus.

4) Effect of CCGS on soil potassium with different CCGS content after leaching

As shown in Figure 18, before and after leaching, the content of available potassium changed significantly with different CCGS content, and the difference increased with the increase of CGS content. The results showed that the addition of CGS had a weak effect on soil available potassium, and the higher the content of CGS, the weaker the effect. Taking planted forest as the expected goal of improvement, it can be found that when the amount of CGS is 10–15%, the retention effect of available potassium is better than that of the planted forest sample, and the content is close to that of the planted forest sample.

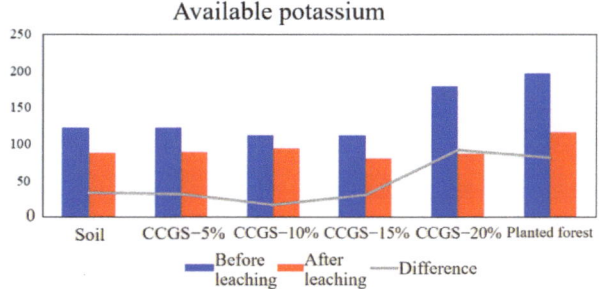

Figure 18. Effect of CCGS on available potassium.

(6) Salt control performance
1) Cations

It can be seen from Figure 19 that the addition of CGS increased the content of magnesium ions, potassium ions and sodium ions in the soil. The calcium ions, magnesium ions, potassium ions and sodium ions in the soil before evaporation and after adding CGS were higher than those after evaporation. The content of calcium ion, magnesium ion and potassium ion increased after evaporation in the treated group of planted forest samples, while sodium ion decreased. The addition of CGS was able to reduce the content of calcium ion and potassium ion in soil after evaporation but had no effect on other cations.

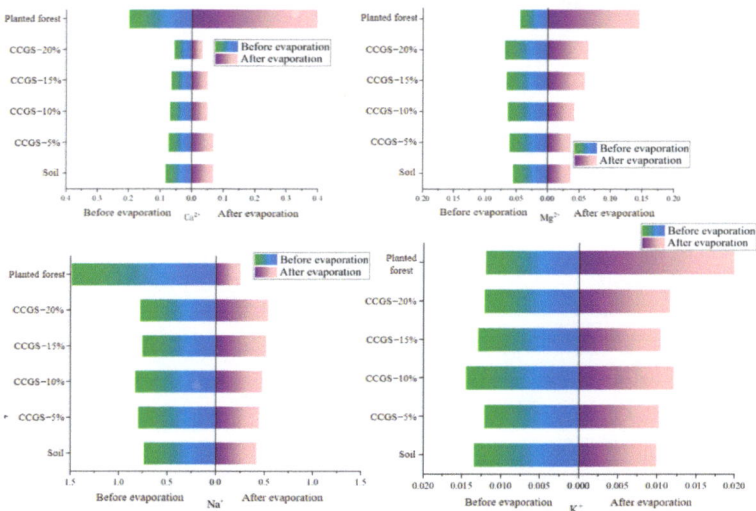

Figure 19. Changes of cation.

2) Anions

From Figure 20, it can be seen that the addition of CCGS has a weak effect on the anion content in the soil, but the carbonate ions appear in the soil after evaporation and the soil mixed with CGS, and the evaporation brings the carbonate ions. However, the content of the ions decreases with the increase of the content of CCGS. The chloride ions and bicarbonate ions in the soil before evaporation and the soil mixed with CGS are lower than those after evaporation. The content of sulfate ion decreased with the addition of CCGS. There was no carbonate ion before and after evaporation in the treatment group of planted forest. The addition of CGS had a poor effect on the weakening of soil anion content compared with planted forest samples.

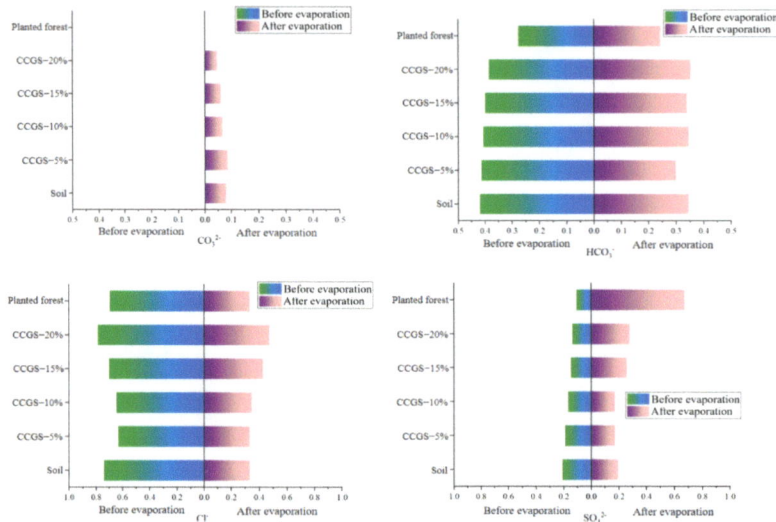

Figure 20. Changes of anions.

In summary, the addition of CCGS increases the ion content, but mainly acts on soil cations, and has a relatively weak effect on soil anions. The sum of the eight ions in the soil before and after evaporation is reduced, as shown in Figures 21 and 22.

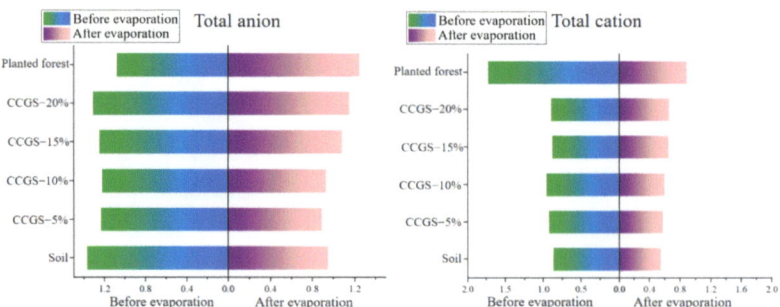

Figure 21. Changes of anion and cation.

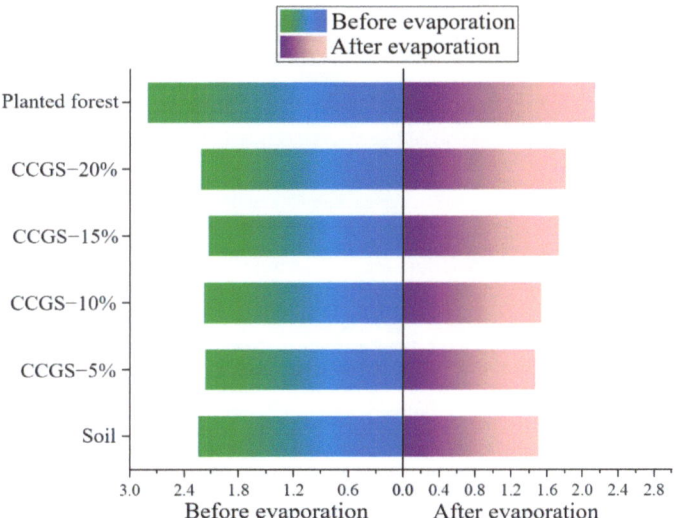

Figure 22. Changes of eight ions.

6. Conclusions

There are very few studies on the application of CCGS in soil improvement. In this paper, the characteristics of CCGS and its feasibility in soil improvement were studied, which fills the gap in related research. The following conclusions were obtained:

(1) CCGS produced by Shenhua Xinjiang Chemical Co., Ltd. presents honeycomb holes with high roughness. The particle sizes of CCGS are mainly between 20–500 μm;

(2) The raw coal is bituminous coal, the coal quality of Heishan coal is beneficial to gasification, and the characteristic pollutants in the CCGS are closely related to the raw coal;

(3) There are no radioactive pollutants in the CCGS, and the content of various pollutants does not exceed the standard, which can be used for environmentally friendly applications;

(4) The CCGS is applicable for soil improvement. The effect of CCGS on soil particle size and texture improvement is limited. The CCGS has a certain effect on soil water retention performance, and increases with the increase of CCGS content, while the pH and conductivity values decrease; the improvement effect of SOM and available potassium was remarkable; the higher the CCGS content, the stronger the effect on maintaining soil available nitrogen, ammonium nitrogen and available phosphorus, but the effect is smaller. CCGS can increase the ion content, especially the soil cation. The soil anion effect is relatively weak: before and after evaporation, the soil's total eight ions decreased.

Author Contributions: Conceptualization, R.Z., X.L. and K.Z.; methodology, all authors; validation, X.L. and P.W.; formal analysis, X.L. and P.W.; investigation, X.L. and K.Z.; resources, R.Z. and X.L.; data curation, P.X. and H.Z.; writing—original draft preparation, R.Z., X.L., K.Z. and P.W.; writing—review and editing, P.W.; visualization, X.L.; supervision, R.Z. project administration, K.Z.; funding acquisition, K.Z. All authors have read and agreed to the published version of the manuscript.

Funding: This research was funded by [National Natural Science Foundation of China] grant number [42177037].

Data Availability Statement: Data is available from the authors upon reasonable request.

Conflicts of Interest: The authors declare no conflict of interest.

References

1. Ministry of Natural Resources. *China Mineral Resources Report*; Geological Publishing House: Beijing, China, 2021.
2. Shuai, H. *Intrinsic Characteristics of CGS and Phase Evolution during CRN Process*; Xi'an University of Architecture and Technology: Xi'an, China, 2015.
3. Zhu, J.F.; Li, J.; Yan, L.; Shang, Y.; Wang, Y.; Li, Q.; Wang, J. Research progress and application prospect of coal gasification slag resource utilization. *Clean Coal Technol.* **2021**, *27*, 11–21.
4. Yuan, H. *Fundamental Research on Intrinsic Characteristics and Application of Coal Gasification Slag*; Xi'an University of Architecture and Technology: Xi'an, China, 2020.
5. Yang, S.; Shi, L.J. Component analysis and comprehensive utilization of coal gasification fine slag. *Coal Chem. Ind.* **2013**, *4*, 34–36, 43.
6. Zhao, Y.B.; Wu, H.J.; Zhang, X.B.; Liu, H.G.; Jing, Y.H.; Yuan, Y. Preparation of Porous Ceramics from Coal Gasification Residue. *Clean Coal Technol.* **2016**, *22*, 7–11. [CrossRef]
7. Yin, H.F.; Tang, Y.; Ren, Y. Basic characteristics and application of Texaco gasifier slag. *Coal Convers.* **2009**, *32*, 30–33.
8. Li, G.Y.; Zhang, T.; Huo, L. Basic Performance and Application of LurgiCGS "C". In Proceedings of the First Symposium on Solid Waste Treatment and Eco-Environmental Materials for the Establishment of Solid Waste Branch of China Silicate Society, Beijing, China, August 2015; China Silicate Society: Beijing, China, 2015.
9. Acosta, A.; Aineto, M.; Iglesias, I.; Romero, M.; Rincón, J. Physico-chemical characterization of slag waste coming from GICC thermal power plant. *Mater. Lett.* **2001**, *50*, 246–250. [CrossRef]
10. Wu, T.; Gong, M.; Lester, E.; Wang, F.; Zhou, Z.; Yu, Z. Characterisation of residual carbon from entrained-bed coal water slurry gasifiers. *Fuel* **2007**, *86*, 972–982. [CrossRef]
11. Xu, S.Q.; Zhou, Z.J.; Gao, X.X.; Yu, G.; Gong, X. The gasification reactivity of unburned carbon present in gasification slag from entrained-flow gasifier. *Fuel Process. Technol.* **2009**, *90*, 1062–1070. [CrossRef]
12. Hu, W.H. *Basic Research on Activation Separation and Resource Utilization of Aluminum-Silicon Components in Coal Gasification Slag*; University of Chinese Academy of Sciences: Hangzhou, China, 2019.
13. Shang, Z.F.; Ma, J.L.; Zhang, J.; Xu, D.Y.; Zhang, L.Y.; Zhou, J.Q.; Duan, X.Y.; Zhang, X.M. Research status and utilization technology prospect of CGS. *Solid Waste Pollut. Control. Technol.* **2017**, *7*, 712–717.

Article

Experimental Investigation on Pyrolysis of Domestic Plastic Wastes for Fuel Grade Hydrocarbons

Praveen Kumar Ghodke [1], Amit Kumar Sharma [2], Krishna Moorthy [3], Wei-Hsin Chen [4,5,6], Alok Patel [7,*] and Leonidas Matsakas [7]

[1] Department of Chemical Engineering, National Institute of Technology Calicut, Kozhikode 673601, Kerala, India
[2] Center for Alternate Energy Research (CAER), Department of Chemistry, University of Petroleum and Energy Studies (UPES), Dehradun 248007, Uttarakhand, India
[3] Department of Mechanical Engineering, University of Petroleum and Energy Studies (UPES), Dehradun 248007, Uttarakhand, India
[4] Department of Aeronautics and Astronautics, National Cheng Kung University, Tainan 701, Taiwan
[5] Research Center for Smart Sustainable Circular Economy, Tunghai University, Taichung 407, Taiwan
[6] Department of Mechanical Engineering, National Chin-Yi University of Technology, Taichung 411, Taiwan
[7] Biochemical Process Engineering, Division of Chemical Engineering, Department of Civil, Environmental, and Natural Resources Engineering, Luleå University of Technology, SE-971 87 Luleå, Sweden
* Correspondence: alok.kumar.patel@ltu.se; Tel.: +46-(0)-920-491570

Abstract: Plastics usage is rising daily because of increased population, modernization, and industrialization, which produces a lot of plastic garbage. Due to their various chemical structures, long chain polymeric compositions, and thermal/decomposition behavior, it is challenging to recycle these plastic wastes into hydrocarbon fuels. In the current work, domestic plastic waste was pyrolyzed at 473 to 973 K in a fixed bed reactor and compared with the three virgin plastics LDPE (low-density polyethylene), HDPE (high-density polyethylene), and PP (polypropylene), as well as a mixture of the three (virgin mixed plastics). The pyrolysis results showed that maximum liquid hydrocarbons obtained from HDPE, LDPE, PP, mixed plastic, and domestic waste were 64.6 wt.%, 62.2 wt.%, 63.1 wt.%, 68.6 wt.%, and 64.6 wt.% at 773 K, respectively. The composition of liquid fuels was characterized using FTIR and GC-MS, which showed a wide spectrum of hydrocarbons in the C8–C20 range. Furthermore, liquid fuel characteristics such as density, viscosity, fire and flash point, pour point, and calorific value were examined using ASTM standards, and the results were found to be satisfactory. This study provides an innovative method for recycling waste plastics into economical hydrocarbon fuel for use in transportation.

Keywords: domestic plastic waste; pyrolysis; TGA; GC-MS; alternate fuel

1. Introduction

The demand for plastic has increased due to its attractive applications like packaging, utensils, and other industrial uses. According to Central Pollution Control Board, CPCB's latest report, the generation of plastic waste in India for 2018–2019 was around 9.46 million tons per year [1]. As a result, today's biggest concern is how to properly dispose of plastic waste. There are several popular methods used to dispose of plastics, depending on local regulations: landfilling and open dumping, ocean dumping, incineration, and recycling [2,3]. However, these methods result in several economic and environmental concerns. [4–6]. The researcher's focus has been switched in recent years to the recovery of energy from plastic wastes, which not only solves the issue of managing plastic waste but also generates energy as a value-added product. As a result, a simple, effective, and low-cost technique for resolving plastic pollution and converting it into useful energy products is required. A prospective method for meeting the energy needs of the industrial, transportation, and agricultural sectors as well as solid waste management is the thermochemical conversion of mixed plastic waste (MPW) to fuel. Numerous investigations have been conducted on the pyrolysis of various forms of unmixed plastic materials [7–11]. However, municipal/domestic plastic waste primarily consists of low-density polyethylene (LDPE), high-density polyethylene (HDPE), polyethylene terephthalate (PET), polypropylene (PP), polystyrene (PS), and poly (vinyl chloride) (PVC) [12–16]. Hence, mixed-waste separation and material variability are significant obstacles to the broader use of the technique. Until now, no commercial plants have been available to convert domestic/municipal plastic waste into fuel due to its thermal decomposition behavior, making it challenging to convert usable fuel into a single reactor. The information on plastic waste conversion's technological aspects is scanty and needs to be investigated deeply in order to utilize plastic waste for fuel.

Pyrolysis is one of the important thermochemical conversion technologies for the transformation of plastic waste into valuable products like liquid fuel, gas fuel, and carbon black [17,18]. It is an endothermic response where volatile matter of input plastic waste decomposes to produce condensable vapors, non-condensable gases, and solid pyro-char (fixed carbon and inorganic compounds such as glass, metals, ash, etc.). The inorganic chemicals from pyrolysis are unaltered and can be employed as additives for other polymers, chemical modification or recovery, or road construction [19–21].

Most of the studies have reported on using single-type plastic waste. For instance, Hazrat 2014 performed the pyrolysis of high-density polyolefin in the temperature range 473–853 K and observed that the obtained liquid product contained hydrocarbon of waxes, gums, and coke along with light oils [22]. The batch process of virgin plastic (PE, PP, PS, and PET) to crude liquid fuel was also studied in Parr mini autoclave at 773 K and found yields of 90–95 wt.%, 5–10 wt.% and 1 wt.% of liquids, gases, and solid residue respectively [23]. At the same time, low-temperature pyrolysis of used plastic in a batch reactor with a mixture of LDPE and PP of 3 mm in length had a standard yield of 48.6 wt.% at 548 K of liquid products with the non-catalytic pyrolysis technique [24]. In a different experiment, scientists looked at the catalytic and non-catalytic pyrolysis of PS with LDPE, HDPE, PP, and PET plastics in a batch microreactor at 725 K and 5−6.0 MPa of N2 gas pressure over a 1 h residence period. Each plastic mixture with PS was subjected to three reactions, and it was found that the 1:1 mix ratio produced the highest output of liquid hydrocarbon fuel [25,26]. The outcomes of earlier research were compared to those of other studies, which carried out experiments in a batch autoclave reactor using HDPE plastic as feedstock and recorded a maximum output of 70 wt.% at 753 K in 20 min of residence time [27]. The capacity of a mixture of PP and PE plastics to produce hydrocarbon fuels by thermal cracking at various temperatures in horizontal tubular reactors was also explored by some researchers, and it was determined that yields rely on the makeup of the plastic feed and residence time [28]. These studies showed that pyrolysis is the best technique to convert plastic waste to fuel. However, very few studies are available on the effect of operating temperatures on converting domestic plastic into usable alternate fuels [29]. Hence, this study aims to pyrolyze domestic plastic waste at different temperatures for maximum hydrocarbon yield and to compare it with virgin HDPE, LDPE, PP, and mixed virgin plastic (MVP). The study's main objective was to identify domestic plastic waste's decomposition behavior and temperature, compared to that of virgin plastics and mixed virgin plastic. In addition, reaction products were characterized to see their feasibility as alternative fuels such as gasoline, diesel, or jet fuel.

2. Materials and Methods

2.1. Materials

Virgin low-density polyethylene (LDPE), high-density polyethylene HDPE), polypropylene (PP), and polyethylene terephthalate (PET) were obtained from local vendorAldrich made, Dehradun, Uttarakhand, India. Virgin mixed plastic was made by considering domestic plastic waste (PP 27 wt.%, LDPE 60 wt.%, HDPE 10 wt.%, and PET 3 wt.%) composition. Domestic plastic wastes were collected from campus bins. It was observed that domestic plastic waste contains, on average (50–60 wt.% LDPE, 30–35 wt.% PP, 10–12 wt.% HDPE, and 1–3 wt.% PET) which are shredded into small pieces and sieved into a particle size of 3–5 mm as virgin plastic available.

2.2. Characterization of Feedstock

2.2.1. Proximate and Ultimate Analysis

Proximate analysis was performed to assess the combustion properties, including moisture content, volatile matter, fixed carbon, and ash. A bomb calorimeter was used to examine the calorific value. To determine the elemental composition of domestic plastic waste, mixed virgin plastics, and individual virgin plastics (LDPE, HDPE, and PP), as well as hydrocarbon fuels, a CHNS analyzer (varioMICRO CHNS, Elementar Analysensysteme GmbH, Germany) was used. Properties of LDPE, HDPE, PP, mixed virgin plastic (MVP), and domestic plastic waste (DPW) are depicted in Table 1.

Table 1. Characteristic properties of different plastic feedstocks (dry basis).

Properties	Virgin Plastic			Mixed Virgin Plastic	Domestic Plastic Waste
	PP	HDPE	LDPE		
Volatile matter (wt.%)	99.9	97.7	98.78	98.72	93.45
Fixed carbon (wt.%)	0.09	2.12	1.12	1.17	5.34
Ash (wt.%)	0.01	0.18	0.1	0.11	1.21
Bulk Density (kg m^{-3})	0.574	0.584	0.552	0.56	0.862
Conradson Carbon residue	0.2	0.68	0.61	0.51	1.34
Heating value (MJ kg^{-1})	41.1	42.1	45.7	42.04	40.42
Carbon (wt.%)	83.49	85.26	85.85	84.88	84.43
Hydrogen (wt.%)	16.13	14.65	14.15	14.83	12.45
Nitrogen (wt.%)	0.28	0.09	0	0.26	2.71
Sulfur (wt.%)	0.1	0	0	0.03	0.41
H/C ratio	0.19	0.17	0.16	0.17	0.15

It was observed from Table 1 that all plastics feedstock contains high amounts of volatile matter > 97% and less percentages of fixed carbon, which can be inferred to achieve 97% conversion. Plastic feedstock measures higher heating values than diesel, petrol, and natural gas. From the ultimate analysis of plastic, it was observed that virgin polypropylene has a high H/C ratio, whereas domestic plastic waste has 0.15 H/C ratio equivalent to HDPE (Table 1). The lesser the H/C ratio, the lesser will be the heating value of the feedstock. The bulk density of plastic was determined in accordance with ASTM D1895B, and the results revealed that LDPE was the lightest of all the feedstocks selected for the pyrolysis process.

Table 1 shows that domestic plastic wastes have a carbon residue of 5.34 wt.%, compared to mixed virgin plastic's 1.17 wt.% which indicates that the carbon in domestic plastic trash may have a complicated structure. According to ASTM standards, the heating value of liquid hydrocarbon fuels and plastic feedstock was evaluated using a bomb calorimeter.

2.2.2. Thermogravimetric Analysis (TGA)

A thermogravimetric analyzer (SII 6300 EXSTAR, Seiko Instruments Inc., Tokyo, Japan) was used to assess the mass loss of plastic feedstock in order to understand how the composition of the feedstock changed with time and temperature. Over a temperature range of 303 K to 1173 K, nitrogen was employed as an inert gas at a flow rate of 150 mL min^{-1}. Differential thermogravimetric analysis was derived and analyzed in further sections. A uniform sample weight of up to 10 mg was used in all TGA analysis.

2.3. Experimental Set Up and Procedure

The experiments were conducted in fixed-bed reactor under inert environment. The primary reactor consisted of a cylindrical quartz column with an internal diameter of 75 mm and a height of 420 mm. The preheating of the feed gas was made possible by the heating zone's proximity to the inlet. The samples used in all of the studies weighed around 50 g. Initially, the reactor was purged with inert gas, i.e., nitrogen, at a flow rate of 500 mL min^{-1}. The ideal heating rate for all tests was 10 °C min^{-1} from room temperature to the desired temperature, and the desired temperature was maintained for 60 min to ensure reaction completion. Three bottle-jacketed water-cooling condenser units, each with a 500 cc capacity, condensed the volatiles released during the pyrolysis process from the plastic waste into liquid form. The bottle condensers were held at a temperature of 6 °C and connected in series. Non-condensable gases leave the system by the available vent, are collected in the bladder, and undergo qualitative analysis thereafter. Each feedstock was pyrolyzed at 473 K to 973 K to optimize the best yield of liquid, solid, and gaseous products. After the completion of the experiment, residue and condensed liquid was measured, and the yields in weight percentage were calculated. Each experiment was repeated twice, and average values are shown in the manuscript. The methodology adopted in this investigation is shown in Figure 1.

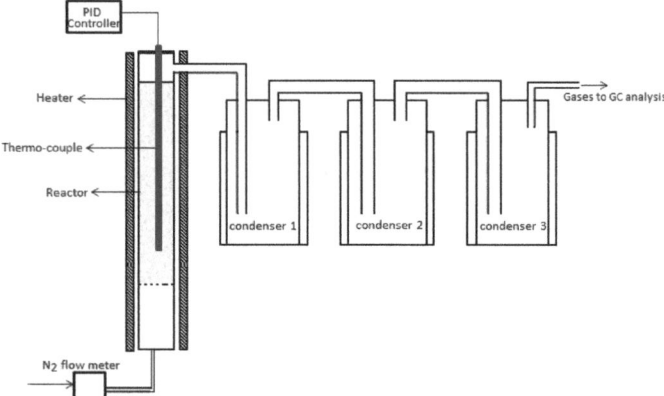

Figure 1. Process pathway for production of hydrocarbon fuels from domestic plastic waste and virgin plastics.

2.4. Product Analysis

The chemical characteristics of solid feedstock and liquid product were analyzed for FTIR to understand the functional group. The usual KBr (potassium bromide) approach was employed to record the IR spectra in the 400–4000 cm^{-1} range at a resolution of 4 cm^{-1} using the Perkin Elmer's FTIR spectrometer. The detailed chemical composition of liquid hydrocarbons was performed using GC-MS and FTIR analysis techniques. Perkin Elmer's GC-MS equipped with DB-5ms capillary column with i.d. 0.25 mm and length of 30 m was used to identify the chemical composition, and unknown compounds were matched with standard NIST 11 libraries. Helium was used as a carrier gas at a flow rate of 1.5 mL min^{-1}, with a split ratio of 50:1, and 70 eV ionization energy was applied to detect the mass. To assure the elution of any potential high boiling compounds, the temperature of the GC oven was initially kept at 348 K for 10 min, increased to 573 K at a heating rate of 10 K min^{-1}, and held for 25 min. GC with a thermal conductivity detector (TCD) and flame ionization detector (FID) was used to collect the non-condensable gases in the balloon and analyze all immediately. With argon serving as a carrier gas, pyrolytic gases were isothermally separated in a molecular sieve-packed column. The temperature of injector and detector was 393 K and 433 K, respectively. All the physical characteristics were determined as per ASTM standards.

3. Results and Discussion

3.1. Characterization of Plastic Feedstock

3.1.1. Thermogravimetric Analysis (TGA) Analysis of Plastic Waste

TGA is a standard technique that demonstrates the sample's behavior concerning time, temperature, and heating rate and helps to get the optimum temperature range for plastic polymer degradation. The TGA analysis curve of domestic plastic waste and virgin plastics under a non-isothermal (10 K/min) range is represented in Figure 2 and the results revealed that the thermal decomposition of LDPE, HDPE, and PP plastic was almost similar. The decomposition of LDPE started at 573 K with an initial mass of 96.24 wt.% and reached up to mass-loss of 3.4 wt.% at 720 K while the degradation of HDPE started with a mass-loss of 94.20% at 613 K and achieved up to 6.57% at 749 K (Figure 2b). Because HDPE has more branching hydrocarbon bonds than LDPE, which indicates stronger internal molecular forces, its degradation range was marginally larger than LDPE's. As a result, it needed a higher temperature to degrade [4]. On the other side, PP started to degrade at 648 K with an initial mass of 95.2 wt.% and reached a maximum of 2.6 wt.% at 750 K (Figure 2c), indicating single-step degradation. The presence of a single DTG peak also supports the fact that the degradation of all these three plastic feedstocks, i.e., LDPE, HDPE, and PP, takes place in a single step.

The temperature at which the maximum degradation rate takes place is called peak temperature (Tmax). In contrast, the temperature at which maximum degradation began is denoted as onset temperature (To), and the temperature at which degradation ended is termed as end temperature (Te). The values of these temperatures vary for different source materials. Since the rate of degradation changes as reaction time (temperature) increases, the changes in product distribution of both gas and liquid phases are also to be expected. In this study, the peak temperature Tmax for LDPE, HDPE, and PP was 703 K, 700 K, and 721 K, respectively, while the end temperature was 720 K, 730 K, and 740 K, respectively. Total mass loss for LDPE, HDPE, and PP was 92.84 wt.%, 88.63% wt.%, and 90.9 wt.%, corresponding to these temperatures. Therefore, the yield of product distribution varied with these feedstocks. In domestic plastic waste and mixed virgin plastic, Tmax was 740 K and 744 K, respectively, higher than individual plastics. In addition, three peaks were detected in the DTG curve (Figure 2d,e), indicating that the degradation of domestic plastic waste and mixed virgin plastic is a significant multiple-reaction process; therefore, total mass loss occurs in more than two reactions. It may be due to the synergistic effect when all three plastic materials degrade together [30]. However, the onset temperature (To) for domestic plastic waste and mixed virgin plastic was observed to be 614 K and 654 K, while the end temperature (Te) was 749 K and 758 K, and the mass loss was higher for mixed virgin (92.20%) compared to domestic plastic waste (89.93%).

The temperature at which domestic plastic waste decomposed was lower than that of mixed virgin plastics. The primary causes may result from a change in the structural composition of domestic plastic waste while molding completed goods from virgin plastic. Binders, fillers, and coloring chemicals may disintegrate mixed plastic waste more quickly than unprocessed virgin plastics by lowering the temperature. Based on To and Te, it can be predicted that the pyrolytic zone for both domestic plastic waste and mixed virgin plastic lies in the range of 600 to 754 K temperature. These data were found to be similar to other studies carried out by different researchers [8,30,31].

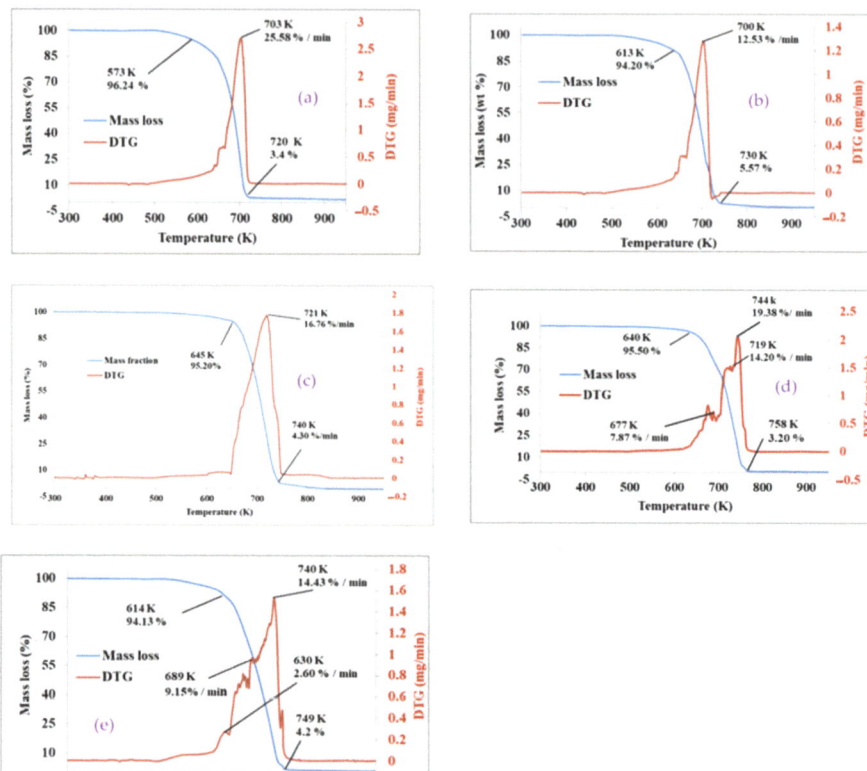

Figure 2. Thermogravimetric (TG) and differential thermogravimetric (DTG) analysis of (**a**) LDPE (**b**) HDPE (**c**) PP (**d**) Mixed virgin plastic (**e**) Domestic plastic waste.

3.1.2. FTIR Analysis of Plastic Feedstock

Figure 3 shows FTIR studies of virgin plastics and domestic plastic waste. Large monomers are combined to produce polymer compounds for use in plastics. Some polymers are supported by oxygen doping, whereas others have olefinic composition. However, domestic plastic waste contains fillers, binders, and additives that FTIR spectra can identify regarding the hydrocarbon composition's stretching frequencies. Figure 3 shows that =C−H, −C−H, and C−C stretching frequencies ranged between 2900 and 3000 cm^{-1}, which indicates the existence of hydrocarbon groups like alkanes, alkenes, and alkynes. Long-chain, closely packed hydrocarbons, and closed, densely packed hydrocarbon molecules are responsible for the behavior. Above 3000 cm^{-1}, wave numbers are slightly skewed. Domestic plastic waste also contains groups that contain oxygen at frequencies between 2600 and 2900 cm^{-1}. The comprehensive summary of the FTIR analysis of domestic plastic waste and mixed virgin plastic are shown in Table 2. Table 2 provides comprehensive details regarding the various functional groups of hydrocarbons and their behavior, strength, and mode of vibration.

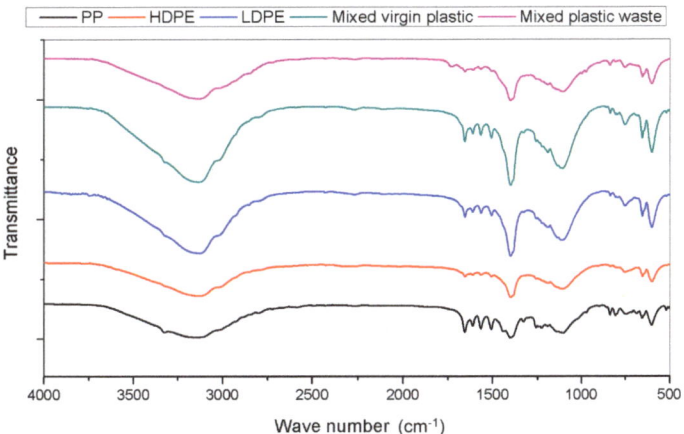

Figure 3. Fourier transformed Infrared spectra of plastic feedstock.

Table 2. Summary of functional group analysis of plastic feedstock.

Wavelength	Remark
3200–3000 cm^{-1}	=C–H stretch, –C–H stretch, CH$_3$, CH$_2$ & CH (strong)
2962 cm^{-1}	–C–H stretch, CH$_3$, CH$_2$ & CH (strong)
1650 cm^{-1}	C=C stretch
1458, 1377 cm^{-1}	–C–H bending, C=C bending.
Below 1000 cm^{-1}	=C–H bending and fingerprint region

3.2. Product Distribution of Pyrolysis Reaction with Domestic Plastic Waste, PP, LDPE, HDPE, and Mixed Virgin Plastic

The product distribution of pyrolysis reaction with domestic plastic waste, PP, LDPE, HDPE, and mixed virgin plastic is depicted in Figures 4 and 5. The temperature range for the pyrolysis of these plastics was 573 K to 973 K with a constant heating rate of 10 K min^{-1}. Liquid hydrocarbon fuel, non-condensable gases (pyrolysis gases), and solid residue (pyro char) were the main products of the reaction. The results showed that the yield of gaseous products was increased with the rising of temperature while liquid product yield increased with a specific temperature, and after that, it was found to be decreased with increasing temperature. As shown in Figure 5a, LDPE's liquid hydrocarbons fuel yield increased from 4.3% (473 K) to 64.6% (773 K) due to the devolatilization reactions being supported by higher temperatures. When the temperature increased beyond 773 K, the liquid product yield was reduced from 64.6% (773 K) to 30.8% (973 K). This may be due to secondary thermal cracking, which results in decomposition of these liquid hydrocarbons into non-condensable hydrocarbons. In addition, higher temperature favors the cracking of the large hydrocarbon molecules into small molecular products [32]. Therefore, the yield of gaseous hydrocarbons was found to be increased with increasing temperature. The poor yield of liquid and gaseous hydrocarbons at lower temperatures was due to incomplete reaction.

Figure 4. Different alternate fuels produced from (**a**) PP (**b**) LDPE (**c**) HDPE (**d**) Mixed virgin plastic (**e**) Domestic plastic waste (all products shown are produced at optimum temperature condition).

Figure 5b shows the product distribution of HDPE virgin plastic pyrolysis. HDPE liquid hydrocarbons yield was observed maximum (62.2 wt.%) at 773 K. In contrast, gaseous hydrocarbon was maximum (68.6 wt.%) at 973 K. The trend of solid, liquid, and gaseous hydrocarbon yield was almost similar to LDPE pyrolysis products. However, LDPE produced a higher amount of liquid products compared to HDPE and PP. The results of PP pyrolysis are shown in Figure 5c and demonstrated that the maximum value of liquid and gaseous hydrocarbons was 63.1 wt.% and 66.8 wt.% at the temperature of 773 K and 973 K, respectively. At higher temperatures, condensables undergo secondary reactions in which large molecules further break down to smaller molecules, thereby reducing the condensate and increasing the non-condensable gases [33]. Solid residue decreases with increasing temperature and almost produces a fixed amount of 4.2 g to 1.5 g at 773 K onwards. These data were also supported by TGA analysis. The liquid hydrocarbons were lesser than LDPE but higher than HDPE. A similar study was conducted on virgin high-density polyethylene (HDPE) pyrolysis at temperature and pressure ranges of 450–504 °C and 0.1–2 bar in a continuous pilot-scale plant [34]. The findings demonstrated that even at low temperatures and pressures in the examined ranges, the chain end scission mechanism is the primary mechanism in the HDPE pyrolysis process. The oil produced from the pyrolysis of virgin HDPE at a temperature of 464 °C and sub-atmospheric pressure of 0.1 bar results in the highest linear hydrocarbon concentration (93.2 wt.%). Furthermore, the share of cyclic and branched hydrocarbons was improved up to 17.4 wt.% at higher pressure and temperature compared to 6.8 wt.% at vacuum pressure and lower temperature.

In addition, to see the combined effect of PP LDPE, and HDPE pyrolysis, all these three virgin plastics were mixed into a particular ratio, and results were compared with mixed virgin plastic and domestic plastic waste. It was noted that the mixed virgin plastic composition was almost identical to that of domestic plastic garbage collected from university campuses. The pyrolysis results of mixed virgin plastic and domestic plastic waste are shown in Figure 5d,e. Pyrolysis of mixed virgin plastic was carried out to identify the fuel quality and compare it with the real-time quality of domestic plastic waste. It was observed that liquid hydrocarbon fuel from HDPE virgin plastic was waxy oil while PP and LDPE virgin plastic pyrolysis resulted in a clear liquid. In the case of mixed virgin plastic, liquid hydrocarbons were again completely in liquid form, which may be because waxy oil from HDPE is soluble in other liquid hydrocarbons fuel at room temperature. As illustrated in Figure 4d, the mixed virgin plastic yielded maximum 68.6% liquid product at 723 K temperature, while domestic plastic waste resulted in 64.5%. In addition, the liquid products yield was higher for mixed virgin plastic compared to individual virgin plastic. The reason behind this may be due to the synergetic effect of decomposition of LDPE, HDPE, and PP simultaneously during pyrolysis reaction [35]. On the other hand, gaseous hydrocarbon yield was reached up to 64 wt.% at 973 K.

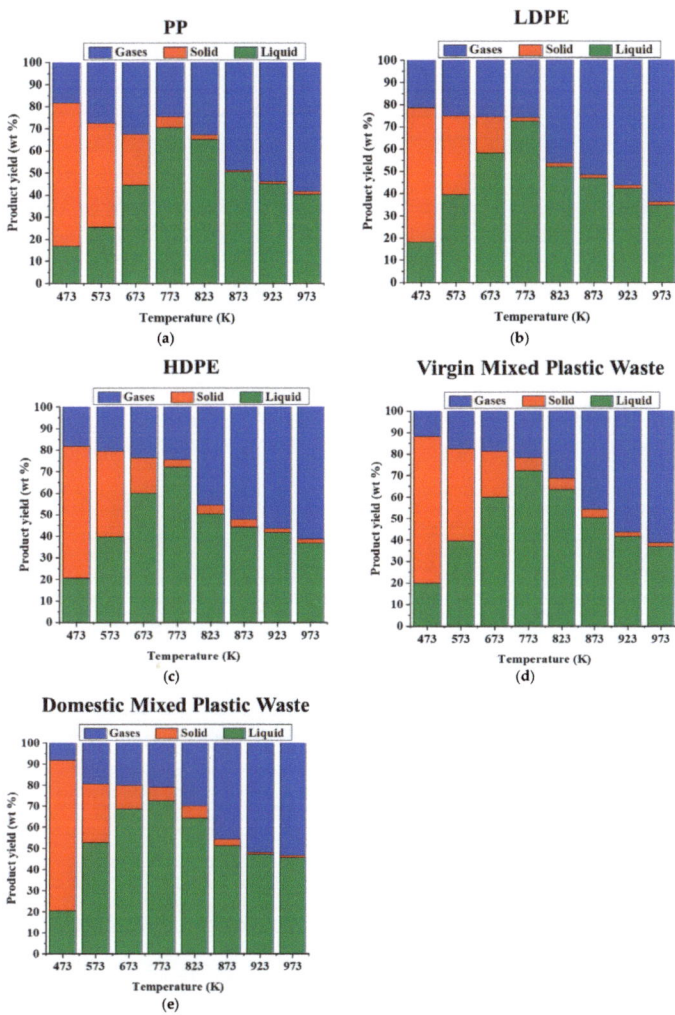

Figure 5. Product yield obtained from pyrolysis of (**a**) PP, (**b**) LDPE, (**c**) HDPE, (**d**) MVP, (**e**) DPW.

Domestic plastic waste behaves quite differently in pyrolysis than mixed virgin plastics because it contains a variety of other polymers in traces (1–5%), as well as coloring agents, additives, and other materials. In the narrow temperature range of 723–773 K, the highest yield of liquid product was reported to be 60.3 wt.% to 64.5 wt.% (Figure 5e). However, the maximum yield of liquid and gaseous products was observed to be lower for domestic plastic waste compared to mixed virgin plastic. This may be due to some polymer binders and coloring agents present in domestic plastic waste [35].

3.3. Analysis of Liquid Products Extracted from Plastic Feedstock by Pyrolysis Process

3.3.1. FTIR of Pyrolysis Liquid Fuels

The FTIR spectra of alternative fuel produced by the pyrolysis of plastic feedstock are shown in Figure 6. Chemical bonds absorb specific wavelengths that describe the fuel's structure and molecular bond strength as it interacts with infrared light in the FTIR spectrometer. The spectra of all feedstocks, i.e., PP, LDPE, HDPE, mixed virgin plastic, and domestic plastic waste, were almost similar.

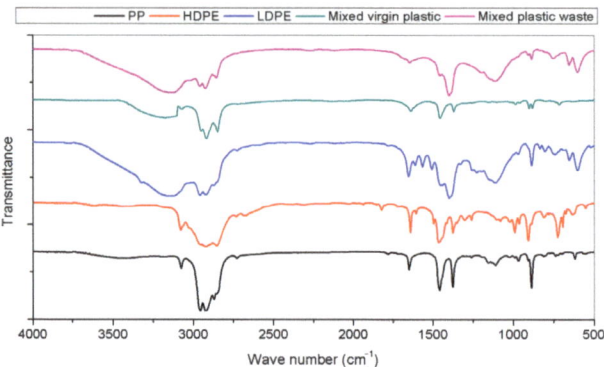

Figure 6. FTIR spectra of liquid hydrocarbon fuel from pyrolysis of LDPE, HDPE, PP, MVP, and DPW.

Figure 6 illustrates the presence of C-H, C=C, and =C−H bonds in the spectra of hydrocarbon fuels. Alkenes were detected at 3138 and 3444 cm^{-1} with a significant peak signal associated with the =C−H stretching vibration. The alkanes in the hydrocarbon fuel have a high −C−H vibrational signature, as indicated by the wavenumber of 2922 cm^{-1}. Alkene was detected by the presence of C=C vibrational bending, C=C bending, and −C−H stretching vibration signals with wavenumbers of 1642, 1466, 1398, and 1376 cm^{-1}. GC−MS analysis was used to determine the precise chemical structural composition because FTIR analysis only gives an impression of the existence of functional groups for the preliminary structure of the chemical composition.

3.3.2. GC-MS Analysis

Utilizing GC-MS, the chemical make-up of liquid hydrocarbons extracted from LDPE, HDPE, PP, mixed virgin plastic, and domestic plastic waste was examined. The findings showed that aliphatic (alkane, alkene, and alkyl compounds) carbon, in the range of C8–C20, made up the majority of the liquid hydrocarbon fuels produced. It was observed from Table 3 that a major constitute of most of virgin plastics and domestic hydrocarbon was 1-Dodecene, 1-Decene, Undecane, Tetradecane and 1-Pentadecene, Pentadecane, 1-Heptadecene, Hexadecane. When individual virgin plastic (LDPE, HDPE, and PP) pyrolyzed, LDPE showed the maximum concentration of 1-Decene (12.43%), Undecane (12.31%), 1-Dodecene (9.13%), Decane (8.58%), 1-Heptadecene (8.56%), and Dodecane (6.65%) while HDPE liquid fuel was with the major constituent of Pentadecane (11.71%), 1-Pentadecene (10.58%), 1-Heptadecene (9.09%), Hexadecane (8.19%), and 1-Dodecene (5.78%). Furthermore, PP liquid fuel was majorly composed of 1-Octadecene (13.46%), 1-Hexadecene (11.61%), 1-Heptadecene (10.06%), Hexadecane (12.46%), and 1-Tetradecene (6.83%). All the virgin plastics liquid hydrocarbons were in the range of C8 to C20 with a major constituent alkene. In the case of mixed virgin plastic, 1-Pentadecene (9.08%), Pentadecane (9.16%), 1-Hexadecene (8.32%), Hexadecane (8.52%), and 1-Decene (6.8%) appeared as significant hydrocarbons.

Table 3. Chemical composition of liquid hydrocarbon fuel obtained from LDPE, HDPE, PP, MVP, and DPW.

Compound	Molecular Formula	LDPE	HDPE	PP	Mixed Virgin	Domestic Plastic Waste (wt.%)
1-Octene	C_8H_{16}	1.78			1.35	0.81
Toluene	$C_{10}H_{20}$	0		4.05	5.26	1.01
Nonane	C_9H_{20}	3.01	2.41		1.08	
1-Nonene	C_9H_{18}	1.06	2.62		3.16	3.52
1-Decene	$C_{10}H_{20}$	12.43	4.14	2.57	6.8	3.84
Decane	$C_{10}H_{22}$	8.58	5.21	2.24	5.42	3.17
cyclodecane	$C_{10}H_{20}$		5.76		3.9	
1-Undecene	$C_{11}H_{22}$		5.47		1.7	6.06
Undecane	$C_{11}H_{24}$	12.31	5.6	3.27	1.2	2.41
1-Dodecene	$C_{12}H_{24}$	9.13	5.78	4.74	4.15	3.61
Dodecane	$C_{12}H_{26}$	6.65	3.65		5.49	12.63
Tridecane	$C_{13}H_{28}$				1.93	5.32
1-Tridecene	$C_{13}H_{26}$	5.32	1.97	5.73	3.58	9.96
1-Tetradecene	$C_{14}H_{28}$	2.02	5.23	6.83		8.31
Tetradecane	$C_{14}H_{30}$	6.55	4.66	5.09	5.83	5.97
1-Pentadecene	$C_{15}H_{30}$	6.12	10.58	3.65	9.08	2.28
Pentadecane	$C_{15}H_{32}$		11.71	6.82	9.16	10.21
1-Hexadecene	$C_{16}H_{32}$	5.08		11.61	8.32	5.24
1-Heptadecene	$C_{17}H_{34}$	8.56	9.09	10.06	5.71	0.17
Hexadecane	$C_{16}H_{34}$	3.61	8.19	12.46	8.52	2.62
Dibutyl adipate	$C_{14}H_{26}O_4$					5.9
Heptadacne	$C_{17}H_{36}$	3.66	5.48	4.38	3.01	3.08
1-Octadecene	$C_{18}H_{36}$	0	2.45	13.46	1.31	
1-Nonadecene	$C_{19}H_{38}$	2.06		1.52	2.02	0.94
Eicosane	$C_{20}H_{42}$	2.07		1.52	2.02	2.94

Domestic plastic waste's composition was almost like mixed virgin plastic. However, it showed a slightly different hydrocarbon composition. Dodecane (12.63%), 1-Tridecene (9.96%), Pentadecane (10.21%), 1-Hexadecene (9.24%), Tetradecane (5.97%), and Tridecane (5.32%) were the major hydrocarbons compared to mixed virgin plastics. In thermo-catalytic pyrolysis, random scission of LDPE, HDPE, and PP occurs, resulting in radicals. After that, β-scission of these radicals takes place to produce a monomer which undergoes a stabilization process by transfer of intramolecular or intermolecular hydrogen. Olefins and dienes are made when the secondary radicals undergo a series of β-scission reactions. Paraffine is produced simultaneously as a result of the intermolecular hydrogen transfers. Due to the abundance of the hydrogen atom in the radical chain at elevated temperatures, the probability of successive β-scission with intramolecular hydrogen transfer is highly expected [35]. In addition, Dibutyl adipate, a specific oxygenated compound utilized generally as a plasticizer in the paint industry, was also identified in domestic liquid hydrocarbon fuels. These findings were in line with those obtained using FTIR.

On the other hand, when mixed virgin plastic and domestic plastic waste were pyrolyzed under the same temperature conditions using mineral clay as a catalyst, the results showed that the catalyst favored the formation of alkanes. Due to catalytic reaction, alkanes increased from 43.66% to 58.55% and from 48.35% to 61.5% in the case of mixed virgin plastic and domestic plastic waste, respectively. In addition, a slight increase in aromatics was also observed. Besides, wax formation was also reduced in liquid products, which may be due to the reason that clay is more acidic in nature and, therefore, leads to crack waxes (C13–C28) into lighter hydrocarbon [36].

3.3.3. Analysis of Physic-Chemical Properties of Liquid Fuels

After obtaining the liquid hydrocarbons fuel, various tests were performed for its characteristic properties such as ultimate and proximate analysis, viscosity, density, fire and flash point, cloud and pour point, and moisture analysis, and are depicted in Table 4. All the techniques were carried out as per the standards mentioned.

Table 4. Characteristics properties of alternate fuel obtained from different plastic.

Parameter	PP	LDPE	HDPE	Mixed Virgin Plastic	Domestic Plastic Waste	Gasoline	Diesel
Appearance	Pale yellow	Pale yellow	Dark brown	Brown	Dark brown	No color	Pale yellow
Moisture (% v/v) (ASTM D95)	0	0	0	0	2.4	0.4–0.5	0.1–0.3
API gravity @ 60 °F (ASTM D287)	33.03	27.48	34.21	36.72	39.6	55	38
Density @ 15 °C g/cc (ASTM D4052—16)	0.86	0.89	0.92	0.91	0.86	0.78	0.807
Kinematic viscosity @ 40 °C (cSt) (ASTM D445)	4.09	3.98	5.08	4.53	4.48	1.17	2–4.5
Gross heat of combustion (MJ/kg) (ASTM D240—17)	45.72	45.59	43.63	44.61	43.92	47.64	45.21
Conradson carbon residue (wt.%) (ASTM D189)	0.12	0.19	0.11	0.15	0.15	0.14	0.35
Ash (wt.%) (ASTM D482)	0.013	0	0	0.11	0.013	0.001	0.01
Pour point (°C) (ASTM D97)	−9	−10	35	30	18	–	6
Flash Point (°C) (ASTM D93)	30	48	29	40	35	42	52
Aniline point (°C)	40	45	50	50	60	71	77.5
Diesel index	42.5	38.01	40.23	38.54	35.34	–	40

Liquid hydrocarbons from virgin HDPE plastic were found to be waxy, whereas PP and LDPE produced a clear liquid. Furthermore, the quality of the hydrocarbon fuel made from domestic plastic waste and mixed virgin plastic in this investigation was comparable to that of standard petroleum fuels, with kerosene and unpleasant odor and a dark brown color. This fuel color may be due to coloring and binding agents in the input feed. On the other hand, the produced hydrocarbon fuels were free-flowing and could be utilized directly for heating applications. Table 4 illustrates various properties such as viscosity, density, fire and flash point, cloud and pour point, and calorific value of the liquid hydrocarbon fuels from LDPE, HDPE, PP, mixed virgin plastic, and domestic plastic waste. Density and viscosity are the main fuel properties which highly affect the engine performance and emissions. Higher density and viscosity may affect the atomization process during combustion, resulting in decreased engine performance [37,38]. The density of liquid hydrocarbon fuels derived from LDPE, HDPE, PP, mixed virgin plastic, and domestic plastic waste was 0.89 g/cc, 0.92 g/cc, 0.86 g/cc, 0.91 g/cc, and 0.86 g/cc, respectively, in comparison to gasoline (0.78 g/cc) and diesel (0.807 g/cc). Similarly, the kinematic viscosity of LDPE (3.98 cSt), HDPE (5.08 cSt), PP (4.09 cSt), mixed virgin plastic (4.53 cSt), and domestic plastic waste hydrocarbon fuels (4.48 cSt) was lower than MVP fuel (4.53 cSt); nonetheless, it was in the range of ASTM standards (2–6 cSt). Other properties such as flash point were also found to be lesser for individual virgin plastics (LDPE—30 °C, HDPE—34 °C, PP—29 °C) compared to mixed virgin plastic (40 °C) and domestic plastic waste (35 °C). The values of flash point for diesel and gasoline were observed to be 52 °C and 42 °C, respectively, which is in agreement with other research [4,29]. On the other hand, the calorific value of mixed virgin plastic and domestic waste plastic was 44.61 MJ kg^{-1} and 43.92 MJ/kg, respectively, compared to diesel (45.21 MJ/kg) and gasoline (47.64 MJ kg^{-1}). Moreover, the calorific value of individual virgin plastics, i.e., LDPE (45.72 MJ kg^{-1}), HDPE (45.59 MJ kg^{-1}), and PP (43.63 MJ kg^{-1}), was also in the range of the values obtained for diesel and gasoline. Calorific value is one of the main properties of fuel that highly affects combustion. Similar results for calorific value of LDPE, HDPE, and PP were also obtained by Budsaereechai et al. 2019 [36]. Table 4 shows a comparison of the pour points of the resulting hydrocarbon fuels and commercial fuels. Due to the high volatility of the sample, the pour point of gasoline was not examined in this study. The pour point of pyrolytic liquid fuels derived from mixed virgin plastic and domestic plastic waste was poorer than that of diesel fuel. The diesel index is a measurement of a diesel fuel's ignition efficiency. It is calculated on the basis of the sample's specific gravity and aniline point. In the present study, the diesel index of plastic hydrocarbon fuels was 42.5 (LDPE), 38.01 (HDPE), 40.23 (PP), 38.54 (mixed virgin plastic), and 35.34 (domestic plastic waste). These values were in good agreement with the standard value of diesel [38]. Based on these fuel properties, it can be observed that liquid hydrocarbon fuels, derived either from virgin plastic or plastic waste, have an excellent potential for use as an alternative fuel.

3.4. Gas Analysis Obtained from Pyrolysis of Plastic Waste

Table 5 summarizes the analysis of the gases produced during the pyrolysis of the plastic feedstock. The findings showed that the gas compositions obtained during the pyrolysis of mixed virgin plastic and household plastic garbage were almost similar. Significant levels of alkane and alkene hydrocarbon gases from C1 to C4 have been found in pyrolytic gases. These gases are produced due to irregular scission of larger hydrocarbon groups at a higher temperature. These gases are also feasible if secondary cracking reactions of condensable gases continue for a longer period of time in the primary reactor. The GC results showed that pyrolytic gases derived from individual virgin plastics have hydrocarbons such as ethene and propene as a major product. In addition, some traces of hydrogen gas are also identified in pyrolytic gases. However, LDPE, HDPE, PP, and mixed virgin plastic showed no CO and CO_2 in pyrolytic gaseous composition. However, small traces of CO and CO_2 were examined in domestic plastic waste, which may be due to impurities, binder, filler, or coloring agent. Butene was also observed in the least amount for all types of plastic pyrolytic gases. Unsaturated hydrocarbons, which are produced by the random scission breakdown of plastic followed by the stabilization of intermediate radicals, were also examined. These hydrocarbons include ethene, propylene, butene, and its derivative [34]. The gross and net calorific values of pyrolytic gases obtained from virgin and domestic plastic wastes were observed in the range of 66.74 MJ m^{-3} to 75.61 MJ m^{-3} which confirm that these pyrolytic gases can be used as fuel gas for heating and engines. The pyrolytic gas compositions obtained from virgin plastics and domestic plastic waste were found to be consistent with other studies carried out by different researchers [30,31,34]. Furthermore, the pyrolytic gases have good potential to utilize in turbines for power generation or to be used directly in boilers as a substitute for coal without any additional pretreatment.

Table 5. Non-condensable gas composition of plastic feedstock (wt.%).

Plastic	LDPE	HDPE	PP	Mixed Virgin Plastic	Domestic Plastic Waste
Hydrogen	0.31	0.46	0.96	1.58	0.45
Carbon dioxide	0	0	0	0	0.82
Carbon monoxide	0	0	0	0	0.44
Methane	7.47	9.28	1.48	6.07	7.6
Ethane	12.1	11.56	14.42	11.69	12.12
Ethene	27.99	26.41	38.65	31.02	27.41
Propane	8.1	8.67	8.87	8.55	8.44
Propene	26.34	26.74	29.9	27.66	26.71
Butane	2.52	1.51	1.67	1.9	1.98
Butene	15.17	15.37	4.05	11.53	14.03
Gross calorific value (MJ nm^{-3})	69.99	69.02	75.61	70.97	69.38
Net calorific value (MJ nm^{-3})	67.49	66.60	71.02	67.84	66.74

4. Conclusions

The pyrolysis of individual and mixed virgin plastic was compared with domestic plastic waste collected from UPES, University. This study has demonstrated the production of various grades of hydrocarbons fuels from individual virgin plastics (LDPE, HDPE, and

PP), mixed virgin plastic, and domestic plastic waste at the temperature range 473 K to 973 K. All types of plastic feedstock showed more similarity with diesel fuel hydrocarbons. Additionally, gas fuel products from pyrolysis of domestic plastic waste and virgin plastic feedstock contain C1–C4 hydrocarbons that have high calorific value compared to other sources (biomass). Hence, catalytic conversions of plastics using inexpensive catalysts provide an innovative and feasible refinery pathway, explicitly targeting jet-fuel-range hydrocarbon fuels.

Author Contributions: Conceptualization, A.K.S. and P.K.G.; methodology, A.K.S. and P.K.G.; validation, A.K.S., P.K.G., A.P. and K.M.; formal analysis, K.M. and P.K.G.; investigation, P.K.G. and A.K.S.; resources, A.K.S.; data curation, P.K.G.; writing—original draft preparation, A.K.S. and P.K.G.; writing—review and editing, A.K.S., A.P., P.K.G. and L.M.; visualization, W.-H.C.; supervision, W.-H.C. and L.M.; project administration, A.K.S. and P.K.G.; funding acquisition, P.K.G. All authors have read and agreed to the published version of the manuscript.

Funding: This work is funded and supported by the Science and Engineering Research Board (SERB), DST, New Delhi—110070 (Project file No. ECR/2017/000185).

Data Availability Statement: Not applicable.

Acknowledgments: This research is dedicated to the late chancellor S. J. Chopra.UPES. The authors are very thankful to Ram Sharma (VC), and D K Avasthi (Dean, R & D) for providing continued support and for providing analysis facilities in UPES, Bidholi campus, Dehradun, UK, India. We are also thankful for Central Instrumentation Centre (CIC), R & D, UPES, for FTIR and GC−MS analysis.

Conflicts of Interest: The authors declare no conflict of interest.

References

1. Rafey, A.; Siddiqui, F.Z. A Review of Plastic Waste Management in India–Challenges and Opportunities. *Int. J. Environ. Anal. Chem.* **2021**, 1–17. [CrossRef]
2. Damodharan, D.; Sathiyagnanam, A.P.; Rana, D.; Saravanan, S.; Rajesh Kumar, B.; Sethuramasamyraja, B. Effective Utilization of Waste Plastic Oil in a Direct Injection Diesel Engine Using High Carbon Alcohols as Oxygenated Additives for Cleaner Emissions. *Energy Convers. Manag.* **2018**, *166*, 81–97. [CrossRef]
3. Tulashie, S.K.; Boadu, E.K.; Dapaah, S. Plastic Waste to Fuel via Pyrolysis: A Key Way to Solving the Severe Plastic Waste Problem in Ghana. *Therm. Sci. Eng. Prog.* **2019**, *11*, 417 424. [CrossRef]
4. Chandran, M.; Tamilkolundu, S.; Murugesan, C. *Conversion of Plastic Waste to Fuel*; Academic Press: Cambridge, MA, USA, 2020; ISBN 9780128178805.
5. Dobó, Z.; Jakab, Z.; Nagy, G.; Koós, T.; Szemmelveisz, K.; Muránszky, G. Transportation Fuel from Plastic Wastes: Production, Purification and SI Engine Tests. *Energy* **2019**, *189*, 116353. [CrossRef]
6. Bharathy, S.; Gnanasikamani, B.; Radhakrishnan Lawrence, K. Investigation on the Use of Plastic Pyrolysis Oil as Alternate Fuel in a Direct Injection Diesel Engine with Titanium Oxide Nanoadditive. *Environ. Sci. Pollut. Res.* **2019**, *26*, 10319–10332. [CrossRef] [PubMed]
7. Honus, S.; Kumagai, S.; Němček, O.; Yoshioka, T. Replacing Conventional Fuels in USA, Europe, and UK with Plastic Pyrolysis Gases—Part I: Experiments and Graphical Interchangeability Methods. *Energy Convers. Manag.* **2016**, *126*, 1128–1145. [CrossRef]
8. Miandad, R.; Barakat, M.A.; Aburiazaiza, A.S.; Rehan, M.; Ismail, I.M.I.; Nizami, A.S. Effect of Plastic Waste Types on Pyrolysis Liquid Oil. *Int. Biodeterior. Biodegrad.* **2017**, *119*, 239–252. [CrossRef]
9. Park, K.B.; Jeong, Y.S.; Guzelciftci, B.; Kim, J.S. Characteristics of a New Type Continuous Two-Stage Pyrolysis of Waste Polyethylene. *Energy* **2019**, *166*, 343–351. [CrossRef]
10. Thahir, R.; Altway, A.; Juliastuti, S.R. Susianto Production of Liquid Fuel from Plastic Waste Using Integrated Pyrolysis Method with Refinery Distillation Bubble Cap Plate Column. *Energy Rep.* **2019**, *5*, 70–77. [CrossRef]
11. Jahnavi, N.; Kanmani, K.; Kumar, P.S.; Varjani, S. Conversion of Waste Plastics into Low Emissive Hydrocarbon Fuel Using Catalyst Produced from Biowaste. *Environ. Sci. Pollut. Res.* **2020**, *28*, 63638–63645. [CrossRef]
12. Achilias, D.S.; Roupakias, C.; Megalokonomos, P.; Lappas, A.A.; Antonakou, V. Chemical Recycling of Plastic Wastes Made from Polyethylene (LDPE and HDPE) and Polypropylene (PP). *J. Hazard. Mater.* **2007**, *149*, 536–542. [CrossRef] [PubMed]
13. Adrados, A.; de Marco, I.; Caballero, B.M.; López, A.; Laresgoiti, M.F.; Torres, A. Pyrolysis of Plastic Packaging Waste: A Comparison of Plastic Residuals from Material Recovery Facilities with Simulated Plastic Waste. *Waste Manag.* **2012**, *32*, 826–832. [CrossRef] [PubMed]
14. Quesada, L.; Calero, M.; Martín-Lara, M.A.; Pérez, A.; Blázquez, G. Characterization of Fuel Produced by Pyrolysis of Plastic Film Obtained of Municipal Solid Waste. *Energy* **2019**, *186*, 115874. [CrossRef]

15. Dogu, O.; Pelucchi, M.; van de Vijver, R.; van Steenberge, P.H.M.; D'hooge, D.R.; Cuoci, A.; Mehl, M.; Frassoldati, A.; Faravelli, T.; van Geem, K.M. The Chemistry of Chemical Recycling of Solid Plastic Waste via Pyrolysis and Gasification: State-of-the-Art, Challenges, and Future Directions. *Prog. Energy Combust. Sci.* **2021**, *84*, 100901. [CrossRef]
16. Dao Thi, H.; Djokic, M.R.; van Geem, K.M. Detailed Group-Type Characterization of Plastic-Waste Pyrolysis Oils: By Comprehensive Two-Dimensional Gas Chromatography Including Linear, Branched, and Di-Olefins. *Separations* **2021**, *8*, 103. [CrossRef]
17. Pal, S.; Kumar, A.; Sharma, A.K.; Ghodke, P.K.; Pandey, S.; Patel, A. Recent Advances in Catalytic Pyrolysis of Municipal Plastic Waste for the Production of Hydrocarbon Fuels. *Processes* **2022**, *10*, 1497. [CrossRef]
18. Ragaert, K.; Delva, L.; van Geem, K. Mechanical and Chemical Recycling of Solid Plastic Waste. *Waste Manag.* **2017**, *69*, 24–58. [CrossRef]
19. Dai, L.; Fan, L.; Duan, D.; Ruan, R.; Wang, Y.; Liu, Y.; Zhou, Y.; Yu, Z.; Liu, Y.; Jiang, L. Production of Hydrocarbon-Rich Bio-Oil from Soapstock via Fast Microwave-Assisted Catalytic Pyrolysis. *J. Anal. Appl. Pyrolysis* **2017**, *125*, 356–362. [CrossRef]
20. Abdy, C.; Zhang, Y.; Wang, J.; Yang, Y.; Artamendi, I.; Allen, B. Pyrolysis of polyolefin plastic waste and potential applications in asphalt road construction: A technical review. *Resour. Conserv. Recycl.* **2022**, *180*, 106213. [CrossRef]
21. Rajamohan, S.; Kasimani, R. Analytical Characterization of Products Obtained from Slow Pyrolysis of Calophyllum Inophyllum Seed Cake: Study on Performance and Emission Characteristics of Direct Injection Diesel Engine Fuelled with Bio-Oil Blends. *Environ. Sci. Pollut. Res.* **2018**, *25*, 9523–9538. [CrossRef]
22. Hazrat, M.A.; Rasul, M.G.; Khan, M.M.K.; Azad, A.K.; Bhuiya, M.M.K. Utilization of Polymer Wastes as Transport Fuel Resources—A Recent Development. *Energy Procedia* **2014**, *61*, 1681–1685. [CrossRef]
23. Williams, P.T.; Slaney, E. Analysis of Products from the Pyrolysis and Liquefaction of Single Plastics and Waste Plastic Mixtures. *Resour. Conserv. Recycl.* **2007**, *51*, 754–769. [CrossRef]
24. Shah, S.H.; Khan, Z.M.; Raja, I.A.; Mahmood, Q.; Bhatti, Z.A.; Khan, J.; Farooq, A.; Rashid, N.; Wu, D. Low Temperature Conversion of Plastic Waste into Light Hydrocarbons. *J. Hazard. Mater.* **2010**, *179*, 15–20. [CrossRef]
25. Siddiqui, M.N.; Redhwi, H.H. Pyrolysis of Mixed Plastics for the Recovery of Useful Products. *Fuel Process. Technol.* **2009**, *90*, 545–552. [CrossRef]
26. Ahmad, N.; Ahmad, N.; Maafa, I.M.; Ahmed, U.; Akhter, P.; Shehzad, N.; Amjad, U.e.s.; Hussain, M. Thermal Conversion of Polystyrene Plastic Waste to Liquid Fuel via Ethanolysis. *Fuel* **2020**, *279*, 118498. [CrossRef]
27. Abbas, A.S.; Shubar, S.D.A. Pyrolysis of High-Density Polyethylene for the Production of Fuel-like Liquid Hydrocarbon. *Iraqi J. Chem. Pet. Eng.* **2008**, *99*, 23–29.
28. Miskolczi, N.; Bartha, L.; Deák, G.; Jóver, B. Thermal Degradation of Municipal Plastic Waste for Production of Fuel-like Hydrocarbons. *Polym. Degrad. Stab.* **2004**, *86*, 357–366. [CrossRef]
29. Rajendran, K.M.; Chintala, V.; Sharma, A.; Pal, S.; Pandey, J.K.; Ghodke, P. Review of Catalyst Materials in Achieving the Liquid Hydrocarbon Fuels from Municipal Mixed Plastic Waste (MMPW). *Mater. Today Commun.* **2020**, *24*, 100982. [CrossRef]
30. Singh, R.K.; Ruj, B. Time and Temperature Depended Fuel Gas Generation from Pyrolysis of Real World Municipal Plastic Waste. *Fuel* **2016**, *174*, 164–171. [CrossRef]
31. Zhang, Y.; Duan, D.; Lei, H.; Villota, E.; Ruan, R. Jet Fuel Production from Waste Plastics via Catalytic Pyrolysis with Activated Carbons. *Appl. Energy* **2019**, *251*, 113337. [CrossRef]
32. Peng, Y.; Wang, Y.; Ke, L.; Dai, L.; Wu, Q.; Kirk, C.; Yuan, Z.; Zou, R.; Liu, Y.; Roger, R. A review on catalytic pyrolysis of plastic wastes to high-value products. *Energy Con. Manag.* **2022**, *254*, 115243. [CrossRef]
33. Ruiz, M.; Martin, E.; Blin, J.; Van De Steene, L.; Broust, F. Understanding the Secondary Reactions of Flash Pyrolysis Vapors inside a Hot Gas Filtration Unit. *Energy Fuels* **2017**, *31*, 13785–13795. [CrossRef]
34. Abbas-Abadi, M.S.; Zayoud, A.; Kusenberg, M.; Roosen, M.; Vermeire, F.; Yazdani, P.; Van Waeyenberg, J.; Eschenbacher, A.; Hernandez, F.J.A.; Kuzmanović, M.; et al. Thermochemical recycling of end-of-life and virgin HDPE: A pilot-scale study. *J. Anal. Appl. Pyrolysis* **2022**, *166*, 105614. [CrossRef]
35. Das, P.; Tiwari, P. Valorization of Packaging Plastic Waste by Slow Pyrolysis. *Resour. Conserv. Recycl.* **2018**, *128*, 69–77. [CrossRef]
36. Budsaereechai, S.; Hunt, A.J.; Ngernyen, Y. Catalytic Pyrolysis of Plastic Waste for the Production of Liquid Fuels for Engines. *RSC Adv.* **2019**, *9*, 5844–5857. [CrossRef] [PubMed]
37. Pal, S.; Chintala, V.; Sharma, A.K.; Ghodke, P.; Kumar, S.; Kumar, P. Effect of Injection Timing on Performance and Emission Characteristics of Single Cylinder Diesel Engine Running on Blends of Diesel and Waste Plastic Fuels. *Mater. Today Proc.* **2019**, *17*, 209–215. [CrossRef]
38. Sharma, A.K.; Sharma, P.K.; Chintala, V.; Khatri, N.; Patel, A. Environment-Friendly Biodiesel/Diesel Blends for Improving the Exhaust Emission and Engine Performance to Reduce the Pollutants Emitted from Transportation Fleets. *Int. J. Environ. Res. Public Health* **2020**, *17*, 3896. [CrossRef] [PubMed]

Disclaimer/Publisher's Note: The statements, opinions and data contained in all publications are solely those of the individual author(s) and contributor(s) and not of MDPI and/or the editor(s). MDPI and/or the editor(s) disclaim responsibility for any injury to people or property resulting from any ideas, methods, instructions or products referred to in the content.

Article

Thermal Stability for the Continuous Production of γ-Valerolactone from the Hydrogenation of N-Butyl Levulinate in a CSTR

Wenel Naudy Vásquez Salcedo [1,2], Bruno Renou [2] and Sébastien Leveneur [1,*]

[1] INSA Rouen Normandie, University Rouen Normandie, Normandie Université, LSPC, UR 4704, F-76000 Rouen, France
[2] INSA Rouen-Normandie, UNIROUEN, CNRS, CORIA, Normandie University, F-76000 Rouen, France
* Correspondence: sebastien.leveneur@insa-rouen.fr

Abstract: γ-valerolactone can be a game-changer in the chemical industry because it could substitute fossil feedstocks in different fields. Its production is from the hydrogenation of levulinic acid or alkyl levulinates and can present some risk of thermal runaway. To the best of our knowledge, no studies evaluate the thermal stability of this production in a continuous reactor. We simulated the thermal behavior of the hydrogenation of butyl levulinate over *Ru/C* in a continuous stirred-tank reactor and performed a sensitivity analysis. The kinetic and thermodynamic constants from Wang et al.'s articles were used. We found that the risk of thermal stability is low for this chemical system.

Keywords: simulation; GVL; thermal stability; hydrogenation

Citation: Vásquez Salcedo, W.N.; Renou, B.; Leveneur, S. Thermal Stability for the Continuous Production of γ-Valerolactone from the Hydrogenation of N-Butyl Levulinate in a CSTR. *Processes* **2023**, *11*, 237. https://doi.org/10.3390/pr11010237

Academic Editor: Antoni Sánchez

Received: 7 December 2022
Revised: 8 January 2023
Accepted: 9 January 2023
Published: 11 January 2023

Copyright: © 2023 by the authors. Licensee MDPI, Basel, Switzerland. This article is an open access article distributed under the terms and conditions of the Creative Commons Attribution (CC BY) license (https://creativecommons.org/licenses/by/4.0/).

1. Introduction

The shift from fossil raw materials to renewable raw materials in the chemical industry is mandatory to make this industry sustainable and decrease its negative environmental impact. Among renewable raw materials, lignocellulosic biomass (LCB), that is not in competition with the food sector, is an excellent candidate because it could avoid the dilemma of food versus fuel that led to the alimentary crisis in the late 2000s. Even if there is divergence on the role of biofuel production in explaining the food shortage [1,2], non-food-use raw materials for chemical, biofuel, or material production should be favored [3].

LCB is available worldwide and can be obtained from agricultural wastes, such as maize stover, straw, wheat straw, sugarcane bagasse, rice husk, etc.; forestry residues including remaining wood harvestings, such as roots, branches, and leaves; dedicated crops on marginal land that is not suitable for food growth (e.g., miscanthus, switchgrass, eucalyptus, etc.); and the paper industry [4,5].

LCB consists of three main elements: cellulose and hemicellulose, which are polymers of sugars, and lignin, a polymer of aromatic compounds. The percentage of these three elements varies with species, location, and seasons, making it challenging to develop the same pretreatment or valorization process for all LCB raw materials. Nevertheless, these raw materials can lead to the production of fuels, materials, and chemicals.

The sugar fraction valorization can produce valuable platform molecules or building blocks such as levulinic acid/levulinate, furfural, GVL, HMF, etc. [3,6,7]. The potential use of GVL in fuels, materials, and chemicals is enormous [8–13]. GVL was found to be a suitable solvent for the dissolution of lignin, hemicellulose, cellulose, or fructose [14–19]. GVL can reduce CO exhaust, unburned fuel, and smoke [20]. GVL updated to hydrocarbons can be a temporary solution for jet fuels [21]. The valorization of GVL into alpha methylene can lead to an excellent substitute for acrylate [22,23].

GVL is produced from the hydrogenation of levulinic acid or alkyl levulinates. There are three main approaches: molecular hydrogen, catalytic transfer hydrogenation via the use of alcohol, or the in situ decomposition of formic acid [24–26]. The most common approach is using molecular hydrogen over Ru on activated carbon.

There are two types of catalytic systems in GVL production: homogeneous and heterogeneous. The advantage of homogeneous systems is their high catalytic performance [27,28]. However, separation processes need to be implemented to separate the catalyst from the final products, while heterogeneous catalysts are easy to remove and can be recycled [29,30].

In heterogeneous systems, the most common catalysts for GVL production from levulinic acid and alkyl levulinates are ruthenium (Ru), rhodium (Rh), palladium (Pd), platinum (Pt), gold (Au), and rhenium (Re) in which the noble metal Ru exhibits a high selectivity [8]. Manzer studied the hydrogenation of levulinic acid over a series of metal catalysts (Ir, Rh, Pd, Ru, Pt, Re, and Ni) supported on carbon (metal loading was equal to 5%) wherein a 5 wt.% *Ru/C* catalyst had the highest performance in terms of conversion and selectivity [23]. The catalytic activity of *Ru/C* and some other solid catalysts show promising results for the hydrogenation of butyl levulinate [31–34].

We have demonstrated that the hydrogenation of levulinic acid or alkyl levulinates presents some risk of thermal runaway when the thermal mode is adiabatic and in batch conditions [35,36]. One way to decrease the thermal risk is to work in continuous mode in a steady-state regime [37]. Nevertheless, one needs to assess the thermal stability of such continuous reactor [38,39]. In the literature we can find studies about thermal stability, dynamic stability, and sensitivity assessments in continuous reactors for reactions such as the hydrolysis of acetic anhydride, polystyrene production in CSTRs, and light-cycle oil hydrotreatment [40–43]. To the best of our knowledge, such a study has not been conducted for the continuous production of GVL.

In this paper, we focused on evaluating the thermal stability of GVL production from butyl levulinate over *Ru/C* and included a sensitivity approach. We modeled the thermal behavior of an ideal continuous stirred-tank reactor (CSTR) and used the kinetic and thermodynamic constants from Wang et al. [35,44]. A CSTR was chosen because its mixing is more efficient than other continuous reactors, which is vital for a gas–liquid–solid system.

2. Materials and Methods
2.1. Kinetics

Wang et al. showed that the hydrogenation of BL over *Ru/C* is a two-step reaction (Figure 1). BHP stands for butyl 4-hydroxypentanoate, and it is an intermediate. They performed this study by using GVL as a solvent.

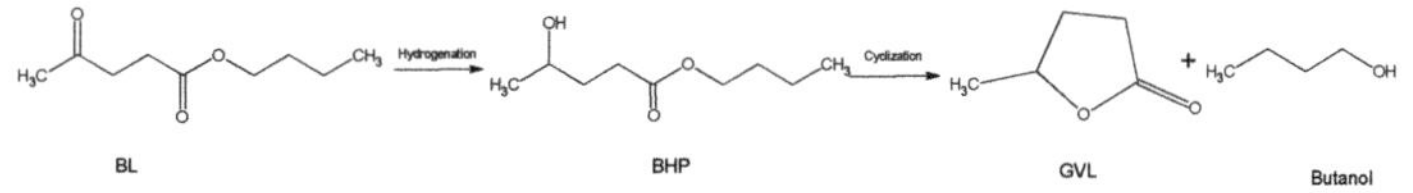

Figure 1. Reaction scheme for BL hydrogenation.

The rate expression for the hydrogenation step is derived as follows:

$$R_1 = k_1 \cdot [BL]_{Liq} \cdot [H_2]_{Liq} \cdot \omega_{Ru/C} \tag{1}$$

The rate expression for the cyclization is:

$$R_2 = k_2 \cdot [BHP]_{Liq} \tag{2}$$

where $\omega_{Ru/C}$ is the catalyst loading in kg/L.

The kinetic and thermodynamic constants from the articles of Wang et al. [35,44] were used (Table 1).

Table 1. Kinetic and thermodynamic constants.

	Values	Units
k_1 (T = 403.15 K)	$3.09 \cdot 10^{-6}$	$m^6 \cdot mol^{-1} \cdot kg^{-1} \cdot s^{-1}$
Ea_1	9.68	$kJ \cdot mol^{-1}$
ΔH_{R1}	−38.66	$kJ \cdot mol^{-1}$
k_2 (T = 403.15 K)	$1.88 \cdot 10^{-4}$	s^{-1}
Ea_2	10.25	$kJ \cdot mol^{-1}$
ΔH_{R2}	6.50	$kJ \cdot mol^{-1}$

2.2. Mass and Energy Balances

In this study, the flow distribution was assumed to be ideal. Thus, the material balance for a compound j can be written:

$$\frac{dC_j}{dt} = \frac{C_{j_{in}} - C_{j_{out}}}{\tau} + \sum_i v_{j,i} R_i \quad (3)$$

where i represents the reaction index, τ is the space-time, $v_{j,i}$ represents the stoichiometry coefficient of compound j in reaction i, and R_i is the reaction rate.

In a previous study by our group [44], we showed that the kinetics of hydrogen mass transfer from the gas to the liquid phase can be considered fast when GVL is the solvent. Thus, the hydrogen concentration in the liquid phase (reaction mixture) can be assumed to be constant. The solubility of hydrogen in GVL solvent was calculated from the following relationships:

$$C_{H2} = P_{H_2} \cdot He\left(T_{Ref} = 373.15K\right) \cdot exp\left(\frac{-\Delta H_{Sol.}}{R} \cdot \left(\frac{1}{T_R} - \frac{1}{373.15}\right)\right) \quad (4)$$

where P_{H_2} is the hydrogen pressure in the reactor, $He\left(T_{Ref} = 373.15K\right) = 1.86 \text{ mol} \cdot m^{-3} \cdot bar^{-1}$ is Henry's constant at 373.15 K, and $\Delta H_{Sol.} = 5936.8 \text{ J} \cdot mol^{-1}$ is the enthalpy of solubilization [44].

For an ideal CSTR, the energy balance of the reactionary phase can be written as:

$$\left[(\rho \hat{C}_P)_{liq} + (\rho \hat{C}_P)_{ins}\right] \frac{dT_r}{dt} = \frac{\sum C_{j_{in}} \overline{C}_{P_j}}{\tau}(T_{in} - T_r) + Ua(T_c - T_r) - \sum_i R_i \Delta H_i \quad (5)$$

where ρ is the volumic mass, $\hat{C}_P$ is the specific heat capacity, T_r is the reactionary media temperature, T_C is the temperature of the heat carrier in the jacket, Ua is the global heat transfer coefficient, ins represents the reactor insert, and ΔH_i is the enthalpy of reaction i. Data for heat capacities and volumetric mass were found in the literature [45,46].

The flow distribution of the heat carrier fluid is ideal; thus, the energy balance is:

$$\rho_c \hat{C}_{P_c} \frac{dT_c}{dt} = \frac{\rho_c \hat{C}_{P_c}}{\tau_c}(T_{c_0} - T_c) + Ua(T_r - T_c) \quad (6)$$

where ρ_c and $\hat{C}_{P_c}$ are the volumic mass and heat capacity of the heat carrier, and T_{c_0} is the heat carrier temperature at the inlet.

Figure 2 is a schematic representation of the reactor setup.

In this study, we will consider the steady-state regime; thus, Equations (3), (5), and (6) become:

$$\frac{dT_c}{dt} = \frac{dT_R}{dt} = 0 \text{ K} \cdot s^{-1} \text{ and } \frac{dC_j}{dt} = 0 \text{ mol} \cdot L^{-1} \cdot s^{-1} \quad (7)$$

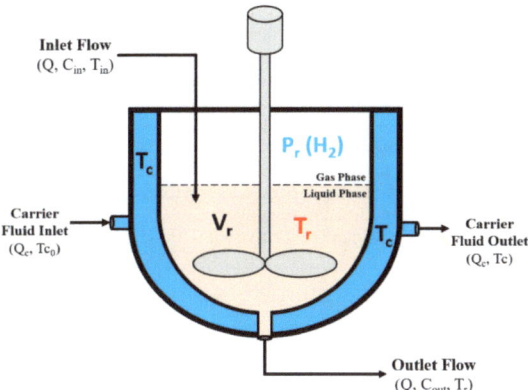

Figure 2. Reactor setup.

2.3. Operating Conditions

The simulation was performed under isobaric conditions within a reaction temperature range of 300–600 K. Table 2 shows the operating conditions used during the simulation. The inlet concentrations, catalyst loading, and temperature were in the same ranges as the ones from Wang et al. [44].

Table 2. Operating conditions used in this study.

Inlet Parameters	Values	Units
C_{BL_0}	4840	mol·m^{-3}
C_{BHP_0}	0	mol·m^{-3}
C_{GVL_0}	2080	mol·m^{-3}
C_{BuOH_0}	0	mol·m^{-3}
ω_{Cat}	10	kg·m^{-3}
T_r	300 to 600	K
T_{in}	333.15	K
P_{H_2}	25	bar
τ	2000	s
Ua	17,000	W·m^{-3}·K^{-1}

2.4. Thermal Stability Criterion

To assess the stationary thermal stability, the van Heerden criterion was calculated during the course of the reaction. The van Heerden criterion is a stability-based criterion defined as [47–49]:

$$\frac{dQ_{Removal}}{dt} > \frac{dQ_{Generated}}{dt} \tag{8}$$

where $Q_{Removal}$ is the amount of energy exchange between the reactionary media and the heat carrier fluid, and $Q_{Generated}$ is the amount of energy released during the reaction.

The van Heerden criterion is necessary to satisfy stationary stability and states that the energy removed from a reactionary system must be higher than the energy generated by the system.

$\frac{dQ_{Removal}}{dt}$ and $\frac{dQ_{Generated}}{dt}$ were calculated from the material and energy balances.

2.5. Simulation and Parametric Sensitivity

MATLAB R2021b software was used to make the simulation and to solve the mathematical equations presented during thermal analysis. The ODE15s routine was used to solve stiff differential equations. The FSOLVE routine was used to solve the system of nonlinear equations and the energy and mass balance in the steady-state regime. The EIG routine was used to calculate the eigenvalues and eigenvectors of the Jacobian matrix.

Parametric sensitivity analysis studies the relationship between the system behavior according to changes in the inlet parameters. As mentioned by Varma et al. [50], if a slight variation in the input parameter values can lead to a significant change, then the chemical system is qualified as sensitive.

The parametric sensitivity is defined as follows:

$$S\left(\vec{y},\phi\right) = \frac{d\vec{y}}{d\phi} \tag{9}$$

For a dynamic system, we have that:

$$\frac{dS\left(\vec{y},\phi\right)}{dt} = J \cdot S\left(\vec{y},\phi\right) + \frac{d\vec{f}}{d\phi} \tag{10}$$

Solving the expression above for $S\left(\vec{y},\phi\right)$ in the steady state, we obtain:

$$\frac{dS\left(\vec{y},\phi\right)}{dt} = 0 \tag{11}$$

$$S\left(\vec{y},\phi\right) = -J^{-1} \cdot \frac{d\vec{f}}{d\phi} \text{ with } \frac{d\vec{f}}{d\phi} = \begin{pmatrix} \frac{df_1}{d\phi} \\ \vdots \\ \frac{df_n}{d\phi} \end{pmatrix} \tag{12}$$

To compare the sensitivity of one output variable according to different parameters, we can define the normalized parametric sensitivity as follows:

$$S_n(y,\phi_j) = \frac{\phi_j}{y}\frac{dy}{d\phi_j} \tag{13}$$

3. Results and Discussion

3.1. Effect of Space-Time on Conversion

Figure 3 shows the effect of temperature on BL conversion at different space-times. As the reaction temperature and space-time increase, the BL conversion increases. A space-time value of 2000 s was found to be a good compromise between time and conversion since the space-time increase does not significantly improve the conversion. We can realize from Figure 3, comparing the space-times equal to 2000 s and 10,000 s, that the difference in the BL conversion is less than 15%, while space-time is multiplied by a factor of 5.

3.2. Comparison of Heat Flow Rate Exchange Due to Chemical Reactions

By solving the energy balance in the reactionary medium, one obtains:

$$T_c = T_r + \frac{1}{Ua}\sum_i R_i \Delta H_i - \frac{\sum C_{j_{in}} \overline{C}_{P_j}}{\tau \cdot Ua}(T_{in} - T_r) \tag{14}$$

Figure 4 shows the heat flow rates due to chemical reactions in the temperature range of 300–600 K. We plotted the heat flow rate generated in watts per cubic meters for different space-times from 100 s to 10,000 s. Based on the results presented in Figure 4, we can conclude that the energy release per unit of time per unit of volume decreases if we increase the space-time. Such results are expected for an ideal CSTR.

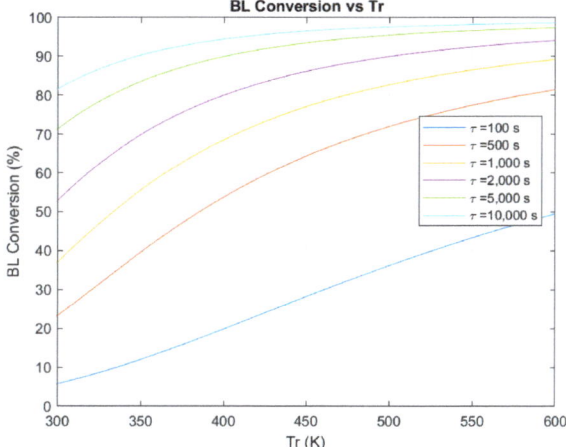

Figure 3. BL conversion as a function of T_r for different space-times.

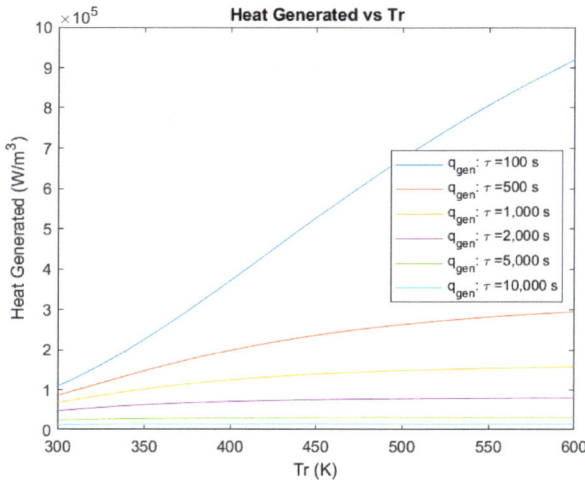

Figure 4. Heat flow as a function of T_r for different space-times.

Figure 5 represents the application of the van Heerden criterion to determine if the reactionary system is stable from the thermal point of view operating at a steady-state regime. This criterion solves the energy balance and determines if T_r is related to T_c by a one-to-one function (injective function). When the one-to-one function relates T_r and T_c, there is no multiplicity of steady states; consequently, the system is stable.

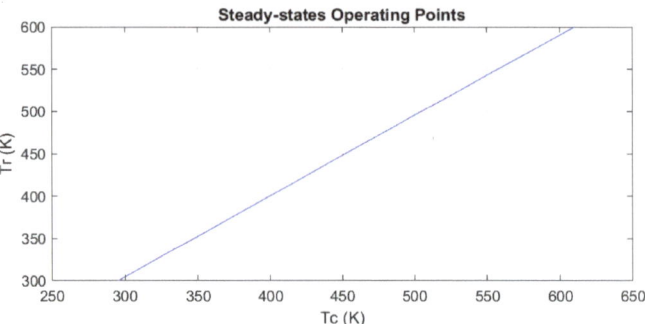

Figure 5. Reactor temperature vs. jacket temperature.

From Figure 5, we can realize that T_r and T_c are related by a one-to-one function in the range 300 K < T_r < 600 K. Thus, we can conclude that there is no multiplicity of steady-states and also that the reactionary system can stably operate in a steady-state regime.

3.3. Parametric Sensitivity

In this part, we evaluate the parametric sensitivity of the BL concentration in the outlet flow, the GVL concentration in the outlet flow, and the reactor temperature. We decided to focus on these three variables since they represent the main reagent, the main product, and the variable linked to thermal stability.

The parameters considered for this evaluation were C_{BL_0}, k_{hyd}, k_{cyc}, Ua, τ, ω_{Cat}, and T_{in}.

Figure 6 shows the normalized parametric sensitivity of the BL concentration in the outlet flow as a function of the reaction temperature. From Figure 6, we can notice that the final BL concentration is more sensitive to the inlet BL concentration, space-time, and catalyst loading. This means that variations in these parameters significantly change the final BL concentration.

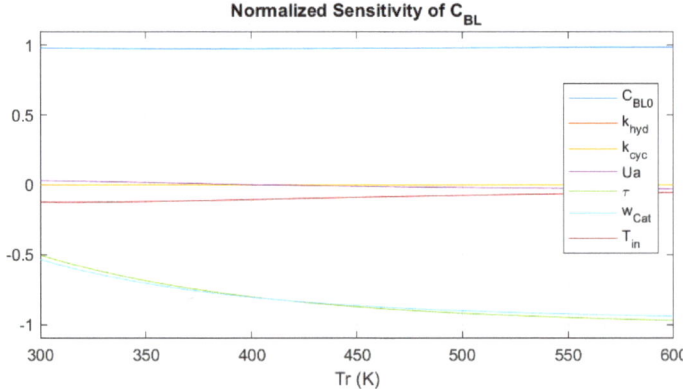

Figure 6. Parametric sensitivity for the outlet BL concentration.

Figure 7 represents the normalized parametric sensitivity of the GVL concentration in the outlet flow as a function of the reaction temperature. Based on the results, we found that the GVL concentration is more sensitive to variations in the inlet BL concentration, the space-time, and the cyclization rate constant. If any of these parameters increase, then the GVL production also increases. From Figure 7, we can also realize that GVL's sensitivity to these parameters gains importance as we increase the reaction temperature.

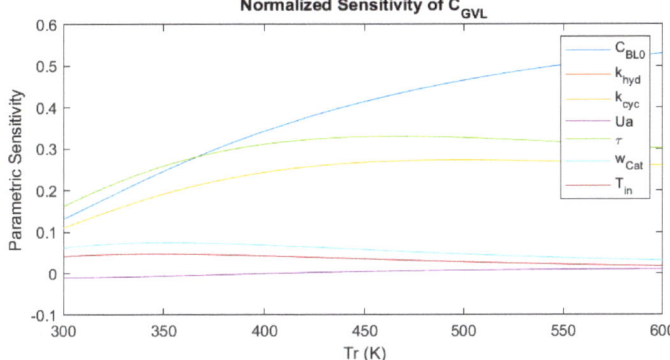

Figure 7. Parametric sensitivity for the outlet GVL concentration.

Figure 8 represents the normalized parametric sensitivity of the reaction temperature in the range of temperatures from 300 K to 600 K. Figure 8 shows how sensitive the reaction temperature is to the operating parameters. We found that reaction temperature is more sensitive to variations in the inlet temperature, the inlet BL concentration, space-time, and the heat transfer coefficient. Based on these results, we can conclude that the inlet BL concentration, the hydrogenation and cyclization rate constants, the heat transfer Ua, the space-time τ, the catalyst loading $\omega_{Ru/C}$, and the inlet temperature T_{in} have a low impact on the reaction temperature within the temperature range of 300–600 K. This low influence explains the low risk of thermal instability for this reaction in a CSTR.

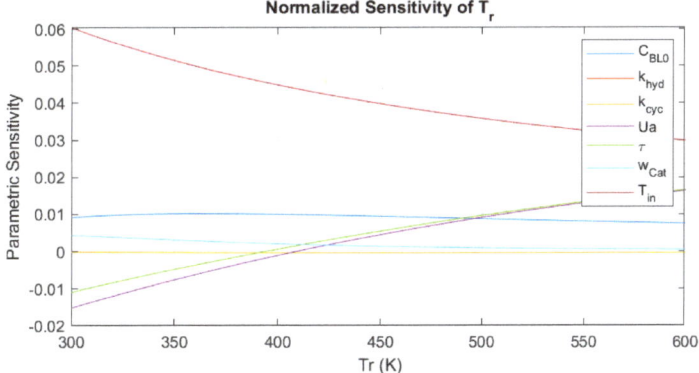

Figure 8. Results: Parametric sensitivity for the reactor temperature (T_r).

3.4. Dynamic Thermal Stability

In this part, we seek to evaluate the dynamic response of the system to perturbations near stationary conditions. For this purpose, we applied the linear dynamic model of perturbation.

Considering our dynamical model:

$$\frac{dy_i}{dt} = f_i(y_1, y_2, \ldots, y_n, \phi, t) \tag{15}$$

where y_i represents the variables of the system, and ϕ represents the other parameters.

$$y_i = C_{BL}, C_{BHP}, C_{GVL}, C_{BuOH}, T_r, T_c \tag{16}$$

Let us define a small perturbation (x_i) on the whole set of variables as follows:

$$x_i = y_i - y_{i,s} \tag{17}$$

Therefore:

$$y_i = y_{i,s} + x_i \tag{18}$$

Now we can define the perturbed dynamical model as follows:

$$\frac{d(y_{i,s} + x_i)}{dt} = f_i(y_{1,s} + x_1, y_{2,s} + x_2, \ldots, y_{n,s} + x_n, \phi, t) \tag{19}$$

As we have an interest in making a linear analysis, we used the 1st-order Taylor expansion of the perturbed dynamical model to obtain:

$$\frac{d(y_{i,s} + x_i)}{dt} = f_i(y_{1,s}, y_{2,s}, \ldots, y_{n,s} + x_n, \phi, t) + \left(\frac{\partial f_i}{\partial y_1}\right)_s \cdot x_1 + \left(\frac{\partial f_i}{\partial y_2}\right)_s \cdot x_2 + \cdots + \left(\frac{\partial f_i}{\partial y_n}\right)_s \cdot x_n \tag{20}$$

Under stationary conditions:

$$\frac{d(y_{i,s} + x_i)}{dt} = 0 \tag{21}$$

$$f_i(y_{1,s}, y_{2,s}, \ldots, y_{n,s} + x_n, \phi, t) = 0 \tag{22}$$

Therefore, the linear model of perturbation under stationary conditions is:

$$\frac{dx_i}{dt} = \left(\frac{\partial f_i}{\partial y_1}\right)_s \cdot x_1 + \left(\frac{\partial f_i}{\partial y_2}\right)_s \cdot x_2 + \cdots + \left(\frac{\partial f_i}{\partial y_n}\right)_s \cdot x_n \tag{23}$$

Developing the linear model of perturbation under stationary conditions for a system with n variables, we have:

$$\begin{cases} \frac{dx_1}{dt} = \left(\frac{\partial f_1}{\partial y_1}\right)_s \cdot x_1 + \left(\frac{\partial f_1}{\partial y_2}\right)_s \cdot x_2 + \cdots + \left(\frac{\partial f_1}{\partial y_n}\right)_s \cdot x_n \\ \vdots \\ \frac{dx_i}{dt} = \left(\frac{\partial f_i}{\partial y_1}\right)_s \cdot x_1 + \left(\frac{\partial f_i}{\partial y_2}\right)_s \cdot x_2 + \cdots + \left(\frac{\partial f_i}{\partial y_n}\right)_s \cdot x_n \\ \vdots \\ \frac{dx_n}{dt} = \left(\frac{\partial f_n}{\partial y_1}\right)_s \cdot x_1 + \left(\frac{\partial f_n}{\partial y_2}\right)_s \cdot x_2 + \cdots + \left(\frac{\partial f_n}{\partial y_n}\right)_s \cdot x_n \end{cases} \tag{24}$$

In a matrix formalism, we can define the linear dynamical model of perturbation as follows:

$$\dot{X} = J \cdot X$$

where

$$X = \begin{pmatrix} x_1 \\ \vdots \\ x_n \end{pmatrix}; \quad \dot{X} = \begin{pmatrix} \frac{dx_1}{dt} \\ \vdots \\ \frac{dx_n}{dt} \end{pmatrix}; \quad J = \begin{pmatrix} \frac{df_1}{dy_1} & \cdots & \frac{df_1}{dy_n} \\ \vdots & \ddots & \vdots \\ \frac{df_n}{dy_1} & \cdots & \frac{df_n}{dy_n} \end{pmatrix} \quad (25)$$

Solving the linear system leads to these solutions for all the perturbations around the stationary point:

$$\begin{cases} x_1 = \sum_{m=1}^{n} a_m \cdot U_{1,m} \cdot e^{\lambda_m t} \\ \vdots \\ x_i = \sum_{m=1}^{n} a_m \cdot U_{i,m} \cdot e^{\lambda_m t} \\ \vdots \\ x_n = \sum_{m=1}^{n} a_m \cdot U_{n,m} \cdot e^{\lambda_m t} \end{cases} \quad (26)$$

where U_i is the ith eigenvector of J associated to the eigenvalue λ_i. The condition of asymptotic stability is:

$$\forall k \lim_{t \to \infty} x_k = 0 \quad (27)$$

This leads to the following:

$$\lambda_i \in \mathbb{C} \cdot \Re e(\lambda_i) < 0 \quad (28)$$

To evaluate the dynamic thermal stability, we defined the Jacobian matrix of the dynamic model in the range of temperature of 300 K to 600 K and calculated the eigenvalues of the Jacobian matrix for each temperature value. The eigenvalues are plotted in Figure 9.

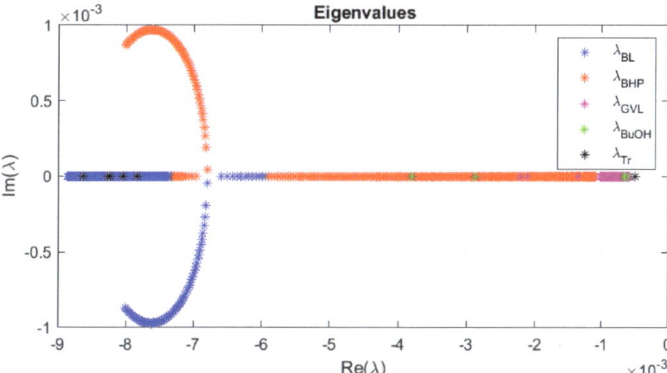

Figure 9. Dynamic Stability—Eigenvalues.

Figure 9 shows the eigenvalues obtained from the Jacobian matrix of the reactionary system in the range of temperature from 300 K to 600 K. This Jacobian matrix was generated from the material and energy balances. It is considered that there are dynamic thermal instabilities in the system when there are eigenvalues whose real parts are positive (Re(λ) > 0). From Figure 9, we can conclude that the CSTR reactor is dynamically stable in the temperature range of 300 K to 600 K since the real parts of all eigenvalues are negative. Visualizing the eigenvalues also helps to identify which variable is responsible for instabilities when the system is not dynamically stable.

4. Conclusions

This article deals with the safety production of GVL from the hydrogenation of butyl levulinate over *Ru/C* in a continuous stirred-tank reactor (CSTR) in a steady-state regime. The kinetic and thermodynamic constants determined from Wang et al.'s articles were used to simulate the thermal behavior in a CSTR. The van Heerden criterion showed that the risk of thermal instability is low for this reaction system with the operating conditions used in this study.

The sensitivity analysis demonstrated that the kinetic constants, global heat transfer, inlet concentrations, space-time, inlet temperature, and catalyst loading have a low impact on the reaction temperature. Nevertheless, the inlet concentration of BL, space-time, and cyclization rate constant have a non-negligible impact on the outlet concentration of GVL.

A continuation of this study could be the study of thermal stability during the transient phase and for non-ideal flow in continuous reactors.

Author Contributions: Conceptualization, W.N.V.S. and S.L.; methodology, W.N.V.S.; formal analysis, W.N.V.S.; investigation, W.N.V.S.; writing—original draft preparation, W.N.V.S., B.R. and S.L.; writing—review and editing, W.N.V.S., B.R. and S.L.; supervision, B.R. and S.L. All authors have read and agreed to the published version of the manuscript.

Funding: This study was conducted in the framework of the PROMETEE project, funded by Rouen Metropole. The authors thank the Ministry of High Education, Science and Technology of Dominican Republic (MESCyT).

Data Availability Statement: Data available on request.

Conflicts of Interest: The authors declare no conflict of interest.

References

1. Filip, O.; Janda, K.; Kristoufek, L.; Zilberman, D. Food versus fuel: An updated and expanded evidence. *Energy Econ.* **2019**, *82*, 152–166. [CrossRef]
2. Timilsina, G.R.; Shrestha, A. How much hope should we have for biofuels? *Energy* **2011**, *36*, 2055–2069. [CrossRef]
3. Isikgor, F.H.; Becer, C.R. Lignocellulosic biomass: A sustainable platform for the production of bio-based chemicals and polymers. *Polym. Chem.* **2015**, *6*, 4497–4559. [CrossRef]
4. Gunasekaran, M.; Kumar, G.; Karthikeyan, O.P.; Varjani, S. Lignocellulosic biomass as an optimistic feedstock for the production of biofuels as valuable energy source: Techno-economic analysis, Environmental Impact Analysis, Breakthrough and Perspectives. *Environ. Technol. Innov.* **2021**, *24*, 102080. [CrossRef]
5. Nahak, B.K.; Preetam, S.; Sharma, D.; Shukla, S.K.; Syväjärvi, M.; Toncu, D.C.; Tiwari, A. Advancements in net-zero pertinency of lignocellulosic biomass for climate neutral energy production. *Renew. Sustain. Energy Rev.* **2022**, *161*, 112393. [CrossRef]
6. Melero, J.A.; Iglesias, J.; Garcia, A. Biomass as renewable feedstock in standard refinery units. Feasibility, opportunities and challenges. *Energy Environ. Sci.* **2012**, *5*, 7393–7420. [CrossRef]
7. Di Menno Di Bucchianico, D.; Wang, Y.; Buvat, J.C.; Pan, Y.; Casson Moreno, V.; Leveneur, S. Production of levulinic acid and alkyl levulinates: A process insight. *Green Chem.* **2022**, *24*, 614–646. [CrossRef]
8. Ye, L.; Han, Y.; Feng, J.; Lu, X. A review about GVL production from lignocellulose: Focusing on the full components utilization. *Ind. Crops Prod.* **2020**, *144*, 112031. [CrossRef]
9. Xu, R.; Liu, K.; Du, H.; Liu, H.; Cao, X.; Zhao, X.; Qu, G.; Li, X.; Li, B.; Si, C. Falling Leaves Return to Their Roots: A Review on the Preparation of γ-Valerolactone from Lignocellulose and Its Application in the Conversion of Lignocellulose. *ChemSusChem* **2020**, *13*, 6461–6476. [CrossRef]
10. Alonso, D.M.; Wettstein, S.G.; Dumesic, J.A. Gamma-valerolactone, a sustainable platform molecule derived from lignocellulosic biomass. *Green Chem.* **2013**, *15*, 584–595. [CrossRef]
11. Tang, X.; Zeng, X.; Li, Z.; Hu, L.; Sun, Y.; Liu, S.; Lei, T.; Lin, L. Production of γ-valerolactone from lignocellulosic biomass for sustainable fuels and chemicals supply. *Renew. Sustain. Energy Rev.* **2014**, *40*, 608–620. [CrossRef]
12. Fábos, V.; Lui, M.Y.; Mui, Y.F.; Wong, Y.Y.; Mika, L.T.; Qi, L.; Cséfalvay, E.; Kovács, V.; Szucs, T.; Horváth, I.T. Use of Gamma-Valerolactone as an Illuminating Liquid and Lighter Fluid. *ACS Sustain. Chem. Eng.* **2015**, *3*, 1899–1904. [CrossRef]
13. Kerkel, F.; Markiewicz, M.; Stolte, S.; Müller, E.; Kunz, W. The green platform molecule gamma-valerolactone—Ecotoxicity, biodegradability, solvent properties, and potential applications. *Green Chem.* **2021**, *23*, 2962–2976. [CrossRef]
14. Di Menno Di Bucchianico, D.; Buvat, J.C.; Mignot, M.; Casson Moreno, V.; Leveneur, S. Role of solvent the production of butyl levulinate from fructose. *Fuel* **2022**, *318*, 123703. [CrossRef]
15. Luo, Y.; Li, Z.; Zuo, Z.; Su, Z.; Hu, C. A Simple Two-Step Method for the Selective Conversion of Hemicellulose in Pubescens to Furfural. *ACS Sustain. Chem. Eng.* **2017**, *5*, 8137–8147. [CrossRef]

16. Yuan, C.; Shi, W.; Chen, P.; Chen, H.; Zhang, L.; Hu, G.; Jin, L.; Xie, H.; Zheng, Q.; Lu, S. Dissolution and transesterification of cellulose in γ-valerolactone promoted by ionic liquids. *New J. Chem.* **2019**, *43*, 330–337. [CrossRef]
17. Xue, Z.; Zhao, X.; Sun, R.C.; Mu, T. Biomass-derived γ-valerolactone-based solvent systems for highly efficient dissolution of various lignins: Dissolution behavior and mechanism study. *ACS Sustain. Chem. Eng.* **2016**, *4*, 3864–3870. [CrossRef]
18. Motagamwala, A.H.; Won, W.; Maravelias, C.T.; Dumesic, J.A. An engineered solvent system for sugar production from lignocellulosic biomass using biomass derived γ-valerolactone. *Green Chem.* **2016**, *18*, 5756–5763. [CrossRef]
19. Di Menno Di Bucchianico, D.; Cipolla, A.; Buvat, J.C.; Mignot, M.; Casson Moreno, V.; Leveneur, S. Kinetic Study and Model Assessment for n-Butyl Levulinate Production from Alcoholysis of 5-(Hydroxymethyl)furfural over Amberlite IR-120. *Ind. Eng. Chem. Res.* **2022**, *61*, 10818–10836. [CrossRef]
20. Yan, K.; Yang, Y.; Chai, J.; Lu, Y. Catalytic reactions of gamma-valerolactone: A platform to fuels and value-added chemicals. *Appl. Catal. B Environ.* **2015**, *179*, 292–304. [CrossRef]
21. Bond, J.Q.; Alonso, D.M.; Wang, D.; West, R.M.; Dumesic, J.A. Integrated catalytic conversion of γ-valerolactone to liquid alkenes for transportation fuels. *Science* **2010**, *327*, 1110–1114. [CrossRef]
22. Al-Naji, M.; Puértolas, B.; Kumru, B.; Cruz, D.; Bäumel, M.; Schmidt, B.V.K.J.; Tarakina, N.V.; Pérez-Ramírez, J. Sustainable Continuous Flow Valorization of γ-Valerolactone with Trioxane to α-Methylene-γ-Valerolactone over Basic Beta Zeolites. *ChemSusChem* **2019**, *12*, 2628–2636. [CrossRef]
23. Manzer, L.E. Catalytic synthesis of α-methylene-γ-valerolactone: A biomass-derived acrylic monomer. *Appl. Catal. A Gen.* **2004**, *272*, 249–256. [CrossRef]
24. Kuwahara, Y.; Kaburagi, W.; Osada, Y.; Fujitani, T.; Yamashita, H. Catalytic transfer hydrogenation of biomass-derived levulinic acid and its esters to γ-valerolactone over ZrO2 catalyst supported on SBA-15 silica. *Catal. Today* **2017**, *281*, 418–428. [CrossRef]
25. Kuwahara, Y.; Kango, H.; Yamashita, H. Catalytic Transfer Hydrogenation of Biomass-Derived Levulinic Acid and Its Esters to γ-Valerolactone over Sulfonic Acid-Functionalized UiO-66. *ACS Sustain. Chem. Eng.* **2017**, *5*, 1141–1152. [CrossRef]
26. Liu, M.; Li, S.; Fan, G.; Yang, L.; Li, F. Hierarchical Flower-like Bimetallic NiCu catalysts for Catalytic Transfer Hydrogenation of Ethyl Levulinate into γ-Valerolactone. *Ind. Eng. Chem. Res.* **2019**, *58*, 10317–10327. [CrossRef]
27. Oklu, N.K.; Makhubela, B.C.E. Highly selective and efficient solvent-free transformation of bio-derived levulinic acid to γ-valerolactone by Ru(II) arene catalyst precursors. *Inorg. Chim. Acta* **2018**, *482*, 460–468. [CrossRef]
28. Chalid, M.; Broekhuis, A.A.; Heeres, H.J. Experimental and kinetic modeling studies on the biphasic hydrogenation of levulinic acid to γ-valerolactone using a homogeneous water-soluble Ru-(TPPTS) catalyst. *J. Mol. Catal. A Chem.* **2011**, *341*, 14–21. [CrossRef]
29. Agirrezabal-Telleria, I.; Hemmann, F.; Jäger, C.; Arias, P.L.; Kemnitz, E. Functionalized partially hydroxylated MgF2 as catalysts for the dehydration of d-xylose to furfural. *J. Catal.* **2013**, *305*, 81–91. [CrossRef]
30. Han, J.; Ye, L.; Gu, X.; Zhu, P.; Lu, X. Lignin-based solid acid catalyst for the conversion of cellulose to levulinic acid using γ-valerolactone as solvent. *Ind. Crops Prod.* **2019**, *127*, 88–93. [CrossRef]
31. Li, F.; France, L.J.; Cai, Z.; Li, Y.; Liu, S.; Lou, H.; Long, J.; Li, X. Catalytic transfer hydrogenation of butyl levulinate to Γ-valerolactone over zirconium phosphates with adjustable Lewis and Brønsted acid sites. *Appl. Catal. B Environ.* **2017**, *214*, 67–77. [CrossRef]
32. Guo, H.; Ding, S.; Zhang, H.; Wang, C.; Peng, F.; Xiong, L.; Chen, X.; Ouyang, X. Improvement on the catalytic performances of butyl levulinate hydrogenation to γ-valerolactone over self-regenerated CuNiCoB/Palygorskite catalyst. *Mol. Catal.* **2021**, *504*, 111483. [CrossRef]
33. Delgado, J.; Vasquez Salcedo, W.N.; Bronzetti, G.; Casson Moreno, V.; Mignot, M.; Legros, J.; Held, C.; Grénman, H.; Leveneur, S. Kinetic model assessment for the synthesis of γ-valerolactone from n-butyl levulinate and levulinic acid hydrogenation over the synergy effect of dual catalysts Ru/C and Amberlite IR-120. *Chem. Eng. J.* **2022**, *430*, 133053. [CrossRef]
34. Capecci, S.; Wang, Y.; Casson Moreno, V.; Held, C.; Leveneur, S. Solvent effect on the kinetics of the hydrogenation of n-butyl levulinate to γ-valerolactone. *Chem. Eng. Sci.* **2021**, *231*, 116315. [CrossRef]
35. Wang, Y.; Plazl, I.; Vernières-Hassimi, L.; Leveneur, S. From calorimetry to thermal risk assessment: γ-Valerolactone production from the hydrogenation of alkyl levulinates. *Process Saf. Environ. Prot.* **2020**, *144*, 32–41. [CrossRef]
36. Wang, Y.; Vernières-Hassimi, L.; Casson-Moreno, V.; Hébert, J.P.; Leveneur, S. Thermal Risk Assessment of Levulinic Acid Hydrogenation to γ-Valerolactone. *Org. Process Res. Dev.* **2018**, *22*, 1092–1100. [CrossRef]
37. Fei, Y.; Sun, B.; Zhang, F.; Xu, W.; Shi, N.; Jiang, J. Inherently safer reactors and procedures to prevent reaction runaway. *Chin. J. Chem. Eng.* **2018**, *26*, 1252–1263. [CrossRef]
38. Aguilar-López, R.; Mata-Machuca, J.L.; Godinez-Cantillo, V. A tito control strategy to increase productivity in uncertain exothermic continuous chemical reactors. *Processes* **2021**, *9*, 873. [CrossRef]
39. Abusrafa, A.E.; Challiwala, M.S.; Wilhite, B.A.; Elbashir, N.O. Thermal assessment of a micro fibrous fischer tropsch fixed bed reactor using computational fluid dynamics. *Processes* **2020**, *8*, 1213. [CrossRef]
40. Jayakumar, N.S.; Agrawal, A.; Hashim, M.A.; Sahu, J.N. Experimental and theoretical investigation of parametric sensitivity and dynamics of a continuous stirred tank reactor for acid catalyzed hydrolysis of acetic anhydride. *Comput. Chem. Eng.* **2011**, *35*, 1295–1303. [CrossRef]
41. Gómez García, M.Á.; Dobrosz-Gómez, I.; Ojeda Toro, J.C. Thermal stability and dynamic analysis of the acetic anhydride hydrolysis reaction. *Chem. Eng. Sci.* **2016**, *142*, 269–276. [CrossRef]

42. Nguyen, S.T.; Hoang, N.H.; Hussain, M.A. Analysis of the Steady-State Multiplicity Behavior for Polystyrene Production in the CSTR. *Chem. Prod. Process Model.* **2017**, *12*, 20170027. [CrossRef]
43. Schweitzer, J.M.; López-García, C.; Ferré, D. Thermal runaway analysis of a three-phase reactor for LCO hydrotreatment. *Chem. Eng. Sci.* **2010**, *65*, 313–321. [CrossRef]
44. Wang, Y.; Cipolletta, M.; Vernières-Hassimi, L.; Casson-Moreno, V.; Leveneur, S. Application of the concept of Linear Free Energy Relationships to the hydrogenation of levulinic acid and its corresponding esters. *Chem. Eng. J.* **2019**, *374*, 822–831. [CrossRef]
45. Ariba, H.; Wang, Y.; Devouge-Boyer, C.; Stateva, R.P.; Leveneur, S. Physicochemical Properties for the Reaction Systems: Levulinic Acid, Its Esters, and γ-Valerolactone. *J. Chem. Eng. Data* **2020**, *65*, 3008–3020. [CrossRef]
46. Lu, X.; Wang, Y.; Estel, L.; Kumar, N.; Grénman, H.; Leveneur, S. Evolution of specific heat capacity with temperature for typical supports used for heterogeneous catalysts. *Processes* **2020**, *8*, 911. [CrossRef]
47. Aris, R. On stability criteria of chemical reaction engineering. *Chem. Eng. Sci.* **1969**, *24*, 149–169. [CrossRef]
48. Van Heerden, C. Autothermic Processes. *Ind. Eng. Chem.* **1953**, *45*, 1242–1247. [CrossRef]
49. Kummer, A.; Varga, T. What do we know already about reactor runaway?—A review. *Process Saf. Environ. Prot.* **2021**, *147*, 460–476. [CrossRef]
50. Varma, A.; Morbidelli, M.; Wu, H. *Parametric Sensitivity in Chemical Systems*; Cambridge University Press: Cambridge, UK, 1999; ISBN 0521019842.

Disclaimer/Publisher's Note: The statements, opinions and data contained in all publications are solely those of the individual author(s) and contributor(s) and not of MDPI and/or the editor(s). MDPI and/or the editor(s) disclaim responsibility for any injury to people or property resulting from any ideas, methods, instructions or products referred to in the content.

Article

Estimation of ^{137}Cs Distribution and Recovery Using Various Types of Sorbents in the Black Sea Surface Layer

Nikolay A. Bezhin [1,2,*], Dmitriy A. Kremenchutskii [1], Evgeniy V. Slizchenko [1], Ol'ga N. Kozlovskaia [1], Iuliia G. Shibetskaia [1], Vitaliy V. Milyutin [3] and Ivan G. Tananaev [2,3,4]

[1] Department of Marine Biogeochemistry, Marine Hydrophysical Institute, Russian Academy of Sciences, Kapitanskaya Str., 2, 299011 Sevastopol, Russia
[2] Department of Chemistry and Chemical Engineering, Sevastopol State University, Universitetskaya Str., 33, 299053 Sevastopol, Russia
[3] Frumkin Institute of Physical Chemistry and Electrochemistry, 31 Leninsky Prospect, 4, 119071 Moscow, Russia
[4] Radiochemistry Laboratory, Vernadsky Institute of Geochemistry and Analytical Chemistry of the Russian Academy of Sciences (GEOKHI RAS), Kosygin Str., 19, 119991 Moscow, Russia
* Correspondence: nabezhin@mail.sevsu.ru

Abstract: Monitoring ^{137}Cs in seawater is necessary for the timely detection of radioactive contamination. The possibility of sorption and the sorption efficiency of ^{137}Cs from seawater were studied for the first time during several cruises of the R/V (research vessel) Professor Vodyanitsky using various types of sorbents based on transition metal ferrocyanides (Anfezh, Niket, Uniket, FSS, FD-M, FIC, Termoxid 35, NKF-C) and zirconium phosphate (Termoxid 3A). The influence of the seawater flow rate and volume of the sorbent used for the recovery of ^{137}Cs was estimated. The ferrocyanide sorbents Niket, Uniket, Termoxid 35, and FIC showed the best sorption efficiency (60–100%) at a seawater flow rate of 2–4 column volumes per minute. The data obtained during three cruises on the R/V Professor Vodyanitsky were analyzed. A detailed (28 sampling points) spatial distribution of ^{137}Cs in the Black Sea along the southern coast of Crimea was studied using the sorbents that showed the best characteristics. An increase in ^{137}Cs activity in the study area was not found, and the average activity was 9.01 ± 0.87 Bq/m^3.

Keywords: ^{137}Cs; seawater; sorbents; sorption; Black Sea; ferrocyanide sorbents

Citation: Bezhin, N.A.; Kremenchutskii, D.A.; Slizchenko, E.V.; Kozlovskaia, O.N.; Shibetskaia, I.G.; Milyutin, V.V.; Tananaev, I.G. Estimation of ^{137}Cs Distribution and Recovery Using Various Types of Sorbents in the Black Sea Surface Layer. Processes 2023, 11, 603. https://doi.org/10.3390/pr11020603

Academic Editor: Antoni Sánchez

Received: 25 January 2023
Revised: 14 February 2023
Accepted: 15 February 2023
Published: 16 February 2023

Copyright: © 2023 by the authors. Licensee MDPI, Basel, Switzerland. This article is an open access article distributed under the terms and conditions of the Creative Commons Attribution (CC BY) license (https://creativecommons.org/licenses/by/4.0/).

1. Introduction

The problem of marine ecosystem pollution is given considerable attention all over the world [1].

The constant monitoring of marine areas for technogenic radionuclides and other pollutants is necessary to identify the sources of pollutants in time to prevent negative impacts on living organisms.

One of the consequences of the accident at the Chornobyl nuclear power plant (26 April 1986) is the contamination of the Black Sea with technogenic radionuclides, the main of which is ^{137}Cs, with a half-life of approximately 30 years.

Information about ^{137}Cs content in seawater is needed to determine its accumulation coefficients in hydrobionts. ^{137}Cs, having similar properties to potassium, accumulates in muscle tissue.

The distribution of ^{137}Cs after the Chornobyl disaster was studied in many expeditions. The main works discussing the results of expeditionary studies include the research conducted by K.O. Buesseler et al. [2] and V.N. Egorov et al. [3]. Staneva et al. [4] performed a mathematical modeling of ^{137}Cs distribution, and the current state of the issue was described in several articles by S. Gulin et al. [5,6] and R. Delfanti et al. [7]. Many methods for the radioanalytical determination of ^{137}Cs have been developed [8]. Currently, improved sorption materials are being developed worldwide. For cesium recovery, many sorbents based on potassium [9,10] and calcium [11] aluminosilicates, as well as ferrocyanides with various supporting materials (polyacrylonitrile fiber [12], zeolite [13,14], silica gel [15], etc.), have been synthesized.

While copper hexacyanoferrate was used in some of the first studies on the recovery of ^{137}Cs from seawater [16], at present, mixed nickel–potassium hexacyanoferrate on an acrylate support KFeNiCN-PAN [17] is more widely used. The fiber impregnated with hexacyanoferrate has a developed specific surface, which increases the speed and efficiency of the extraction of radionuclides from seawater; therefore, this type of material can be considered the most promising. At the same time, the high sorption efficiency of ^{137}Cs from seawater is shown by sorbents based on cellulose support and silica gel, for example, a Russian-made sorbent of the FSS [18].

Sorption materials intended for the recovery, concentration, and isolation of ^{137}Cs from radioactively contaminated seawater are of considerable interest [19], for example, resorcinol–formaldehyde resin [20]. Its advantage is the possibility of repeated use after elution and regeneration. Another option is chitosan–ferrocyanide sorbents [21]. They were successfully tested under expeditionary conditions during radioecological monitoring of the Barents and Kara Seas. These sorbents also show a high sorption efficiency for ^{137}Cs [22].

This paper continues the work performed in a series of articles [18,22–24] devoted to the recovery of cesium, including ^{137}Cs, from seawater by various types of sorbents based on transition metal ferrocyanides (Anfezh, Niket, Uniket, FSS, FD-M, Termoxid 35, NKF-C, FIC), resorcinol–formaldehyde polymer (Axionit RCs), and zirconium phosphate (Termoxid 3A).

In previous articles, we determined the distribution coefficients for cesium and plotted output sorption curves for different seawater flow rates. The dynamic exchange capacity (DEC) and total dynamic exchange capacity (TDEC) of sorbents were determined [22,23]. A study was performed on the physicochemical regularities (isotherm and kinetics) of cesium sorption from seawater. The obtained dependences of the sorption parameters on time were described using the models of intraparticle diffusion; the pseudo-first and pseudo-second orders, the Elovich model, the dependence of sorption parameters on the equilibrium concentration of the metal in the solution; and the Langmuir, Freundlich, and Dubinin–Raduskevich sorption isotherms [24].

The purpose of this study was to evaluate the sorption efficiency of ^{137}Cs by various types of sorbents to select the most effective sorbents and develop a technique for ^{137}Cs recovery from seawater, allowing us to analyze the current radioecological state of the Black Sea, namely its ^{137}Cs contamination after the Chornobyl disaster.

A systematic assessment of the distribution of ^{137}Cs is necessary to identify fresh sources of this radionuclide. In the absence of a fresh source, the distribution of ^{137}Cs in the surface layer is homogeneous [18] because this radionuclide is practically not adsorbed onto suspended matter. Therefore, when assessing the distribution of ^{137}Cs, it is necessary to indicate the time parameters and number of research cruises. This will make it possible to compare the results of ^{137}Cs distribution obtained in different time intervals and identify possible changes.

This paper presents the results of three expedition studies: the 113 (4–29 June 2020), 116 (22 April–17 May 2021), and 121 (19 April–14 May 2022) cruises of the R/V Professor Vodyanitsky. Sorbents that showed the best characteristics for cesium recovery, including ^{137}Cs, from seawater under laboratory conditions were selected for expeditionary studies [18,22–24].

2. Materials and Methods

2.1. Sorbents

Commercially available sorbents based on transition metal ferrocyanides (Anfezh, Niket, Uniket, FSS, FD-M, FIC, Termoxid 35, NKF-C), and zirconium phosphate (Termoxid 3A) were used to recover ^{137}Cs from seawater. Table 1 provides their characteristics.

Table 1. Characteristics of sorbents used to recover ^{137}Cs from seawater.

Sorbent; Technical Conditions (TC)[1]	Manufacturer	View	Granulation, mm	Bulk Density, g/mL	Sorbent Composition		Reference
					Support	Sorption-Active Phase: Content, Mass %	
Anfezh; TC 2165-003-26301393-99	SPE Eksorb Ltd. (Yekaterinburg, Russia)	blue irregular granules	0.1–1.0	0.25–0.4	cellulose	ferric potassium ferrocyanide; not less than 10	[25–27]
Niket; TC 2165-008-26301393-2005		green irregular granules	0.1–2.5	0.5–0.7	cellulose	nickel potassium ferrocyanide; not less than 10	[23,28]
Uniket; TC 2165-012-26301393-2010		dark-blue irregular granules	0.1–2.5	0.8–1.2	cellulose	ferric potassium ferrocyanide; not less than 10	[23,29]
FSS; TC 2641-012-57989206-2012	Frumkin IPCE RAS (Moscow, Russia)	green irregular granules	0.2–3.0	0.5–0.6	silica gel	nickel potassium ferrocyanide; 8–10	[18]
FD-M; TC 2641-019-57983206-2012		brown irregular granules	0.5–1.0	0.1–0.2	phosphorylated wood	copper potassium ferrocyanide; 5.0–5.5	[23,30]
FIC; laboratory sample		blue irregular granules	0.1–1.0	0.25–0.4	activated carbon	iron ferrocyanide; not less than 10	–
Termoxid 35; TC 2641-006-12342266-2004	JSC "Inorganic Sorbents" (Zarechny, Sverdlovsk region, Russia)	dark-green spherical granules	0.4–1.5	1.1–1.2	zirconium hydroxide	nickel potassium ferrocyanide; 30–35	[31–33]
Termoxid 3A; TC 2641-004-12342266-2004		white spherical granules	0.4–1.0	1.05–1.10	–	zirconium phosphate	[33]
NKF-C	UrFU (Yekaterinburg, Russia)	light-brown irregular granules	0.2–0.6	0.25–0.4	cellulose	nickel potassium ferrocyanide; not less than 10	[6]

[1] Technical conditions (TC) are issued as a document establishing technical requirements that a specific product, material, substance, or group must conform with. They also specify the procedures to determine whether those requirements have been met.

2.2. Seawater Sampling

Water samples from the sea surface layer (up to 3 m) were taken at various stations during cruises 113 (4–29 June 2020), 116 (22 April–17 May 2021), and 121 (19 April–14 May 2022) of the R/V Professor Vodyanitsky along the southern coast of Crimea in the Black and Azov Seas.

Samples were taken using a Unipump Bavlenets BV 0.12-40-U5 submersible vibration pump (Subline Service LLC, Moscow, Russia), pumped through a polypropylene filter with a pore size of 1 μm FCPS1M series (Aquafilter Europe Ltd., Lodz, Poland), which served to remove suspended particles from the water, after which the samples filled plastic containers with a volume of 250 L located on board the vessel.

2.3. Sorption of ^{137}Cs

Sorption of ^{137}Cs was carried out by a single-column method by passing 250 L of seawater from a tank using a LongerPump WT600-2J peristaltic pump (Longer Precision Pump Co., Baoding, China) through a column filled with 50 or 100 mL of the sorbent (Figure 1).

To evaluate the yield in the seawater sample, stable cesium was added as a tracer at a concentration of 2.5 mg/L. In the process of sorption, every 10–20 L, samples of the passed seawater were taken into plastic test tubes for further evaluation of the yield.

After elution, the sorbent was squeezed out to remove excess seawater and dried in a SNOL-3.5.5.3.5/3.5-I2 oven (LLC "NPF TermIKS", Moscow, Russia) at a temperature of 70–80 °C.

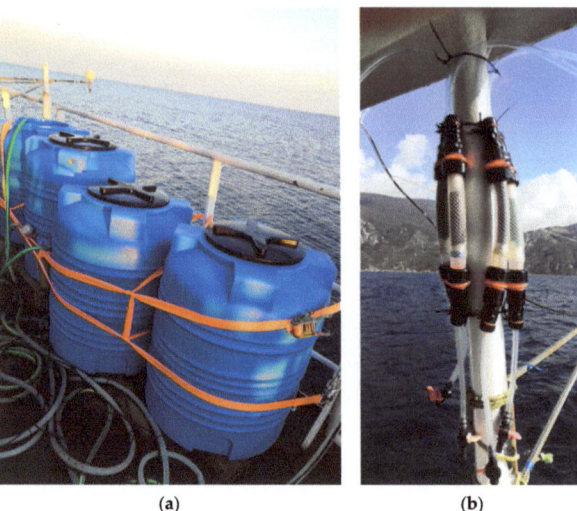

Figure 1. Sorption of ^{137}Cs from seawater: (**a**) sampling barrels; (**b**) columns with sorbents.

2.4. Determination of ^{137}Cs Activity in Sorbent Samples

Measurement of the specific activity of ^{137}Cs in sorbent samples was carried out in Petri dishes on a low-background spectrometric setup MKS-01A "MULTIRAD" (LLC "NTC Amplitude", Zelenograd, Russia) with a gamma spectrometric tract "MULTIRAD-gamma" with a NaI(Tl) scintillation detector (diameter 63 mm, height 63 mm, resolution 7% for ^{137}Cs peak, MDA (Minimum Detectable Activity) was 0.47 Bq/m^3). Spectrometric data were registered and processed using the Progress software on the operational system Windows 10. The time for recording the activity of a single sample averaged 24 h. The efficiency of recording ^{137}Cs activity in the samples was calibrated using a certified source with a known specific activity. The error in measuring the activity of each sample (σ) usually did not exceed 10%. The spectra of sorbents after cesium recovery are shown in Figure S1 in the supplementary materials.

2.5. Determination of Cesium Concentration

The concentration of stable cesium to evaluate output was determined on a KVANT-2 atomic absorption spectrophotometer (LLC "Kortek", Moscow, Russia) in an air–acetylene flame in the emission mode at a wavelength of 852.1 nm. The sorption efficiency (*E*, %) of ^{137}Cs from seawater was calculated from stable cesium using the formula [34,35]:

$$E = \frac{V \cdot C_0 - \sum V_p \cdot C_p}{V \cdot C_0} \cdot 100\%, \tag{1}$$

where C_0 is the initial cesium concentration, mg/L; V is the total volume of seawater passed through the sorbent, L; C_p is the cesium concentration in a portion of seawater passed through the sorbent, mg/L; and V_p is the volume of a portion of seawater passed through the sorbent, L.

3. Results and Discussion

3.1. Evaluation of the Sorption Efficiency of ^{137}Cs by Various Sorbents

The possibility and efficiency of ^{137}Cs sorption from seawater by various types of sorbents were studied during cruises 113 (4–29 June 2020) and 116 (22 April–17 May 2021) of the R/V Professor Vodyanitsky.

Table 2 shows the results of our study on the influence of the sorbent volume on the sorption efficiency of ^{137}Cs. We found that the sorption efficiency of ^{137}Cs increased with an increase in the volume of the sorbent, which is associated with an increase in the contact area of the phases. So, for example, when using 50 mL of the FIC sorbent, the sorption efficiency is 60%, and when using 100 mL, it is 91.6%.

Table 2. Dependence of sorption efficiency (E, %) of ^{137}Cs on volume (mass) of sorbent (seawater flow rate 4 CV/min (column volumes per minute)).

Sorbent	Niket	Uniket	Termoxid 35	FIC	FSS	Anfezh	NKF-C	FD-M	Termoxid 3A
Sorbent volume V, mL	50	50	50	50	50	50	50	50	50
Mass of sorbent m, g	46.5	34.5	60.0	17.5	28.6	15.0	13.0	13.0	56.5
Sorption efficiency E, %	93.0	78.9	67.4	60.0	27.3	26.0	16.3	16.1	5.44
Sorbent volume V, mL	100	100	100	100	100	100	100	100	100
Mass of sorbent m, g	93.0	69.0	120	35.0	57.2	30.0	26.0	26.0	113
Sorption efficiency E, %	99.3	94.8	96.5	91.6	42.1	41.7	23.2	22.5	8.07

The same volumes of sorbents were compared; however, the studied sorbents have different bulk densities and, accordingly, different masses. Tables 1 and 2 show that sorbents with a lower bulk density (Anfezh, FD-M, FSS, NKF-C) have a lower cesium sorption efficiency due to their lower mass and, accordingly, a smaller phase contact area.

The exceptions are the Termoxid 3A sorbent, which, despite its high bulk density, shows a low cesium sorption efficiency, and the FIC sorbent, which, despite its low bulk density, shows a high cesium sorption efficiency. This can be explained by the high availability of sorption centers due to the developed porous structure of activated carbon, which supports the FIC sorbent.

Cesium sorption mechanisms are as follows:

- Sorbents based on transition metal ferrocyanides (Anfezh, Niket, Uniket, FSS, FD-M, FIC, Termoxid 35, NKF-C) [22,36]:

$$n\text{Cs}^+ + \text{K}_{1.33}\text{Me}^{II}{}_{1.33}[\text{Fe(CN)}_6] = n\text{K}^+ + \text{K}_{1.33-n}\text{Cs}_n\text{Me}^{II}{}_{1.33}[\text{Fe(CN)}_6],$$

- Sorbents based on zirconium phosphate (Termoxid 3A) [22,37]:

$$2n\text{Cs}^+ + \text{Zr(HPO}_4)_2 \, m\text{H}_2\text{O} = 2n\text{H}^+ + \text{Zr(Cs}_n\text{H}_{1-n}\text{PO}_4)_2 \, m\text{H}_2\text{O}.$$

There is no direct relationship between the mechanisms and sorption efficiency. The sorption efficiency is determined by the sorbents' capacities up to breakthrough and saturation, which depend on the sorption kinetics. The parameters for the studied sorbents were determined in our previous articles [23,24].

Figure 2 shows the effect of the seawater flow rate on the sorption efficiency of ^{137}Cs with 50 mL of sorbents.

The sorption efficiency of ^{137}Cs decreases with an increase in the flow rate due to a decrease in the contact time between seawater and the sorbent. Therefore, at a speed of 2 CV/min, 100 mL of seawater is passed through 50 mL of sorbent in 1 min, and at a speed of 8 CV/min, 400 mL of seawater is passed; therefore, the sorption efficiency decreases.

The optimum flow rate of seawater for the studied sorbents is 2–4 CV/min. For this range of rates, the ferrocyanide sorbents Niket, Uniket, Termoxid 35, and FIC have the best sorption efficiency (60–100%), while the sorption efficiency of ^{137}Cs by other sorbents is less than 30%.

A considerable technical task under expeditionary conditions is to achieve high-speed seawater percolation through a fixed sorbent bed to reduce the analysis time. This requirement is best met by the Uniket, FSS, and FIC sorbents with coarse grains. The use of highly dispersed sorbents, such as Anfezh, becomes difficult with an increase in the percolation speed [23,24].

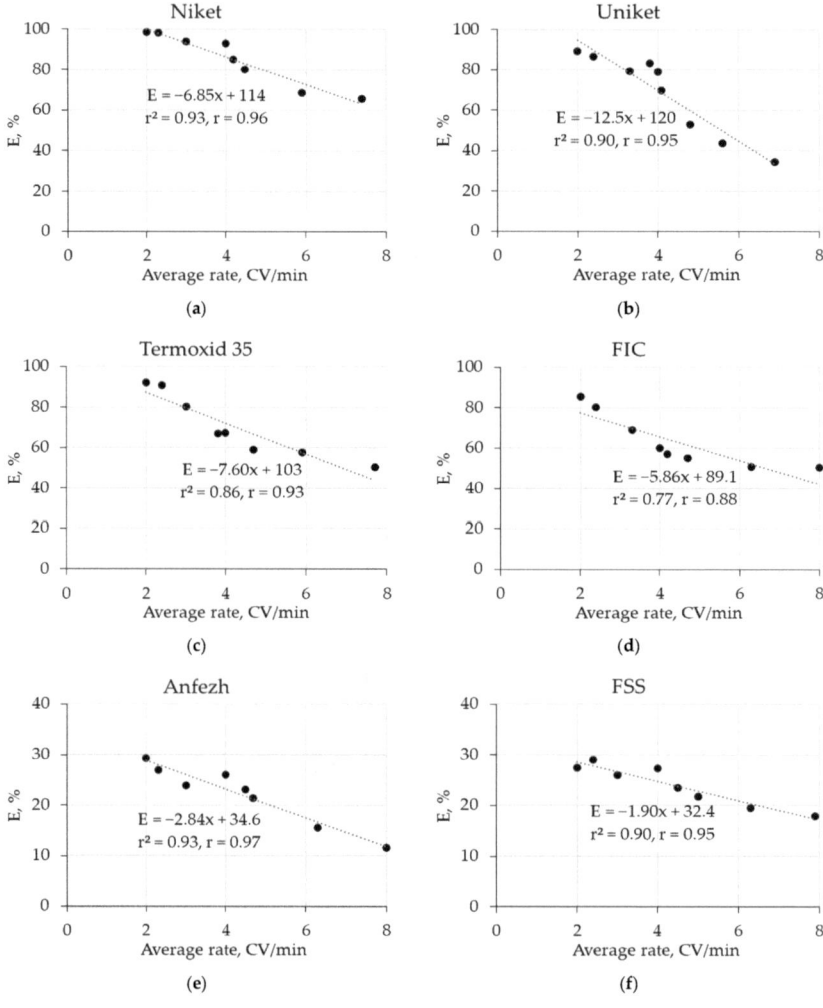

Figure 2. Cont.

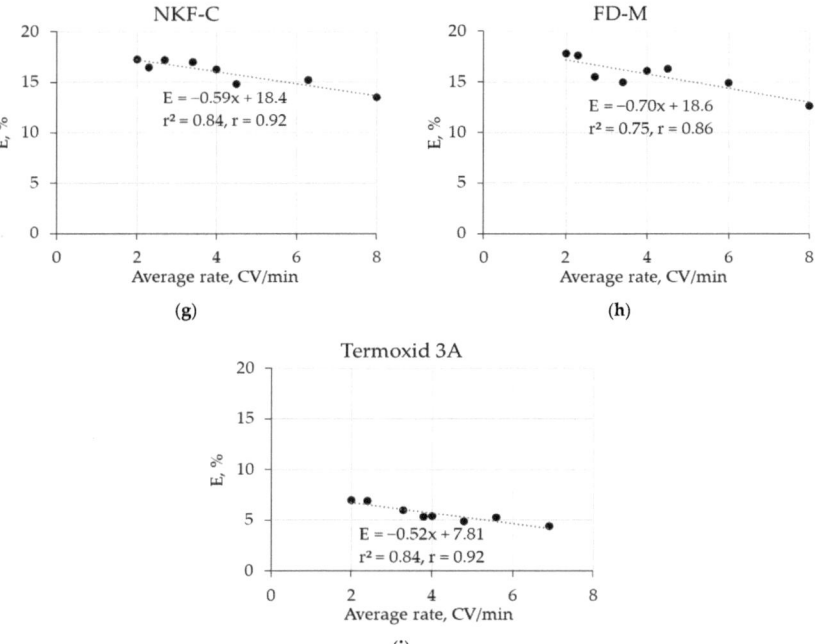

Figure 2. Dependence of sorption efficiency (E, %) of ^{137}Cs on average rate of passage of seawater by sorbents: (**a**) Niket; (**b**) Uniket; (**c**) Termoxid 35; (**d**) FIC; (**e**) Anfezh; (**f**) FSS; (**g**) NKF-C; (**h**) FD-M; (**i**) Termoxid 3A (volume of sorbents—50 mL; the volume of seawater—250 L).

Based on the results obtained, we developed a procedure for recovering ^{137}Cs from seawater using commercially available ferrocyanide sorbents (Figure 3):

1. Pump 250 L of seawater into a container on board the vessel while simultaneously filtering seawater through a polypropylene filter with a pore diameter of 1 µm;
2. Add a sample of cesium nitrate to the seawater in the container to a concentration of 2–3 mg/L of cesium to assess the sorption efficiency, then leave for 5–6 h to equalize the concentration of cesium in the entire volume of the container;
3. Load 50 mL of Niket, Uniket, Termoxid 35, FIC sorbent, or 100 mL of FSS or Anfezh sorbent into the column;
4. Pass 250 L of prepared seawater through the column with the sorbent at a speed of 2–4 CV/min;
5. Periodically (every 10–20 L), take a sample of seawater passed through the sorbent to assess the sorption efficiency of stable cesium;
6. After sorption, dry the sorbent in an oven at a temperature of 70–80 °C and place it in a Petri dish;
7. Determine the activity of ^{137}Cs in the sorbent on a scintillation gamma spectrometer with an exposure of at least 24 h to achieve a measurement error of no more than 10%.

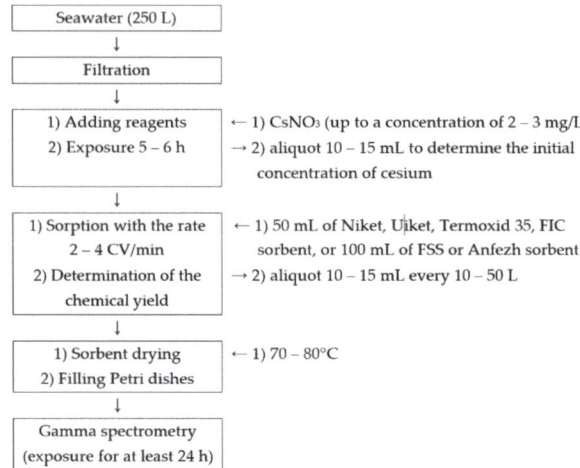

Figure 3. Scheme of method developed for ^{137}Cs sorption.

This technique is applied in further studies on the concentration of ^{137}Cs from seawater.

Figure 4 shows the values of the specific activity of ^{137}Cs in the surface layer of the Black and Azov Seas, which were obtained by studying the sorption efficiency during cruises 113 and 116 of the R/V Professor Vodyanitsky. Increased values of ^{137}Cs activity are observed in the western part of the study area due to the proximity of the source of entry—the Dnieper River (Ukraine) [38].

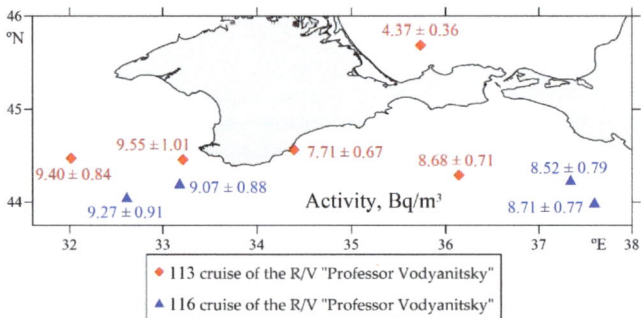

Figure 4. Specific activity values of ^{137}Cs (Bq/m^3) in surface layer of Black and Azov Seas (along the southern coast of Crimea), obtained during cruises 113 (4–29 June 2020) and 116 (22 April–17 May 2021) of R/V Professor Vodyanitsky.

3.2. Surface Distribution of ^{137}Cs in the Black Sea in Spring 2022

To analyze the current radioecological state of the Black Sea, including its contamination with ^{137}Cs after the Chornobyl accident, an analysis of ^{137}Cs concentration was carried out by the developed method presented above. The sorbents that showed the best parameters of sorption efficiency of ^{137}Cs during cruises 113 and 116 of the R/V Professor Vodyanitsky were used. During cruise 121 of the R/V Professor Vodyanitsky

(19 April–14 May 2022), 28 seawater samples were taken and processed at 28 stations. The layout of the stations is shown in Figure 5.

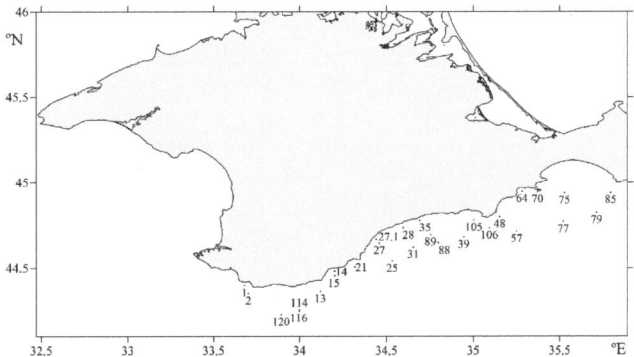

Figure 5. Location of sampling stations during cruise 121 (19 April–14 May 2022) of R/V Professor Vodyanitsky (along the southern coast of Crimea, stations numbering during the cruise retained).

Table 3 shows the results obtained.

Table 3. Parameters of samples and stations during study of the distribution of ^{137}Cs in cruise 121 (19 April–14 May 2022) of R/V Professor Vodyanitsky.

Station Number	Coordinates of Sampling Points		Sorbent	E, %	A_{sp} ^{137}Cs, Bq/m^3
	Northern Latitude	Eastern Longitude			
1	44.39808	33.67864	Termoxid 35	67.3	8.73 ± 0.89
2	44.35120	33.70265	Uniket	69.8	8.73 ± 0.88
13	44.36246	34.12065	Termoxid 35	82.1	9.75 ± 0.79
14	44.48178	34.20170	Uniket	78.7	10.0 ± 0.98
15	44.45617	34.20333	FIC	64.4	9.50 ± 0.95
21	44.50590	34.31795	FIC	69.2	9.62 ± 1.27
25	44.54041	34.53309	Termoxid 35	79.9	9.04 ± 1.07
27	44.64467	34.45784	FIC	64.0	9.06 ± 0.94
27.1	44.66783	34.43950	Niket	95.0	8.41 ± 0.79
28	44.73593	34.59710	FIC	56.5	8.57 ± 0.83
31	44.62115	34.65419	Termoxid 35	79.8	9.13 ± 0.75
35	44.77496	34.69233	FIC	63.5	7.60 ± 0.86
39	44.67979	34.94443	Niket	93.8	9.12 ± 0.96
48	44.79867	35.15200	Termoxid 35	80.1	8.85 ± 0.75
57	44.71315	35.24935	FIC	66.5	7.33 ± 0.68
64	44.94662	35.28064	Uniket	75.0	8.62 ± 0.81
70	44.94445	35.36925	FIC	66.9	9.21 ± 1.01
75	44.93706	35.52754	Termoxid 35	78.1	9.03 ± 0.75
77	44.77019	35.52102	FIC	64.8	9.03 ± 0.92
79	44.82319	35.71791	Niket	92.7	8.62 ± 0.83
85	44.93957	35.80088	FIC	59.3	9.66 ± 0.90
88	44.64783	34.79639	Termoxid 35	80.3	9.09 ± 0.80
89	44.69392	34.75217	FIC	64.3	10.4 ± 0.91
105	44.77917	35.00317	Termoxid 35	76.2	9.69 ± 0.84
106	44.73351	35.09265	Termoxid 35	73.5	9.09 ± 0.85
114	44.25389	33.99746	FIC	55.7	9.07 ± 0.76
116	44.24846	33.99762	Termoxid 35	78.4	9.07 ± 0.82
120	44.22626	33.89136	FIC	59.5	8.28 ± 0.78

Figure 6 shows the distribution of ^{137}Cs in the surface layer of the Black Sea along the southern coast of Crimea. The value of ^{137}Cs activity varied over space in the range of 7.33–10.4 Bq/m^3 and averaged 9.01 ± 0.87 Bq/m^3. Thus, the spatial variability of the cesium concentration field in the study area was within the error range of the method for determining this parameter.

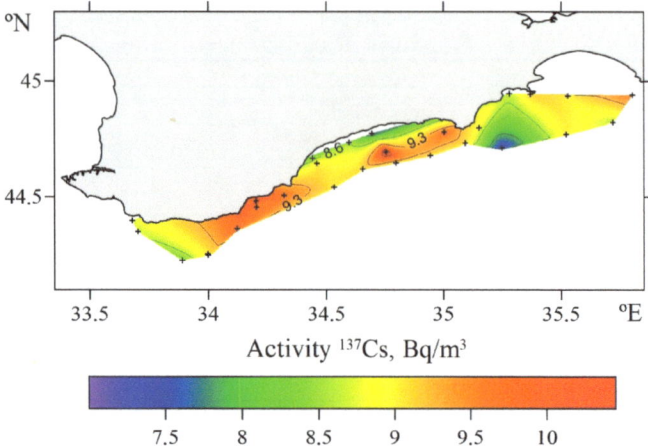

Figure 6. Distribution of ^{137}Cs in surface layer of Black Sea (along the southern coast of Crimea), obtained during cruise 121 (19 April–14 May 2022) of R/V Professor Vodyanitsky.

According to the literature data, ^{137}Cs activity in the Black Sea was 20.0 ± 1.1 Bq/m^3 in 2007 [7], 17.1 ± 0.9 Bq/m^3 in 2013 [6], and 14.4 ± 1.3 Bq/m^3 in 2015 [39]. The data obtained are consistent with the published data [6,7,39], taking into account the half-life for the decrease in ^{137}Cs inventory, which, according to [38], is 8.6 years for the period 1987–2011. The decrease in ^{137}Cs activity in the surface layer of the Black Sea is associated with its radioactive decay and penetration into the underlying layers [38]. Thus, an increase in ^{137}Cs activity in the study area was not determined.

During cruise 121, a limited area of the Black Sea along the southern coast of Crimea was available for study; the sampling and measurement of samples were not carried out at the western part of the Black Sea, where elevated values of ^{137}Cs activity are usually observed due to the proximity of the source of cesium, the Dnieper River (Ukraine) [38].

According to the Radiation Safety Norms–99/2009 [40] of Russia, the allowable concentrations (intervention levels) of ^{137}Cs in seawater are 11 Bq/L; therefore, the current levels of ^{137}Cs in the surface water of the Black Sea are below the maximum allowable.

4. Conclusions

Systematic monitoring of ^{137}Cs content in seawater is necessary for the timely detection of sources of radioactive contamination entering the environment, allowing for decision makers to take measures to prevent negative impacts on living organisms.

The possibility of ^{137}Cs recovery from seawater and its sorption efficiency were studied using various types of sorbents based on transition metal ferrocyanides (Anfezh, Niket, Uniket, FSS, FD-M, Termoxid 35, NKF-C, FIC) and zirconium phosphate (Termoxid 3A). We found that the sorption efficiency of ^{137}Cs decreased with an increase in the flow rate due to a decrease in the contact time of seawater with the sorbent. The optimum flow rate of seawater for the studied sorbents is 2–4 CV/min. The ferrocyanide sorbents Niket, Uniket, Termoxid 35, and FIC showed the best sorption efficiency (60–100%). Based on the results obtained, a procedure was developed for recovering ^{137}Cs from seawater.

To analyze the current radioecological state of the Black Sea, namely its contamination with ^{137}Cs after the Chornobyl accident, in the spring of 2022, the spatial distribution of ^{137}Cs in the Black Sea along the southern coast of Crimea was studied using the developed methodology and sorbents that showed the best characteristics. The value of ^{137}Cs activity varied over space in the range of 7.33–10.4 Bq/m^3 and averaged 9.01 ± 0.87 Bq/m^3. The data obtained are consistent with the literature data, taking into account the half-life for the decrease in ^{137}Cs inventory; an increase in ^{137}Cs activity in the study area was not found. The current levels of ^{137}Cs in the surface water of the Black Sea are below the maximum allowable level.

Further research is needed in the coastal ecosystems of the Black Sea, which are accumulators of anthropogenic radionuclides.

Supplementary Materials: The following supporting information can be downloaded at: https://www.mdpi.com/article/10.3390/pr11020603/s1, Figure S1: Spectra of sorbents after cesium recovery.

Author Contributions: Conceptualization, N.A.B. and I.G.T.; methodology, N.A.B.; validation, N.A.B., D.A.K., and V.V.M.; formal analysis, O.N.K. and D.A.K.; investigation, N.A.B., I.G.S., and E.V.S.; resources, N.A.B., D.A.K., and V.V.M.; data curation, E.V.S., I.G.S., and O.N.K.; writing—original draft preparation, N.A.B., D.A.K., V.V.M., and I.G.T.; writing—review and editing, all authors; visualization, N.A.B. and O.N.K.; supervision, I.G.T.; project administration, N.A.B.; funding acquisition, N.A.B. and I.G.T. All authors have read and agreed to the published version of the manuscript.

Funding: The purchase of sorbents and evaluation of the sorption efficiency of ^{137}Cs was carried out with the financial support of the Russian Foundation for Basic Research within the framework of project No. 19-33-60007 (competition "Perspective"). The collection and measurement of large-volume samples was carried out within the framework of the state task of the Ministry of Science and Higher Education of the Russian Federation (topic "Oceanological processes» No. FNNN-2021-0004). The distribution of ^{137}Cs was studied within the framework of Sevastopol State University project No. 42-01-09/169/2021-7.

Institutional Review Board Statement: Not applicable.

Informed Consent Statement: Not applicable.

Data Availability Statement: Not applicable.

Acknowledgments: The authors are grateful to Illarion I. Dovhyi for valuable advice in writing the article.

Conflicts of Interest: The authors declare no conflict of interest.

References

1. Kotelyanets, E.A.; Gurov, K.I.; Tikhonova, E.A.; Kondratev, S.I. Pollutants in Bottom Sediments in the Balaklava Bay (the Black Sea). *Phys. Oceanogr.* **2019**, *26*, 414–424. [CrossRef]
2. Buesseler, K.O.; Livingston, H.D. Time-Series Profiles of ^{134}CS, ^{137}CS and ^{90}SR in the Black Sea. In *Sensitivity to Change: Black Sea, Baltic Sea and North Sea. NATO ASI Series (Series 2: Environment)*; Özsoy, E., Mikaelyan, A., Eds.; Springer: Dordrecht, The Netherlands, 1997; Volume 27, pp. 239–251. [CrossRef]
3. Egorov, V.N.; Povinec, P.P.; Polikarpov, G.G.; Stokozov, N.A.; Gulin, S.B.; Kulebakina, L.G.; Osvath, I. ^{90}Sr and ^{137}Cs in the Black Sea after the Chernobyl NPP accident: Inventories, balance and tracer applications. *J. Environ. Radioact.* **1999**, *43*, 137–155. [CrossRef]
4. Staneva, J.V.; Buesseler, K.O.; Stanev, E.V.; Livingston, H.D. The application of radiotracers to a study of Black Sea circulation: Validation of numerical simulations against observed weapons testing and Chernobyl ^{137}Cs data. *J. Geophys. Res.* **1999**, *104*, 11099–11114. [CrossRef]
5. Gulin, S.B.; Mirzoyeva, N.Y.; Egorov, V.N.; Polikarpov, G.G.; Sidorov, I.G.; Proskurnin, V.Y. Secondary radioactive contamination of the Black Sea after Chernobyl accident: Recent levels, pathways and trends. *J. Environ. Radioact.* **2013**, *124*, 50–56. [CrossRef] [PubMed]
6. Gulin, S.B.; Egorov, V.N.; Duka, M.S.; Sidorov, I.G.; Proskurnin, V.Y.; Mirzoyeva, N.Y.; Bey, O.N.; Gulina, L.V. Deep-water profiling of ^{137}Cs and ^{90}Sr in the Black Sea. A further insight into dynamics of the post-Chernobyl radioactive contamination. *J. Radioanal. Nucl. Chem.* **2015**, *304*, 779–783. [CrossRef]
7. Delfanti, R.; Özsoy, E.; Kaberi, H.; Schirone, A.; Salvi, S.; Conte, F.; Tsabaris, C.; Papucci, C. Evolution and fluxes of ^{137}Cs in the Black Sea/Turkish Straits System/North Aegean Sea. *J. Mar. Syst.* **2014**, *135*, 117–123. [CrossRef]

8. Lehto, J.; Hou, X. *Chemistry and Analysis of Radionuclides. Laboratory Techniques and Methodology*; Wiley-VCH: Weinheim, Germany, 2011; 426p.
9. Yarusova, S.B.; Shichalin, O.O.; Belov, A.A.; Azon, S.A.; Buravlev, I.Y.; Golub, A.V.; Mayorov, V.Y.; Gerasimenko, A.V.; Papynov, E.K.; Ivanets, A.I.; et al. Synthesis of amorphous $KAlSi_3O_8$ for cesium radionuclide immobilization into solid matrices using spark plasma sintering technique. *Ceram. Int.* **2021**, *48*, 3808–3817. [CrossRef]
10. Ohara, E.; Soejima, T.; Ito, S. Removal of low concentration Cs(I) from water using Prussian blue. *Inorg. Chim. Acta* **2021**, *514*, 120029. [CrossRef]
11. Le, Q.T.N.; Cho, K. Caesium adsorption on a zeolitic imidazolate framework (ZIF-8) functionalized by ferrocyanide. *J. Colloid Interface Sci.* **2021**, *581*, 741–750. [CrossRef]
12. El-Shazly, E.A.A.; Dakroury, G.A.; Someda, H.H. Sorption of ^{134}Cs radionuclide onto insoluble ferrocyanide loaded silica-gel. *J. Radioanal. Nucl. Chem.* **2021**, *329*, 437–449. [CrossRef]
13. Bondar, Y.; Olkhovyk, O.; Kuzenko, S. Nanocomposite adsorbent based on polyacrylonitrile fibers for rapid and selective removal of Cs radionuclides. *J. Radioanal. Nucl. Chem.* **2021**, *330*, 1221–1231. [CrossRef]
14. Gordienko, P.S.; Yarusova, S.B.; Shabalin, I.A.; Slobodyuk, A.B.; Nekhlyudova, E.A.; Shichalin, O.O.; Papynov, E.K.; Kuryavyi, V.G.; Polyakova, N.V.; Parot'kina, Y.A. Synthesis of Calcium Aluminosilicates from Nanostructured Synthetic Na Zeolites and Study of Their Sorption Properties. *Russ. J. Inorg. Chem.* **2022**, *67*, 1393–1399. [CrossRef]
15. Panasenko, A.E.; Shichalin, O.O.; Yarusova, S.B.; Ivanets, A.I.; Belov, A.A.; Dran'kov, A.N.; Azon, S.A.; Fedorets, A.N.; Buravlev, I.Y.; Mayorov, V.Y.; et al. A novel approach for rice straw agricultural waste utilization: Synthesis of solid aluminosilicate matrices for cesium immobilization. *Nucl. Eng. Technol.* **2022**, *54*, 3250–3259. [CrossRef]
16. Mann, D.R.; Casso, S.A. In situ chemisorption of radiocesium from seawater. *Mar. Chem.* **1984**, *14*, 307–318. [CrossRef]
17. Breier, C.F.; Pike, S.M.; Sebesta, F.; Tradd, K.; Breier, J.A.; Buesseler, K.O. New applications of KNiFC-PAN resin for broad scale monitoring of radiocesium following the Fukushima Dai-ichi nuclear distaster. *J. Radioanal. Nucl. Chem.* **2016**, *307*, 2193–2200. [CrossRef]
18. Dovhyi, I.I.; Kremenchutskii, D.A.; Bezhin, N.A.; Kozlovskaia, O.N.; Milyutin, V.V.; Kozlitin, E.A. Distribution of ^{137}Cs in the Surface Mixed Layer of the Black Sea in summer 2017. *Phys. Oceanol.* **2020**, *36*, 387–396. [CrossRef]
19. Avramenko, V.A.; Egorin, A.M.; Papynov, E.K.; Sokol'nitskaya, T.A.; Tananaev, I.G.; Sergienko, V.I. Processes for treatment of liquid radioactive waste containing seawater. *Radiochemistry* **2017**, *59*, 407–413. [CrossRef]
20. Egorin, A.M.; Palamarchuk, M.S.; Tokar', E.A.; Tutov, M.V.; Azarova, Y.A.; Tananaev, I.G.; Avramenko, V.A. Sorption of ^{137}Cs from seawater onto resorcinol–formaldehyde resin. *Radiochemistry* **2017**, *59*, 160–165. [CrossRef]
21. Egorin, A.; Tokar, E.; Zemskova, L.; Didenko, N.; Portnyagin, A.; Azarova, Y.; Palamarchuk, M.; Tananaev, I.; Avramenko, V. Chitosan-ferrocyanide sorbents for concentrating Cs-137 from seawater. *Sep. Sci. Technol.* **2017**, *52*, 1983–1991. [CrossRef]
22. Dovhyi, I.I.; Bezhin, N.A.; Tananaev, I.G. Sorption methods in marine radiochemistry. *Russ. Chem. Rev.* **2021**, *90*, 1544–1565. [CrossRef]
23. Bezhin, N.A.; Dovhyi, I.I.; Milyutin, V.V.; Kaptakov, V.O.; Kozlitin, E.A.; Egorin, A.M.; Tokar', E.A.; Tananaev, I.G. Study of sorbents for analysis of radiocesium in seawater samples by one-column method. *J. Radioanal. Nucl. Chem.* **2021**, *327*, 1095–1103. [CrossRef]
24. Bezhin, N.A.; Dovhyi, I.I.; Tokar, E.A.; Tananaev, I.G. Physical and chemical regularities of cesium and strontium recovery from the seawater by sorbents of various types. *J. Radioanal. Nucl. Chem.* **2021**, *330*, 1101–1111. [CrossRef]
25. Leppänen, A.-P.; Kasatkina, N.; Vaaramaa, K.; Matishov, G.G.; Solatie, D. Selected anthropogenic and natural radioisotopes in the Barents Sea and off the western coast of Svalbard. *J. Environ. Radioact.* **2013**, *126*, 196–208. [CrossRef] [PubMed]
26. Remez, V.P.; Sapozhnikov, Y.A. The rapid determination of caesium radionuclides in water systems using composite sorbents. *Appl. Radiat. Isot.* **1996**, *47*, 885–886. [CrossRef]
27. Remez, V.P.; Zheltonozhko, E.V.; Sapozhnikov, Y.A. The Experience of Using ANFEZH Sorbent for Recovery of Radioactive Caesium from Sea Water. *Radiat. Prot. Dosim.* **1998**, *75*, 77–78. [CrossRef]
28. Semenishchev, V.S.; Pyankov, A.A.; Remez, V.P.; Afonin, Y.D.; Nikiforov, A.F. Study of physicochemical and sorption properties of nickel and iron hexacyanoferrates to cesium. *Sorpt. Chromatogr. Process* **2020**, *20*, 54–63. (In Russian) [CrossRef]
29. Matel, L.; Dulanska, S.; Silikova, V. Composite sorbents for radionuclide separation. In *XXXIX Days of Radiation Protection. Proceedings of Presentations and Posters*; Slovenska Zdravotnicka Univerzita: Bratislava, Slovakia, 2018; p. 578.
30. Nada, A.M.A.; Moussa, W.M.; El-Mongy, S.A.; El-Sayed, E.S.A. Physicochemical Studies of Cation Ion Exchange Wood Pulp. *Aust. J. Basic Appl. Sci.* **2009**, *3*, 9–16.
31. Sharygin, L.M.; Muromskii, A.Y. Inorganic Sorbent for Ion-Selective Purification of Liquid Radioactive Wastes. *At. Energy* **2000**, *89*, 658–662. [CrossRef]
32. Sharygin, L.M.; Muromskii, A.Y. Inorganic Sorbent for Selective Treatment of Liquid Radioactive Wastes. *Radiochemistry* **2004**, *46*, 185–189. [CrossRef]
33. Voronina, A.V.; Noskova, A.Y.; Semenishchev, V.S.; Gupta, D.K. Decontamination of seawater from ^{137}Cs and ^{90}Sr radionuclides using inorganic sorbents. *J. Environ. Radioact.* **2020**, *217*, 106210. [CrossRef]
34. Pincam, T.; Jampeetong, A. Treatment of Anaerobic Digester Effluent Using Typha angustifolia L.: Growth Responses and Treatment Efficiency. *J. Water Environ. Technol.* **2020**, *18*, 105–116. [CrossRef]

35. Kadko, D. Upwelling and primaryproduction during the U.S. GEOTRACES East Pacific Zonal Transect. *Glob. Biogeochem. Cycles* **2017**, *31*, 218–232. [CrossRef]
36. Tananaev, I.V.; Seifer, G.B.; Kharitonov, Y.Y.; Kuznetsov, V.G.; Korolkov, A.P. *Chemistry of ferrocyanides*; Nauka: Moscow, Russia, 1971; 320p. (In Russian)
37. Lokshin, E.P.; Ivanenko, V.I.; Avsaragov, H.-M.B.; Melnik, N.A.; Vladimirova, V.V.; Kalinnikov, V.T. Purification of water-salt solutions with Ti(IV) and Zr(IV) phosphates. *At. Energy* **2002**, *92*, 118–123. (In Russian) [CrossRef]
38. Gulin, S.B.; Egorov, V.N. Radioactive Tracers in the Black Sea: A Tool for Environmental Assessment and Ecological Regulation. In *Genetics, Evolution and Radiation*; Korogodina, V., Mothersill, C., Inge-Vechtomov, S., Seymour, C., Eds.; Springer: Cham, Germany, 2016; pp. 303–313.
39. Mirzoeva, N.Y.; Gulin, S.B.; Miroshnichenko, O.N. Radionuclides of strontium and cesium. In *Black Sea System*; Lisitsyn, A.P., Ed.; Scientific World: Moscow, Russia, 2018; Volume 7.2, pp. 605–624. (In Russian)
40. *Radiation Safety Standards (RSS-99/2009)*; Sanitary Rules and Norms 2.6.1.2523-09. Federal Center for Hygiene and Epidemiology of Rospotrebnadzor: Moscow, Russia, 2009; 88p. (In Russian)

Disclaimer/Publisher's Note: The statements, opinions and data contained in all publications are solely those of the individual author(s) and contributor(s) and not of MDPI and/or the editor(s). MDPI and/or the editor(s) disclaim responsibility for any injury to people or property resulting from any ideas, methods, instructions or products referred to in the content.

Article

Management of Agricultural Water Containing Acetimidothioic Acid Pesticide through Catalytic Oxidation to Facilitate Reclaimed Water Recycling for Sustainable Food Production

Ehssan Ahmed Hassan [1,2,*], Maha A. Tony [3,4], Hossam A. Nabwey [3,5,*] and Mohamed M. Awad [5,6]

1. Department of Biology, College of Science and Humanities, Prince Sattam Bin Abdul Aziz University, Alkharj 11942, Saudi Arabia
2. Department of Zoology, Faculty of Science, Suez Canal University, Ismailia 41522, Egypt
3. Basic Engineering Science Department, Faculty of Engineering, Menoufia University, Shebin El-Kom 32511, Egypt
4. Advanced Materials/Solar Energy and Environmental Sustainability (AMSEES) Laboratory, Faculty of Engineering, Menoufia University, Shebin El-Kom 32511, Egypt
5. Department of Mathematics, College of Science and Humanities in Al-Kharj, Prince Sattam Bin Abdulaziz University, Al-Kharj 11942, Saudi Arabia
6. Department of Mathematics, Faculty of Science, Suez Canal University, Ismailia 41522, Egypt

* Correspondence: e.basiouny@psau.edu.sa (E.A.H.); eng_hossam21@yahoo.com (H.A.N.)

Abstract: Agro-industrial discharge contains acetimidothioic acid, which is commercially named "Lanox 90" and is a widely applied insecticide in greenhouses, and the result is wastewater loaded with this insecticide. Treating such wastewater is a must to reduce the environmental impact as well as to facilitate the opportunity for water recycling. Thus, the present work introduced Montmorillonite (MMT) clay as a novel Fenton reaction source to treat wastewater loaded with Lanox 90 insecticide as a benign sustainable strategy. Scanning electron microscopy (SEM) supported with energy-dispersive X-ray spectroscopy (EDX) and Fourier-transform infrared spectroscopy (FTIR) were used to characterize the MMT sample. Response surface methodology based on Box–Behnken analysis was selected to optimize the parametric circumstances. The optimized parameters of the proposed technique were obtained at a pH of 2.6 with the addition of 0.8 and 854 mg/L of MMT and H_2O_2, respectively, to attain the highest predicted Lanox 90 removal rate of 97%. Analysis of variance (ANOVA) was used to examine the statistical data and displayed a significant quadratic model. Ultimately, the results reveal that the oxidation system is exothermic and has a non-spontaneous nature, and the reaction kinetics are categorized according to the second-order reaction kinetic rate. The results of the current study indicate the importance of MMT for treating wastewater. These results confirm the possibility of using oxidation technique as a suitable candidate for greenhouse effluent management to enhance the efficiency of water recycling for smart irrigation.

Keywords: agricultural wastewater; water recycle; Montmorillonite; Fenton oxidation; catalyst recycle

Citation: Hassan, E.A.; Tony, M.A.; Nabwey, H.A.; Awad, M.M. Management of Agricultural Water Containing Acetimidothioic Acid Pesticide through Catalytic Oxidation to Facilitate Reclaimed Water Recycling for Sustainable Food Production. *Processes* **2023**, *11*, 792. https://doi.org/10.3390/pr11030792

Academic Editor: Antoni Sánchez

Received: 8 February 2023
Revised: 5 March 2023
Accepted: 6 March 2023
Published: 7 March 2023

Copyright: © 2023 by the authors. Licensee MDPI, Basel, Switzerland. This article is an open access article distributed under the terms and conditions of the Creative Commons Attribution (CC BY) license (https://creativecommons.org/licenses/by/4.0/).

1. Introduction

Nowadays, there is a persistent need for culturing through greenhouses due to the need for fruits and vegetables that are out of season. This technique assures protected conditions of crops to attain a high-quality yield. Additionally, the requirement of sustainable agricultural technology motivates the development of improved advanced greenhouses [1]. Such technology includes the enhancement in infrastructure to reclaim water in a semi-closed recycling system for the double benefits of conserving natural resources and the treatment of waste effluents to attain a sustainable food production world through efficient use of hydric resources [2]. The persistent existence of pesticides in greenhouse effluents causes grave environmental damage and raises concerns even at miniscule concentrations. In this regard, the pertinent option is to treat agricultural effluent wastewater [3].

Lanox 90, or S-methyl-N((methylcarbamoyl)oxy) thioactimidate, is signified as one of the most widely applied insecticides in greenhouse farming for the protection of ornamental plants. In this context, water is loaded with Lanox 90. Lanox 90 is one of the members of the carbamate family and is characterized by a main functional group of -NH(CO)O-. Such functional group principally attributes to its high solubility in water, which reaches 57.9 g/L (at 20 °C), and low affinity for soils [4]. These combined characteristics make it noxious for both surface and groundwater and cause damage to the ecosystem. Therefore, the World Health Organization (WHO) as well as the Environmental Protection Agency, USA (EPA), have signified it as a restricted very toxic and hazardous material.

The so-called conventional treatment methodologies, including biological treatments and physical separation through membranes, are insufficient for insecticide elimination due to the recalcitrant and bio-accumulative characteristics of insecticides [5]. To reach an acceptable quality of processed water, the search for an efficient way of treatment is engaging both the academia and the industrial world. In recent years, great attention has been paid toward dealing with active light processes called advanced oxidation systems, which are based on complete mineralization [6]. Such systems are able to oxidize pollutants to obtain risk-free end products of CO_2, H_2O, and inorganics compounds. Photo-Fenton reaction is one of the advanced oxidation systems that is based on the production of ($\cdot$OH) radicals, which are categorized as highly reactive species as a result of the interaction between H_2O_2 and iron-based salts under ultraviolet illumination through a cyclic reaction to reach pollutant oxidation. This system has shown promising results in the removal of agricultural effluents containing pesticide according to the literature [6,7]. Although a high yield of Fenton's reaction is attained, the disadvantages also have to be taken into consideration. These disadvantages include the reaction precursors are expensive as well as the reaction needs a fixed pH. Additionally, the final iron sludge is a concern [8].

Currently, great efforts are focused on the improvement of photocatalysis through changing catalysts' characteristics to enhance the efficiency of their photocatalytic activity. Aluminum and iron metal are considered to be the most abundant metallic elements on the Earth's crust. Due to its chemical properties and amorphous nature, Montmorillonite, which contains aluminum, iron, and silicon, and has a porous structure and a high specific surface, is considered a replacement of iron precursors in the Fenton's reaction, specially due to its nature occurrence, which helps in reducing the operating cost. Such material is an excellent adsorbent material, although, to date, it has not been used as a source of photocatalytic reaction [9].

Response surface methodology (RSM) is a powerful scheme for photocatalytic process optimization that includes multiple variables [4,8,10]. Such methodology is applied to explore the most effective parameters in a catalytic reaction, especially in a Fenton process, since it is a multivariable dependent reaction. A 3-level factorial design, or the so-called Box–Behnken design, is a statistical model that provides a powerful experimental tool and has been increasingly applied to optimize Fenton's parameters [11,12]. This optimization tool plays a key role in the success of the photo-Fenton system. Nevertheless, it has not been well exploited to optimize Montmorillonite-based Fenton reaction.

MMT has been applied as a catalyst/adsorption source according to previous data cited in the literature [9]. However, MMT has not been used as a catalytic source to initiate the Fenton reaction, especially in the treatment of pesticide-loaded wastewater from agricultural streams. MMT in the Fenton's reaction leads to a greener photocatalytic reaction for the Fenton's test. Thus, the current investigation is a preliminary project dealing with oxidation by the photo-Fenton reaction based on the use of MMT as a naturally abundant clay for treating synthetic waters polluted via one of the most extensively applied pesticides in greenhouse farming; MMT is used as a novel Fenton's source from an environmentally benign material. An analysis of the removal of the pesticide while mineralizing its intermediates and an evaluation of the final effluent toxicity with the remaining pesticide were performed for the purpose of recycling the reclaimed water for greenhouse plants' use. Additionally, the reaction parameters were optimized to maximize toxin removals.

2. Experimental Materials and Methodology

2.1. Experimental Materials

2.1.1. Lanox 90 Aqueous Effluent

Lanox 90 (L90) was applied in the current study as a commercial-grade insecticide to simulate wastewater effluent from greenhouses. L90 was supplied by an agricultural insecticide and chemical company and applied as received without further modification or treatments. The synthetic wastewater was created by preparing a stock of the aqueous solution (1000-ppm) of L90, which was then subjected to dilution, as required, to attain various L90 concentrations. Thereafter, the desired concentration was used and subjected to ultraviolet treatments at a volume of 100 mL.

2.1.2. Montmorillonite-Based Photo-Fenton Catalyst

Montmorillonite, which is a naturally abundant clay substance, was selected to be the source of aluminum metal to substitute for iron in the photo-Fenton reaction. MMT was collected from the Eastern Desert in the upper part of Egypt near El Minia city at the location coordinates of 28° north and 30° east. In this regard, MMT was collected from the deposit, and the clay was taken to the laboratory for preparation by drying in an electric furnace (105 °C) for seven days to maintain it dry and to remove any excess moisture. Consequently, MMT was exposed to grinding through a ball mill to attain an acceptable powder material. The resulting powder was used as the source of the Fenton's catalyst.

2.2. Experimental Methods

2.2.1. Wastewater Treatment Test

Acetimidothioic acid, which is commercially referred to as Lanox 90, was purchased from a central agricultural pesticide and chemical company, El-Menoufia, in Egypt. The synthetic acetimidothioic acid (Lanox 90) aqueous medium (100 mL) was poured into a 250 mL container, and certain amounts of MMT and hydrogen peroxide (30% w/v) as the sources of the photocatalyst were added to the container prior to being subjected to ultraviolet (UV) illumination. The pH of the aqueous Lanox 90 matrix was found to be 7.2, which was then adjusted, when needed, to the needed values through the addition of diluted H_2SO_4 or NaOH solutions, which were of analytical grade and were supplied by Sigma-Aldrich, Darmstadt, Germany. The solution was then magnetically stirred to keep the suspension homogenous and the catalyst well dispersed. Then, the solution was periodically analyzed to investigate L90 removals. Figure 1 summarizes the treatment steps and the suggested treatment sequence.

2.2.2. Experimental Design

Response surface methodological analysis (RSM) was applied to optimize the complex system's performance based on the Box–Behnken (BB) design. The BB design was selected as a multivariate nonlinear model for optimizing the response surface that influenced the system's variables, namely H_2O_2, MMT catalyst concentrations, and pH of the aqueous medium. These variables were chosen to investigate their effects on Lanox 90 oxidation as a dependent response.

2.2.3. Kinetic Modeling

In order to investigate the kinetics of Lanox 90 oxidation in wastewater using the modified Fenton oxidation technique, the data were regressed based on the simple zero (Equation (1)), first (Equation (2)), and second (Equation (3)) kinetic orders [12] as follows:

$$\left(\frac{dc}{dt}\right) = -k_o \qquad (1)$$

$$\left(\frac{dc}{dt}\right) = -k_1 C \qquad (2)$$

$$\left(\frac{dc}{dt}\right) = -k_2 C^2 \tag{3}$$

where C is the Lanox 90 concentration in wastewater; C_t is the Lanox 90 concentration in wastewater at time t; C_o is the initial concentration of Lanox 90 organics in wastewater, and t is the reaction time. Additionally, k_0, k_1, and k_2 represent the kinetic rate constants of the zero-, first- and second-order reaction kinetics, respectively. Then, integrating Equations (1)–(3) leads to the linearized solutions for the zero, first, and second kinetic orders, as displayed in Equations (4)–(6), respectively.

$$(C_t = C_o - k_o t) \tag{4}$$

$$((C_t = C_o - e^{k_1 t}) \tag{5}$$

$$(\left(\frac{1}{C_t}\right) = \left(\frac{1}{C_0}\right) - k_2 t) \tag{6}$$

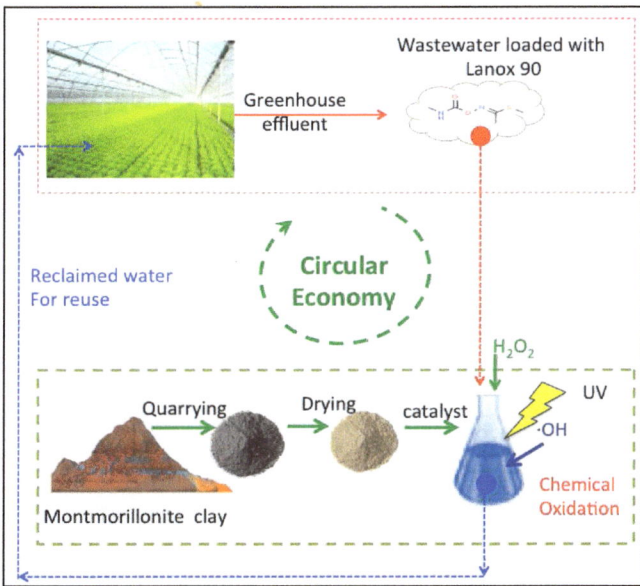

Figure 1. Graphical representation of agricultural wastewater effluent management.

2.3. Analytical Methods

The Lanox 90 solution containing the catalyst after treatment was subjected to periodic analysis at the time intervals of 10 min each. L90 was inspected in the solution at the maximum wavelength of 231 nm using a UV–visible spectrophotometer (model, Unico UV-2100 spectrophotometer, Columbus, OH, USA). The solution was kept under the photocatalytic equipment test till a steady state was achieved or complete Lanox 90 removal was attained. Prior to analysis, the catalyst was removed from the aqueous matrix through filtration using syringe filters with a size of 0.45 mm. Additionally, the pH of the aqueous solution was examined and adjusted when required using a digital pH meter (model AD1030, Adwa instrument, Szeged, Hungary).

2.4. Statistical Analyses

Statistical software (SAS Institute, New York, NY, USA, V STAT 15.1) was used to investigate the full matrix of the factorial experimental design. Moreover, the Mathematica software (V 5.2) was applied to investigate the optimal numerical variables. To further understand the effect of the interacting variables and their response, surface analysis was conducted to analyze the affinity of such interactions. The 3-D response surface and 2-D contour plots were created using the MATLAB R2017a software. Moreover, to check the model, ANOVA was performed to examine the pattern and the acceptance of the model. The ANOVA results, including the sum of squares, mean squares, estimated coefficient, standard error, and the corresponding F-value and p-values were examined using a t-test. Generally, an RSM model is accepted as a significant model if its F-value is greater than the critical value while the p-value is small (<0.05). Moreover, the R^2 (the coefficient of determination) is also used to confirm the fitness of the examined model. In RSM statistics, a model is accepted when $R^2 > 80\%$ [7].

2.5. Characterization Study

The morphology of the sample (MMT) was examined and imaged using a field-emission scanning electron microscope (SEM) (FE-SEM, Quanta FEG 250, The Netherlands). The applied magnifications were $\times 8000$ and $\times 60,000$. This was augmented with energy-dispersive X-ray spectroscopy (EDX) to investigate the main oxides present in the MMT sample via an examination of the energy-dispersive spectrum. Additionally, Fourier-transform infrared spectroscopy (FTIR) (Jasco, FT/IR-4100, type A, Tokyo, Japan) of the MMT sample was carried out to investigate the kind of functional group responsible for the photocatalytic reaction.

3. Results and Discussions

3.1. Characterization of Montmorillonite Catalyst

3.1.1. SEM Images of Montmorillonite

The scanning electron microscopic (SEM) images were investigated to highlight the morphology of the naturally occurring catalyst. The scanning electron micrographs of the MMT sample indicate its morphology at different magnifications. Figure 2 shows that the layered structure of the material has a smooth surface with agglomerated regularly shaped particles, which have an average particle size in the range of 3.514 μm. The MMT surface signifies the existence of a lot of asymmetric open pores with voids. Additionally, the chemical elemental composition showing the weight ratio of the main elements on the surface was examined via an energy-dispersive X-ray spectroscopy test (EDX). The results of the elemental analysis displayed in Table 1 show that MMT possesses mainly SiO_2. Additionally, the presence of the oxides of Al_2O_3 and Fe_2O_3 is observed, showing its importance as a Fenton source. Such results are in accordance with what has been previously reported by various authors [9,12,13] for this type of clay mineral. The Fenton reaction could be conducted through various metals, especially iron and aluminum, which initiate the reaction. The presence of iron and aluminum oxides react with hydrogen peroxide and produce OH radicals, which drive the oxidization of Lanox 90 molecules. In addition, the surface morphology of the clay leads to the occurrences of adsorption in combination with the oxidation reaction. Additionally, a low loss of ignition (L.O.I.) value (6%) indicates the presence of organic matter and carbonate content, as well as combined water in the MMT clay. These results show the suitability of the material to be a catalyst and an adsorbent surface due to the presence of voids as well as the increase in surface area of the substance, according to the ignition of organic matter.

Figure 2. SEM images of the Montmorillonite (MMT) sample at different magnifications: (**i**) 4000× and (**ii**) 50,000×.

Table 1. Chemical constituents of Montmorillonite as inferred by EDX *.

Oxides	SiO_2	Al_2O_3	Fe_2O_3	CaO	MgO	K_2O	Na_2O	SO_3	L.O.I.
Weight %	62.3	18.2	10.1	4.0	1.0	1.0	0.09	0.02	6.0

* L.O.I.: Loss of Ignition.

3.1.2. FTIR Spectroscopy of Montmorillonite

Fourier-transform infrared (FTIR) transmittance spectrum analysis is a significant technique for identifying the existence of different forms of minerals; MMT as a source of photocatalyst was analyzed for its FTIR performances. Due to the presence of numerous elements, besides the presence of the main intensive absorption bands of clay, there are considerable coupled vibrations. Si–O stretching vibrations (silanol) are observed at 1032.6 cm^{-1}, identifying the existence of quartz [13]. Furthermore, the Montmorillonite spectra show bands at 528.4 cm^{-1} and 781.9 cm^{-1} that are related to the stretching vibrations representing Si-O-Al group, which might validate the presence of illite [14,15]. The interlayer hydrogen bonding at 3694.9 cm^{-1}, 3438.4 cm^{-1}, and 1638.2 cm^{-1} indicates the probability of hydroxyl linkage. The band at 1032.6 cm^{-1} verifies the existence of illite. The band near 781.9 cm^{-1} is attributed to the presence of Al-Mg-OH bonding. This spectrum confirms the presence of "Montmorillonite" clay [16]. Additionally, Al bonding is present at 820 cm^{-1} in the spectrum, and Si-O-Fe bonding is present at 446.1 cm^{-1} [16].

3.2. Lanox 90 Oxidation

3.2.1. Assessment of Various Oxidation Processes

The effects of various oxidation systems on Lanox 90 treatment were evaluated and compared with the MMT-based Fenton system to investigate its efficacy in removing Lanox 90 from greenhouse wastewater. The results in Figure 3 show that in the absence of MMT, while the used H_2O_2 is recorded to be 800 mg/L, the extent of Lanox 90 oxidation barely reaches 24%. However, by solely using MMT, the decrease in Lanox 90 load is around 60% within 50 min of irradiation time. Such results show the influence of the adsorption equilibrium due to the existence of CaO, MgO, and illite, which possess porous adsorption surfaces. However, the addition of Montmorillonite augmented with UV irradiance leads to a removal rate of 76%, confirming the role of the material as a photocatalyst. Additionally, MMT combined with H_2O_2 shows a removal rate of 91%; this verifies the role of dark Fenton test in Lanox 90 oxidation. In order to better understand the oxidation capability, further combination of Montmorillonite/H_2O_2/UV oxidation was checked, and the oxidation efficiency reaches 97% of Lanox 90 removals. These results might be because of the augmentation of the sorption and photocatalytic systems [17,18].

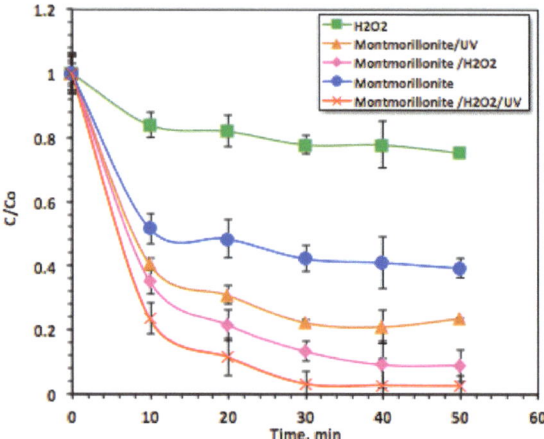

Figure 3. Effects of different oxidation systems on Lanox 90 elimination.

Even through hydrogen peroxide is considered a powerful oxidant, the oxidation of Lanox 90 is not significant when using this reagent. However, when Montmorillonite/H_2O_2 is augmented with UV, the excited Lanox 90 molecules convert O_2 to $O_2^\bullet$ since Lanox 90 absorbs ultraviolet light. Then, the autoprotolysis of H_2O generates protons, which then leads to $O_2^\bullet$ radicals to produce superoxide radicals ($OOH^\bullet$). Such radicals could ultimately completely oxidize Lanox 90 molecules to harmless end products, including CO_2 and H_2O, as well as mineral acids [18]. The catalytic oxidation reaction of Lanox 90 molecules in the existence of Montmorillonite, under UV illumination, commonly incorporates the separation of electron/hole pairs existing on Montmorillonite and subsequent reduction–oxidation reactions. The adsorbed molecular O_2 species might scavenge electrons and H_2O or adsorbed Lanox 90 molecules, which could trap the holes. Subsequently, L90 insecticide molecules could be oxidized directly by the effect of photogenerated oxidants. Additionally, H_2O_2 addition in the presence of Montmorillonite and ultraviolet illumination enhances the photodegradation rate of L90 since the direct dissociation of H_2O_2 under UV illumination produces $OH^\bullet$ radicals, which could oxidize L90 molecules to CO_2, H_2O, and mineral acids [19].

3.2.2. Tailoring Montmorillonite for the Fenton-Based System
Effect of Lanox 90 Loading

The effect of initial Lanox 90 insecticide concentration in the aqueous effluent on oxidation by the Montmorillonite photo-Fenton system is shown in Figure 4. The initial H_2O_2 concentration was added (800 mg/L) to the MMT catalyst loading that was kept at 1 g/L at a pH of 3.0. The maximum L90 removal efficiency was attained at 97% oxidation after 50 min for the Lanox 90 loading of 50, 100, 200, and 400 mg/L. The removal efficacy of Lanox 90 reduced slowly when the Lanox 90 loading was increased, and the oxidation of L90 ranged from 99 to 71% as the Lanox 90 loading increased in the solution. This could be attributed to the quantity of MMT and H_2O_2 being constant in the low (50 mg/L) and high concentrations (400 mg/L); thus, H_2O_2 and MMT, which are the main elements accountable for the formation of highly oxidized •OH radicals, were categorized as not being sufficient to generate enough hydroxyl radicals. Additionally, the amount of vacant active sites on the MMT surface was not sufficient to adsorb higher initial L90 loads in the aqueous matrix. The high loads of L90 occupying the active sites of MMT could result in a decline of reactive •OH radicals. Numerous authors [20,21] have reported a similar trend when treating various pollutants via catalytic oxidation systems.

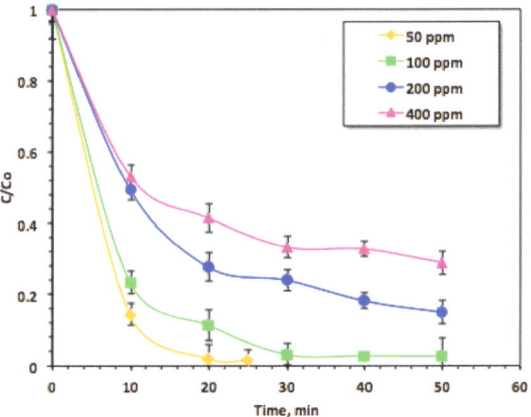

Figure 4. Effect of initial Lanox 90 loading on the Montmorillonite photo-Fenton oxidation system.

Effect of Montmorillonite Concentration

To further investigate the effect of MMT on the photo-Fenton system, the influence of its concentration was investigated, and the results are shown in Figure 5. The MMT concentration was changed over the range of 0.5 to 1.5 g/L, whereas all the other variables were kept at constant values (pH of 7.2 and H_2O_2 at 800 mg/L). The oxidation tendency increases with increasing catalyst concentration, while further catalyst concentration increase results in a reduction in the oxidation efficacy, which reaches almost complete removal (98%) when 1.0 g/L of MMT was added to the aqueous matrix. Additionally, Al and Fe ions react with hydrogen peroxide to form more highly reactive hydroxyl radicals and metals ions. Such non-selective hydroxyl radicals attack the Lanox 90 molecules and strongly mineralize them. However, further increase in MMT leads to a reduction in the treatment efficacy due to the shadowing effect in the media. Excess MMT causes a turbid solution, which prevents ultraviolet radiation from penetrating the aqueous matrix and obeys the UV transmittance. Additionally, extreme metal ions that are in excess in the medium act as a scavenger of hydroxyl radicals rather than as a generator [5].

Effect of H_2O_2 Concentration

Hydrogen peroxide's effect on Lanox 90 removal in the Montmorillonite-based photo-Fenton system was investigated by varying the hydrogen peroxide concentration, and the results of the experiments are displayed in Figure 6. As expected, elevating the H_2O_2 concentration from 100 mg/L to 400 mg/L enhances Lanox 90 oxidation. However, further elevation in the reagent to an optimal concentration (800 mg/L) results in a reduction in the treatment efficacy. The oxidation declines to 83% when the H_2O_2 concentration increases to more than 800 mg/L. Thus, 800 mg/L is recorded as the optimal H_2O_2 concentration. This could be because excessive dosing of such reagent leads to a decline in Lanox 90 treatment since perhydroxyl radical (HO_2) is generated due to excess hydrogen peroxide, rather than highly oxidized OH radicals. Thus, the overall oxidation rate is reduced.

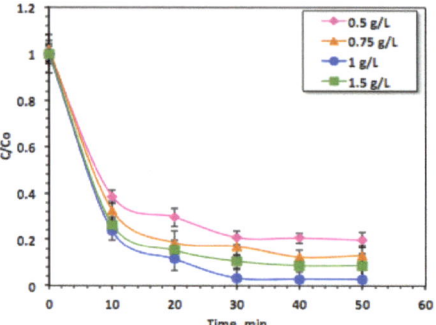

Figure 5. Effect of Montmorillonite catalyst concentration on the photo-Fenton reaction.

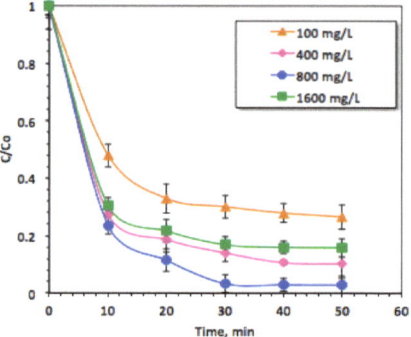

Figure 6. Effect of H_2O_2 concentration on the photo-Fenton system.

Effect of Aqueous Effluent pH

pH is categorized as a significant variable in the photo-Fenton reaction since pH affects H_2O_2 decomposition and hydrolytic speciation of metal ions. Hence, to evaluate the effect of the aqueous environment's pH on oxidation, the initial pH values of the aqueous matrix were varied from 3.0 to 7.2, and the data are expressed as a decline in Lanox 90 concentration. Figure 7 verifies that an acidic pH (3.0) shows a maximum oxidation of Lanox 90 efficiency. It is important to note that the pH value of the aqueous solution achieves the highest oxidation efficacy, which reaches 97%, during 50 min of UV irradiation and that Lanox 90 is almost totally oxidized into different intermediates. Increasing the pH value results in the creation of radicals that inhibit the oxidation reaction, instead of the generation of highly oxidized (OH) radicals. Additionally, the yield of Lanox 90 removal could be associated with the fraction of soluble metals that are responsible for inducing H_2O_2 to produce (OH) radicals in the aqueous medium, which declines within an acidic pH range [9,22].

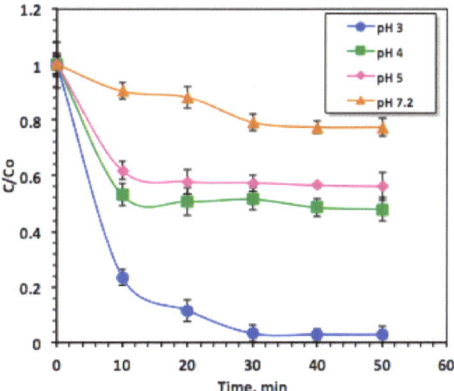

Figure 7. Effect of pH of the aqueous matrix on the photo-Fenton system.

3.2.3. RSM Model's Optimization of Operating Parameters

Model Establishment

To attain a higher removal efficiency in a reasonable time with a minimal concentration of reagents, the 3-level factorial design, also known as the Box–Behnken model design, was correlated. A Box–Behnken design based on RSM with triplicates at the central values was applied. The following independent variables were chosen: (i) H_2O_2 concentration; (ii) MMT catalyst concentration; and (iii) pH value. Their levels were selected as a support of the introductory work, and the selected levels are displayed in Table 2.

Table 2. Boundaries of model design for the coded and natural experimental domains and the corresponding levels' spacing.

Experimental Variable	Symbols		Range and Levels		
	Natural	Coded	−1	0	1
H_2O_2 (mg/L)	ε_1	ζ_1	700	800	900
MMT (mg/L)	ε_2	ζ_2	0.75	1.0	1.25
pH	ε_3	ζ_3	2.0	3.0	4.0

Furthermore, the analysis using the SAS software suggested the full matrix of the factorial experimental design, as seen in Table 3, at the coded and un-coded levels. A 15-factorial design was performed, and the second-order polynomial model was investigated according to Equation (7):

$$Y(\%) = 92.66 + 3.62\varepsilon_1 - 6.255\varepsilon_2 - 3.875\varepsilon_3 - 6.456\varepsilon_1^2 + \varepsilon_1\varepsilon_2 - 9.75\varepsilon_1\varepsilon_3 - 5.20\varepsilon_2^2 + 4.0\,\varepsilon_2\varepsilon_3 - 14.45\,\varepsilon_3^2 \quad (7)$$

where Y is the predicted Lanox 90 removal rate depending on the parameters' response (%); $i = 1, 2, 3$ and $j = 1, 2, 3$; βo, βi, βii, and βij are the model regression coefficient variables; and ζi is the input used to calculate the coded variable. In order to simplify the model calculations, the natural parameters of the operating system (ε_i) were converted to coded variables (ζi).

ANOVA Test

An ANOVA test was applied to evaluate the model. The R^2 and p-value were recorded to investigate the model's adequacy. A small p-value of 0.008 is obtained. Moreover, the R^2 is 96%, which supports the proposed model. Thus, a good correlation is achieved for the predicted model of Lanox 90 removal through the modified photo-Fenton test. Such results are in agreement with the previous work of Elsayed and his co-workers [10], who found a correlation coefficient of 99% for their optimized parameters for the oxidation of dye species using a chitin biopolymer system. Additionally, they recorded a p-value of 0.00054 for their model. Additionally, Nour et al. [7] found a p-value of 0.027552, which is accepted for significance of their suggested model that optimizing the variables using RSM model.

Table 3. Box–Behnken factorial design in terms of coded and natural variables and the corresponding Lanox 90 removal rate affecting effluent oxidation.

Exp. No.	Variables						Response (Y)
	H_2O_2 Concentration		MMT Concentration		pH Value		% L90 Removal
	Coded	Natural	Coded	Natural	Coded	Natural	
1	−1	700	−1	0.75	0	3.0	82
2	−1	700	1	1.25	0	3.0	72
3	1	900	−1	0.75	0	3.0	88
4	1	900	1	1.25	0	3.0	82
5	0	800	−1	0.75	−1	2.0	92
6	0	800	−1	0.75	1	4.0	71
7	0	800	1	1.25	−1	2.0	67
8	0	800	1	1.25	1	4.0	62
9	−1	700	0	1.0	−1	2.0	60
10	1	900	0	1.0	−1	2.0	86
11	−1	700	0	1.0	1	4.0	77
12	1	900	0	1.0	1	4.0	64
13	0	800	0	1.0	0	3.0	92
14	0	800	0	1.0	0	3.0	93
15	0	800	0	1.0	0	3.0	93

Response Surface Plots

The 3-D response surface and 2-D contour plots of Lanox 90 removal efficacy are displayed in Figures 8–10, showing the three pairs of selected variables. According to the data displayed in Figures 8–10, Lanox 90 removal efficacy steadily increases with an elevation in both H_2O_2 and MMT catalyst. This could be attributed to the presence of highly reactive species (·OH radicals) in the aqueous reaction medium with an increase in the concentrations of the reagents [9]. However, when reaching a certain limit of concentration for the reagents, Lanox 90 removal and oxidation declines. An explanation for this phenomenon is that excess reagents might act as a scavenger of OH radicals rather than a generator [23]. It is known that hydroxyl radicals are the drivers of such oxidation removal rate. Furthermore, it can be observed from the plots that Lanox 90 elimination is extremely sensitive to the variation in pH value in the assessment of the other examined parameters. This phenomenon is in agreement with the probability values (p-values) achieved for each variable from the ANOVA test. It is important to remark that an acidic pH value is essential to conduct such oxidation.

Numerical Optimization

Additionally, after the experimental work was conducted, the optimal results were predicted. The estimated optimal values are 854 and 0.8 mg/L for hydrogen peroxide and MMT, respectively, and the corresponding optimal pH is a pH value of 2.6 with a predicted response of 97% removal rate. Afterward, three additional replicates of the experimental work were performed to validate the predicted model, which reached a response of 98%. Thus, the numerical optimization maximized Lanox 90 oxidation, which is mainly based on OH radicals. Thus, OH radicals are increased through using the optimal reagent values and pH conditions, which exceeds the overall reaction rate.

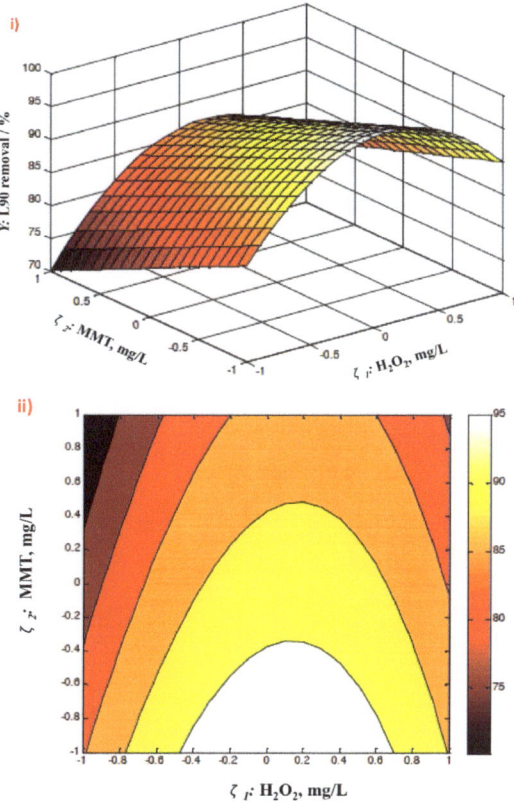

Figure 8. Factorial model design's optimal results: (**i**) 3-D surface plot and (**ii**) 2-D contour plot of the (Y) response and the interacting effect of H_2O_2 and Montmorillonite catalyst concentration.

3.2.4. Temperature Effect on Kinetics and Thermodynamic Parameters

To proceed to real-life and practical applications, it is critical to investigate the influence of temperature on the treatment process. An investigation of the influence of temperature on reaction kinetics was conducted by changing the temperature from 26 °C (room temperature) to 40, 50, and 60 °C. The results shown in Figure 11i demonstrate that the removal rate declines to 43% as the temperature is elevated to 60 °C, when compared to a removal rate of 97% at room temperature (26 °C). Even though the oxidation reaction could be more effective at an elevated temperature, H_2O_2 decomposes into oxygen and water at a high temperature. This results in an inhibition in the overall Lanox 90 oxidation reaction rate. Various reports in the literature [24–27] confirm the small terminal effect of reaction rate in comparison to other influencing parameters on the Fenton reaction. Some previous studies stated that 38 °C is the optimal operating temperature for the Fenton reaction [28,29].

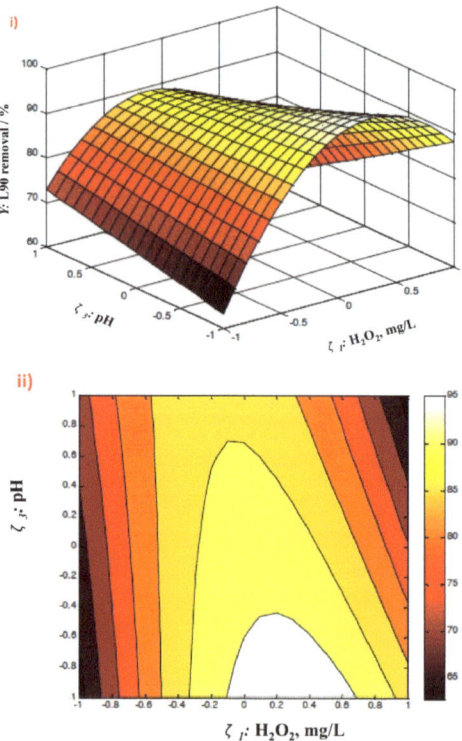

Figure 9. Factorial model design's optimal results: (**i**) 3-D surface plot and (**ii**) 2-D contour plot of the (Y) response and the interacting effect of H_2O_2 and pH.

To investigate the impact of the Lanox 90 oxidation system, kinetic modeling study is essential to define the reaction rate constants. At various operating temperatures for the Montmorillonite-based Fenton system, the empirical and theoretical values of the zero-, first-, and second-order kinetic models were assessed and compared using the linearized form of Equations (1)–(3). Then, the correlation coefficient of determination values (R^2) were compared and used to estimate the best-fit model. Commonly, the best-fit model is associated with the highest R^2 value between the empirical and theoretical data [30,31]. Thus, the correlation was compared, and the zero- and first-order models were rejected for having lower R^2 values, which displayed values of 0.61 to 0.88, respectively. The highest R^2 value corresponds to the second-order kinetic model (0.91–0.98), as seen in Table 4. Hence, this model is selected to represent the data. This model specifies the reaction between Lanox 90 and the MMT-based photo-Fenton system, indicating that the reaction between Lanox 90 and the reagents is temperature dependent. The second-order model shows that it is not affected so much by random errors [32]. Furthermore, the half-life time ($t_{1/2}$), as displayed in Table 4, increases with an increase in the temperature. This could be attributed to the increase in temperature hindering the catalytic activity of the MMT substance since its surface activity is affected by the temperature change [32,33].

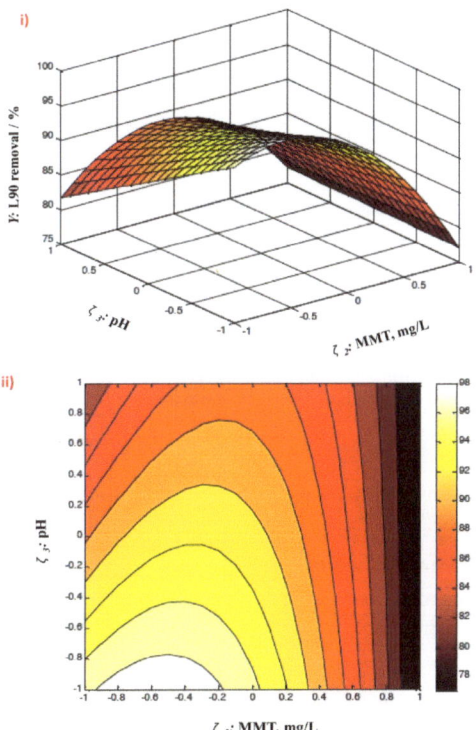

Figure 10. Factorial model design's optimal results: (**i**) 3-D surface plot and (**ii**) 2-D contour plot of the (Y) response and the interacting effect of Montmorillonite catalyst concentration and pH.

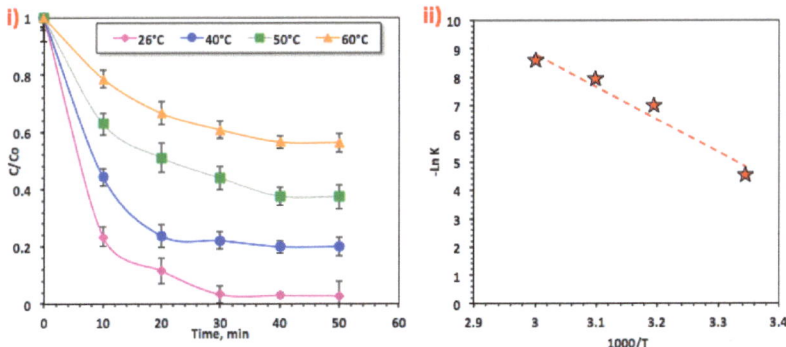

Figure 11. Effect of temperature on the reaction: (**i**) effect of temperature on the aqueous matrix in the photo-Fenton system, and (**ii**) plot of (−Ln K) vs. 1000/T.

Table 4. Fitted kinetic reaction data for agricultural effluent oxidation reaction *.

Kinetic Oder-Model	Boundaries	Temperature			
		299 K	313 K	323 K	333 K
Zero-order	k_0 (min^{-1})	1.48	1.33	1.11	0.82
	$t_{1/2}$ (min)	31.45	36.89	44.24	60.12
	R^2	0.61	0.64	0.78	0.84
First-order	k_1 (min^{-1})	0.073	0.03	0.019	0.011
	$t_{1/2}$ (min)	61.32	36.86	23.1	9.49
	R^2	0.88	0.76	0.88	0.88
Second-order	k_2 (L·mg^{-1}min^{-1})	0.0101	0.001	0.0004	0.0002
	$t_{1/2}$ (min)	1.06	10.18	25.46	50.93
	Rr^2	0.91	0.92	0.99	0.98

* k_0, k_1, and k_2: kinetic rate constants of the zero-, first-, and second-order kinetic models; C_o and C_t: Lanox 90 loadings at initial time and time t; t: time; R^2: coefficient of determination; and $t_{1/2}$: half-life time.

To further examine the influence of temperature on the Lanox 90 treatments, thermodynamic values of activation were evaluated using the Arrhenius equation (Equation (8)):

$$lnk_2 = lnA - \frac{E_a}{RT} \quad (8)$$

where A is the pre-exponential factor constant; R is the universal gas constant based on the second-order kinetic model used to estimate the energy of activation; and Ea is from the linear plot of lnk_2 versus $1/T$ (Figure 11ii). Furthermore, the thermodynamic activation parameters of oxidation were estimated by using the Eyring equation (Equation (9)):

$$k_F = \frac{k_B T}{h} e^{(-\frac{\Delta G^\#}{RT})} \quad (9)$$

where k_B and h are the Boltzmann and Planck's constants. Additionally, the enthalpy ($\Delta H^\#$) and the entropy ($\Delta S^\#$) of activation could be determined from the following equations [24]:

$$\Delta H^\# = E_a - RT \quad (10)$$

$$\Delta S^\# = \left(\Delta H^\# - \Delta G^\#\right)/T \quad (11)$$

The results from these equations were calculated and are shown in Table 5. The positive Gibbs free energy ($\Delta G^\# > 0$) and the negative values of entropy ($\Delta S^\#$) show the non-spontaneous nature of the oxidation reaction. Additionally, the negative values of entropy verify the exothermic nature of such reaction. These results verify the decline in the degree of freedom of Lanox 90 molecules and maintain high hydroxyl radical species yield. Similar data in the literature confirm the non-spontaneous behavior of the oxidation removal test [34,35]. Additionally, the results exhibited in Table 5 show the reaction proceeds at 95.86 kJ/mol. This high activation energy of more than 40 kJ/mol demonstrates the high-energy barrier that is required to complete the oxidation reaction of Lanox 90 molecules. Such a high level of Ea (activation energy) is well matched with the results reported in previously published articles [36,37].

3.2.5. Comparison of Data with the Literature

A comparison of different data presented in the literature for treating Lanox 90 and the results obtained in the current investigation (Montmorillonite-based Fenton's system) was conducted, and the results are shown in Table 6. Promisingly, photo-Fenton reaction in its heterogeneous form shows almost complete oxidation rate in all examined systems. However, in the current investigation, a lower reaction time and the use of an efficient superior treatment are needed since the catalyst is a naturally abundant material. It is noteworthy to mention that the other systems support the use of fresh iron precursor or catalyst source associated with naturally occurring, environmentally benign catalyst as in the current study. Moreover, the catalyst's sustainability supports its use in a Fenton reaction since it is a naturally occurring and abundant material and is, thus, a cost-effective substance for Lanox 90 insecticide reduction.

Table 5. Thermodynamic data for agricultural effluent oxidation using Montmorillonite-based photo-Fenton reaction *.

Temperature	E_A = 95.86 kJ/mol		
	$\Delta H^{\#}$	$\Delta S^{\#}$	$\Delta G^{\#}$
299 K	0.038	−205.12	61.33
313 K	0.036	−186.27	58.30
323 K	0.035	−178.92	57.79
333 K	0.034	−173.41	57.74

* Activation energy (Ea), variation in activation enthalpy $\Delta H^{\#}$ (kJ/mol), variation in activation entropy $\Delta S^{\#}$ (J/mol·K), and variation in the free energy of activation $\Delta G^{\#}$ (kJ/mol).

Table 6. Comparison of different oxidation systems for treating Lanox 90.

Treatment Process	Effluent Characteristics and Treatment Conditions	Initiation Source	Performance Efficiency	Ref.
Montmorillonite-based Fenton's system	Catalyst: 1 g/L, H_2O_2: 800 mg/L, pH: 6, and 26 °C	UV	97%	Current work
Alum sludge/magnetite-modified Fenton	Catalyst: 50 mg/L, H_2O_2: 130 mg/L, and pH: 6	UV	99%	[20]
Silica-supported iron Fenton system	23 °C, pH 3, H_2O_2 0.015 M, Fe^{2+} 5.0 × 10^{-4} M, and 90 min	UV	98%	[31]
Heterogeneous Fenton-like copper nanoparticle-microwave system	L90 100 ppm; n-CuO 75 mg/L, H_2O_2 395 mg/L, and pH 6.5	MW	91%	[38]
Heterogeneous photo-Fenton-like magnetite nanoparticles	L90 50 mg/L, pH 3, iron 40 mg/L, H_2O_2 50 mg/L, and 60 min	UV	90%	[37]
Catalytic photooxidation-based ZnO system	L90 16 ppm, pH 5.6, ZnO 2000 mg/L, and 240 min	UV	80%	[39]
Heterogeneous solar photo-Fenton-like system	L90 50 mg/L, pH 3, iron 44 mg/L, H_2O_2 52 mg/L, and 170 min	Solar energy	96.5%	[20]

3.2.6. Assessment of Catalytic Oxidation Cycles of Montmorillonite

The life cycle of a catalytic oxidation system is one of the most important stages to assess in catalytic reactions. MMT recyclability was investigated by recycling the MMT material after Fenton oxidation. After each use, the material was collected via filtration and subjected to repeated cleaning with distilled water three times before drying in an electric furnace (105 °C) for one hour. Then, the recovered material was further used to remove Lanox 90 from wastewater, and the final Lanox 90 residual in the wastewater was monitored to check the material's ability to treat wastewater after successive use. The initial and final amounts of Lanox 90 residual were compared to check the treatment adequacy of the material, and the removal percentage was recorded.

The data shown in Figure 12 reveal the sustainability of the material; even though the oxidation efficacy lowers from 97 to 62%, the substance could still treat Lanox 90 pollutant. However, it is noteworthy to mention that the substance becomes loaded with Lanox 90 molecules, which reduces its activity. Additionally, the activity of the material till the fourth cycle indicates its stability. These data are in accordance with the results reported in a previous study [38], which investigated a copper catalyst for successive use and the treatment efficiency reached 65% after six cycles of use in comparison to 91% for the first catalyst use. Additionally, Ashour and Tony [9] investigated the recyclability of clay material, which showed a decline in the adsorption capacity, reaching 7%, when compared to fresh clay use. Such reduction is associated with the material being loaded with pollutants, which results in a reduction in the vacancies for adsorbing further pollutants.

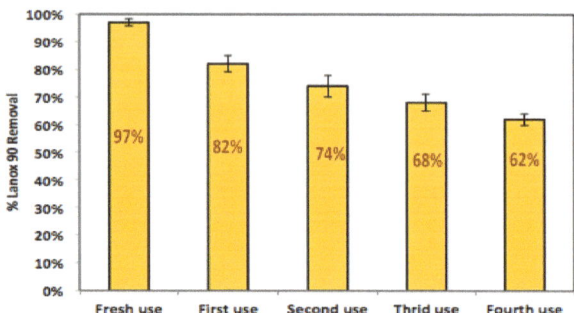

Figure 12. Catalyst's recyclability activity on Lanox 90 oxidation.

Furthermore, the dissolution of the MMT clay was investigated at an acidic pH value (2.6), and the concentrations of aluminum and iron released were recorded to be 0.043 mg/L and 0.11 mg/L, respectively. Additionally, the amount of catalyst loss after one cyclic use was estimated to be 1.02%.

4. Conclusions

The present investigation reports for the first time the ability to use Montmorillonite (MMT), a naturally occurring material, to be a source of mineral for photocatalytic reaction. This study introduces its potential for agricultural wastewater reclaiming and recycling for further irrigation option. The results demonstrated that 97% of Lanox 90 could be removed from the aqueous medium using the optimized operating parameters achieved by the response surface methodology at the concentration of 854 and 0.8 mg/L for H_2O_2 and MMT, respectively, at a pH of 2.6. The catalyst's recyclability showed a reasonable activity, reaching 62% after the fourth reuse. The kinetic investigation revealed that the reaction acted according to the second-order reaction rate. The thermodynamic parameters were categorized as exothermic and followed a non-spontaneous nature. Additionally, the reaction was conducted at a high-energy barrier. The promising results of the present work can lead to the introduction of such a system to real-life world for an environmental symbiosis approach.

Author Contributions: Conceptualization, E.A.H. and M.A.T.; methodology, E.A.H., M.A.T., H.A.N. and M.M.A.; software, H.A.N. and M.M.A.; validation, E.A.H. and M.A.T.; investigation, E.A.H., M.A.T., H.A.N. and M.M.A.; resources E.A.H., M.A.T., H.A.N. and M.M.A.; writing—original draft preparation, E.A.H., M.A.T., H.A.N. and M.M.A.; writing—review and editing, E.A.H., M.A.T., H.A.N. and M.M.A.; project administration E.A.H. All authors have read and agreed to the published version of the manuscript.

Funding: Prince Sattam Bin Abdulaziz University for funding this research work through the project number (PSAU/2022/01/23497).

Data Availability Statement: Data are available upon request.

Acknowledgments: The authors thank the Prince Sattam Bin Abdulaziz University for funding this research work through the project number (PSAU/2022/01/23497).

Conflicts of Interest: The authors declare no conflict of interest.

References

1. Petchwattana, N.; Naknaen, P.; Narupai, B. A circular economy use of waste wood sawdust for wood plastic composite production: Effect of bio-plasticiser on the toughness. *Int. J. Sustain. Eng.* **2020**, *13*, 398–410. [CrossRef]
2. Wu, J.; Ding, T.; Sun, J. Neurotoxic potential of iron oxide nanoparticles in the rat brain striatum and hippocampus. *Neurotoxicology* **2013**, *34*, 243–253. [CrossRef] [PubMed]
3. Ashour, E.A.; Tony, M.A.; Purcell, P.J. Use of agriculture-based waste for basic dye sorption from aqueous solution: Kinetics and isotherm studies. *Am. J. Chem. Eng.* **2014**, *2*, 92. [CrossRef]
4. Tony, M. Win-win wastewater treatment to sustain world: Porous adsorbents from waste waterworks sludge for phenol remediation. In Proceedings of the Anaerobic Digestion Conference AD16, Delft, The Netherlands, 23–27 June 2019; The International Water Association, IWA: London, UK, 2019.
5. Gu, L.; Zhu, N.; Guo, H.; Huang, S.; Lou, Z.; Yuan, H. Adsorption and Fenton-like degradation of naphthalene dye intermediate on sewage sludge derived porous carbon. *J. Hazard. Mater.* **2013**, *246–247*, 145–153. [CrossRef]
6. Phan, T.T.N.; Nikoloski, A.N.; Bahri, P.A.; Li, D. Facile fabrication of perovskite-incorporated hierarchically mesoporous/macroporous silica for efficient photoassisted-Fenton degradation of dye. *Appl. Surf. Sci.* **2019**, *491*, 488–496. [CrossRef]
7. Nour, M.M.; Tony, M.A.; Nabwey, H.A. Immobilization of magnetic nanoparticles on cellulosic wooden sawdust for competitive Nudrin elimination from environ-mental waters as a green strategy: Box-Behnken Design optimization. *Int. J. Environ. Res. Public Health* **2022**, *19*, 15397. [CrossRef]
8. Nguyen, T.T.; Huynh, K.A.; Padungthon, S.; Pranudta, A.; Amonpattaratkit, P.; Tran, L.B.; Phan, P.T.; Nguyen, N.H. Synthesis of natural flowerlike iron-alum oxide with special interaction of Fe-Si-Al oxides as an effective catalyst for heterogeneous Fenton process. *J. Environ. Chem. Eng.* **2021**, *9*, 105732. [CrossRef]
9. Ashour, E.A.; Tony, M.A. Eco-friendly removal of hexavalent chromium from aqueous solution using natural clay mineral: Activation and modification effects. *SN Appl. Sci.* **2020**, *2*, 2042. [CrossRef]
10. Elsayed, S.A.; El-Sayed, I.E.; Tony, M.A. Impregnated chitin biopolymer with magnetic nanoparticles to immobilize dye from aqueous media as a simple, rapid and efficient composite photocatalyst. *Appl. Water Sci.* **2022**, *12*, 252. [CrossRef]
11. Ling, Y.; Long, M.; Hu, P.; Chen, Y.; Huang, J. Magnetically separable core–shell structural γ-Fe$_2$O$_3$@Cu/Al-MCM-41 nanocomposite and its performance in heterogeneous Fenton catalysis. *J. Hazard. Mater.* **2014**, *264*, 195–202. [CrossRef]
12. Tireli, A.A.; Guimarães, I.D.R.; Terra, J.C.D.S.; da Silva, R.R.; Guerreiro, M.C. Fenton-like processes and adsorption using iron oxide-pillared clay with magnetic properties for organic compound mitigation. *Environ. Sci. Pollut. Res.* **2015**, *22*, 870–881. [CrossRef]
13. Van der Marel, H.W.; Beutelspacher, H. Atlas of Infrared Spectroscopy of Clay Minerals and Their Admixtures. Elsevier Publishing Company: Amsterdam, The Netherlands, 1976.
14. Tinti, A.; Tugnoli, V.; Bonora, S.; Francioso, O. Recent applications of vibrational mid-Infrared (IR) spectroscopy for studying soil components: A review. *J. Central Eur. Agric.* **2015**, *16*, 141299. [CrossRef]
15. Bukalo, N.N.; Ekosse, G.-I.E.; Odiyo, J.O.; Ogola, J.S. Fourier transform infrared spectroscopy of clay size fraction of cretaceous-tertiary kaolins in the Douala sub-basin, Cameroon. *Open Geosci.* **2017**, *9*, 407–418. [CrossRef]
16. Vaculikova, L.; Plevova, E. Identification of clay minerals and micas in sedimentary rocks. *Acta Geodyn. Geomater.* **2005**, *2*, 163.
17. Tony, M.A.; Lin, L.-S. Performance of acid mine drainage sludge as an innovative catalytic oxidation source for treating vehicle-washing wastewater. *J. Dispers. Sci. Technol.* **2021**, *43*, 50–60. [CrossRef]
18. Nassar, M.Y.; Ahmed, I.S.; Samir, I. A novel synthetic route for magnesium aluminate (MgAl$_2$O$_4$) nanoparticles using sol–gel auto combustion method and their photocatalytic properties. *Spectrochim. Acta Part A Mol. Biomol. Spectrosc.* **2014**, *131*, 329–334. [CrossRef]
19. Nassar, M.Y.; Abdelrahman, E.A. Hydrothermal tuning of the morphology and crystallite size of zeolite nanostructures for simultaneous adsorption and photocatalytic degradation of methylene blue dye. *J. Mol. Liq.* **2017**, *242*, 364–374. [CrossRef]
20. Thabet, R.H.; Fouad, M.K.; Ali, I.A.; El Sherbiny, S.A.; Tony, M.A. Synthesis, characterization and potential application of magnetized nanoparticles for photocatalysis of Levafix CA reactive azo-dye in aqueous effluent. *Water Environ. J.* **2022**, *36*, 245–260. [CrossRef]
21. Tony, M.A.; Lin, L.-S. Iron coated-sand from acid mine drainage waste for being a catalytic oxidant towards municipal wastewater remediation. *Int. J. Environ. Res.* **2021**, *15*, 191–201. [CrossRef]
22. Tony, M.A. An industrial ecology approach: Green cellulose-based bio-adsorbent from sugar industry residue for treating textile industry wastewater effluent. *Int. J. Environ. Anal. Chem.* **2021**, *101*, 167–183. [CrossRef]
23. Guanghua, W.; Dong, W.; Wenbing, L.; Yunzhou, L.; Kun, C. Synthesis, characterization and Fenton-like degradation for Orange II of magnetic bentonite. *Chin. J. Environ. Eng.* **2014**, *8*, 1857–1862.
24. Ahmadi, M.; Behin, J.; Mahnam, A.R. Kinetics and thermodynamics of peroxydisulfate oxidation of Reactive Yellow 84. *J. Saudi Chem. Soc.* **2016**, *20*, 644–650. [CrossRef]
25. Toosi, F.S.; Hosseiny, M.; Joghataei, A.; Toosi, F.S. The Application of Sio2 Nanoparticles for Anionic Dye Removal from Aqueous Solution. *Arch. Hyg. Sci.* **2017**, *6*, 136–144.
26. Buthiyappan, A.; Raman, A.A.A.; Daud, W.M.A.W. Development of an advanced chemical oxidation wastewater treatment system for the batik industry in Malaysia. *RSC Adv.* **2016**, *6*, 25222–25241. [CrossRef]

27. Deng, Y.; Englehardt, J.D. Treatment of landfill leachate by the Fenton process. *Water Res.* **2006**, *40*, 3683–3694. [CrossRef]
28. Pintor, A.M.; Vilar, V.J.; Boaventura, R.A. Decontamination of cork wastewaters by solar-photo-Fenton process using cork bleaching wastewater as H_2O_2 source. *Sol. Energy* **2011**, *85*, 579–587. [CrossRef]
29. Ioannou, L.A.; Fatta-Kassinos, D. Solar photo-Fenton oxidation against the bioresistant fractions of winery wastewater. *J. Environ. Chem. Eng.* **2013**, *1*, 703–712. [CrossRef]
30. Lopez-Lopez, C.; Martín-Pascual, J.; Martínez-Toledo, M.V.; González-López, J.; Hontoria, E.; Poyatos, J.M. Effect of the operative variables on the treatment of wastewater polluted with phthalo blue by H_2O_2/UV process. *Water Air Soil Pollut.* **2013**, *224*, 1725. [CrossRef]
31. Tony, M.A.; Lin, L.-S. Attenuation of organics contamination in polymers processing effluent using iron-based sludge: Process optimization and oxidation mechanism. *Environ. Technol.* **2022**, *43*, 718–727. [CrossRef]
32. Repo, E.; Mäkinen, M.; Rengaraj, S.; Natarajan, G.; Bhatnagar, A.; Sillanpää, M. Lepidocrocite and its heat-treated forms as effective arsenic adsorbents in aqueous medium. *Chem. Eng. J.* **2012**, *180*, 159–169. [CrossRef]
33. Singh, C.; Chaudhary, R.; Gandhi, K. Preliminary study on optimization of pH, oxidant and catalyst dose for high COD content: Solar parabolic trough collector. *Iran. J. Environ. Health Sci. Eng.* **2013**, *10*, 13. [CrossRef] [PubMed]
34. Pourali, P.; Behzad, M.; Arfaeinia, H.; Ahmadfazeli, A.; Afshin, S.; Poureshgh, Y.; Rashtbari, Y. Removal of acid blue 113 from aqueous solutions using low-cost adsorbent: Adsorption isotherms, thermodynamics, kinetics and regeneration studies. *Sep. Sci. Technol.* **2021**, *56*, 3079–3091. [CrossRef]
35. Lv, Q.; Li, G.; Sun, H.; Kong, L.; Lu, H.; Gao, X. Preparation of magnetic core/shell structured γ-Fe_2O_3@ Ti-tmSiO$_2$ and its application for the adsorption and degradation of dyes. *Microporous Mesoporous Mater.* **2014**, *186*, 7–13. [CrossRef]
36. Sidney Santana, C.; Nicodemos Ramos, M.D.; Vieira Velloso, C.C.; Aguiar, A. Kinetic evaluation of dye decolorization by Fenton processes in the presence of 3-hydroxyanthranilic acid. *Int. J. Environ. Res. Public Health* **2019**, *16*, 1602. [CrossRef]
37. Chen, J.; Zhu, L. Heterogeneous UV-Fenton catalytic degradation of dyestuff in water with hydroxyl-Fe pillared bentonite. *Catal. Today* **2007**, *126*, 463–470. [CrossRef]
38. Tony, M.A.; Mansour, S.A. Microwave-assisted catalytic oxidation of methomyl pesticide by Cu/Cu$_2$O/CuO hybrid nanoparticles as a Fenton-like source. *Int. J. Environ. Sci. Technol.* **2020**, *17*, 161–174. [CrossRef]
39. Tomašević, A.; Mijin, D.; Gašic, S.; Kiss, E. The influence of polychromatic light on methomyl degradation in TiO$_2$ and ZnO aqueous suspension. *Desalination Water Treat.* **2014**, *52*, 4342–4349. [CrossRef]

Disclaimer/Publisher's Note: The statements, opinions and data contained in all publications are solely those of the individual author(s) and contributor(s) and not of MDPI and/or the editor(s). MDPI and/or the editor(s) disclaim responsibility for any injury to people or property resulting from any ideas, methods, instructions or products referred to in the content.

Article

Prediction of Oxygen Content in Boiler Flue Gas Based on a Convolutional Neural Network

Zhenhua Li, Guanghong Li and Bin Shi *

School of Chemistry, Chemical Engineering and Life Sciences, Wuhan University of Technology, Wuhan 430070, China
* Correspondence: shibin@whut.edu.cn; Tel.: +86-189-8619-5381

Abstract: As one of the core pieces of equipment of the thermal power generation system, the economic and environmental performance of a boiler determines the energy efficiency of the thermal power generation unit. The oxygen content in boiler flue gas is an important parameter reflecting the combustion status of the furnace, and accurate prediction of flue gas oxygen content is of great significance for online boiler optimization. In order to solve the online prediction problem of the oxygen content in boiler flue gas, a CNN is applied to build a time series prediction model, which takes the time series samples within a fixed time window as the input of the model and uses several feature extraction modules containing convolutional, activation, and pooling layers for feature extraction and compression, and the model output is the oxygen content in boiler flue gas. Since the oxygen content in boiler flue gas is not only correlated with other variables but also influenced by its own historical trend, the input of the CNN model is improved, and an oxygen content in boiler flue gas time series prediction model (TS-CNN) is established, which takes the historical values of the boiler flue gas oxygen content as the input of the model. The comparison test results show that the R^2 and $RMSE$ of the TS-CNN model are 0.8929 and 0.1684, respectively. The prediction accuracy is higher than the CNN model, LSSVM model, and BPNN model by 18.6%, 31.2%, and 54.6%, respectively.

Keywords: oxygen content in boiler flue gas; convolutional neural network; feature extraction; online prediction

---

Citation: Li, Z.; Li, G.; Shi, B. Prediction of Oxygen Content in Boiler Flue Gas Based on a Convolutional Neural Network. *Processes* **2023**, *11*, 990. https://doi.org/10.3390/pr11040990

Academic Editor: Antoni Sánchez

Received: 7 February 2023
Revised: 14 March 2023
Accepted: 20 March 2023
Published: 24 March 2023

Copyright: © 2023 by the authors. Licensee MDPI, Basel, Switzerland. This article is an open access article distributed under the terms and conditions of the Creative Commons Attribution (CC BY) license (https://creativecommons.org/licenses/by/4.0/).

1. Introduction

Under the background of China's "poor in oil, deficient in natural gas, but rich in coal" energy structure, thermal power generation is still an important part of China's electric power resources production. A boiler is one of the core devices of thermal power generation, and its economic and environmental performance determines the energy efficiency of the whole generator unit [1]. The oxygen content in boiler flue gas is an important parameter that reflects the combustion state of the boiler furnace and is also a key indicator to measure whether the fuel burns adequately. The air/coal ratio required for efficient combustion in the furnace can be reasonably deduced from the oxygen content in the flue gas. Therefore, the timely and accurate measurement of oxygen content in flue gas is of great significance for realizing efficient and stable boiler operation [2,3]. The measurement for oxygen content in boiler flue gas can be divided into direct measurement and soft measurement. At present, zirconia sensors are mostly used to measure the oxygen content in the flue gas in coal-fired power plants in China. However, this method has the disadvantages of moderate lag, decreased measurement accuracy with the aging of sensors, high cost of hardware replacement, short device service life, etc., which struggles to meet the actual needs of power plants [4–6].

In recent years, with the continuous development of computer software and hardware, the soft-sensing technology driven by historical data has been widely applied in the fields of boiler combustion optimization, boiler condition monitoring and control, etc. [7–9]. Among them, the prediction of oxygen content in boiler flue gas based on modeling methods, such as machine learning, has been studied extensively. Research by Ma [10], Zhang [11], and Geng [12] verified the effectiveness of using the BP neural network and its improved algorithm to establish a soft-sensing model for oxygen content in the flue gas. Su [13], Zhang [14], and Li [15] studied the application of a support vector machine (SVM) and a least squares support vector machine (LS-SVM) in the prediction of oxygen content in boiler flue gas, respectively, and used intelligent optimization algorithms to optimize the parameters of the model, improving the accuracy and stability of the model. However, in this traditional soft-sensing model based on machine learning, the feature that the correlation between the various parameters of boilers will change with different operating conditions is ignored in the selection of modeling variables. In order to solve the above problems, Tang [16–18] et al. successively proposed several dynamic correction models for NO_x emission concentration of boilers based on an extreme learning machine and a measurement model for oxygen content in flue gas based on a deep belief network. The core idea of their modeling is that there are large differences in the model feature variables under different load conditions, and this method has been verified through comparison.

Compared with traditional machine learning algorithms, deep learning algorithms such as a convolutional neural network (CNN), feedforward neural network, deep belief network, recurrent neural network, and its modified version of long- and short-time memory networks have strong advantages in the learning and expression ability of data characteristics [19–21]. A CNN has been successfully applied in the field of boiler combustion process monitoring with complex variables because of its powerful feature extraction and feature expression capabilities. Wang [22], Liu [23], and Han [24] used the convolution operation of the CNN model to extract the flame image features of boiler furnaces and predict the furnace combustion state, boiler combustion efficiency, and other indicators of power plants. However, in the above research, the furnace flame images of the boilers are taken as the input of the model. Before practical application, it is necessary to transform the original boilers to obtain the furnace flame images. For such a boiler system with time delay, high nonlinearity, and multivariable coupling features, the two-dimensional matrix composed of time series samples in a fixed time window can also be used as the object of convolution operation to realize the feature extraction and compression of input sample space on the premise of avoiding variable screening and time delay analysis. Xing [25] et al. converted the historical NO_x emission data and boiler combustion process data sample into model training samples and adopted the convolution layer and pooling layer for extraction of input features to establish a NO_x emission prediction model based on CNN-LSTM. Taking the time series samples in a fixed time window as the input of the convolutional network, Li [26] and Jia [27] established the NO_x emission prediction model and the multi-step prediction model of main steam temperature based on the convolutional neural network, respectively, verifying the effectiveness of the CNN processing timing prediction.

In summary, in this paper, a 130 t/h circulating fluidized bed boiler actually running in a petrochemical enterprise in Shandong is the research object, and in view of the multivariable, nonlinearity, and large time delay characteristics of the boiler, the time series samples in the fixed time window were taken as the input of model, and feature extraction was conducted for input samples by use of convolution operation. On this basis, a prediction model of oxygen content in boiler flue gas based on a convolutional neural network was proposed.

2. Data Acquisition and Analysis

2.1. Data Acquisition

In the SIS system of the power plant, 12,000 historical operation samples of the 130 t/h circulating fluidized bed boiler were collected from 2:19 p.m. on 26 November 2020 to 10:14 a.m. on 29 November 2020. As shown in Table 1, a single sample consists of oxygen content in boiler flue gas and 23 variables. In order to make the established model more consistent with the actual production process, the historical samples collected cover 60–100% of the load conditions, including most of the key variables of the boiler during operation.

Table 1. Variables of the 130 t/h CFB boiler.

Variable Name	Unit	Scope
Main steam flow rate	t/h	[90.84, 162.25]
Main steam temperature	°C	[452.63, 470.31]
Main steam pressure	MPa	[4.45, 5.04]
Boiler load	t/h	[92.40, 140.22]
Drum pressure	MPa	[4.95, 5.51]
Furnace chamber differential pressure	Pa	[683.05, 1292.18]
Lower furnace temperature	°C	[854.78, 946.58]
Furnace outlet gas temperature	°C	[793.60, 919.27]
Furnace outlet air pressure	kPa	[−607.46, −203.32]
Economizer inlet temperature	°C	[269.64, 290.63]
Economizer inlet pressure	kPa	[−2767.96, −1463.91]
Secondary fan outlet temperature	°C	[4.07, 13.34]
Primary fan outlet temperature	kPa	[7.34, 8.46]
Secondary fan outlet pressure	kPa	[2.64, 5.64]
Feed water pressure	MPa	[5.36, 6.03]
Feed water temperature	°C	[149.52, 156.53]
Exhaust outlet temperature	°C	[123.43, 132.61]
Primary air volume	Nm^3/h	[94,450.76, 102,729.19]
Secondary air volume	Nm^3/h	[69,768.91, 136,108.61]
Feed water flow	t/h	[85.39, 160.62]
Total coal feed flow	t/h	[14.09, 23.66]
Current of 1# induced draft fan	A	[23.86, 32.37]
Current of 2# induced draft fan	A	[21.84, 33.74]
Oxygen content in boiler flue gas	%	[3.62, 7.09]

The scope in the above table represents the upper and lower bounds of each variable.

2.2. Data Analysis

Boiler operation is a process of multivariable coupling and state accumulation. That is, different operating conditions correspond to different key variables. Moreover, the current state is not simply described as the values of several variables at a certain moment, but the accumulation of states in the past period of time. Generally, the mapping relationship between the input and output of the current system is described in Formulas (1) and (2):

$$X_n = \begin{pmatrix} x_{n-l+1,1} & \cdots & x_{n-l+1,m} \\ \vdots & \ddots & \vdots \\ x_{n,1} & \cdots & x_{n,m} \end{pmatrix} \quad (1)$$

$$y_n = f(X_n) \quad (2)$$

However, during the boiler combustion operation, the oxygen content in the boiler flue gas is affected not only by other relevant variables but also by its own historical change trends. Therefore, the mapping relationship between the input and output of the system is revised in Formulas (3) and (4) in this paper:

$$X_n = \begin{pmatrix} x_{n-l+1,1} & \cdots & x_{n-l+1,m} & y_{n-l+1} \\ \vdots & \ddots & \vdots & \vdots \\ x_{n,1} & \cdots & x_{n,m} & y_n \end{pmatrix} \quad (3)$$

$$y_{n+1} = f(X_n) \quad (4)$$

where X_n is a sample set composed of l historical samples of the boiler at the moment n, l is the length of the time window, m is the number of boiler variables, $x_{i,j}$ is the value of the variable i of the sample j, and y_i is the oxygen content in the flue gas of the sample n.

The size of X_n will increase with the increase in the time window length l, which means a huge scale of input parameters. When such data are processed with a traditional regression learning algorithm, it will take a long time and reduce the generalization performance of the model due to too many parameters to be trained. Therefore, it is necessary to extract the sample features before model training. According to the common variable screening methods, it is often necessary to manually set a threshold and screen the modeling variables based on the correlation between each variable and the target variable. Such methods usually have higher requirements for threshold selection. Different from the above methods, the convolutional neural network can automatically learn the features required for regression tasks from the training sample data, which can improve the model accuracy and training efficiency without relying on the artificial selection of features.

3. Basic Principles of the Convolutional Neural Network

A complete convolutional neural network consists of five basic units: input layer, convolution layer, activation layer, pooling layer, and full connection layer.

3.1. Convolution Layer

The convolution operation is a special feature extraction algorithm that gives practical significance to the convolutional neural network. The convolution layer can extract high-level features with translation invariance from all input parameters through matrix operation and can express the original features effectively. Different from the convolution function in the mathematical sense, for the input matrix A and the convolution kernel of size $r \times c$, the convolution operation is as shown in Formulas (5)–(7), and $G_{i,j}$ is the output matrix.

$$A = \begin{pmatrix} a_{1,1} & \cdots & a_{1,m} \\ \vdots & \ddots & \vdots \\ a_{n,1} & \cdots & a_{n,m} \end{pmatrix} \tag{5}$$

$$W = \begin{pmatrix} w_{1,1} & \cdots & w_{1,c} \\ \vdots & \ddots & \vdots \\ w_{r,1} & \cdots & w_{r,c} \end{pmatrix} \tag{6}$$

$$G_{i,j} = (A \times W)_{i,j} = \sum_{u=1}^{r} \sum_{v=1}^{c} (a_{i+u-1,j+v-1} w_{u,v}) + b_{i,j} \tag{7}$$

An example of a two-dimensional convolution operation is shown in Figure 1. The input matrix of the original 4×4 is transformed into the output matrix of 3×3 under the convolution operation of the convolution kernel that is 2×2 in size.

The type of extracted features depends on the size and number of convolution kernels. For the same input matrix, each convolution kernel corresponds to one feature. The size of the convolution kernel is significantly smaller than that of the input matrix, which greatly reduces the scale of the parameters to be trained in the model, thereby reducing the complexity of the model. As shown in Figure 2, different features can be extracted by increasing the number of convolution kernels. Each convolution kernel corresponds to one output channel, the outputs of all channels are summarized into the final feature map, and the output of each layer is used as the input matrix for the next layer.

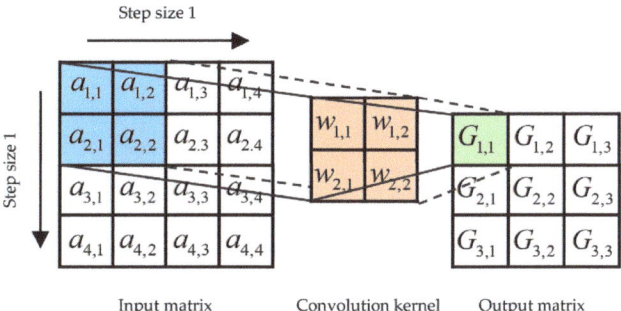

Figure 1. Example of the 2D convolution operation.

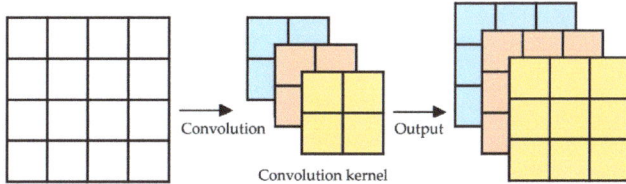

Figure 2. Example of the multi-channel convolution operation.

3.2. Activation Layer

The matrix operation of the convolution layer is a linear operation, which is challenging when dealing with nonlinear problems. When modeling complex systems such as boilers, it is usually necessary to carry out nonlinear mapping of features to make the trained model more in line with the actual production situation. In this paper, the Relu function is selected as the activation layer after the convolution layer. For the output matrix G of the convolution layer, the calculation rule for activating it into the feature matrix H by the Relu function is as follows:

$$H_{i,j} = \varphi(G_{i,j}) = max(0, G_{i,j}) \qquad (8)$$

3.3. Pooling Layer

The role of the pooling layer is feature dimension reduction. For the input feature matrix, there are following two pooling methods. Maximize pooling, which selects the maximum value from a definition window as a new feature and mean pooling, which selects the mean from a definition window as a new feature. In this paper, the maximum pooling is selected as the pooling layer, as shown in Figure 3. A window with a size of 2×2 and a moving step of 2 compresses the features.

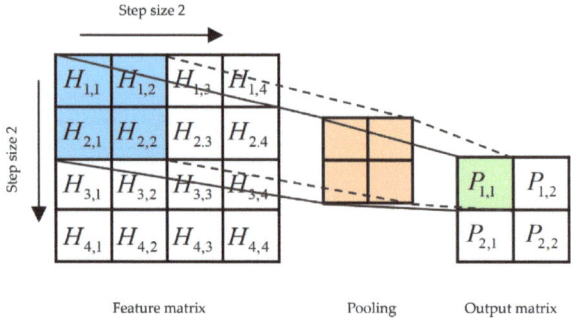

Figure 3. Example of max pooling.

3.4. Full Connection Layer

After feature extraction of the input matrix, the full connection layer is used for parameter training according to the extracted features to achieve the fitting task of the target variables. The structure of the full connection layer is shown in Figure 4. The feature map is flattened and used as the input of the full connection layer, and after passing through several layers of neurons, it is output by the regression layer for the calculation of results. The relationship between the output and input of a single neuron is shown in Formula (9):

$$u_i^t = \sum_{j=1}^{n^{t-1}} \left(w_{i,j}^{t,t-1} \cdot u_j^{t-1} \right) + b_i^t \qquad (9)$$

where u_i^t, u_j^{t-1} represents the output of the neuron i of the layer t and the output of neuron j of the layer $t-1$, respectively, $w_{i,j}^{t,t-1}$ represents the connection weight between the neuron i of the layer t and the neuron j of the layer $t-1$, n^{t-1} represents the number of neurons on the layer $t-1$, and b_i^t represents the bias term of the neuron i of the layer t.

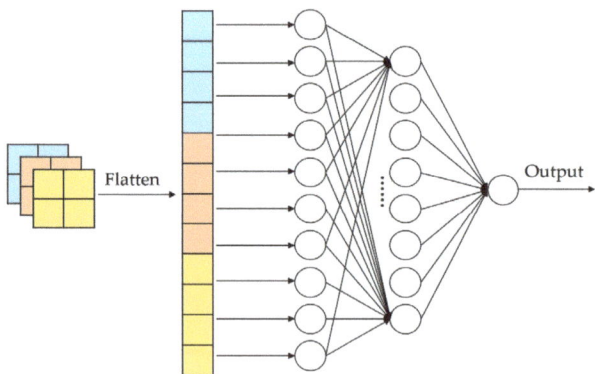

Figure 4. The fully connected layer.

In summary, the model parameters that require optimization calculation in the training process of the CNN model mainly include the convolution kernel parameters of the convolution layer, the weight and bias term of the full connection layer, etc. the basic procedure of model parameters training is as follows: first, the training set samples are divided into a number of small batch sample sets in each iteration in order to avoid model over-fitting, and then the model parameters are adjusted in the negative gradient direction of the small batch training error by using the gradient descent algorithm. Training will be terminated while the preset convergence precision or the maximum number of iterations are reached. finally, the training results of the model are output, and the output model is tested for performance through the test set samples.

4. Case Analysis
4.1. Data Pre-Processing

In order to study the effectiveness of the CNN in dealing with time series prediction, the actual operation data of the CFB boiler were collected for training and model testing. Parts of the data examples are shown in Table 2. The combustion of the boiler is typically impacted by changes in coal composition, and if the data used for modeling do not change accordingly, the accuracy of the model will be affected. In the proposed mode, the data utilized for modeling are l historical samples from the boiler's historical moment $n - l + 1$ to the present moment n. These data are constantly being updated, which can complement new data created by the system after the coal type is changed in a timely manner and increase the model's accuracy. The effect of coal quality on model accuracy can be ignored while the time span of the data collected is short.

Table 2. Sample example.

Variable	Unit	Sample 1	Sample 2	Sample 12,000	Variable	Unit	Sample 1	Sample 2	Sample 12,000
Main steam flow rate	t/h	111.38	113.38	128.15	Primary fan outlet temperature	kPa	7.57	7.58	8.00
Main steam temperature	°C	464.18	464.18	464.76	Secondary fan outlet pressure	kPa	3.00	2.98	4.50
Main steam pressure	MPa	4.90	4.88	4.89	Feed water pressure	MPa	5.62	5.61	5.81
Boiler load	t/h	103.12	103.52	128.13	Feed water temperature	°C	151.84	151.94	153.75
Drum pressure	MPa	5.22	5.21	5.37	Exhaust outlet temperature	°C	124.88	124.91	128.18
Furnace chamber differential pressure	kPa	0.75	0.74	1.00	Primary air volume	Nm^3/h	97,230.77	97,406.60	94,989.02
Lower furnace temperature	°C	899.78	899.68	914.63	Secondary air volume	Nm^3/h	77,714.29	80,263.73	108,131.9
Furnace outlet gas temperature	°C	839.41	839.12	882.20	Feed water flow	t/h	98.11	98.29	111.91
Furnace outlet air pressure	Pa	−257.02	−255.80	−479.24	Total coal feed flow	t/h	15.73	15.78	19.95
Economizer inlet temperature	°C	270.70	270.70	282.42	Current of 1# induced draft fan	A	26.43	26.50	28.37
Economizer inlet pressure	kPa	−1.589	−1.58	−2.11	Current of 2# induced draft fan	A	21.94	21.96	26.58
Secondary fan outlet temperature	°C	12.19	12.11	9.21	Oxygen content in boiler flue gas	%	5.57	5.63	4.79

In order to ensure the prediction accuracy and stability of the model, it was necessary to conduct abnormal value processing and noise reduction processing for the collected historical operation data of the boiler. First of all, the abnormal data were detected using the

3sigam criterion and interpolated by the mean value method, and denoising of each variable was conducted by use of the wavelet denoising method. Then, the first 10,000 samples were normalized to [0, 1] by Formula (10), and the last 2000 samples were normalized based on the statistics of the first 10,000 samples. Finally, the time window l was set to 24 and sample reforming was performedm according to Formulas (3) and (4), to obtain 11,976 sets of new samples. Then, the first 9976 sets of samples were set as the training set and the last 2000 sets of samples were set as the test set. The training set was used to solve the most appropriate model parameters, and the test set was used to test the generalization performance of the model.

$$x' = \frac{x - x_{min}}{x_{max} - x_{min}} \quad (10)$$

Taking the boiler load of this boiler as an example, Figure 5 shows the results of data pre-processing.

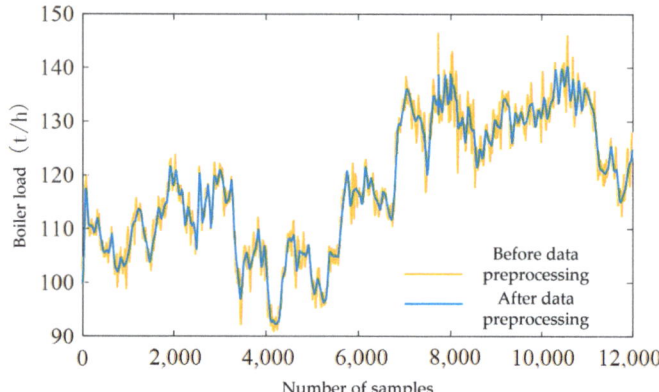

Figure 5. The result of data preprocessing.

4.2. Model Evaluation Indicators

In order to evaluate the prediction accuracy and generalization performance of the model, the decision coefficient R^2 and the root mean square error $RMSE$ were selected as evaluation indicators, and the evaluation indicators were used for comparing the prediction performance of different models. R^2 and $RMSE$ are defined as follows:

$$R^2 = \frac{\left\{\sum \left[(y_i - \bar{y}_i) \cdot (\hat{y}_i - \bar{\hat{y}}_i)\right]\right\}^2}{\sum (y_i - \bar{y}_i)^2 \cdot \sum (\hat{y}_i - \bar{\hat{y}}_i)^2} \quad (11)$$

$$RMSE = \sqrt{\frac{1}{n} \sum (y_i - \hat{y}_i)^2} \quad (12)$$

where y_i, $\bar{y}_i$, $\hat{y}_i$, and $\bar{\hat{y}}_i$, respectively, represent the oxygen content in the flue gas of the sample boiler, the mean of true values, the predicted value, and the mean of predicted values.

4.3. Modeling and Result Analysis

The framework of the prediction model for oxygen content in flue gas based on the CNN is shown in Figure 6, and the hyper-parameter values are shown in Table 3. The hyperparameters of the TS-CNN model include the maximum number of iterations, the sample size of the minimum training batch, the initial learning rate, the learning rate decline factor, the learning rate decline frequency interval, the discard rate, the optimization algorithm, etc. The optimal values of the hyper-parameters are determined through several experiments as well as empirical values. Cross-validation was performed throughout the test. A total of 80% of the data in the training set were used to create a new training set and the remaining 20% of the data were utilized as a validation set, and each iteration was accompanied by one validation of the model parameters.

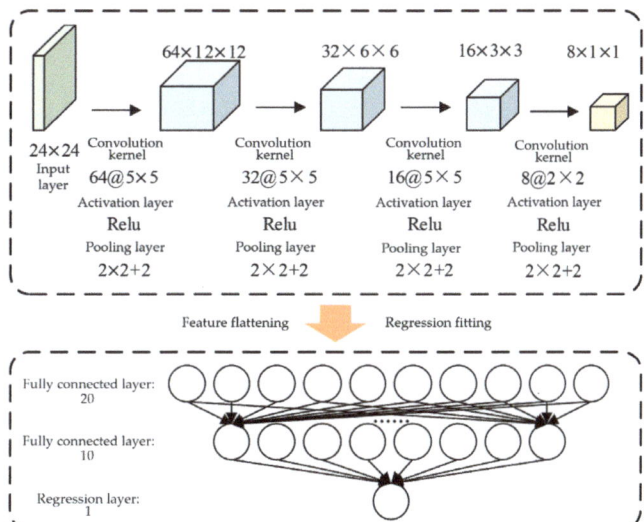

Figure 6. Framework of the CNN-based model.

Table 3. Parameters for CNN-based model.

Hyper-Parameter	Name	Value
Maximum number of iterations	MaxEpochs	50
Sample size of the minimum training batch	miniBatchSize	25
Initial learning rate	InitialLearnRate	0.003
Learning rate decline factor	LearnRateDropFactor	0.2
Learning rate decline frequency interval	LearnRateDropPeriod	8
Discard rate	dropout	0.2
Optimization algorithm	Gradient descent with momentum (SGDM)	

The feature extraction module includes four convolution layers, an activation layer, and a pooling layer, respectively. The eight extracted features were flattened and then input into the full connection layer, and there are two full connection layers in total, with 20 and 10 neurons on each layer, respectively, and the last layer is regression layer.

In order to verify the effectiveness of the CNN in the prediction of oxygen content in the flue gas, the following four groups of experiments were designed with different modeling algorithms:

(1) Time series prediction model (TS-CNN), $y_{n+1} = f(X_n)$;

(2) Conventional prediction model (CNN), $y_n = f(X_n)$;
(3) BP neural network model (BPNN) with a single hidden layer and 10 neurons;
(4) Least squares support vector machine model with model parameter $\gamma = 100$, $\sigma^2 = 3$ (LSSVM).

According to Pearson's correlation coefficient between variables and oxygen content in the flue gas, boiler load with a correlation coefficient greater than 0.6, lower furnace temperature, furnace outlet temperature, feed water flow, and total feed coal flow were taken as input variables of tests (3) and (4).

The training results of the TS-CNN model and the test results of each model are shown in Figure 7a,b, respectively. It can be seen in Table 4 that the TS-CNN model has the best fitting effect, followed by the CNN model, which indicates that the use of convolution operation for feature extraction of the input matrix can effectively improve the generalization performance of the model. The BPNN model and LSSVM model both have a poor fitting effect, and their prediction curves deviate from the real curves seriously after the 100th test point. The main reasons for the above results are as follows. (1) The boiler has the state accumulation feature, (2) the oxygen content in the boiler flue gas is not only related to other variables but also affected by its own historical change trends, and (3) the feature extraction module in the CNN can extract time sequence features from the input matrix.

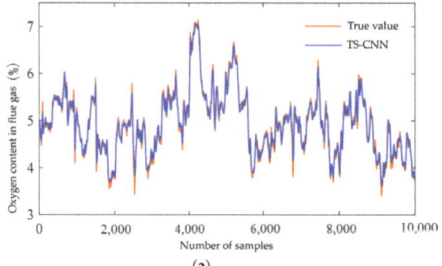
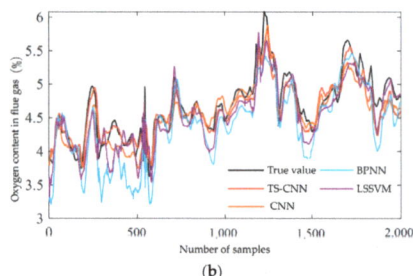

Figure 7. (**a**) Training results of the TS-CNN model. (**b**) Testing results of different models.

Table 4. R^2 and $RMSE$ for each model.

		TS-CNN	CNN	BPNN	LSSVM
Training set	R^2	0.9838	0.9798	0.9636	0.9660
	$RMSE$	0.0903	0.0986	0.1283	0.1240
Test set	R^2	0.8929	0.8443	0.7963	0.8251
	$RMSE$	0.1684	0.2070	0.3707	0.2448

5. Conclusions

The boiler system is a complicated nonlinear system with a time lag, where the current value of each operational variable does not accurately describe the current operating state of the boiler, which may be the accumulation of states over a period of time in the past. In order to improve the prediction accuracy of oxygen content in the flue gas, a prediction model for oxygen content in the boiler flue gas based on the CNN was proposed. First of all, the original data were pre-processed using the 3sigam criterion and wavelet denoising. Then, the data were analyzed, and the time series samples in a fixed time window were taken as the input of the model. Additionally, the effect of historical trends of oxygen content in the flue gas on the performance of the model was studied. Considering the boiler flue gas oxygen content may also be affected by its own historical trend, the historical values of the boiler flue gas oxygen content were added to the input of the model for the prediction of the boiler flue gas oxygen content in the next moment. To solve the low efficiency problem of model training caused by too large of a scale of features, a convolution kernel was used to extract the effective features from the input matrix, and a pooling layer was used for dimension reduction in the features. Finally, the TS-CNN model was tested by the actual operating data. The R^2 and $RMSE$ of the TS-CNN model were 0.8929 and 0.1684, respectively, and its prediction accuracy was improved by 18.6%, 31.2%, and 54.6% compared with that of the CNN model, LSSVM model, and BPNN model, respectively. The test results show that the proposed model can effectively predict the oxygen content in the boiler flue gas.

Since all boilers are characterized by complex nonlinearities and time lags, the method proposed in this paper may also be potentially applicable to predict the flue gas oxygen content of a wide range of boilers. In our future research, we will also make an effort to confirm the performance of the proposed method for predicting the flue gas oxygen content of different types of boilers.

Author Contributions: Conceptualization and project administration, B.S.; methodology, Z.L. and G.L.; writing—original draft, Z.L and G.L.; supervision, review, and editing, B.S. All authors have read and agreed to the published version of the manuscript.

Funding: This research was funded by the National Natural Science Foundation of China, funding number 21878238.

Data Availability Statement: The data that support the findings of this study are available from the corresponding author upon reasonable request.

Conflicts of Interest: The authors declare no conflict of interest.

References

1. Da, B.-W. *Strategies for Clean Coal Technologies and Carbon Reduction Investment of Coal-Electric Supply Chain under Cap-and-Trade Model*; China University of Mining and Technology: Xuzhou, China, 2021.
2. Liu, C.-L.; Li, S.-N. Soft measurement of flue gas oxygen content based on LS-SVM and simplex. *J. Eng. Therm. Energy Power* **2010**, *25*, 292–296.
3. Zhao, C.-Y. Discussion on logic calculation of oxygen content in boiler flue gas for 300MW unit. *North China Electr. Power* **2007**, *8*, 12–15.
4. Luo, J.; Wu, L. Research status of soft measurement technology of typical thermal parameters for utility boilers. *Therm. Power Gener.* **2015**, *44*, 1–9+13.
5. Liu, F.-G.; Hao, W.-D.; Yang, J.-Z.; Guo, Y.-Q.; Zhang, Q.-G.; Hou, F.-J. Economic analyze for utility boiler operated in different oxygen content outlet furnace and it's optimization. *Proc. CSEE* **2003**, *23*, 172–176.
6. Peng, X.; Lv, Y.-K. Study on analytical solutions on optimal economics of power boiler based on flue gas oxygen content. *Electr. Power Sci. Eng.* **2009**, *25*, 40–44.
7. Liang, T.; Jin, Y.-J.; Jiang, W.; Liu, Z.-H. Optimization of NO$_x$ emissions from coal-fired boilers based on improved MVO and WLSSVM. *China Meas. Test* **2021**, *47*, 148–154.
8. Xie, L.; Mao, G.-M.; Jin, X.-M.; Su, H.-Y. Predictive control and economic performance optimization of CFBB combustion process. *CIESC J.* **2016**, *67*, 695–700.
9. Chui, E.-H.; Gao, H. Estimation of NO$_x$ emissions from coal-fired utility boilers. *Fuel* **2010**, *89*, 2977–2984. [CrossRef]
10. Ma, L.Y.; Wang, Y.; Zuo, X. ANN-based soft sensing of oxygen content in boiler air-flue gas system. In Proceedings of the 2019 Chinese Control and Decision Conference, Nanchang, China, 3–5 June 2019.
11. Zhang, W.; Chen, C.-B.; Wang, J.-C.; Li, J.-C.; Hao, S.-J. Prediction of the oxygen content in flue gas of power plant based on PSO-elman model. *Autom. Instrum.* **2020**, *35*, 75–79+85.
12. Geng, M.-Y.; Hu, R.; Li, L. Prediction of oxygen content in boiler flue gas of thermal power unit. *J. Univ. Shanghai Sci. Technol.* **2021**, *43*, 319–324+359.
13. Su, T.; Pan, H.-G.; Huang, X.-D.; Shao, X.-Q.; Ma, B. Soft sensor of flue gas oxygen content based on improved PSO-SVM in coal-fired power plant. *J. Xi'an Univ. Sci. Technol.* **2020**, *40*, 342–348.
14. Zhang, Y.-F.; Wang, J.-C.; Shi, Y.-H.; Fei, L. Soft sensors model based on state constrained moving window. *Control. Eng. China* **2014**, *21* (Suppl. 1), 115–117+120.
15. Li, J.-Q.; Zhang, Y.-Y.; Niu, C.-L. Prediction of the oxygen content in flue gas of power plant based on PSO-LSSVM model. *J. Eng. Therm. Energy Power* **2018**, *33*, 49–55. [CrossRef]

16. Tang, Z.-H.; Chai, X.-Y.; Cao, S.-X.; Mou, Z.-H.; Pang, X.-Y. Deep learning modeling for the NO$_x$ emissions of coal-fired boiler considering time-delay characteristics. *Proc. CSEE* **2020**, *40*, 6633–6644.
17. Tang, Z.-H.; Li, Y.; Kusiak, A. A deep learning model for measuring oxygen content of boiler flue gas. *IEEE Access* **2020**, *8*, 12268–12278. [CrossRef]
18. Tang, Z.-H.; Zhu, D.-Y.; Li, Y. Data driven based dynamic correction prediction model for NOx emission of coal fired boiler. *Proc. CSEE* **2022**, *42*, 5182–5193.
19. Li, G.Q.; Qi, X.B.; Chan, K.-C.-C.; Chen, B. Deep bidirectional learning machine for predicting NO$_x$ emissions and boiler efficiency from a coal-fired boiler. *Energy Fuels* **2017**, *31*, 11471–11480. [CrossRef]
20. Pan, H.; Su, T.; Huang, X.-D.; Wang, Z. LSTM-based soft sensor design for oxygen content of flue gas in coal-fired power plant. *Trans. Inst. Meas. Control* **2021**, *43*, 78–87. [CrossRef]
21. Hu, H.-Z.; Zhang, J.-B.; Liu, H.-Q.; Li, M.-D.; Yang, Q.-Y. Power plant boiler combustion efficiency modeling approach based on convolutional neural networks. *J. Xi'an Jiaotong Univ.* **2019**, *53*, 10–15.
22. Wang, Z.-Y.; Song, C.-F.; Chen, T. Deep learning based monitoring of furnace combustion state and measurement of heat release rate. *Energy* **2017**, *131*, 106–112. [CrossRef]
23. Liu, Y.; Fan, Y.; Chen, J.-H. Flame images for oxygen content prediction of combustion systems using DBN. *Energy Fuels* **2017**, *31*, 8776–8783. [CrossRef]
24. Han, Z.-Z.; Li, J.; Zhang, B.; Hossain, M.-M.; Xu, C.-L. Prediction of combustion state through a semi-supervised learning model and flame imaging. *Fuel* **2020**, *289*, 119745. [CrossRef]
25. Xing, H.-T.; Guo, J.-L.; Liu, S.-A.; Yan, B.; Yang, Y.-Y. NO$_x$ emission forecasting based on CNN-LSTM hybrid neural network. *Electron. Meas. Technol.* **2022**, *45*, 98–103.
26. Li, N.; Hu, Y. The deep convolutional neural network for NOx emission prediction of a coal-fired boiler. *IEEE Access* **2020**, *8*, 85912–85922. [CrossRef]
27. Jia, X.-J.; Sang, Y.-C.; Li, Y.-J.; Du, W.; Zhang, G.-L. Short-term forecasting for supercharged boiler safety performance based on advanced data-driven modelling framework. *Energy* **2022**, *239*, 122449. [CrossRef]

Disclaimer/Publisher's Note: The statements, opinions and data contained in all publications are solely those of the individual author(s) and contributor(s) and not of MDPI and/or the editor(s). MDPI and/or the editor(s) disclaim responsibility for any injury to people or property resulting from any ideas, methods, instructions or products referred to in the content.

Review

Bibliometric Analysis of Constructed Wetlands with Ornamental Flowering Plants: The Importance of Green Technology

José Luis Marín-Muñiz [1], Irma Zitácuaro-Contreras [1], Gonzalo Ortega-Pineda [1], Luis Manuel Álvarez-Hernández [1], Karina Elizabeth Martínez-Aguilar [1], Aarón López-Roldán [1] and Sergio Zamora [2,*]

[1] El Colegio de Veracruz, Xalapa 91000, Veracruz, Mexico; jmarin@colver.info (J.L.M.-M.)
[2] Facultad de Ingeniería, Construcción y Habitad, Universidad Veracruzana, Bv. Adolfo Ruíz Cortines 455, Costa Verde, Boca del Rio 94294, Veracruz, Mexico
* Correspondence: szamora@uv.mx; Tel.: +52-442-226-6337

Abstract: The use of constructed wetlands (CWs) for wastewater treatment has earned high interest around the world. However, innovations to improve its removal efficiency and adoption have been suggested in the last decades. For instance, the use of ornamental flowering plants (OFP), which make wetland treatment systems more aesthetic and is an option for the production of commercial flowers while the water is cleansed. The objectives of this study were to identify through a bibliometric analysis (2000–2022) the main OFP that have been used in CWs and their functionality as phytoremediators (removal effects), as well as the authors, collaborations, main investigations, and the countries where such investigations have been carried out. To this respect, 10,254 studies on CWs were identified. The United States and China were the leading countries in the use of this eco-technology. Subsequently, regarding the use of OFP, the analysis revealed 92 studies on this matter in which Mexico has three researchers who lead the use of OFP in CWs (almost 40% of publications of CWs with OFP), where the main species studied include *Canna hybrids*, *Zantedeschia aethiopica*, *Strelitzia reginae*, *Iris species*, *Spathiphyllum* sp., and *Anturium* sp. These species may remove between 30–90% of pollutants of organic compounds, 30–70% of heavy metals and drugs, and about 99.9% of pathogens. Thus, this study may help researchers to identify OFP for new CWs design, and to know new future research directionsand collaboration approaches in this area using multipurpose alternatives like those of CWs with OFP. More research can still be carried out on the use of CWs with OFP in temperate climates, as well as evaluating the influence of different substrates and water flow on the growth of these plants.

Keywords: bibliometric study; ornamental plants; treatment wetlands; wastewater

1. Introduction

Constructed wetlands (CWs), also called treatment wetlands, are a nature-based solution that emulates natural wetlands processes (physical, chemical, and biological) in order to optimize and treat different types of wastewater. CWs consist of shallow cells or channels with an impermeable layer and structures to control the water level, flow direction, and hydraulic retention time. Substrate, microorganisms, and plants are the principal components of CWs [1–3].

According to the water flow, CWs can be classified as free water surface (shallow open waters, where plants are rooted in a soil layer on the bottom; these systems are the most similar to natural wetlands) or subsurface CWs (shallow watertight beds, filled with porous media, plants are rooted in the water-saturated beds, water is loaded in the inlet of the bed and therefore it flows below the surface in a horizontal or vertical pattern) [4,5].

Common substrates in CWs include mineral or plastic materials. In a recent study, nine substrates were evaluated (zeolite, anthracite, shale, vermiculite, ceramic filter material, gravel, steel slag, bio-ceramic and combination substrate-isopyknic layered anthracite, bio-ceramic and zeolite), corroborating this combination of substrates was the best scheme among nine materials. Zeolite was ideal for better nitrogen removal [6].

In other studies, some plastic substrates were used as filter material in CWs (plastic rings and PET residues) [7]. However, some microplastics could be released in certain time, being a later problem, depending on the intended use of the treated water [8,9].

The importance of CWs for wastewater treatment lies at the multiple types of wastewater they can clean. Some reviews regarding the use of CWs for removal of pesticides from agricultural runoff and drainage [10], industrial wastewater [11], emerging contaminants [12], acid mine drainage [13], leachate [14], or wastewaters to community or municipal level [15–20] have been developed, corroborating the functionality of CWs for the removal of pollutants.

In order to increase the removal efficiency of the ecotechnology, some innovations have been proposed in recent years. For instance, intermittent flows of water to be treated in wetlands (tidal flow CWs, partially saturated CWs, or integration of hydraulic or aeration machinery into constructed wetlands [21,22]). The combination of different types of wetlands or flows has also been an option to improve concentrations of pollutants through CWs (hybrid CWs) [23].

Furthermore, about plants in CWs, the common vegetation of natural wetlands (*Cyperus papyrus*, *Phragmites australis*, *Typha* and *Scirpus* spp.) [24] that is also used in CWs has been changed or combined with terrestrial ornamental flowering plants (OFP) (herbaceous perennial ornamental plants including the use of species with different colored flowers), evaluating their adaptation to conditions of water saturation to be treated and their functionality as water purification [1,25,26].

OFP harvesting can be an economic entity for CW operators, providing social and economic benefits such as the improvement of system landscapes and a better habitat quality [25–27]. The economic potential using CWs with OFP has recently been analyzed [28]. To this respect, 21 species of phytoremediation plants were identified. *Anthurium andreanum* and *Zantedeschia aethiopica* stand out for their commercial value, reported in 2018 to be USD 272,875 and 30,318, respectively, at the national level.

In addition, several studies have reported that ornamental macrophytes species have an excellent capacity to enter flooding mechanisms, but each one had different physiological development. These conditions favor the removal of pollutants in different ways, demonstrating removals between 40–90% of organic and inorganic compounds [28–30]. Other studies have also demonstrated that the polyculture of OFP in CWs may enhance the release of root exudates, which might stimulate the uptake of nitrogen and phosphate compounds [31,32].

For this reason, recent studies have considered the use of OFP as the main vegetation for CWs. However, some questions remain unanswered: What are the main studies on CWs using OFP and who has carried them out? What is the main vegetation of OFP used in CWs and how many pollutants are removed? In order to answer these questions, this research was carried out and the main objective was to identify through a bibliometric analysis (BA) the use of CWs around the world (2000–2022), to know the main OFP that have been used in CWs and their functionality as phytoremediators (removal effects), as well as the authors, collaborations, main investigations, and the countries where such investigations have been carried out.

A bibliometric analysis (BA) is a scientific computer-assisted review methodology that can identify core research or authors, as well as their relationship, by covering all the publications related to a given topic or field [33]. For the BA, bibliographic tools such as DIMENSIONS are used and software tools such as VOSviewer, a computer program used for network analysis; it draws maps of scientific knowledge to show the interrelationships between literature [34].

Scientometric studies on CWs or climate change have previously been carried out. For example, Colares et al. [35] provided a BA regarding the use of floating CWs. Zhang et al. [36] reported a BA to summarize the impact between water management and CWs. Moondra et al. [37] explored a BA for the use of CWs in wastewater treatment. However, specific bibliometric studies to analyze the use of ornamental plants in CWs are scarce. Santos et al. [38] used a BA to create comparative trends of publications about global warming/climate emergency. Thus, this study may contribute more knowledge in this research area in which a selection of OFP is presented in order to complement the design of new CWs and help readers to establish new collaborations in the field.

2. Materials and Methods

The first step of this study was to know the types of names with which an ecological wastewater treatment system has been used in publications around the world from 2000 to 2023. This period of time was selected in the early 2000s when the amount of publications on this topic took an important standout and continuity as a research area in the face of wastewater contamination problems [2,18,39].

The procedure used to discover the name used for ecological wastewater treatment was to detect the number of publications using the term "constructed wetland", "artificial wetland", "treatment wetland", "wetland biofilter", "engineering wetland", "ecotechnology wetland" in the title and abstracts. This was performed byusing the DIMENSIONS program. This number of publications with the terms described were used to generate word clouds using the software WordArt [40].

Dimensionsisan integrated database that allows researchers to search and analyze grants, patents, clinical trials, policy documents, and publications (https://app.dimensions.ai/ (accessed on 10 February 2023)). This program has been described like a new scholarly search database that focuses on the broader set of use cases that academics now face. Compared to other databases, it has a free version that includes a searchable publications index and links to all the other different entities [41].

The second step was to identify the scientometric analysis; these were based on papers regarding the use of CWs around the world and collaborations about the topic in journals registered on the DIMENSIONS bibliometric database during the period 2000–2023, using the title and abstract codes "constructed wetlands" and other similar names ("constructed wetland", "CW", "CWs", "constructed wetlands", "artificial wetlands", "treatment wetlands"). For ornamental plant, other similar names were "ornamental plants"and"flowering plants". In addition, studies on the use of ornamental plants in CWs were consulted in the DIMENSIONS program. Search example: "Constructed wetland AND ornamental plants"; co-occurrence, and collaboration with countries and affiliations were also performed on the full search results, which were exported from DIMENSIONS to a CSV file.

The recovered manuscripts were properly organized using Microsoft Excel, while the maps were made with VOSviewer. Thanks to this program, it was possible to identify the different thematic areas, the journals indexed, the main studies, the countries, the main authors, and collaborations.

Once the main authors who have conducted research on the use of ornamental plants in CWS were identified with DIMENSIONS, the third step was to individually corroborate all the studies, not only on DIMENSIONS, but also on Google Scholar. Subsequently, they were sent by each of their authors individually via email and corroborated.

3. Results and Discussion

3.1. Importance of CWs as a Green Technology

Regarding the background of the use of CWs, it should be noted that subsurface CWs were first researched in Germany in 1954 by Dr. Seidel. In 1960, this was described as the "root method" by Dr. Kickuth [2,3,19]. Later on, they were called artificial wetlands [20], which, to date, is not used, as the word 'artificial'can be understood as something useless or of little use. Figure 1 presents the word cloud generated for the different names using ecological wastewater treatment. Based on such a word cloud, the most employed concepts have been *Treatment wetlands* and *Constructed wetlands*, increasing over time in terms of occurrence in articles. However, other terms have been incorporated to a lesser extent such as *wetland biofilters* and *bioengineered wetlands* (Figure 1; [1–5]). These data showed coincidences regarding the fact that recent book publications are already titled as treatment wetlands [42–44].

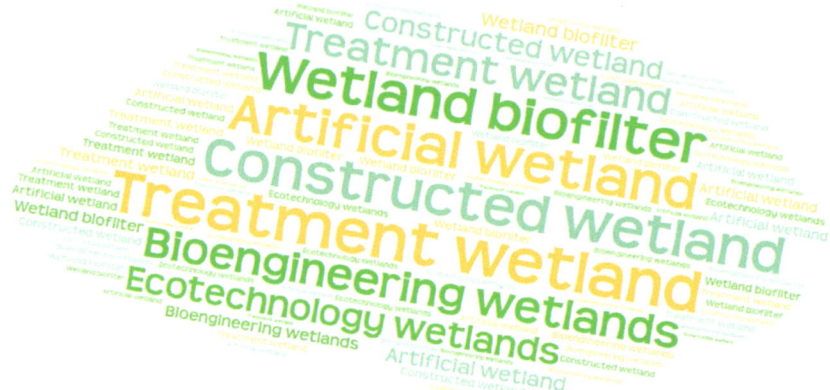

Figure 1. Word cloud of names used for wastewater treatment with ecological engineering systems.

On the other hand, recently, more attention has been paid to CWs as part of a circular economy in the rural and urban environments as these systems are a good fit for the new concept of sponge cities [2]. Many factors indicate that the future of rural and urban water systems is shifting towards solutions that are resource oriented, integrated, sustainable, distributed, and nature-based. The treatment of wastewater will be replaced by the production of goods, an optimized system like CWs will allow reaching multiple targets (wastewater treatment and water reuse, ornamental plant production, compost with plant biomass, bioelectricity generation, scenic landscaping), instead of having a separate infrastructure for every purpose [44–46].

Some authors, through the assessment of the sustainability (based on the development of a composite indicator embracing economic, environmental, and social issues) [47], and life cycle analysis studies using wastewater treatment like constructed wetlands, have identified that such systems combine low costs, high efficiencies in removal of pollutants (40–99%), and lower environmental impact (environment friendly) [48,49].

3.2. Use of CWs around the World and Collaborations in the Field

It has been described that CWs are widely recognized as efficient and cost-effective solutions to wastewater problems [1–3]. Such affirmation was confirmed with the analysis on the use of this technology around the world (Figure 2), in which a wide distribution of publications on the topic was detected in 89 countries. This demonstrates the importance that CWs have as a research area facing the problem of water pollution. Despite this, there is still a wastewater treatment deficit; only 39% of the global population has used a safely managed sanitation service [50].

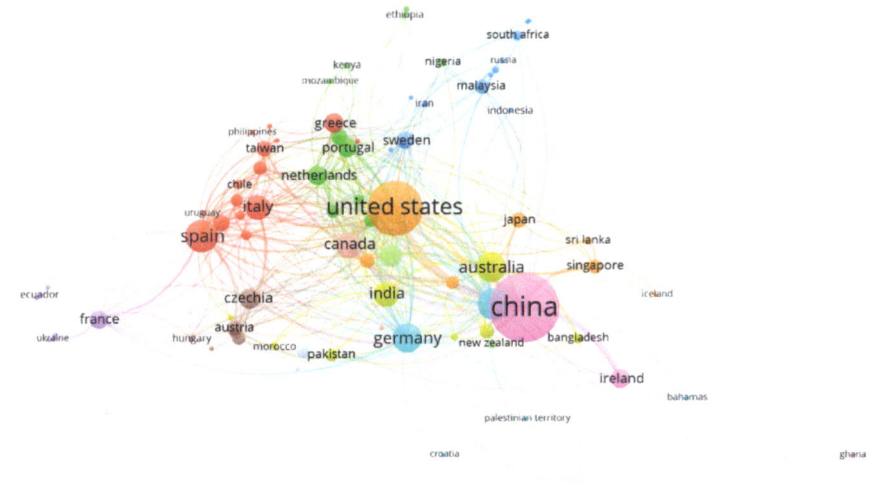

Figure 2. Publications on CWs by countries during 2000–2023 around the world.

In Figure 2, the largest circles represent the largest publications by country, where the United States and China are the main countries, leading with 6.9% and 4.4%, respectively, followed mainly by European countries. Regarding Mexico, it is already represented on the map with an extensive collaboration between publications from European, American, and Latin countries, but only representing 1%, which suggests it is a country that has just recently used CWs compared to countries like China and the USA.

The findings regarding the main countries where research on CWs is carried out is consistent with those reported by Zhao [51], who describes that China and the USA lead the new strategies with technical principles that include penetration, detention, storage, purification, usage, and drainage, where the CWs are key technical solutions for water purification. Reyes et al. [52] also identified China and the USA by means of a BA among the countries that had the most number of treatment wetlands, specifically for stormwater. Thus, greater efforts to replicate this alternative by other countries are pertinent. Some studies stress the need for integration among the water field actors to include and accept the use of CW technology in public policies without risk aversion [53].

Moreover, through bibliometric studies, the importance of ecotechnology in the face of water scarcity has been discussed [36], reporting that CWs focus on water management in three different ways: rainwater management, wastewater treatment, and ecological water purification. Furthermore, the influencing factors of CWs for water management, as well as their additional benefits are also discussed, which demonstrates that CWs must be designed and maintained in future research, and should be more involved in water management so that they may become sustainable through CWs.

The productivity by authors about the publications of CWs around the world was analyzed with the BA, and approximately 10,254 posts on CWs were found worldwide. The size of the circles on the map (Figure 3) is proportional to the number of articles that the author leads in that area, regardless of whether they are technical research or literature review texts. Furthermore, it is observed that the main authors according to the number of publications and citations include Jan Vymazal from Czech University of Life Science Prague, Czechia (110 publications; 9977 citations), Jian Zang of Shandong University of

Science and Technology, China (93; 3442), Joan García from Universitat Politécnica de Catalunya, Spain (77; 4286), and Hans Brix from Aarthus University, Denmark (64; 4262).

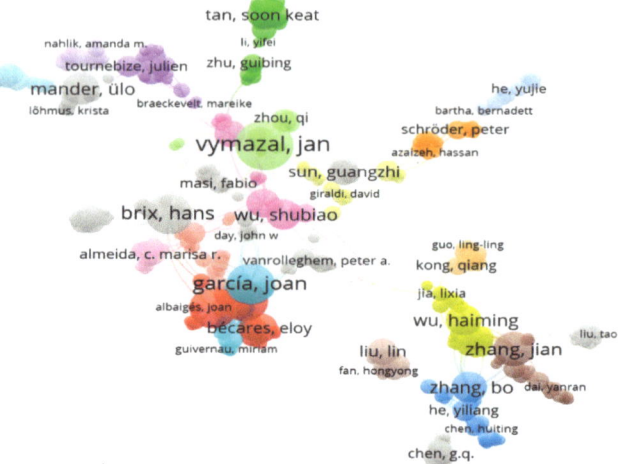

Figure 3. Researcher collaboration co-occurrence map on CWs studies during 2000–2023 around the world.

Although the detected authors are from geographically distant countries, the closeness between circles on the map indicates their intellectual relationship in terms of co-authorship in that area of research. The authors that are close to each of the main ones detected indicate mutual collaborations.

It should be noted that there is a paucity of comparative data with bibliometric studies on the general use of CWs. However, in a BA about the authors and institutions boarding topics on the relationship between water management and CWs, Zhang et al. [36] showed that in terms of the most productive authors according to the number of publications are M. Scholz, C.M. Cooper, and R. Kroeger. This refers to the fact that there is a great variety of scientists on CWs, but there is also a wide specialization of topics, which may include: agricultural, domestic, or industrial wastewater, regression models, greenhouse gases, circular economy, plant growth, clogging, different flows, and hybrid systems, among others.

3.3. CWs Using Ornamental Flowering Plants and Collaborations in the Topic

Once the use of CWs in the world was detected, a search regarding the use of ornamental plants during the treatment of wastewater by means of CWs was needed owing to the importance that this type of vegetation provides in the aesthetic appearance of ecotechnology, as an economic resource, and for its better adoption and appropriation.

Regarding the use of ornamental plants in subsurface flow constructed wetlands, the scientometric study on DIMENSIONS found 92 publications related to the use of ornamental plants in CWs during wastewater treatment. Figure 4 shows the countries with the highest number of publications on the topic, according to the size of the circles that represent each country. Mexico stands out with the highest number of publications (24.2%), followed by India (12%), China (11%), Brazil (8.8%), and the United States (7.7%).

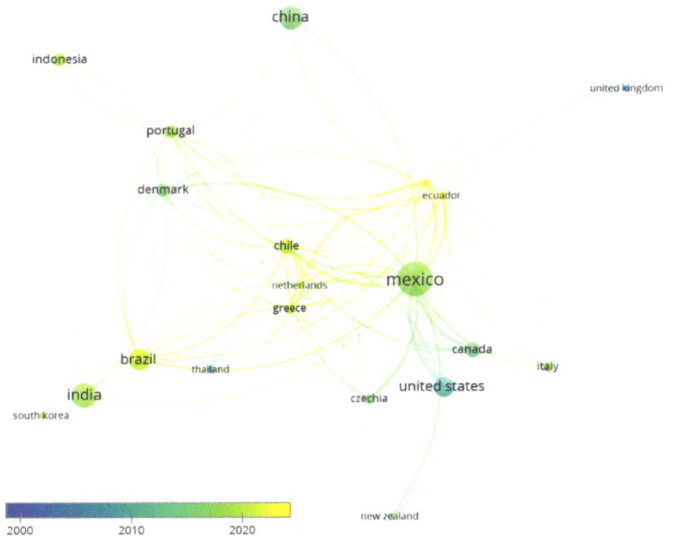

Figure 4. Network visualization of the main countries in the investigation on wastewater treatment with CWs and ornamental plants.

It should be noted that on this map, the color of the circles, on a scale from blue to yellow (2000–2023), indicates that although Mexico leads the largest publications on treatment wetlands using ornamental plants, those that began with this type of inclusion of plants were countries like the United States, Thailand, and the United Kingdom (blue tones). Later on, Mexico, and recently Chile and Brazil were as the most representative (yellow tones). The link between the circles (countries) indicates the co-authorship.

It is evident that there is cooperation between Mexico and all the countries on the map, however, there is a greater emphasis in relation to Latin American countries. For such region, Rodríguez-Domínguez et al. [53] showed that this area is a heterogeneous territory where CWs arean excellent option to solve the wastewater problems using a largevariety of OFP, and these vegetation can influence the interest or the impact of the technology either by beautification or integration in the place of establishment, which coincides with the fact that Mexico is one of those countries with wide use of CWs with OFP as found in this BA.

It is important to describe that countries with a large portion of land in the tropical and subtropical area such as Mexico, India, China, and Brazil have a greater biodiversity of vegetation species due to the prevailing climatic conditions. This has favored the greater use of variety of ornamental plants as an alternative treatment in CWs. However, more studies are needed both as monocultures or polycultures of ornamental plants as this favors diversity and a better removal in the system [30,54,55], as well as different designs of CWs that may reinforce what has been detected so far.

When the importance of Mexico as a leader in publications on wetlands constructed with ornamental plants was detected, the collaboration between the main authors in this area of research was analyzed. Three main authors stand out (Figure 5a): 1. Dr. Florentina Zurita, Centro Universitario de la Ciénega, University of Guadalajara, 2. Dr. José Luis Marín-Muñiz, El Colegio de Veracruz, 3. Dr. Luis Carlos Sandoval Herazo, National Technology of Mexico/Technological Institute of Misantla. It is worth mentioning that each of these authors has built extensive networks of independent collaboration, as well as joint work.

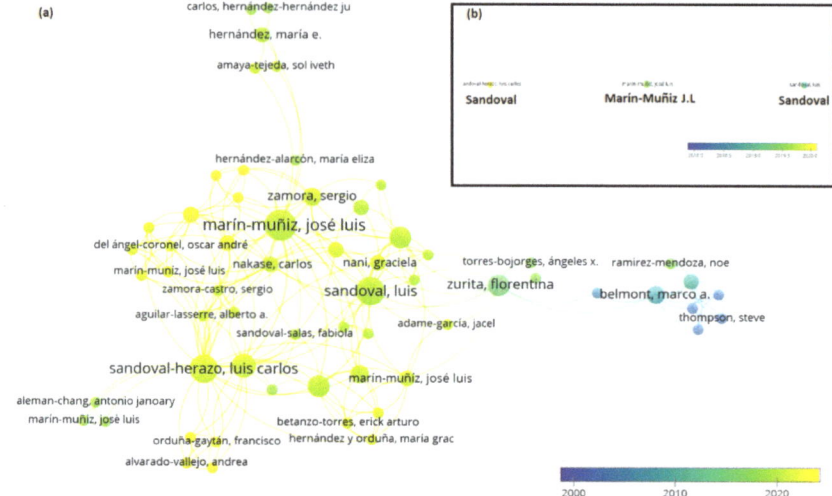

Figure 5. Researcher collaboration co-occurrence map regarding studies on CWs with ornamental plants during 2000–2023 (**a**), and during 2018–2023 (**b**).

When the analysis of collaborations between the authors who carry out research on ornamental plants in CWs was reduced from the period 2018 to 2023 (Figure 5b), that is, to detect in recent years who continue to focus on such studies, the collaboration of projects between the researchers Sandoval and Marín-Muñiz stand out as the main ones, in view of which further research on the topic is pertinent, considering different study regions, climate, diversity of plant species, and greater national and international collaborations to achieve greater details of the effect of ornamental plants in the wastewater treatment with wetlands.

A recent study [39] also identified these aforementioned three authors as leaders in the use of ornamental plants in CWs with Scopus data. The study pointed out that ornamental plants in CWs have leaned towards Canna, Iris, Heliconia and Zantedeschia in the last two decades, however, it did not highlight the works addressed by each of the leading authors. Table 1 describes the main findings of their studies, including the ornamental plants used, the removal percentages according to the organic loading rate based on biological oxygen demand (BOD_5), chemical oxygen demand (COD), total nitrogen (TN) or total phosphorous (TP), ammonium ($N-NH_4$), phosphates ($P-PO_4$), total suspended solids (TSS), coliforms (CF), or *Escherichia coli* (*E. coli*), and the citations for every study.

Table 1 also shows the ornamental plants used, and a total of 25 publications were detected by Zurita's research, three of them in collaboration with Sandoval and three more collaborating in a triad with Marín-Muñiz and Sandoval. On the other hand, Marín-Muñiz's research presents a total of 23 publications, three of them in collaboration in a triad and 11 of them in joint work with Sandoval. For his part, Sandoval presents a total of 21 studies, three of them in triad with Marín-Muñiz and Zurita, three more in which he only collaborates with Zurita, and 11 in collaboration with Marín-Muñiz.

Some deficiencies that could be mentioned for the three researchers in terms of their studies is that their investigations began at the microcosm level or on a pilot scale. It is until recent years that they already apply the design factors learned on a large scale to favor high efficiencies of removal of contaminants in CWs. It is also observed that there is a lack of greater international collaboration comparing different plant species, as well as design conditions according to climatic conditions.

In column 5 of Table 1, the number of times the publication has been cited (based on statistics from Google Scholar) is showed, and the top 3 for every author and collaboration is reported in bold. The most highly cited reference was a paper written by F. Zurita, cited 358 times. In these research topics, this paper was one of the first in Mexico and represents a wetland treatment study treating domestic wastewater with commercial flowers in vertical and horizontal conditions. This was followed by a review of CWs using OFP co-authored with L.C. Sandoval and J.L. Marín-Muñiz (cited 107 times). The third study with more citations was on hybrid CWs by F. Zurita (74 times). The top 4 and 5 were with the same number of citations (65 every), one written by F. Zurita regarding CWs with OFP treating domestic wastewater on a laboratory scale. The other were co-authored between J.L Marín-Muñiz and L.C. Sandoval addressing the issue of the OFP used in CWs with different substrates as filter.

Data reported by the authors (Table 1) revealed that CWs using OFP are efficient in the removal of pollutants as the ranges oscillated between 60–98% for BOD_5 and COD, TN and TP 40–95%, pathogens 62–99%, and nitrogen and phosphorous compounds 30–80%. In addition, arsenic was observed in some studies by Zurita, with removals between 79 and 91%, and drugs like carbamazepine (36–63%) and ibuprofen (71%) were reduced in CWs with OFP. These data provided part of the answer to the second question that guided this study.

The use of plants in CWs for pollutant removal has been applied in different countries around the world (Figure 2). A comparison by Sandoval et al. [26] on the average removal of pollutants with CWs using OFP and typical plants of natural wetlands showed that the removal percentages were similar across all plant genera for TSS (62–86%; n = 26; p = 0.236), COD (41–72%; n = 49), BOD_5 (51–82%; n = 38), TP (49–66%; n = 44), NH_4-N (62–82%; n = 24), NO_3-N (63–93%; n = 34), and TN (48–72%; n = 32). Hernández et al. [56] compared removals of nitrogen in CWs with the OFP *Zantedeschia* a. vs. typical plants of wetlands (*Typha* sp., *Cyperus papyrus*) corroborating similar removals (40–45 mg L^{-1}) without finding differences. This highlights the importance, in terms of phytoremediation, that OFPs have added to their aesthetic and commercial value, as previously mentioned.

Some treatment mechanisms for pollutant and pathogen in CWs include sedimentation and filtration (for the removal of particulate organic matter, biological degradation), ammonification, nitrification, denitrification and plant uptake by nitrogen compounds, adsorption–precipitation reactions and plant uptake for phosphorus, sedimentation, filtration, predation for pathogens and sedimentation, filtration, adsorption, ion exchange, and precipitation and biological degradation through plants and microbiological metabolism for heavy metal removals [21–23,29–31].

Water in CWs is the vehicle for the entry and distribution of nutrients within the system, as well as a support for plant material and establishment of bacterial colonies. Its main function is to provide the necessary nutrients for the development and metabolism of bacteria, which has an impact on the processes of removal, biodegradation, and biotransformation of the substances that enter it [57].

The removal of pollutants showed are similar to those used in CWs with typical plants of natural wetlands [26–28], and similar to removals by conventional wastewater treatments [58,59], but without the need for electrical requirements or specialized labor. The main requirements in CWs include vegetation harvesting, flow control, clogging monitoring, and proper management of pretreatment systems.

Table 1. Classification of publications regarding CWs using ornamental plants according to the three researchers detected with the co-occurrence map by VOSviewer (quantity of individual publications + collaborations among them).

Study Title	Study Type	Ornamental Plants Used	Pollutant Removal (%)	Citation	Reference
Florentina Zurita Martínez (Total sum of studies: 25)					
1. Performance of laboratory-scale wetlands planted with tropical ornamental plants to treat domestic wastewater	Experi-mental	Zantedeschia aethiopica, Anthurium andreanum, Strelitzia reginae, Hemerocallis dumortieri, Canna hybrids	COD > 75, BOD_5 and TN > 70, TP > 66	65	[60]
2. Stress detection by laser-induced fluorescence in Zantedeschia aethiopica planted in subsurface-flow treatment wetlands	Experi-mental	Zantedeschia aethiopica	COD: 78, BOD_5: 80, TN: 49, TP: 41	34	[61]
3. Treatment of domestic wastewater and production of commercial flowers in vertical and horizontal subsurface-flow constructed wetlands	Experi-mental	Zantedeschia aethiopica, Strelitzia reginae, Anturium andreanum, Agapanthus africanus	COD and BOD_5: >80, TP >50	358	[62]
4. Seeking a way to promote the use of constructed wetlands for domestic wastewater treatment in developing countries	Experi-mental	Zantedeschia aethiopica, Anthurium andreanum, Strelitzia reginae, Hemerocallis dumortieri, Canna hybrids	COD: 80, BOD_5: 78, TN: 73, TP: 50	55	[63]
5. Municipal wastewater treatment in Mexico: current status and opportunities for employing ecological treatment systems	Review	X	X	48	[64]
6. Preliminary study on the potential of arsenic removal by subsurface flow constructed mesocosms	Experi-mental	Zantedeschia aethiopica, Anemopsis californica	Arsénic: 79–91	40	[65]
7. Comparative study of three two-stage hybrid ecological wastewater treatment systems for producing high nutrient, reclaimed water for irrigation reuse in developing countries	Experi-mental	Zantedeschia aethiopica, Strelitzia reginae, Canna indica	TN: 20–57, TP: 0, E. coli: 99.9	74	[66]
8. Wastewater disinfection in three hybrid constructed wetlands	Experi-mental	Zantedeschia aethiopica, Strelitzia reginae	CF/E. coli.: 99.93–99.99	16	[67]
9. Performance of three pilot-scale hybrid constructed wetlands for total coliforms and Escherichia coli removal from primary effluent—a 2-year study in a subtropical climate	Experi-mental	Zantedeschia aethiopica, Strelitzia reginae, Canna indica	E. coli: 80–99.9	35	[68]

Study Title	Study Type	Ornamental Plants Used	Pollutant Removal (%)	Citation	Reference
10. Efficiency of three hybrid wetland systems for carbamazepina removal	Experi-mental	Zantedeschia aethiopica, Iris sibirica, Thypha latifolia, Strelitzia r.	Carbamazepine: 36–60	9	[69]
11. Carbamazepine removal in three pilot-scale hybrid wetlands planted with ornamental species	Experi-mental	Thypha latifolia, Iris sibirica, Zantedeschia aethiopica	Carbamazepine: 59–63	50	[70]
12. Evaluation of three pilot-scale hybrid wetland systems for nitrogen removal.	Experi-mental	Zantedeschia aethiopica, Canna indica	$N-NH_4$: 84, TN: 58	18	[71]
13. Nitrogen removal in pilot-scale partially saturated vertical wetlands with and without an internal source of carbon	Experi-mental	Strelitzia reginae	TN: 72–73	35	[72]
14. Addition of Corn Cob in the Free Drainage Zone of Partially Saturated Vertical Wetlands Planted with I. sibirica for Total Nitrogen Removal—A Pilot-Scale Study	Experi-mental	Iris sibirica	BOD_5: 91–92, COD: 67,–75, TN: 66–68	1	[73]
15. Changes in the nitrification-denitrification capacity of pilot-scale partially saturated vertical flow wetlands (with corncob in the free-drainage zone) after two years of operation	Experi-mental	Iris sibirica	BOD_5: 96, COD: 84, TN: 51–53	3	[74]
16. Capacity of two ornamental species (Iris sibirica and Zantedeschia aethiopica) to take up, translocate, and accumulate carbamazepine under hydroponic conditions	Experi-mental	Iris sibirica, Zantedeschia aethiopica	X	8	[75]
17. Resistance evaluation of Canna indica, Cyperus papyrus, Iris sibrica, and Typha latifolia to phytotoxic charafteristics of dilutes tequila vinasses in wetland microcosms	Experi-mental	Canna indica, Cyperus papyrus, Iris sibrica, Typha latifolia	X	1	[76]
18. Method for treating domestic wastewater through the use of ornamental plants	Experi-mental (patent)	Anthurium andreanum, Hemerocallis dumortieri, iris laevigata, pseudacorus, Lysichitum americanum, camtschatcense, Agapantus umbellatus/africanus	COD: 75, BOD_5: 70, TP: 66	2	[77]
19. Ornamental plants	Book review	X	X	40	[44]

Study Title	Study Type	Ornamental Plants Used	Pollutant Removal (%)	Citation	Reference
	Luis Carlos Sandoval Herazo (21)				
1. Effect of *Canna hybrids* in partially saturated constructed wetlands for swine water treatments	Experi-mental	*Canna hybrids*	COD: 66, TP: 23, CF: 62	9	[78]
2. Influence of light intensity on growth and flowering ornamental plants in constructed wetlands	Experi-mental	*Lavandula* sp., *Anthurium* sp., *Zantedeschia aethiopica*, *Spathiphyllum wallisii*	COD: 60–85,	0	[79]
3. Evaluation of the performance of vertical partially saturated constructed wetlands for sewage treatment swine	Experi-mental	*Canna hybrids*, *Iris germánica*	COD: 90, $N-NH_4$: 78	11	[80]
4. Plant biomass production in constructed wetlands treating swine wastewater in tropical climates	Experi-mental	*Typha latifolia*, *Canna hybrids*	COD: 84, TN: 94, TP: 82	4	[81]
	José Luis Marín-Muñiz (23)				
1. Removal of wastewater pollutant in artificial wetlands implemented in Actopan, Veracruz, Mexico	Experi-mental	*Typha* spp.	BOD_5: 80, $N-NO_3$: 60	14	[82]
2. Constructed wetlands in Mexico for wastewater treatment, ornamental plant production, and water reuse	Review	X	X	29	[83]
3. Influence of different porous media and ornamental vegetation on wastewater pollutant removal in vertical subsurface flow wetland microcosms	Experi-mental	*Zantedeschia aethiopica*, *Alpinia purpurata*	BOD_5: 80, $N-NO_3$: 40, $P-PO_4$: 40	23	[84]
4. Greenhouse Gas Emissions and Treatment Performance in Constructed Wetlands with Ornamental Plants: Case Studies in Veracruz, Mexico	Experi-mental	*Alpinia p.*, *Typha* sp., *Hedychium coronarium*, *Canna hybrids*, *Anturium a.*, *Lillium* sp., *Zantedeschia a.*, *Cyperus papyrus/alternifolius*	$N-NH_4$: 50, $P-PO_4$: 61–81, TN: 47	2	[85]
5. Plant growth and pollutant removal from wastewater in domiciliary constructed wetland microcosms with monoculture and polyculture of tropical ornamental plants	Experi-mental	*Alpinia purpurata*, *Hedychium coronarium*, *Canna hybrids*	$N-PO_4$: 68–80, $N-NH_4$: 60–80	22	[54]
6. Evaluation of the growth of vegetation planted in artificial wetland: effect of planting position	Experi-mental	*Canna hybrids*, *Typha* sp., *Sphatyphylum wallisii*, *Heliconia* sp.	ND	1	[86]

Study Title	Study Type	Ornamental Plants Used	Pollutant Removal (%)	Citation	Reference
7. Ornamental vegetation used in phytoremediation and its environmental, economic and social potential	Review	X	X	1	[87]
8. Environmental conditions for the optimal development of ornamental and phytoremedial plants	Experi-mental	*Alpinia purpurata, Zingiber spectabile*	N-NH$_4$: 60, P-PO$_4$: 72	1	[88]
9. The circular economy as a proposal for the reuse of swine sewage	Experi-mental	*Canna hybrids, Cyperus alternifolius*	COD: 59, TN: 50, TP: 39	1	[89]
Collaborations between F. Zurita, L.C. Sandoval, and J.L Marín-Muñiz					
1. Influence of a new ornamental species (*Spathiphyllum blandum*) on the removal of COD, nitrogen, phosphorus and fecal coliforms: a mesocosm wetland study with pet and tezontle substrates	Experi-mental	*Spathiphyllum blandum*	COD: 78–81, P-PO$_4$: 51–53	8	[90]
2. Effect of *Spathiphyllum blandum* on the removal of ibuprofen and conventional pollutants from polluted river water, in fully saturated constructed wetlands at mesocosm level	Experi-mental	*Spathiphyllum blandum*	COD: 72, TN: 39, TP: 63, and 71 ibuprofen	6	[91]
3. Partially saturated vertical constructed wetlands and free-flow vertical constructed wetlands for pilot-scale municipal/swine wastewater treatment using *Heliconia latispatha*	Experi-mental	*Heliconia latispatha*	COD: 82–93, TN: 58–1, TP: 37–60	1	[21]
Collaborations between F. Zurita and L.C. Sandoval					
1. Nitrogen removal from domestic wastewater and the development of tropical ornamental plants in partially saturated mesocosm-scale constructed wetlands	Experi-mental	*Canna hybrids, Zantedeschia aethiopica*	COD: 58–97, TN: 65–95, TP: 82	13	[92]
2. Treatment of swine effluent mixed with domestic wastewater and vegetation development in monoculture and polyculture horizontal subsurface flow wetlands	Experi-mental	*Heliconia latispatha, Typha latifolia, Cyperus alternifolius*	TP: 44–63, TN: 64–68, COD: 68	2	[93]

Study Title	Study Type	Ornamental Plants Used	Pollutant Removal (%)	Citation	Reference
3. Development of *Heliconia latispatha* in constructed wetlands, for the treatment of swine/domestic wastewater in tropical climates, with PET as a substitute for the filter medium	Experi-mental	*Heliconia latispatha*	COD: 56, TP: 41, TSS: 55	2	[94]
Collaborations between Marín-Muñiz and Sandoval					
1. Effects of the use of ornamental plants and different substrates in the removal of wastewater pollutants through microcosms of constructed wetlands	Experi-mental	*Lavandula* sp., *Spathiphyllum wallisii*, *Zantedeschia aethiopica*	BOD_5: 58, $P-PO_4$: 38, $N-NO_3$: 40	65	[95]
2. Role of Wetland Plants and Use of Ornamental Flowering Plants in Constructed Wetlands for Wastewater Treatment: A Review	Review	X	X	107	[26]
3. Effect of ornamental plants, seasonality, and filter media material in fill-and-drain constructed wetlands treating rural community wastewater	Experi-mental	*Canna indica*, *Pontederia sagittata*, *Spathiphyllum wallisii*	COD: 82, $N-NO_3$: 65, $P-PO_4$: 68	21	[96]
4. Evaluation of wastewater treatment by microcosms of vertical subsurface wetlands in partially saturated conditions planted with ornamental plants and filled with mineral and plastic substrates	Experi-mental	*Anthurium* sp., *Zantedeschia aethiopica*, *Spathiphyllum wallisii*	BOD_5: 55–70, $N-NO_3$: 28–44, $P-PO_4$: 25–45	24	[97]
5. Impact of ornamental vegetation type and different substrate layers on pollutant removal in constructed wetland mesocosms treating rural community wastewater	Experi-mental	*Spathiphyllum wallisii*, *Hedychium coronarium*	COD: 75–92, $N-NO_3$: 41–45	22	[98]
6. Wastewater treatment by constructed wetland eco-technology: Influence of mineral and plastic materials as filter media and tropical ornamental plants	Experi-mental	*Canna indica*, *Cyperus papyrus*, *Hedychium coronarium*	COD: 91, $N-NO_3$: 41, $P-PO_4$: 54	32	[99]
7. Effects of Ornamental Plant Density and Mineral/Plastic Media on the Removal of Domestic Wastewater Pollutants by Home Wetlands Technology	Experi-mental	*Alpinia purpurata*, *Canna hybrids*, *Hedychium coronarium*	COD: 88, $P-PO_4$: 27, $N-NO_3$: 28	4	[100]

Study Title	Study Type	Ornamental Plants Used	Pollutant Removal (%)	Citation	Reference
8. Environmental, economic, and social potentialities of ornamental vegetation cultivated in constructed wetlands of Mexico	Review	X	X	7	[28]
9. Bioelectricity Generation and Production of Ornamental Plants in Vertical Partially Saturated Constructed Wetlands.	Experi-mental	*Zantedeschia aethiopica, Canna hybrids*	BOD_5: 98, $P-PO_4$: 25	4	[46]
10. Wetlands with ornamental plants, filled with plastic reused as sustainable wastewater treatment	Experi-mental	*Canna hybrids*, *Typha* sp.	COD: 90–95, TSS: 50–70	2	[101]
11. Treatment wetlands in Mexico for control of wastewater contaminants: a review of experiences during the last twenty-two years	Review	X	X	1	[3]

Note: X= does not include these data. In the citation column, the numbers in bold are the top 5 of the most cited publications.

In Figure 4 and Table 1, the first question that guided this study is answered.

The main plants used by the authors of the largest studies on CWs with OFP include *Canna hybrids* (19 cases), *Zantedeschia aethiopica* (18 cases), *Strelitzia reginae* (8 cases), *Iris* species (8 cases), *Spathiphyllum* species (7 cases), and *Anturium* sp. (6 cases). The use of OFP combines the function of phytoremediation and landscape benefits of CWs. There are several landscape plants, however, only a few are utilized in CWs. Thus, future research should be aimed at increasing the public participation in the maintenance of CWs for their adoption and appropriation, which may lead to longer lifespans and environmental services. These data provided the second part of the answer to the second question that guided this study.

This review shows the feasibility to produce flowers and treat water at the same time with nature-based systems and ecological engineering like that of CWs. Thus, future studies conducted in order to evaluate the health of the plants and to discover if they are suffering stress from the flooding due to wastewater conditions, pests, degree of toxicity at different concentrations of wastewater, competition between species, or uses of vegetation of wetlands, are necessary.

It is important to highlight that macrophytes are the main source of oxygen in CWs through a process that occurs in the rizosphera zone called radial oxygen loss [102]. The plant roots are the house of many microorganisms, because they provide a source of microbial attachment [24] and release an excretion of carbon that contributes to the denitrification process, which increases the removal of pollutants in anoxic or anaerobic conditions [26,27].

Another mechanism of the plants in CWs is the reduction in the velocity of water flow, sedimentation, decreased resuspension, and uptake of nutrients. In the case of roots and rhizomes in the sediment, the physical effects include stabilizing the sediment surface, less erosion, nutrient absorption, prevention of medium clogging (in subsurface conditions), and improved hydraulic conductivity. Aerial plant tissue favors the light attenuation (reduced growth of photosynthesis), reduced wind velocity, storage of nutrients, and aesthetic pleasing appearance of the system [24–27,103].

On the other hand, it is important to know that the removal of organic matter in CWs is mediated by several microbial reactions, where the products of some of these reactions include greenhouse gases such as methane, carbon dioxide, and nitrous oxide [104]. However, some studies have revealed that these emissions are minimum in CWs, and the amount of OFP does not influence the methane (4.5–11 g m^{-2} d^{-2}), nitrous oxide (0–2.3 g m^{-2} d^{-2}), and carbon dioxide emissions (0.4–7.4) as these are affected mainly by the substrate and water flow [56,85,105].

A study in tropical conditions comparing GHG emissions in CWs planted with *Zantedeschia aethiopica* compared with the zones near the inflow planted with *Typha* sp. and *Cyperus gigantus* (native plants of natural wetlands), showed higher methane emissions in the zone with OFP. The authors related this with differences in the radial oxygen loss between the plant species [85].

Other studies in constructed wetlands treating heavy metals or different leachates [106–109] have also demonstrated the feasibility of using this eco-technology. This demonstrates the multiple pollutants that CWs can clean, and therefore, the use of OFP detected in this study as phytoremediators should now be investigated for all of these types of contaminants.

4. Conclusions

This study initially presents a bibliometric analysis regarding the use of CWs around the world. To this respect, China and USA are the countries with the most significant use of this technology. Subsequently, the use of ornamental plants in CWS is identified. It is worth emphasizing that Mexico is the leader regarding the number of publications on this topic.

The findings suggest that the most used ornamental flowering plants in CWs are *Canna hybrids*, *Zantedeschia aethiopica*, *Strelitzia reginae*, *Iris species*, *Spathiphyllum* sp., and *Anturium* sp. This may serve as the basis for further research on CW systems, principally in tropical and subtropical areas where these plant species are present. This study also revealed that such OFP have an excellent function in water purification with removals of organic matter that oscillate between 30–90%, heavy metals and drugs 30–70%, or about 99.9% in elimination of pathogens.

In addition, the bibliometric analysis revealed the main authors that use this technology with OFP. This will serve to carry out future collaborations with them as well as to continue promoting the use of this sustainable technology and taking advantage of the circular economy. Thus, new studies conducted to evaluate the health of the plants and their artisanal uses are necessary, as well as the integration of decision makers, creators of public policies, and communities in the construction and operation of CWs, which is an emerging need.

Author Contributions: Conceptualization, J.L.M.-M.; methodology, S.Z.; software, I.Z.-C.; validation, S.Z. and J.L.M.-M.; formal analysis, S.Z.; investigation, J.L.M.-M.; resources, S.Z., L.M.Á.-H., K.E.M.-A. and A.L.-R.; data curation, S.Z.; writing—original draft preparation, J.L.M.-M.; writing—review and editing, I.Z.-C. and G.O.-P.; visualization, A.L.-R.; supervision, J.L.M.-M.; project administration, G.O.-P. and S.Z.; funding acquisition, A.L.-R., L.M.Á.-H. and K.E.M-A. All authors have read and agreed to the published version of the manuscript.

Funding: This research received no external funding.

Institutional Review Board Statement: Not applicable.

Informed Consent Statement: Not applicable.

Data Availability Statement: The data presented in this study are available on request from the corresponding author.

Acknowledgments: The authors acknowledge researchers Florentina Zurita (Centro Universitario de la Ciénega, University of Guadalajara) and Luis Carlos Sandoval (National Technology of Mexico/Technological Institute of Misantla) by the corroboration of information.

Conflicts of Interest: The authors declare no conflict of interest.

References

1. Kadlec, R.H.; Knight, R.L. *Treatment Wetlands*, 1st ed.; CRC Pess LLC: Boca Raton, FL, USA, 1996.
2. Vymazal, J. The historical development of constructed wetlands for wastewater treatment. *Land* **2022**, *11*, 174. [CrossRef]
3. Marín-Muñiz, J.L.; Sandoval, L.C.; López-Méndez, M.C.; Sandoval-Herazo, M.; Meléndez-Armenta, R.; González-Moreno, R.; Zamora, S. Treatment wetlands in Mexico for control of wastewater contaminants: A review of experiences during the last twenty-two years. *Processes* **2023**, *11*, 359. [CrossRef]
4. Masi, F.; Rizzo, A.; Regelsberger, M. The role of constructed wetlands in a new circular economy, resource oriented, and ecosystem services paradigm. *J. Environ. Manag.* **2018**, *216*, 275–284. [CrossRef]
5. Bakhshoodeh, R.; Alavi, N.; Oldham, C.; Santos, R.M.; Babaei, A.A.; Vymazal, J.; Paydary, P. Constructed wetlands for landfill leachate treatment: A review. *Ecol. Eng.* **2020**, *146*, 105725. [CrossRef]
6. Wu, J.; Xu, D.; He, J.; Wu, Z. Comprehensive evaluation of substrates in vertical flow constructed wetlands for domestic wastewater treatment. *Water Pract. Technol.* **2015**, *10*, 625–632. [CrossRef]
7. Zaboon, B.; Al-Abbawy, D.; Yaseen, D. Improving wastewater reclamation using constructed wetlands by artificial plastic biofilm carriers. *J. Ecol. Eng.* **2022**, *23*, 241–253. [CrossRef]
8. Bakhshoodeh, R.; Santos, R.M. Comparative bibliometric trends of microplastics and perfluoroalkyl and polyfluoroalkyl substances: How these hot environmental remediation research topics developed over time. *RSC Adv.* **2022**, *12*, 4973–4987. [CrossRef]
9. Bydalek, F.; Ifayemi, D.; Reynolds, L.; Barden, R.; Kasprzyk-Hordern, B.; Wenk, J. Microplastic dynamics in a free water surface constructed wetland. *Sci. Total Environ.* **2023**, *858*, 160113. [CrossRef]
10. Vymazal, J.; Březinová, T. The use of constructed wetlands for removal of pesticides from agricultural runoff and drainage: A review. *Environ. Int.* **2015**, *75*, 11–20. [CrossRef]
11. Vymazal, J. Constructed wetlands for treatment of industrial wastewaters: A review. *Ecol. Eng.* **2014**, *73*, 724–751. [CrossRef]
12. Sánchez, M.; Ruiz, I.; Soto, M. The potentital of constructed wetland systems and photodegradation processes for the removal of emerging contaminants-a review. *Environments* **2022**, *9*, 116. [CrossRef]
13. Pat-Espadas, A.; Loredo, R.; Amabilis-Sosa, L.; Gómez, G.; Vidal, G. Review of constructed wetlands for acid mine drainage treatment. *Water* **2018**, *10*, 1685. [CrossRef]
14. Bakhshoodeh, R.; Alavi, N.; Majlesi, M.; Paydary, P. Compost leachate treatment by a pilot-scale subsurface horizontal flow constructed wetland. *Ecol. Eng.* **2017**, *105*, 7–14. [CrossRef]
15. Morales, G.; López, D.; Vera, I.; Vidal, G. Constructed wetlands with ornamental plants for removal of organic matter and nutrients contained in sewage. *Theoria* **2013**, *22*, 3346.
16. Machado, A.I.; Beretta, M.; Fragoso, R.D.A.; Duarte, E.D.C.N.F.D.A. Overview of the state of the art of constructed wetlands for decentralized wastewater management in Brazil. *J. Environ. Manag.* **2017**, *187*, 560–570. [CrossRef]
17. Vazquez, A.M.; Samudio-Segrero, A.; Nakayama, H.D.; Cantero-García, I. Sub-surface flow constructed wetland for the treatment of sewage generated in a municipal park. *Global J. Environ. Sci. Manag.* **2023**, *9*, 545–558. [CrossRef]
18. García-García, P.L.; Ruelas-Monjardín, L.; Marín-Muñíz, J.L. Constructed wetlands: A solution to water quality issues in Mexico? *Water Policy* **2016**, *18*, 654–669. [CrossRef]
19. Hernández, M.E. Ecological engineering for controlling water pollution in Latin America. In *Ecological Dimensions for Sustainable Socio Economic Development*; Yañez-Arancibia, A., Yáñez-Arancibia, A., Dávalos-Sotelo, R., Day, J.W., Reyes, E., Eds.; WIT Press: Southampton, UK, 2013.
20. Shutes, R.B.E. Atificial wetlands and water quality improvement. *Environ. Int.* **2001**, *26*, 441–447. [CrossRef]
21. Fernández, J.A.F.; Martínez-Resédiz, G.; Zurita, F.; Marín-Muñiz, J.L.; Méndez, M.C.L.; Zamora, S.; Sandoval Herazo, L.C. Partially saturated vertical constructed wetlands and free-flow vertical constructed wetlands for pilot-scale municipal-swine wastewater treatment using *Heliconia latispatha*. *Water* **2022**, *14*, 3860. [CrossRef]
22. Borkar, R.P.; Mahatme, P.S. Tidal flow constructed wetland: An overview. *Res. Inventory Int. J. Eng. Sci.* **2015**, *5*, 31–34.
23. Abbasi, H.; Xie, J.; Hussain, S.; Lu, X. Nutrient removal in hybrid constructed wetlands: Spatial-seasonal variation and the effect of vegetation. *Water Sci. Technol.* **2019**, *79*, 1985–1994. [CrossRef] [PubMed]
24. Vymazal, J. Plants used in constructed wetlands with horizontal subsurface flow: A review. *Hydrobiologia* **2011**, *20*, 133–156. [CrossRef]
25. Hernández, M.E. Humedales ornamentales con participación comunitaria para el saneamiento de aguas municipales en México. *Rinderesu* **2016**, *1*, 1–12.
26. Sandoval, L.; Zamora-Castro, S.A.; Vidal-Álvarez, M.; Marín-Muñiz, J.L. Role of Wetland Plants and Use of Ornamental Flowering Plants in Constructed Wetlands for Wastewater Treatment: A Review. *Appl. Sci.* **2019**, *9*, 685. [CrossRef]
27. Lara-Acosta, M.; Lango-Reynoso, F.; Castañeda-Chávez, M. Use of tropical macrophytes in wastewater treatment. *Agroproductividad* **2022**, *15*, 131–140. [CrossRef]
28. Zitácuaro-Contreras, I.; Vidal-ÁLvarez, M.; Hernández y Orduña, M.; Zamora-Castro, S.; Betanzo-Torres, E.; Marín-Muñíz, J.; Sandoval-Herazo, L. Environmental, economic, and social potentialities of ornamental vegetation cultivated in constructed wetlands of Mexico. *Sustainability* **2021**, *13*, 6267. [CrossRef]
29. Vymazal, J. *The Role of Natural and Constructed Wetlands in Nutrient Cycling and Retention on the Landscape*; Springer: New York, NY, USA, 2015; p. 326. [CrossRef]

30. Karathanasis, A.D.; Potter, C.L.; Coyne, M.S. Vegetation effects on fecal bacteria, BOD, and suspended solid removal in constructed wetlands treating domestic wastewater. *Ecol. Eng.* **2003**, *20*, 157–169. [CrossRef]
31. Wu, F.Y.; Chung, A.K.; Tam, A.K.; Wong, M.H. Root exudates of wetland plants influenced by nutrient status and types of plant cultivation. *Int. J. Phytoremed.* **2012**, *14*, 543–553. [CrossRef]
32. Canarini, A.; Kaiser, C.; Merchant, A.; Richter, A.; Wanek, W. Root exudation of primary metabolites: Mechanisms and their roles in plant responses to environmental stimuli. *Front. Plant Sci.* **2019**, *10*, 157. [CrossRef]
33. Nicolaisen, J. Bibliometrics and Citation Analysis: From the Science Citation Index to Cybermetrics. *J. Am. Soc. Inf. Sci. Tecnol.* **2010**, *61*, 205–207. [CrossRef]
34. Van, E.J.; Waltman, L. Software survey: VOSviewer, a computer program for bibliometric mapping. *Scientometrics* **2010**, *84*, 523–538. [CrossRef]
35. Colares, G.; Dell'Osbel, N.; Wiesel, P.; Oliveira, G.; Lemos, P.; Silva, F.; Lutterbeck, C.; Kist, L.; Machado, E. Floating treatment wetlands: A review and bibliometric analysis. *Sci. Total Environ.* **2020**, *714*, 136776. [CrossRef] [PubMed]
36. Zang, Y.; You, X.; Huang, S.; Wang, M.; Dong, J. Knowledge atlas on the relationship between water management and constructed wetlands-a bibliometric analysis based on citespace. *Sustainability* **2022**, *14*, 8288. [CrossRef]
37. Moondra, N.; Christian, R.; Jariwala, N. Bibliometric analysis of constructed wetlands in wastewater treatment. *Recent Trends Civil Eng.* **2020**, *77*, 1021–1028.
38. Santos, R.M.; Bakhshoodeh, R. Climate change/global warming/climate emergency versus general climate research: Comparative bibliometric trends of publications. *Heliyon* **2021**, *7*, e08219. [CrossRef]
39. García-Ávila, F.; Avilés-Añazco, A.; Cabello-Torres, R.; Guanuchi-Quito, A.; Cadme-Galabay, M.; Gutiérrez-Ortega, H.; Alvarez-Ochoa, R.; Zhindón-Arévalo, C. Application of ornamental plants in constructed wetlands for wastewater treatment: A scientometric analysis. *Case Stud. Chem. Environ. Eng.* **2023**, *7*, 100307. [CrossRef]
40. Nezhyva, L.; Palamar, S.; Marienko, M. Clouds of words as a didactic tool in literary education of primary school children. *CEUR Workshop Proc.* **2022**, *3085*, 381–393. Available online: https://ceur-ws.org/Vol-3085/paper29.pdf (accessed on 10 December 2022). [CrossRef]
41. Hook, D.; Porter, S.; Herzong, C. Dimensions: Building context for search and evaluation. *Front. Res. Metr. Anal.* **2018**, *3*, 23. [CrossRef]
42. Dotro, G.; Langergraber, G.; Molle, P.; Nivala, J.; Puigaget, J.; Stein, O.; Sperling, M. *Treatment Wetlands*; IWA: London, UK, 2017.
43. Kadlec, R.H.; Wallace, S.D. *Treatment Wetlands*, 2nd ed.; CRC Pess LLC: Boca Raton, FL, USA, 2009.
44. Alarcón, M.T.; Zurita, F.; Lara-Borrro, J.; Vidal, G. *Humedales de Tratamiento: Alternativa de Saneamiento de Aguas Residuales en América Latina*; Pontificia Universidad Javeriana: Bogotá, Colombia, 2018; Available online: https://cimav.repositorioinstitucional.mx/jspui/handle/1004/2022 (accessed on 20 January 2023). (In Spanish)
45. Brix, H.; Koottatep, T.; Fryd, O.; Laugesen, C. The flower and the butterfly constructed wetland system at Koh Phi Phi-system design and lesson learned during implementation and operation. *Ecol. Eng.* **2011**, *37*, 729–735. [CrossRef]
46. González-Moreno, H.; Marín-Muñiz, J.L.; Sánchez-DelaCruz, E.; Nakase, C.; Ángel Coronel, O.; Reyes Gonzalez, D.; Nava-Valente, N.; Sandoval-Herazo, L. Bioelectricity Generation and Production of Ornamental Plants in Vertical Partially Saturated Constructed Wetlands. *Water* **2021**, *13*, 143. [CrossRef]
47. Molinos-Senante, M.; Gómez, T.; Garrido-Baserba, M.; Caballero, R.; Sala-Garrido, R. Assessing the sustainability of small wastewater treatment systems: A composite indicator approach. *Sci. Total Environ.* **2014**, *497–498*, 607–617. [CrossRef]
48. Lutterbeck, C.; Kist, L.T.; Lopez, D.A.R.; Zerwes, F.V.; Machado, Ê.L. Life cycle assessment of integrated wastewater treatment systems with constructed wetlands in rural areas. *J. Clean. Prod.* **2017**, *148*, 527–536. [CrossRef]
49. López-Serrano, M.J.; Lakho, F.H.; Van Hulle, S.W.H.; Batlles-delaFuente, A. Life cycle cost assessment and economic analysis of a decentralized wastewater treatment to achieve water sustainability within the framework of circular economy. *Oeconomia Copernic.* **2023**, *14*, 103–133. [CrossRef]
50. Jean-Martin, B.; Buchauer, K.; Gambrill, M. *Wastewater Treatment and Reuse: A Guide to Help Small Towns Select Appropiate Options*; World Bank: Washington, DC, USA, 2022.
51. Zhao, Y.; Ji, B.; Liu, R.; Ren, B.; Wei, T. Constructed treatment wetland: Glance of development and future perspectives. *Water Cycle* **2020**, *1*, 104–112. [CrossRef]
52. Reyes, N.; Geronimo, F.; Guerra, H.; Kim, L. Bibliometric analysis and comprehensive review of stormwater treatment wetlands: Global research trends and existing knowledge gaps. *Sustainability* **2023**, *15*, 2332. [CrossRef]
53. Rodríguez-Domínguez, M.; Konnerup, D.; Brix, H.; Arias, C. Constructed wetlands in Latin America and the Caribbean: A review of experiences during the last decade. *Water* **2020**, *12*, 1744. [CrossRef]
54. Marín-Muñiz, J.L.; Hernández, M.E.; Gallegos-Pérez, M.P.; Amaya-Tejeda, S.I. Plant growth and pollutant removal from wastewater in domiciliary constructed wetland microcosms with monoculture and polyculture of tropical ornamental plants. *Ecol. Eng.* **2020**, *147*, 105658. [CrossRef]
55. Calheiros, C.S.C.; Bessa, V.S.; Mesquita, B.R.; Brix, H.; Rangel, A.O.S.S.; Castro, P.M.L. Constructed wetland with a polyculture of ornamental plants for wastewater treatment at a rural tourism facility. *Ecol. Eng.* **2015**, *79*, 1–7. [CrossRef]
56. Hernández, M.; Galindo-Zetina, M.; Hernández-Hernández, J.C. Greenhouse gas emissions and pollutant removal in treatment wetlands with ornamental plants under subtropical conditions. *Ecol. Eng.* **2018**, *114*, 88–95. [CrossRef]

57. Masoud, A.; Alfarra, A.; Sorlini, S. Constructed wetlands as a solution for sustainable sanitation: A comprehensive review on integrating climate change resilience and circular economy. *Water* **2022**, *14*, 3232. [CrossRef]
58. Restrepo, A.; Rodríguez, D.; Peñuela, G. Eficiencia de un reactor SBR para la remoción de la materia orgánica presente en el agua residual de una industria de teñido de flores. *Rev. Ion* **2021**, *34*, 47–59. (In Spanish) [CrossRef]
59. Pérez, J.; Aldana, G.; Rojano, R. Upflow anaerobic sludge blanket reactor (UASB) performance through sludge age load and kinetic coefficients. *Rev. Int. Cont. Amb.* **2016**, *32*, 281–291. [CrossRef]
60. Zurita, F.; de Anda, J.; Belmont, M.A. Performance of laboratory-scale wetlands planted with tropical ornamental plants to treat domestic wastewater. *Water Qual. Res. J. Can.* **2006**, *41*, 410–417. [CrossRef]
61. Zurita, F.; De Anda, J.; Cervantes-Martínez, J. Stress detection by laser-induced fluorescence in Zantedeschia aethiopica planted in subsurface-flow treatment wetlands. *Ecol. Eng.* **2018**, *33*, 110–118. [CrossRef]
62. Zurita, F.; De Anda, J.; Belmont, M.A. Treatment of domestic wastewater and production of comercial flowers in vertical and horizontal subsurface-flow constructed wetlands. *Ecol. Eng.* **2009**, *35*, 861–869. [CrossRef]
63. Zurita, F.; Belmont, M.A.; De Anda, J.; White, J.R. Seeking a way to promote the use of constructed wetlands for domestic wastewater treatment in developing countries. *Water Sci. Technol.* **2011**, *63*, 654–659. [CrossRef] [PubMed]
64. Zurita, F.; Roy, E.; White, J. Municipal wastewater treatment in Mexico: Current status and opportunities for employing ecological treatment systems. *Environ. Technol.* **2012**, *33*, 1151–1158. [CrossRef]
65. Zurita, F.; Del Toro-Sánchez, C.; Gitiérrez-Lomelí, M.; Ridriguez-Sahagún, A.; Castellanos-Hernández, O.; Ramírez-Martínez, G.; White, J. Preliminary study on the potential of arsenic removal by subsurface flow constructed mesocosms. *Ecol. Eng.* **2012**, *47*, 101–104. [CrossRef]
66. Zurita, F.; White, J.R. Comparative study of three two-stage hybrid ecological wastewater treatment systems for producing high nutrient, reclaimed water for irrigation reuse in developing countries. *Water* **2014**, *6*, 213–228. [CrossRef]
67. Zurita, F.; Rojas, D.; Carreón, A.; Gutiérrez-Lomelí, M. Wastewater disinfection in three hybrid constructed wetlands. *Interciencia* **2015**, *40*, 409–415. Available online: https://www.redalyc.org/articulo.oa?id=33938675008 (accessed on 6 January 2023).
68. Zurita, F.; Carreón-Álvarez, A. Performance of three pilot-scale hybrid constructed wetlands for total coliforms and Escherichia coli removal from primary effluent—A 2-year study in a subtropical climate. *J. Water Health* **2015**, *13*, 446–458. [CrossRef]
69. Tejeda, A.; López, Z.; Rojas, D.; Barrera, A.; Zurita, F. Eficiencia de tres sistemas de humedales híbridos para la remoción de carbamazepina. *Tecnol. Y Cienc. Del Agua.* **2015**, *6*, 19–31. Available online: https://www.scielo.org.mx/scielo.php?script=sci_arttext&pid=S2007-24222015000600019 (accessed on 4 May 2022). (In Spanish).
70. Tejeda, A.; Torres-Bojorges, Á.X.; Zurita, F. Carbamazepine removal in three pilot-scale hybrid wetlands planted with ornamental species. *Ecol. Eng.* **2017**, *98*, 410–417. [CrossRef]
71. Torres, A.; Hernández, N.; Fausto, A.; Zurota, F. Evaluación de tres sistemas de humedales híbridos a escala piloto para la remoción de nitrógeno. *Rev. Int. Cont. Amb.* **2017**, *33*, 37–47. (In Spanish) [CrossRef]
72. Martínez, N.; Tejeda, A.; Del Toro, A.; Sánchez, M.; Zurita, F. Nitrogen removal in pilot-scale partially saturated vertical wetlands with and without and internal source of carbon. *Sci. Total Environ.* **2018**, *645*, 524–532. [CrossRef]
73. Del Toro, A.; Tejeda, A.; Zurita, F. Addition of corn cob in the free drainage zone of partially saturated vertical wetlands planted with *I. sibirica* for total nitrogen removal—A pilot-scale study. *Water* **2019**, *11*, 2151. [CrossRef]
74. Del Toro Farías, A.; Zurita Martínez, F. Changes in the nitrification-denitrification capacity of pilot-scale partially saturated vertical flow wetlands (with corncob in the free-drainage zone) after two years of operation. *Int. J. Phytoremediation* **2021**, *23*, 829–836. [CrossRef]
75. Tejeda, A.; Zurita, F. Capacity of two ornamental species (*Iris sibirica* and *Zantedeschia aethiopica*) to take up, translocate, and accumulate carbamazepine under hydroponic conditions. *Water* **2020**, *12*, 1272. [CrossRef]
76. Del Toro, A.; Tejeda, A.; Ramos, J.; Ibarra, E.; Zurita, F. Resistencia de la *Canna indica, Cyperus papyrus, Iris sibirica y Typha latifolia* a vinazas tequileras en mesocosmos de humedales. In *Book of Abstracts V Panamerican Conference of Wetland Systems for Treatment and Improvement of Water Quality*; Hupanam: Santa Catarina, Brasil, 2021; Available online: https://hupanam.com/wp-content/uploads/2022/05/Caderno-V-HUPANAM-5o.-Wetlands-BR.pdf (accessed on 2 December 2022). (In Spanish)
77. De Anda, J.; Zurita, F.; Belmont, M. Método para Tratar Aguas Residuales Domésticas Mediante el Uso de Plantas Ornamentales. Patent No. 338619. 2016. Available online: https://ciatej.repositorioinstitucional.mx/jspui/handle/1023/362 (accessed on 1 January 2023). (In Spanish)
78. Mateo, N.; Nani, G.; Montiel, W.; Nakase, C.; Salazar-Salazar, C.; Sandoval, L. Efecto de *Canna hybrids* en humedales construidos parcialmente saturados para el tratamiento de aguas porcinas. *Rinderesu* **2019**, *4*, 59–68.
79. Sandoval-Herazo, L.C.; Alavarado-Lassman, A.; Nani, G.; Nakase-Rodriguez, C. Influence of light intensity on growth and flowering ornamental plants in constructed wetlands. *REB&S* **2020**, *2*, 27–36. [CrossRef]
80. Sandoval-Herazo, M.; Nani, G.; Sandoval, L.; Rivera, S.; Fernández-Lambert, G.; Alvarado-Lassman, A. Evaluación del desempeño de humedales construidos verticales parcialmente saturados para el tratamiento de aguas residuales porcinas. *Trop. Subtrop. Agroec.* **2020**, *23*, 38. (In Spanish)
81. Sandoval-Herazo, M.; Martínez-Reséndediz, G.; Fernández, E.; Fernández-Lambert, G.; Sandoval, L.C. Plant biomass production in constructed wetlands treating swine wastewater in tropical climates. *Fermentation* **2021**, *7*, 296. [CrossRef]

82. Marín-Muñiz, J.L. Removal of wastewater pollutant in artificial wetlands implemented in Actopan, Veracruz, Mexico. *Rev. Mex. Ing. Quím.* **2016**, *15*, 553–563. Available online: http://www.redalyc.org/articulo.oa?id=62046829021 (accessed on 30 January 2023). (In Spanish) [CrossRef]
83. Marín-Muñiz, J.L. Humedales construidos en México para el tratamiento de aguas residuales, producción de plantas ornamentales y reúso del agua. *Agroproductividad* **2017**, *10*, 90–95. Available online: https://revista-agroproductividad.org/index.php/agroproductividad/article/view/1028 (accessed on 30 January 2023). (In Spanish).
84. Marín-Muñiz, J.L.; García-González, M.; Ruelas-Monjardín, L.; Moreno-Casasola, P. Influence of different porous media and ornamental vegetation on wastewater pollutant removal in vertical subsurface flow wtland microcosms. *Environ. Eng. Sci.* **2018**, *35*, 88–94. [CrossRef]
85. Hernández, M.E.; Marín-Muñiz, J.L. Greenhouse Gas Emissions and Treatment Performance in Constructed Wetlands with Ornamental Plants: Case Studies in Veracruz, Mexico. In *Artificial or Constructed Wetlands a Suitable Technology for Sustainable Water Management*; Durán-Domínguez, M., Navarro-Frómeta, A., Bayona, J., Eds.; CRC Press: Boca Raton, FL, USA; Taylor & Francis Group: Abingdon, UK, 2018; pp. 163–177.
86. López-Alba, J.E.; Marín-Muñiz, J.L.; Zamora, S.; Celis, M. Evaluación del crecimiento de plantas sembradas en humedal artificial: Efecto del posicionamiento de sembrado. *J. Basic Sci.* **2022**, *8*, 104–111. (In Spanish)
87. Zitácuaro-Contreras, I.; Marín-Muñiz, J.L.; Celis, M.; Vidal, M.; León, X.; Zamora, S. Vegetación ornamental utilizada en fitorremediación y sus potencialidades ambientales, económicas y sociales. *J. Basic Sci.* **2022**, *8*, 133–145. Available online: https://revistas.ujat.mx/index.php/jobs/article/view/5353 (accessed on 2 January 2023).
88. Boyás, T.; Álvarez-Contreras, L.; Marín-Muñiz, J.L.; Celis-Pérez, M.; Zamora-Castro, S.; Landa, M. Condiciones ambientales para el óptimo desarrollo de plantas ornamentales y fitorremediadoras. *J. Basic Sci.* **2022**, *8*, 96–103. Available online: http://revistas.ujat.mx/index.php/jobs (accessed on 5 June 2022). (In Spanish).
89. Martínez-Aguilar, K.E.; Marín-Muñiz, J.L. La economía circular como una propuesta para la reutilización de aguas residuales porcinas. In *Reconstrucción de una Economía Social Para Lograr el Desarrollo Sustentable*; Ortega, G., Rodríguez, E., Eds.; Martí/Códice, México, 2022; pp. 61–75. Available online: https://umarti.edu.mx/index.php/download/libro/ (accessed on 5 February 2023). (In Spanish)
90. Sandoval, L.; Zurita, F.; Del Ángel-Coronel, O.; Adame-García, J.; Marín-Muñiz, J.L. Influence of a new ornamental species (*Spathiphyllum blandum*) on the removal of COD, nitrogen, phosphorus and fecal coliforms: A mesocosm wetland study with pet and tezontle substrates. *Water Sci. Technol.* **2020**, *81*, 961–970. [CrossRef]
91. Sandoval, L.; Marín-Muñiz, J.L.; Adame-García, J.; Fernández-Lambert, G.; Zurita, F. Effect of *Spathiphyllum blandum* on the removal of ibuprofen and conventional pollutants from polluted river water, in fully saturated constructed wetlands at mesocosm level. *J. Water Health* **2020**, *18*, 224–228. [CrossRef]
92. Nakase, C.; Zurita, F.; Nani, G.; Reyes, G.; Fernández-Lambert, G.; Cabrera-Hernández, A.; Sandoval, L. Nitrogen removal from domestic wastewater and the development of tropical ornamental plants in partially saturated mesocosm-scale constructed wetlands. *Int. J. Environ. Res. Public Health* **2019**, *16*, 4800. [CrossRef] [PubMed]
93. Sandoval, L.C.; Zurita, F.; Nani, G.; Del Ángel-Coronel, O.; Aguilar, F. Treatment of swine effluent mixed with domestic wastewater and vegetation development in monoculture and polyculture horizontal subsurface flow wetlands. *Ecol. Eng.* **2021**, *173*, 106432. [CrossRef]
94. Fernández-Echeverría, E.; Sandoval-Herazo, L.C.; Zurita, F.; Betanzo-Torres, E.; Sandoval-Herazo, M. Development of *Heliconia latispatha* in constructed wetlands, for the treatment of swine/domestic wastewater in tropical climates, with PET as a substitute for the filter medium. *Rev. Mex. Ing. Quím.* **2022**, *21*, IA2811. [CrossRef]
95. Sandoval-Herazo, L.; Alvarado-Lassman, A.; Marín-Muñiz, J.L.; Méndez-Contreras, J.; Zamora-Castro, S. Effects of the use of ornamental plants and different substrates in the removal of wastewater pollutants through microcosms of constructed wetlands. *Sustainability* **2018**, *10*, 1594. [CrossRef]
96. Zamora-Castro, S.; Marín-Muñiz, J.L.; Sandoval, L.; Vidal-Álvarez, M.; Carrión-Delgado, J. Effect of ornamental plants, seasonality, and filter media material in fill-and-drian constructed wetlands treating rural community wastewater. *Sustainability* **2019**, *11*, 2350. [CrossRef]
97. Sandoval, L.; Marín-Muñiz, J.L.; Zamora-Castro, S.; Sandoval-Salas, F.; Alvarado-Lassman, A. Evaluation of wastewater treatment by microcosms of vertical subsurface wetlands in partially saturated conditions planted with ornamental plants and filled with mineral and plastic substrates. *Int. J. Environ. Res. Public Health* **2019**, *16*, 167. [CrossRef]
98. Zamora, S.; Sandoval, L.; Marín-Muñiz, J.L.; Fernández-Lambert, G.; Hernández-Orduña, M. Impact of ornamental vegetation type and different substrate layers on pollutant removal in constructed wetland mesocosms treating rural community wastewater. *Processes* **2019**, *7*, 531. [CrossRef]
99. Zamora, S.; Marín-Muñíz, J.L.; Nakase-Rodríguez, C.; Fernández-Lambert, G.; Sandoval, L. Wastewater treatment by constructed wetland eco-technology: Influence of mineral and plastic materials as filter media and tropical ornamental plants. *Water* **2019**, *11*, 2344. [CrossRef]
100. Sandoval-Herazo, L.C.; Alvarado-Lassman, A.; López-Méndez, M.C.; Martínez-Sibaja, A.; Aguilar-Lasserre, A.A.; Zamora-Castro, S.; Marín-Muñiz, J.L. Effects of Ornamental Plant Density and Mineral/Plastic Media on the Removal of Domestic Wastewater Pollutants by Home Wetlands Technology. *Molecules* **2020**, *25*, 5273. [CrossRef]

101. Marín-Muñiz, J.L.; Sandoval, L.; Zamora-Castro, S.; Celis-Pérez, M. Humedales con plantas ornamentales y relleno de plástico reutilizado como tratamiento sustentable de aguas residuales. *J. Basic Sci.* **2022**, *8*, 146–153. Available online: http://revistas.ujat.mx/index.php/jobs (accessed on 5 January 2023). (In Spanish).
102. Wang, Q.; Hu, Y.; Xie, H.; Yang, Z. Constructed wetlands: A review on the role of radial oxygen loss in the rhizosphere by macrophytes. *Water* **2018**, *10*, 678. [CrossRef]
103. Thamke, S.; Khan, A. Constructed wetlands-Natural treatment of wastewater. *Int. J. Eng. Res. Technol.* **2021**, *10*, 204–212. Available online: http://www.ijert.org (accessed on 7 December 2022).
104. Mander, Ü.; Dotro, G.; Ebie, Y.; Towprayoon, S.; Chiemchaisri, C.; Nogueira, S.; Jamsranjav, B.; Kasak, K.; Truss, J.; Tournebize, J.; et al. Greenhouse gas emission in constructed wetlands for wastewater treatment: A review. *Ecol. Eng.* **2014**, *66*, 19–35. [CrossRef]
105. Lazzerini, G.; Lucchetti, S.; Nicese, F.P. Analysis of greenhouse gas emissions form ornamental plant production: A nursery level approach. *Urban For. Urban Green.* **2014**, *13*, 517–525. [CrossRef]
106. Bakhshoodeh, R.; Alavi, N.; Soltani-Mohammadi, A.; Ghanavati, H. Removing heavy metals from Isfahan composting leachate by horizontal subsurface flow constructed wetland. *Environ. Sci. Poll. Res.* **2016**, *23*, 12384–12391. [CrossRef]
107. Bakhshoodeh, R.; Soltani-Mohammadi, A.; Alavi, N.; Ghanavati, H. Treatment of high polluted leachate by subsurface flow constructed wetland with vetiver. *Amirk. J. Civ. Eng.* **2017**, *49*, 139–148. [CrossRef]
108. Bakhshoodeh, R.; Alavi, N.; Paydary, P. Composting plant leachate treatment by a pilot-scale, three-stage, horizontal flow constructed wetland in central Iran. *Environ. Sci. Poll. Res.* **2017**, *24*, 23803–23814. [CrossRef]
109. Qasaimeh, A.; Alsharie, H.; Masoud, T. A review on constructed wetlands components and heavy metal removal form wastewater. *J. Environ. Prot.* **2015**, *6*, 710–718. [CrossRef]

Disclaimer/Publisher's Note: The statements, opinions and data contained in all publications are solely those of the individual author(s) and contributor(s) and not of MDPI and/or the editor(s). MDPI and/or the editor(s) disclaim responsibility for any injury to people or property resulting from any ideas, methods, instructions or products referred to in the content.

Article

Comparative Analysis of Three WEEE Management Scenarios Based on LCA Methodology: Case Study in the Municipality of Iasi, Romania

Simona Cecilia Ghiga [1], Isabela Maria Simion [2,*], Cătălina Filote [1], Mihaela Roșca [3], Raluca Maria Hlihor [3,*] and Maria Gavrilescu [1,4,*]

1. Department of Environmental Engineering and Management, "Cristofor Simionescu" Faculty of Chemical Engineering and Environmental Protection, "Gheorghe Asachi" Technical University of Iasi, 73 Prof. D. Mangeron Blvd., 700050 Iasi, Romania; sghiga@gmail.com (S.C.G.); catalina.filote@gmail.com (C.F.)
2. Research Department, "Ion Ionescu de la Brad" Iasi University of Life Sciences, 3 Mihail Sadoveanu Alley, 700490 Iasi, Romania
3. Department of Horticultural Technologies, Faculty of Horticulture, "Ion Ionescu de la Brad" Iasi University of Life Sciences, 3 Mihail Sadoveanu Alley, 700490 Iasi, Romania; mihaelarosca@uaiasi.ro
4. Academy of Romanian Scientists, 3 Ilfov Street, 050044 Bucharest, Romania
* Correspondence: simion.i@uaiasi.ro (I.M.S.); raluca.hlihor@uaiasi.ro (R.M.H.); mgav@tuiasi.ro (M.G.)

Abstract: The increasing consumption of electrical and electronic equipment (EEE), correlated with the fast innovation pace in this field, generates a large amount of annual waste. The current established management practices cannot keep up with it, and the results are of increased significance given the negative effects on the environment and human health. Thus, the current study aimed to analyze the environmental impact of three different scenarios of waste electrical and electronic equipment (WEEE) management, following population awareness campaigns regarding its collection in the Municipality of Iasi, Romania. Data processing was carried out considering Life Cycle Assessment (LCA) methodology with the established functional unit for each scenario according to the collected amount. The results were quantified using the CML2001 and ReCiPe methods and showed that the highest environmental impact was obtained for scenario II (S2) (1.59×10^{-7} pers. equiv. using the CML2001 method and 32.7 pers. equiv. using the ReCiPe method), while the lowest for scenario I (S1) (6.42×10^{-8} pers. equiv. using the CML2001 method and 13.8 pers. equiv. using the ReCiPe method). The process with the highest contribution to the total environmental impact was the collection stage for all scenarios, with the exception of scenario S2, in which case the highest value was generated for the landfill process following the application of the ReCiPe method (39.93%). The current study provides value to a critical issue in the environmental area and supports the development of sustainable WEEE management processes.

Keywords: e-waste; Life Cycle Assessment; environmental impact; energy; waste management; recovery

Citation: Ghiga, S.C.; Simion, I.M.; Filote, C.; Roșca, M.; Hlihor, R.M.; Gavrilescu, M. Comparative Analysis of Three WEEE Management Scenarios Based on LCA Methodology: Case Study in the Municipality of Iasi, Romania. *Processes* **2023**, *11*, 1305. https://doi.org/10.3390/pr11051305

Academic Editor: Farooq Sher

Received: 15 March 2023
Revised: 12 April 2023
Accepted: 19 April 2023
Published: 23 April 2023

Copyright: © 2023 by the authors. Licensee MDPI, Basel, Switzerland. This article is an open access article distributed under the terms and conditions of the Creative Commons Attribution (CC BY) license (https://creativecommons.org/licenses/by/4.0/).

1. Introduction

The rapid development of electrical and electronic equipment (EEE) over the last decades, together with the incapacity of current e-waste management systems to keep up with its disposal, generates serious concerns worldwide [1]. E-waste, also known as waste electrical and electronic equipment (WEEE), contains both hazardous and non-hazardous substances that can cause critical effects on the environment and human health. These consequences can be generated during different life cycle stages of the WEEE management system, from the collection of the waste up to its disposal and recycling [2]. Hazardous substances and materials contained by e-waste are heavy metals, plastics, brominated flame retardants, chlorofluorocarbons (CFCs) and hydrochlorofluorocarbons (HCFCs), etc. [3–6]. Heavy metals such as Pb, Hg, Cd and As [7] can inhibit plant growth and negatively affect animal and human health since they are able to bioaccumulate in living organisms [8,9]. It is thus difficult and costly to remove them [9]. Some elements have a higher impact than others. For example, lithium and fluorine from Li-ion batteries can contribute the most to negative environmental effects (80–90%), while phosphorous has a lower contribution (20%) [10].

Furthermore, it is not only household electronic and electrical devices that can end up as waste. The renewable energy sector, namely that of solar power, has been raising concerns over the increase in waste photovoltaic panels, which is estimated to reach 60–78 million tons by 2050 [11]. Thus, efficient WEEE management systems are important in order to avoid the negative effects of improper landfilling as well as to minimize the environmental burden of the management system itself.

Unfortunately, although WEEE generation is a significant environmental issue, only 66% of the world has implemented e-waste policies. Since the enforced rules, programs and rate of WEEE recycling differ around the world, it can be difficult to compare the amounts of generated and collected WEEE. Furthermore, it is not only the collected and recycled WEEE that should be considered, but also WEEE that is informally collected, recycled outside of the take-back systems, and illegally exported, but their quantification is an even greater challenge [12]. The ineffectiveness of global WEEE management systems is also proven by the issue of large exports from the developed to the developing countries that are even less equipped to tackle e-waste, causing health problems to the native population and environment [13].

The best enforced WEEE legislation and management systems are in countries or regions such as Japan and countries of the European Union, while most developing countries do not even have a WEEE management system [14]. In Italy for example, the collection system is based on five categories of e-waste, while in Norway there are fourteen total WEEE categories that are followed, four being additional to the ones established by the EU directives [15,16]. In Sweden, although some WEEE management processes are delegated to the private sector, the main responsibility is attributed to the local authorities, which manage all household wastes. By comparison, most European countries have in place a system that assigns the main responsibility to the producers, which are organized in Producer Responsibility Organizations (PROs) [16]. Therefore, although the informal recycling of WEEE can cause major issues in the environment and human health, formal recycling requires a careful analysis in order to understand the key points that can be improved from a sustainability perspective. Furthermore, the negative environmental impacts of WEEE management can be attributed not only to informal recycling, but also to an inefficient application of a formal system. It is thus important to optimize the processes included in WEEE management systems in order to reduce the overall environmental burden.

A pivotal player in the WEEE management scheme is represented by the collection centers, where the pathway of an EEE is decided, whether it is reuse, remanufacturing, repair or recycling ([17]). These institutions or organizations are required to abide by standards and laws. In the European Union, the current EU legislation, namely Directive 2002/06/EC and Directive 2012/19/EU, imposed restrictions regarding the use of certain toxic substances in EEE, established WEEE collection targets and introduced the Extended Producer Responsibility (EPR), which placed the responsibility for the whole e-waste life cycle management in the hands of producers [18,19].

Life Cycle Assessment (LCA) is an established methodology for the analysis of the environmental performance of products and processes and can be used as an input in decision-making regarding the choice of waste management systems or strategic decisions regarding the priority of resource use [20]. LCA enables the identification of opportunities that can bring improvements in the quality of the environment. This methodology is standardized at the international level, and considers the Ecoinvent database [21], which is one of the most effective and complete databases for identifying and evaluating environmental impacts. The LCA methodology facilitates the identification of environmental burdens of a product or system and ultimately enables problem solving and the optimization of key sustainability issues, including WEEE management. The LCA methodology is also recommended at the level of the European Union for quantifying the environmental impact of products and processes [22]. So far, a number of significant research studies have addressed this area. The LCA analysis of the waste treatment steps and recycling of lithium batteries [23], e-waste recycling for metal recovery from high-grade WEEE [24], the end-of-life stage of cooking hoods [25], WEEE management in a full-scale Italian facility [26], the WEEE transportation network in the Reggio Emilia district of Northern Italy [18], the e-waste management system in Bologna, Municipality of Emilia Romagna region [14], and the remanufacturing of computers [27] have been covered.

Although developed countries from the European Union such as Germany and Sweden have no problem with meeting the established-by-law collection targets, in Romania this is still an issue [28]. The sustainability of the Romanian WEEE management system can definitely be improved, either in terms of increasing the collected amounts of e-waste and/or optimizing the established collecting practices. Carbon footprint of WEEE management systems in EU countries such as Italy, Sweden, Germany, Bulgaria, as well as Romania were calculated recently for the time period 2007–2014 [28]. The results showed that all these countries, including Romania, have reduced their carbon footprint. The study also highlighted that out of these five countries, Romania occupies the second place among the largest exporters of WEEE outside its territory [28]. The current study aims to analyze the environmental performance of three WEEE management scenarios in the Municipality of Iasi, Romania using LCA methodology. This research study thus highlights key processes and resources where the environmental burden can be improved for WEEE management in Romania, with applicability to other countries as well that follow the same system. This is performed using two different established LCA methods and GaBi Education software. The carried-out research adds value through the comparison of three different scenarios (S1, S2, S3) of WEEE management. Moreover, two of the analyzed scenarios (S2, S3) include a phase of raising awareness among the local population regarding the importance of WEEE collection, a process which to our knowledge has not been yet included in LCA studies of WEEE management.

The main objectives set for the LCA analysis are: (1) the qualitative and quantitative analysis of WEEE flow in the Municipality of Iasi, Romania; (2) the development of management alternatives for WEEE and the evaluation of their impact taking into account the amount and composition of the collected e-waste; (3) the evaluation of the impact on the environment generated by the implementation of WEEE management systems by applying the LCA methodology; (4) carrying out a comparative analysis of some WEEE management systems using the CML2001 and ReCiPe methods; (5) the identification of an environmentally favorable WEEE management alternative.

2. Materials and Methods

2.1. Life Cycle Assessment Methodology

The environmental impact analysis of WEEE management scenarios in the Municipality of Iași, Romania was carried out using the LCA methodology (Figure 1) following the four stages as established by ISO 14040 and ISO 14044 standards [22,29]:

- goal and scope definition—consists of the establishment of a reference that will be considered for the overall analysis in order to follow a clear pathway;
- inventory analysis—consists of data gathering and categorizes the available information into inputs or outputs for the analyzed system;
- impact assessment—represents the phase in which the results concerning the generated environmental impact are obtained;
- interpretation—the phase in which the results are interpreted in a clear, concise and accurate manner according to the established goal and scope in order to be further used by researchers, policy and decision makers.

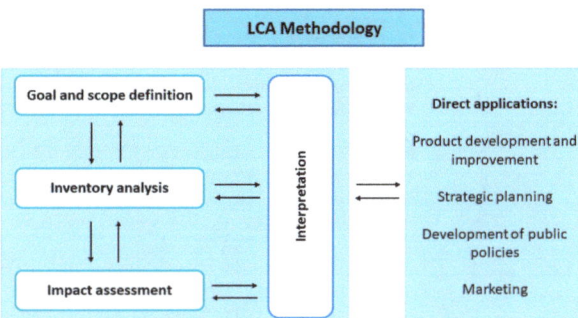

Figure 1. Stages of the Life Cycle Assessment (LCA) methodology.

2.2. Scope and Functional Unit

The functional unit is represented by the WEEE amount collected during population awareness campaigns in the Municipality of Iasi, Romania in 2018–2019, respectively: for scenario I, S1—20,818 kg, for scenario II, S2 and scenario III, S3—29,691 kg. All the input and output data regarding these three analyzed scenarios (energy consumption, raw materials, emissions, etc.) were related to the established functional units (Figure 2).

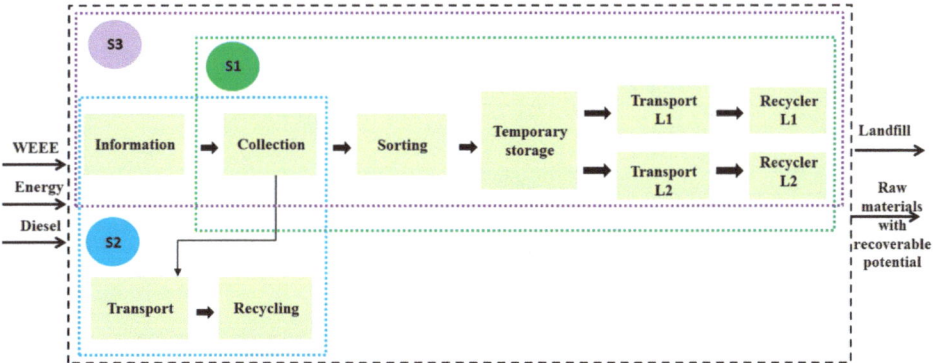

Figure 2. System boundaries of WEEE management systems—all considered scenarios (L1—recycling location Apahida, Romania; L2—recycling location Jilava, Romania).

2.3. System Description

The system boundary defines which processes will be included in or excluded from the system. Often, a combination of different criteria must be used to properly define the boundaries. In terms of system characteristics, the cutoff approach was applied, in which the flow of recyclable parts is considered only up to the process of their recovery, excluding their upcycling or reuse into new products [30]. This means that, in the current study, a cradle-to-cradle approach of the system was defined for the analyzed scenarios, with the first process included in the system being the collection step for scenario I (S1), while the information step was further included for scenarios II (S2) and III (S3). The cradle-to-cradle approach involves the recovery of materials from a waste product through recycling in a closed-loop system [31].

The stages included in the three scenarios are as follows:

- Information—involves the activity of education and awareness through several communication channels. In this sense, the following steps are usually taken: the creation of promotional material layout, printing, press conferences, the distribution of materials by volunteers or specially authorized companies, press layouts, radio, TV and the 1:1 approach.
- Collection—consists of taking over WEEE from individuals and legal entities following requests received in local and national call centers, loading them into specially authorized cars, as well as transporting them to the temporary storage depot.
- Transport—the distance traveled by the van loaded with WEEE to the unloading point, temporary storage or recycling storage.
- Sorting—the handling–storage procedure according to the legal provisions based on categories and codes of electrical and electronic equipment waste.
- Temporary storage—involves keeping WEEE in specially authorized warehouses in order to collect some quantities and send them to recyclers.
- Recycling—can be manual or mechanical. The mechanical method involves the procedure of shredding or breaking. Unlike the manual method, the mechanical method cannot effectively recover precious metals. For this reason, disassembly is manually performed in many cases. This represents the operations of disassembly, processing, and the recovery of waste [32]. In Romania, recycling facilities do not represent the standard known model. They usual perform e-waste preparation for the further recycling and recovery of some parts, and disposal activities [33].

The stages were chosen according to the waste management situation in recent years. In scenario I (S1), the amount of waste collected without the population being informed and updated with the new WEEE management rules was considered. Currently, the implicit organization applies new standards by which it brings new changes in the stages of the management system. Due to the changes in legal provisions, the organization in partnership with the local authorities built a center for the collection and temporary storage of WEEE. The extent of WEEE recovery and the cost of recycling required the transport of WEEE to different recyclers based on categories, and groups were transported in batches of 10–12 tons.

Scenario II (S2) considered 4 stages including a stage of informing the population with the aim of collecting a larger amount of waste compared to S1. In this scenario, it was also considered that the sorting stage was carried out within the transport stage at the time of unloading waste to the recycler. The information stage was taken into account from the desire to meet the collection targets imposed by the European Union, namely 45% of the number of electrical and electronic products sold on the market in a specific year for the time period 2017–2020 [34], and to increase the collection rate of WEEE removed from use. This stage involved a campaign that took place over a period of two weeks, being carried out only through the print media and radio. Due to the lack of local infrastructure, the quantity taken from individuals and legal entities was loaded unsorted into a single haul destined for a single recycler.

Scenario III (S3) was the most complex scenario and was applied by the organization included in the study for taking over the responsibility of producers, within the scope of the Municipality of Iași. Local partners in this campaign were: Iași City Hall, the Local Sanitation Operator, Environmental Protection Agency, the Environmental Guard Commissariat and the student leagues. Attempts to make costs and consumption more efficient have led to the finding that information, education and awareness can contribute in the long term to increasing the WEEE collection rate. The information phase was provided by flyers, on the street and in mailboxes, print and online media, radio and the Facebook page. The information campaign took place two weeks before the collection campaign. The involvement of student organizations had a positive impact on the population. They were trained and divided into teams, managing in this way the approach of a large number of people. The advantage of this campaign was the fact that the organizers made available to citizens a free WEEE pick-up service from home by calling or by placing orders online and directly with volunteers. In the same campaign, fixed points were set up where citizens could bring used or non-functional electrical equipment. To encourage and stimulate the population to conscientiously dispose of this equipment, a raffle with fixed prizes or bonuses was also organized. The amount collected during this campaign was 29,691 kg.

2.4. Life Cycle Inventory

The life cycle inventory phase (LCI) consists of the collection of input (natural resources, primary materials, types of energy, products) and output information (emissions, energy, products and by-products) for all processes included in the system boundaries. In the current study, several different sources of data were used, including databases incorporated in GaBi Education software such as Ecoinvent, collected data from the accredited collector RoRec Association and two local recyclers. Input data regarding the collected WEEE amount per category considered in the study is summarized in Table 1. In terms of energy, the electricity consumption was 11,033 MJ for S1, 18,782 MJ for S2 and 12,968 in the case of S3. As far as the transport component is concerned, diesel consumption was equal for S1 and S2, 2500 kg, while S3 had a quantity of 1500 kg.

Table 1. LCI data for the analyzed scenarios of WEEE management through LCA methodology.

Input Data	Amount per Scenario (%)		
	S1	S2	S3
Air (air-conditioned)	1.59	1.59	1.59
Boiler household	0.64	0.64	0.64
Computer case	1.81	1.81	1.81
Cooking machines	8.41	8.43	8.43
Electric hobs	0.04	0.04	0.04
Hoods	0.03	0.03	0.03
Keyboard and mouse	0.10	0.10	0.10
Kitchen appliances	1.61	1.62	1.62
Large appliances for waste heat	0.43	0.40	0.40
Measuring device	0.64	0.64	0.64
Microwave ovens	2.32	2.32	2.32
Monitors CRT	1.66	1.66	1.66
Monitors LCD	0.19	0.19	0.19
Other IT equipment	0.07	0.07	0.07
Personal care appliances	0.67	0.67	0.67
Photocopiers	2.09	2.09	2.09
Printers	0.51	0.52	0.52
Radio sets	0.15	0.15	0.15
Refrigerating appliances	40.35	40.25	40.25
Television CRT	13.08	13.12	13.12
Television LCD	1.72	1.72	1.72
Vacuums cleaner	1.11	1.11	1.11
Washing machines	20.71	20.76	20.76
Writing machines	0.06	0.06	0.06

2.5. GaBi Education Software

The inventory data (input and output data for the used scenarios) were processed in GaBi Education software. GaBi Education software is a modular system that includes plans, processes, flows, as well as their functions, which is why the system can be considered with a clear and transparent structure [35]. The databases used by the system are independent of each other, being responsible for saving all the information related to an analyzed system [36].

In order to evaluate the impact of the scenarios proposed as WEEE management alternatives according to the LCA methodology, two specific evaluation methods with different categories of impact were chosen to highlight the favorable scenario from the point of view of environmental protection. The CML2001 and ReCiPe methods were considered due to the annually updated database and the fact that they are the most used and recognized methods in Europe and the United States.

3. Results

3.1. Life Cycle Assessment of the Environmental Impact of WEEE Management System in Romania Using CML2001 Method

The results of the environmental impact assessment of S1, S2 and S3 using CML2001 method are depicted in Figure 3.

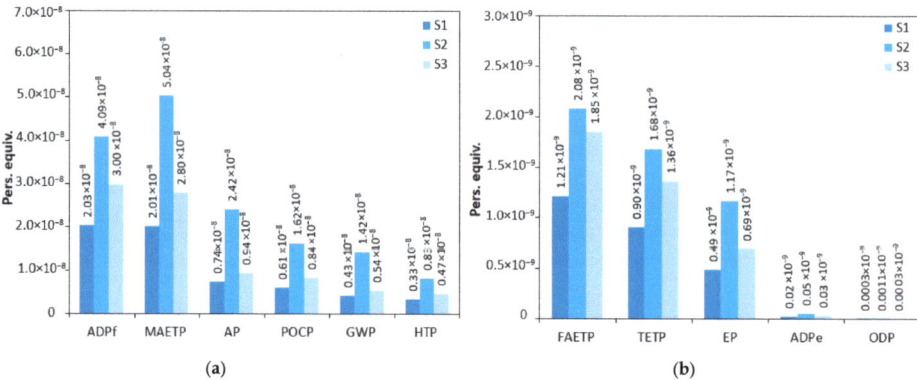

Figure 3. Environmental impact assessment of WEEE management system in the Municipality of Iasi, Romania using CML2001 method—all scenarios: (**a**) ADPf: abiotic depletion—fossil; MAETP: marine aquatic ecotoxicity potential; AP: acidification potential; POCP: photochemical ozone creation potential; GWP: global warming potential—100 years; HTP: human toxicity potential; (**b**) FAETP: freshwater aquatic ecotoxicity potential; TETP: terrestrial ecotoxicity potential; EP: eutrophication potential; ADPe: abiotic depletion—elements; ODP: ozone layer depletion potential, steady state.

It can be observed that the obtained impact category values for S1 and S3 followed the hierarchy: ADPf > MAETP > AP > POCP > GWP > HTP > FAETP > TETP > EP > ADPe > ODP. In the case of S2 though, the highest value was generated for the impact category marine aquatic ecotoxicity potential (MAETP).

The total generated environmental impact identified by the CML2001 method was higher for S2 (1.59×10^{-7} pers. equiv.), followed by S3 (8.98×10^{-8} pers. equiv.) and finally, S1 (6.42×10^{-8} pers. equiv.). The same pattern was identified for all analyzed impact categories, however. Furthermore, the obtained results show positive values for each impact category. Positive impacts show the negative effects on the environment and human health, while negative values highlight the benefits that are brought in terms of sustainability [24].

3.2. Life Cycle Assessment of the Environmental Impact of WEEE Management System in Romania Using ReCiPe Method

The results of the environmental impact assessment of S1, S2 and S3 using ReCiPe method are depicted in Figure 4.

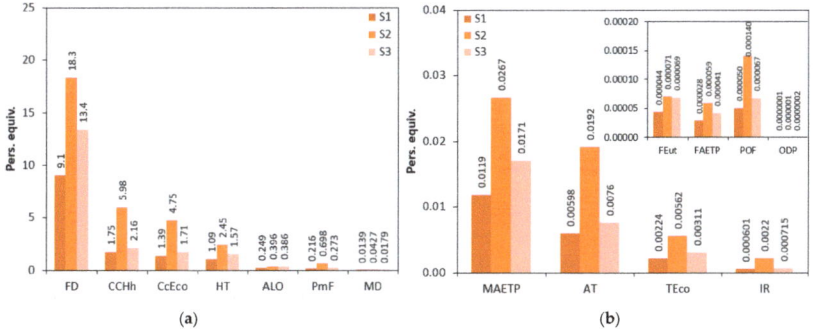

Figure 4. Environmental impact assessment of WEEE management system in the Municipality of Iasi, Romania using ReCiPe method—all scenarios: (**a**) FD: fossil depletion; CCHh: climate change human health, including biogenic carbon; CcEco: climate change ecosystems, including biogenic carbon; HT: human toxicity; ALO: agricultural land occupation; PmF: particulate matter formation; MD: metal depletion; (**b**) MAETP: marine ecotoxicity potential; AT: terrestrial acidification; TEco: terrestrial ecotoxicity; IR: ionizing radiation; FEut: freshwater eutrophication; FAETP: freshwater ecotoxicity; POF: photochemical oxidant formation; ODP: ozone depletion.

The obtained impact category values for S1 followed the hierarchy: FD > CCHh > CcEco > HT > ALO > PmF > MD > MAETP > AT > TEco > IR > FEut > FAETP > POF > ODP.

In the case of S2, the order was slightly different: FD > CCHh > CcEco > HT > PmF > ALO > MD > MAETP > AT > TEco > IR > POF > FEut > FAETP > ODP.

In S3, the hierarchy was: FD > CCHh > CcEco > HT > ALO > PmF > MD > MAETP > AT > TEco > IR > FEut > POF > FAETP > ODP.

The results show that for all the analyzed system boundaries, the highest impact was obtained for the fossil depletion (FD) impact category. Its observed environmental impact value was in fact significantly higher than the rest of the impact categories. It was approximately three times higher than the values generated for climate change human health (CCHh), climate change ecosystems (CcEco) and human toxicity (HT). Additionally, for all analyzed scenarios, the lowest environmental impact was identified in case of ozone depletion (ODP) category. Similar to the results obtained using CML2001 method, for all analyzed impact categories through the ReCiPe method, the total generated impact value is higher for S2 (32.7 pers. equiv.), followed by S3 (19.6 pers. equiv.) and lastly, by S1 (13.8 pers. equiv.). The results also show positive values for each impact category, proving that there are only negative effects on the environment and human health.

3.3. Comparative Analysis of Life Cycle Assessment Results and Possibilities for System Improvement

Although the issues concerning WEEE management have been known and addressed for more than a decade, and given the advancement of the LCA methodology in recent years, a review study by Withanage and Habib [37] analyzing the application of Life Cycle Assessment in this area identified only 31 studies, out of which most were focused on the recycling and recovery processes. Only a small part of the known literature is concentrated on the full cycle from collection to recycling. This highlights a serious gap in the research of the sustainability of WEEE management [37]. It is also important to note that LCA is the methodology for environmental impact assessment, which has been mostly applied from all available methods for WEEE management analysis [38].

Raising awareness regarding the importance of proper WEEE disposal is very important as studies show that this can have a considerable impact on the efficiency of waste management [39]. In Romania, there is, for example, a lack of information concerning the existence and location of WEEE collection centers, as well as the environmental legislation attributed to e-waste management [33]. Since most published articles evaluated the sustainability of WEEE management from collection to recycling or only focused on the recycling part, in the current study one of our objectives was to focus through our research on the processes preceding the recycling stage. Furthermore, we also included in the system boundaries a stage considering raising the awareness among local communities with the purpose of increasing people's involvement in contributing to the e-waste collection system, and thus reducing the amount of WEEE that enters the informal landfills, which is improperly handled and can affect the environment and human health. This is why the current study also considered in S2 and S3 the information process for the comparative analysis.

As far as the contribution of each process included in the system boundaries is concerned, the results illustrated in Figure 5 for the CML2001 method show that for S1, the highest percentage was attributed to the collection step (47.78%), followed by recycling (25.77%) and sorting (13.75%). The lowest values were identified for the temporary storage of the collected e-waste (0.13%), landfilling (0.65%) and transport (11.83%). The hierarchy of the process contribution to the total environmental impact of S1 was collection > recycling > sorting > transport > landfill > temporary storage. In the case of S2 (Figure 6), the highest contribution among all the involved processes was also for the collection step (32.13%). However, the obtained percentage for landfill (25.77%) was higher than that of recycling (18.20%) and transport (5.87%) in comparison with S1. The lowest value was generated in the case of the information process (0.01%). So, in the case of the results obtained for S2 using CML2001, the hierarchy was collection > landfill > recycling > transport > information. The results obtained for S3 showed a similar trend (Figure 7). The collection process (56.96%) had the highest contribution to the total environmental impact, while the lowest was identified for the sorting step (0.09%). Similar to S1, the recycling stage (18.50%) had a higher contribution than the transport (8.45%) and landfill (1.22%) processes. Thus, for S3 the identified order of the process contribution to the total generated impact was collection > recycling > temporary storage > transport > landfill > information > sorting.

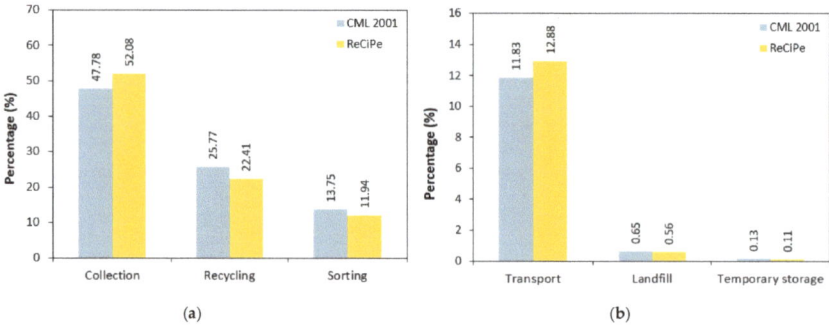

Figure 5. Process contribution to the total environmental impact of WEEE management according to S1 (CML2001 and ReCiPe methods): (**a**) Collection, Recycling, Sorting; (**b**) Transport, Landfill, Temporary storage.

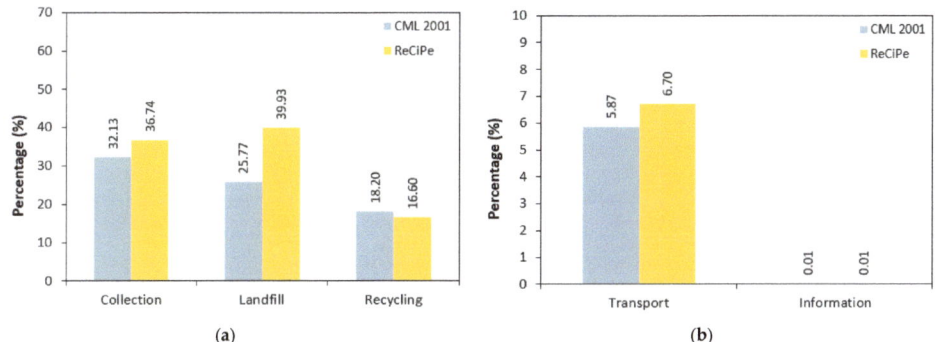

Figure 6. Process contribution to the total environmental impact of WEEE management according to S2 (CML2001 and ReCiPe methods): (**a**) Collection, Landfill, Recycling; (**b**) Transport, Information.

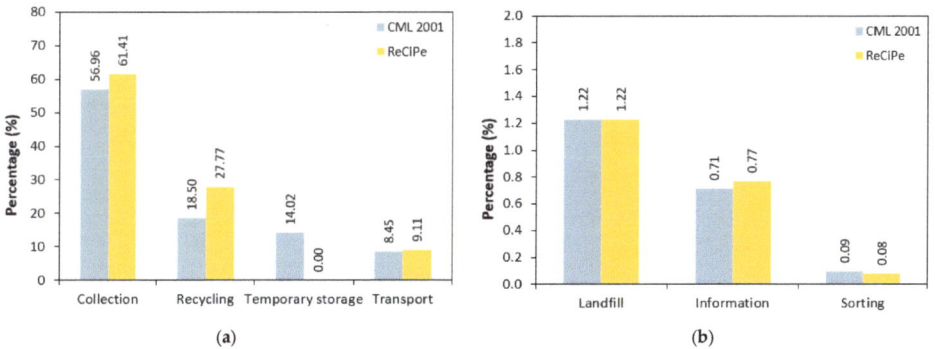

Figure 7. Process contribution to the total environmental impact of WEEE management according to S3 (CML2001 and ReCiPe methods): (**a**) Collection, Recycling, Temporary storage, Transport; (**b**) Landfill, Information, Sorting.

The results obtained by applying the ReCiPe method also showed the highest contribution to the total environmental impact of the collection step in almost all the analyzed scenarios. With a few exceptions, the hierarchy of the percentages per process was similar to the one identified when the CML2001 method was used. One difference is the fact that the highest value was obtained for the landfill stage (39.93%) for S2. Another difference is that in the case of S1, the transport process (12.88%) generated a higher contribution to the total impact in comparison with the sorting step (11.94%).

The obtained percentage contribution values for S1 through the ReCiPe method followed the hierarchy of collection > recycling > transport > sorting > landfill > temporary storage. In case of S2, the order was landfill > collection > recycling > transport > information. Finally, for S3, the hierarchy was collection > recycling > temporary storage > transport > landfill > information > sorting.

The differences between the two applied LCA methods were determined by the different characterization factors included by the methods and the fact that CML2001 is a problem-oriented methodology, while the ReCiPe method considers the cause as well as the effect [40].

To compare, a study analyzing the environmental impact of the treatment, disposal, collection and external transport of municipal waste containing various types of waste, including WEEE, found that the highest contribution to the total environmental impact was for the treatment and disposal phase (72.3%), followed by collection (18.3%) and external transport (9.4%). The research was carried out in the context of a small town in Italy with a population of 16,820 inhabitants. A functional unit of 1 ton of waste was used and the ReCiPe method was applied in order to quantify the environmental impact [20].

Results regarding the percentage contribution to the total environmental impact obtained using Impact 2002+ method in another research study showed a 75% value for the mechanical processing of WEEE in the context of a Swiss take-back and recycling system [41].

The impact category with the highest value for the applied scenarios was represented by FD (fossil depletion potential), followed by CCHh (climate changes associated with the deterioration of human health). The negative influence of these impact categories resulting from the application of the three scenarios was due to the consumption of diesel and electricity.

The LCA methodology is able to provide an overview considering the environmental aspects of different waste management practices as well as of the materials used and the emissions released into the environment. In order to analyze the contribution of the most important resources to the sustainability outcome of WEEE management as described in the Romanian case study, the percentage of electricity consumption and transportation to the total environmental impact was calculated as well, for both the CML2001 and ReCiPe methods.

The results obtained using the CML2001 method are depicted in Figure 8a. The generated data show that the highest electricity consumption was attributed to S1 (80.6%), followed by S2 (62%) and S3 (33.9%), respectively. The hierarchy for the transport contribution was the opposite though, the lowest value being identified for S1 (19.4%). For S2, the transport value was 38%, while for S3 it was 66.1%. Furthermore, it is worth comparing the energy consumption of laptop and home computer manufacturing with the total electricity consumption of their recycling. Thus, 1266 MJ are consumed for the conversion of heavy metals for laptop manufacturing, 5832 MJ are necessary for using an office laptop, while 1867 MJ of energy are estimated for the remanufacturing process [22].

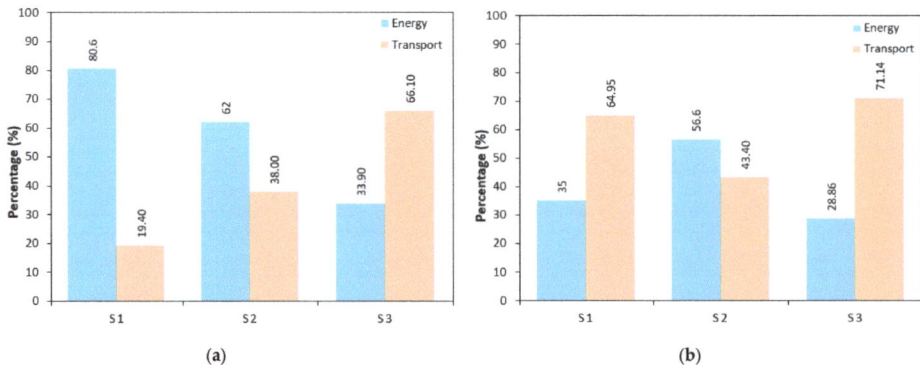

Figure 8. Electricity and transport contribution to the total environmental impact of WEEE management systems: (**a**) CML2001 method; (**b**) ReCiPe method.

The results obtained using the ReCiPe method are depicted in Figure 8b. In this case, the highest value for electricity contribution was obtained for S2 (56.6%). For S1, a percentage of 35% was identified and for S3, the lowest contribution was observed (28.86%).

As far the contribution of transport is concerned, the obtained data showed the lowest value for S2 (43.4%), while the highest was generated in the case of S3 (71.14%). For S1, the calculated percentage was 64.95%.

The proximity of recycling facilities to the collection centers, but at the same time that of the collection centers to the inhabited areas, is very important in order to reduce the environmental burden of transportation [20]. The development of strategies and policies that consider building local infrastructure in order to minimize the distance between these key points in the WEEE management system could significantly improve the impact on the environment.

Although the concepts of sustainability and a circular economy are similar in terms of the global model, interdisciplinarity, the integration of non-economic aspects and the reduction of environmental impact, the main difference lies in the fact that the circular economy exclusively involves ensuring a closed cycle of resources and secondary products obtained from the analyzed system, while sustainability entails a more extensive perspective, depending on the objectives, components and sub-processes included in the study [42]. From an environmental point of view, it is estimated that approximately 48% of emissions could be reduced through the implementation of circular economy principles [43]. Reducing the environmental impact can also thus be achieved by moving from a linear economy to a circular economy. To adapt the circular economy concept to WEEE management, actions are needed at different levels and processes within WEEE management systems. On the one hand, from the early stages, more precisely, starting with the WEEE collection process, it is important that it is carried out in the most efficient way to be able to ensure the recovery of the largest possible amount of materials that can be recycled.

The basic principles of a circular economy include the 3Rs (reduction, reuse, recycling) at the global level, and the 4Rs relative to the territory of the European Union. The 4Rs additionally include the recovery process [44]. Among these, the concept of a circular economy especially encourages reuse and remanufacturing compared to recycling, both for economic and environmental reasons. However, the reuse rate of collected WEEE is very low, 2%. In contrast, the recycling percentage of electrical and electronic waste is around 68% [45]. Thus, the technology applied for the manufacture of electrical and electronic devices represents another aspect that requires special attention in order to increase the possibility of the recovery of materials with added value, such as metals, and to decrease the concentration of toxic substances in the composition of EEE [46]. Additionally, innovation in terms of technology for the recovery of materials from the WEEE structure will allow increasing the level of inclusion of the principles of a circular economy within the management systems of this type of waste. The current available recycling methods are physical, chemical, pyrometallurgical and hydrometallurgical [47].

Although there are no environmental savings recorded through the application of LCA methodology for the analyzed scenarios, the recovery of valuable materials from e-waste contributes to the reduction in mining and industrial production activities, which can greatly harm the environment and human health. Energy savings quantified through the recovery of metals such as aluminum, copper and iron are estimated at 95%, 85% and 74%, respectively. In case of plastics, it is approximated at >80% [48]. The plastic fraction of e-waste is quite high, approximately 20–30% of the total WEEE quantities [49]. A study analyzing the WEEE management in Italy according to the five categories of e-waste established by law showed that metal, plastic and glass recycling offered the highest benefits in terms of materials recovery [39,40]. Though the collection targets are not yet fulfilled fully in Romania, the recycling rates increased from 11% in 2007 to 87% in 2014 [28]. It is thus an important aspect of the whole WEEE management system regarding sustainability [50,51]. In the e-waste management scenarios considered in the current study, several important metal and plastic parts were recovered during the recycling stage. These were considered as output data in the LCA analysis. The related data are included in Table 2.

Table 2. Recovered parts from the collected e-waste.

Recovered Part	Recovered Amount per Scenario (% of Total Recovered Parts)		
	S1	S2	S3
Aluminum scrap	2.92	3.22	3.05
Copper scrap	4.90	4.91	4.50
Iron scrap	3.81	4.12	3.89
Plastic	23.63	21.84	26.23
Steel scrap	47.95	52.73	49.86
Waste glass	16.74	13.11	12.40
Wood	0.04	0.04	0.04

Finally, to complete the perspective on our results, it should be pointed out that the performed study has several limitations. The data availability is one aspect to be considered. In Romania, there is, for example, a lack of information concerning the existence and location of WEEE collection centers, the amount of collected waste, as well as the environmental legislation attributed to e-waste management. Another issue is the fact that the available studies used different LCA methods, and more importantly, many did not normalize the obtained results in the used software in order to enable a leaner comparison between different data generated in the published research. The difficulty of including a scenario on WEEE management that encompasses the full end-of-life stage and thus can fulfill the circular economy principles is another aspect to consider. There are few recycling facilities in Romania, and even these do not carry out a full recycling process, only recovering some larger parts. Other elements such as precious metals are not put back in the cycle at this phase. Romania is not the only European country in which this occurs. Norway for example, which is one of the European territories with the best WEEE management systems, partly ensures WEEE treatment in other countries due to the limited number of facilities [16].

Furthermore, though in our study we included a wide range of types of collected WEEE, there are other components such as solar panels, batteries from electric cars and other types of WEEE that have rarely been considered together with household items, from both the personal and private sectors, and could be included in future studies to give a broader view on the overall environmental impact of a municipality. We therefore recommend the extended research of other types of WEEE, the increase in available data from collection centers and recycling facilities, a more unified approach to applying LCA and related software, as well as the inclusion of raising awareness among the population phase in the study of WEEE management across different countries and regions around the world. Since the full recycling or recovery of valuable materials from WEEE can take place in a different territory than the one for collection and treatment, and given the issues related to the developing world, cross-country collaborations are key for more efficient research and the innovation of WEEE management in the context of a circular economy and a more sustainable future. The main aspects that should be tackled to address the global WEEE issue and implement efficient management systems are preventing or minimizing WEEE generation in order to reduce the e-waste streams, innovating recycling technology as well as the manufacturing processes in order to improve resource recovery, raising awareness among the population, optimizing WEEE treatment, reducing energy consumption, and the efficient implementation of all established roles and processes that are part of a WEEE management system.

4. Conclusions

The current study aimed to analyze the sustainability of WEEE management in the Municipality of Iasi, Romania through three different scenarios implemented in the period 2018–2019. The research analysis was carried out by applying a standardized LCA methodology, in GaBi Education software, through the application of two methods, CML2001 and ReCiPe. One innovative aspect of the performed analysis was the inclusion in the system boundaries of raising awareness among the local community. There are a few limitations that were acknowledged in the current study, such as the lack of data from collection centers and the difficulty in comparing the calculated environmental impact with other studies due to the different ways of applying the methodology and processing the generated results. The results showed that this process has a low environmental impact among all the included processes. The highest contribution to the total obtained impact was that of the collection stage in all three scenarios, this showing that the environmental burden could be reduced through the implementation of sustainable transport routes for gathering all the e-waste. In terms of impact categories, the highest value was determined through the CML2001 method for the marine aquatic ecotoxicity potential (MAETP) impact category in S2 and for the abiotic depletion fossil (ADPf) impact category in the cases of S1 and S3. By comparison, the ReCiPe method results showed a lower value for ozone depletion (ODP) and a higher one for fossil depletion (FD) for all three scenarios, which indicates that a reduction in fossil fuel consumption is required.

Author Contributions: Conceptualization, M.G., S.C.G. and I.M.S.; methodology, S.C.G. and C.F.; software, S.C.G. and I.M.S.; validation, I.M.S., M.R., R.M.H. and M.G.; formal analysis, S.C.G., C.F. and M.R.; investigation, S.C.G.; resources, S.C.G.; data curation, S.C.G.; writing—original draft preparation, S.C.G. and C.F.; writing—review and editing, I.M.S., M.R., R.M.H. and M.G.; visualization, R.M.H. and M.G.; supervision, M.G. All authors have read and agreed to the published version of the manuscript.

Funding: This research received no external funding.

Institutional Review Board Statement: Not applicable.

Informed Consent Statement: Not applicable.

Data Availability Statement: Not applicable.

Acknowledgments: The authors would like to acknowledge the support of Sphera with providing the student version of GaBi Education software.

Conflicts of Interest: The authors declare no conflict of interest.

References

1. Isernia, R.; Passaro, R.; Quinto, I.; Thomas, A. The Reverse Supply Chain of the E-Waste Management Processes in a Circular Economy Framework: Evidence from Italy. *Sustainability* **2019**, *11*, 2430. [CrossRef]
2. Ghiga, S.C.; David, M.; Minut, M.; Comanita-Ungureanu, E.-D.; Cozma, P.; Gavrilescu, M. Reducing Health and Ecological Risks by Using WEEE as Secondary Sources for Critical Raw Materials. In Proceedings of the 2020 International Conference on e-Health and Bioengineering (EHB), Iasi, Romania, 29–30 October 2020; pp. 1–4. [CrossRef]
3. Sansotera, M.; Navarrini, W.; Talaeemashhadi, S.; Venturini, F. Italian WEEE management system and treatment of end-of-life cooling and freezing equipments for CFCs removal. *Waste Manag.* **2013**, *33*, 1491–1498. [CrossRef]
4. Julander, A.; Lundgren, L.; Skare, L.; Grandér, M.; Palm, B.; Vahter, M.; Lidén, C. Formal recycling of e-waste leads to increased exposure to toxic metals: An occupational exposure study from Sweden. *Environ. Int.* **2014**, *73*, 243–251. [CrossRef]
5. Malandrino, O.; Sica, D.; Testa, M.; Supino, S. Policies and Measures for Sustainable Management of Solar Panel End-of-Life in Italy. *Sustainability* **2017**, *9*, 481. [CrossRef]
6. Butturi, M.A.; Marinelli, S.; Gamberini, R.; Rimini, B. Ecotoxicity of Plastics from Informal Waste Electric and Electronic Treatment and Recycling. *Toxics* **2020**, *8*, 99. [CrossRef]
7. Khairunnash, A.; Muhammad, I.; Diva Rayyan, R.; Aulia, A.; Aulia Qisthi, M.; Agnia, P.; Intan, Q.; Abdulmadjid, S.N.; Kana, P. Heavy Metal Contamination in Aquatic and Terrestrial Animals Resulted from Anthropogenic Activities in Indonesia: A Review. *Asian J. Water Environ. Pollut.* **2022**, *19*, 1–8.

8. Filote, C.; Hlihor, R.-M.; Simion, I.M.; Rosca, M. Life Cycle Assessment (LCA) Application for Heavy Metals Removal from Wastewaters using Conventional and Microbial Sorbents. In Proceedings of the 2021 International Conference on e-Health and Bioengineering (EHB), Iasi, Romania, 18–19 November 2021; pp. 1–4. [CrossRef]
9. Filote, C.; Roşca, M.; Simion, I.M.; Hlihor, R.M. Continuous Systems Bioremediation of Wastewaters Loaded with Heavy Metals Using Microorganisms. *Processes* **2022**, *10*, 1758. [CrossRef]
10. Wang, L.; Wu, H.; Hu, Y.; Yu, Y.; Huang, K. Environmental Sustainability Assessment of Typical Cathode Materials of Lithium-Ion Battery Based on Three LCA Approaches. *Processes* **2019**, *7*, 83. [CrossRef]
11. Ziemińska-Stolarska, A.; Pietrzak, M.; Zbiciński, I. Application of LCA to Determine Environmental Impact of Concentrated Photovoltaic Solar Panels—State-of-the-Art. *Energies* **2021**, *14*, 3143. [CrossRef]
12. Kuehr, R. E-waste seen from a global perspective. In *Waste Electrical and Electronic Equipment (WEEE) Handbook*; Elsevier: Amsterdam, The Netherlands, 2019; pp. 1–16. [CrossRef]
13. Morris, A.; Metternicht, G. Assessing effectiveness of WEEE management policy in Australia. *J. Environ. Manag.* **2016**, *181*, 218–230. [CrossRef]
14. Chen, Y.; Li, S.; Tan, Q.; Li, J.; Miao, Y. Study on WEEE collection and recycling scheme in typical Asia-Pacific countries. *Math. Probl. Eng.* **2019**, *18*, 6669989.
15. Elia, V.; Gnoni, M.G.; Tornese, F. Assessing the Efficiency of a PSS Solution for Waste Collection: A Simulation Based Approach. *Procedia CIRP* **2016**, *47*, 252–257. [CrossRef]
16. Ylä-Mella, J.; Román, E. Waste electrical and electronic equipment management in Europe. In *Waste Electrical and Electronic Equipment (WEEE) Handbook*; Elsevier: Amsterdam, The Netherlands, 2019; pp. 483–519. [CrossRef]
17. Bruno, G.; Diglio, A.; Passaro, R.; Piccolo, C.; Quinto, I. Measuring spatial access to the recovery networks for WEEE: An in-depth analysis of the Italian case. *Int. J. Prod. Econ.* **2021**, *240*, 108210. [CrossRef]
18. Gamberini, R.; Gebennini, E.; Manzini, R.; Ziveri, A. On the integration of planning and environmental impact assessment for a WEEE transportation network—A case study. *Resour. Conserv. Recycl.* **2010**, *54*, 937–951. [CrossRef]
19. Gamberini, R.; Gebennini, E.; Rimini, B. An innovative container for WEEE collection and transport: Details and effects following the adoption. *Waste Manag.* **2009**, *29*, 2846–2858. [CrossRef]
20. De Feo, G.; Ferrara, C.; Iuliano, C.; Grosso, A. LCA of the Collection, Transportation, Treatment and Disposal of Source Separated Municipal Waste: A Southern Italy Case Study. *Sustainability* **2016**, *8*, 1084. [CrossRef]
21. Roland, H.; Bo, W. *Implementation of Life Cycle Impact Assessment Methods*; Data v2.2; Swiss Centre for Life Cycle Inventories: Zurich, Switzerland, 2010.
22. Backes, J.G.; Traverso, M. Application of Life Cycle Sustainability Assessment in the Construction Sector: A Systematic Literature Review. *Processes* **2021**, *9*, 1248. [CrossRef]
23. Yu, Y.; Chen, B.; Huang, K.; Wang, X.; Wang, D. Environmental Impact Assessment and End-of-Life Treatment Policy Analysis for Li-Ion Batteries and Ni-MH Batteries. *Int. J. Environ. Res. Public. Health* **2014**, *11*, 3185–3198. [CrossRef] [PubMed]
24. Bigum, M.; Brogaard, L.; Christensen, T.H. Metal recovery from high-grade WEEE: A Life Cycle Assessment. *J. Hazard. Mater.* **2012**, *207–208*, 8–14. [CrossRef]
25. Reale, F.; Buttol, P.; Cortesi, S.; Mengarelli, M.; Masoni, P.; Scalbi, S.; Zamagni, A. Dealing with LCA modeling for the end of life of mechatronic products. *Environ. Eng. Manag. J.* **2015**, *14*, 1691–1704. [CrossRef]
26. Fiore, S.; Ibanescu, D.; Teodosiu, C.; Ronco, A. Improving waste electric and electronic equipment management at full-scale by using material flow analysis and Life Cycle Assessment. *Sci. Total Environ.* **2019**, *659*, 928–939. [CrossRef]
27. Mann, A.; Saxena, P.; Almanei, M.; Okorie, O.; Salonitis, K. Environmental Impact Assessment of Different Strategies for the Remanufacturing of User Electronics. *Energies* **2022**, *15*, 2376. [CrossRef]
28. Ibanescu, D.; Cailean (Gavrilescu), D.; Teodosiu, C.; Fiore, S. Assessment of the waste electrical and electronic equipment management systems profile and sustainability in developed and developing European Union countries. *Waste Manag.* **2018**, *73*, 39–53. [CrossRef]
29. Friðriksson, G.B.; Johnsen, T.; Bjarnadóttir, H.J.; Sletnes, H. *Guidelines for the Use of LCA in the Waste Management Sector*; Technical Report; Linuhonnun Consulting: Reykjavík, Iceland, 2002.
30. Nordelöf, A.; Poulikidou, S.; Chordia, M.; de Oliveira, F.B.; Tivander, J.; Arvidsson, R. Methodological Approaches to End-Of-Life Modelling in Life Cycle Assessments of Lithium-Ion Batteries. *Batteries* **2019**, *5*, 51. [CrossRef]
31. Cao, C. Sustainability and life assessment of high strength natural fibre composites in construction. In *Advanced High Strength Natural Fibre Composites in Construction*; Elsevier: Amsterdam, The Netherlands, 2017; pp. 529–544. [CrossRef]
32. de Oliveira, C.R.; Bernardes, A.M.; Gerbase, A.E. Collection and recycling of electronic scrap: A worldwide overview and comparison with the Brazilian situation. *Waste Manag.* **2012**, *32*, 1592–1610. [CrossRef]
33. Pacesila, M.; Ciocoiu, C.N.; Colesca, S.E.; Burcea, S.G. Current Trends in WEEE Management in Romania. *Theor. Empir. Res. Urban Manag.* **2016**, *11*, 46–59.
34. Government of Romania, Ministry of Regional Development and Public Administration. OUG No. 5 from 2 April 2015 Regarding Electrical and Electronic Equipment Waste. Available online: https://legislatie.just.ro/Public/DetaliiDocument/167211 (accessed on 1 March 2023). (In Romanian).
35. Herrmann, I.T.; Moltesen, A. Does it matter which Life Cycle Assessment (LCA) tool you choose?—A comparative assessment of SimaPro and GaBi. *J. Clean. Prod.* **2015**, *86*, 163–169. [CrossRef]

36. Pieragostini, C.; Mussati, M.C.; Aguirre, P. On process optimization considering LCA methodology. *J. Environ. Manag.* **2012**, *96*, 43–54. [CrossRef] [PubMed]
37. Withanage, S.V.; Habib, K. Life Cycle Assessment and Material Flow Analysis: Two Under-Utilized Tools for Informing E-Waste Management. *Sustainability* **2021**, *13*, 7939. [CrossRef]
38. Rocha, T.B.; Penteado, C.S.G. Life Cycle Assessment of a small WEEE reverse logistics system: Case study in the Campinas Area, Brazil. *J. Clean. Prod.* **2021**, *314*, 128092. [CrossRef]
39. Siddiqi, M.M.; Naseer, M.N.; Wahab, Y.A.; Hamizi, N.A.; Badruddin, I.A.; Hasan, M.A.; Chowdhury, Z.Z.; Akbarzadeh, O.; Johan, M.R.; Kamangar, S. Exploring E-Waste Resources Recovery in Household Solid Waste Recycling. *Processes* **2020**, *8*, 1047. [CrossRef]
40. Ismail, H.; Hanafiah, M.M. Evaluation of e-waste management systems in Malaysia using life cycle assessment and material flow analysis. *J. Clean. Prod.* **2021**, *308*, 127358. [CrossRef]
41. Hischier, R.; Wäger, P.; Gauglhofer, J. Does WEEE recycling make sense from an environmental perspective? *Environ. Impact Assess. Rev.* **2005**, *25*, 525–539. [CrossRef]
42. Geissdoerfer, M.; Savaget, P.; Bocken, N.M.P.; Hultink, E.J. The Circular Economy—A new sustainability paradigm? *J. Clean. Prod.* **2017**, *143*, 757–768. [CrossRef]
43. Kirchherr, J.; Piscicelli, L.; Bour, R.; Kostense-Smit, E.; Muller, J.; Huibrechtse-Truijens, A.; Hekkert, M. Barriers to the Circular Economy: Evidence from the European Union (EU). *Ecol. Econ.* **2018**, *150*, 264–272. [CrossRef]
44. Kirchherr, J.; Reike, D.; Hekkert, M. Conceptualizing the circular economy: An analysis of 114 definitions. *Resour. Conserv. Recycl.* **2017**, *127*, 221–232. [CrossRef]
45. Parajuly, K.; Wenzel, H. Product Family Approach in E-Waste Management: A Conceptual Framework for Circular Economy. *Sustainability* **2017**, *9*, 768. [CrossRef]
46. Cesaro, A.; Marra, A.; Kuchta, K.; Belgiorno, V.; Van Hullebusch, E.D. WEEE management in a circular economy perspective: An overview. *Glob. NEST J.* **2018**, *20*, 743–750. [CrossRef]
47. de Oliveira Neto, J.F.; Silva, M.M.; Florencio, L.; Miranda, R.; Santos, S.M. Quantification and characterization of waste electrical and electronic equipment disposal: a case study from Brazil. *Environ. Eng. Manag. J.* **2021**, *20*, 1555–1567. [CrossRef]
48. Cherrington, R.; Makenji, K. Mechanical methods of recycling plastics from WEEE. In *Waste Electrical and Electronic Equipment (WEEE) Handbook*; Elsevier: Amsterdam, The Netherlands, 2019; pp. 283–310. [CrossRef]
49. Ardolino, F.; Cardamone, G.F.; Arena, U. How to enhance the environmental sustainability of WEEE plastics management: An LCA study. *Waste Manag.* **2021**, *135*, 347–359. [CrossRef]
50. Biganzoli, L.; Falbo, A.; Forte, F.; Grosso, M.; Rigamonti, L. Mass balance and Life Cycle Assessment of the waste electrical and electronic equipment management system implemented in Lombardia Region (Italy). *Sci. Total Environ.* **2015**, *524–525*, 361–375. [CrossRef] [PubMed]
51. Khan, M.A.R.; Motalib, M.A.; Saadat, A.H.M. Mobile phone and spent laptop waste: Generation, dissemination and flow pattern analysis. *Environ. Eng. Manag. J.* **2022**, *21*, 1339–1349. [CrossRef]

Disclaimer/Publisher's Note: The statements, opinions and data contained in all publications are solely those of the individual author(s) and contributor(s) and not of MDPI and/or the editor(s). MDPI and/or the editor(s) disclaim responsibility for any injury to people or property resulting from any ideas, methods, instructions or products referred to in the content.

Article

Enhanced Treatment of Basic Red 46 by Ozonation in a Rotating Packed Bed with Liquid Detention

Peng Xu [1], Tianyang Wu [1], Yang Xiang [1], Jimmy Yun [2,3] and Lei Shao [1,*]

[1] Research Center of the Ministry of Education for High Gravity Engineering and Technology, Beijing University of Chemical Technology, Beijing 100029, China; 2021200065@buct.edu.cn (P.X.); 2020200061@mail.buct.edu.cn (T.W.); xiangy@mail.buct.edu.cn (Y.X.)
[2] School of Chemical Engineering, The University of New South Wales, Sydney, NSW 2052, Australia; jimmy.yun@unsw.edu.au
[3] College of Chemical and Pharmaceutical Engineering, Hebei University of Science and Technology, Shijiazhuang 050018, China
* Correspondence: shaol@mail.buct.edu.cn; Tel.: +86-10-6442-1706

Abstract: This study investigated the use of ozone in a rotating packed bed (RPB) with liquid detention for the treatment of Basic Red 46 (BR-46). Liquid detention means that liquid accumulates at the lower section to a certain level in the RPB, which leads to longer liquid residence time and greater liquid holdup in the packing and cavity in the RPB. The experimental results showed that the presence of liquid detention in the RPB significantly enhanced the BR-46 treatment effect and ozone absorption rate. With 200 mL of liquid detention in the RPB, the decolorization rate, COD degradation rate, and ozone absorption rate were 34.7%, 62.8%, and 80.0% higher than those without liquid detention. The effects of the rotational speed of the RPB, ozone concentration, initial BR-46 concentration, liquid and gas flow rates on BR-46 degradation were also investigated, and it was found that the high-gravity environment is beneficial to the degradation of BR-46. These results suggest that with the utilization of the liquid detention phenomena in the high-gravity devices, the applications of the high-gravity technology can be extended to the processes where a long liquid residence time is required.

Keywords: liquid detention; Basic Red 46; ozonation; rotating packed bed; degradation

Citation: Xu, P.; Wu, T.; Xiang, Y.; Yun, J.; Shao, L. Enhanced Treatment of Basic Red 46 by Ozonation in a Rotating Packed Bed with Liquid Detention. *Processes* **2023**, *11*, 1345. https://doi.org/10.3390/pr11051345

Academic Editor: Monika Wawrzkiewicz

Received: 30 March 2023
Revised: 20 April 2023
Accepted: 25 April 2023
Published: 26 April 2023

Copyright: © 2023 by the authors. Licensee MDPI, Basel, Switzerland. This article is an open access article distributed under the terms and conditions of the Creative Commons Attribution (CC BY) license (https://creativecommons.org/licenses/by/4.0/).

1. Introduction

Azo dyes are the largest category of commercial synthetic dyes, accounting for 70% of the total number of textile dyes. They are extensively used in the food, pharmaceutical, paper, cosmetic, textile, and leather industries due to their wide range of colors and structures [1]. Azo dyes are organic compounds that have one or more azo bonds (–N = N–) in a molecule [2]. However, they have been reported to have adverse effects on ecosystems and human health and are present in aqueous environments, sediments, soils, and drinking water supplies [3]. Basic Red 46 (BR-46) is a cationic azo dye that is widely used in coloring nylon, acrylic, and wool fabrics. It is known to be difficult to degrade BR-46 through chemical oxidation, photocatalysis, and biodegradation [4]. Compared to anionic dyes, cationic dyes are more toxic and can enter cells easily by reacting with negatively charged surfaces of cell membranes and gathering in the cytoplasm [5]. Therefore, the removal of these dyes prior to discharge in wastewater has become an important issue.

Advanced oxidation processes (AOPs) based on highly reactive radicals have been shown to be robust technologies for treating organic contaminants in wastewater, providing nearly total degradation [6]. Ozone is a powerful oxidizer with a high oxidation potential of 2.07 V, which directly participates in the reaction with organic matters under acidic conditions (direct oxidation), while alkaline conditions are conducive to forming •OH from ozone, and •OH-based oxidation is considered to be an advanced oxidation process (indirect oxidation) [7,8]. Under acidic conditions, ozone selectively attacks organic matters, while •OH reacts with organic matters without selectivity under alkaline conditions [9]. The ozonation process is affected by pH, ozone flow rate and initial organic matter concentration [10].

Over the past few decades, AOPs have been demonstrated to enhance the degradation of various organic compounds [11]. Well-known advanced oxidation technologies mainly include O_3/H_2O_2, O_3/UV, O_3/US, Fenton, and AOPs based on persulfate [12–16]. It was found that the degradation of dyes by ozone-based AOPs exhibited the benefits of high reactivity, environmental friendliness and easy operation with ubiquitous air sources [17–19]. However, the ozone oxidation process is significantly affected by the ozone–liquid mass transfer rate due to the low solubility of ozone in water. Thus, a reactor with high gas–liquid mass transfer efficiency is needed to improve the ozone oxidation process [20].

The concept of mass transfer intensification using the rotating packed bed (RPB) was first introduced by Ramshaw [21]. In the RPB, high centrifugal acceleration derived from a rotating rotor disperses the liquid into thinner films and smaller droplets, which enhances gas–liquid mass transfer and intrinsically improves fast reaction processes [22]. The RPB is considered as a reactor that can increase the amount of ozone dissolved per unit time and make wastewater treatment more effective [23].

Recently, we found that the liquid detention phenomena in the RPB can significantly enhance the gas–liquid mass transfer. The phenomena are illustrated in Figure 1. When liquid is detained in the RPB, it will accumulate at the bottom and immerse the lower part of the rotor. In addition, some of the detained liquid will be carried by the rotating rotor to the upper part of the rotor and cavity. Thus, both the liquid residence time and liquid holdup in the RPB increase when the liquid is detained. A longer liquid residence time and greater liquid holdup in the RPB can facilitate the process of ozone mass transfer, suggesting that the phenomena can be used to enhance ozone AOPs for the treatment of organic wastewater.

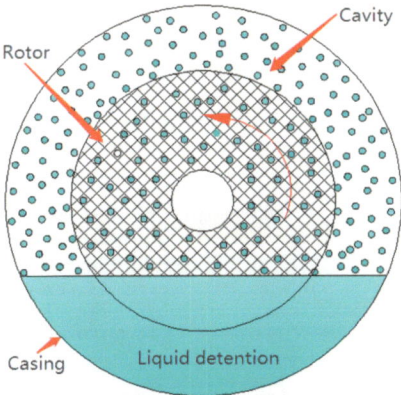

Figure 1. Schematic diagram of liquid detention phenomena in RPB.

Herein, we investigated the effect of liquid detention on ozonation of BR-46 in an RPB for the first time. This work indicates that the RPB with liquid detention enhanced the ozonation efficiency of BR-46 and the absorption rate of ozone, thus providing a novel means for the intensification of organic wastewater treatment by AOPs in high-gravity devices.

2. Materials and Methods

2.1. Materials and Procedure

The experiment used BR-46 (strength: 250%) provided by Shanghai Huayuan Century Trading Co., Shanghai, China. The simulated BR-46 wastewater was prepared by dissolving BR-46 in deionized water. The pH value of the wastewater was measured using a PHSJ-3F pH Meter (Shanghai INESA Scientific Instrument Co., Ltd., Shanghai, China). Table 1 provides the specifications of the RPB.

Table 1. Specifications of the RPB.

Item	Value
Inner diameter of packing	40 mm
Outer diameter of packing	120 mm
Thickness of packing	15 mm
Material of packing	Stainless steel wire mesh
Specific surface area of packing	522 m^2/m^3
Porosity of packing	97%
Inner diameter of casing	180 mm

The experimental setup is presented in Figure 2. Before the experiment, the liquid outlet valve was adjusted to ensure that the inlet and outlet liquid flow rates were equal under the preset experimental conditions. Then, ozone generated from oxygen by a 3S-A10 Ozone Generator (Tonglin High-Tech Technology Co., Ltd., Beijing, China) was introduced into the RPB. Once the ozone concentration at the gas inlet reached the required level, the RPB was turned on before the BR-46 wastewater was pumped into the center of the rotor by a peristaltic pump.

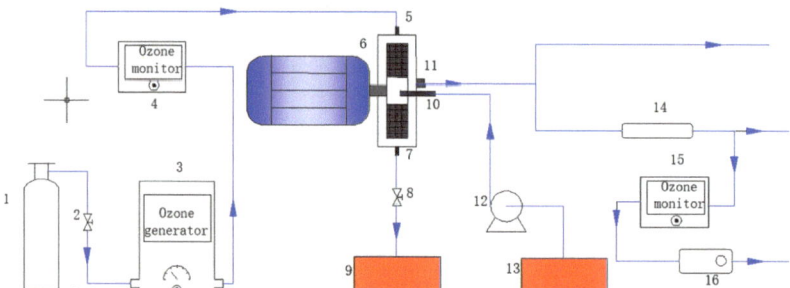

Figure 2. Experimental Setup. (1) Oxygen cylinder; (2) oxygen flowmeter; (3) ozone generator; (4) ozone monitor; (5) gas inlet; (6) RPB; (7) liquid outlet; (8) liquid outlet valve; (9) treated wastewater tank; (10) liquid inlet; (11) gas outlet; (12) pump; (13) original wastewater tank; (14) drying tube; (15) ozone monitor; (16) pump.

When the required amount of liquid was detained in the RPB, the plug of the liquid outlet line was immediately removed to keep the detained liquid in the RPB at a certain level during the experiment. The gas and liquid flows were in counter-current contact in the packing of the RPB, resulting in the absorption of ozone into the liquid stream and degradation of BR-46 by ozone. Finally, the liquid and gas flow exited the RPB through the liquid and gas outlets, respectively. Sampling was conducted from the liquid outlet line when the outlet ozone concentration was stable, and the BR-46 concentration and COD were measured immediately.

2.2. Analytical Methods

The concentration of BR-46 in the wastewater was determined using a DR6000 UV–Vis Spectrophotometer (Hach Corp., Loveland, CO, USA) at a wavelength of 532 nm. The COD in the wastewater was determined using a 5B-6C Multi-parameter Water Quality Analyzer (Lianhua Technology, Beijing, China). The inlet and outlet ozone concentrations were monitored by two detectors (UV300B, Guangzhou Limei Ozone Co., Ltd., Guangzhou, China, and UVOZ-1200, Shandong Zhipu Measurement and Control Technology Co., Ltd., Zibo, China), respectively. The decolorization rate, COD degradation rate, and ozone absorption rate were calculated by the following Equations (1)–(3), respectively:

$$D_B = \frac{C_0 - C_1}{C_0} \times 100\% \tag{1}$$

where D_B represents the decolorization rate of BR-46 wastewater, while C_0 and C_1 represent the initial and final BR-46 concentrations before and after treatment, respectively, (mg/L).

$$R_{COD} = \frac{COD_0 - COD_1}{COD_0} \times 100\% \tag{2}$$

where R_{COD} represents the COD degradation rate, while COD_0 and COD_1 represent the initial and final COD of the BR-46 wastewater before and after treatment, respectively, (mg/L).

$$A_B = \frac{\omega_0 - \omega_1}{\omega_0} \times 100\% \tag{3}$$

where A_B represents the ozone absorption rate, while ω_0 and ω_1 represent the ozone concentration at the inlet and outlet of RPB, respectively, (mg/L).

3. Results and Discussion

3.1. Effect of Liquid Detention

In the degradation of BR-46 by ozonation, ozone and •OH first break the –N = N– bond of BR-46 to produce various intermediates, which are further attacked by ozone and •OH to eventually produce N_2, NO_3^-, CO_2, H_2O, etc. [24,25].

Figure 3 shows the effect of liquid detention volume (V) on the ozonation of BR-46 in the liquid detention range of 0–300 mL. The results indicate that the presence of liquid detention in the RPB enhances the treatment efficiency of BR-46 and increases the absorption rate of ozone. In the absence of liquid detention in the RPB, the decolorization rate, COD degradation rate, and ozone absorption rate were 61.3%, 18.3%, and 40.1%, respectively. However, with 200 mL of liquid detention, the decolorization rate, COD degradation rate, and ozone absorption rate increased to 82.6%, 29.8%, and 72.2%, respectively, which were 34.7%, 62.8%, and 80.0% higher than those without liquid detention, suggesting that liquid detention in the RPB can significantly enhance the absorption of ozone and the degradation of BR-46.

As shown in Figure 1, liquid detention means that liquid does not flow out of the RPB immediately, but accumulates and stays at the lower section of the RPB for a certain time after it is ejected from the rotor. Thus, the liquid residence time in the RPB greatly extends. Furthermore, some of the detained liquid will be carried by the rotating rotor to the upper part of the rotor, causing an increase in liquid holdup in the packing of the rotor and the cavity of the RPB. The increase in the liquid residence time and holdup is conducive to the absorption of ozone and thus the degradation of BR-46.

However, a further increase in the liquid detention to more than 200 mL resulted in a lower treatment effect, which may be ascribed to the reduced gas flow channel and accelerated gas flow rate as a result of the excessive liquid detention, thereby leading to the decreased ozone absorption rate and reduced treatment effect of BR-46.

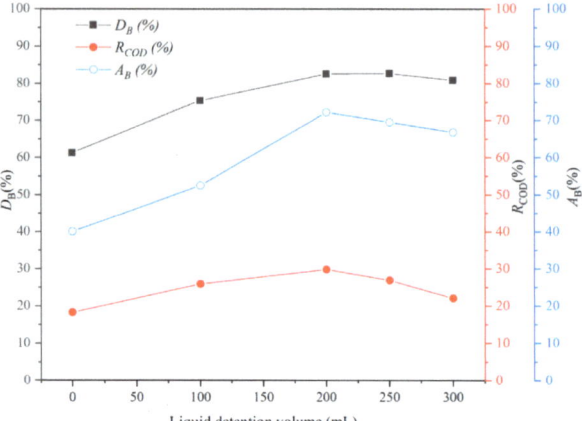

Figure 3. Effect of liquid detention volume on BR-46 degradation. Ozone concentration (C) = 20 mg/L; gas flow rate (G) = 75 L/h; liquid flow rate (L) = 15 L/h; rotational speed (R) = 800 rpm; initial BR-46 concentration (C_{BR-46}) = 300 mg/L.

3.2. Effect of Rotational Speed of RPB

Figure 4 illustrates the impact of the rotational speed of the RPB on the degradation efficiency of BR-46 in the rotational speed range of 200–1000 rpm. With an increase in rotational speed from 200 rpm to 600 rpm, the decolorization rate, COD degradation rate, and ozone absorption rate increased from 78.0%, 28.8%, and 40.1% to 95.3%, 33.7%, and 63.2%, respectively. When the rotational speed exceeded 600 rpm, the decolorization rate, COD degradation rate, and ozone absorption rate remained steady at approximately 95%, 33%, and 63%, respectively.

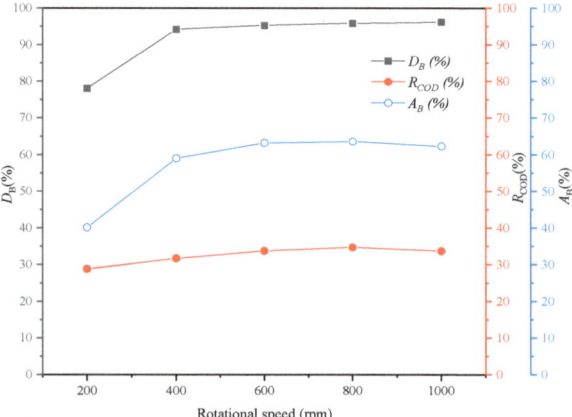

Figure 4. Effect of rotational speed on BR-46 degradation. V = 200 mL; G = 75 L/h; L = 15 L/h; C = 30 mg/L; C_{BR-46} = 300 mg/L.

The reason behind this is that a higher rotational speed increases the turbulence of the liquid in the RPB, leading to its dispersion into thinner films and smaller droplets, thus increasing the area of gas–liquid mass transfer. As a result, more ozone dissolves in the wastewater, leading to the higher degradation efficiency of BR-46.

However, the liquid residence time in the packing decreases with an increasing rotational speed, which is unfavorable for the degradation of BR-46. When the rotational speed increases over 600 rpm, the unfavorable effect of reduced liquid residence time offsets the favorable effect of increased dispersion of the BR-46 solution, resulting in almost stable ozone absorption rate, decolorization rate, and COD degradation rate. Liu et al. [26] also observed similar phenomena in the inactivation of E. coli by ozone in an RPB.

3.3. Effect of Gaseous Ozone Concentration

Figure 5 shows the effect of ozone concentration in a gas stream on the ozonation of BR-46 in the gaseous ozone concentration range of 10–50 mg/L. The results indicate that as the ozone concentration increased from 10 mg/L to 50 mg/L, the decolorization rate and COD degradation rate increased, while the ozone absorption rate decreased. At an ozone concentration of 30 mg/L, the decolorization rate, COD degradation rate, and ozone absorption rate were 97.0%, 29.4%, and 57.7%, respectively. The amount of ozone dissolved in wastewater increases with the increase in gaseous ozone concentration, leading to an increase in the amount of ozone reacting with the wastewater and promoting the degradation of BR-46. However, with the increase in ozone concentration, more ozone entering the RPB is discharged without participating in a reaction, resulting in a decrease in the ozone absorption percentage. Similar phenomena have also been observed by other researchers [27].

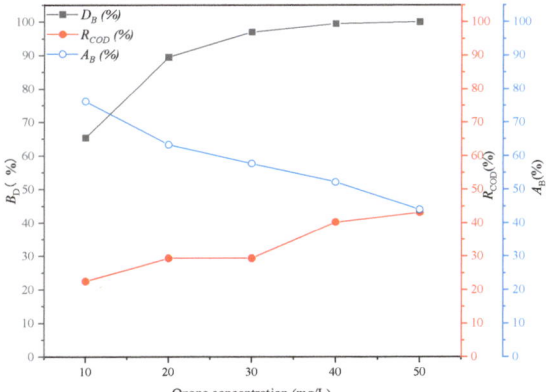

Figure 5. Effect of ozone concentration on BR-46 degradation. $V = 200$ mL; $G = 75$ L/h; $L = 15$ L/h; $R = 800$ rpm; $C_{BR\text{-}46} = 300$ mg/L.

3.4. Effect of Initial BR-46 Concentration

Figure 6 shows the effect of the initial BR-46 concentration on the degradation efficiency of BR-46 in the BR-46 concentration and COD range of 92.8–512.0 mg/L and 57.2–255.8 mg/L, respectively. As the initial concentration increased from 100 mg/L to 500 mg/L, the decolorization rate and COD degradation rate decreased from 100% and 50.0% to 85.4% and 27.6%, respectively, while the ozone absorption rate increased from 31.8% to 63.7%. This is because the increase in BR-46 concentration increases the mass transfer driving force and promotes ozone absorption. However, with the constant ozone concentration, the increase in BR-46 concentration results in the insufficiency of oxidants, leading to the reduction in the degradation efficiency of BR-46. It was found that the degradation of Bisphenol A by ozone in an RPB also followed the same rules [28].

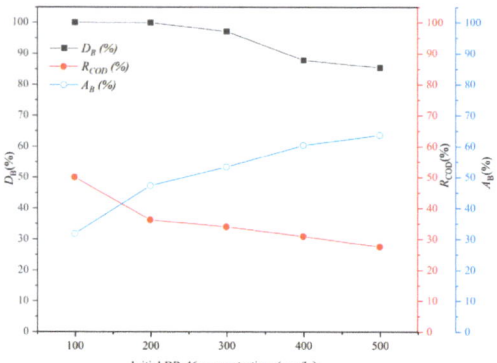

Figure 6. Effect of initial BR-46 concentration on BR-46 degradation. V = 200 mL; G = 75 L/h; L = 15 L/h; R = 800 rpm; C = 30 mg/L.

3.5. Effect of Liquid Flow Rate

Figure 7 shows the effect of the liquid flow rate on the degradation efficiency of BR-46 in the liquid flow rate range of 5–25 L/h. As the liquid flow rate increased from 5.0 to 25 L/h, the decolorization rate and COD degradation rate decreased from 100% and 44.9% to 80.9% and 28.4%, respectively, while the ozone absorption rate increased from 41.0% to 71.2%. The decrease in the residence time of liquid in the RPB due to the increase in liquid flow rate leads to the discharge of the BR-46 solution with underreaction with ozone, resulting in a decrease in the decolorization rate and COD degradation rate. However, the increase in the gas–liquid interfacial area due to the elevation of the liquid flow rate promotes ozone absorption, leading to an increase in the ozone absorption rate. Similar observations have also been reported for the ozonation of amaranth in a rotating zigzag bed [20].

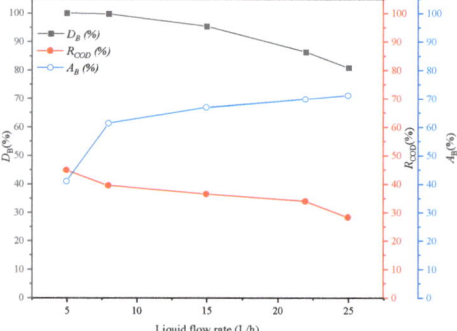

Figure 7. Effect of liquid flow rate on BR-46 degradation. V = 200 mL; G = 75 L/h; R = 800 rpm; C = 30 mg/L; C_{BR-46} = 300 mg/L.

3.6. Effect of Gas Flow Rate

Figure 8 demonstrates the effect of the gas flow rate on the degradation efficiency of BR-46 in the gas flow rate range of 30–90 L/h. With an increase in the gas flow rate from 30 L/h to 90 L/h, the decolorization rate and COD degradation rate increased from 65.4% and 24.0% to 97.0% and 37.0%, respectively, while the ozone absorption rate decreased from 94.0% to 55.8%.

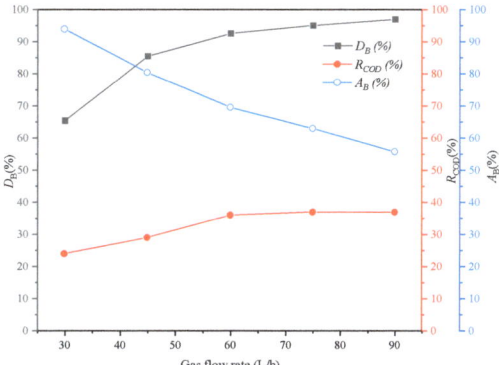

Figure 8. Effect of gas flow rate on BR-46 degradation. V = 200 mL; R = 600 rpm; L = 15 L/h; C = 30 mg/L; C_{BR-46} = 300 mg/L.

The increase in the gas flow rate leads to an increase in the turbulence of the gas and liquid phases, enabling more ozone to dissolve in the wastewater, thereby increasing the decolorization rate and COD degradation rate. However, a higher gas flow rate leads to a higher flow speed of the ozone gas in the RPB, resulting in shorter gas–liquid contact time and thus a decreased ozone absorption rate. The phenomena agree with the observations of Wang et al. on Bisphenol A ozonation in an RPB [28].

4. Conclusions

This study investigated the ozonation of BR-46 in the RPB with liquid detention under various process conditions. The experimental results showed that the presence of liquid detention in the RPB enhanced the ozone absorption rate and the ozonation of BR-46. With 200 mL of liquid detention, the decolorization rate, COD degradation rate, and ozone absorption rate were 34.7%, 62.8%, and 80.0% higher than those without liquid detention, respectively, suggesting that liquid detention in the RPB can significantly promote ozone absorption and BR-46 degradation. It is deduced that the liquid detention leads to the increase in liquid residence time and holdup in the RPB, which is conducive to the absorption of ozone and thus the degradation of organic matters. It was also found that the decolorization rate, COD degradation rate, and ozone absorption rate increased from 78.0%, 28.8%, and 40.1% to 95.3%, 33.7%, and 63.2%, respectively, with an increase in the rotational speed of the RPB from 200 rpm to 600 rpm. These results indicated that the utilization of the liquid detention phenomena in the high-gravity technology can overcome the shortcomings of insufficient liquid residence time in this technology and extend its applications to kinetics-limited processes.

Author Contributions: Conceptualization, L.S.; methodology, P.X.; validation, T.W.; formal analysis, Y.X.; investigation, P.X.; resources, J.Y.; data curation, T.W.; writing—original draft preparation, P.X.; writing—review and editing, J.Y.; supervision, L.S.; project administration, L.S.; funding acquisition, L.S. All authors have read and agreed to the published version of the manuscript.

Funding: This research was funded by the National Natural Science Foundation of China, grant number 22178021.

Data Availability Statement: Not applicable.

Acknowledgments: The authors gratefully acknowledge the financial support from the National Natural Science Foundation of China (No. 22178021).

Conflicts of Interest: The authors declare no conflict of interest.

References

1. Sen, S.K.; Raut, S.; Bandyopadhyay, P.; Raut, S. Fungal decolouration and degradation of azo dyes: A review. *Fungal Biol. Rev.* **2016**, *30*, 112–133. [CrossRef]
2. Kong, S.; Zhang, W.; Gao, S.; Chen, D. Immobilized CeO_2 for adsorption of azo dye. *J. Exp. Nanosci.* **2019**, *14*, 107–115. [CrossRef]
3. Shi, Y.; Yang, Z.; Xing, L.; Zhang, X.; Li, X.; Zhang, D. Recent advances in the biodegradation of azo dyes. *World J. Microb. Biot.* **2021**, *37*, 1–18. [CrossRef] [PubMed]
4. Torres-Luna, J.A.; Giraldo-Gómez, G.I.; Sanabria-González, N.R.; Carriazo, J.G. Catalytic degradation of real-textile azo-dyes in aqueous solutions by using Cu–Co/halloysite. *Bull. Mater. Sci.* **2019**, *42*, 137. [CrossRef]
5. Kapoor, R.T.; Sivamani, S. Adsorptive Potential of Orange Peel Biochar for Removal of Basic Red Dye and Phytotoxicity Analysis. *Chem. Eng. Technol.* **2023**, *46*, 756–765. [CrossRef]
6. Guo, Y.; Zeng, Z.; Zhu, Y.; Huang, Y.; Cui, Y.; Yang, J. Catalytic oxidation of aqueous organic contaminants by persulfate activated with sulfur-doped hierarchically porous carbon derived from thiophene. *Appl. Catal. B Environ.* **2018**, *220*, 635–644. [CrossRef]
7. Malik, S.N.; Ghosh, P.C.; Vaidya, A.N.; Mudliar, S.N. Hybrid ozonation process for industrial wastewater treatment: Principles and applications: A review. *J. Water Process Eng.* **2020**, *35*, 101193. [CrossRef]
8. Toro, C.A.T.; Dagostin, J.L.A.; Vasques, É.C.; Spier, M.R.; Igarashi-Mafra, L.; Dantas, T.L.P. Effectiveness of ozonation and catalytic ozonation (iron oxide) in the degradation of sunset yellow dye. *Can. J. Chem. Eng.* **2020**, *98*, 2530–2544. [CrossRef]
9. Otieno, B.; Apollo, S.; Kabuba, J.; Naidoo, B.; Simate, G.; Ochieng, A. Ozonolysis pre-treatment of waste activated sludge for solubilization and biodegradability enhancement. *J. Environ. Chem. Eng.* **2019**, *7*, 102945. [CrossRef]
10. Otieno, B.; Apollo, S.; Kabuba, J.; Naidoo, B.; Ochieng, A. Ozonolysis post-treatment of anaerobically digested distillery wastewater effluent. *Ozone Sci. Eng.* **2019**, *41*, 551–561. [CrossRef]
11. Dang, T.T.; Do, V.M.; Trinh, V.T. Nano-catalysts in ozone-based advanced oxidation processes for wastewater treatment. *Curr. Pollut. Rep.* **2020**, *6*, 217–229. [CrossRef]
12. Ouali, S.; Biard, P.F.; Loulergue, P.; You, R.; Nasrallah, N.; Maachi, R.; Szymczyk, A. Water treatment intensification using a monophasic hybrid process coupling nanofiltration and ozone/hydrogen peroxide advanced oxidation. *Chem. Eng. J.* **2022**, *137*, 135263. [CrossRef]
13. Li, R.; Siriwardena, D.; Speed, D.; Fernando, S.; Holsen, T.M.; Thagard, S.M. Treatment of azole-containing industrial wastewater by the fenton process. *Ind. Eng. Chem. Res.* **2021**, *60*, 9716–9728. [CrossRef]
14. Tichonovas, M.; Krugly, E.; Jankunaite, D.; Racys, V.; Martuzevicius, D. Ozone-UV-catalysis based advanced oxidation process for wastewater treatment. *Environ. Sci. Pollut. Res.* **2017**, *24*, 17584–17597. [CrossRef] [PubMed]
15. Zhang, H.; Zhang, Y.; Qiao, T.; Hu, S.; Liu, J.; Zhu, R.; Yang, K.; Li, S.; Zhang, L. Study on ultrasonic enhanced ozone oxidation of cyanide-containing wastewater. *Sep. Purif. Technol.* **2022**, *303*, 122258. [CrossRef]
16. Qi, F.; Zeng, Z.; Wen, Q.; Huang, Z. Enhanced organics degradation by three-dimensional (3D) electrochemical activation of persulfate using sulfur-doped carbon particle electrode: The role of thiophene sulfur functional group and specific capacitance. *J. Hazard. Mater.* **2021**, *416*, 125810. [CrossRef]
17. Wang, J.; Yuan, R.; Feng, Z.; Ma, F.; Zhou, B.; Chen, H. The advanced treatment of textile printing and dyeing wastewater by hydrodynamic cavitation and ozone: Degradation, mechanism, and transformation of dissolved organic matter. *Environ. Res.* **2022**, *215*, 114300. [CrossRef]
18. Muniyasamy, A.; Sivaporul, G.; Gopinath, A.; Lakshmanan, R.; Altaee, A.; Achary, A.; Chellam, P.V. Process development for the degradation of textile azo dyes (mono-, di-, poly-) by advanced oxidation process-Ozonation: Experimental & partial derivative modelling approach. *J. Environ. Manag.* **2020**, *265*, 110397. [CrossRef]
19. Parsa, J.B.; Negahdar, S.H. Treatment of wastewater containing Acid Blue 92 dye by advanced ozone-based oxidation methods. *Sep. Purif. Technol.* **2012**, *98*, 315–320. [CrossRef]
20. Wu, T.; Zhang, H.; Liu, Z.; Liu, T.; Jiang, P.; Arowo, M.; Shao, L. Amaranth wastewater treatment by intensified ozonation in a rotating zigzag bed. *J. Water Process Eng.* **2022**, *49*, 102984. [CrossRef]
21. Gao, W.; Song, Y.; Jiao, W.; Liu, Y. A catalyst-free and highly efficient approach to ozonation of benzyl alcohol to benzoic acid in a rotating packed bed. *J. Taiwan Inst. Chem. Eng.* **2019**, *103*, 1–6. [CrossRef]
22. Han, R.; Fang, X.; Song, Y.; Wang, L.; Lu, Y.; Ma, H.; Xiao, H.; Shao, L. Study on the oxidation of ammonium sulfite by ozone in a rotating packed bed. *Chem. Eng. Process.* **2022**, *173*, 108820. [CrossRef]
23. Yang, P.; Luo, S.; Liu, H.; Jiao, W.; Liu, Y. Aqueous ozone decomposition kinetics in a rotating packed bed. *J. Taiwan Inst. Chem. Eng.* **2019**, *96*, 11–17. [CrossRef]

24. Karimi-Shamsabadi, M.; Behpour, M. Comparing photocatalytic activity consisting of Sb_2S_3 and Ag_2S on the TiO_2–SiO_2/TiO_2 nanotube arrays-support for improved visible-light-induced photocatalytic degradation of a binary mixture of basic blue 41 and basic red 46 dyes. *Int. J. Hydrogen Energy* **2021**, *46*, 26989–27013. [CrossRef]
25. Berkani, M.; Kadmi, Y.; Bouchareb, M.K.; Bouhelassa, M.; Bouzaza, A. Combination of a Box-Behnken design technique with response surface methodology for optimization of the photocatalytic mineralization of CI Basic Red 46 dye from aqueous solution. *Arab. J. Chem.* **2020**, *13*, 8338–8346. [CrossRef]
26. Liu, T.; Wang, D.; Liu, H.; Zhao, W.; Wang, W.; Shao, L. Rotating packed bed as a novel disinfection contactor for the inactivation of E. coli by ozone. *Chemosphere* **2019**, *214*, 695–701. [CrossRef] [PubMed]
27. Qiao, J.; Luo, S.; Yang, P.; Jiao, W.; Liu, Y. Degradation of nitrobenzene-containing wastewater by ozone/persulfate oxidation process in a rotating packed bed. *J. Taiwan Inst. Chem. Eng.* **2019**, *99*, 1–8. [CrossRef]
28. Wang, L.; Yun, J.; Zhang, H.; Si, J.; Fang, X.; Shao, L. Degradation of Bisphenol A by ozonation in rotating packed bed: Effects of operational parameters and co-existing chemicals. *Chemosphere* **2021**, *274*, 129769. [CrossRef]

Disclaimer/Publisher's Note: The statements, opinions and data contained in all publications are solely those of the individual author(s) and contributor(s) and not of MDPI and/or the editor(s). MDPI and/or the editor(s) disclaim responsibility for any injury to people or property resulting from any ideas, methods, instructions or products referred to in the content.

Article

Development of Geopolymer Mortars Using Air-Cooled Blast Furnace Slag and Biomass Bottom Ashes as Fine Aggregates

Yolanda Luna-Galiano *, Carlos Leiva Fernández, Rosario Villegas Sánchez and Constantino Fernández-Pereira

Departamento de Ingeniería Química y Ambiental, Escuela Técnica Superior de Ingeniería, Universidad de Sevilla, Camino de los Descubrimientos s/n, 41092 Seville, Spain; cleiva@us.es (C.L.F.); rvillegas@us.es (R.V.S.); pereira@us.es (C.F.-P.)
* Correspondence: yluna@us.es; Tel.: +34-954481180

Abstract: The aim of this study is to compare the mechanical and physical properties of different geopolymer mortars made with granulated blast furnace slag as a geopolymer source material, NaOH (8 M) as the activating solution, and three different types of fine aggregates (air-cooled blast furnace slag, biomass bottom ashes, and silica sand). The samples were made with an aggregate/geopolymer ratio of 3/1, and physical (density and mercury intrusion porosimetry), mechanical (compressive and flexural strength), and acid attack resistance were determined. When air-cooled blast furnace slag is used, the mechanical and acid attack properties are improved compared with silica sand and biomass bottom ashes because of the existence of amorphous phases in this slag, which increase the geopolymer reaction rate despite the particle size being higher than other aggregates. It can be highlighted that the use of ACBFS as a fine aggregate in geopolymer mortars produces better properties than in cement Portland mortar.

Keywords: geopolymer mortar; air-cooled blast furnace slag; olive pomace bottom ash; mechanical properties; porosity; leaching; acid attack resistance

---

Citation: Luna-Galiano, Y.; Leiva Fernández, C.; Villegas Sánchez, R.; Fernández-Pereira, C. Development of Geopolymer Mortars Using Air-Cooled Blast Furnace Slag and Biomass Bottom Ashes as Fine Aggregates. *Processes* **2023**, *11*, 1597. https://doi.org/10.3390/pr11061597

Academic Editor: Antoni Sánchez

Received: 24 March 2023
Revised: 19 May 2023
Accepted: 20 May 2023
Published: 23 May 2023

Copyright: © 2023 by the authors. Licensee MDPI, Basel, Switzerland. This article is an open access article distributed under the terms and conditions of the Creative Commons Attribution (CC BY) license (https://creativecommons.org/licenses/by/4.0/).

1. Introduction

The European Union presents the circular economy as a viable alternative to the prevailing model of production and consumption worldwide, especially in developed countries or in those where excessive means of production are used, which encourage compulsive and sometimes unnecessary consumption, blurring the idea of acquiring goods and services for their necessity [1].

This new paradigm requires a significant shift in current production and consumption systems. The shift must be toward regenerative systems that are designed to conserve the value of resources (materials, water, soil, and energy) and products while exponentially diminishing raw material and energy inputs. This will reduce waste generation and negative impacts, hence decreasing negative externalities for the environment, climate, and human health [2].

The construction sector is one of the main polluters. For example, the cement industry is responsible for the emissions of 2 gigatons of carbon dioxide (CO_2) per year, which is more than 5% of the total world emissions, and it is expected that by 2050, the emissions will be 5 gigatons [1]. There are numerous lines of investigation researching the replacement of cement with geopolymers [3]. Geopolymerization is a term coined by Joseph Davidovits in the 1980s to designate synthetic inorganic polymers of aluminosilicates resulting from the chemical reaction known as geopolymerization [4]. Geopolymers have the advantages of low CO_2 emissions during production, high chemical and thermal resistance, and satisfactory mechanical properties, all at room temperature and at extreme temperatures. The geopolymerization reaction takes place under highly alkaline conditions between an aluminosilicate powder and an activating solution (alkaline hydroxide and/or alkaline silicate) at ambient or slightly above ambient conditions (<60 °C), to obtain a new synthetic alkaline aluminosilicate of a polymeric chain structure.

Many wastes (coal fly ashes, blast furnace slag, construction and demolition wastes, municipal solid waste incineration ashes, metallurgical and mining waste, etc.) [5–9] have been studied as raw materials for the manufacturing of geopolymeric materials such as concrete, mortars, building components, insulation, and fire-resistant coatings [10–13].

Slags developed during the manufacturing of pig iron are referred to as "blast furnace" slags and are produced by the smelting of various fluxes mixed with gangue minerals. The raw material quality, as well as the design and operation, determine the quality and quantity of slag. Several types of slags are produced. Granulated blast furnace slag, air-cooled blast furnace slag, expanded or foamed slag, and pelletized slag are the various names for these products [14].

Granulated BFS is obtained by cooling the liquid slag by dropping it on a powerful jet of cold water, thereby making it expand, and using the water jet as a transport vehicle to the decantation basins. During this process (granulation), the slag vitrifies. The principal use of granulated blast furnace slags is for cement production [15,16], but GBFS can also be used as a raw material to obtain geopolymers [7,17], showing good physical and mechanical properties.

Air-cooled blast furnace slag (ACBFS) is also a material derived from iron and steel production, which is obtained by slow cooling of the liquid slag in large facilities. The material crystallizes, forming different components, leaving only a small part in a glassy state. The principal uses of this material are cements with soil-cement additions [18], geopolymers [19], base layers of roads [20], and sound absorption materials [21]. Previous studies [15] have analyzed the use of ACBFS as a fine aggregate, but the results are worse than for natural aggregates. In 2016, 430,000,000 tons of slag were produced, 66% of which were granulated blast furnace slags and 34% air-cooled blast furnace slags [14].

Olive pomace is used as biomass because of its high energy content and low cost; around 30% of it is used to create power. In Spain, the combustion of olive pomace produces more than 50,000 tons of ash each year [22].

Bottom and fly ash are two types of ash created during the combustion process of solid fuel. Bottom ash is created on the grate in the boiler's initial combustion chamber, and it presents a higher percentage of unburned biomass. Previous studies have used these bottom ashes in bricks [23,24], cement manufacture [25], road binders [26], geopolymers [27], fine aggregates in mortars [28], fire resistance materials [29], and fertilizers [30], but the percentage of recycling is very low.

Although ACBFS and olive pomace bottom ash (OPBA) has previously been used as sources of aluminum and silicon to produce geopolymers and as a fine aggregate for mortars using Portland cement, the results have not been promising [15,19,27,28]. The aim of this study is to compare the mechanical and physical properties of two types of geopolymeric mortars made with BFS as geopolymeric precursor, NaOH (8 M) as activating solution, and ACBFS and OPBA as fine aggregates. This work presents two important benefits: (1) the environmental benefit by means of the valorization of three wastes/byproducts in this construction material, fulfilling the European regulation regarding circular economy, and (2) the respective cost savings because of not landfilling these wastes.

2. Materials and Methods

2.1. Materials

Mortars were made with three fine aggregates and a geopolymer cement as the binder. The geopolymer cement is made by means of the activation of granulated blast furnace slag (BFS) with NaOH (8 M). The fine aggregates are standard silica sand, air-cooled blast furnace slag, and olive pomace bottom ash.

Both granulate (BFS) and air-cooled (ACBFS) blast furnace slag come from EDERSA (Gijón, Asturias, Spain). Biomass bottom ashes came from an energy generation process that uses only olive pomace in an inclined grill oven from Villanueva del Arzobispo (Jaén, Spain). Figure 1 shows an image of the four raw materials.

Figure 1. Solid wastes and natural silica aggregates.

The chemical composition of BFS and ACBFS is practically the same, as can be seen in Table 1. Both materials comprise four main components: lime, silica, alumina, and magnesia, which constitute more than 95%. The chemical composition of the slags varies depending on the steelmaking process employed and varies between 27–50% of SiO_2; 5–33% of Al_2O_3; 30–50% of CaO, and between 1–21% of MgO [19].

Table 1. Chemical composition, specific gravity, and loss on ignition of the materials.

Chemical Composition (% Weight)	BFS	Natural Aggregate	ACBFS	OPBA
CaO	43.46	0.59	42.14	16.5
SiO_2	35.82	86.5	34.76	45.4
Al_2O_3	11.60	5.83	9.12	10.4
MgO	7.59	0.13	6.06	5.0
SO_3	-	0.04	1.77	-
TiO_2	-	0.13	0.76	-
K_2O	0.36	2.37	0.54	17.2
Fe_2O_3	1.01	1.33	0.42	4.2
MnO_2	-	-	0.41	-
Na_2O	0.21	0.87	0.19	1.7
BaO	-	-	0.11	-
P_2O_5	-	0.07	-	-
MnO	-	0.03	-	-
Specific gravity (g/cm^3)	2.93	2.71	2.91	2.05
Loss on ignition (%)	1.47	1.34	1.49	9.30

According to EN 196-1 [31], natural silica fine aggregate (NA) (standard sand) is processed mainly from what used to be lakes and rivers where large silica sand sediments are found. SiO_2 exceeds 85% of its chemical composition.

As can be seen, CaO, SiO_2, Al_2O_3, and K_2O are the main components of olive pomace bottom ash (OPBA). In addition, OPBA presents a high unburned content, which leads to the particles presenting a low specific gravity.

The XRD analysis of BFS, ACBFS, and OPBA was carried out using a D8 Advance A25 instrument (BRUKER) (40 kV and 30 mA). The DIFFRAC-EVA software (BRUKER) was used for phase identification. The software works with a reference database ICDD PDF4.2022 version of JCPS. Phase identification and accurate quantitative phase analysis (amorphous and crystalline contents) are based on the reference intensity ratio (RIR) method [32,33]. Figure 2 shows the diffractograms of the three raw materials.

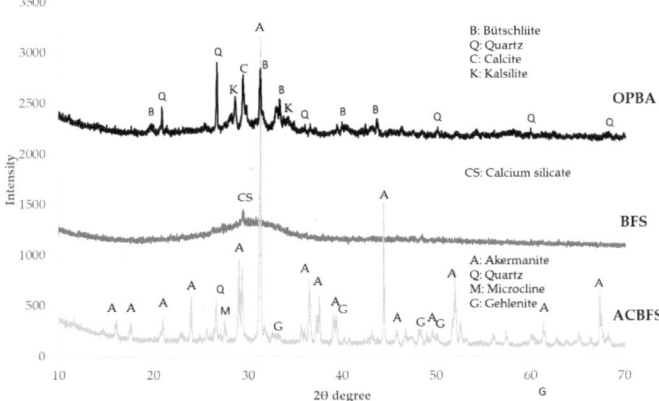

Figure 2. X-ray diffraction of BFS, ACBFS and OPBA.

Curves of BFS and OPBA were moved 1000 and 2000, respectively, from the real intensity to improve the visualization of the curves. The XRD pattern of BFS showed a broad peak in almost all 2θ ranges which is characteristic of an amorphous material (60.4%). BFS only presented a peak corresponding to calcium silicate. ACBFS presented an amorphous content of 20.5%. The main crystalline phases were akermanite, quartz, microcline, and gehlenite. OPBA showed an amorphous content of 39.6%. Quartz, bütschliite, calcite, and kalsilite were identified as the main crystalline phases. As can be seen, BFS has a large amount of vitreous content, which made it a perfect raw material for the geopolymerization reaction. On the other hand, ACBFS, which comes from the same process but with a slow cooling in the air, showed a lower content of vitreous phase than BFS.

The particle size was examined using a Mastersizer 3000 particle size analyzer. The particle size distribution of the three fine aggregates is depicted in Figure 3. OPBA presents a particle size between 0–1500 μm with an average particle size of 387 μm. NA presents a particle size between 250–1500 μm, with an average particle size of 680 μm while ACBFS presents a wider size range than SS (0–2000 μm), but with a slightly lower average particle size (660 μm) than NA. Previous research shows that BFS presents a smaller particle size (50–100 μm) compared to the three fine aggregates [16].

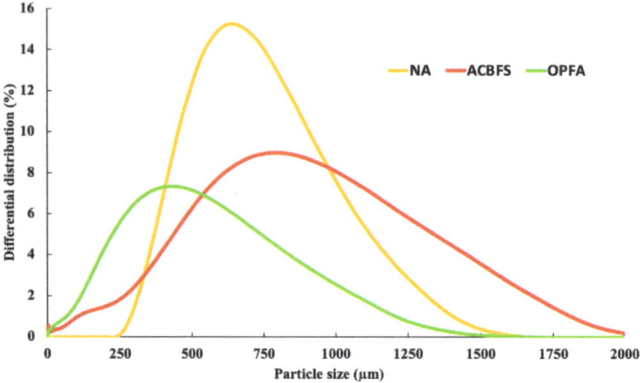

Figure 3. Particle size distribution of the fine aggregates.

2.2. Methods

2.2.1. Geopolymeric Mortar Preparation

Three different geopolymeric mortars were manufactured at room temperature using a mixer (KitchenAid). The solid phase (BFS and fine aggregates) was mixed for 4 min at low speed. Next, the liquid phase (activating solution, superplasticizer, and water) was added to the solid phase, and all materials were mixed for a further 10 min. Table 2 shows the different dosages. The geopolymer binder was prepared using BFS as the source material and NaOH 8 M as the activating solution. In all cases, a superplasticizer (SP) based on polycarboxylic ether-based superplasticizer (MasterEase 5025) was added. NaOH/BFS, fine aggregate/BFS, and SP/BFS ratios were kept constant in all the mortars. Previous tests were performed to calculate the accurate ratios of water to obtain a thixotropic material with the same workability, as can be seen in Table 3. Mixtures with OPBA required a higher H_2O/BFS ratio, due to the higher LOI content, lower specific gravity, and fine particle size, which increase the absorption of water during the mixing. Mixtures with SS showed the lowest H_2O/BFS ratio since SS presents the highest specific gravity (lower porosity).

Table 2. Ratios of geopolymeric mortars.

Fine Aggregates	NaOH/BFS	Fine Aggregate/BFS	SP/BFS	H_2O/BFS
M-NA	0.3	3	0.078	0.027
M-CBFS	0.3	3	0.078	0.168
M-OPBA	0.3	3	0.078	0.503

Table 3. Density and strength of mortars.

Fine Aggregates	Density (kg/m^3)	Compressive Strength (MPa)	Flexural Strength (MPa)
M-NA	2313 ± 24	17.6 ± 1.1	2.5 ± 0.2
M-CBFS	2316 ± 34	18.9 ± 0.9	2.7 ± 0.1
M-OPBA	1712 ± 15	14.9 ± 0.7	2.0 ± 0.1

The solid phase (blast furnace ash and fine aggregates) was mixed for 4 min in a mixing machine. Next, activating solutions SP and H_2O were added to the previous mixture and mixed for 15 min. The resulting paste was placed in molds and was vibrated on the vibrating machine for 1.5 min. The setting time of the mortars was less than 15 h at room temperature, results were similar to other works [34], then, 24 h after their manufacture, the samples were unmolded, wrapped in transparent film, and left to cure for a total of 28 days at 20 °C.

2.2.2. Mortar Characterization

The density of the mortars was evaluated in accordance with EN 1936 [35] for samples cured for 28 days.

The pore size distribution in the range of 1 to 300 μm was studied using mercury intrusion porosimetry (MIP-PoreMaster 60GT). The surface tension was 480 mN/m, the contact angle was 140°, and the maximum pressure was 413 MPa.

After 28 days, flexural and compressive tests were performed on parallelepipeds 160 × 40 × 40 mm, using a Tinius Olsen-TO317EDG, in accordance with EN 1015-11 [36]. For these tests, 5 parallelepipeds of each mortar were used, and the 2 pieces after the flexural test (10 per composition) were subjected to compressive tests.

Resistance to acid attack is measured by evaluating the compressive strength of the samples after immersion in 1 M sulfuric acid and water for 15 days (Figure 4), in accordance with previous studies [37].

Figure 4. Samples in sulfuric acid.

For the test, four samples of each mortar were left to cure during a 28-day period. Two of the samples were immersed in 1 M sulfuric acid, while the other two were left out in the air. Acid samples were removed after 15 days. Then, they were dried at room temperature for 2 days, and compressive strength was determined.

2.2.3. Leaching Study

According to EN 998-2 [38], mortars require the study of emissions of dangerous substances, using standardized European tests and considering the different existing national and regional provisions, although the said standard does not have any specific tests or limits that must be met.

There are more than 55 different leaching tests for different conditions and materials. Leaching tests can be classified mainly as static, dynamic, and tank tests.

In static tests, the leaching solution is a single addition that is not updated during the test. The most used batch leaching tests are EN 12457-4 [39] and TCLP [40].

The leaching solution is recovered during dynamic experiments. This approach is unsuitable for monolithic materials, such as cement-based materials, unless the material size is reduced to the standard size required before testing.

The tank test method involves rinsing the monolithic material in reagent water in a tank. The most common tank tests are NEN 7345 [41] and EPA-1315 [42] and require more than 60 days of testing.

In static tests, the leaching solution is a single addition which is not updated during the test. EN-12457-4 [39] is the most frequently used leaching test in Europe, and it is used to classify wastes in accordance with the EU Landfill Directive [43]. The test is quite basic. It is based on a single stage leaching at a liquid/solid ratio of 10/1 for materials with particle size distributions less than 10 mm. The liquid/solid mixture was rotated at 15 rpm for 24 h. This study made use of deionized water. The Research, Technology, and Innovation Center of the University of Seville (CITIUS) provided an ICP spectrometer (Agilent Technologies, Madrid, Spain). Each leaching was subjected to two leaching tests.

Furthermore, this test is utilized in various European national and regional leaching regulations to evaluate waste use in construction applications. For example, Portugal [44], Italy [45], and some Spanish regions (Cantabria [46] and Basque Country [47]) have imposed leaching limits for the valorization of wastes as part of construction materials based on the results of this test.

3. Results and Discussion

3.1. Physical and Mechanical Properties

In Table 3, physical and mechanical properties (density, compressive, and flexural strength) are shown. With respect to density, geopolymer mortars prepared with NA and ACBFS presented similar values. Geopolymer mortar prepared with OPBA presented a very low density (almost half compared with the other two).

To explain the results, porosity and pore size distribution were also analyzed. Porosities of geopolymer mortars are: 0.5 (M-NA), 0.8 (M-ACBFS), and 3.22 mL/g (M-OPBA). Figure 5 shows the pore size distribution of the geopolymer mortars. M-OPBA presented a high proportion of sorption pores (<0.1 µm) due to the presence of hydrated phases [48] and the internal porosity of these bottom ashes because of the high quantity of unburned matter (Table 1) present in the OPBA aggregate. Capillary pores are also visible in the graph (ranging in size from 0.1 to 100 µm). They are the pores generated within the binder and in the aggregate/binder interface. Water movement causes primary porosity due to absorption into the surrounding masonry unit or evaporation to the air. Because of its high water/solid ratio, M-OPBA has more capillary holes due to its high-water requirement (Table 2). For these reasons, the M-NA mortar shows the lowest number of capillary pores.

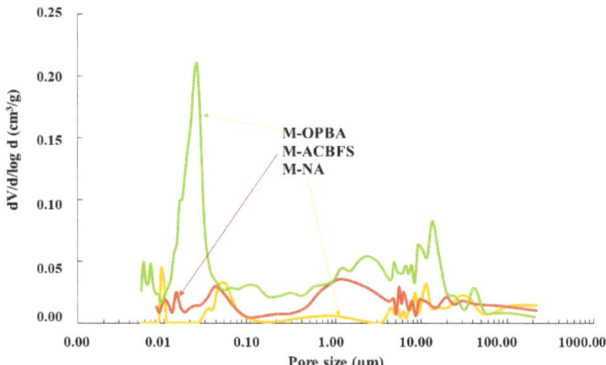

Figure 5. Pore size distribution of the mortars.

Coarse pores present sizes higher than 100 μm. Aggregates with high particle sizes produce higher pores between particles. Consequently, M-OPBA mortars present a lower coarse pore content compared with M-ACBFS and M-NA.

M-ACBFS mortar presented the highest compressive strength values (slightly higher than M-NA and much higher than M-OPFA).

XRD of the three mortars was carried out and diffractograms are presented in Figure 6.

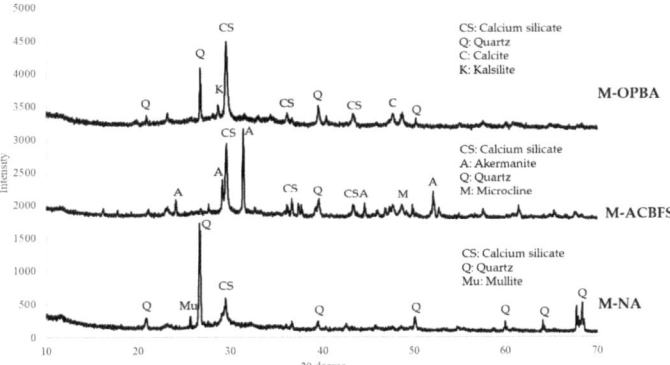

Figure 6. Mortars diffractograms.

Curves of M-ACBFS and M-OPBA were moved 1700 and 3000, respectively, from the real intensity to improve the visualization of the curves. As can be seen, calcium silicate appears in all curves; the crystalline phase comes from the BFS. Calcite, quartz, and kalsilite from the OPBA stayed in the M-OPBA. However, the Bütschliite completely disappeared. Akermanite, quartz and, microcline from the ACBFS remained in the M-ACBFS (reduction of the akermanite peak is important) and the gehlenite disappeared. M-NA presented peaks of quartz and mullite, which comes from the natural aggregate (standard sand). Amorphous content of M-NA, M-ACBFS, and M-OPBA was determined by DIFFRACT.EVA software and the results were 34.2, 36.3, and 41.9%, respectively. Considering that the amorphous content in the M-NA (34.2%) is due to the BFS attack (NA was contacted with the activating solution and no reaction was displayed (wet sand behavior was observed)) and comparing the amorphous content of the three mortars (M-ACBFS = 36.3% and M-OPBA = 41.9%), it can be confirmed that the aggregates ACBFS and OPBA have been attacked during the geopolymerization reaction, contributing to the development of the amorphous phase of the final material.

Although M-ACBFS presented higher porosity than M-NA, the CS of M-ACBFS was slightly higher due to the greater amorphous content of M-ACBFS lead by the contribution of BFS and ACBFS (materials with amorphous content of 60.4 and 20.5%, respectively) to the geopolymerization reaction, which creates a final mortar with a higher content of geopolymer gel and better CS. In addition, BFS and ACBFS are similar materials with the same source; therefore, compatibility and adhesion between the geopolymer gel, the unreacted BFS and ACBFS, could be right to improve the CS [19].

M-OPBA mortars presented the worst mechanical properties. This mortar showed the highest amorphous content (41.9%) of the three mortars; therefore, the contribution of OPBA to the amorphous content of the M-OPBA is greater than the ACBFS and NA in their respective mortars. However, this higher contribution does not correspond with the CS results. This could be due to the effect of the smallest particle size and unburned content of OPBA, which produces greater requirements of water to obtain a workable material, with a final result of a low-density mortar with a lower CS.

According to EN 998-2 [38], M-NA and M-ACBFS could be classified as M-15 to be used as masonry mortars, and M-OPBA is slightly below M-15 and can be classified as M-10. On the other hand, all mortars present a compressive strength higher than 12.4 MPa at 28 days, and they can be classified as type S mortars according to ASTM C270 for masonry mortars [49].

The flexural strength followed the same trend as density and compressive strengths. The mortars made with NA and ACBFS, which contained less water, obtained the highest flexural strength results. On the other hand, the OPBA mortar presents a high porosity; therefore, the flexural test showed the worst results. As previously mentioned, the use of ACBFS produced a higher geopolymerization process and slightly increased the flexural strength.

3.2. Acid Attack Test

Compressive strength results after air contact and acid immersion for a further 15 days are shown in Figure 7. All the compressive strength results after the acid attack are lower than air. The main effect of the sulfuric acid attacks in the matrix was the generation of gypsum inside the pores and all around the sample (Figure 8), which causes pore spalling and results in worse mechanical properties for all the mortars [26]. This decrement is directly related to the macropores present in the mortars; M-OPBA presents a high proportion of macropores (Figure 5) and presents a higher percentage of diminution (41% of reduction), while M-NA presents a low amount of macropores, and its diminution is lower (23% of reduction).

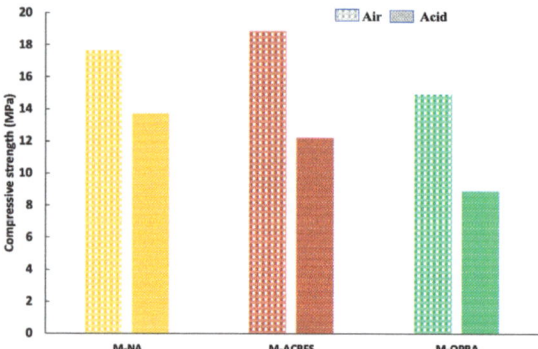

Figure 7. Compressive strength after acid attack.

Figure 8. M-ACBFS after immersion in sulfuric acid and air for 15 days.

3.3. Leaching Study

EN-12457-4 [39] has been used to characterize the leaching behavior of the different solid materials. According to the EU Landfill Directive [41], this test is used to classify wastes [43].

Table 4 shows the results of the leaching test of BFS, ACBFS, OPBA, and NA. Three categories are defined by the Landfill Directive: inert, non-hazardous, and hazardous wastes. Results show that ACBFS, BFS, and NA can be considered an inert waste. Because the values of Se, Sb, and Ni are higher than inert limits but lower than non-hazardous standards, OPBA can be classified as non-hazardous waste.

Table 4. Leaching results of different solid materials of EN 12457-4 (mg/kg, dry basis).

	BFS	NA	OPBA	ACBFS	Inert Waste	Non-Hazardous Waste	Hazardous Waste
As	<0.2	<0.2	1.8	<0.2	0.5	2	25
Zn	<0.25	<0.25	<0.25	<0.25	4	50	200
V	0.19	-	-	0.16	-	-	-
Sn	<0.25	-	-	<0.25	-	-	-
Se	<0.04	<0.04	0.4	0.07	0.1	0.5	7
Sb	<0.05	<0.05	0.2	<0.05	0.06	0.7	5
Pb	<0.2	<0.2	9.3	<0.2	0.5	10	50
Ni	<0.05	<0.05	1.3	<0.05	0.4	10	40
Mo	<0.2	<0.2	1.8	<0.2	0.5	10	30
Hg	<0.01	<0.01	<0.01	<0.01	0.01	0.2	2
Cu	<0.1	<0.1	6.7	<0.1	2	50	100
Cr	<0.1	<0.1	<0.1	<0.1	0.5	10	70
Co	<0.02	<0.02	<0.02	<0.02	-	-	-
Cd	<0.02	<0.02	<0.02	<0.02	0.04	1	5
Ba	13.1	0.82	0.3	0.7	20	100	300

Portugal [44] and Italy [45] have national requirements, whereas Spain (Cantabria [46] and Basque Country [47]) present regional regulations for waste recycling in construction materials in accordance with the results of EN 12457-4. Table 5 shows the comparison of the results with the different international and regional requirements.

Table 5. Leaching results of EN 12457-4 compared with different international and regional requirements (mg/kg, dry basis).

Element	Portugal [43]	Italy [44]	Cantabria [45]	Basque Country [46]	BFS	OPBA	ACBFS
Zn	4	0.03	4	1.2	<0.25	<0.25	<0.25
V	-	-	-	1.3	0.19	-	0.16
Sn	-	-	-	-	<0.25	-	<0.25
Se	0.1	0.1	0.1	0.007	<0.04	0.4	0.07
Sb	0.06	-	0.06	-	<0.05	0.2	<0.05
Pb	0.5	0.5	0.5	-	<0.2	9.3	<0.2
Ni	0.4	0.1	0.4	0.8	<0.05	1.3	<0.05
Mo	0.5	-	0.5	1.3	<0.2	1.8	<0.2
Hg	0.01	0.01	0.01	-	<0.01	<0.01	<0.01
Cu	2	0.5	2	-	<0.1	6.7	<0.1
Cr (total)	0.5	0.5	0.5	2.6	<0.1	<0.1	<0.1
Co	-	-	-	-	<0.02	<0.02	<0.02
Cd	0.04	0.05	0.04	0.009	<0.02	<0.02	<0.02
Ba	20	10	20	17	13.1	0.3	0.7
As	0.5	0.5	0.5	-	<0.2	1.8	<0.2

In Portugal, waste recycling is permitted as long as the limit for inert waste [42] in waste components is not exceeded. According to Portuguese law, BFS and ACBFS could be reused, but not OPBA. According to the Italian requeriments [45], OPBA cannot be used due to excessive As, Mo, Pb, Se, Ni, Sb, and Cu levels. BFS has a greater Ba leaching content, whereas ACBFS matches the standards of the Italian law.

In Spain, there are no specified national limitations for heavy metals leaching of wastes as raw materials. Nonetheless, there is regional legislation based on EN 12457-4 results, that allows us to determine whether a waste can be recycled in construction applications, such as Cantabria and Basque Country legislations. BFS and ACBFS can be recycled in construction materials in Cantabria and Basque Country under these conditions. Most of the metals in OPBA leaching exceed the Cantabria and Basque Country limits.

4. Conclusions

The results of some physical, leaching, and mechanical properties of two different recycled aggregates, air cooled blast furnace slag and olive pomace bottom ash in geopolymeric mortars has been analyzed.

Although OPBA shows amorphous content which is slightly activated by the alkaline solution, as can be observed with the amorphous content of the M-OPBA, in the M-OPBA prevails the effect of the smallest particle size and unburned content of the OPBA, which produces greater requirements of water to obtain a workable material, with the final result of a low-density mortar with lower CS.

Regarding mechanical properties, geopolymeric mortars with ACBFS have 7% more compressive and flexural strength than those made with OPBA and even with NA. This result could be due to two reasons. On one hand, ACBFS presents an amorphous content, which, although it is lower than BFS, it is significant enough to participate in the geopolymerization reaction. On the other hand, chemical similarities between BFS and ACBFS could improve the compatibility and adhesion between the geopolymer paste, the unreacted BFS and ACBFS, upgrading the final mechanical properties.

Leaching studies have also been performed to determine the environmental safety use of these wastes. According to those findings, OPBA has leaching values greater than several Spanish, Portuguese, and Italian criteria, but the use of ACBFS has not presented any leaching problems.

According to EN 998-2 [38], M-NA and M-ACBFS could be classified as M-15 to be used as masonry mortars while, as M-OPBA strength is slightly below the M-15 limit, it must, therefore, be classified as M-10.

Author Contributions: Conceptualization, Y.L.-G. and C.F.-P.; methodology, C.L.F.; validation, Y.L.-G. and C.L.F.; formal analysis, Y.L.-G., C.F.-P., C.L.F. and R.V.S.; investigation, Y.L.-G. and C.L.F.; resources, C.F.-P.; writing—original draft preparation, Y.L.-G. and C.F.-P.; writing—review and editing, Y.L.-G. and R.V.S.; supervision, C.F.-P.; project administration, Y.L.-G. All authors have read and agreed to the published version of the manuscript.

Funding: The Junta de Andalucia's (Spain) Ministry of Development, Infrastructure, and Territory Planning (grant number: US.20-14) and the Spanish National Plan 2017–2020 under grant number: PID2019-110928RB-C33 provided funding for this project.

Data Availability Statement: Data available on request due to restrictions eg privacy or ethical.

Acknowledgments: CITIUS-University of Seville Innovation, Technology and Research Centre.

Conflicts of Interest: The authors declare no conflict of interest.

References

1. Peceño, B.; Bakit, J.; Cortes, N.; Alonso-Fariñas, B.; Bonilla, E.; Leiva, C. Assessing Durability Properties and Economic Potential of Shellfish Aquaculture Waste in the Construction Industry: A Circular Economy Perspective. *Sustainability* **2022**, *14*, 8383. [CrossRef]
2. Alonso-Fariñas, B.; Rodríguez-Galán, M.; Arenas, C.; Torralvo, F.A.; Leiva, C. Sustainable management of spent fluid catalytic cracking catalyst from a circular economy approach. *Waste Manag.* **2020**, *110*, 10–19. [CrossRef]
3. Lu, X.; Liu, B.; Zhang, Q.; Wen, Q.; Wang, S.; Xiao, K.; Zhang, S. Recycling of Coal Fly Ash in Building Materials: A Review. *Minerals* **2023**, *13*, 25. [CrossRef]
4. Davidovits, J. Geopolymers: Inorganic polymeric new materials. *J. Therm. Anal. Calorim.* **1991**, *37*, 1633–1656. [CrossRef]

5. Xu, H.; Van Deventer, J.S.J. Effect of source materials on geopolymerisation. *Eng. Chem. Res.* **2003**, *42*, 1698–1716. [CrossRef]
6. Luna-Galiano, Y.; Leiva, C.; Arenas, C.; Arroyo, F.; Vilches, L.F.; Villegas, R.; Fernández-Pereira, C. Behaviour of Fly Ash-Based Geopolymer Panels Under Fire. *Waste Biomass Valorization* **2017**, *8*, 2485–2494. [CrossRef]
7. Luna Galiano, Y.; Fernández Pereira, C.; Pérez, C.M.; Suarez, P. Influence of BFS content in the mechanical properties and acid attack resistance of fly ash based geopolymers. *Key Eng.* **2016**, *663*, 50–61. [CrossRef]
8. Lu, N.; Ran, X.; Pan, Z.; Korayem, A.H. Use of Municipal Solid Waste Incineration Fly Ash in Geopolymer Masonry Mortar Manufacturing. *Materials* **2022**, *15*, 8689. [CrossRef]
9. Zhao, Y.; Yang, C.; Yan, C.; Yang, J.; Wu, Z. Design and Properties of Coal Gangue-Based Geopolymer Mortar. *Buildings* **2022**, *12*, 1932. [CrossRef]
10. Andreola, F.; Barbieri, L.; Lancellotti, I.; Bignozzi, M.C.; Sandrolini, F. New blended cement from polishing and grazing ceramic sludge. *Int. J. Appl. Ceram.* **2010**, *7*, 546–555. [CrossRef]
11. Lancellotti, I.; Kamseu, E.; Michelazzi, M.; Barbieri, L.; Corradi, A.; Leonelli, C. Chemical stability of geopolymers containing municipal solid waste incinerator fly ash. *Waste Manag.* **2010**, *30*, 673–679. [CrossRef]
12. Rapazote, J.G.; Laginhas, C.; Teixeira-Pinto, A. Developed of building materials through alkaline activation of construction and demolition waste (CDW)-Resistance to acid attack. *Adv. Sci. Technol.* **2010**, *69*, 159–163. [CrossRef]
13. Vaou, V.; Panias, D. Thermal insulating foamy geopolymers from perlite. *Miner. Eng.* **2010**, *23*, 1146–1151. [CrossRef]
14. Tripathy, S.K.; Dasu, J.; Murthy, Y.R.; Kapure, G.; Pal, A.R.; Filippov, L.O. Utilization perspective on water quenched and air-cooled blast furnace slags. *J. Clean. Prod.* **2020**, *262*, 121354. [CrossRef]
15. Ríos, J.D.; Vahí, A.; Leiva, C.; Martínez-De la Concha, A.M.; Cifuentes, H. Analysis of the utilization of air-cooled blast furnace slag as industrial waste aggregates in self-compacting concrete. *Sustainability* **2019**, *11*, 1702. [CrossRef]
16. Ríos, J.D.; Arenas, C.; Cifuentes, H.; Vilches, L.F.; Leiva, C. Development of a paste for passive fire protection mainly composed of granulated blast furnace slag. *Environ. Prog. Sustain. Energy* **2020**, *39*, e13382. [CrossRef]
17. Azad, N.M.; Samarakoon, S.M.S.M.K. Utilization of Industrial By-Products/Waste to Manufacture Geopolymer Cement/Concrete. *Sustainability* **2021**, *13*, 873. [CrossRef]
18. Abdel-Ghania, N.T.; El-Sayedb, H.A.; El-Habak, A.A. Utilization of by-pass cement kiln dust and air-cooled blast-furnace steel slag in the production of some "green" cement products. *HBRC J.* **2018**, *14*, 408–414. [CrossRef]
19. Tole, I.; Rajczakowska, M.; Humad, A.; Kothari, A.; Cwirzen, A. Geopolymer Based on Mechanically Activated Air-cooled Blast Furnace Slag. *Materials* **2020**, *13*, 1134. [CrossRef] [PubMed]
20. Ahn, B.-H.; Lee, S.-J.; Park, C.-G. Physical and Mechanical Properties of Rural-Road Pavement Concrete in South Korea Containing Air-Cooled Blast-Furnace Slag Aggregates. *Appl. Sci.* **2021**, *11*, 5645. [CrossRef]
21. Arenas, C.; Ríos, J.D.; Cifuentes, H.; Vilches, L.F.; Leiva, C. Sound absorbing porous concretes composed of different solid wastes. *Eur. J. Environ. Civ. Eng* **2020**, *26*, 3805–3817. [CrossRef]
22. Skevi, L.; Baki, V.A.; Feng, Y.; Valderrabano, M.; Ke, X. Biomass Bottom Ash as Supplementary Cementitious Material: The Effect of Mechanochemical Pre-Treatment and Mineral Carbonation. *Materials* **2022**, *15*, 8357. [CrossRef]
23. Pérez-Villarejo, L.; Eliche-Quesada, D.; Carrasco-Hurtado, B.; Sánchez-Soto, P.J. Valorization of Olive Biomass Fly Ash for Production Eco Friendly Ceramic Bricks. *Encycl. Renew. Sustain. Mater.* **2020**, *5*, 285–294. [CrossRef]
24. Eliche-Quesada, J.; Leite-Costa, J. Use of bottom ash from olive pomace combustion in the production of eco-friendly fired clay bricks. *Waste Manag.* **2016**, *48*, 323–333. [CrossRef]
25. Rosales, M.; Rosales, J.; Agrela, F.; de Rojas, M.I.S.; Cabrera, M. Design of a new eco-hybrid cement for concrete pavement, made with processed mixed recycled aggregates and olive biomass bottom ash as supplementary cement materials. *Constr. Build. Mater.* **2022**, *358*, 129417. [CrossRef]
26. Peceño, B.; Hurtado-Bermudez, S.; Alonso-Fariñas, B.; Villa-Alfageme, M.; Más, J.L.; Leiva, C. Recycling Bio-Based Wastes into Road-Base Binder: Mechanical, Leaching, and Radiological Implications. *Appl. Sci.* **2023**, *13*, 1644. [CrossRef]
27. Cabrera, M.; Díaz-López, J.L.; Agrela, F.; Rosales, J. Eco-Efficient Cement-Based Materials Using Biomass Bottom Ash: A Review. *Appl. Sci.* **2020**, *10*, 8026. [CrossRef]
28. Beltrán, M.G.; Barbudo, A.; Agrela, F.; Jiménez, J.R.; de Brito, J. Mechanical performance of bedding mortars made with olive biomass bottom ash. *Constr. Build. Mater.* **2016**, *112*, 699–707. [CrossRef]
29. Leiva, C.; Gómez-Barea, A.; Vilches, L.F.; Ollero, P.; Vale, J.; Fernández-Pereira, C. Use of biomass gasification fly ash in lightweight plasterboard. *Energy Fuels* **2007**, *21*, 361–367. [CrossRef]
30. Nogales, R.; Delgado, G.; Quirantes, M.; Romero, M.; Romero, E.; Molina-Alcaide, E. Characterization of Olive Waste Ashes as Fertilizers. In *Recycling of Biomass Ashes*; Insam, H., Knapp, B., Eds.; Springer: Berlin/Heidelberg, Germany, 2011. [CrossRef]
31. EN 196-1; Methods of Testing Cement—Part 1: Determination of Strength. Spanish Association for Standardization and Certification: Madrid, Spain, 2018.
32. Available online: http://www.icdd.com (accessed on 16 May 2023).
33. Gates-Rector, S.; Blanton, T. The Powder Diffraction File: A quality materials characterization database. *Powder Diffr.* **2019**, *34*, 352–360. [CrossRef]
34. El-Mir, A.; El-Hassan, H.; El-Dieb, A.; Alsallamin, A. Development and Optimization of Geopolymers Made with Desert Dune Sand and Blast Furnace Slag. *Sustainability* **2022**, *14*, 7845. [CrossRef]

35. *EN 1936*; Natural Stone Test Methods—Determination of Real Density and Apparent Density, and of Total and Open Porosity. Spanish Association for Standardization and Certification: Madrid, Spain, 2007.
36. *EN 1015-11*; Methods of Test for Mortar for Masonry—Part 11: Determination of Flexural and Compressive Strength of Hardened Mortar. Spanish Association for Standardization and Certification: Madrid, Spain, 2020.
37. Leiva, C.; Arenas, L.F.V.; Vilches, L.F.; Arroyo, F.; Luna-Galiano, Y. Assessing durability properties of noise barriers made of concrete incorporating bottom ash as aggregates. *Eur. J. Environ. Civ. Eng.* **2019**, *23*, 1485–1496. [CrossRef]
38. *EN 998-2*; Specification for Mortar for Masonry—Part 2: Masonry Mortar. Spanish Association for Standardization and Certification: Madrid, Spain, 2018.
39. *EN 12457-4*; Characterisation of Waste—Leaching—Compliance Test for Leaching of Granular Waste Materials and Sludges—Part 4: One Stage Batch Test at a Liquid to Solid Ratio of 10 l/kg for Materials with Particle Size below 10 mm (without or with Size Reduction). Spanish Association for Standardization and Certification: Madrid, Spain, 2003.
40. US EPA. Toxicity Characteristics Leaching Procedure, Method 1311. Test Methods for the Evaluation of Solid Waste. 1992. Available online: https://www.epa.gov/sites/default/files/2015-12/documents/1311.pd (accessed on 10 March 2023).
41. *NEN 7375*; Leaching Characteristics—Determination of the Leaching of Inorganic Components from Moulded or Monolitic Materials with a Diffusion Test—Solid Earthy and Stony Materials. NEN (Netherlands Standardization Institute): Delf, The Netherlands, 2005.
42. US EPA. Method 1315: Mass Transfer Rates of Constituents in Monolithic or Compacted Granular Materials Using a Semi-Dynamic Tank Leaching Procedure. In *Test Methods for Evaluating Solid Waste, Physical/Chemical Methods*; US Environmental Protection Agency: Washington, DC, USA, 1986.
43. Council Directive 1999/31/EC of 26 April 1999 on the landfill of Waste. Official Journal L 182, 16/07/1999 P. 0001–0019. European Commission, 1999. Available online: http://data.europa.eu/eli/dir/1999/31/oj (accessed on 8 March 2022).
44. *DL 183/2009*; Waste Disposal at Landfills. Transposition to the Portuguese Law of Council. Directive 1999/31/CE, April 26. Portuguese Official Journal, Portuguese Mint and Official Printing Office: Lisbon, Portugal, 2009.
45. Ministero dell'Ambiente e Della Tutela Del Territorio. Decreto 5 Aprile 2006, n 186. Regolamento Recante Modifiche al Decreto Ministeriale 5 Febbraio 1998 «Individuazione Dei Rifiuti Non Pericolosi Sottoposti Alle Procedure Semplificate Di Recupero, ai Sensi Degli Articoli 31 e 33 Del Decreto Legislativo 5 Febbraio 1997, n. 22». Gazzeta Ufficiale, GU Serie Generale n.115 Del 19-05-2006, Italia, Roma. 2006. Available online: https://www.gazzettaufficiale.it/eli/id/2006/05/19/006G0202/sg (accessed on 10 March 2023).
46. Decreto 100/2018 de Valorización de Escorias en la Comunidad Autónoma de Cantabria. Cantabria, Spain, 2019. Available online: https://boc.cantabria.es/boces/verAnuncioAction.do?idAnuBlob=333276 (accessed on 8 March 2022).
47. Decreto 34 del País Vasco por el que se Regula la Valorización y Posterior Utilización de Escorias Procedentes de la Fabricación de Acero en Hornos de arco Eléctrico, en el Ámbito de la Comunidad Autónoma del País Vasco. País Vasco, Spain, 2003. Available online: https://www.legegunea.euskadi.eus/eli/es-pv/d/2003/02/18/34/dof/spa/html/webleg00-contfich/es/ (accessed on 8 March 2022).
48. Soares, I.; Nobre, F.X.; Vasconcelos, R.; Ramírez, M.A. Study of Metakaolinite Geopolymeric Mortar with Plastic Waste Replacing the Sand: Effects on the Mechanical Properties, Microstructure, and Efflorescence. *Materials* **2022**, *15*, 8626. [CrossRef] [PubMed]
49. *ASTM C270-19*; Standard Specification for Mortar for Unit Masonry. ASTM International: West Conshohocken, PA, USA, 2019.

Disclaimer/Publisher's Note: The statements, opinions and data contained in all publications are solely those of the individual author(s) and contributor(s) and not of MDPI and/or the editor(s). MDPI and/or the editor(s) disclaim responsibility for any injury to people or property resulting from any ideas, methods, instructions or products referred to in the content.

Article

Removal of Organic Contaminants in Gas-to-Liquid (GTL) Process Water Using Adsorption on Activated Carbon Fibers (ACFs)

Roghayeh Yousef [1], Hazim Qiblawey [1] and Muftah H. El-Naas [2,*]

[1] Department of Chemical Engineering, College of Engineering, Qatar University, Doha P.O. Box 2713, Qatar; rd1105246@student.qu.edu.qa (R.Y.); hazim@qu.edu.qa (H.Q.)
[2] Gas Processing Center, Qatar University, Doha P.O. Box 2713, Qatar
* Correspondence: muftah@qu.edu.qa

Citation: Yousef, R.; Qiblawey, H.; El-Naas, M.H. Removal of Organic Contaminants in Gas-to-Liquid (GTL) Process Water Using Adsorption on Activated Carbon Fibers (ACFs). *Processes* **2023**, *11*, 1932. https://doi.org/10.3390/pr11071932

Academic Editor: Maria Jose Martin de Vidales

Received: 1 June 2023
Revised: 17 June 2023
Accepted: 21 June 2023
Published: 27 June 2023

Copyright: © 2023 by the authors. Licensee MDPI, Basel, Switzerland. This article is an open access article distributed under the terms and conditions of the Creative Commons Attribution (CC BY) license (https://creativecommons.org/licenses/by/4.0/).

Abstract: Gas-To-Liquid (GTL) processing involves the conversion of natural gas to liquid hydrocarbons that are widely used in the chemical industry. In this process, the Fischer–Tropsch (F-T) approach is utilized and, as a result, wastewater is produced as a by-product. This wastewater commonly contains alcohols and acids as contaminants. Prior to discharge, the treatment of this wastewater is essential, and biological treatment is the common approach. However, this approach is not cost effective and poses various waste-related issues. Due to this, there is a need for a cost-effective treatment method. This study evaluated the adsorption performance of activated carbon fibers (ACFs) for the treatment of GTL wastewater. The ACF in this study exhibited a surface area of 1232.2 m^2/g, which provided a significant area for the adsorption to take place. Response surface methodology (RSM) under central composite design was used to assess the effect of GTL wastewater's pH, initial concentration and dosage on the ACF adsorption performance and optimize its uptake capacity. It was observed that ACF was vitally affected by the three studied factors (pH, initial concentration and dosage), where optimum conditions were found to be at a pH of 3, 1673 mg/L initial concentration and 0.03 g of dosage, with an optimum uptake of 250 mg/L. Kinetics and isotherm models were utilized to fit the adsorption data. From this analysis, it was found that adsorption was best described using the pseudo-second order and Freundlich models, respectively. The resilience of ACF was shown in this study through conducting a regeneration analysis, as the results showed high regeneration efficiency (~86%) under acidic conditions. The results obtained from this study show the potential of using ACF under acidic conditions for the treatment of industrial GTL wastewater.

Keywords: industrial water treatment; activated carbon fibers; optimization; isotherm models; kinetics models; adsorption regeneration; GTL process

1. Introduction

To counteract climate change, there has been a vast focus on the Fischer–Tropsch (F-T) process to produce liquid hydrocarbon products [1]. This is reasoned for F-T's ability to operate at lower carbon dioxide (CO_2) emissions than regular fossil fuel production processes [2]. Along with that, fossil fuels from the F-T process have lower contents of sulfur and aromatics in comparison to fossil fuels from conventional processes [3]. These lower contents are advantageous towards the environment [2] as they are favored by end-users [4]. However, there is a side effect of this process, where wastewater is produced as a by-product in huge quantities [5], and this by-product is expected to grow even further [6,7].

Wastewater produced from the F-T process is known as Gas-To-Liquid (GTL) water [8]. For every ton of liquid fuel obtained from the F-T process, 1–1.3 tons of wastewater is produced as a by-product. The source of this GTL wastewater is mainly from the reaction units [9], and this water mainly contains dissolved organic matter. This organic matter is usually constituted of acids, alcohols, acetates, ketones and aldehydes [10,11]. The adversity of the presence of these contaminants is usually portrayed through measuring their chemical oxygen demand (COD) or total organic carbon (TOC) [12,13]. Commonly, the COD of GTL wastewater mixture consists of 76% and 10% of short- and long-chain alcohols, respectively, with the rest being acids and hydrocarbons [8]. Due to the organic mixed nature of this wastewater, there are limited treatment approaches. Given that, the conventional treatment approach is anaerobic biodegradation. This treatment in the GTL process does not achieve complete removal of these contaminants before discharge [14–16]. Hence, there is a need to explore new methods to achieve better removal levels, where discharge regulations are expected to become even sterner [7].

As the current treatment method delivers undesirable removal, a more robust treatment approach is needed to achieve better treatment of GTL wastewater. Advanced biological treatment methods for contaminant removal have been of interest in the literature to enhance the current treatment approach [8]. Such methods were observed to be cell immobilization [17,18] and bio-nanotechnology [19,20]. Regardless of their effectiveness, these methods exhibit several drawbacks. These drawbacks were reported to be mainly cost related, linked to the cost of chemicals and the considerable solid waste produced [8,21]. Based on this, a low-cost approach with less waste and appealing removal is needed for GTL wastewater treatment.

Although the literature is mostly focused on developing advanced aerobic biological methods, exploring alternative cost-effective treatment methods is of value to enhance GTL wastewater treatment. Such methods need to be able to tackle various contaminants at the same time, while exhibiting minimal solid waste and operational costs. From the different methods of treatment discussed in the literature for wastewater treatment, adsorption is known to bring in these attributes: low cost and waste [22,23]. In addition to that, the best material reported to exhibit these attributes using the adsorption technique is known to be activated carbon [6]. This is due to its high efficiency and reusability, as it is reported to last for several adsorption cycles through means of regeneration [6,24]. Based on the advantages brought by activated carbon and the lack of work on GTL wastewater adsorption in the literature, there is a need to explore this area as it is of great economic value. Hence, the objective of this study is to investigate the effectiveness of inexpensive activated carbon fibers (ACFs) for the treatment of GTL wastewater as an inexpensive alternative method to costly biological treatment. To report the output of this investigation, the ACF was characterized and tested against actual GTL wastewater using different investigation approaches. These approaches consisted of response surface methodology (RSM) to determine the optimal conditions for the adsorption medium, equilibrium studies that were used to discuss the adsorption mechanism and a regeneration study to report the recyclable nature of the ACF used.

2. Materials and Method

2.1. Materials

GTL wastewater samples for the study were collected from a local GTL plant. The main characteristics of this water have been reported in a previous study by Surkatti et al. [25]. To ensure the stability of the system, the GTL wastewater samples were pretreated using aeration to remove any volatile organic components such as short-chain alcohols. Analysis of the GTL wastewater is shown in Figure 1.

2.2. Adsorbents

Activated carbon fibers (ACFs), obtained from Zhejiang Xingda in China, were utilized as adsorbent materials. The ACF was selected based on a screening process, where several types of adsorbents were tested for the removal of organic pollutants in GTL wastewater. These adsorbents are as shown in Table 1. Out of these types, ACF showed superior performance in terms of reducing the COD and TOC content.

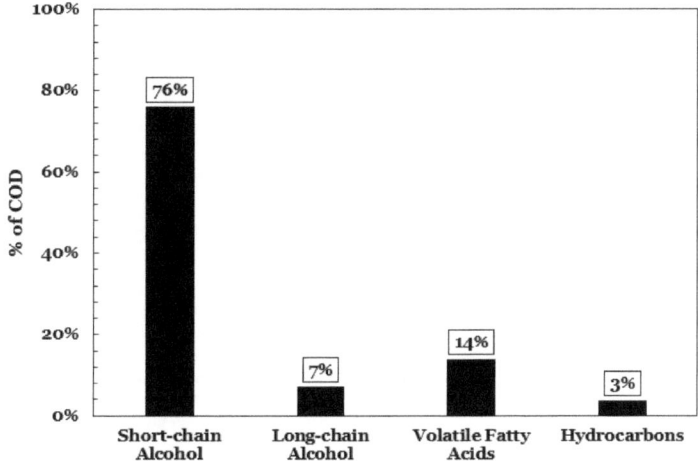

Figure 1. F-T wastewater compositions by COD readings [8].

Table 1. Screened adsorbents for GTL wastewater treatment.

Sample	Uptake (mg/g)	Source
Powder AC	ND *	Commercial
Fibrous AC	81	[26]
ACF	116.5	Zhejiang Xingda
Date-Pit	ND *	Produced in house
Steel Dust	ND *	Produced in house
Wood	ND *	Produced in house

* ND: no detectable uptake was observed.

2.3. Activated Carbon Fibers Characterization

To characterize the ACF, functional groups were obtained using transform infrared spectroscopy (FTIR) analysis that was performed on a range from 400 to 5000 cm^{-1}. Transmission electron microscopy (TEM—EDX) was used to observe the internal form of the adsorbent using Transmission Electron Microscopy Model: TECNAI G2 TEM, TF20, Thermo Fisher Scientific, Waltham, MA, USA. The choice of TEM instead of the SEM is due to the sample size. Depending on the sample size, it was reported by many studies that it is ideal to use TEM to view the internal details of the adsorbent [27–30]. The X-ray diffraction (XRD) trims were obtained using Rigaku MiniFlex-600 equipped with a Cu X-ray tube. The readings from the device provide diffraction peaks that define the structures present using their distinct fingerprint. The intensity and width of the peak can be used to identify the quantity of the structures present. Surface area and pore volume were obtained using Brunauer Emmett Teller (BET, Micromeritics, Tristar II series, USA).

2.4. Batch Adsorption and Response Surface Methodology

For the adsorption studies, a shaker of Labnet model was used. This shaker was used at a 200 rpm rotational speed and 293 K temperature for all the experiments. The factors under investigation consisted of GTL wastewater pH and initial concentration, in addition to adsorbent dosage. GTL wastewater of 50 mL in a sealed jar was used in all the batch experiments unless it is otherwise mentioned. For each experiment where an adsorbent was inserted into the GTL wastewater, a corresponding GTL wastewater of the same concentration without an adsorbent was placed in the shaker. This was performed to unify the conditions where concentration readings are taken. The concentration readings are measured with an HAC—UV spectrophotometer using COD reagents. The samples were inserted into HAC LCK514 cuvettes and were heated for 2 h to ensure the completion of the reaction between the GTL wastewater sample and the reagent. The cuvettes were then transferred to HAC 3900 to measure the COD content that is reported in milligrams per liter (mg/L).

These concentration measurements are used to quantify the uptake capacity using Equation (1). This is to show the effect of the GTL wastewater pH, initial concentration and ACF dosage.

$$q_e = \frac{(C_i - C_e)}{m} V \qquad (1)$$

where q_e is the adsorption capacity in milligrams per gram (mg/g), C_i is the initial concentration in mg/L, C_e is the equilibrium capacity in mg/L, V is the volume of the adsorption system in L and m is the mass of the ACF adsorbent.

The factors under investigation were three, and they are as shown in Table 2. The Minitab software generated 20 experimental runs under central-composite type of design. The results obtained from the RSM analysis were fitted using a polynomial shown in Equation (2) to acquire the investigated factors at their optimized conditions.

$$Y = \beta_0 + \sum_{i=1}^{4}(\beta_i X_i) + \sum_{i=1}^{4}\sum_{j=1}^{4}(\beta_i X_i X_j) + \sum_{i=1}^{4}\left(\beta_{ii} X_i^2\right) + \varepsilon \qquad (2)$$

where Y is the measured response (adsorption capacity—q_e); β_0, β_i, β_{ij} and β_{ii} are the coordinates of constant, linear, interaction and quadratic, respectively. X_i is the independent factor that affects the measured response and ε is the error posed by the model. To gain the interactions between the factors and the measured response, analysis of variance (ANOVA) was utilized. The significance of the factors in the model on the response was assessed using the Fisher value ratio (F-value) and probability value (p-value) and the correlation between them was constructed based on the correlation coefficient (R^2).

Table 2. Parameters for designing the 3-factor RSM for GTL wastewater treatment

Independent Factor	Factorial and Center Level			Axial Level	
	Low (−1)	Center (0)	High (+1)	Lowest (−α)	Highest (+α)
pH	2.64	6	9.36	4	8
Initial Concentration (mg/L)	327.28	1000	1672.7	600	1400
ACF Dosage (g)	0.032	0.3	0.37	0.1	0.3

Based on the results obtained, another set of 12 experimental RSM runs was conducted for two factors to confirm the results obtained from the first RSM. The runs obtained are under the same levels and they are shown in Table 3.

Table 3. Parameters for designing the 2-factor RSM for GTL wastewater treatment.

Independent Factor	Factorial and Center Level			Axial Level	
	Low (−1)	Center (0)	High (+1)	Lowest (−α)	Highest (+α)
pH	1.79	2.5	3.21	2	3
Initial Concentration (mg/L)	434.31	1000	1565.69	600	1400

2.5. Kinetic and Isotherm Modeling

For reporting the kinetic behavior of the GTL wastewater adsorption system, the adsorption process was conducted at room temperature, using 250 mL of GTL at 1000 ppm concentration. The pH was set at the original pH conditions which are (3.2) of 1000 ppm. A total of 0.25 g of ACF was used in the system, and a 10–180 min of contact time was considered. The output of this experiment was assessed using the below models.

$$\text{Pseudo-first order}: q_t = q_e\left(1 - e^{-k_1 t}\right) \tag{3}$$

$$\text{Pseudo-second order}: q_t = \frac{k_2 q_e^2 t}{1 + k_2 q_e t} \tag{4}$$

$$\text{Intraparticle diffusion}: q_t = K_{int}\sqrt{t} \tag{5}$$

where q_t is the uptake capacities of the ACF at the time of measurement in (mg/g), q_e is the equilibrium uptake capacity q_e in (mg/g) of the ACF where t is the time of the measurement (min). k_1 is the rate of adsorption factor (min^{-1}), k_2 is the rate constant of the Pseudo-second order model (g/mg.min), K_{int} is the intraparticle diffusion constant (mg/g min$^{0.5}$) [31,32].

In order to obtain the adsorption isotherms, batch experiments were carried out for a duration of 24 h. These experiments were conducted at room temperature, where an ACF dosage of 0.1 g was used in a 100 mL volume of GTL wastewater. The initial concentration of the GTL wastewater ranged between 300–1640 ppm and the output of these runs were fitted using the below models.

$$\text{Langmuir}: q_e = \frac{q_m k_1 C_e}{1 + k_1 C_e} \tag{6}$$

$$\text{Freundlich}: q_e = k_f C_e^{\frac{1}{n}} \tag{7}$$

$$\text{Exponential}: q_e = a\left(1 - e_e^{bC_e}\right) \tag{8}$$

$$\text{Dubinin-Radushkevick (D-R)}: q_e = q_e \exp\left(-\beta\left[RTln\left(1+\frac{1}{C_e}\right)\right]^2\right), E = \frac{1}{\sqrt{2\beta}} \tag{9}$$

where q_e is the uptake capacity of ACF at equilibrium in mg/g, q_m is the maximum uptake capacity in mg/g, k_1 is the Langmuir isotherm constant in L/mg, k_f is the Freundlich constant in mg/g (L/g)^n, 1/n is the heterogeneity factor, a and b are the exponential isotherm model constants in mg/g and g/mg, respectively, β is the activity coefficient of the D-R model in mol^2/kJ^2, R is the gas constant, T is the absolute temperature in (K) and E is the free energy of sorption in kJ/mol [33,34].

2.6. ACF Regeneration

The ACF adsorbents were regenerated using ethanol, which has been reported to achieve the best performance for the regeneration of activated carbon [35] (El-Naas et al., 2010). A specific mass of the saturated adsorbent (about 0.1 g) was tested in a series of batch experiments with 1000 ppm COD GTL wastewater. After each batch experiment, the uptake capacity is calculated and ACF was treated with 100 mL of 100% ethanol and placed on the shaker for a period of 2 h. The ACF was washed using distilled water and later dried in the oven at 105 °C for 24 h. The results from these runs are then translated into regeneration efficiency that is described below:

$$Regeneration\ Efficiency\ (\%) = \frac{q_r}{q_1} 100\% \tag{10}$$

where q_1 is the uptake capacity in mg/g obtained from the first cycle of batch adsorption and q_r is the uptake capacity in the succeeding cycles in mg/g.

3. Results and Discussion

3.1. TEM—EDX and BET Analysis

Figure 2 shows the TEM imaging for the ACF used in this study. From the figure, it can be seen that the activated carbon fibers are cylindrical in shape, which is similar to other fibrous activated carbon used in the literature [27,28]. In addition, the surface of the adsorbent shown is rough, as indicated by the stripes in Figure 2b. These stripes enable the adsorbent to enhance the trapping of small organic molecules [36,37], and this serves the objective of this study: removing organic material from GTL wastewater. With the rough surfaces, various smears are observed on the ACF. These indicate the modification of the adsorbent, where similar smear patterns were observed in the literature [38–40]. This confirms the treatment of the ACF shown in the map—EDX in Figure 3. From this map, it is seen that the used ACF consists of 87.97, 10.08 and 1.95 wt% of carbon, oxygen and phosphorous, respectively. In addition to this, the BET analysis revealed a surface area of 1232.3 m^2/g and BET average pore diameter of 21.4 A. The distribution of the BET pore volume is shown in Figure 4.

Figure 2. TEM test for ACF (**a**) at 5000× magnification and (**b**) at 10,000× magnification.

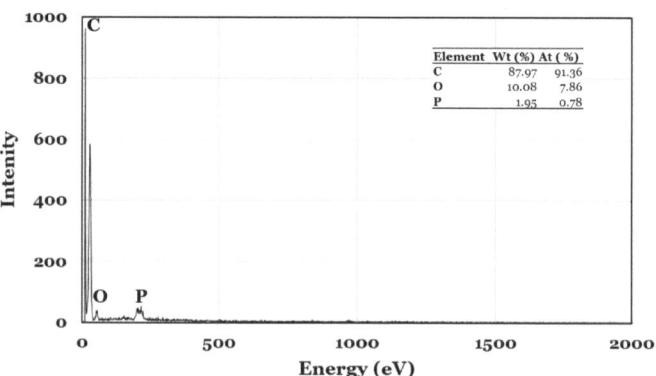

Figure 3. Map—EDX for ACF.

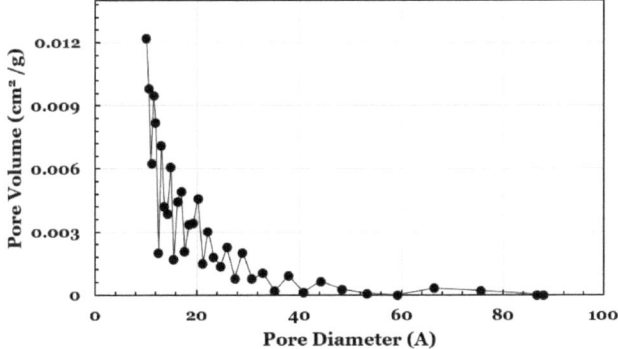

Figure 4. BET performed on ACF to showcase the pore volume distribution.

3.2. X-ray Diffraction Analysis (XRD)

In addition to the discussed ACF characteristic analysis above, the ACF has undergone an XRD analysis. The results from this analysis confirmed the characterization of this study's adsorbent as fibrous activated carbon (ACF) when compared to the ACF XRD readings present in the literature [41,42]. The XRD reading in Figure 5 shows two broad diffraction peaks that correspond to 23° and 43.4°. These two peaks are representations of the 002 and 100 reflections of carbon that are observed in other studies [43,44]. These two planes confirm the presence of amorphous carbon in the adsorbent used in this study [45].

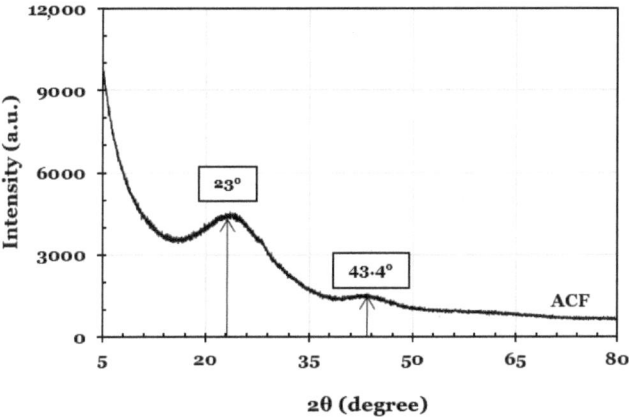

Figure 5. XRD analysis of ACF used in this study.

3.3. RSM Analysis of Statistical Model

RSM is a widely used method in the experimental field to design tests for obtaining desired optimized conditions using a set of experiments. These experimental sets are obtained through stating key variables, in which they are optimized to reach the maximum desirable response [46,47]. As stated in the methods section, the response here is the uptake of contaminants in GTL wastewater. Using the RSM results for the experiments, at the specified conditions, the maximum observed uptake was 111 mg/g while the minimum case was where no uptake took place. From these results and the proposed independent factors, the obtained mathematical equation is as shown below:

$$\begin{aligned}Uptake = {}& 171.8 - 34.65\,pH + 0.0975 C_i - 568 Dosage + 1.599 pH^2 \\& - 0.000017 C_i^2 + 436 Dosage^2 - 0.0035 pH\,C_i \\& + 51.6 pH\,Dosage - 0.0402 C_i Dosage\end{aligned} \quad (11)$$

To learn about the importance level of the model, ANOVA is utilized as a method that is generated after analyzing the RSM output. From the ANOVA, the p-value and F-value are obtained, in which they represent the adequacy of the model through being small and large in value, respectively [48]. As shown in Table 4, the metric to measure the significance of the variables was the p-value < 0.05 along with the F-value < 247.7 for DF 1 or <8.667 for DF 3. This shows that the model obtained poses a 95% level of confidence for the experimental data, hence its adequacy. Furthermore, for the three tested factors, the p-value and the F-value obtained showed that their effect on the uptake is significant. All the interactions in the model were observed to be significant as well. To determine the quality of the model, the correlation coefficient (R^2) is used as an indication. For the model shown in Equation (11), the obtained R^2 was 0.9341 and this shows the strength of the model in determining the uptake of GTL wastewater contaminants using the independent factors.

Table 4. Analysis of variance (ANOVA) for response quadratic model for adsorption uptake.

Source	DF	Adj SS	Adj MS	F-Value	p-Value	Remarks
Model	9	10,854.9	1206.10	15.74	0.000	
Linear	3	8936.2	2978.74	38.88	0.000	
pH	1	4077.1	4077.08	53.21	0.000	Significant
Ci	1	2746.5	2746.48	35.84	0.000	Significant
Dosage	1	2112.7	2112.67	27.57	0.000	Significant
Square	3	983.3	327.77	4.28	0.035	Significant
pH×pH	1	589.7	589.73	7.70	0.020	
Ci×Ci	1	100.5	100.53	1.31	0.279	
Dosage×Dosage	1	274.1	274.05	3.58	0.088	
2 Way Interaction	3	935.4	311.79	4.07	0.040	Significant
pH×Ci	1	62.6	62.62	0.82	0.387	
pH×Dosage	1	852.1	852.09	11.12	0.008	
Ci×Dosage	1	20.7	20.66	0.27	0.615	
Error	10	766.2	76.62			
Lack-of-Fit	5	755.6	151.12	71.13	0.000	
Pure Error	5	10.6	2.12			

In order to obtain a comprehensive view of the RSM model using the stated experimental conditions, the three (C_i, pH and dosage) independent factors were examined in the form of plots. To determine the effect of each independent factor, the three-dimensional (3D) and contour plots were obtained as shown in Figure 6. From the plots and Table 4, it is observed that the three examined factors have a significant effect on the response, while their squares do not. This non-effect is also observed through the two-way interaction between the factors. This finding was based on the p-value and F-value obtained.

In this GTL wastewater system, pH showed influence over the uptake and was examined for the range of 2.6–9.4. To explain the behavior of the ACF under various pH conditions, it is essential to first gain an overview of the adsorption mechanism for AC. As suggested in the literature, the mechanism of adsorption occurs via multiple complex mechanisms. These adsorption mechanisms can take place due to: (1) accumulation of GTL wastewater on the surface of the ACF, (2) adsorption due to functional group polarity and (3) π–π interactions between the different layers of the adsorbent and the adsorbate [49]. As the nature of GTL wastewater consists of aliphatic compounds, the latter mechanism is not expected to take place in this study (mechanism 3). Due to this, electrostatic interactions are considered to be playing the major role between the ions in the GTL wastewater and the ACF surface [50]. As ACF is amphoteric in nature, adsorption is influenced by the pH of the system [51]. To examine the effect of pH on the interaction between GTL wastewater and ACF, drops of 0.1 M NaOH or 0.1 M HCl were used. From Figure 6, the effect of this modification can be observed, and it is concluded that at low pH, higher uptake is attained at different initial GTL wastewater concentrations and ACF dosages. The low performance of the adsorbent at high pH is explained by the competition on the ACF active sites that occurs between the OH^- ions present in the GTL wastewater and the added electrons. Furthermore, at high pH, the occurrence of soluble complexes is possible, which can also hinder the uptake capabilities of the ACF [52].

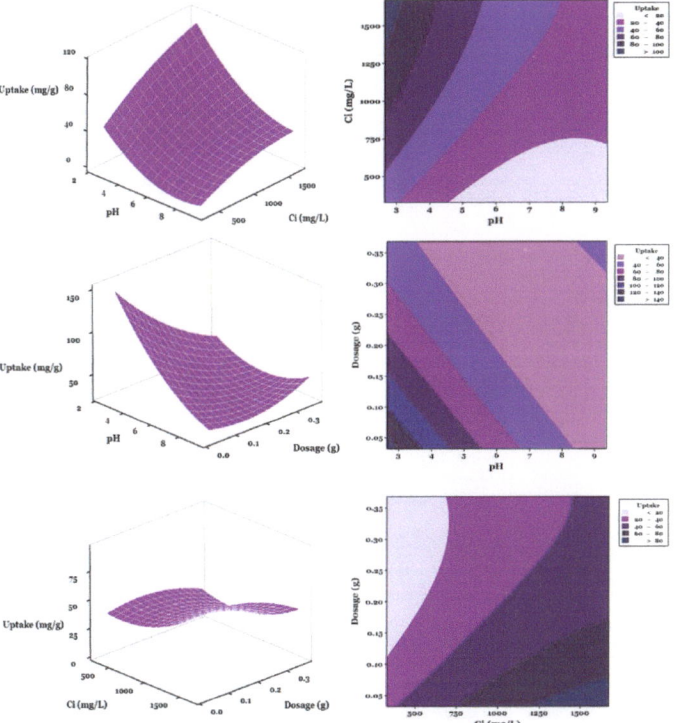

Figure 6. 3D surface and contour plots for three-factor (pH, C_i and dosage) RSM.

As pH was part of the RSM analysis, initial GTL wastewater concentration was also examined using the series of batch experiments. The effect of initial concentration on the GTL wastewater is as shown in Figure 6. From this figure, it is seen that uptake is mostly optimal at high concentrations. The reason for this is the presence of more OH^- groups from the GTL wastewater in the system at high concentrations. This increased presence of OH^- was reported in the literature to increase adsorption due to the increase of mass transfer forces [53]. Based on this, more uptake takes place under high concentrations in GTL wastewater using ACF and it is due to the increase in the driving force of the mass transfer.

Similar to the initial concentration effect, dosage exhibited similar behavior in terms of uptake. As observed in Figure 6, the uptake of the GTL wastewater system increased with the increase of the dosage. This is simply explained by the presence of more active sites where more adsorption took place. However, this increase is expected to be hindered when a mass transfer limitation is faced [53].

As discussed above, GTL wastewater is favorable for treatment with ACF under acidic conditions. The most-favored conditions were around an optimum pH of 3 in the three-factor RSM, which is GTL wastewater's pH without any modification. This optimum condition is ideal for the GTL wastewater, as it is acidic in nature and hence will not require pre-treatment prior to the adsorption process. Based on this, an economic benefit is introduced by the ACF adsorbent studied, as there will be no requirement for pH modification and extra treatment costs are avoided. Most adsorbents in the literature operate at basic or neutral pH [6,54,55], whereas the ACF used in this study can withstand acidic conditions. This shows the effectiveness of this adsorbent to handle and operate efficiently at acidic environments. The confirmation of this advantage was also shown through the two-factor RSM analysis (Figure 7), where the adsorption system was also optimal at pH close to 3, and this is due to the reasons explained previously.

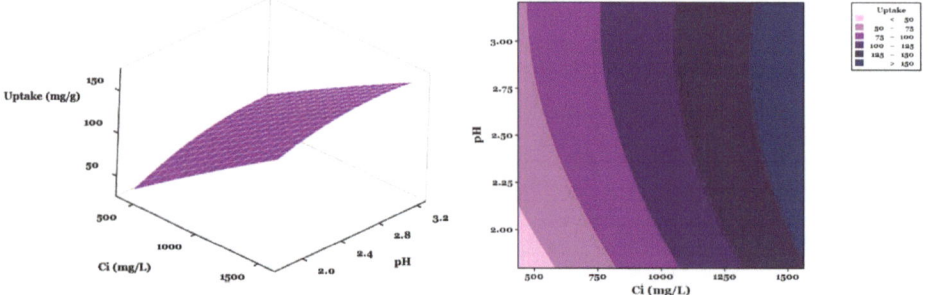

Figure 7. 3D surface and contour plots for two factor (pH and C_i) RSM.

3.4. Model Optimization and Validation

From the developed RSM model, the response was optimized to determine the best conditions for maximum uptake. The output of the optimization is shown in Table 5, where uptake is seen to be optimum at an acidic pH, high concentration and low dosage. These data were validated experimentally, where the obtained uptake was seen to be higher than expected. This better performance is expected due to the increase in mass driving force due to the high concentration and small dosage.

Table 5. RSM model validation using repeated experiments.

	pH	C_i (mg/L)	Adsorbent (g)	Actual Uptake (mg/g)	Predicted (mg/g)
Trial 1	2.6	1672.7	0.03	248.4	177.5
Trial 2	2.6	1672.7	0.03	250.0	177.5

To assess the adequacy of the model, the response obtained from the model was validated experimentally. The assessment's results are as shown in Figure 8, where can be seen that the experimental data are close to the uptake obtained from the model. With these results, it can be concluded that the obtained model to determine the uptake is adequate for GTL wastewater contaminant removal using ACF.

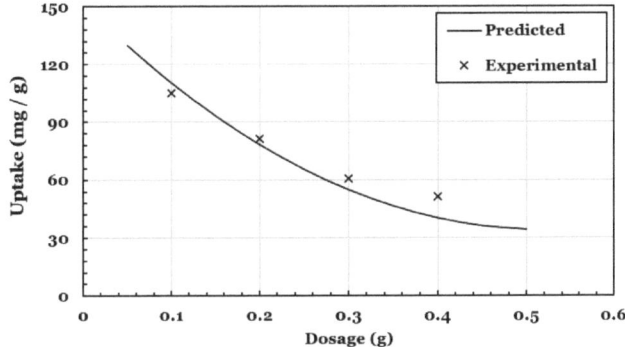

Figure 8. Model v at C_i 1000 mg/L and 3.0 pH.

3.5. Kinetic and Isotherm Studies

To determine the adsorption rate, experimental data were collected at the identified conditions in the methods section. The collected data were fitted into three kinetic models: pseudo-first order, pseudo-second order and intraparticle diffusion. The choice of these models is based on their common presence in the literature. The data obtained from this analysis are shown in Figures 9–11 and Table 6 using the kinetic models stated in the methods section. Using the R^2 obtained via fitting the models, the fitting adequacy of each model was assessed. Figure 9 shows the linearized plotting of the pseudo-first order model where the slope and the intercept were used to obtain the equilibrium uptake Q_e and rate constant k_1. The R^2 for this model was of 96%, which indicates that the kinetics of GTL wastewater follow the pseudo-first order model. Similarly, in Figure 10, the linearized pseudo-second order plot was constructed using t/Q_t versus time. The experimental data in this plot were very close to the predicted values, and this is represented by the 98% R^2 value. On the other hand, for the intraparticle diffusion in Figure 11, the linearized plot of Q_t versus $time^{0.5}$ showed a correlation of 84%. This low R^2 indicates that the adsorption system of GTL wastewater and ACF do not follow the intraparticle model.

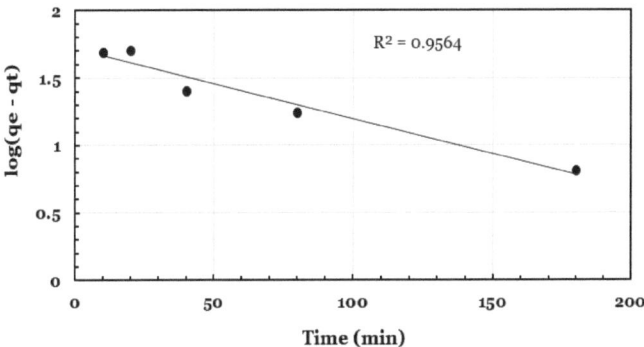

Figure 9. First-order kinetic model for GTL wastewater treatment using ACF.

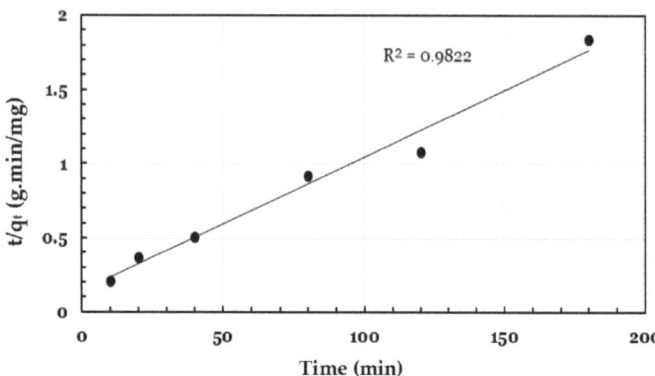

Figure 10. Second-order kinetic model for GTL wastewater treatment using ACF.

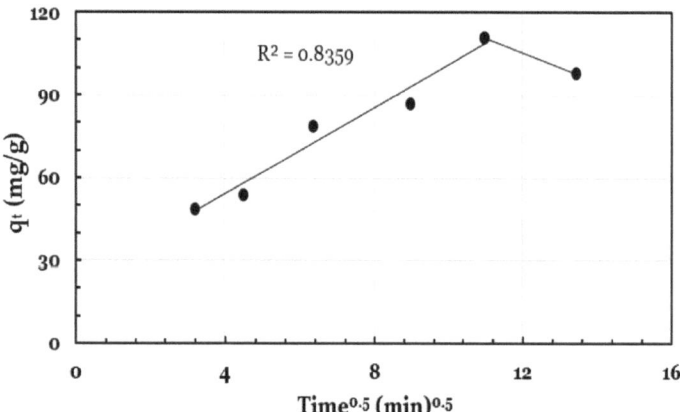

Figure 11. Intraparticle diffusion kinetic model for GTL wastewater treatment using ACF.

Table 6. Kinetic models fitted for ACF/GTL wastewater adsorption process.

Kinetic Model	Parameters	Value
Pseudo-first order	q_e (mg/g)	51.8
	k_1 (min^{-1})	0.01
	R^2	0.96
Pseudo-second order	q_e (mg/g)	111
	k_2 (min^{-1})	0
	R^2	0.98
Intraparticle diffusion	K_{int} (mg/g min$^{0.5}$)	5.66
	I (mg/g)	35.1
	R^2	0.84

The illustration in Figure 11 of the intraparticle diffusion shows that multistage adsorption occurs in the GTL wastewater/ACF system. The figure indicates the presence of two stages for how adsorption takes place. The first stage is the external diffusion of the adsorbate into the ACF surface where the adsorbate is instantaneously adsorbed. This is reflected in the steep slope observed at the beginning of the treatment time. The later stage is when the adsorption rate is slow, and this represents the slow motion of the adsorbate in the system from the large pore to the small ones. Overall, the observed behavior from Figure 11 indicates that the adsorption process for the GTL wastewater system into ACF is not only intraparticle controlled [56,57].

Out of all the examined models, the pseudo-second order model was observed to be the better representative of the kinetics of the GTL wastewater/ACF system. Based on this, the system's adsorption mechanism follows chemisorption.

In addition to the kinetics, an isotherm analysis was conducted to assess the applicability of Langmuir (Equation (6)), Freundlich (Equation (7)), exponential (Equation (8)) and D-R (Equation (9)) isotherm models. Using the nonlinear regression approach—the sum of square errors (SSE), R^2 and the Akaike Information Criterion (AIC) [35], the quality of fitting for each model was determined. The AIC is a method used for comparison between different models in which the lowest value yielded from the following formula is considered the best model:

$$AIC = 2p + Nln\left(\frac{SSE}{N}\right) \qquad (12)$$

where p is the number of independent parameters in the tested model, N is the number of data points. For a small sample size (N/p < 40), the second-order AIC (AIC_c) is used. AIC_c is defined as follows:

$$AIC_c = AIC + \left[\frac{2p\,(p+1)}{N-p-1}\right] \qquad (13)$$

The following difference in the AIC_c using the model's AIC_c and minimum AIC_c (AIC_{cmin}) for all the models is used to find the Akaike weight (w_i), where the highest value recommends the best model:

$$\Delta AIC_c = AIC_{c(i)} - AIC_{cmin} \qquad (14)$$

$$w_i = \frac{exp\left(-\frac{1}{2}\Delta AIC_{c(i)}\right)}{\sum_{i=1} exp\left(-\frac{1}{2}\Delta AIC_{c(i)}\right)} \qquad (15)$$

Figure 12 shows the fitting of these models against experimental data with isotherm parameters of each model in Table 7. From this table, the best fit that is close to experimental data is seen to be exhibited by the Freundlich isotherm model, with R^2 being at 97%, SSE being the lowest (228) and w_i being the highest at 0.79. Overall, from the tested models, the Langmuir and Freundlich models best fitted the isotherm obtained experimentally. This can be reflected in Figure 12, as it shows that the adsorption mechanism is non-ideal, reversible, monolayer and multilayer. The maximum adsorbed contaminants on the monolayer (q_m) were found to be 322 mg/g, while k_F, representing the bond between GTL wastewater contaminants and the surface layer of the ACF, was 2.7 [6,58–61]. From these findings, it can be concluded that the ACF adsorbent is a desirable material for the treatment of GTL wastewater. Furthermore, the results obtained in the table were used to determine the mean free energy of sorption—E (Equation (9)). The value was found to be 6 kJ/mol, which is lower than the typical range of bonding energy for ion-exchange mechanisms, that is, between 8–16 kJ/mol [35,62,63]. This implies that ion exchange does not play a major role in the treatment of GTL wastewater using ACF and chemical/physical adsorption are the main followed adsorption mechanisms.

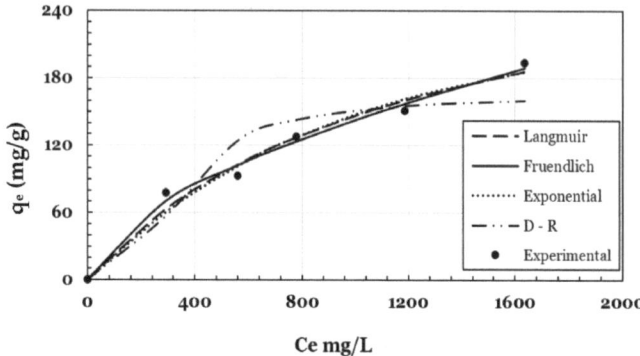

Figure 12. Nonlinear isotherm regression for GTL wastewater/ACF adsorption process.

Table 7. Isotherm models fitted for ACF/GTL wastewater adsorption process.

Isotherm Model	Parameters	Value	R^2	SSE	AIC	AIC_C	w_i
Freundlich	k_F (mg/g) N	2.69 1.74	0.97	228.3	23.1	29.1	0.79
Langmuir	q_m (mg/g) k_1 (L/mg)	322.25 0.0008	0.95	470.1	26.7	32.7	0.13
Exponential	a (mg/g) b (g/mg)	225.05 0.0011	0.94	569.1	27.7	33.7	0.08
D-R	qe (mg/g) β (mol^2/kJ^2)	165.7 0.014	0.68	2791.3	35.6	41.6	0.002

Studies related to GTL wastewater treatment using the adsorption technique are scarce in the literature. To make a comparison for where the ACF use in this study stands, similar industrial wastewater studies were used. Table 8 contains a summary of industrial wastewater studies using the adsorption technique. Through comparing the stipulated values in the table, the ACF used for GTL wastewater treatment shows a very competitive result in comparison to other adsorbents used in similar studies.

Table 8. Comparison of uptake capacities for various industrial wastewater.

Adsorbent	Contaminant	Uptake (mg/g)	Source
ACF	GTL wastewater	250	This work
Commercial Activated Carbon	Organic compounds from a Bio-Process	303	[64]
Wood Biochar	Organic compounds from a Bio-Process	166.63	[64]
Date-Pit Activated Carbon	Industrial wastewater (Phenol)	56.9	[35]
Rice Husk Activated Carbon	Petroleum refinery wastewater	28	[65]

3.6. Regeneration Study

In order to examine the adsorbent's reliability, three cycles of regeneration were conducted for the GTL wastewater/ACF system. As observed in Figure 13, adsorption stayed persistent through all the cycles, while two cycles showed a regeneration efficiency averaging around 85.5%. Regardless, the cycles showed that the adsorbent can withstand regeneration cycles, and this reflects on the resilience of this ACF for multiple adsorption cycles under acidic conditions for GTL wastewater treatment.

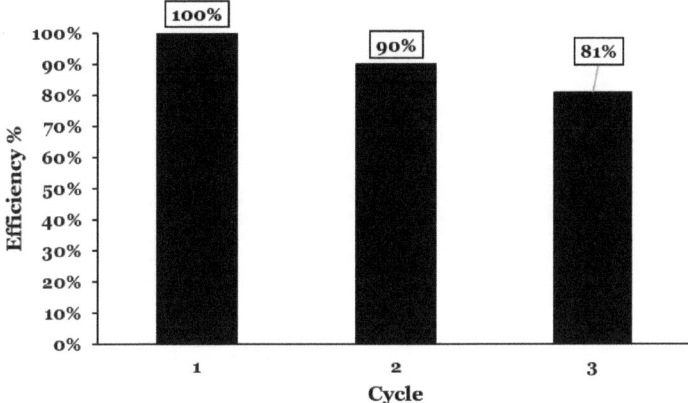

Figure 13. Regeneration cycles for batch experiments of GTL wastewater treatment using ACF.

4. Conclusions

In this study, ACF was used for the removal of GTL wastewater contaminants using the adsorption technique. The feasibility of this technique was optimized through the RSM approach, where three factors were considered as independent variables: pH, Ci and dosage. From the performed analysis, it was concluded that the three factors affected the uptake significantly, while the RSM model was validated experimentally. In addition, the kinetics and isotherm modeling analysis showed that the ACF/GTL wastewater system followed pseudo-second order and Langmuir/Freundlich models, respectively. Following that, the potential of the ACF was shown through conducting a regeneration study, where the adsorbent showed resilience in terms of offering high efficiencies through multiple cycles, while operating in an acidic environment. Hence, the outcome of this study shows the ability of ACF to be an effective adsorbent to treat acidic GTL wastewater.

Author Contributions: Conceptualization, M.H.E.-N. and H.Q.; methodology, R.Y. and M.H.E.-N.; formal analysis, R.Y.; investigation, R.Y.; writing—original draft preparation, R.Y.; writing, reviewing and editing, H.Q. and M.H.E.-N.; visualization, R.Y.; supervision, H.Q. and M.H.E.-N.; funding acquisition, R.Y. and H.Q. All authors have read and agreed to the published version of the manuscript.

Funding: This publication was made possible by GSRA grant, ID# GSRA5-1-0531-18104, from the Qatar National Research Fund (a member of Qatar Foundation). The authors would like to thank the Central Laboratories Unit (CLU) at Qatar University for carrying out the TEM imaging.

Data Availability Statement: Not applicable.

Conflicts of Interest: The authors declare no conflict of interest.

References

1. Schulz, H. Short history and present trends of Fischer–Tropsch synthesis. *Appl. Catal. A Gen.* **1999**, *186*, 3–12. [CrossRef]
2. Knottenbelt, C. Mossgas "gas-to-liquid" diesel fuels—An environmentally friendly option. *Catal. Today* **2002**, *71*, 437–445. [CrossRef]
3. Kim, Y.H.; Jun, K.-W.; Joo, H.; Han, C.; Song, I.K. A simulation study on gas-to-liquid (natural gas to Fischer–Tropsch synthetic fuel) process optimization. *Chem. Eng. J.* **2009**, *155*, 427–432. [CrossRef]
4. Gard. Low-Sulphur Fuels Explained—GARD. 2013. Available online: https://www.gard.no/web/updates/content/20734083/low-sulphur-fuels-explained (accessed on 9 June 2022).
5. Enyi, G.C.; Nasr, G.G.; Burby, M. Economics of wastewater treatment in GTL plant using spray technique. *Int. J. Energy Environ.* **2013**, *4*, 561–572.

6. Yousef, R.; Qiblawey, H.; El-Naas, M.H. Adsorption as a process for produced water treatment: A review. *Processes* **2020**, *8*, 1657. [CrossRef]
7. Pedenaud, P. TOTAL Experience to Reduce Discharge of Hydrocarbons Through Produced Water. In Proceedings of the SPE International Health, Safety & Environment Conference, Abu Dhabi, United Arab Emirates, 2–4 April 2006; p. SPE-98490-MS. [CrossRef]
8. Surkatti, R.; El-Naas, M.H.; Van Loosdrecht, M.C.M.; Benamor, A.; Al-Naemi, F.; Onwusogh, U. Biotechnology for Gas-to-Liquid (GTL) Wastewater Treatment: A Review. *Water* **2020**, *12*, 2126. [CrossRef]
9. Zacharia, R.; El-Naas, M.H.; Al-Marri, M.J. Photocatalytic Oxidation of Non-Acid Oxygenated Hydrocarbons. In *Water Management*; CRC Press: Boca Raton, FL, USA, 2018; pp. 287–302.
10. Saravanan, N.P.; Van Vuuren, M.J. Process Wastewater Treatment and Management in Gas-to-Liquids Industries. In Proceedings of the SPE Oil and Gas India Conference and Exhibition, Mumbai, India, 20–22 January 2010; p. SPE-126526-MS. [CrossRef]
11. Majone, M.; Aulenta, F.; Dionisi, D.; D'Addario, E.N.; Sbardellati, R.; Bolzonella, D.; Beccari, M. High-rate anaerobic treatment of Fischer–Tropsch wastewater in a packed-bed biofilm reactor. *Water Res.* **2010**, *44*, 2745–2752. [CrossRef]
12. Kurniawan, T.A.; Chan, G.Y.; Lo, W.-H.; Babel, S. Physico–chemical treatment techniques for wastewater laden with heavy metals. *Chem. Eng. J.* **2006**, *118*, 83–98. [CrossRef]
13. Damjanović, L.; Rakić, V.; Rac, V.; Stošić, D.; Auroux, A. The investigation of phenol removal from aqueous solutions by zeolites as solid adsorbents. *J. Hazard. Mater.* **2010**, *184*, 477–484. [CrossRef]
14. Müller, N.; Worm, P.; Schink, B.; Stams, A.J.M.; Plugge, C.M. Syntrophic butyrate and propionate oxidation processes: From genomes to reaction mechanisms. *Environ. Microbiol. Rep.* **2010**, *2*, 489–499. [CrossRef]
15. Veil, J.A.; Puder, M.G.; Elcock, D.; Redweik, R.J. *A White Paper Describing Produced Water from Production of Crude Oil, Natural Gas, and Coal Bed Methane*; Argonne National Lab: Lemont, IL, USA, 2004. [CrossRef]
16. Judd, S.; Qiblawey, H.; Al-Marri, M.J.; Clarkin, C.; Watson, S.; Ahmed, A.; Bach, S. The size and performance of offshore produced water oil-removal technologies for reinjection. *Sep. Purif. Technol.* **2014**, *134*, 241–246. [CrossRef]
17. Gebara, F. Activated sludge biofilm wastewater treatment system. *Water Res.* **1999**, *33*, 230–238. [CrossRef]
18. Banerjee, A.; Ghoshal, A.K. Biodegradation of an actual petroleum wastewater in a packed bed reactor by an immobilized biomass of Bacillus cereus. *J. Environ. Chem. Eng.* **2017**, *5*, 1696–1702. [CrossRef]
19. Dyal, A.; Loos, K.; Noto, M.; Chang, S.W.; Spagnoli, C.; Shafi, K.V.P.M.; Ulman, A.; Cowman, M.; Gross, R.A. Activity of *Candida rugosa* Lipase Immobilized on γ-Fe_2O_3 Magnetic Nanoparticles. *J. Am. Chem. Soc.* **2003**, *125*, 1684–1685. [CrossRef]
20. Peng, Q.; Liu, Y.; Zeng, G.; Xu, W.; Yang, C.; Zhang, J. Biosorption of copper(II) by immobilizing Saccharomyces cerevisiae on the surface of chitosan-coated magnetic nanoparticles from aqueous solution. *J. Hazard. Mater.* **2010**, *177*, 676–682. [CrossRef]
21. Campos, J.C.; Borges, R.M.H.; Filho, A.M.O.; Nobrega, R.; Sant'Anna, G.L., Jr. Oilfield wastewater treatment by combined microfiltration and biological processes. *Water Res.* **2002**, *36*, 95–104. [CrossRef]
22. Jiménez, S.; Micó, M.; Arnaldos, M.; Medina, F.; Contreras, S. State of the art of produced water treatment. *Chemosphere* **2018**, *192*, 186–208. [CrossRef]
23. Arthur, J.; Bruce, P.; Langhus, G.; Patel, C. *Technical Summary of Oil & Gas Produced Water Treatment Technologies*; All Consulting, LLC: Tulsa, OK, USA, 2005.
24. Ahmaruzzaman, M. Adsorption of phenolic compounds on low-cost adsorbents: A review. *Adv. Colloid Interface Sci.* **2008**, *143*, 48–67. [CrossRef]
25. Surkatti, R.; Al Disi, Z.A.; El-Naas, M.H.; Zouari, N.; Van Loosdrecht, M.C.M.; Onwusogh, U. Isolation and Identification of Organics-Degrading Bacteria From Gas-to-Liquid Process Water. *Front. Bioeng. Biotechnol.* **2021**, *8*, 603305. [CrossRef]
26. Mochida, I.; Korai, Y.; Shirahama, M.; Kawano, S.; Hada, T.; Seo, Y.; Yoshikawa, M.; Yasutake, A. Removal of SOx and NOx over activated carbon fibers. *Carbon* **2000**, *38*, 227–239. [CrossRef]
27. Reza, M.; Kontturi, E.; Jääskeläinen, A.-S.; Vuorinen, T.; Ruokolainen, J. Transmission Electron Microscopy for Wood and Fiber Analysis—A Review. *Bioresources* **2015**, *10*, 6230–6261. [CrossRef]
28. YLiu, Y.; Hou, H.; He, X.; Yang, W. Mesporous 3C-SiC Hollow Fibers. *Sci. Rep.* **2017**, *7*, 1893. [CrossRef]
29. Williams, D.B.; Carter, C.B. *The Transmission Electron Microscope BT—Transmission Electron Microscopy: A Textbook for Materials Science*; Williams, D.B., Carter, C.B., Eds.; Springer: Boston, MA, USA, 1996; pp. 3–17.
30. Hirsch, P.B. *Electron Microscopy of Thin Crystals*; Butterworths: Oxfordshire, UK, 1965.
31. Black, R.; Sartaj, M.; Mohammadian, A.; Qiblawey, H.A.M. Biosorption of Pb and Cu using fixed and suspended bacteria. *J. Environ. Chem. Eng.* **2014**, *2*, 1663–1671. [CrossRef]
32. Ewis, D.; Benamor, A.; Ba-Abbad, M.M.; Nasser, M.; El-Naas, M.; Qiblawey, H. Removal of Oil Content from Oil-Water Emulsions Using Iron Oxide/Bentonite Nano Adsorbents. *J. Water Process. Eng.* **2020**, *38*, 101583. [CrossRef]
33. Albatrni, H.; Qiblawey, H.; Al-Marri, M.J. Walnut shell based adsorbents: A review study on preparation, mechanism, and application. *J. Water Process. Eng.* **2022**, *45*, 102527. [CrossRef]
34. Al-Ghouti, M.A.; Sayma, J.; Munira, N.; Mohamed, D.; Da'na, D.A.; Qiblawey, H.; Alkhouzaam, A. Effective removal of phenol from wastewater using a hybrid process of graphene oxide adsorption and UV-irradiation. *Environ. Technol. Innov.* **2022**, *27*, 102525. [CrossRef]

35. El-Naas, M.H.; Al-Zuhair, S.; Alhaija, M.A. Removal of phenol from petroleum refinery wastewater through adsorption on date-pit activated carbon. *Chem. Eng. J.* **2010**, *162*, 997–1005. [CrossRef]
36. Xu, C.; Niu, Y.; Popat, A.; Jambhrunkar, S.; Karmakar, S.; Yu, C. Rod-like mesoporous silica nanoparticles with rough surfaces for enhanced cellular delivery. *J. Mater. Chem. B* **2014**, *2*, 253–256. [CrossRef]
37. Nakashima, Y.; Fukushima, M.; Hyuga, H. Fiber template approach toward preparing one-dimensional silica nanostructure with rough surface. *Adv. Powder Technol.* **2021**, *32*, 1099–1105. [CrossRef]
38. Huang, L.; Zhang, X.; Xu, M.; Chen, J.; Shi, Y.; Huang, C.; Wang, S.; An, S.; Li, C. Preparation and mechanical properties of modified nanocellulose/PLA composites from cassava residue. *AIP Adv.* **2018**, *8*, 25116. [CrossRef]
39. Qiao, W.; Yoon, S.; Korai, Y.; Mochida, I.; Inoue, S.; Sakurai, T.; Shimohara, T. Preparation of activated carbon fibers from polyvinyl chloride. *Carbon* **2004**, *42*, 1327–1331. [CrossRef]
40. Beyene, D.; Chae, M.; Dai, J.; Danumah, C.; Tosto, F.; Demesa, A.G.; Bressler, D.C. Characterization of Cellulase-Treated Fibers and Resulting Cellulose Nanocrystals Generated through Acid Hydrolysis. *Materials* **2018**, *11*, 1272. [CrossRef]
41. Li, Y.; Zhang, M. 6—Mechanical properties of activated carbon fibers. In *Woodhead Publishing Series in Textiles*; Chen, J.Y., Chen, T., Eds.; Woodhead Publishing: Oxford, UK, 2017; pp. 167–180.
42. Shi, G.; Liu, C.; Wang, G.; Chen, X.; Li, L.; Jiang, X.; Zhang, P.; Dong, Y.; Jia, S.; Tian, H.; et al. Preparation and electrochemical performance of electrospun biomass-based activated carbon nanofibers. *Ionics* **2019**, *25*, 1805–1812. [CrossRef]
43. Zhang, F.; Xie, F.; Xu, H.; Liu, J.; Oh, C.W. Characterization of Pd/TiO_2 embedded in multi-walled carbon nanotube catalyst with a high photocatalytic activity. *Kinet. Catal.* **2013**, *54*, 297–306. [CrossRef]
44. Jin, Z.; Yan, X.; Yu, Y.; Zhao, G. Sustainable activated carbon fibers from liquefied wood with controllable porosity for high-performance supercapacitors. *J. Mater. Chem. A* **2014**, *2*, 11706–11715. [CrossRef]
45. Makarov, I.S.; Golova, L.K.; Vinogradov, M.I.; Levin, I.S.; Shandryuk, G.A.; Arkharova, N.A.; Golubev, Y.V.; Berkovich, A.K.; Eremin, T.V.; Obraztsova, E.D. The Effect of Alcohol Precipitants on Structural and Morphological Features and Thermal Properties of Lyocell Fibers. *Fibers* **2020**, *8*, 43. [CrossRef]
46. Box, G.E.P.; Wilson, K.B. On the Experimental Attainment of Optimum Conditions BT—Breakthroughs in Statistics: Methodology and Distribution; Kotz, S., Johnson, N.L., Eds.; Springer: New York, NY, USA, 1992; pp. 270–310.
47. Khuri, A.I. A general overview of response surface methodology. *Biom. Biostat. Int. J.* **2017**, *5*, 87–93. [CrossRef]
48. Saini, S.; Chawla, J.; Kumar, R.; Kaur, I. Response surface methodology (RSM) for optimization of cadmium ions adsorption using C16-6-16 incorporated mesoporous MCM-41. *SN Appl. Sci.* **2019**, *1*, 894. [CrossRef]
49. Ghani, Z.A.; Yusoff, M.S.; Zaman, N.Q.; Zamri, M.F.M.A.; Andas, J. Optimization of preparation conditions for activated carbon from banana pseudo-stem using response surface methodology on removal of color and COD from landfill leachate. *Waste Manag.* **2017**, *62*, 177–187. [CrossRef]
50. Liu, L.; Yang, W.; Zhang, H.; Yan, X.; Liu, Y. Ultra-High Response Detection of Alcohols Based on CdS/MoS2 Composite. *Nanoscale Res. Lett.* **2022**, *17*, 7. [CrossRef]
51. Biesheuvel, M. Activated carbon is an electron-conducting amphoteric ion adsorbent. *arXiv* **2015**, arXiv:1509.06354.
52. Timothy, A. Adsorption of Chromium Ion from Industrial Effluent Using Activated Carbon Derived from Plantain (*Musa paradisiaca*) Wastes. *Am. J. Environ. Prot.* **2016**, *4*, 7–20.
53. Inglezakis, V.J.; Balsamo, M.; Montagnaro, F. Liquid–Solid Mass Transfer in Adsorption Systems—An Overlooked Resistance? *Ind. Eng. Chem. Res.* **2020**, *59*, 22007–22016. [CrossRef]
54. Girish, C.R.; Murty, V.R. Mass Transfer Studies on Adsorption of Phenol from Wastewater Using *Lantana camara*, Forest Waste. *Int. J. Chem. Eng.* **2016**, *2016*, 5809505. [CrossRef]
55. Pestman, R.; Chen, W.; Hensen, E. Insight into the Rate-Determining Step and Active Sites in the Fischer–Tropsch Reaction over Cobalt Catalysts. *ACS Catal.* **2019**, *9*, 4189–4195. [CrossRef]
56. Pholosi, A.; Naidoo, E.B.; Ofomaja, A.E. Intraparticle diffusion of Cr(VI) through biomass and magnetite coated biomass: A comparative kinetic and diffusion study. *South Afr. J. Chem. Eng.* **2020**, *32*, 39–55. [CrossRef]
57. Albatrni, H.; Qiblawey, H.; Almomani, F.; Adham, S.; Khraisheh, M. Polymeric adsorbents for oil removal from water. *Chemosphere* **2019**, *233*, 809–817. [CrossRef]
58. Freundlich, H.M.F. Over the Adsorption in Solution. *J. Phys. Chem.* **1906**, *57*, 385–471.
59. Bikerman, J.J.B.T.-P.C. (Ed.) CHAPTER II–Physical Chemistry of Liquid Surfaces. In *Physical Surfaces*; Elsevier: Amsterdam, The Netherlands, 1970; Volume 20, pp. 44–116.
60. Foo, K.Y.; Hameed, B.H. Insights into the modeling of adsorption isotherm systems. *Chem. Eng. J.* **2010**, *156*, 2–10. [CrossRef]
61. Langmuir, I. The constitution and fundamental properties of solids and liquids. II. liquids.1. *J. Am. Chem. Soc.* **1917**, *39*, 1848–1906. [CrossRef]
62. Ho, Y.S.; Porter, J.F.; McKay, G. Equilibrium Isotherm Studies for the Sorption of Divalent Metal Ions onto Peat: Copper, Nickel and Lead Single Component Systems. *Water Air Soil Pollut.* **2002**, *141*, 1–33. [CrossRef]
63. Ozcan, A.; Ozcan, A.S.; Tunali, S.; Akar, T.; Kiran, I. Determination of the equilibrium, kinetic and thermodynamic parameters of adsorption of copper(II) ions onto seeds of Capsicum annuum. *J. Hazard. Mater.* **2005**, *124*, 200–208. [CrossRef]

64. de Caprariis, B.; De Filippis, P.; Hernandez, A.D.; Petrucci, E.; Petrullo, A.; Scarsella, M.; Turchi, M. Pyrolysis wastewater treatment by adsorption on biochars produced by poplar biomass. *J. Environ. Manage.* **2017**, *197*, 231–238. [CrossRef]
65. Mohammad, Y.S.; Shaibu-Imodagbe, E.M.; Igboro, S.B.; Giwa, A.; Okuofu, C.A. Adsorption of Phenol from Refinery Wastewater Using Rice Husk Activated Carbon. *Iran. J. Energy Environ.* **2014**, *5*, 393–399. [CrossRef]

Disclaimer/Publisher's Note: The statements, opinions and data contained in all publications are solely those of the individual author(s) and contributor(s) and not of MDPI and/or the editor(s). MDPI and/or the editor(s) disclaim responsibility for any injury to people or property resulting from any ideas, methods, instructions or products referred to in the content.

Article

Determination of Soil Agricultural Aptitude for Sugar Cane Production in Vertisols with Machine Learning

Ofelia Landeta-Escamilla [1,*], Alejandro Alvarado-Lassman [1,*], Oscar Osvaldo Sandoval-González [1], José de Jesús Agustín Flores-Cuautle [2], Erik Samuel Rosas-Mendoza [2], Albino Martínez-Sibaja [1], Norma Alejandra Vallejo Cantú [1] and Juan Manuel Méndez Contreras [1]

[1] Tecnológico Nacional de México, Instituto Tecnológico de Orizaba, Av. Oriente 9, 852, Col. Emiliano Zapata, Orizaba 94320, Mexico; oscar.sg@orizaba.tecnm.mx (O.O.S.-G.); albino.ms@orizaba.tecnm.mx (A.M.-S.); norma.vc@orizaba.tecnm.mx (N.A.V.C.); juan.mc@orizaba.tecnm.mx (J.M.M.C.)

[2] Programa de Investigadoras e Investigadores por México del CONACYT, Av. Insurgentes Sur 1582, Ciudad de México 03940, Mexico; jose.fc@orizaba.tecnm.mx (J.d.J.A.F.-C.); erik.rm@orizaba.tecnm.mx (E.S.R.-M.)

* Correspondence: ofelia.le@orizaba.tecnm.mx (O.L.-E.); alejandro.al@orizaba.tecnm.mx (A.A.-L.)

Abstract: Sugarcane is one of the main agro-industrial products consumed worldwide, and, therefore, the use of suitable soils is a key factor to maximize its production. As a result, the need to evaluate soil matrices, including many physical, chemical, and biological parameters, to determine the soil's aptitude for growing food crops increases. Machine learning techniques were used to perform an in-depth analysis of the physicochemical indicators of vertisol-type soils used in sugarcane production. The importance of the relationship between each of the indicators was studied. Furthermore, and the main objective of the present work, was the determination of the minimum number of the most important physicochemical indicators necessary to evaluate the agricultural suitability of the soils, with a view to reducing the number of analyses in terms of physicochemical indicators required for the evaluation. The results obtained relating to the estimation of agricultural capability using different numbers of parameters showed accuracy results of up to 91% when implementing three parameters: Potassium (K), Calcium (Ca) and Cation Exchange Capacity (CEC). The reported results, relating to the estimation of the physicochemical parameters, indicated that it was possible to estimate eleven physicochemical parameters with an average accuracy of 73% using only the data of K, Ca and CEC as input parameters in the Machine Learning models. Knowledge of these three parameters enables determination of the values of soil potential in regard to Hydrogen (pH), organic matter (OM), Phosphorus (P), Magnesium (Mg), Sulfur (S), Boron (B), Copper (Cu), Manganese (Mn), and Zinc (Zn), the Calcium/Magnesium ratio (Ca/Mg), and also the texture of the soil.

Keywords: land use; vertisols; machine learning; soil agricultural aptitude; sugar cane

1. Introduction

To achieve efficient and safe methods of food production it is important to improve agricultural techniques and adapt farming practices to attend to the needs of the soil and its appropriate management. There are multiple factors to achieve good crop management and to optimize it, which require continuous evaluation for appropriate decisions to be made. Additionally, predicting suitable areas to grow food in faces the issue of uncertainty in the quality of the soil and the corresponding practices required to improve the health of the soil to ensure it can fulfill the demands for global food necessities. World sugarcane production in 2018 was 2,042,654 thousand tons, of which 56,842 thousand tons were from Mexico (the seventh highest sugarcane producing country) [1]. The state of Veracruz in Mexico contributes 38% of the sugarcane production [2].

The agricultural aptitude of soil to obtain above 80 t/ha of sugarcane requires, among others, the following: available Nitrogen above 300 kg/ha, Phosphorus (P) above 40 ppm, Potassium (K) above 468 ppm, and potential of Hydrogen (pH) between 6.6 and 7.3 amo [3,4]. These parameters have to be maintained and monitored because the properties of soil vary greatly due to agricultural cropping patterns [5]

The challenge is still the optimization of the parameters that determine soil capability to produce food using a minimum of physicochemical parameters. A strategy that has proved to improve decision making in agriculture is the use of Artificial Intelligence (AI), which analyzes big volumes of data [6] to solve nonlinear problems where there may be no mathematical representations and to obtain models based on experience in cases of supervised learning. AI has been employed in regard to many fruit, vegetable and cereal crops, such as potato, lemon, and wheat [7]. In regard to maize, AI exhibited good predictive capacity, obtaining the lowest root mean square error (RMSE) and the highest determination coefficient (R^2) [8]. In general, all of the results obtained provided accurate descriptive data [6]. The evaluated areas have included fertilizer efficiency, prediction of rainfall, crop production, soil preparation, crop pattern, and precision agriculture [9].

In this AI field, several models, such as the Decision Tree model (DT), have been implemented to evaluate the population dynamics of soil organisms and how these dynamics are affected by changes in different biological and physicochemical environmental attributes and agricultural practices. AI has also been used to relate morphological, physical and chemical soil properties to soil structure by creating a framework for Soil Quality assessment, resulting in an adequate index that reproduces the effect of the interactions between physicochemical variables, the arrangement of soil fragments and biological activity in the soil [10].

Principal Component Analysis (PCA) was used to evaluate soil variables and concluded that Magnesium (Mg), Calcium (Ca), potential of Hydrogen (pH), Silt, Clay, and Potassium (K) are the main variables determining Soil Quality [11]. These methods appear to be more sensitive to disturbances for management practices [12]. Other research, that included 18 parameters and different soils, in terms of crop, residue and fertilization, showed that the created indicator was most affected by the Nitrogen–Phosphorus–Potassium (NPK) rate, and that other parameters failed to correlate yield significantly. Additionally, the PCA synthesized the data [13].

Other research proposed two Soil Quality Index (SQI) approaches, applying PCA and Expert Opinion (EO), by which 24 physical and chemical parameters were evaluated in the surface and the control sections (0–100 cm) in soil. The results indicated five principal components for the first methodology and six indicators for the second, the latter performing better in both the surface and control section evaluations [14].

Regression methods, such as Relative Risk (RR), which is an alternative approach to partial least squares regression (SIMPLS), Principal Component Regression (PCR), and Partial Least Squares Regression (PLSR), were applied to synthesize ten physical and chemical variables in soils, and it was concluded that the PLSR method was the most robust [15,16]. Furthermore, Deep Autoencoders (DAs) have been applied to satellite images to determine change detection in burnt areas, in mapping forests [17] and in landslide susceptibility prediction [18]. Excellent classification results in three of the projects [17,19] indicated that DL is an adequate tool in evaluating complex matrices of variables. In Table 1 a comparative analysis of state-of-the-art research, separated into configuration, target and main contribution, is presented.

Table 1. Comparative table of different state-of-the-art research separated into configuration, target and main contribution.

Name/Ref.	Configuration	Target	Main Contribution
[20]	Comparative assessment of the cubist model and the quantile random forest models	Soil fertility index map	The topographic covariates had strong predictive ability for all the soil properties along with the bioclimatic variables.
[21]	Visible near-infrared spectroscopy and machine learning models, such as Partial Least Square Regression (PLSR), Support Vector Machine (SVM), and Wavelet Neural Network (WNN)	Soil organic carbon	A combination of the techniques was most suitable in pre-processing data with different models.
[22]	Visible near-infrared spectroscopy (VIRS) and machine learning (PLSR), Support Vector Machine (SVM), Artificial Neural Networks (ANN), cubist combined with VIRS	Soil organic matter	The combination of algorithms resulted in more precise calibration–validation models.
[23]	Successive projections algorithm (SPA), competitive adaptive weight weighting algorithm (CARS), and the combination of Smart Process Automation (SPA) and (CARS)	Soil organic matter	The combination of algorithms resulted in more precise calibration–validation models.
[24]	Kriging interpolation, density-based spatial clustering of applications and noise (DBSCAN) validated with random forest (RF) algorithms	Soil fertility degradation (SFD)	Implementing Random Forest and clustering provided an accuracy above 95%.
[25]	SVM model paired with 7 Gaussian Process, Random forest (RF) and multi-linear regression (MLP)	Permeability of soil (PS)	The parameters of time and water head were the most effective to estimate permeability of soil.
[26]	Artificial intelligence model based on ANN	Hydraulic conductivity (Ks)	The model predicts Ks by means of soil parameters, such as silt, clay, organic matter, bulk density, pH, and electrical conductivity.
[27]	Architectural model	Soil fertility	The model predicted organic matter and clay
[28]	Extreme Learning Machine model with different activation functions	Available phosphorus, available potassium, Organic carbon (OC), B, and pH	The model predicted four of the five parameters evaluated.
[29]	Various machine learning techniques (K-Nearest)	Land susceptibility zonation (LSZ)	The susceptibility maps of the Landslid model paired with the extreme learning adaptive neuro fuzzy inference system (LSM-ELANFIS-VII) provided the most accurate results.
[30]	Neighbor Naïve Bayes (KNN), Multinomial Logistic Regression,	Soil nutrient quality	Two models were accurate and some uncertainties in the process are to be studied.
[31]	ANN and RF	Mustard crop yield	The parameters used were pH, electrical conductivity (EC), OC, Nitrogen (N), P, K, S, Cu, iron (Fe), Zinc (Zn) and Mn and the most accuracy was obtained with the KNN and the ANN.
[32]	Evaluation of soil nutrient content through machine learning models	Soil nutrient quality	Two models were accurate and some uncertainties in the process are to be studied.

Therefore, the present research aimed to ascertain, by comparing algorithms, the technique requiring the least parameters to achieve accurate results in determining the capability of soils. Additionally, the results provide correlations among physicochemical variables which could help farmers determine soil amendments faster to increase crop yields.

2. Materials and Methods

2.1. Study Case

Veracruz is the state of Mexico that has the most sugar mills (20) in the country. The experimental sites included those having the most sugar mills in a region called the High Mountains in Veracruz, Mexico. Till June 2021 this region had 326,706 ha of sugarcane and a total production of 19,134,311 tons, earning $45,984.21 USD per ton [2]. The area has 57 municipalities with an approximate area of 6053 km^2. The soils sampled covered 0.5% of the total surface planted with sugar cane. The soil is classified as Vertisol (Vp) according to the World Soil Resources Report [1]. Figure 1 shows the selected soil and other classifications of soils presented in the studied area.

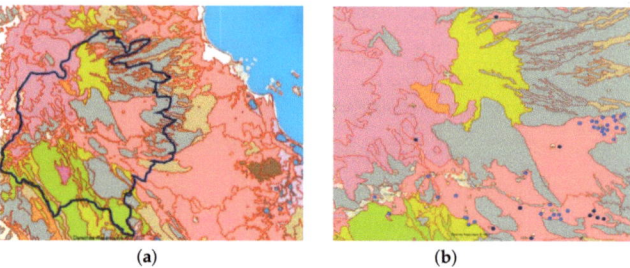

Figure 1. Types of soils present in the studied area include Andosol (purple), Leptosol (grey), Acrisol (green), Vertisol (pink), Umbrisol (mauve), Luvisol (chartreuse), Phaeozem (brown), Cambisol (orange), Chernozem (dark brown) and Arenosol (white) (**a**) and the samples location (blue spots) (**b**).

Specifically, the obtained soil samples were collected at the municipalities of Atoyac (18°55′00.0″ N 96°46′00.0″ W), Camaron de Tejeda (19°01′00.0″ N 96°37′00.0″ W), Carrillo Puerto (18°47′00.0″ N 96°34′00.0″), Coetzala (18°47′00.0″ N 96°55′00.0″ W), Ixtaczoquitlan (18°51′04.6″ N 97°03′04.4″ W), Cordoba (18°51′018.300″ N 96°57′002.200″ W), and El Naranjal (18°47′038.100″ N 96°55′030.5″ W), which are areas that traditionally cultivate sugarcane and include fertilizers, pesticides, herbicides and fuel in the processes of cultivation and harvesting [33].

2.2. Soil Sampling and Physicochemical Determinations

The sampling procedure implemented to obtain the soil samples was the one described in the standard SESDPROC-300-R3 (Environmental Protection Agency, 2014) and three samples were obtained from each site. One from 0 to 10 cm, another from 10 to 20 cm and a third from 20 to 30 cm. All of the samples were subjected to laboratory analysis to measure the following 27 physicochemical parameters: texture (%sand, %silt, and %clay); physical parameters: pH, electric conductivity, apparent density, field capacity 1/3 bar, and permanent wilting point 15 Bar; OM, CEC, Sodium (Na), CS for Na, and Hydrogen (H); macronutrients: phosphorus (P), Potassium (K), Calcium (Ca), Nitrogen–Nitrate (N_2–NO_3), K/Mg ratio, Ca/Mg ratio, Magnesium (Mg), Sulfur (S), CS for K, CS for Ca and CS for Mg; micronutrients: Boron (B), Copper (Cu), Iron (Fe), Manganese (Mn), and Zinc (Zn) . The textural analysis was performed using the Bouyoucos hydrometer, pH was measured by the 1:1 method ASTM D4972-13, electrical conductivity (EC) was measured by the conductimetry method, and apparent density was measured by the method proposed by the United States Department of Agriculture (USDA). The Walkley and Black method [34] (FAO, 2019) was conducted with the aim of determining the amount of OM expressed regarding total organic carbon. Atomic absorption spectrometry was used to determine the global composition of Na, K, Mg, and Ca in the soils. The composites were digested in hot HCl and deionized distilled water solution (2:1 ratio) and, afterwards, the solution was filtered and submitted for analysis. Exchangeable Cations, Nitrogen, Phosphorous, and S Exchangeable cations were measured using silver thiourea, following the method described by Pleyser and Juo [35]. Total nitrogen was measured by the Kjheldhal method, phosphorous was measured by colorimetry, and S was measured by turbidimetry.

2.3. Soil Aptitude Evaluation

The results obtained from the parameters measured by the laboratory were separated into 4 different groups, based on data from the literature of the desirable variables in the soil for higher production of sugarcane (16 variables were by this system) [4,36,37]. The four groups were the following: (1) unsuitable, (2) low, (3) media, and (4) high. Afterwards, the results were summarized in a final evaluation of three groups (good, medium and bad) using the following criteria: (1) Samples with 13% or less unsuitable values and eight parameters or more (out of 16) scoring high were considered to have good quality soils; (2) Samples with 62.5% of parameters in either medium, high or both were included in the medium group; (3) Samples having seven parameters in either unsuitable or low, or in the sum of both, were classified in the bad quality group. It must be mentioned that no samples were included in two groups with these rules.

2.4. Machine Learning

To achieve the objective of the present study and for better comprehension of the process, all the experiments evaluated with machine learning methodologies were segmented into four categories, listed and explained below. Figure 2 presents the schematic diagram of the methodology used in the present work.

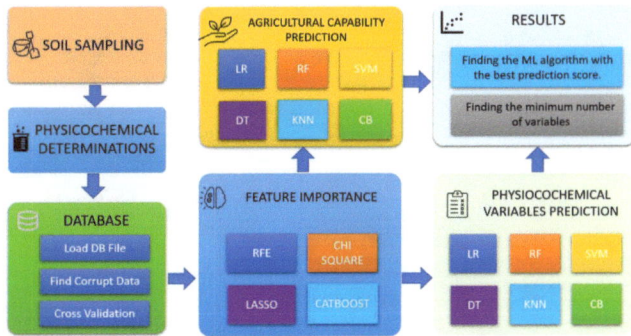

Figure 2. Schematic diagram of the applied methodology.

2.5. Feature Importance Analysis

The Recursive Feature Elimination (RFE), Chi Square, Least Absolute Shrinkage and Selection operator (LASSO) and Catboost (CB) algorithms were implemented to determine, in detail, the most relevant physicochemical parameters, by executing different machine learning models. The database from the laboratory analysis used for the experiments contained one hundred soil samples of the studied area. This database included the 28 parameters listed in the soil sampling physicochemical determination and the soil aptitude evaluation. All these parameters were evaluated with the four algorithms mentioned to determine the feature importance. The experiments and analysis of the data were developed in Python programming language using Sci-Kit learn libraries.

2.6. Agricultural Capability Prediction

Through the identification of relevant variables, another experiment was carried out to predict the aptitude of soil to grow sugarcane, with the objective of ascertaining how many variables could determine the capability of soil. Reducing the number of variables in the determination of the physicochemical parameters determining soil quality could decrease time and costs. The tests were implemented using 27, 8, 5 and 3 variables, according to the variables that showed higher importance in the Feature Importance Analysis executed. For the first experiment, all 27 variables were used and the capability of soil was the predicted variable. For the second experiment, 8 variables were used as inputs in the methodology (Soil pH, K, Ca, B, Zn, N_2-NO_3 CEC, CS for H, CS for Na) and the capability of soil was the predicted variable. For the experiment with five elements (K, Ca, Zn, CEC y CS for Na), the feature performance results obtained in the experiments were used. Finally, the experiments with three variables (K, Ca y CEC) were used to predict the capability of soil. These experiments were carried out by using the following machine learning techniques: linear regression (LR), Decision Tree (DT), Random Forest (RF), K Nearest Neighbor (KNN), Support Vector Machine (SVM) and Catboost (CB). To implement these methodologies, a cross validation of the data was executed to ensure the separation of the training data from the test data to avoid having significant variance that could lead to an error in the accuracy determination of each method. Another fundamental segment was the tuning of the hyperparameters, by implementing algorithms, such as Grid Search and Random Search, to find which variables were the more adequate hyperparameters to obtain better accuracy in predictions. Figure 3 shows the schematic diagram of the prediction of agricultural capability and the determination of physicochemical variables.

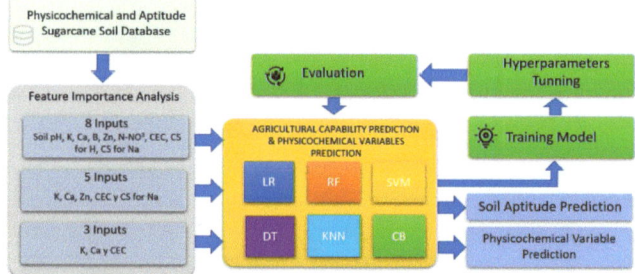

Figure 3. Schematic diagram of the prediction of agricultural capability and the determination of relevant physicochemical variables.

2.7. Physicochemical Variables Prediction

The last segment of the experimentation was focused on the determination of the physicochemical parameters in soil through the values of some of the parameters of higher importance. The present segment estimates a great variety of physicochemical parameters from a reduced number of known parameters. Three experiments were executed using different numbers of parameters, selected by relevance, and determined using different machine learning techniques, such as LR, DT, RF, KNN, SVM and CB. A prediction of different physicochemical parameters was determined. The first test was executed using the elements of Soil pH, Potassium, Ca, B, Zn, Nitrogen-Nitrate, CEC, CS H, CS for Na with the objective of predicting OM, P, Mg, S, Cu, Mn, Ca/Mg and Texture. In the second experiment, potassium, Ca, Zn, CEC, and CS for N were considered with the objective of predicting OM, P, Mg, S, B, Cu, Mn, Ca/Mg and texture. Finally, in the third experiment, three parameters were used, K, Ca, and CEC, to predict the values of the parameters of soil pH, OM, P, Mg, S, B, Cu, Mn, Zn, Ca/Mg and Texture. The results obtained enabled the accuracy of each ML technique for the prediction of each physicochemical property of soil to be ascertained. It also enabled determination of the accuracy of the predictions from a certain number of parameters (8, 5 and 3 elements).

3. Results

3.1. Soil Aptitude Evaluation

The results of the soil aptitude evaluation clearly indicated that pH, organic matter, phosphorus, potassium, calcium, conductivity, zinc, and nitrogen–nitrate marked important differences between bad and good soil aptitudes. Similarly, in the results indicating bad aptitude evaluation, a greater presence of elements such as sulfur, CS for H, CS for Na was found. The Figure 4 shows the results obtained from the physicochemical properties of the soils with respect to their soil aptitude classification.

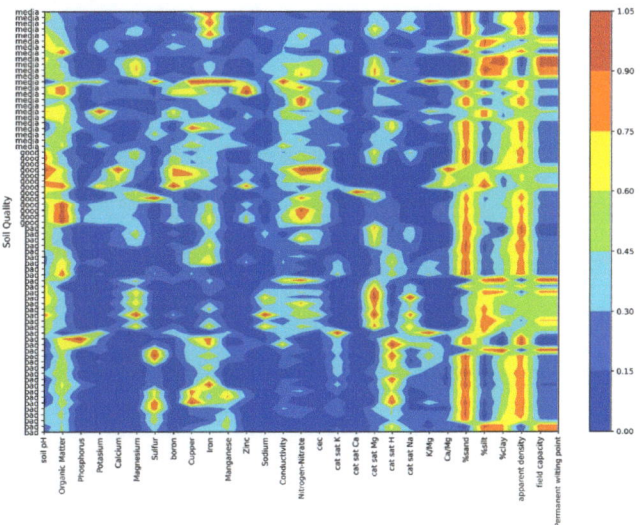

Figure 4. Soil Aptitude Evaluation.

3.2. Feature Importance Results

The physicochemical analyses performed in the previous section offered the possibility to determine the impact of each variable individually with respect to soil aptitude. However, it was important to perform an analysis of the behavior of each variable with respect to the others in order to know how they were interconnected and related to the soil aptitude evaluation. The results of this relevancy analysis indicated that K, Ca, Zn, CEC, and CS for Na were the parameters recognized by the four techniques (RFE, CHI SQUARE, LASSO, CB) as the relevant parameters in determining the soil aptitude of vertisol soil. There were also parameters, such as pH, B, N_2–NO_3 and CS H, where 3 techniques concurred in their importance (RFE, CHI SQUARE and LASSO). Figure 5 shows the results obtained by these 4 methods. These parameters of importance were used in the following experiments, wherein accuracy in the determination of soil aptitude using a reduced number of parameters was evaluated with data presented in this study.

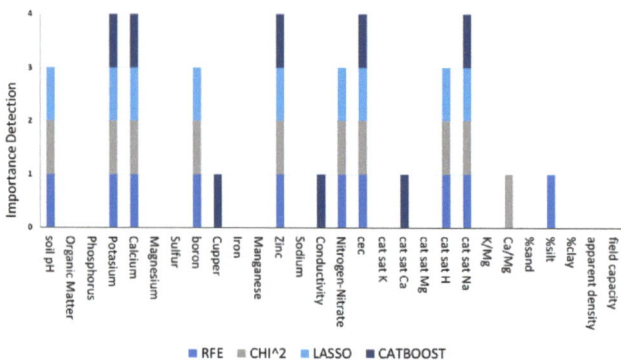

Figure 5. Feature Importance using RFE, Chi Square, LASSO and CB.

3.3. Agricultural Capability Prediction Results

The results found after implementing the ML algorithms showed the average of the accuracy results of the 6 algorithms with respect to the identification of the soil capability. After specifically analyzing the results by algorithm type, the following observations were made: by using 27 parameters as the input parameters in the ML algorithms, the highest average accuracy was obtained with CB 93%; when using 8 parameters the highest average accuracy was obtained with RF 91%; when using 5 parameters the highest average accuracy was achieved with LR 91%; when using 3 parameters there were two algorithms with the highest average accuracy, these being LR and KNN (91%). Figure 6 shows the best scores related to the accuracy of the ML algorithms in the soil quality prediction.

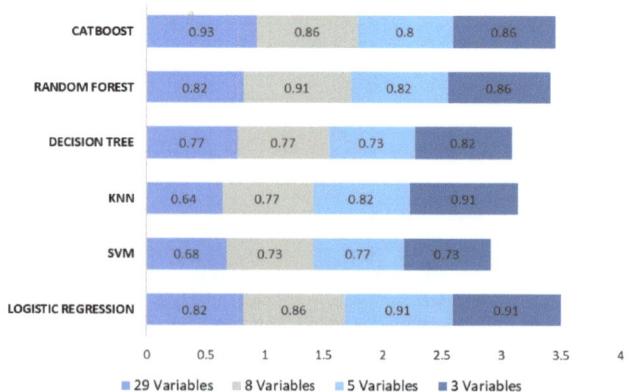

Figure 6. Features Importance using RFE, Chi Square, LASSO and CB.

3.4. Physicochemical Parameters Prediction Results

The experiments carried out in this section were focused on ascertaining the accuracy with which it was possible to determine the physicochemical parameters of soil from a reduced number of elements as input variables of the ML algorithms. In the first experiment, 8 elements (Soil pH, K, Ca, B, Zn, N_2–NO_3, CEC, CS H, CS Na) were used as the input parameters and it was possible to predict OM, P, Mg, S, Cu, Mn, Ca/Mg and Texture. Figure 7 shows the results focused on the evaluation of accuracy of the 6 machine learning algorithms executed in the predictions. It can be appreciated, from Figure 7, that, for each component to be predicted there was an algorithm that had the best accuracy and for each element to be predicted there was an algorithm presenting the best accuracy. Mostly, the CB algorithm presented the best accuracy globally with 71.5%. The one with the least accurate results was the DT algorithm with 58% accuracy. The parameters that could be predicted were OM (90% using CB), texture (77% using CB) and Mn (77% using LR) and the parameter with the least accurate result was P with 0.55 accuracy using LR. Figure 6 provides a graphic with the results of the best predictions for each element. To the left of the name of each element is the name of the ML algorithm executed with which the best result was obtained.

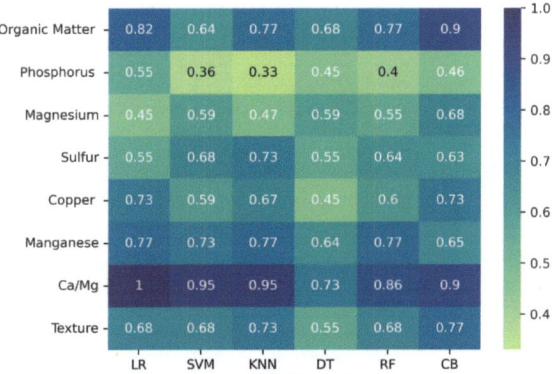

Figure 7. Accuracy of the Ml algorithms using 8 input variables.

In the second experiment, 5 elements (K, Ca, Zn, CEC and CS N) were implemented as inputs and it was possible to predict OM, P, Mg, S, B, Cu, Mn, Ca/Mg and texture. Figure 8 shows the results focusing on the evaluation of accuracy of the 6 ML algorithms used in the prediction. It can be appreciated from Figure 8 that, for each component being estimated or predicted, there was an algorithm that had great accuracy. Therefore, Figure 8 indicates which algorithm presented the best accuracy in prediction for each element. Broadly, 10 parameters were predicted with the KNN algorithm, which had the best global accuracy with 73.11%, and the least global accuracy was obtained with CB (64%). The parameters predicted with more accuracy were Ca/Mg (100% using KNN), B (86% using RF) and OM (86% using LR), and the parameter with less accuracy was P with 45% using LR. Figure 8 provides a graphic with the results of the predictions with the best accuracy for each element. To the left of the name of each element is the ML algorithm executed in which the best accuracy was obtained.

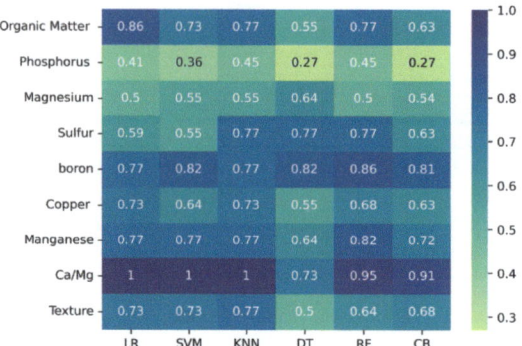

Figure 8. Accuracy of the ML algorithms using 5 input variables.

In the third experiment, 3 elements (K, Ca and CEC) were used as inputs for the evaluation and it was possible to predict soil pH, OM, P, Mg, S, B, Cu, Mn, Zn and Ca/Mg. Figure 9 shows the results focusing on the evaluation of the accuracy of the 6 ML algorithms used in the prediction. The general average of the prediction of the 12 parameters was best executed by the KNN algorithm, with a global accuracy of 68%, and the least accurate global result was obtained with the DT algorithm, with 68% accuracy. The parameters that could be predicted with higher accuracy were Ca/Mg (91% using SVM) and S (0.86 using RF) and the least accurate prediction was for P (36% using SVM). Figure 9 provides a graphic with the results of the best predictions for each element. To the left of the name of each element is the ML algorithm with which the best accuracy was obtained.

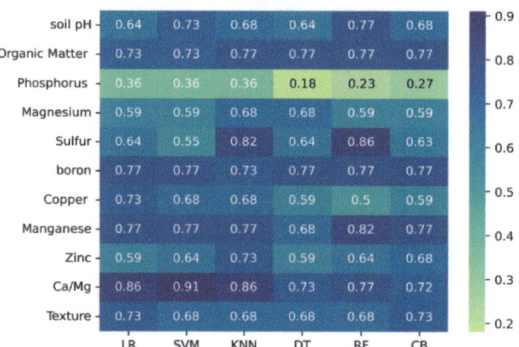

Figure 9. Accuracy of the ML algorithms using 3 input variables.

Figure 10 provides a radial graphic with the accuracy of the ML algorithms using 8, 5 and 3 elements as inputs. The average accuracy was 76% for 8 elements as inputs, 76% for 5 elements as inputs and 73% for 3 elements as inputs.

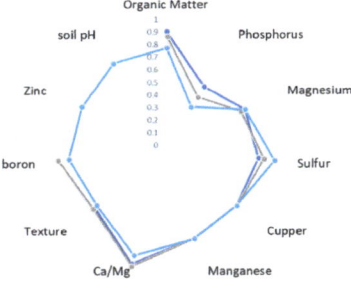

Figure 10. The average accuracy using 8, 5 and 3 elements as an input variables.

4. Discussion

The discussion of the present study is divided into three segments: relevant parameters, agricultural capability prediction and physicochemical parameters prediction. This study indicates that the four implemented techniques, RFE, CHI SQUARE, LASSO and CB, determined K, Ca, Zn, CEC and CS for Na as being the most relevant parameters for vertisol-type soil, and pH, B, N and CS H were determined to be relevant by three techniques (RFE, CHI SQUARE, and LASSO). Meanwhile, [27] determined available Phosphorus (P), available Potassium (K), organic carbon (OC), boron (B) and pH as being relevant for a village-wise soil by implementing Extreme Learning Machine (ELM) and [20] established that the relevant parameters were OC, N, pH, CEC, base saturation and exchangeable cation, when implementing quantile regression forest (QRF) and the cubist model (CB). It is important to implement various techniques to validate the parameters to be used.

In the segment regarding the agricultural capability prediction, the present research evaluated the relevance of different numbers of parameters, and had good accuracy results for the different techniques (77% to 93%) for specific technique and number of parameters. Other authors have also evaluated the prediction ability of different models, with accuracy results in the range of 85 to 95% [38,39] reported when implementing three algorithms, with Random forest having the highest accuracy (72%), which was below the results obtained in the present study, and, furthermore, the number of samples was not mentioned and neither was the percentage of data used for training the model.

From the results, it is possible to have higher accuracy in agricultural capability prediction using only three parameters for vertisol soils cultivated with sugarcane, these being those with higher significance, namely, K, Ca and CEC. Most of the producers add N, P and K fertilizers to soils because these have commonly been considered to increase yield, without evaluating the present state of the soils. It is remarkable that, from the present study, for one parameter to remain relevant is needs to connect with the rest of the parameters. Additionally, the CEC is connected to the presence of organic matter, which is known not only to be a relevant parameter to increase yield, but also soil structure, availability of other cations and pH. Finally, Ca is also relevant, as its presence complements the physical parameters and pH and the possible presence of complex structures that could affect or impact absorption and availability of minerals.

It can also be observed that with three parameters it is possible to have a system capable of great accuracy in predicting soil aptitude. The impact these results can have is relevant because the results indicate that it is not necessary to analyze all the parameters to determine the ability of soil to grow sugar cane. By implementing ML algorithms using K, Ca, and CEC as input parameters one can, with high accuracy, ascertain soil aptitude.

The third aspect to discuss is that the present study evaluated the possibility of predicting parameters from other soil physicochemical parameters. It was observed that 10 parameters were likely to be predicted with the KNN algorithm, which had the best global accuracy of 73%, while the least global accuracy was obtained with CB (64%). The parameters predicted with more accuracy were Ca/Mg (1.0 using KNN), B (86% using RF) and OM (86% using LR) and the parameter with least accuracy was P with 45%, using LR. Other authors have aimed to predict different parameters, with accuracy ranging from 86% to 97%, such as the following: exchangeable sodium percentage with different models (ANN (89%) and Adaptive Neuro Fuzzy Inference System (92%)) [40], OM with different models (Kennard-Stone (KS), Successive Projections Algorithm (SPA), Competitive adaptive weight weighting algorithm (CARS) and their combination).

5. Conclusions

The present study evaluated the potential of different ML algorithms in predicting the agricultural aptitude of soils with the least number of parameters and to determine if it was possible to predict some other parameters to reduce the amount of soil analysis in laboratories. After presenting the results, it can be concluded that the capability of Vertisol soils in sugarcane production can be determined with three parameters and excellent accuracy is obtained by using the KNN and LR algorithms. When evaluating the prediction parameters from other parameters, many excellent prediction results were obtained for different ML algorithms. These correlations can have an impact in developing countries on the methodologies implemented to determine the agricultural capability of soils, so as to help in increasing crop yields and coping with the environmental states of soils.

Author Contributions: Conceptualization, O.L.-E., N.A.V.C. and O.O.S.-G.; methodology, J.M.M.C., J.d.J.A.F.-C. and A.A.-L.; validation, J.M.M.C., J.d.J.A.F.-C., O.L.-E. and O.O.S.-G.; formal analysis, A.M.-S. and O.O.S.-G.; investigation, J.M.M.C., E.S.R.-M. and A.A.-L.; writing—original draft preparation, J.d.J.A.F.-C., O.L.E., N.A.V.C. and O.O.S.-G.; writing—review and editing, J.d.J.A.F.-C., A.A.-L., E.S.R.-M., A.M.-S., O.L.-E. and O.O.S.-G.; visualization, J.M.M.C., A.A.-L. and A.M.-S.; supervision, O.O.S.-G. and O.L.-E. All authors have read and agreed to the published version of the manuscript.

Funding: This research was funded by the Consejo Nacional de Ciencia y Tecnología (CONACYT), Sectorial fund of environmental, grant number 26282.

Informed Consent Statement: This work does not contain any studies with human participants performed by any of the authors.

Data Availability Statement: Dataset is uploaded on GitHub Repository name: Physicochemical-Analysis-Sugarcane-Soils, https://github.com/oosg/Physicochemical-Analysis-Sugarcane-Soils.git, accesed on 29 June 2023.

Acknowledgments: We are grateful to Tecnológico Nacional de México and CONACYT for the scholarships granted to the students for this project.

Conflicts of Interest: The authors declare no conflict of interest.The funders had no role in the design of the study; in the collection, analyses, or interpretation of data; in the writing of the manuscript, or in the decision to publish the results.

Abbreviations

The following abbreviations are used in this manuscript:

Ca	Calcium
Ca/Mg	Calcium/Magnesium
CARS	Competitive adaptive weight weighting algorithm
CB	CatBoost
CEC	Cation exchange capacity
CS H	Cationic Saturation for Hydrogen
CS N	Cationic Saturation for Nitrogen
Cu	Copper
DBSCAN	Density-Based Spatial Clustering of Applications with Noise
DL	Deep Learning
DT	Decision Tree
EO	Expert opinion
K	Potassium
KNN	K nearest neighbor
LASSO	least absolute shrinkage and selection operator
LR	Linear Regression
Mg	Magnesium
ML	Machine Learning
Mn	Manganese
N2-NO3	Nitrogen - Nitrate
NPK	Amount of Nitrogen, Phosphorus and Potassium
OC	Organic Carbon
OM	Organic Matter
P	Phosphorus
PCA	Principal Component Analysis
PCR	Principal Component Regression
pH	Potential of hydrogen
PLSR	Partial Least Squares Regression
RF	Random Forest
RFE	Recursive Feature Elimination
RR	Relative Risks
S	Sulfur
SIMPLS	An alternative approach to partial least squares regression
SPA	Smart Process Automation
SQI	Soil Quality Indexes
SVM	Support Vector Machine
VIRS	Visible near Infrared Spectroscopy
WNN	Wavelet Neural Network
Zn	Zinc

References

1. FAO. *International Soil Classification System for Naming Soils and Creating Legends for Soil Maps*; World Soil: Rome, Italy, 2015; p. 203. Available online: https://www.fao.org/3/i3794en/I3794en.pdf (accessed on 28 June 2023).
2. Secretaría de Agricultura, Ganadería, Desarrollo Rural, Pesca y Alimentación. Reporte Final de Producción de Caña y Azucar Zafra 2017/2018. 2018. Available online: https://www.gob.mx/cms/uploads/attachment/file/371833/REPORTE_FINAL_.pdf (accessed on 28 June 2023).
3. Durán, R.Q.; Sánchez, A.G.; Lombana, A.C.; Arboleda, F.M.; Aguas, J.S.T.; González, J.A.C.; Murillo, C.A.O. *Grupos Homogéneos de Suelos del área Dedicada al Cultivo de la caña de Azúcar en el valle del río Cauca (Segunda Aproximación)*; Publicación Cenicaña: Cali, Colombia, 2008.
4. Rivera, N.A.; Vargas, L.A.O.; Mendoza, G.G. Evaluación de aptitud de tierras al cultivo de caña de azúcar en la Huasteca potosina, México, por técnicas geomáticas. *Rev. Geogr. Norte Gd.* **2013**, *55*, 141–156. [CrossRef]
5. Chami, D.E.; Daccache, A.; Moujabber, M.E. What are the impacts of sugarcane production on ecosystem services and human well-being? A review. *Ann. Agric. Sci.* **2020**, *65*, 188–199. [CrossRef]
6. Sánchez, P.; Ortiz, C.; Gutiérrez, M.; Gómez, J. Local Land Classification and its Relationship with Sugarcane Crop in the South of Veracruz. *Terra* **2002**, *20*, 359–369.

7. Romero, J.R.; Roncallo, P.F.; Akkiraju, P.C.; Ponzoni, I.; Echenique, V.C.; Carballido, J.A. Using classification algorithms for predicting durum wheat yield in the province of Buenos Aires. *Comput. Electron. Agric.* **2013**, *96*, 173–179. [CrossRef]
8. Dorado, H.; Delerce, S.; Jimenez, D.; Cobos, C. Finding optimal farming practices to increase crop yield through global-best harmony search and predictive models, a data-driven approach. In *Lecture Notes in Computer Science (Including Subseries Lecture Notes in Artificial Intelligence and Lecture Notes in Bioinformatics)*; Springer: Berlin/Heidelberg, Germany, 2018; 11289 LNAI, pp. 15–29. [CrossRef]
9. Sethy, P.K.; Panigrahi, G.R.; Barpanda, N.K.; Behera, S.K.; Rath, A.K. *Application of Soft Computing in Crop Management*; Springer: Singapore, 2018; Volume 695, pp. 633–646. [CrossRef]
10. Moncada, M.P.; Gabriels, D.; Cornelis, W.M. Data-driven analysis of soil quality indicators using limited data. *Geoderma* **2014**, *235–236*, 271–278. [CrossRef]
11. Shankar, S.V.; Radha, M.; Kumaraperumal, R.; Gowsar, S.N. Statistical evaluation of physico-chemical properties of Soils of Coimbatore district using Dimensionality Reduction Technique S.Vishnu. *Int. Arch. Appl. Sci. Technol.* **2019**, *10*, 84–89. [CrossRef]
12. Tesfahunegn, G.B. Soil quality assessment strategies for evaluating soil degradation in Northern Ethiopia. *Appl. Environ. Soil Sci.* **2014**, *2014*, 646502. [CrossRef]
13. Armenise, E.; Redmile-Gordon, M.A.; Stellacci, A.M.; Ciccarese, A.; Rubino, P. Developing a soil quality index to compare soil fitness for agricultural use under different managements in the mediterranean environment. *Soil Tillage Res.* **2013**, *130*, 91–98. [CrossRef]
14. Vasu, D.; Singh, S.K.; Ray, S.K.; Duraisami, V.P.; Tiwary, P.; Chandran, P.; Nimkar, A.M.; Anantwar, S.G. Soil quality index (SQI) as a tool to evaluate crop productivity in semi-arid Deccan plateau, India. *Geoderma* **2016**, *282*, 70–79. [CrossRef]
15. de Paul Obade, V.; Lal, R. A standardized soil quality index for diverse field conditions. *Sci. Total Environ.* **2016**, *541*, 424–434. [CrossRef]
16. Lal, R. Restoring soil quality to mitigate soil degradation. *Sustainability* **2015**, *7*, 5875–5895. [CrossRef]
17. Shao, Z.; Zhang, L.; Wang, L. Stacked Sparse Autoencoder Modeling Using the Synergy of Airborne LiDAR and Satellite Optical and SAR Data to Map Forest Above-Ground Biomass. *IEEE J. Sel. Top. Appl. Earth Obs. Remote Sens.* **2017**, *10*, 5569–5582. [CrossRef]
18. Faming, H.; Jing, Z.; Chuangbing, Z.; Yuhao, W.; Jinsong, H.; Li, Z. A deep learning algorithm using a fully connected sparse autoencoder neural network for landslide susceptibility prediction. *Landslides* **2020**, *17*, 217–229. [CrossRef]
19. de Bem, P.P.; de Carvalho Júnior, O.A.; de Carvalho, O.L.F.; Gomes, R.A.T.; Fontes Guimarães, R. Performance Analysis of Deep Convolutional Autoencoders with Different Patch Sizes for Change Detection from Burnt Areas. *Remote Sens.* **2020**, *12*, 2576. [CrossRef]
20. Hounkpatin, K.O.; Bossa, A.Y.; Yira, Y.; Igue, M.A.; Sinsin, B.A. Assessment of the soil fertility status in Benin (West Africa)—Digital soil mapping using machine learning. *Geoderma Reg.* **2022**, *28*, e00444. [CrossRef]
21. Xu, M.; Chu, X.; Fu, Y.; Wang, C.; Wu, S. Improving the accuracy of soil organic carbon content prediction based on visible and near-infrared spectroscopy and machine learning. *Environ. Earth Sci.* **2021**, *80*, 326. [CrossRef]
22. Dong, Z.; Wang, N.; Liu, J.; Xie, J.; Han, J. Combination of machine learning and VIRS for predicting soil organic matter. *J. Soils Sediments* **2021**, *21*, 2578–2588. [CrossRef]
23. Wang, Z.; Wang, G.; Ren, T.; Wang, H.; Xu, Q.; Zhang, G. Assessment of soil fertility degradation affected by mining disturbance and land use in a coalfield via machine learning. *Ecol. Indic.* **2021**, *125*, 107608. [CrossRef]
24. Singh, B.; Sihag, P.; Pandhiani, S.M.; Debnath, S.; Gautam, S. Estimation of permeability of soil using easy measured soil parameters: Assessing the artificial intelligence-based models. *ISH J. Hydraul. Eng.* **2021**, *27*, 38–48. [CrossRef]
25. Vaheddoost, B.; Guan, Y.; Mohammadi, B. Application of hybrid ANN-whale optimization model in evaluation of the field capacity and the permanent wilting point of the soils. *Environ. Sci. Pollut. Res.* **2020**, *27*, 13131–13141. [CrossRef]
26. Helfer, G.A.; Barbosa, J.L.V.; dos Santos, R.; da Costa, A.B. A computational model for soil fertility prediction in ubiquitous agriculture. *Comput. Electron. Agric.* **2020**, *175*, 105602. [CrossRef]
27. Suchithra, M.S.; Pai, M.L. Improving the prediction accuracy of soil nutrient classification by optimizing extreme learning machine parameters. *Inf. Process. Agric.* **2020**, *7*, 72–82. [CrossRef]
28. Pandith, V.; Kour, H.; Singh, S.; Manhas, J.; Sharma, V. Performance Evaluation of Machine Learning Techniques for Mustard Crop Yield Prediction from Soil Analysis. *J. Sci. Res.* **2020**, *64*, 394–398. [CrossRef]
29. Peethambaran, B.; Anbalagan, R.; Kanungo, D.P.; Goswami, A.; Shihabudheen, K.V. A comparative evaluation of supervised machine learning algorithms for township level landslide susceptibility zonation in parts of Indian Himalayas. *Catena* **2020**, *195*, 104751. [CrossRef]
30. Wu, C.; Chen, Y.; Hong, X.; Liu, Z.; Peng, C. Evaluating soil nutrients of Dacrydium pectinatum in China using machine learning techniques. *Forest Ecosyst.* **2020**, *7*, 30. [CrossRef]
31. Inazumi, S.; Intui, S.; Jotisankasa, A.; Chaiprakaikeow, S.; Kojima, K. Artificial intelligence system for supporting soil classification. *Results Eng.* **2020**, *8*, 100188. [CrossRef]
32. Yang, M.; Xu, D.; Chen, S.; Li, H.; Shi, Z. Evaluation of machine learning approaches to predict soil organic matter and pH using vis-NIR spectra. *Sensors* **2019**, *19*, 263. [CrossRef] [PubMed]

33. Meza-Palacios, R.; Aguilar-Lasserre, A.A.; Morales-Mendoza, L.F.; Pérez-Gallardo, J.R.; Rico-Contreras, J.O.; Avarado-Lassman, A. Life cycle assessment of cane sugar production: The environmental contribution to human health, climate change, ecosystem quality and resources in México. *J. Environ. Sci. Health-Part A Toxic Hazard. Subst. Environ. Eng.* **2019**, *54*, 668–678. [CrossRef]
34. FAO. Standard operating procedure for soil organic carbon Walkley-Black method. *Glob. Soil Lab. Netw.* **2019**, *1*, 1–25.
35. Pleysier, J.L.; Juo, A.S.R. A single-extraction method using silver-thiourea for measuring exchangeable cations and effective CEC in soil with variable charges. *Soil Sci.* **1980**, *129*, 205–211.
36. Chaves, M. Nutrición y Fertilización de la Caña de Azúcar en Costa Rica. In *XI Congreso Nacional Agronómico/III Congreso Nacional de Suelos*; Sistema Integrado de Información Documental Centroamericano: San José, Costa Rica, 1999; pp. 193–214.
37. *Norma Oficial Mexicana NOM-021-RECNAT-2000, Que Establece las Especificaciones de Fertilidad, Salinidad y Clasificación de Suelos, Estudios, Muestreo y anáLisis*; Diario Oficial de la Federación: Ciudad de México, México, 2002; pp. 1–65. Available online: https://faolex.fao.org/docs/pdf/mex50674.pdf (accessed on 28 June 2023).
38. Wu, X.; Wang, Q.; Liu, M.; Wu, Y. In-situ soil moisture sensing. *ACM Trans. Sens. Netw.* **2012**, *8*, 1–30. [CrossRef]
39. Kumar, T.G.K.; Shubha, C.; Sushma, S.A. *Random Forest Algorithm for Soil Fertility Prediction and Grading Using Machine Learning*; Blue Eyes Intelligence Engineering and Sciences Publication: Bhopal, India, 2019; Volume 9, pp. 1301–1304. [CrossRef]
40. Keshavarzi, A.; Bagherzadeh, A.; Omran, E.S.E.; Iqbal, M. Modeling of soil exchangeable sodium percentage using easily obtained indices and artificial intelligence-based models. *Model. Earth Syst. Environ.* **2016**, *2*, 130. [CrossRef]

Disclaimer/Publisher's Note: The statements, opinions and data contained in all publications are solely those of the individual author(s) and contributor(s) and not of MDPI and/or the editor(s). MDPI and/or the editor(s) disclaim responsibility for any injury to people or property resulting from any ideas, methods, instructions or products referred to in the content.

Article

Complex Agent for Phosphate Sequestration from Digested Sludge Liquor: Performances and Economic Cost Analysis

Shi Yan [1], Li Nie [1,*], Juan Ren [2], Wei Wang [3,4], Jingtao Xu [5], Ning Wang [5] and Qian Zhao [5,*]

[1] School of Business Administration, Shandong University of Finance and Economics, Jinan 250014, China; 20053821@sdufe.edu.cn
[2] Jinan Urban Planning and Design Institute, Jinan 250001, China; renjuan379@126.com
[3] Shandong Institute of Geological Sciences, Jinan 250013, China; veily91@163.com
[4] Key Laboratory of Gold Mineralization Processes and Resources Utilization, Key Laboratory of Metallogenic-Geologic Processes and Comprehensive Utilization of Minerals Resources in Shandong Province, Jinan 250013, China
[5] School of Municipal and Environmental Engineering, Shandong Jianzhu University, Jinan 250101, China; xujingtao@sdjzu.edu.cn (J.X.); wangning@sdjzu.edu.cn (N.W.)
* Correspondence: 20068472@sdufe.edu.cn (L.N.); zhaoqian@sdjzu.edu.cn (Q.Z.)

Abstract: Phosphorus (P) management in the "water-energy-resource-nexus" in wastewater treatment plants (WWTPs) remains a longstanding challenge. P adsorption from the P-enriched digested sludge liquor (DSL) is a comparatively more practical and economically viable approach for P recovery in WWTPs. However, high concentrations of impurities in DSL might pose a negative and interferential effect on P adsorption, hindering the application of sorbents or precipitation methods. Given such a situation, highly efficient and cost-effective sorbent towards P reclamation from DSL is highly needed. Therefore, this study aims to develop a novel complex agent containing aluminum coagulant and superparamagnetic nano-sorbent (SNS) that can be used in magnetic seeding coagulation for P recovery. The complex agents with different PACl: SNS ratios showed varied turbidity removal rates and P recovery efficiencies and the optimal ratio was 15 mg PACl: 15 g SNS. PAC and SNS showed significant interaction because PAC could enhance P adsorption by shielding the interferential effect of colloidal impurities. In addition, the complex is highly regenerative, with turbidity and P removal rate stably maintained at 70–80% after 10 adsorption/regeneration cycles. The cost–benefit analysis of the dosing complex agent showed a dosing cost of 0.154 EUR/m3, admittedly much higher than the conventional magnetic seeding coagulation, which could probably be covered by the profit if the expensive and rare P product is reclaimed. This work indicated that the complex agent was superior due to its high adsorption capacity, easy separation, and repeated dosing, and therefore had the potential for P recovery from DSL.

Keywords: phosphorus recovery; digested sludge liquor; magnetic seeding coagulation; superparamagnetic nano-sorbents; economic cost

Citation: Yan, S.; Nie, L.; Ren, J.; Wang, W.; Xu, J.; Wang, N.; Zhao, Q. Complex Agent for Phosphate Sequestration from Digested Sludge Liquor: Performances and Economic Cost Analysis. *Processes* **2023**, *11*, 2050. https://doi.org/10.3390/pr11072050

Academic Editor: Antoni Sánchez

Received: 7 June 2023
Revised: 4 July 2023
Accepted: 7 July 2023
Published: 9 July 2023

Copyright: © 2023 by the authors. Licensee MDPI, Basel, Switzerland. This article is an open access article distributed under the terms and conditions of the Creative Commons Attribution (CC BY) license (https://creativecommons.org/licenses/by/4.0/).

1. Introduction

Nowadays, phosphorus (P) resource management is like a missing piece of the puzzle in the "water-energy-resource- nexus" in wastewater treatment plants (WWTPs). P pollutants in the domestic wastewater, with total phosphorus (TP) of 5–15 mg/L and annually discharged amount of 3.78 million tons globally, have been generally recovered with low fraction [1,2]. More than 90% of phosphorus in sewage is channeled into waste bio-sludge discharged from the biological process, especially from the enhanced biological phosphorus removal-centered bio-treatment facilities, resulting in high loads of P-enriched sewage sludge for digestion, dewatering, and final disposal [3]. Indeed, most of the P in the sewage sludge would be released into the liquid phase again under anaerobic conditions in a digester, generating P-rich digested sludge liquor (DSL), the total phosphorus in which was 87–478 mg/L at a pH of 4–5 [1]. It is more practical and economically viable to grasp P from the P-enriched sludge liquor than that from raw wastewater due to its large volume and low P concentration. As the WWTPs are undergoing a paradigm shift of treatment processes towards great environmental and economic sustainability, the current simple-removal philosophy for total phosphorus pollutants needs to be re-examined and P recovery addressed, especially considering the energy-intensive and water-consuming mining of phosphate rock [2].

The most viable option for P recovery is struvite (magnesium ammonium phosphate, $MgNH_4PO_4 \cdot 6H_2O$) or hydroxyapatite (CaP) crystallization. By adding Ca^{2+} and Mg^{2+} to the sludge liquor containing ammonia nitrogen and phosphate, struvite crystals formed and could be separated from the wastewater for later agricultural use as a slow-release fertilizer. The stable and effective Ca/struvite precipitation has been firmly established in Western European countries. In particular, many technologies, such as the DHV Crystalactor^{TM}, Pelletiser FIX-Phosand P-RoC®, etc., have gained success in the market [4–6]. Temperature-, Mg/P-, N/P-, and pH-controlling strategies are no easy tasks for optimal crystal formation and crystal growth. For instance, Guadie et al. found that the optimal conditions for forming struvite crystals were in neutral or slightly acidic environments, while there was almost no struvite crystal formation in phosphate once the pH value increased beyond 10.5 [7]. Aside from the P pollutants, DSL might also contain high concentrations of suspended solids (1000–2400 mg/L) [8]. Therefore, the large amount of organic matter in the sludge liquor might have an adverse effect on the crystallization process, producing low-quality P end-product.

Actually, the magnetic adsorption and separation method might be a "one stone two birds" strategy for P recovery from DSL. On one hand, the superparamagnetic nano-sorbent (SNS) developed based on the layered double hydroxide (LDH) or metallic oxides could provide a new idea for the rapid and efficient recovery of phosphate. SNS is composed of superparamagnetic nanomagnetic cores (Fe_3O_4 magnetite embedded in a porous SiO_2 matrix) and an LDH surface, which serves as the active phosphate adsorption center, while the Fe_3O_4 magnetic core serves as the carrier. SNS is easy to be separated from the liquid phase in a magnetic field. After being modified with various transitional metals, SNS could sequestrate P with high adsorption capacity [9–11]. Selectively, SNS has been found to exhibit high selectivity in the presence of competing ions due to the stronger complexation between phosphate and LDH loaded on SNS. In addition, SNS could be easily regenerated using NaOH or KOH. As revealed by Drenkova-Tuhtan et al., a high P removal rate (>90%) could be achieved even after 60 adsorption–desorption cycles [12]. On the other hand, magnetic particles combined with flocculation, i.e., the newly emerging magnetic seeding coagulation process attracting great attention for offering advantages of high turbidity removal, settleability improvement, and low energy consumption compared to the traditional coagulation process. The coagulants (polyamine chloride or polyferric chloride, PACl or PFC) mixed with magnetic seeds could remove more turbidities than the sole use of PACl. For example, the magnetic seeds could improve the aggregation and precipitation of nanoparticles from palm oil wastewater treatment, swine wastewater, textile wastewater, etc. [13–15]. Therefore, as for the treatment of P-enriched waste sludge, there is a need to rethink the management strategy of this coagulation process and to consider whether the seeds in the magnetic seeding coagulation process could be replaced with SNS. As such, magnetic coagulation and SNS adsorption have complementary advantages and can be combined or integrated, with phosphate being "recovered" rather than "removed".

In recent years, comprehensive studies have been conducted for the synthesis of superparamagnetic P nano-sorbents. Nano-size core-shell Fe_3O_4@LDHs composites with good super-paramagnetism were prepared by Yan et al., and the batch experiments results revealed an adsorption capacity of 36.9 mg/g by Fe_3O_4@Zn-Al-LDH, with P recovered after 10 s separation from aqueous solution by introducing an external magnetic field [16]. Instead of LDH synthesis, the magnetic nanoparticles composed of zirconium-iron oxides were prepared and the P adsorption capacity could be enhanced with the decrease in Fe/Zr molar ratios. This nano-sorbent showed high adsorption and strong selectivity toward phosphate with co-existing ions such as Cl^-, SO_4^{2-}, NO_3^-, etc., and the selectivity could be improved by doping transitional metals such as Zr, La, Se, or Hf [17,18]. Drenkova-Tuhtan et al. reported a pilot study of the reliability of superparamagnetic ZnFeZr nano-sorbent treating P-containing wastewater, with a P recovery rate of >90% and effluent phosphate concentration of <0.05 mg/L [3]. The novel magnetically recoverable magnetite/lanthanum hydroxides were also investigated for phosphate sequestration in a lake. However, the phosphate sorption efficiency could be significantly attenuated by 34–45% compared to that in water solution due to the interference from lake sediment substances [4]. Similarly, the impurities in sludge liquor might not only have an interferential effect on the P adsorption, but also result in the inactive adsorption sites during the sorbent regeneration. By now, little information is available for the integration of PACl and SNS and little research has been conducted for simultaneous SS removal and P recovery by dosing this type of complex agent. The role of PACl in the complex agent has not been investigated from the perspective of P recovery.

In this study, complex agents were prepared by combining aluminum coagulant (PACl) and SNS and used for P recovery from DSL. The novel agents were characterized in terms of P adsorption capacity, turbidity removal, and reusability. The coupling mechanism between PACl and SNS and the economic cost were also discussed. The specific objectives were to (1) prepare the complex agent and investigate the turbidity removal, P adsorption performances, and reusability; (2) investigate the effect of dissolved organic matter (DOM) in the DSL and elucidate the interaction mechanism between PACL and SNS in the complex agent; and (3) evaluate the economic cost of dosing the complex agent and make a comparison with the conventional magnetic seeding coagulation.

2. Materials and Methods

2.1. Complex Agent and DSL Characteristics

Complex agents were prepared by mixing PACl ($AlCl_3 \cdot 6H_2O$) and synthesized SNSs with different mass ratios. These super-paramagnetic nanoparticles were prepared using the co-precipitation method. Firstly, the $Fe_3O_4@SiO_2$ superparamagnetic nano or ultrafine particles were synthesized. Then, by calcination of Mg/Al LDH by dissolving $MgCl_2 \cdot H_2O$ and $AlCl_3 \cdot H_2O$ in a basic solution, La-LDH crystals were formed. Thereafter, the La-LDH was surface-modified by lanthanum-hydroxides loading with the pH maintained at 10. Finally, after crystallization in an 80 °C bath and washing with boiling deionized water and anhydrous ethanol repeatedly till the pH reached neutral, the MgAl-La-LDH loaded onto the $Fe_3O_4@SiO_2$ particles and SNSs were dried and finally harvested. The detailed procedures have been revealed by Zhao et al. [18]. Afterward, the surface configurations of the complex agent and SNSs were analyzed with a scanning electron microscope (SEM, ZEISS Gemini SUPRA55, Germany).

DSL was obtained from the lab-scale mesophilic digester (operating at 35 °C), which was fed with excess activated sludge in the WWTP treating domestic sewage in Shandong Jianzhu University. The detailed composition of DSL is shown in Table 1. Orthophosphate was the main component of the total dissolved P. In addition, according to ICP-AES analysis, the content of Zn was detected as 0.3~0.5 mg/L, while the concentration of other heavy metals, such as Cu, Pb, As, Cd, Cr, and Zn, was below the detecting limit.

Table 1. Typical water quality parameters or components of DSL.

Term	DSL
Total dissolved P (mg/L)	22.6 ± 1.4
Orthophosphate (mg/L)	20.3 ± 0.9
HCO_3^- (mg $CaCO_3$/L)	57.2 ± 0.7
Cl^- (mg/L)	47.6 ± 2.8
SO_4^{2-} (mg/L)	5.2 ± 0.3
SS (mg/L)	135 ± 18
Zn^{2+} (mg/L)	0.4 ± 0.1
Extracellular protein (mg/L)	20.5 ± 1.3
Polysaccharide (mg/L)	28.4 ± 0.7
pH	6.4 ± 0.2

Note: All the values in the table are written as "mean ± standard deviation".

2.2. Adsorption and Clarification Batch Experiments

The complex agents, with PACl and SNS ingredients at different mass ratios (25 mg:5 g, 20 mg:10 g, 15 mg:15 g, 10 mg:25 g, and 5 mg:30 g), were respectively dosed into 5 jars containing 100 mL DSL at room temperature. These jars were capped and vigorously shaken in a shaker at 120 rpm for 12 h to reach saturation (pre-determined in the previous P adsorption-equilibrium test). Afterward, the supernatant was decanted through a magnet and filtered with a 0.45 μm filter, the TP concentration was determined according to the standard molybdenum blue method, and turbidity was assayed using a turbidimeter (HACH TU5200) [19]. The P removal performance was determined by calculating the ratio of the P loading amount (mg P/g) to the original P amount in DSL.

The adsorption capacity for phosphate at different equilibrium concentrations could be described by adsorption isotherms. The isotherm test was conducted by exposing 0.5–2.5 g dry mass of complex agent (with the PACl: SNS ratio as 15 mgPACl: 15 g SNS) to a 100 mL aqueous solution containing phosphate with a concentration of 20 mg P/L at room temperature. After 12 h agitation in a shaker at 120 rpm, q_e (mg/g), i.e., the amount of phosphate loaded per unit mass of the complex agent at the equilibrium, the maximum adsorption capacity can be determined. To fit the equilibrium data, Langmuir and Freundlich isotherm models were used, with equations defined as follows:

$$q_e = q_m K_L C_e / (1 + K_L C_e) \quad (1)$$

$$q_e = k_f C_e^{1/n} \quad (2)$$

in which Ce (mg/L) is the phosphate equilibrium concentration. kf ((mg/g)/(mg/L)1/n) and KL (L/mg) are the Freundlich and Langmuir adsorption equilibrium constants, respectively. q_m represents the maximum adsorption capacity (mg/g). n is a constant indicating the Freundlich isotherm curvature. Each sample was assayed in triplicates. Results are shown as the means and standard deviations (error bars) of 3 replicates per point.

The extracellular protein and polysaccharide were determined by the Lowry method and anthrone colorimetry [20,21], respectively. The pH value was measured with a pH electrode (Leici PHS-25). Cl^- and SO_4^{2-} concentrations were quantified using IC (ICS-5000+, Thermo Scientific) (Jackson). All the assays were conducted in triplicate. The raw DSL-filtered samples before and after batch tests were also analyzed by the dimensional excitation-emission matrix (EEM) fluorescence technique using a fluorescence spectrophotometer (F-4500, Hitachi, Japan). An excitation range of 200–400 nm and an emission range of 220–550 nm were employed.

2.3. Desorption and Regeneration Experiments

P recovery rates and the reusability of the magnetic seeds, i.e., SNS in the complex agent, were tested within 10 treatment/reuse (adsorption/desorption) cycles. The desorption experiment, i.e., the PACl regeneration experiment in cycle 1, was conducted with

100 mL DSL dosed with a complex agent containing PACl and SNSs (15 mg:15 g). After 12 h agitation and 15 min sedimentation, 1 mL supernatant was taken to determine the turbidity and orthophosphate content, with P adsorption capacity (q_0) and turbidity removal rate calculated. The SNSs in the exhausted agent were separated with a magnet, rinsed with deionized water, and regenerated in 100 mL 2M NaOH solution for 12 h. 2M NaOH solution, as a generative agent, was prepared in advance, and OH^- in NaOH caused the outer-sphere complexation (phosphate and SNS) to proceed in converse, leading to new "adsorption sites" for phosphate in the next cycle of adsorption [11]. Then, the amount of phosphate in the supernatant (i.e., the desorption amount) was determined, with the P recovery rate calculated. Afterward, these SNSs were rinsed, dried, and mixed with 15 mg PACl before dosing into another 100 mL DSL. Thus, cycle 2 of adsorption started, with the P adsorption capacity in cycle 2 (q_1) being calculated. Therefore, the SNS regeneration efficiency in cycle 1 was determined by calculating the ratio of q_0/q_1. Procedures were repeated in cycles 3–10, with ratios of q_i/q_0 calculated. The desorption and regeneration tests were performed in triplicate.

2.4. Chemicals

$AlCl_3 \cdot 6H_2O$, NaOH, $FeCl_3 \cdot 6H_2O$, $FeSO_4 \cdot 7H_2O$, $NaHCO_3$, and lanthanum oxides were purchased from the Sinopharm Chemical Reagent Co., Ltd. (Beijing, China). Ethanol (CH_3CH_2OH), hydrochloric acid (HCl), anthrone, and chemicals used in the Lowry method were purchased from Aladdin (Shanghai, China).

2.5. Method of Calculation on Dosing Cost

The cost of dosing commercial magnetic powder and coagulants should be the product of dosage and the market uni-price. For SNS dosing, the cost should be the product of dosage and the manufacturing cost (sum of the reagents involved and the main expensive processing). As for complex agents, the cost should be calculated as the sum of the cost of SNSs and coagulant dosage. Lost amounts, especially for magnetic sorbents, should also be taken into account.

3. Results

3.1. Structural Characterizations of the Complex Agent

The SEM pattern of the complex agent and SNS are presented in Figure 1a,b, respectively. Both the complex agent and SNS composites had relatively regular shapes and smooth surfaces, without any noticeable difference between them. This could be explained by the dominantly high content of SNS in the complex agent. Maybe the complex agent showed seemingly little pores, which was probably due to the presence of powdered PACl. The complex agent for both bare SNS and the complex agent showed unclear core-shell structure, with a diameter ranging from 10 to 50 nm.

Figure 1. SEM image of (**a**) complex agent and (**b**) SNS.

3.2. TP and Turbidity Removal Performance by Complex Agent

Figure 2 exhibits the effect of the ratio of PACl and SNS mass in the mixtures on the turbidity removal rate and TP recovery efficiency. The turbidity removal performance varied with the PACl: SNS ratio in the dosed mixtures, with removal rates of 82.4%, 90.4%, 93.5%, 77.3%, and 70.2% after dosing 25 mg:5 g, 20 mg:10 g, 15 mg:15 g, 10 mg:25 g, and 5 mg:30 g of PACl: SNS, respectively. A dramatic decrease in removal efficiency was observed when dosing less than 10 mg/L of PACl, while, comparatively, more turbidities were removed when dosing >15 mg/L of PACl in the presence of PACl. 15 mg:15 g achieved the highest turbidity removal efficiency, because, at those dosages, the PACl played the primary role in the coagulation of colloidal or solid matter, while the SNS served as the magnetic seeds which benefited floc aggregation and precipitation. This result was consistent with the results reported by Lv et al. [22], who believed that the applied magnetic field could achieve effective sedimentation of the looser flocs and less production of fragments compared to the sole coagulation process, therefore resulting in improved turbidity removal rate. A dramatic decrease in the turbidity removal efficiency was observed when dosing 5 and 10 mg/L of PACl, although the component SNS simultaneously dosed was >25 g. This could be explained by the relatively high concentration of flocs in DSL and low concentration of coagulant dosed, which resulted in fewer opportunities for particle collision, and finally a lower coagulation efficiency [23]. According to previous literature, magnetic nanomaterials could affect sludge properties and extracellular polymer behavior by aggregating colloids into large flocs and greatly improve the separation performance of sludge and water. As a result, magnetic nanomaterials combined with macroscopic magnetic fields could promote a sludge dewatering effect and provide a relatively clarified supernatant for P sequestration [24,25].

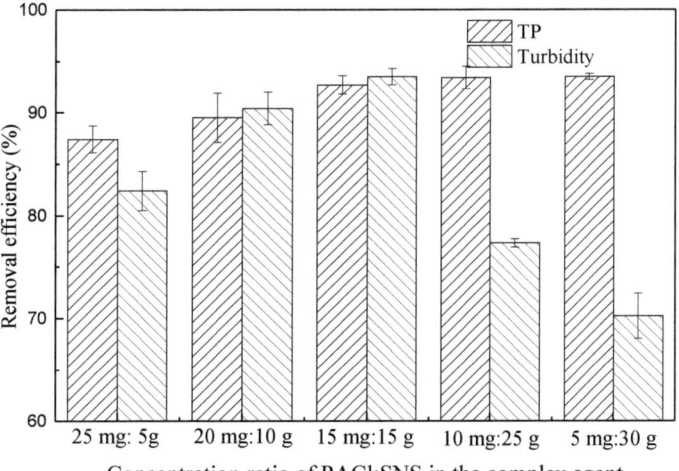

Figure 2. TP recovery and turbidity removal efficiency by complex agent-treating DSL.

As for the TP removal performance, the complex agent achieved removal efficiencies of >85% no matter how much the PACl and SNS ingredients were in the dosing mixtures. This could be explained by the similar P removal efficiency of PACl and SNS in spite of different mechanisms. PACl was precipitated with phosphorus while SNS grasped phosphorus by the means of adsorption or complexation reaction. After dosing the agent containing 15 mg

PACL and 15 g PACl, 93.5% of turbidity and phosphorus were simultaneously removed. During this process, The SNS particles instantly absorbed phosphate, and residual DOM and colloidal particles in the sludge liquor clustered with PACl, with the floc size increasing with the SNS particles as magnetic seeding.

Figure 3 presents the phosphate adsorption isotherm with complex agent/sole SNS plotted against different equilibrium P concentrations. The previous literature revealed that isotherm figures of P adsorption by SNS were more propitious to the Freundlich equation [11]. This tied well with the Freundlich-fitting curve in this study (R^2 = 0.951) in comparison with Langmuir-fitting results (R^2 = 0.883), which assumed multilayer covering is an adsorbent heterogeneous surface in which adsorption energy declined depending on the surface covering. However, the Freundlich model did not fit the data for the phosphate adsorption equilibrium experiment using the complex agent, with a coefficient of determination of R^2 = 0.8653. This explained the complicated P removal process driven by the complex agent. The P precipitation by the coagulant component and the P adsorption process by SNS could not be described by a pure adsorption model.

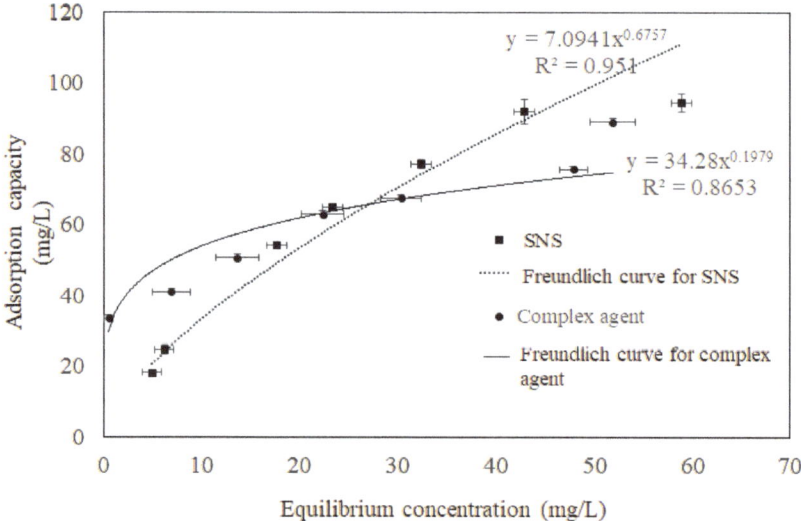

Figure 3. Phosphate adsorption isotherm with complex agent and sole SNS.

3.3. Reusability of Complex Agent

TP and turbidity removal performance by the complex agent during 10 cycles of treatment/reuse cycles is shown in Figure 4. The reusability test of SNS-PACl mixtures confirmed the effective recovery of SNS from flocs after applying a magnetic field, generating a 45% lower volume of particles compressed with PACl compared to that without SNS. During 10 cycles of SNSs recovery and PACl replenishment, the constantly stable turbidity removal performance was observed, with the removal percentage at the 10th cycle maintained at 70–80% of the original level in the 1st cycle. The DOC in the liquor followed similar patterns as turbidity, with concentration ranging from 814.8 mg/L to 903.2 mg/L. The relatively sharp reduction in turbidity removal rate after cycle 5 indicated that the 5th cycle might be the optimal cycle for this process. It was noteworthy that sole SNS without PACl also removed a small proportion of turbidity, which could be explained by the enmeshment and sweeping effect.

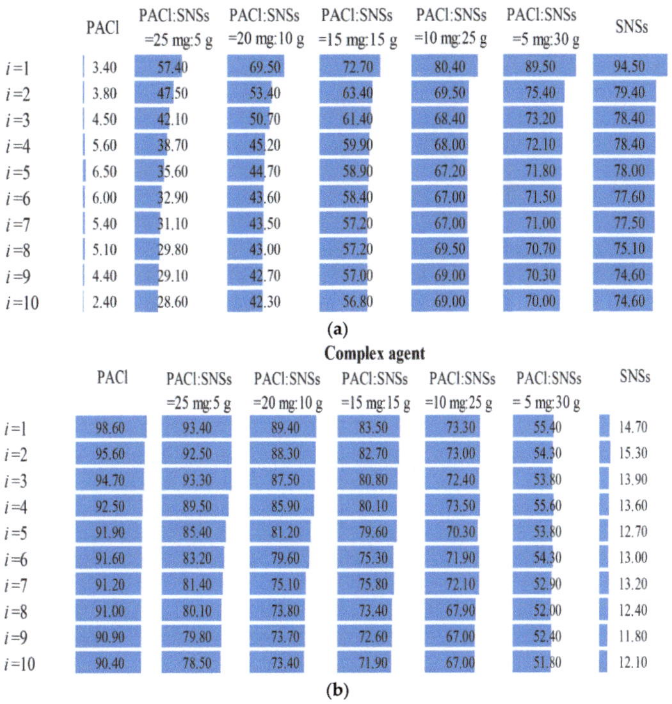

	PACl	PACl:SNSs =25 mg:5 g	PACl:SNSs =20 mg:10 g	PACl:SNSs =15 mg:15 g	PACl:SNSs =10 mg:25 g	PACl:SNSs =5 mg:30 g	SNSs
$i=1$	3.40	57.40	69.50	72.70	80.40	89.50	94.50
$i=2$	3.80	47.50	53.40	63.40	69.50	75.40	79.40
$i=3$	4.50	42.10	50.70	61.40	68.40	73.20	78.40
$i=4$	5.60	38.70	45.20	59.90	68.00	72.10	78.40
$i=5$	6.50	35.60	44.70	58.90	67.20	71.80	78.00
$i=6$	6.00	32.90	43.60	58.40	67.00	71.50	77.60
$i=7$	5.40	31.10	43.50	57.20	67.00	71.00	77.50
$i=8$	5.10	29.80	43.00	57.20	69.50	70.70	75.10
$i=9$	4.40	29.10	42.70	57.00	69.00	70.30	74.60
$i=10$	2.40	28.60	42.30	56.80	69.00	70.00	74.60

(a)

Complex agent

	PACl	PACl:SNSs =25 mg:5 g	PACl:SNSs =20 mg:10 g	PACl:SNSs =15 mg:15 g	PACl:SNSs =10 mg:25 g	PACl:SNSs =5 mg:30 g	SNSs
$i=1$	98.60	93.40	89.40	83.50	73.30	55.40	14.70
$i=2$	95.60	92.50	88.30	82.70	73.00	54.30	15.30
$i=3$	94.70	93.30	87.50	80.80	72.40	53.80	13.90
$i=4$	92.50	89.50	85.90	80.10	73.50	55.60	13.60
$i=5$	91.90	85.40	81.20	79.60	70.30	53.80	12.70
$i=6$	91.60	83.20	79.60	75.30	71.90	54.30	13.00
$i=7$	91.20	81.40	75.10	75.80	72.10	52.90	13.20
$i=8$	91.00	80.10	73.80	73.40	67.90	52.00	12.40
$i=9$	90.90	79.80	73.70	72.60	67.00	52.40	11.80
$i=10$	90.40	78.50	73.40	71.90	67.00	51.80	12.10

(b)

Figure 4. The variation of P (**a**) and turbidity (**b**) removal performance of complex agent during 10 cycles of treatment/reuse with complex agent.

During the treatment/reuse cycles, the P recovery amount was very low, indicating that the phosphorus removed by PACl could hardly be recovered. This small amount of P can be explained by the residual P as well as the P re-dissolved from the PACl flocs in the base solution during the regeneration process. In contrast, the P recovery performance was improved after the dosing of complex agents, with recovery efficiency increasing with the proportion of SNSs in the agent. The inner ligand complexation of phosphate with the LDH group on the surface of SNS, no matter in the form of $H_2PO_4^-$ or HPO_4^-, has been considered a reversible reaction under alkaline conditions [11]. Though the P recovery rates dropped from 94.5% to 79.4% after the 1st cycle, they were maintained at 74.6–78.4% during the 2nd to 10th cycles. The complex agent with PACl: SNSs of 15 mg:15 g achieved a high recovery rate of both TP and turbidity (Figure 3). It also could be concluded that the phosphate preferred to be absorbed on SNS rather than precipitating with PACl because the inner complexation exhibited higher binding energy and stability. As such, it suggested mutually beneficial effects of the complexing agent containing SNS and PACl with a ratio of 1:3, because PACl removed all the impurities while SNS grasped the phosphate.

With the PACl-dominated complex agent, the P recovery rates decreased with regeneration cycles more dramatically than that with the SNS-dominated agent. It was presumably due to the deterioration of the coagulation effect caused by the caustic soda washing during regeneration. Though washed with deionized water, cycles of caustic regeneration might cause the pH value to fluctuate and reach 7.5 or above, under which scenario the hydrolysate of the coagulant was mainly negatively charged and could not agglomerate through adsorption and electro-neutralization [26,27]. Limited amounts of PACl cannot facilitate the precipitate's enmeshment, leading to more P-adsorption interferential impurities, and therefore poorer P recovery performance.

3.4. Mechanism

Significant improvement in DOC removal (from 47% to 52%) was determined for the samples that were dosed with PACl-dominated complexing agents. The EEM spectra showed peak A at Ex/Em of 275/290–320 nm (Figure 5), indicating the presence of soluble microbial by-product-like substances for all the samples, while peak B at 350/430 nm (humic acid-like substances related to hydrophobic acids) was observed exclusively for the raw sludge liquor. These peaks were often found in the EEM spectra of bio-sludge EPS [28] The hydrophobic acids could be almost completely removed by the sole SNS, while the PACl ingredient in the complexed agent removed the soluble microbial by-product-like substances, with removal efficiencies increasing with the content of PACl. This was consistent with the DOC removal performance and P recovery rates shown in Section 3.1, suggesting that PACl removed most of the potential P-adsorption-competing matter, i.e., probably the soluble microbial by-product-like substances. In addition, our previous study showed that SNS exhibited high selectivity towards phosphate in the presence of ions [29], but the hydrophobic PACl ids adhering to or absorbed on the SNS in this study might interfere with the phosphate adsorption. The addition of alum salts contributed to the removal of impurities, providing a comparatively simplified solution matrix for P adsorption.

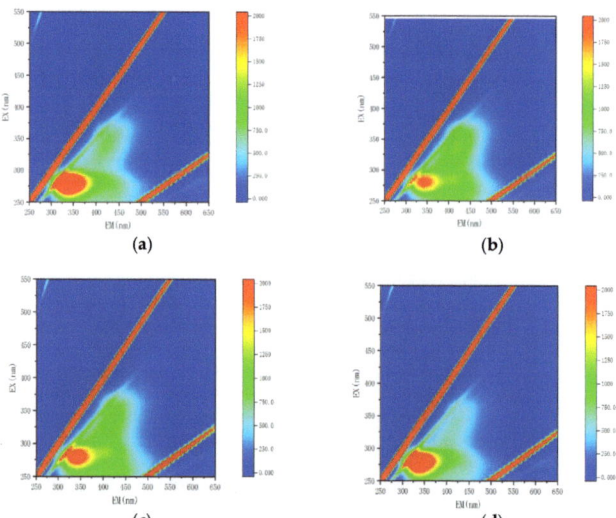

Figure 5. Profile of EEM for raw DSL (**a**) after treatment with complex agent containing PACl: SNS of 25 mg:5 g, (**b**) 15 mg:15 g, (**c**) and 5 mg:30 g (**d**).

It has been confirmed that SNS showed high selective capture ability and strong regeneration performance for phosphate even in the presence of coexisting ions such as nitrate, chloride ion, sulfate, etc. [10,18]. However, the LDH on the SNS surface exhibited strong affinity with the protein or soluble microbial by-product-like colloids in the DOM components. As revealed by Gondim et al., human immunoglobulin G and serum albumin can be absorbed on the non-calcined Mg-Al LDH, and maximum IgG and HSA adsorption uptake occurred in phosphate buffer solution, suggesting that proteins and protein-like substances might interfere with the phosphate adsorption [30]. In addition, other biomacromolecules, including colloidal and soluble microbial products, and extracellular polymeric substances such as polysaccharides, short-chain fatty acids, nucleic acids, and humic acids might be also selectively adsorbed on the LDH-based sorbents, with "active sites" for phosphate decreasing. Once the cationic polymer PACl was added to the liquor, the negatively charged colloidal DOM would change from negative to almost neutral, and PACl cumulated into larger flocs (Figure 6), greatly assisting in the reduction of turbidity [31]. In addition, the induced PACl also acted as the nucleus to produce Al-DOM complexes. In the colloids-free solution, the SNS not only efficiently and rapidly adsorbed the phosphate ions, but also served as nuclei for aggregating by bridging these small aggregates into SNS-Al-DOM clusters, therefore reclaiming P, and meanwhile facilitating the clarification.

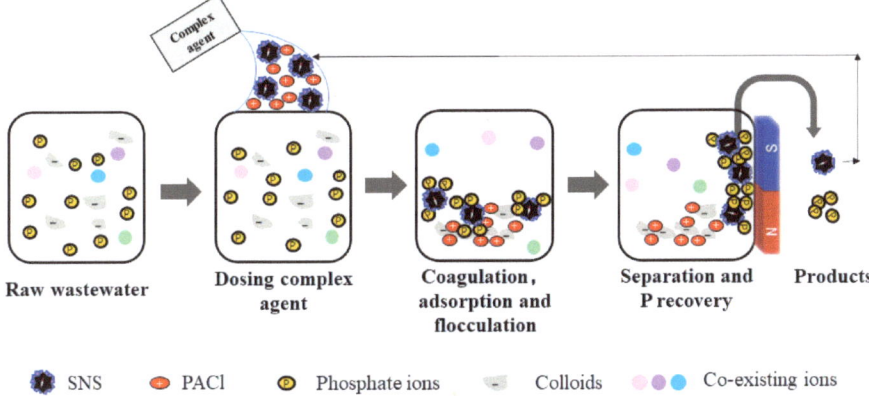

Figure 6. Coupling mechanism of PACl and SNS in the complex agent for P recovery from DSL.

3.5. Economic Analysis

Magnetic seeding coagulation has been regarded as cost-effective because inducing magnetic seeds in coagulation or clarified tank would promote the stable growth and rapid sedimentation of flocs, resulting in higher floc settling rate, faster settling velocity, shorter hydraulic retention, smaller tank size, and lower overall costs. It shows its necessity and feasibility for settling basins or facilities in cold areas where heating or insulation measures are required [32]. Our field investigation on the drinking water treatment plants in Weifang City revealed that 99% of magnetic seeds could be reclaimed, with the cost of the magnetic powder loss of only 0.00076–0.002 EUR/m^3. Together with the cost of the coagulant dosing of 0.013 EUR/m^3, the total cost of the conventional magnetic seeding coagulation was equivalent to about 0.015 EUR/m^3, generating the clarified effluent containing TP of less than 0.05 mg/L, SS of less than 0.8 mg/L, and turbidity of less than 1NTU.

In this study, the magnetic seeds played a dual role in nucleating sites and P recovery. Based on the calculation of the previous test, the P adsorption capacity was in the range of 26.38–46.58 mg P/g SNS. An average of 24.9 g P could be produced after dosing 12.6 g SNS due to the decreasing adsorption capacity, i.e., the exhaustion of SNS after adsorption-regeneration cycles, with an agent synthesis cost of 0.14 EUR/g SNS. Considering the TP concentration of 20 g/m^3 in the sludge liquor and SNS dosing amount of 10.12 g SNS/m^3, 20 P could be reclaimed from 1 cubic liquor at a cost of the sole SNSs estimated to be

10.12 g SNS/m^3 ×0.14 EUR/g SNS = 1.4 EUR /m^3. Thus, the total dosing expense of the complex agent should be 0.14 EUR/m^3 (for PACL) + 1.4 EUR/m^3 (for SNS) = 1.54 EUR/m^3, which could be extremely higher than the cost of the conventional magnetic seeding coagulation. The reclaimed crude P solution shows potential in producing phosphoric acid fertilizer or even some high-end industrial products such as glyphosate, glufosinate ammonium, or yellow phosphorus, which can compromise the high cost of SNS dosing. Considering the reclaimed 20 g/m^3 could be processed and produced as glufosinate ammonium ($C_5HN_2O_4P$, P of 15.6% in w/w) with a market price of 11,400 EUR/ton, the profit would be about 20 g/m^3 × 1 ton/1,000,000 g ÷ 15.6% × 11,400 EUR/ton = 1.46 EUR/m^3, which could almost cover the cost of 0.154 EUR/m^3 due to the complex agent dosing. In addition, the environmental benefits would be more significant if taking into account PACl's role in avoiding eutrophication. The comparison of cost and environmental benefit between the magnetic seeding coagulation process and complex agent are shown in Table 2.

Table 2. Comparison of dosing cost and environmental benefit between magnetic seeding coagulation and complex agent.

	Magnetic Seeding Coagulation	Complex Agent
Cost (EUR/m^3)	0.015	1.54
Profit (EUR/m^3)	0	1.46
Net cost (EUR/m^3)	0.015	0.08
Environmental benefit	Low	High

4. Conclusions

This work investigated the performance of the complex agent consisting of PACl and SNS-treating DSL. The adsorption/clarification experiments demonstrated that both the turbidity removal and P recovery performance varied with the PACl: SNS ratio in the dosed agent, with PACl: SNS of 15 mg:15 g achieving the highest turbidity removal efficiency and comparatively high P recovery rate. In addition, constantly stable turbidity removal performance and regeneration efficiency could be maintained at 70–80% of the original level at the 10th cycle in the treatment/reuse (adsorption/desorption) batch tests. The 5th cycle might be the optimal cycle for this process using these materials because the turbidity removal rate dropped more significantly after cycle 5. The EEM profile indicated that induced Al species neutralized the negatively charged colloidal DOM, providing an almost interferential-substances-free solution for the P recovery by SNS, while the SNS not only rapidly grasped the phosphate in large capacity, but also served as nuclei for the flocs aggregating by bridging these small aggregates into SNS-Al-DOM clusters. In spite of the high cost of SNS dosing, the economic cost calculation indicated that the complex agent would be promising if the reclaimed crude P solution can be processed and produced further for some high-end industrial products with higher added value after replacing the conventional magnetic seeding coagulation. It is expected that this study may foster further development and application of sustainable and efficient complex agents for P recovery from municipal wastewater or DSL with the ultimate aim of holistic water–energy–resource management in robust WWTPs.

Author Contributions: Conceptualization, S.Y., L.N. and Q.Z.; methodology, S.Y. and Q.Z.; software, J.X.; validation, W.W. and Q.Z.; formal analysis, N.W.; investigation, J.R. and W.W.; resources, J.R. and W.W.; writing—original draft preparation, S.Y., L.N. and Q.Z.; writing—review and editing, J.R., W.W., J.X. and N.W.; supervision, W.W. and J.R.; funding acquisition, L.N. and Q.Z. All authors have read and agreed to the published version of the manuscript.

Funding: This work was supported by the National Natural Science Foundation of China Project (grant number 51708338, 2017), Key Technology Research and Development Program of Shandong (2022CXGC021001), Shandong Province Natural Science Foundation (ZR2020ME228), Youth Innovation Technology Project of Higher School in Shandong Province (2019KJD003) and the Introduction and Cultivation Plan for Young Innovative Talents of Colleges and Universities by the Education Department of Shandong Province.

Data Availability Statement: The data presented in this study are available on request from the corresponding author.

Acknowledgments: The authors would like to thank the School of Business Management at Shandong University of Finance and Economics and the key lab at the School of Municipal and Environmental Engineering, Shandong Jianzhu University.

Conflicts of Interest: The authors declare no conflict of interest.

Abbreviations

AAO	anaerobic–anoxic–oxic
DOM	dissolved organic matter
EEM	dimensional excitation-emission matrix
PFC	polyferric chloride
SNS	superparamagnetic nano-sorbent
WWTPs	wastewater treatment plants
CaP	hydroxyapatite
DSL	digested sludge liquor
PACl	polyaluminum chloride
P	phosphorus
TP	total phosphorus

References

1. Bareha, Y.; Saoudi, M.; Santellani, A.-C.; Le Bihan, A.; Picard, S.; Mebarki, C.; Cunha, M.; Daumer, M.-L. Use of fermentation processes for improving the dissolution of phosphorus and its recovery from waste activated sludge. *Environ. Technol.* **2020**, *43*, 1307–1317. [CrossRef] [PubMed]
2. Liu, Y.J.; Gu, J.; Liu, Y. Energy self-sufficient biological municipal wastewater reclamation: Present status, challenges and solutions forward. *Bioresour. Technol.* **2018**, *269*, 513–519. [CrossRef] [PubMed]
3. Monea, M.C.; Löhr, D.K.; Meyer, C.; Preyl, V.; Xiao, J.; Steinmetz, H.; Schönberger, H.; Drenkova-Tuhtan, A. Comparing the leaching behavior of phosphorus, aluminum and iron from post-precipitated tertiary sludge and anaerobically digested sewage sludge aiming at phosphorus recovery. *J. Clean. Prod.* **2020**, *247*, 119129. [CrossRef]
4. Fang, L.; Liu, R.; Li, J.; Xu, C.; Zhuang, L.; Wang, D. Magnetite/Lanthanum hydroxide for phosphate sequestration and recovery from lake and the attenuation effects of sediment particles. *Water Res.* **2018**, *130*, 243–254. [CrossRef]
5. Li, B.; Boiarkina, I.; Yu, W.; Huang, H.M.; Munir, T.; Wang, G.Q.; Young, B.R. Phosphorous recovery through struvite crystallization: Challenges for future design. *Sci. Total Environ.* **2019**, *648*, 1244–1256. [CrossRef]
6. Petzet, S.; Peplinski, B.; Cornel, P. On wet chemical phosphorus recovery from sewage sludge ash by acidic or alkaline leaching and an optimized combination of both. *Water Res.* **2012**, *46*, 3769–3780. [CrossRef] [PubMed]
7. Guadie, A.; Belay, A.; Liu, W.; Yesigat, A.; Hao, X.; Wang, A. Rift Valley Lake as a potential magnesium source to recover phosphorus from urine. *Environ. Res.* **2020**, *184*, 10936. [CrossRef]
8. Keefer, C.E.; Herman, K. Treatment of supernatant sludge liquor by coagulation and sedimentation. *Sew. Work. J.* **1940**, *12*, 738–744.
9. Fang, K.; Peng, F.; Gong, H.; Zhang, H.; Wang, K. Ammonia removal from low-strength municipal wastewater by powdered resin combined with simultaneous recovery as struvite. *Front. Environ. Sci. Eng.* **2020**, *15*, 8. [CrossRef]
10. Zhao, G.G.; Zhao, Q.; Jin, X.W.; Wang, H.B.; Zhang, K.F.; Li, M.; Wang, N.; Zhao, W.X.; Meng, S.J.; Mu, R.M. Preparation of a novel hafnium-loaded Fe_3O_4@SiO_2 superparamagnetic nanoparticles and its adsorption performance for phosphate in water. *Desalin. Water Treat.* **2021**, *216*, 188–198. [CrossRef]
11. Zhao, Q.; Liu, C.F.; Song, H.Q.; Liu, Y.; Wang, H.B.; Tian, F.Y.; Meng, S.J.; Zhang, K.F.; Wang, N.; Mu, R.M.; et al. Mechanism of phosphate adsorption on superparamagnetic microparticles modified with transitional elements: Experimental observation and computational modelling. *Chemosphere* **2020**, *258*, 127327. [CrossRef]
12. Drenkova-Tuhtan, A.; Schneider, M.; Franzreb, M.; Meyer, C.; Gellermann, C.; Sextl, G.; Mandel, K.; Steinmetz, H. Pilot-scale removal and recovery of dissolved phosphate from secondary wastewater effluents with reusable ZnFeZr adsorbent@ Fe_3O_4/SiO_2 particles with magnetic harvesting. *Water Res.* **2017**, *109*, 77–87. [CrossRef]
13. Chen, Y.; Sui, Q.; Yu, D.; Zheng, L.; Chen, M.; Ritigala, T.; Wei, Y. Development of a Short-Cut Combined Magnetic Coagulation-Sequence Batch Membrane Bioreactor for Swine Wastewater Treatment. *Membranes* **2021**, *11*, 83. [CrossRef] [PubMed]

14. dos Santos, T.R.T.; Mateus, G.A.P.; Silva, M.F.; Miyashiro, C.S.; Nishi, L.; de Andrade, M.B.; Fagundes-Klen, M.R.; Gomes, R.G.; Bergamasco., R. Evaluation of Magnetic Coagulant (α-Fe_2O_3-MO) and its reuse in textile wastewater treatment. *Water Air Soil Pollut.* **2018**, *229*, 92. [CrossRef]
15. Noor, M.H.M.; Azli, M.F.Z.M.; Ngadi, N.; Inuwa, I.M.; Opotu, L.A.; Mohamed, M. Optimization of sonication-assisted synthesis of magnetic Moringa oleifera as an efficient coagulant for palm oil wastewater treatment. *Environ. Technol. Innov.* **2022**, *25*, 102191. [CrossRef]
16. Yan, L.; Yang, K.; Shan, R.R.; Yan, T.; Wei, J.; Yu, S.J.; Yu, H.Q.; Du, B. Kinetic, isotherm and thermodynamic investigations of phosphate adsorption onto core–shell Fe_3O_4@ LDHs composites with easy magnetic separation assistance. *J. Colloid. Interface Sci.* **2015**, *448*, 508–516. [CrossRef]
17. Zhang, C.; Li, Y.; Wang, F.; Yu, Z.; Wei, J.; Yang, Z.; Ma, C.; Li, Z.; Xu, Z.; Zeng, G. Performance of magnetic zirconium-iron oxide nanoparticle in the removal of phosphate from aqueous solution. *Appl. Surf. Sci.* **2017**, *396*, 1783–1792. [CrossRef]
18. Zhao, Q.; Tian, J.Z.; Zhang, K.F.; Wang, H.B.; Li, M.; Meng, S.J.; Mu, R.M.; Liu, L.; Yin, M.M.; Li, J.J.; et al. Phosphate recovery from the P-enriched brine of AnMBR-RO-IE treating municipal wastewater via an innovated phosphorus recovery batch reactor with nano-sorbents. *Chemosphere* **2021**, *284*, 131259. [CrossRef]
19. APHA. *Standard Methods for the Examination of Water and Wastewater*, 20th ed.; American Public Health Association: Washington, DC, USA, 1998.
20. Frølund, B.; Palmgren, R.; Keiding, K.; Nielsen, P.H. Extraction of extracellular polymers from activated sludge using a cation exchange resin. *Water Res.* **1996**, *30*, 1749–1758. [CrossRef]
21. Raunkjær, K.; Hvitved-Jacobsen, T.; Nielsen, P.H. Measurement of pools of protein, carbohydrate and lipid in domestic wastewater. *Water Res.* **1994**, *28*, 251–262. [CrossRef]
22. Lv, M.; Li, D.; Zhang, Z.; Logan, B.E.; van der Hoek, J.P.; Sun, M.; Chen, F.; Feng, Y. Magnetic seeding coagulation: Effect of Al species and magnetic particles on coagulation efficiency, residual Al, and floc properties. *Chemosphere* **2021**, *268*, 129363. [CrossRef]
23. Xue, Y.; Liu, Z.; Li, A.; Yang, H. Application of a green coagulant with PACl in efficient purification of turbid water and its mechanism study. *J. Environ. Sci.* **2019**, *81*, 168–180. [CrossRef]
24. Lakshmanan, R.; Rajarao, G.K. Effective water content reduction in sewage wastewater sludge using magnetic nanoparticles. *Bioresour. Technol.* **2014**, *153*, 333–339. [CrossRef] [PubMed]
25. Triques, C.C.; Fagundes-Klen, M.R.; Suzaki, P.Y.R.; Mateus, G.A.P.; Wernke, G.; Bergamasco, R.; Rodrigues, M.L.F. Influence evaluation of the functionalization of magnetic nanoparticles with a natural extract coagulant in the primary treatment of a dairy cleaning-in-place wastewater. *J. Clean. Prod.* **2020**, *243*, 118634. [CrossRef]
26. Meng, S.; Fan, W.; Li, X.; Liu, Y.; Liang, D.; Liu, X. Intermolecular interactions of polysaccharides in membrane fouling during microfiltration. *Water Res.* **2018**, *143*, 38–46. [CrossRef] [PubMed]
27. Meng, S.; Wang, R.; Zhang, K.; Meng, X.; Xue, W.; Liu, H.; Liang, D.; Zhao, Q.; Liu, Y. Transparent exopolymer particles (TEPs)-associated protobiofilm: A neglected contributor to biofouling during membrane filtration. *Front. Environ. Sci. Eng.* **2021**, *15*, 64. [CrossRef]
28. Li, K.; Qian, J.; Wang, J.F.; Wang, C.; Fan, X.L.; Lu, B.H.; Tian, X.; Jin, W.; He, X.X.; Guo, W.Z. Toxicity of three crystalline TiO_2 nanoparticles in activated sludge: Bacterial cell death modes differentially weaken sludge dewaterability. *Environ. Sci. Technol.* **2019**, *53*, 4542–4555. [CrossRef]
29. Hong, P.N.; Honda, R.; Noguchi, M.; Ito, T. Optimum selection of extraction methods of extracellular polymeric substances in activated sludge for effective extraction of the target components. *Biochem. Eng. J.* **2017**, *127*, 136–146. [CrossRef]
30. Gondim, D.R.; Cecilia, J.A.; Santos, S.O.; Rodrigues, T.N.B.; Aguiar, J.E.; Vilarrasa-Garcia, E.; Rodriguez-Castellon, E.; Azevedo, D.C.S.; Silva, I.J., Jr. Influence of buffer solutions in the adsorption of human serum proteins onto layered double hydroxide. *Int. J. Biol. Macromol.* **2018**, *106*, 396–409. [CrossRef]
31. Sabouhi, M.; Torabian, A.; Bozorg, A.; Mehrdadi, N. A novel convenient approach toward the fouling alleviation in membrane bioreactors using the combined methods of oxidation and coagulation. *J. Water Process Eng.* **2020**, *33*, 101018. [CrossRef]
32. Lapointe, M.; Barbeau, B. Selection of media for the design of ballasted flocculation processes. *Water Res.* **2018**, *147*, 25–32. [CrossRef] [PubMed]

Disclaimer/Publisher's Note: The statements, opinions and data contained in all publications are solely those of the individual author(s) and contributor(s) and not of MDPI and/or the editor(s). MDPI and/or the editor(s) disclaim responsibility for any injury to people or property resulting from any ideas, methods, instructions or products referred to in the content.

Perspective

Mini-Review of Best Practices for Greenhouse Gas Reduction in Singapore's Semiconductor Industry

Shikai Zhu [1], Haoqian Hu [2], Haoyi Yang [3], Yunzhuo Qu [4] and Yuanzhe Li [3,5,6,*]

[1] Business College, Wrexham Glyndŵr University, Wrexham LL11 2AW, UK; s22008875@mail.glyndwr.ac.uk
[2] Institut Supérieur du Commerce, 22 Boulevard du Fort de Vaux, 75017 Paris, France; hqhu245@163.com
[3] NUS College of Design and Engineering, National University of Singapore, Singapore 118429, Singapore; yhy2442939401@gmail.com
[4] College of Polymer Science and Engineering, Sichuan University, Chengdu 610065, China; scupseqyz@163.com
[5] Carbon Neutrality Research Lab, China Academy of Art, Hangzhou 310002, China
[6] School of Civil and Environmental Engineering, University of Auckland, Auckland 1010, New Zealand
* Correspondence: yuanzhe001@e.ntu.edu.sg

Citation: Zhu, S.; Hu, H.; Yang, H.; Qu, Y.; Li, Y. Mini-Review of Best Practices for Greenhouse Gas Reduction in Singapore's Semiconductor Industry. *Processes* **2023**, *11*, 2120. https://doi.org/10.3390/pr11072120

Academic Editors: Antoni Sánchez and Jie Zhang

Received: 15 June 2023
Revised: 12 July 2023
Accepted: 14 July 2023
Published: 16 July 2023

Copyright: © 2023 by the authors. Licensee MDPI, Basel, Switzerland. This article is an open access article distributed under the terms and conditions of the Creative Commons Attribution (CC BY) license (https:// creativecommons.org/licenses/by/ 4.0/).

Abstract: Climate change is an urgent global concern driven by human activities and the subsequent rise in greenhouse gas (GHG) emissions. The semiconductor industry has emerged as a significant contributor to GHG emissions, yet there is a lack of clear guidelines for effective reduction methods specifically tailored to domestic and international semiconductor manufacturing. This mini-review addresses this gap by proposing implementation principles for optimal control technology aimed at mitigating GHG emissions in the semiconductor industry. Drawing upon guidance from the Intergovernmental Panel on Climate Change (IPCC) and established reduction methods, our focus is on the deployment of efficient exhaust gas destruction equipment for removing GHGs from critical processes such as Etching, ThinFilm (including chemical/physical vapor deposition), and Diffusion. By examining and consolidating current best practices, this review provides a foundation for developing comprehensive guidelines and standards that support the semiconductor industry's transition to more sustainable operations. Considering the vast body of literature in this field, we highlight the significance of this study as it contributes to the ongoing research efforts in reducing GHG emissions. The objective of this study is to identify research gaps and motivate further investigations, while also providing practical recommendations for reducing GHG emissions in the semiconductor industry.

Keywords: greenhouse gas management; semiconductor industry; fluorinated compounds; optimal control technology; best practices; reduction methodology

1. Introduction

With the global objective of achieving Net Zero Emissions by 2050, the semiconductor industry plays a crucial role in addressing climate change. As a leading semiconductor manufacturing company in Singapore, our focus on reducing greenhouse gas (GHG) emissions aligns with the industry's commitment to sustainable practices. In line with the Scientific Basis-Based Targets (SBTi), many semiconductor fabs in Singapore have set annual carbon emission reduction targets of 3–4% [1]. To meet these targets, various strategies have been implemented, including the accelerated installation of local scrubbers, the promotion of energy-saving equipment and measures, and the adoption of green electricity equipment. Singapore, as a nation, is actively working towards reducing GHG emissions and has set baseline targets for carbon reduction. In this context, the semiconductor industry in Singapore aims to achieve an emission rate of less than 25,000 tons of carbon dioxide equivalent (t/CO_2e) by 2023 [2], as per the baseline established by the National Environment Agency. To achieve this goal, advanced control technology is being implemented across different phases of semiconductor manufacturing [2,3]. The methodology employed for reducing

GHG emissions draws inspiration from the Clean Development Mechanism (CDM) published methods AM0078 and AM0111 by the Environmental Protection Administration. These methods incorporate the latest abatement and management systems, providing a comprehensive approach to GHG reduction. Additionally, a systematic verification method has been developed to assess the effectiveness of these reduction measures [4,5].

The primary objective of this mini-review is to present the implementation principles of optimal control technology for reducing GHG emissions in the semiconductor industry. By leveraging established reduction methods and guidance from the Intergovernmental Panel on Climate Change (IPCC), this review aims to address the lack of clear guidelines for reducing fluorinated compounds (FCs), N_2O, and NF_3 greenhouse gases in the semiconductor industry. Specifically, this review focuses on the installation of efficient exhaust gas destruction equipment for the removal of FCs and N_2O from critical processes such as Etching, ThinFilm (including chemical/physical vapor deposition), and Diffusion [6,7]. By analyzing current best practices and considering the unique requirements of the semiconductor industry, this review aims to provide actionable insights and recommendations for the reduction of GHG emissions. The remainder of this mini-review is structured as follows: Section 2 provides a comprehensive literature review, highlighting the current state of knowledge on GHG reduction in the semiconductor industry. Section 3 outlines the methodology used in developing the implementation principles for optimal control technology. Section 4 presents the proposed principles and discusses their applicability to the semiconductor industry in Singapore. Finally, Section 5 summarizes the key findings, implications, and recommendations for future research and practice. By undertaking this mini-review, we aim to contribute to the advancement of sustainable practices within the semiconductor industry, specifically focusing on the reduction of GHG emissions. Through collaboration and the adoption of innovative solutions, the industry can play a pivotal role in mitigating climate change and ensuring a greener future.

2. Greenhouse Gas Reduction Strategies in the Semiconductor Industry

The semiconductor industry plays a vital role in technological advancements and innovation, but it is also recognized as one of the major contributors to greenhouse gas (GHG) emissions [8]. As the urgency to address climate change grows, there is a pressing need to identify and implement effective strategies for reducing GHG emissions in semiconductor manufacturing processes [9]. This comprehensive literature review aims to provide an overview of the current knowledge and best practices related to GHG reduction in the semiconductor industry, with a specific focus on Singapore [10]. The current literature review on GHG reduction in the semiconductor industry provides a comprehensive overview of the state of knowledge and best practices in this field. The novelty of this study lies in its specific focus on the semiconductor industry in Singapore, which allows for a detailed examination of the strategies and initiatives implemented in a specific context.

The review also identifies greenhouse gas substitution as a key strategy for reducing net fluorine-gas emissions in the semiconductor industry. The novelty here lies in the evaluation of alternative gases that not only have lower global warming potential (GWP) but also meet the performance and operational requirements of semiconductor manufacturing processes. This assessment considers potential safety and health impacts on fab operations, employee protection, and external environmental impacts.

2.1. Greenhouse Gas Substitution-Phase 1

To further reduce net fluorine-gas emissions in the semiconductor industry, one approach is to replace gases with high global warming potential (GWP) with alternatives that have lower GWP or no GWP. This substitution strategy aims to use gases more efficiently in the plasma process [11]. The gases of particular concern in this context are CF_4, C_2F_6, C_3F_8, c-C_4F_8, CHF_3, CH_2F_2, CH_3F, NF_3, and SF_6. These gases have significant GWP values and contribute to greenhouse gas emissions. CF_4 is commonly used in both Etching and

ThinFilm processes, while CHF_3, CH_2F_2, and C_2F_6 are also used in various semiconductor manufacturing processes [12,13].

When considering alternative chemicals for substitution, it is essential to evaluate their potential safety and health impacts on fab operations, employee protection, and external environmental impacts [8]. The objective is to identify replacement gases that not only offer lower GWP but also maintain the desired performance and operational requirements of the semiconductor manufacturing processes. Table 1 summarizes the GWP values, by-products, and noteworthy remarks for the relevant gas categories. These values are based on the Carbon Pricing Act 2018 (CPA 2018) and the Intergovernmental Panel on Climate Change (IPCC) 2019 assessment [1,2]. It is important to note that CF_4, C_2F_6, and CHF_3 are frequently mentioned due to their significant GWP and their presence as by-products in various semiconductor processes [14].

Table 1. GWP values, by-products, and noteworthy remarks for the relevant gas categories [2].

Gas Category	GWP		By-Product		Remark
	CPA 2018	IPCC 2019	CPA 2018	IPCC 2019	
CO_2	1	1	-	-	
CH_4	28	28	-	-	
N_2O	265	265	-	-	
CHF_3	12,400	12,400	CF_4	CF_4, C_2F_6, C_5F_8	
CH_2F_2	677	677	CF_4, CHF_3	CF_4, C_2F_6, CHF_3	
CH_3F	116	116	-	C_2F_6	
CF_4	6630	6630	-	$C_2F_6, C5F8, CHF_3$	IPCC 2019 differentiate ThimFilm & Etching
C_2F_6	11,100	11,100	CF_4	CF_4, CHF_3	
C_3F_8	8900	11,000	CF_4	CF_4	
C_4F_8	9540	9450	CF_4, C_2F_6	CF_4	
SF_6	23,500	23,500	-	CF_4, C_2F_6, CHF_3	
NF_3	17,200	16,100	CF_4	CF_4	(In-situ & Remote)

Through the Greenhouse Gas Substitution-Phase 1, semiconductor manufacturers can make informed decisions regarding the replacement of high GWP gases with alternatives that have a lower environmental impact. This phase requires careful consideration of the gases' performance, safety implications, and overall reduction potential in greenhouse gas emissions [8,15].

2.2. Advanced Abatement Methodology-Phase 2

The semiconductor industry has developed and commercialized various advanced abatement technologies to reduce fluorine-gas emissions effectively. The focus has been on implementing abatement systems (Figure 1) near the emission source to prevent further contamination and dilution of the gases [9,10].

This approach involves connecting each emission stream to a local scrubber, enabling accurate calculations of FC emissions [9,10]. The connection method between the production system and the abatement system is crucial for achieving precise emission measurements. Venting equipment and process conditions, such as the temperature, fluorinated greenhouse gas inlet concentration, flow rate, pump purge rate, and total inlet flow composition, significantly impact the performance of the venting system [11,12].

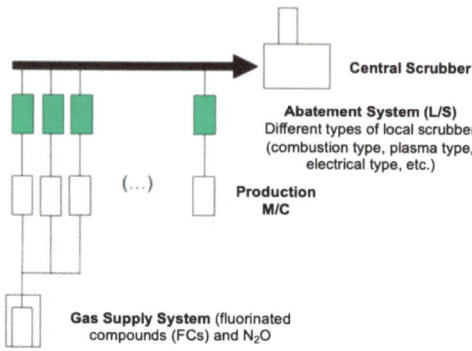

Figure 1. Installation of effective abatement system for the removal of Fluorinated Compound (FCs) and N_2O, such as combustion, electric, or plasma type, etc.

The Table 2 provides an overview of different advanced abatement methods commonly used in the semiconductor industry. These methods focus on the removal of fluorinated compounds (FCs) and N_2O greenhouse gases from various semiconductor manufacturing processes, including Etching, ThinFilm deposition, and Diffusion processes [16]. The combustion-based abatement system involves the installation of efficient combustion-based systems that effectively remove FCs and N_2O. Similarly, the electric-based abatement system utilizes electric-based technologies for emission reduction. Plasma-based abatement systems leverage plasma technology to remove FCs and N_2O. Additionally, other methods, such as UV-based systems, may be employed for FC and N_2O abatement. The primary objective of these abatement methods is to reduce the emissions of specific greenhouse gases, including CF_4, C_2F_6, C_3F_8, $c\text{-}C_4F_8$, CHF_3, CH_2F_2, CH_3F, NF_3, and SF_6. By employing these advanced abatement methods, semiconductor manufacturers can effectively mitigate the environmental impact of their operations and contribute to global efforts in reducing GHG emissions.

Table 2. Overview of advanced abatement methods in the semiconductor industry.

Method	General Practice	Type of GHG Reduction
Combustion-based Abatement System	Installation of efficient combustion-based abatement systems for the removal of fluorinated compounds (FCs) and N_2O from semiconductor manufacturing processes, such as Etching, ThinFilm deposition, and Diffusion processes.	Reduction of emissions of fluorinated compounds (FCs) and N_2O greenhouse gases, including CF_4, C_2F_6, C_3F_8, $c\text{-}C_4F_8$, CHF_3, CH_2F_2, CH_3F, NF_3, and SF_6
Electric-based Abatement System	Implementation of electric-based abatement systems for the removal of FCs and N_2O in semiconductor manufacturing processes.	Reduction of emissions of fluorinated compounds (FCs) and N_2O greenhouse gases, including CF_4, C_2F_6, C_3F_8, $c\text{-}C_4F_8$, CHF_3, CH_2F_2, CH_3F, NF_3, and SF_6
Plasma-based Abatement System	Utilization of plasma-based abatement systems to remove FCs and N_2O from semiconductor manufacturing processes, such as Etching, ThinFilm deposition, and Diffusion processes.	Reduction of emissions of fluorinated compounds (FCs) and N_2O greenhouse gases, including CF_4, C_2F_6, C_3F_8, $c\text{-}C_4F_8$, CHF_3, CH_2F_2, CH_3F, NF_3, and SF_6
Other Abatement Methods (e.g., UV)	Adoption of various additional abatement methods, such as UV-based systems, for the removal of FCs and N_2O in semiconductor manufacturing processes.	Reduction of emissions of fluorinated compounds (FCs) and N_2O greenhouse gases, including CF_4, C_2F_6, C_3F_8, $c\text{-}C_4F_8$, CHF_3, CH_2F_2, CH_3F, NF_3, and SF_6

2.3. Process Optimization-Phase 2 and 3

Process optimization plays a critical role in reducing greenhouse gas consumption and minimizing fluorinated greenhouse gas emissions in semiconductor manufacturing. By modifying process variables such as chamber pressure, temperature, plasma power, cleaning gas flow rate, gas flow time, and gas ratio, it is possible to decrease carbon emissions [6]. Process improvement techniques, including endpoint inspection systems utilizing mass spectrometry, infrared spectroscopy, optical emission spectroscopy, and radio frequency impedance monitoring, provide valuable data for optimizing processes [7]. These techniques have been extensively used for cleaning chemical vapor deposition (CVD) chambers, and they can also be applied to Etching and other fluorinated greenhouse gas plasma operations.

2.4. Remote Plasma Cleaning System-Phase 4

Remote plasma cleaning technology has emerged as an alternative to in situ CVD chamber cleaning. In this approach, a plasma generation unit is installed at the front of the CVD chamber, facilitating the cleaning process [6]. The plasma unit initiates the reaction of NF_3, generating fluorine radicals and ions that chemically react with the deposited material in the processing chamber (Figure 2) [13]. The by-products of this reaction, such as SiF4, are then carried away in gaseous form. Remote plasma cleaning systems can be retrofitted into existing processing tools to replace the original chemistry used for fluorine gas cleaning [14]. Continuous evaluation and sharing of new technologies within the semiconductor industry are essential for further improvement [15]. It is crucial to follow reliable measurement protocols when measuring emissions or assessing the effectiveness of new technologies [16].

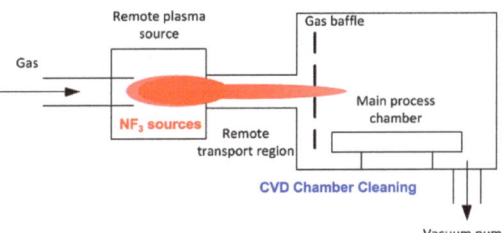

Figure 2. The remote cleaning starts with the reaction of NF_3 in the plasma, and the fluorine radicals and ions generated in the remote plasma unit are guided to the CVD processing chamber.

2.5. Basis of Preparation and Monitoring Plan-Endorsed by ISO14064 and NEA

The basis of preparation (BoP) and monitoring plan (MP) for GHG reduction initiatives in the semiconductor industry are rooted in the "IPCC 2019 Guidelines for National Greenhouse Gas Inventories, Volume 3, Chapter 6" (IPCC GL) and the Fifth Assessment Report (AR5) Global Warming Potential (GWP) values. Estimation methods based on these guidelines provide a framework for calculating emissions, aligning with the objectives and requirements set forth by environmental agencies such as the National Environment Agency (NEA) [7,17]. Adherence to the ISO 14064 standard ensures that GHG reduction efforts in the semiconductor industry comply with internationally recognized protocols [16].

To conclude, this comprehensive literature review has highlighted the current state of knowledge and best practices for GHG reduction in the semiconductor industry. Through greenhouse gas substitution, advanced abatement methodologies, process optimization, and the use of remote plasma cleaning systems, significant progress has been made in reducing emissions of fluorinated compounds and N_2O gases. The basis of preparation and monitoring plans endorsed by ISO 14064 and NEA provide a standardized approach for measuring and managing emissions [18]. Further research and development efforts are essential to continue advancing GHG reduction strategies in the semiconductor industry, ultimately contributing to global sustainability goals. Moreover, this literature review also contributes to the existing knowledge by providing insights into the specific strategies and initiatives implemented in the semiconductor industry in Singapore. The novelty of the study lies in its focus on greenhouse gas substitution, advanced abatement methodologies, process optimization, remote plasma cleaning systems, and adherence to standardized monitoring protocols.

3. Methodology for Developing Implementation Principles of Optimal Control Technology

3.1. Overview of the Control Technology Methodology

3.1.1. Old Control Technology

Early PFC abatement systems were not effective in destroying CF_4 because of its strong C-F molecular bonds. Burn boxes operating at temperatures of 800 degrees Celsius were only up to 27% effective in destroying PFCs. Many times, the destruction of CHF_3, C_2F_6, and C_3F_8 generated CF_4 from the decomposition of the original gases [7]. The semiconductor manufacturing emission factors include fluorinated compounds (FCs) that are not destroyed by the emission reduction system; CO_2 generated as a by-product of the reduction of F-GHGs; CO_2 from the combustion of fossil fuels in the emission reduction system; and CO_2 from electricity use during the operation of the emission reduction system. In the monitoring procedure, the gas concentration at the inlet and outlet of the abatement system will be monitored continuously using two FTIR devices, and the gas velocity at the inlet and outlet of the abatement system will be monitored continuously as well [8,10,13].

The monitoring methodology specifies that the mass of each F-GHG entering and leaving the abatement unit, as well as the inlet and outlet flow rates, should be calculated separately and continuously. The relevant parameters required for the calculation of baseline and project emissions shall be monitored continuously [14]. All measurements shall be carried out using equipment calibrated according to the relevant industry standards.] In addition to following the QA/QC procedures for measuring gas concentrations as described in the baseline chapter and the QA/QC procedures for measuring flows in the US EPA methodology, the project developer should ensure that maintenance and repair procedures follow, at a minimum, the manufacturer's recommendations or the requirements specified in this methodology throughout the monitoring period. A record of the maintenance requirements for the monitoring and abatement equipment should be submitted to the verifier [16].

3.1.2. New Reduction Method

The new methodology is not only applicable to the Etching process, the ThinFilm process, which includes chemical/physical vapor deposition, and Diffusion processes but also to the semiconductor process where FCs and N_2O and NF_3 greenhouse gases are emitted directly into the atmosphere and can also be implied such reduction program. Still, post-production plants should have a history of fluorinated and N_2O greenhouse gas use and utilization rates for three consecutive years prior to the start of the project year; post-production new plants should have a history of fluorinated and N_2O greenhouse gas use and utilization rates for two consecutive years prior to the start of the project year of the installation of the proper abatement system [14–16]. The maximum processing capacity of the abatement must be greater than the historical data on the flow of FCs, N_2O, and NF_3 greenhouse gases into the abatement (including all other by-products and diluted gases). The reduction project should also assess that the lifespan of the abatement system is greater than the project period, and existing equipment that fails due to its age can no longer be used in the case of this method; the removal of equipment has been a previous project in reduction measures and can no longer apply for this method [19].

Fluorinated compounds and the N_2O greenhouse gas usage rate must be the amount of gas used (tons of CO_2e) and wafer production area (m^2) for the installation of exhaust gas destruction treatment equipment, and the wafer size is defined according to the financial annual report of wafer move, including $5''$, $6''$, $8''$, $12''$, $18''$ wafers, etc. The various types of GHGs are requested to follow the global warming potential (GWP) gases announced by US EPA [20].

The comparative table (Table 3) highlights the key differences between the old control technology and the new reduction method. The old control technology was found to have limited effectiveness in destroying CF_4, a greenhouse gas with strong molecular bonds. The abatement systems operating at high temperatures were only up to 27% effective in destroying fluorinated compounds (FCs). Additionally, the monitoring in the old control technology relied on the gas concentration and velocity measurements at the inlet and outlet of the abatement system. In contrast, the new reduction method is applicable to various processes and direct emissions of FCs, N_2O, and NF_3. It takes into account the complete emission stream through the implementation of a SCADA system, enabling the monitoring of the total greenhouse gas (GHG) emissions. The new reduction method also emphasizes the need for a high destruction removal efficiency (DRE) of the abatement system, with a requirement of over 90% for most types of treatment equipment. Furthermore, the calculation of gas usage rates in the new reduction method considers the amount of gas used and the wafer production area, taking into account different wafer sizes. This approach provides a more comprehensive and accurate assessment of GHG emissions. Additionally, the new reduction method requires the abatement system's lifespan to be greater than the project period, ensuring long-term effectiveness and sustainability.

Table 3. Comparative table highlighting the key differences between the old control technology and the new reduction method.

	Old Control Technology	New Reduction Method
Applicability	Limited effectiveness for CF_4 destruction	Applicable to various processes and direct emissions
Emission Types	FCs, CO_2 from reduction, combustion, and electricity	FCs, N_2O, NF_3, CO_2 from reduction and combustion
Monitoring	Gas concentration and velocity monitoring	SCADA system for total GHG monitoring
Baseline Data	Historical data required for assessment	Historical data required for assessment
Abatement System	Less than 27% destruction efficiency for PFCs	DRE > 90% (combustion, electric, or plasma type)
Gas Usage Rate	Not destroyed by emission reduction system	Gas usage rate calculation based on production area
Equipment Lifespan	N/A	Abatement system lifespan > project period
Compliance	Follows industry standards and QA/QC procedures	Compliance with IPCC and US EPA guidelines

It is important to note that the new reduction method complies with international guidelines such as the Intergovernmental Panel on Climate Change (IPCC) and the U.S. Environmental Protection Agency (EPA) mandatory reporting rules. This ensures that the methodology aligns with industry standards and best practices for GHG emissions reduction.

3.2. Important Features of the New Reduction Methods

This method is applicable to the integrated circuit (IC) manufacturing industry. Other targets including semiconductor materials (including chemicals), photomasks, design (including Computer-Aided Design (CAD) software), manufacturing processes, packaging, testing, and equipment may not be applicable to this method. The effectiveness of the damage removal rate of the installed abatement system, which is normally the local scrubber connected to the manufacturing modules, must be considered and referred to the IPCC and US EPA Mandatory Reporting Rule [21]. Moreover, the destruction removal efficiency (DRE) of the treatment equipment should be greater than 90% (combustion, electric, or plasma type). The DRE of the N_2O treatment equipment should be greater than 60%, and the used local scrubbers purchased by external companies should be tested upon completion of installation [22].

The new methodology is such that a facility SCADA system would be connected to the emission stream where the total amount of GHG would be monitored. The pressure transducer is installed for the whole production and abatement process to clean the emission stream for cleaning chemical vapor deposition module tool chambers. The local scrubbers are used to treat the GHG so that less will be emitted into the atmosphere. The process can be seen in Figure 3.

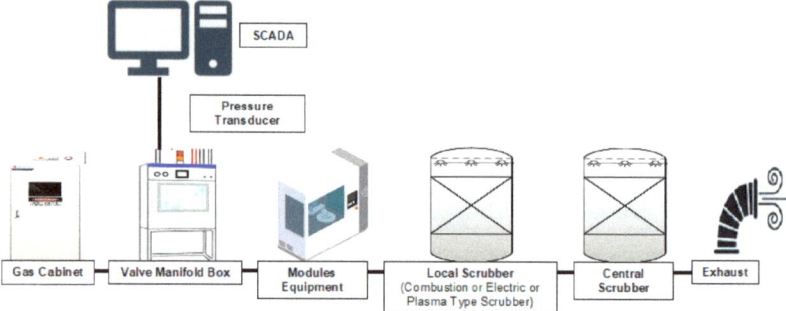

Figure 3. Emission stream diagram for cleaning chemical vapor deposition module tool chambers with pressure transducer.

3.3. Integration of International Standards and Guidelines

To ensure the development of robust and reliable implementation principles, international standards and guidelines were integrated into the methodology. The principles were aligned with the recommendations of the Intergovernmental Panel on Climate Change (IPCC) and the guidelines outlined in the 2019 IPCC Guidelines for National Greenhouse Gas Inventories [23].

Additionally, the principles were developed in accordance with the ISO 14064 standard, which provides guidance on the quantification, monitoring, and reporting of GHG emissions. This integration ensures that the implementation principles are in line with internationally recognized standards and facilitate accurate measurement and reporting of GHG reductions.

3.4. Stakeholder Engagement

The development of the implementation principles involved active engagement with key stakeholders in the semiconductor industry, including semiconductor manufacturers, equipment suppliers, industry associations, and regulatory bodies. Consultations, workshops, and expert interviews were conducted to gather insights, feedback, and recommendations from these stakeholders. Stakeholder engagement played a vital role in understanding the practical challenges and opportunities associated with implementing optimal control technology. It also helped in identifying potential barriers to adoption and exploring strategies for overcoming them.

3.5. Development of Implementation Principles

Based on the information gathered through the methodology described above, the implementation principles for optimal control technology were developed. These principles provide guidance on the selection, installation, operation, and monitoring of control technologies to achieve significant reductions in GHG emissions in the semiconductor industry.

The implementation principles address various aspects, including technology selection criteria, performance indicators, monitoring protocols, and best practices for ongoing maintenance and improvement [24]. They aim to provide a holistic framework that semiconductor manufacturers can follow to effectively implement optimal control technology and drive sustainable GHG reduction in their operations. By employing this comprehensive methodology, the implementation principles for optimal control technology in the semiconductor industry have been developed. These principles serve as a valuable resource for semiconductor manufacturers seeking to enhance their sustainability efforts and contribute to global climate change mitigation.

4. Proposed Principles and Applicability in the Singapore Semiconductor Industry

In this chapter, we further enhance the understanding of the proposed principles for greenhouse gas (GHG) reduction in the semiconductor industry, with a focus on their applicability to the context of Singapore. We also consider important factors related to monitoring, calculation methodology, and implementation considerations for new reduction methods. By incorporating these additional aspects, we aim to provide a comprehensive framework for sustainable semiconductor manufacturing in Singapore.

4.1. Proposed Principles for GHG Reduction

The previously discussed principles for GHG reduction remain relevant, but we now emphasize the implementation of best control technologies for fluorine-gas, PFCs, and HFCs reduction in semiconductor fabs. These technologies have proven effective in reducing emissions and align with the goals set by the World Semiconductor Council (WSC) and the TSIA Semiconductor Fluorine Gas Emission Reduction BAT Implementation Principles. To achieve the desired reduction targets, it is crucial to establish a standard emission rate (NER) and set specific reduction goals. For instance, the WSC expects a 30% reduction in NER, equivalent to a standard emission rate of 0.22 $kgCO_2e/cm^2$ by 2020, based on the 2010 total baseline. Furthermore, the TSIA aligns with the WSC resolution and ensures the implementation of reduction techniques in emission reporting and new plants, including those outside the WSC region.

Additionally, the calculation approach for estimating emissions and by-products should follow the "IPCC 2019 Guidelines for National Greenhouse Gas Inventories, Volume 3: Industrial Processes and Product Use: Chapter 6 Electronics Industry Emission, Tier 2c" formula. This formula takes into account parameters such as the number of fluorinated compounds used, emission factors, destruction rates, creation of by-products, and their corresponding global warming potentials.

4.2. Monitoring Plans and Calculation Approach

To facilitate effective monitoring and reporting, a Monitoring Plan (MP) must be prepared and maintained by corporations exceeding the total GHG emission threshold. The MP should include details on the facility's GHG emission sources and streams, emission quantification methods, quality management procedures, and uncertainty assessment. The NEA's guidelines and the MP Template provide guidance on the key elements to document in the MP, including site details, metering and analysis, emission streams, summary tables, and quality management frameworks [24].

The calculation approach should consider the specific parameters outlined in the Tier 2c formula, as detailed in Table 4. This includes recording data on gas and chemical consumption sourced from facility SCADA systems and wafer move data from modules CIM systems. By accurately measuring and calculating emissions, semiconductor manufacturers can gain insights into their performance and progress towards GHG reduction goals.

Table 4. Specific parameters for IPCC 2019 Tier 2c calculation.

Parameter Monitored	Source of Data	Data Unit	Measured (m), Calculated (c), or Estimated (e)	Recording Frequency	How Is/Was the Data Archived? (Electronic/Paper)	Comments
Gas & Chemical Consumption	Facility SCADA System	kg	Total consumption in pressure (MPa) Average of filled pressure (Default) Total consumption in pressure (MPa)	Monthly	Total consumable mass of each GHG-Calculated weight for yearly basis (kg)	Calculated weight for yearly basis (kg) = $\sum$ Total consumption in pressure (MPa)
Wafer Move	Modules CIM System	pcs	Flow rate (sccm) Supply duration (sec) Supply frequency Wafer move (/year)	Monthly	Fraction usage of individual GHG by machine	Fraction usage = (Flow rate × Supply duration × Supply frequency × Wafer move)/$\sum$ (Flow rate × Supply duration × Supply frequency × Wafer move)

4.3. Implementation Considerations for New Reduction Methods

The implementation of new reduction methods requires careful consideration of several factors. For post-production new plants, historical data on fluorinated and N_2O usage and utilization rates for two consecutive years should be available before initiating the project. The abatement system's processing power must exceed past data on the passage of fluorinated compounds and N_2O, including by-products and diluted gases. It is essential to ensure that the lifespan of the abatement system exceeds the project duration, and that existing equipment is in good working condition or replaced if necessary. Additionally, equipment that has been previously used in reduction measures should be removed to avoid redundancy and inefficiencies.

4.4. Applicability to the Singapore Semiconductor Industry

The proposed principles for GHG reduction and the considerations outlined above are highly applicable to the semiconductor industry in Singapore. Singapore's commitment to environmental sustainability, as reflected in the Sustainable Singapore Blueprint and the Green Plan 2030, aligns with these principles. The advanced infrastructure, strong regulatory frameworks, and collaboration between industry stakeholders create a conducive environment for the implementation of optimal control technologies and the adoption of sustainable practices. By embracing these principles and implementing effective reduction methods, the semiconductor industry in Singapore can lead the way in sustainable semiconductor manufacturing, contributing to national and global environmental goals while maintaining competitiveness in the global market [25].

4.5. Other Consideration Factors for the Implementation of New Reduction Methods

Prior to the start of the project year for the installation of an effective abatement system, post-production new plants shall have a history of fluorinated and N_2O usage and utilization rates for two consecutive years. The abatement's maximum processing power must exceed past data on the passage of FCs and N_2O into the abatement (including all other by-products and diluted gases). The reduction project must also determine whether the lifespan of the abatement system is longer than the project, whether existing equipment has failed or grown too old to be used, and remove equipment if it has been in a previous reduction measures project [19].

4.6. Example of Installing Emission Control Technology with High Destruction Efficiency for C_2F_6

An exemplary case of installing emission control technology with exceptional destruction efficiency for C_2F_6 can be illustrated using the following data:

- FC_g,used (Amount of C_2F_6 used) = 1000 kg.
- D_g for abatement control (combustion/electric heating scrubber) = 0.9.
- D_g for abatement control (wet scrubber) = 0.
- GWP (Global Warming Potential) for C_2F_6 = 9200.

Applying the emission calculation equation $Eg = FC_g,used \times \{(1 - C_g) \times [1 - (A_g \times D_g)] \times GWP_g\}$, we can assess the remarkable impact of implementing emission control technology. With the installation of highly efficient abatement control technology, the total emission of C_2F_6 is calculated to be 2,539,200 kg CO_2e. This impressive achievement signifies a substantial reduction in greenhouse gas emissions, highlighting the effectiveness of the implemented control measures.

In stark contrast, in the absence of abatement control technology, the total emission of C_2F_6 amounts to a staggering 5,520,000 kg CO_2e. This stark contrast emphasizes the significance of installing emission control technology with high destruction efficiency to mitigate environmental impact and significantly reduce greenhouse gas emissions. By successfully implementing such effective emission control measures, we not only demonstrate a commitment to environmental sustainability but also contribute significantly to the preservation of our planet. The substantial reduction achieved in C_2F_6 emissions showcases the positive outcomes that can be achieved when advanced control technologies are applied.

This exemplary case serves as a testament to the remarkable potential for environmental conservation through the adoption of cutting-edge emission control technology. By embracing such initiatives, we pave the way for a greener future and inspire others to follow suit in reducing their environmental footprint.

5. Summary of Key Findings, Implications, and Recommendations for Future Research and Practice

5.1. Summary of Key Findings

This study on semiconductor sustainability manufacturing has yielded several key findings that provide insights into the current state and potential pathways for achieving sustainability goals in the industry [3]. The following are the major findings:

1. Importance of Optimal Control Technologies: The implementation of optimal control technologies for greenhouse gas (GHG) reduction, particularly targeting fluorine-gas, PFCs, and HFCs, is crucial in achieving significant emission reductions. These technologies have demonstrated their effectiveness in reducing emissions and aligning with industry association goals and regulatory requirements.
2. Calculation Approach and Monitoring Plans: The adoption of an accurate and standardized calculation approach, such as the IPCC guidelines, ensures consistent and reliable estimation of emissions and by-products. Furthermore, the development and implementation of robust monitoring plans provide a systematic framework for data collection, analysis, and reporting, enabling better tracking of sustainability performance [5].
3. Applicability to the Singapore Semiconductor Industry: The proposed principles and methodologies discussed in this study are highly applicable to the semiconductor industry in Singapore. The country's supportive infrastructure, regulatory frameworks, and commitment to sustainability create a conducive environment for implementing these principles and achieving sustainable manufacturing practices.

5.2. Implications

The findings of this study have several implications for the semiconductor industry and its stakeholders:

1. Regulatory Compliance: Semiconductor companies in Singapore should prioritize compliance with relevant environmental regulations and standards. By adopting the proposed principles and methodologies, they can demonstrate their commitment to sustainability and align with national and global sustainability initiatives.

2. Collaboration and Knowledge Sharing: Collaboration within the industry, both within Singapore and globally, is essential for sharing best practices, exchanging knowledge, and driving continuous improvement. Active participation in industry associations, forums, and working groups can foster collaboration and advance sustainable manufacturing practices.
3. Continuous Improvement and Innovation: The semiconductor industry should strive for continuous improvement and innovation in GHG reduction technologies and practices. This includes exploring emerging technologies, investing in research and development, and promoting a culture of sustainability within organizations.

5.3. Recommendations for Future Research and Practice

Building upon the findings and implications of this study, the following recommendations are put forth for future research and practice:

1. Longitudinal Studies: Conduct longitudinal studies to monitor the long-term impact of optimal control technologies and sustainable practices on GHG emissions in the semiconductor industry. These studies can provide insights into the effectiveness of the implemented measures and identify areas for further improvement.
2. Technological Advancements: Encourage research and development efforts focused on developing more efficient and environmentally friendly semiconductor manufacturing processes. This includes exploring alternative materials, optimizing resource utilization, and integrating clean energy sources within fabs.
3. Life Cycle Assessment (LCA): Conduct comprehensive life cycle assessments of semiconductor products to evaluate their environmental impact across the entire product life cycle. This holistic approach will facilitate informed decision-making and support the development of sustainable products and processes.
4. Stakeholder Engagement: Engage stakeholders, including employees, customers, suppliers, and the local community, in sustainability initiatives. Foster transparency, communication, and collaboration to build a shared understanding of sustainability goals and leverage collective efforts for sustainable manufacturing [25].
5. Policy Development: Collaborate with policymakers to develop supportive policies and incentives that encourage sustainable manufacturing practices in the semiconductor industry. Policy frameworks should consider the unique challenges and opportunities faced by the industry and provide a conducive environment for sustainable growth.

5.4. Future Trends and Development of the Semiconductor Industry

The semiconductor industry is witnessing a surge in demand due to the increasing popularity of consumer electronics products and the emergence of advanced technologies such as artificial intelligence, machine learning, and the Internet of Things. This growth is driven by factors such as rising household incomes, population growth, digitization, and urbanization [26]. However, the industry may struggle to meet the surging demand sustainably [27].

To achieve the target of net-zero emissions by 2050, semiconductor manufacturing companies must explore greener alternatives and prioritize the use of renewable energy sources. Embracing sustainable practices and investing in cleaner technologies will be essential to meet the future demands of the industry while minimizing environmental impact. Collaborative efforts between industry players, policymakers, and research institutions can drive the development and adoption of sustainable solutions in the semiconductor sector.

6. Conclusions

In conclusion, this study on semiconductor sustainability manufacturing has provided significant insights into the current state and potential pathways for achieving sustainability goals in the industry. The key findings emphasize the importance of optimal control technologies, calculation methodologies, and monitoring plans for greenhouse gas reduction in semiconductor manufacturing processes. By implementing these findings, the industry can align with industry association goals and regulatory requirements, and contribute to national and global sustainability initiatives. The implications of this study are far-reaching. Semiconductor companies in Singapore should prioritize regulatory compliance and demonstrate their commitment to sustainability. Collaboration and knowledge sharing within the industry, both locally and globally, are crucial for driving continuous improvement and advancing sustainable manufacturing practices. Moreover, fostering a culture of continuous improvement and innovation is vital for the industry to stay at the forefront of GHG reduction technologies and practices.

Based on the findings and implications, several recommendations for future research and practice are proposed. Longitudinal studies can monitor the long-term impact of optimal control technologies and sustainable practices, providing insights into effectiveness and areas for improvement. Research and development efforts should focus on technological advancements, exploring alternative materials, optimizing resource utilization, and integrating clean energy sources. Conducting comprehensive life cycle assessments will support informed decision-making and the development of sustainable products and processes. Stakeholder engagement and policy development are also essential to leverage collective efforts and create a conducive environment for sustainable growth.

Looking ahead, the semiconductor industry faces the challenge of meeting growing demand sustainably while striving for net-zero emissions by 2050. To achieve this, companies must explore greener alternatives and prioritize the use of renewable energy sources. Embracing sustainable practices and investing in cleaner technologies will be crucial in minimizing environmental impact. Collaboration among industry players, policymakers, and research institutions will play a pivotal role in driving the development and adoption of sustainable solutions in the semiconductor sector.

Author Contributions: Conceptualization, H.H. and S.Z.; methodology, Y.L.; validation, Y.L., S.Z. and H.H.; formal analysis, Y.L.; investigation, H.H.; resources, Y.L. and Y.Q.; writing—original draft preparation, Y.L.; writing—review and editing, S.Z., H.Y., Y.Q. and H.H.; visualization, S.Z. and H.Y.; supervision, Y.L.; project administration, Y.L. All authors have read and agreed to the published version of the manuscript.

Funding: This research was funded by Enerstay Sustainability Pte Ltd. (Singapore) Grant Call (Call 1/2022) _GHG (Project ID VS1-001), Singapore.

Data Availability Statement: The data that support the findings of this study are available from the corresponding author upon reasonable request.

Conflicts of Interest: All authors declare no Competing Financial or Non-Financial Interests.

References

1. Lee, C.H.; Chang, C.C. Carbon tax in Taiwan: A review and assessment. *Energy Policy* **2018**, *117*, 474–485.
2. Lin, B.; Chiang, J.H. Carbon pricing in Taiwan: Current status and future directions. *J. Clean. Prod.* **2019**, *213*, 512–519.
3. National Climate Change Secretariat. Singapore's Nationally Determined Contribution under the Paris Agreement. 2019. Available online: https://www.climateaction.gov.sg/docs/default-source/default-document-library/ndc-report-2019.pdf (accessed on 10 July 2023).
4. Tan, S.Y.; Tan, E.K. Carbon pricing in Singapore: A review and assessment. *J. Clean. Prod.* **2019**, *212*, 910–921.
5. Wang, Y.C.; Lin, B. Carbon pricing and its impact on the semiconductor industry in Taiwan. *J. Clean. Prod.* **2020**, *254*, 120301.
6. Wong, P.K.; Tan, S.Y. Carbon pricing and its impact on the semiconductor industry in Singapore. *J. Clean. Prod.* **2021**, *275*, 124868.
7. Tietenberg, T.H. Reflections—Carbon Pricing in Practice. *Rev. Environ. Econ. Policy* **2013**, *7*, 313–329. [CrossRef]
8. Metcalf, G.E. Designing a carbon tax to reduce U.S. greenhouse gas emissions. *Rev. Environ. Econ. Policy* **2009**, *3*, 63–83. [CrossRef]
9. Gautier, L. The Role of Multiple Pollutants and Pollution Intensities in the Policy Reform of Taxes and Standards. *B.E. J. Econ. Anal. Policy* **2019**, *19*, 20180186. [CrossRef]
10. Ambec, S.; Cohen, M.A.; Elgie, S.; Lanoie, P. The Porter Hypothesis at 20: Can Environmental Regulation Enhance Innovation and Competitiveness? *Rev. Environ. Econ. Policy* **2013**, *7*, 2–22. [CrossRef]
11. Chen, Y. Taiwan's Plan to Implement Carbon Tax from 2023 to Reduce Emissions. Taipei Times. 2019. Available online: https://www.taipeitimes.com/News/taiwan/archives/2019/06/12/2003716583 (accessed on 10 July 2023).

12. Chu, J. Singapore's Carbon Tax: What It Means for Businesses. Deloitte Insights. 2019. Available online: https://www2.deloitte.com/sg/en/insights/industry/energy-and-resources/singapore-carbon-tax-business-implications.html (accessed on 10 July 2023).
13. Lee, J. Singapore's Carbon Tax: An Overview. Baker McKenzie. 2019. Available online: https://www.bakermckenzie.com/en/insight/publications/2019/01/singapore-carbon-tax-overview (accessed on 10 July 2023).
14. Ministry of the Environment and Water Resources. Singapore's Carbon Pricing Journey. Available online: https://www.mewr.gov.sg/docs/default-source/default-document-library/carbon-pricing-journey.pdf (accessed on 10 July 2023).
15. National Development Council. Taiwan's Carbon Pricing Policy. 2019. Available online: https://www.ndc.gov.tw/En/News/Detail/8781 (accessed on 10 July 2023).
16. International Energy Agency. Carbon Pricing. 2018. Available online: https://www.iea.org/reports/carbon-pricing (accessed on 10 July 2023).
17. Organisation for Economic Co-operation and Development. Carbon Pricing in Practice. 2019. Available online: https://www.oecd.org/environment/indicators-modelling-outlooks/carbon-pricing-in-practice.pdf (accessed on 10 July 2023).
18. Carbon Tax Center. How Carbon Pricing Works. Available online: https://www.carbontax.org/how-carbon-pricing-works/ (accessed on 10 July 2023).
19. World Bank. Carbon Pricing. 2018. Available online: https://www.worldbank.org/en/topic/climatechange/brief/carbon-pricing (accessed on 10 July 2023).
20. International Semiconductor Industry Association. Semiconductor Industry Statistics. 2019. Available online: https://www.semiconductors.org/resources/semiconductor-industry-statistics/ (accessed on 10 July 2023).
21. Li, S.-N.; Shih, H.-Y.; Wang, K.-S.; Hsieh, K.; Chen, Y.-Y.; Chou, J. Preventive Maintenance Measures for Contamination Control. *Solid-State Technol.* **2005**, *48*, 53–57.
22. Li, S.-N.; Lin, C.-N.; Shih, H.-Y.; Cheng, J.-H.; Hsu, J.-N.; Wang, K.-S. Default values appear to be overestimating F-GHG emissions from fabs. *Solid-State Technol.* **2004**, *47*, 4.
23. Li, S.-N.; Chen, Y.-Y.; Shih, H.-Y.; Hong, J.L. Using an Extractive Fourier Transform Infrared (FTIR) Spectrometer for Improving Cleanroom Air Quality in a Semiconductor Manufacturing Plant. *Am. Ind. Hyg. Assoc. J.* **2003**, *64*, 408–414. [CrossRef] [PubMed]
24. Dey, B.K.; Park, J.; Seok, H. Carbon-emission and waste reduction of a manufacturing-remanufacturing system using green technology and autonomated inspection. *RAIRO-Oper. Res.* **2022**, *56*, 2801–2831. [CrossRef]
25. Dey, B.K.; Yilmaz, I.; Seok, H. A Sustainable Supply Chain Integrated with Autonomated Inspection, Flexible Eco-Production, and Smart Transportation. *Processes* **2022**, *10*, 1775. [CrossRef]
26. Liang, Y.L.; Tan, K.T.; Li, Y.Z. Implementation Principles of Optimal Control Technology for the Reduction of Greenhouse Gases in Semiconductor Industry. *E3S Web Conf.* **2023**, *394*, 01031. [CrossRef]
27. Sun, J.X.; Li, Y.Z. Research on Improving Energy Storage Density and Efficiency of Dielectric Ceramic Ferroelectric Materials Based on BaTiO3 Doping with Multiple Elements. *J. Compos. Sci.* **2023**, *7*, 233. [CrossRef]

Disclaimer/Publisher's Note: The statements, opinions and data contained in all publications are solely those of the individual author(s) and contributor(s) and not of MDPI and/or the editor(s). MDPI and/or the editor(s) disclaim responsibility for any injury to people or property resulting from any ideas, methods, instructions or products referred to in the content.

Article

Harnessing Digestate Potential: Impact of Biochar and Reagent Addition on Biomethane Production in Anaerobic Digestion Systems

Alaa Salma *, Nur Maisarah Binti Faeruz, Lydia Fryda and Hayet Djelal *

Unilasalle-Ecole des Métiers de l'Environnement, Cyclann, Campus de Ker Lann, 35 170 Bruz, France; nur_18002269@utp.edu.my (N.M.B.F.); lydia.fryda@unilasalle.fr (L.F.)
* Correspondence: alaa.salma@unilasalle.fr (A.S.); hayet.djelal@unilasalle.fr (H.D.)

Abstract: This article reports on an experiment that aimed to investigate the effects of digestate and cosubstrate input with varying biochar concentrations on methane production in anaerobic digestion processes. The findings revealed distinct trends in methane production among the substrates. Further investigations were conducted to evaluate the effects of different types of biochars on biomethane production from raw cattle manure digestate. Four conditions were tested: one raw digestate condition and three digestate conditions containing 1% of a different biochar type to one another. BC1 (PEFC-certified spruce BC) and BC2 (oak wood BC) showed promising results in enhancing biomethane production. About 884.23 NmL of methane was produced, with a yield and productivity of 22.80 NmL.g^{-1} and 1.62 NmL.g^{-1}.day^{-1} with BC1. However, BC3 (cow and chicken manure digestate BC) demonstrated lower biomethane production compared to raw digestate. Additionally, the study explored the effects of adding reagents to digestate. Hematite and iron chloride salt did not show any positive effects on biomethane production when biochar was introduced, while activated carbon powder significantly improved biomethane production rates by approximately 11.18%.

Keywords: biochar; biomethane production; anaerobic digestion; cattle manure digestate; cosubstrates

Citation: Salma, A.; Binti Faeruz, N.M.; Fryda, L.; Djelal, H. Harnessing Digestate Potential: Impact of Biochar and Reagent Addition on Biomethane Production in Anaerobic Digestion Systems. *Processes* **2023**, *11*, 2284. https://doi.org/10.3390/pr11082284

Academic Editor: Antoni Sánchez

Received: 28 June 2023
Revised: 26 July 2023
Accepted: 26 July 2023
Published: 29 July 2023

Copyright: © 2023 by the authors. Licensee MDPI, Basel, Switzerland. This article is an open access article distributed under the terms and conditions of the Creative Commons Attribution (CC BY) license (https://creativecommons.org/licenses/by/4.0/).

1. Introduction

Anaerobic digestion (AD) is a sustainable technology that can effectively manage organic waste, reduce sludge, and generate renewable energy in the form of biogas and a nutrient-rich residue called digestate [1]. AD offers numerous benefits such as the reduction of greenhouse gas emissions (GHGs), additional income from farmers, recycling of nutrients, and a pollution reduction [2,3]. However, maintaining the stability of AD reactors can be challenging due to the accumulation of toxic inhibitors, unsteady pH, or other key factors [4]. To improve the efficiency of AD technology, different methods such as mechanical [5], physical [6], chemical [7], or biological have been developed [8,9].

Biochar (BC) is a type of charcoal that is produced from biomass, such as wood chips, agricultural waste, manure, and other organic materials [10]. It is produced through a process called pyrolysis, which involves heating the biomass in the absence of oxygen [11]. The quality of the BC produced depends on several factors, including the type of organic matter used, the temperature and duration of pyrolysis, and the conditions in the kiln or container [12].

These materials can be used as a soil amendment, as well as for various other applications [13]. One of the main benefits of BC is its ability to improve soil fertility and plant growth [14,15]. It also has the potential to sequester carbon in the soil, which can help mitigate climate change by reducing the amount of carbon dioxide in the atmosphere [16]. BC has also been shown to have potential in other areas, such as water treatment [17], energy production [18], and the remediation of contaminated soils [19]. Overall, the use of

BC has been a subject of considerable interest and research in the modern age owing to its potential to address a range of environmental and agricultural issues.

BC can be used to address some of the limitations of AD, such as stabilizing carbon, retaining nutrients, high-level Ammonia (NH_3), and buffering pH, while the organic waste material from AD can serve as a feedstock for BC production [20]. The AD process involves a varied assemblage of archaea and bacteria [21]. Direct interspecies electron transfer (DIET) among bacteria and methanogenic archaea has lately been explored to accelerate the syntrophic conversion of various organic compounds to methane [22]. BC, due to its conductive properties, has been found to stimulate DIET and is a possible external additive for enhancing methanogenesis [23]. Various researchers have investigated AD feasibility enhanced by BC, and have demonstrated that BC can notably increase the methane yield of multiple feedstocks [24].

BC can have a positive impact on microbiological activity in AD by creating a more hospitable environment for microorganisms that are involved in the AD process [25]. The porous structure of BC provides a habitat for microorganisms, which can enhance their activity and growth [26]. The high surface area of BC allows for more microorganisms to attach to its surface, which can increase their overall activity [27]. BC can also improve the nutrient availability and retention in the digestate, which is the residue that remains after the AD process is complete [28]. This can provide a sustained source of nutrition for the microorganisms, which can promote their growth and activity [29]. Furthermore, BC can help regulate the pH and moisture content of the digestate, creating a more stable environment for the microorganisms, which can lead to more consistent and efficient microbiological activity [30]. BC can also decrease the lag time required for methane formation, enhance the production and degradation of intermediate acids, and increase the levels of macro- and micronutrients in the digestate [24,31]. Overall, research has shown that the addition of BC to AD systems can increase the population and diversity of microorganisms during the process, which can lead to improved stability and higher yields of biogas [32]. The physicochemical properties of BC, which are attributed to the feedstock types and pyrolysis conditions used for its production, control the variability of these specific effects [33]. Studies on the behavior of different types of BC during AD remain uncommon [31], further research is needed to fully understand its potential in these areas.

The study aims to investigate the impact of BC on biomethane production by working with two different input materials (digestate and a preshredded cosubstrate prior to its integration into the digester). In the first case, BC is introduced along with the digestate, while in the second case, it is introduced with the cosubstrate before it becomes digestate. In addition, we assess the effects of BC concentration and type on methane production and explore the potential benefits of reagent addition such as hematite, iron chloride, and activated carbon powder to enhance biomethane production. The findings aimed to contribute to the optimization of AD processes, with the goal of promoting sustainable waste management practices and renewable energy generation.

2. Materials and Methods

2.1. Digestats, Cosubstrates, Biochars, and Reagents

In the conducted experiment, two different input materials, namely digestate and cosubstrates, were used. The digestate used in the experiment was obtained from the Castel Metha AD plant located in Brittany, France, which operates at a biogas production flow rate of 125 Nm^3/h and is located approximately 20 min away from the laboratory. The primary input for this unit comprised young cattle manure reared on straw, which was stored in opaque containers at room temperature until use. Notably, the Castel Metha unit actively feeds biomethane into the natural gas grid.

The cosubstrates used for the experiment came from the SAS Biogaz-IFF plant, also located in Brittany, France. This unit has a biogas production flow rate of 65 Nm^3/h and is situated approximately 30 min away from the laboratory. The cosubstrate's composition consisted of various components, including cattle slurry (10 m^3 day^{-1}), pig slurry

(5 m³ day⁻¹), cattle manure (4 tons), pig manure (2 tons), poultry manure (3.5 tons), and maize silage (5 tons). In our study, raw digestate and cosubstrates were employed as the control variable.

Furthermore, the experiment involved the utilization of three types of biochars, namely BC1, BC2, and BC3. BC1 was PEFC-certified spruce biochar, BC2 was derived from oak wood by the University of Cassel, and BC3 was digestate biochar sourced from the Netherlands. These biochars were employed in different proportions depending on their specific application. The differences between the three types of biochars are presented in Table 1. Additionally, activated carbon, hematite (Ouenza, 70 km of Tebessa, Algeria), and iron (III) chloride salt were incorporated into the experiment.

Table 1. Type and Characteristics of BC.

BC Type	Source Material	Production Method	Brunauer Emmett-Teller (BET m²/g)	Density (kg/m³)	Ash Content (%)	Production T° (°C)	Residence Time (min)
BC 1	PEFC-certified Spruce	Auger Pyrolysis	420	115	2.5	600	<10
BC 2	Oak Wood	Auger Pyrolysis	160	110	3	400	30
BC 3	Cow and chicken manure digestate	Gasification	105	533	59	650–750	10–20

2.2. Process Monitoring of AMPT II

The Automatic Methanization Potential Test II (AMPT II) is an automated process that involves monitoring various parameters such as substrate and inoculum mass, pH and temperature, monitoring biogas production, and calculating methane yield. Twelve parallel, completely mixed anaerobic digesters are used to conduct batch experiments on anaerobic digestion. Each digester had a working volume of 400 g and was equipped with a gas-sampling bag and a sludge-sampling pore. These digesters are placed in a shaker at a temperature of 37 °C and a speed of 140 rpm for a defined time. Throughout the experiments, the volume of biomethane produced is continuously measured using the Gas-Volume Measuring Device of AMPTS II and recorded in the AMPTS II software (bcp instruments version 1.04) from the start of experiments (day 0) until the last day of experiments. The temperature of the sample incubation unit is maintained at 37 °C to ensure mesophilic conditions. The experiment was conducted in triplicate for each trial.

2.3. Analytical Methods

Physicochemical analyses were conducted in triplicate for each experiment, both at the end of each experiment after centrifuge at 4 °C and 5000 rpm/min for 15 min using centrifugation (ThermoFisher Scientific Heraeus Megafuge, Porton, UK). Six analyses were performed, which included the % of dry matter (% DM), Chemical Oxygen Demand (COD), pH, Complete Alkalimetric Title (CAT), and volatile fatty acids (VFAs).

The protocol of measuring dry matter (DM) involves the following steps:

Three masses were weighed for each essay, including the mass of the empty aluminum container (m0), the mass of the sample with the aluminum container (m1), and finally the mass of the dried sample with the aluminum container (m2) after being placed in the oven for 2 days at 105 °C until it reaches a constant weight. The samples were dried using a drying oven (VWR® DRY-Line®, UK).

The dry matter content is calculated as follows:

$$Dry\ Matter\ (DM\ \%) = (Dry\ weight/\ wet\ weight) \times 100$$

2.3.1. COD Analysis

After centrifugation, the centrifuged samples can be used for COD analysis using COD reagent vials, a thermoreactor (Spectroquant TR 420, Merck, Frankfurt, Germany), and colorimeter (Spectroquant Move 100, Merck, Frankfurt, Germany). A volume of 0.5 mL was extracted from each assay (blank control, control, and essays) and then diluted with 10 mL of distilled water. The resulting mixtures were further diluted with an adapted dilution factor. Next 3 mL of each diluted supernatant was transferred into a COD tube and then placed in the thermoreactor at 150 °C for a period of 2 h. After 2 h, the COD tubes were removed and allowed to cool in a test tube rack for 40 min before reading the results with the colorimeter.

2.3.2. pH Measurement

The pH of samples was determined using a pH meter (pH 3110, pH electrode SenTix® 21, Grosseron, WTW, France) at the start and end of the experiments following centrifugation of the samples at 4 °C and 5000 rpm/min for 15 min.

2.3.3. Complete Alkalimetric Title (CAT) and Volatile Fatty Acid (VFA) Measurement

In this study, the CAT and VFA were measured using an Automatic titrator (ThermoFisher Scientific ™ Orion Star ™ T910 Series Potentiometric Titrators, France). To perform the measurement, 5 mL of supernatant from each of the samples were taken and then diluted to 100 mL with distilled water and mixed thoroughly in glass beakers. The measurement was conducted following the manufacturer's instructions for the automatic titrator. VFA and CAT were determined according to the method described by [34]. Therefore, the VFA/CAT ratio is used to assess the stability and health of the AD system.

3. Results and Discussion

3.1. Experimental Investigation of Digestate and Cosubstrates Input with Different Biochar Concentration in Anaerobic Digestion

The experimental investigation involved the utilization of digestate and cosubstrates as input materials in AD processes, with varying doses of BC 1 (1%, 2%, and 4% based on the mass of the sample) added to the feedstocks. The primary parameter measured in this study was the accumulated biomethane volume after a period of 9 days. Analysis of the obtained data revealed distinct trends in methane production among the different substrates (Figure 1a,b). Specifically, the raw digestate showed higher methane production (around 548.0 ± 49.6 NmL) compared to the cosubstrates (341.5 ± 16.5 NmL). This could be attributed depending on the composition and characteristics of the feedstock use; in terms of complexity and degradability, the cosubstrates with its multiple organic materials would generally be considered more complex and potentially harder to degrade compared to digestate, which primarily consists of raw cattle manure. Moreover, the addition of 1% BC to digestate resulted in similar methane production levels (550.5 ± 22.2 NmL), albeit slightly lower than that of the cosubstrates (299.96 ± 9.7 NmL) when compared to their respective control groups. However, the introduction of 2% and 4% BC doses appeared to inhibit methane production, as the volume of methane generated was noticeably reduced compared to the other experimental conditions. These observations indicate that the influence of BC on methane production varied depending on the substrate used, with the higher BC concentrations negatively impacting methane production.

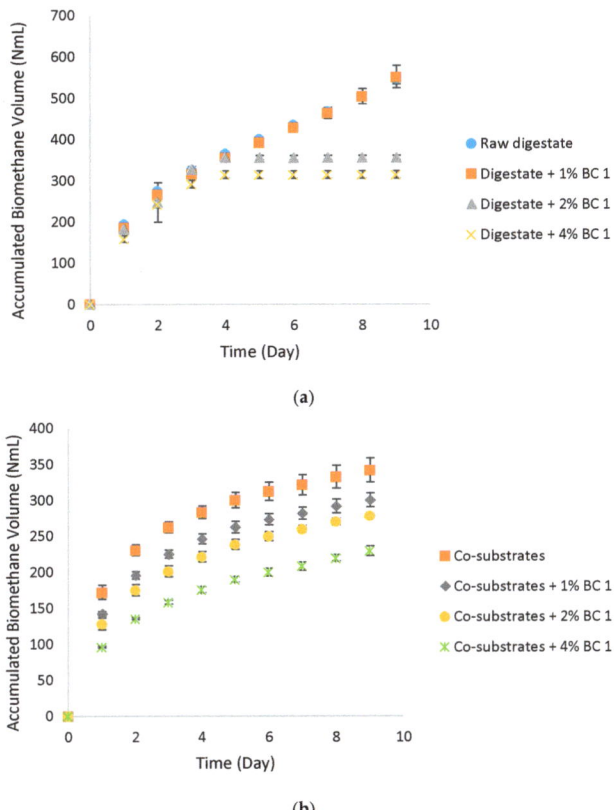

Figure 1. Effect of different doses of BC on biomethane production using digestate (**a**) as a material input and cosubstrates (**b**) as a material input after 9 days of AD.

The addition of 1% BC resulting in similar methane production for raw digestate, although slightly lower than cosubstrates, corresponds to studies suggesting that low concentrations of biochar can enhance anaerobic digestion performance [35]. BC, with its porous structure and high surface area, has the potential to adsorb and retain volatile fatty acids, improving process stability and methane production [30]. However, the slight reduction in methane production compared to cosubstrates could be attributed to variations in substrate composition and biochar's specific interaction with different feedstocks [36].

The inhibitory effect of higher BC concentrations (2% and 4%) on methane production aligns with literature highlighting the potential negative impact of excessive BC doses [37]. High concentrations of BC can lead to increased pH levels, nutrient immobilization, and reduced microbial activity, thereby impeding AD efficiency [32]. These findings emphasize the importance of optimal BC dosing to avoid potential negative consequences on methane production. The compelling results obtained from the experimental investigation strongly warrant further pursuit of experiment focused on digestate as a primary feedstock in AD processes.

3.2. Effects of Different Type of Biochars on Biomethane Production of Digestate

The experiment aimed to evaluate the impact of different types of BC (1, 2, and 3) on biomethane production when added to raw cattle manure digestate. The results varied depending on the type of BC used.

Four different conditions were tested: raw digestate, digestate + 1% BC 1 (PEFC-certified spruce BC), digestate + 1% BC 2 (oak wood BC), and digestate + 1% BC 3 (cow and chicken manure digestate BC). The experiment measured the accumulated biomethane volume against days, as shown in Figure 2a. The results showed that BC1 was the most effective in enhancing biomethane production (884.23 ± 62.0 NmL at the end of experiment), yielding 22.80 NmL·g^{-1} which correspond to a productivity of 1.62 NmL·g^{-1}·day^{-1}. This is likely due to the high porosity and surface area of the spruce BC, which provide more sites for the colonization of methanogenic bacteria that produce biomethane [33]. Interestingly, BC 2 showed a similar performance to BC 1, with some fluctuations in biomethane production. However, as the experiment progressed, BC2 caught up and eventually outperformed BC 1 yield by 2.4%, indicating that adding BC2 can have a positive impact on biomethane production over the long term, although it may not provide immediate benefits. On the other hand, BC 3 showed less performance in biomethane production (around 742.0 ± 22.0 NmL) compared to raw digestate (870.20 ± 37.0 NmL). The yield and productivity of biomethane for BC 3 were 21.66 NmL·g^{-1} and 1.50 NmL·g^{-1}·day^{-1}, while the yield and productivity for raw digestate were 21.25 NmL·g^{-1} and 1.51 NmL·g^{-1}·day^{-1}, respectively (Figure 2b). This could be attributed to the high ash content (see Table 1) and the presence of copper in the BC 3, which may have a negative impact on microbial activity in the AD process.

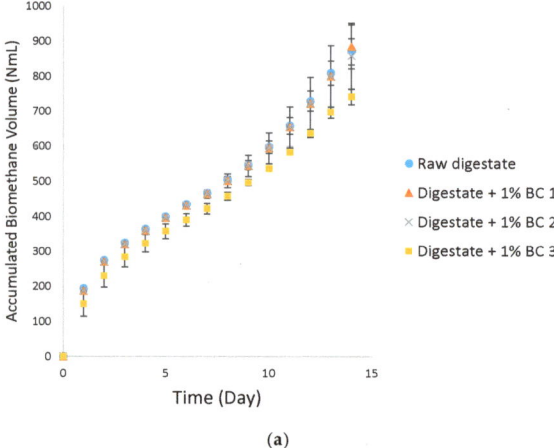

(a)

Figure 2. Cont.

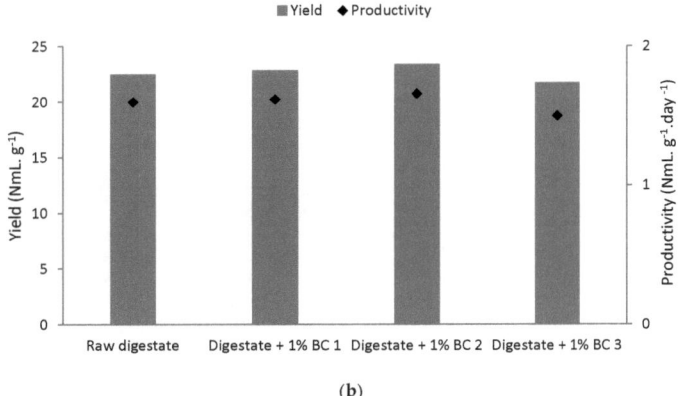

(b)

Figure 2. (a) Effect of different type of biochar on cumulative biomethane (NmL) volume per day. (b) Cumulated biomethane yield and productivity of different biochar in AD.

Table 2 shows the productivity (measured in NmL g^{-1} dry matter day^{-1}), pH, COD, and VFA/CAT ratio values for the four different conditions: raw digestate, digestate + 1% BC 1, digestate + 1% BC 2, and digestate + 1% BC 3.

Table 2. Parameter values at the end of anaerobic digestion after 14 days.

	Methane (NmL)	Yield (NmL·g^{-1} DM)	Productivity (NmL·g^{-1} DM·day^{-1})	DM%	pH		COD (g O$_2$/L)		VFA/CAT	
					t_0	t_f	t_0	t_f	t_0	t_f
Raw digestate	870.20 ± 37.0	22.45	1.60	9.69 ± 0.20	8.36	8.19 ± 0.08	26.23	31.30 ± 5.1	0.49	0.67 ± 0.05
Digestate + 1% BC 1	884.23 ± 62.0	22.80	1.62	10.68 ± 0.1	8.36	8.12 ± 0.10	23.56	33.20 ± 2.4	0.62	0.62 ± 0.03
Digestate + 1% BC 2	856.93 ± 94.0	23.36	1.66	10.16 ± 0.50	8.42	8.07 ± 0.04	24.88	33.00 ± 2.1	0.50	0.59 ± 0.04
Digestate + 1% BC 3	742.0 ± 22.0	21.66	1.50	9.79 ± 0.10	8.61	8.01 ± 0.04	27.80	34.00 ± 0.6	0.33	0.71 ± 0.01

From the Table 2, we can see that the productivity values of all four conditions are relatively similar, ranging from 1.50 to 1.78 NmL g^{-1} dry matter day^{-1}. However, it is worth noting that the addition of BC 2 appears to have a positive impact on productivity and enhance the biomethane production by 9% compared to raw digestate. At the end of the experiment, the pH level decreased for all conditions, but to varying degrees. The pH level of raw digestate decreased from 8.65 to 8.14, while the pH levels for digestate with BC 1, 2, and 3 decreased from 8.36 to 8.12, 8.42 to 8.07, and 8.61 to 8.10, respectively. The decrease in pH level can be an indication of the production of acidic byproducts such as volatile fatty acids (VFAs) during the anaerobic digestion process. It is also possible that the BC addition affected the pH buffering capacity of the digestate, resulting in a less significant decrease in pH level for some conditions.

The COD values for all four conditions show an increase from t_0 (initial time) to t_f (final time). BC 1 and BC 3 show the highest increase in COD values, indicating that they may have a more significant impact on organic matter degradation. During the AD process, microorganisms break down organic compounds, leading to the consumption of oxygen in the sample, which is reflected in higher COD values. In some situations, biochar can support microbial activity, providing a favorable environment for microorganisms to break down organic matter. While this can be beneficial in certain agricultural or composting settings, excessive microbial breakdown of organic matter can lead to increased COD levels in the environment. In terms of process stability, the VFA/CAT ratio results showed varying degrees of effectiveness in enhancing process stability depending on the type of BC used. BC 3 shows the highest VFA/CAT ratio (0.71), indicating a less stable process. Meanwhile, BC 1 (0.62) and BC 2 (0.59) show similar VFA/CAT ratios, which suggests a more stable process.

However, the effect of different types of BC on biomethane production from raw cattle manure digestate can also depend on the conditions used to produce the BC. For example, BC produced at higher temperatures may have a more stable carbon structure that is less accessible to the microbial community responsible for AD, which could reduce biomethane production (BC3). Biochar has gained attention for its potential applications in agriculture and environmental management [25]. One intriguing area of research is its possible effect as an in situ CO_2 adsorbent and its relation to the enhancement of methane production [38]. This discussion aims to explore the hypothesis that the addition of biochar to methane production systems could act as a CO_2 adsorbent, potentially leading to improved methane yields. Biochar's unique physical and chemical properties contribute to its CO_2 adsorption capacity. Its high surface area and porous structure provide ample sites for CO_2 molecules to bind through physisorption and chemisorption mechanisms [33]. The presence of functional groups on the biochar surface also enhances its ability to attract and retain CO_2 molecules. The absence of any improvement in methane production, despite the addition of biochar as an in situ CO_2 adsorbent, could be attributed to several factors [39]. It is possible that the biochar used lacked sufficient CO_2 adsorption capacity or faced competition from other substances for adsorption sites. Moreover, microbial adaptation to CO_2 presence, potential inhibition of methanogens by biochar properties, and altered experimental conditions might have influenced the outcomes. Additionally, complex interactions with the environment, variations in biochar types, and the short-term nature of experiments could have obscured any positive effects on methane production. Understanding these factors is crucial for refining our comprehension of biochar's role in methane production systems.

3.3. Effects of Addition of Reagents on Biomethane Production of Digestate

Numerous studies have been conducted to ascertain the potential benefits of introducing various reagents to biochar to enhance its characteristics and expand its potential applications, particularly in environmental remediation, agriculture, and energy production. This experiment sought to investigate the impact of adding specific reagents (namely, iron (III) oxide (hematite), iron (III) chloride salt, and activated carbon powder) on the biomethane production of digestate. The results presented in Figure 3 demonstrate the effects of these reagents on the accumulated biomethane volume yield and productivity at the end of the process.

Based on the information illustrated in the Figure 3, it appears that the addition of hematite and iron chloride salt did not lead to any positive effects on biomethane production in terms of yield and productivity when compared to the raw digestate (control). This indicates that these additives do not enhance or improve the methane production process when digestate is used as an input material.

The results present in Table 3 show an overall increase in the value of COD at the end of AD. The study also found an increase in volatile fatty acids (VFA) except when 1% biochar 1 + 200 mg hematite was used. However, as we can see in the Table 3, the VFA/CAT ratio increased for all tested substrates, except for 1% biochar 1 + 200 mg iron oxide. It is worth noting that this ratio ranged from 0.4 to 0.8, indicating that the AD process was unstable. Furthermore, the pH values were above the optimal range for AD (6.5–7.5).

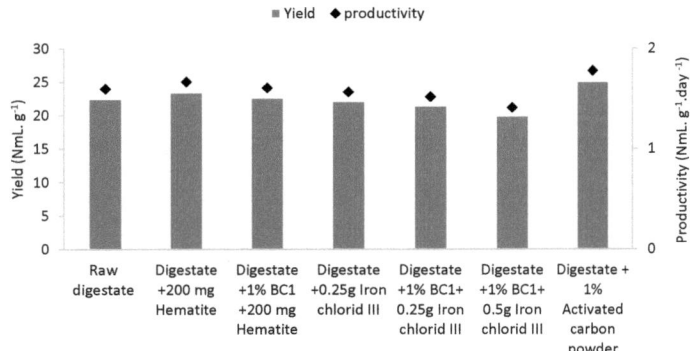

Figure 3. Cumulated biomethane yield and productivity of digestate using biochar and different reagent in anaerobic digestion.

Table 3. Outcomes of a research study examining the impact of reagent addition on biomethane production.

	Methane (Nml)	Yield (NmL·g^{-1} DM)	Productivity (NmL·g^{-1} DM·day^{-1})	% DM	pH		COD (g O$_2$/L)		VFA/CAT	
					t_0	t_f	t_0	t_f	t_0	t_f
Raw digestate	870.20 ± 37.0	22.45	1.60	9.69 ± 0.20	8.36	8.19 ± 0.08	26.23	31.30 ± 5.1	0.49	0.67 ± 0.05
Digestate + 200 mg hematite	885.13 ± 25.6	23.42	1.67	9.13 ± 0.04	8.71	8.09 ± 0.06	25.60	33.00 ± 0.7	0.35	0.54 ± 0.02
Digestate + 1% BC1+ 200 mg hematite	813.13 ± 147.0	22.60	1.61	9.98 ± 0.2	8.42	8.06 ± 0.07	20.76	34.60 ± 0.6	0.56	0.47 ± 0.05
Digestate + 0.25 g iron (III) chloride salt	823.46 ± 171.0	22.03	1.57	9.34 ± 0.10	8.33	7.85 ± 0.07	19.96	31.86 ± 4.9	0.55	0.87 ± 0.03
Digestate + 1% BC1+ 0.25 g iron (III) chloride salt	789.00 ± 191.0	21.38	1.52	10.25 ± 0.09	8.70	7.83 ± 0.01	23.40	32.13 ± 2.0	0.64	0.84 ± 0.10
Digestate + 1% BC1+ 0.5 g iron (III) chloride salt	741.00 ± 114.5	19.86	1.41	10.31 ± 0.07	8.59	7.86 ± 0.07	26.76	32.20 ± 1.4	0.59	0.75 ± 0.08
Digestate + 1% activated carbon powder	947.53 ± 74.0	25.02	1.78	10.46 ± 0.28	8.36	8.12 ± 0.05	21.80	30.54 ± 1.2	0.51	0.61 ± 0.01

The incorporation of hematite (iron (III) oxide), a source of iron, into digestate has been found to enhance the activity and growth of methanogens, which are responsible for methane production during AD, thereby increasing biomethane production [40]. Notably, the introduction of 200 mg hematite with 1% BC1 to the digestate did not result in any significant improvement in biomethane volume (813.13 NmL) compared to the digestate with hematite (885.13 NmL). This phenomenon may be attributed to several factors, such as the dependence of the optimal amount of iron supplementation on multiple variables or the presence of sufficient iron in the digestate that precludes any significant enhancement [40,41]. Consequently, further inquiry is warranted to ascertain the underlying cause of the lack of improvement in biomethane production following the addition of iron (III) oxide. Based on the results presented in Table 3, it can be observed that the addition of activated carbon powder to digestate leads to a substantial improvement in biomethane production. Specifically, the biomethane production rate increases by about 11.18% when compared to the raw digestate. Activated carbon is a highly porous material that can adsorb organic compounds, including inhibitory substances that can inhibit the growth of methanogens [42]. By removing these inhibitory substances, activated carbon can improve the activity and growth of methanogens, leading to increased biomethane production. Haut du formulaireBas du formulaire.

In addition, the study investigated the potential benefits of adding iron (III) chloride to digestate to increase biomethane production. Two different concentrations of iron chloride (0.25 g and 0.5 g) were tested, and the results showed that there was no significant improvement in biomethane production when compared to raw digestate (control). However, the addition of iron chloride did increase the VFA values (from 1.42 to 2.19 and from 134 to 2.02), while there was a significant decrease in pH (from 8.70 to 7.83 and from 8.59 to 7.86) for both concentrations tested, respectively. These observations suggest that the benefits of adding iron III chloride salt may not always be observed contrary to the findings reported in previous studies [43]. This could be explained by the high organic loading rates (OLR) in the digester that may inhibit microbial activity due to the accumulation of VFAs, resulting in a drop in pH and lower availability of iron for methanogenic microorganisms [4]. Further analysis and experimentation may be necessary to fully understand the reasons behind the lack of positive impact. Factors such as additive concentration or dosage, experimental conditions, or other variables could have influenced the results.

4. Conclusions

This paper aimed to harness digestate potential and evaluate the impact of different types of biochar on biomethane production when added to raw cattle manure digestate. The results showed that the addition of BC had varying effects on biomethane production, depending on the type of biochar used. BC 1 (PEFC-certified spruce) was found to be the most effective in enhancing biomethane production, followed by BC 2 (oak wood). However, BC 3 (cow and chicken manure digestate) showed less performance in biomethane production compared to raw digestate. Furthermore, the addition of activated carbon powder to digestate can significantly improve biomethane production, while hematite and iron chloride salt addition did not result in any positive impact on biomethane production. Moreover, the study found an overall increase in the value of COD and the VFA/CAT ratio, indicating an unstable anaerobic digestion process. In general, the results suggest that cattle manure digestate can be reused as a potential substrate for the AD process and that the addition of BC may possess a positive impact on biomethane production, yet the type of biochar used must be carefully considered to guarantee optimal results. Thus, it is imperative to conduct further research to thoroughly investigate the underlying factors and optimize the relevant conditions to enhance biomethane production from digestate.

Author Contributions: Conceptualization, A.S., L.F. and H.D.; Validation, L.F. and H.D.; Formal analysis, A.S. and N.M.B.F.; Writing—original draft, A.S.; Writing—review & editing, A.S. and H.D.; Funding acquisition, H.D. All authors have read and agreed to the published version of the manuscript.

Funding: Région Bretagne "Dispositif SAD" (Stratégie d'Attractivité Durable) 2022.

Data Availability Statement: Not applicable.

Acknowledgments: The authors express their gratitude to the Brittany Region for the financial support provided through the "Dispositif SAD" (Stratégie d'Attractivité Durable) 2022. Special thanks are extended to Patrick BOURSAULT from the anaerobic digestion Unit Castel Metha (Brittany, France), as well as Aureli LEPAGE and Ludovic PERRIN from the Biogaz-IFF unit for providing the input material samples.

Conflicts of Interest: The authors declare no conflict of interest.

References

1. Zouaghi, L.Y.S.K.; Djelal, H.; Salem, Z. Anaerobic co-digestion of three organic wastes under mesophilic conditions: Lab-scale and pilot-scale studies. *Environ. Dev. Sustain.* **2021**, *23*, 9014–9028. [CrossRef]
2. Vasco-Correa, J.; Khanal, S.; Manandhar, A.; Shah, A. Anaerobic digestion for bioenergy production: Global status, environmental and techno-economic implications, and government policies. *Bioresour. Technol.* **2018**, *247*, 1015–1026. [CrossRef]
3. Seruga, P.; Krzywonos, M.; den Boer, E.; Niedźwiecki, Ł.; Urbanowska, A.; Pawlak-Kruczek, H. Anaerobic Digestion as a Component of Circular Bioeconomy—Case Study Approach. *Energies* **2022**, *16*, 140. [CrossRef]
4. Harirchi, S.; Wainaina, S.; Sar, T.; Nojoumi, S.A.; Parchami, M.; Parchami, M.; Varjani, S.; Khanal, S.K.; Wong, J.; Awasthi, M.K.; et al. Microbiological insights into anaerobic digestion for biogas, hydrogen or volatile fatty acids (VFAs): A review. *Bioengineered* **2022**, *13*, 6521–6557. [CrossRef]
5. Pilli, S.; Pandey, A.K.; Katiyar, A.; Pandey, K.; Tyagi, R.D.; Pilli, S.; Pandey, A.K.; Katiyar, A.; Pandey, K.; Tyagi, R.D. *Pre-Treatment Technologies to Enhance Anaerobic Digestion*; IntechOpen: London, UK, 2020; ISBN 978-1-83962-707-1.
6. Hajji, A.; Rhachi, M. The effect of thermochemical pretreatment on anaerobic digestion efficiency of municipal solid waste under mesophilic conditions. *Sci. Afr.* **2022**, *16*, e01198. [CrossRef]
7. Lee, J.; Ryu, D.-Y.; Jang, K.H.; Lee, J.W.; Kim, D. Influence of Different Pretreatment Methods and Conditions on the Anaerobic Digestion Efficiency of Spent Mushroom Substrate. *Sustainability* **2022**, *14*, 15854. [CrossRef]
8. Singh, B.; Kovács, K.L.; Bagi, Z.; Nyári, J.; Szepesi, G.L.; Petrik, M.; Siménfalvi, Z.; Szamosi, Z. Enhancing Efficiency of Anaerobic Digestion by Optimization of Mixing Regimes Using Helical Ribbon Impeller. *Fermentation* **2021**, *7*, 251. [CrossRef]
9. Uddin, M.M.; Wright, M.M. Anaerobic digestion fundamentals, challenges, and technological advances. *Phys. Sci. Rev.* **2022**. [CrossRef]
10. Amalina, F.; Razak, A.S.A.; Krishnan, S.; Sulaiman, H.; Zularisam, A.W.; Nasrullah, M. Biochar production techniques utilizing biomass waste-derived materials and environmental applications—A review. *J. Hazard. Mater. Adv.* **2022**, *7*, 100134. [CrossRef]
11. Mulabagal, V.; Baah, D.A.; Egiebor, N.O.; Sajjadi, B.; Chen, W.-Y.; Viticoski, R.L.; Hayworth, J.S. Biochar from Biomass: A Strategy for Carbon Dioxide Sequestration, Soil Amendment, Power Generation, CO2 Utilization, and Removal of Perfluoroalkyl and Polyfluoroalkyl Substances (PFAS) in the Environment. In *Handbook of Climate Change Mitigation and Adaptation*; Lackner, M., Sajjadi, B., Chen, W.-Y., Eds.; Springer International Publishing: Cham, Switzerland, 2022; pp. 1023–1085, ISBN 978-3-030-72579-2.
12. Rodriguez, J.A.; Ferreira Lustosa Filho, J.; Carrijo Azevedo Melo, L.; de Assis, I.R.; Senna de Oliveira, T. Influence of pyrolysis temperature and feedstock on the properties of biochars produced from agricultural and industrial wastes. *J. Anal. Appl. Pyrolysis* **2020**, *149*, 104839. [CrossRef]
13. Kamali, M.; Sweygers, N.; Al-Salem, S.; Appels, L.; Aminabhavi, T.M.; Dewil, R. Biochar for soil applications-sustainability aspects, challenges and future prospects. *Chem. Eng. J.* **2021**, *428*, 131189. [CrossRef]
14. Ding, Y.; Liu, Y.; Liu, S.; Li, Z.; Tan, X.; Huang, X.; Zeng, G.; Zhou, L.; Zheng, B. Biochar to improve soil fertility. A review. *Agron. Sustain. Dev.* **2016**, *36*, 36. [CrossRef]
15. Zeghioud, H.; Fryda, L.; Djelal, H.; Assadi, A.; Kane, A. A comprehensive review of biochar in removal of organic pollutants from wastewater: Characterization, toxicity, activation/functionalization and influencing treatment factors. *J. Water Process. Eng.* **2022**, *47*, 102801. [CrossRef]
16. Kalu, S.; Kulmala, L.; Zrim, J.; Peltokangas, K.; Tammeorg, P.; Rasa, K.; Kitzler, B.; Pihlatie, M.; Karhu, K. Potential of Biochar to Reduce Greenhouse Gas Emissions and Increase Nitrogen Use Efficiency in Boreal Arable Soils in the Long-Term. *Front. Environ. Sci.* **2022**, *10*, 914766. [CrossRef]
17. Wang, X.; Guo, Z.; Hu, Z.; Zhang, J. Recent advances in biochar application for water and wastewater treatment: A review. *PeerJ* **2020**, *8*, e9164. [CrossRef]
18. Xiao, L.; Lichtfouse, E.; Kumar, P.S.; Wang, Q.; Liu, F. Biochar promotes methane production during anaerobic digestion of organic waste. *Environ. Chem. Lett.* **2021**, *19*, 3557–3564. [CrossRef]
19. Murtaza, G.; Ahmed, Z.; Eldin, S.M.; Ali, I.; Usman, M.; Iqbal, R.; Rizwan, M.; Abdel-Hameed, U.K.; Haider, A.A.; Tariq, A. Biochar as a Green Sorbent for Remediation of Polluted Soils and Associated Toxicity Risks: A Critical Review. *Separations* **2023**, *10*, 197. [CrossRef]
20. Rowan, M.; Umenweke, G.C.; Epelle, E.I.; Afolabi, I.C.; Okoye, P.U.; Gunes, B.; Okolie, J.A. Anaerobic co-digestion of food waste and agricultural residues: An overview of feedstock properties and the impact of biochar addition. *Digit. Chem. Eng.* **2022**, *4*, 100046. [CrossRef]
21. Lim, J.W.; Park, T.; Tong, Y.W.; Yu, Z. The microbiome driving anaerobic digestion and microbial analysis. In *Advances in Bioenergy*; Elsevier: Amsterdam, The Netherlands, 2020; Volume 5, pp. 1–61. [CrossRef]

22. Park, J.-H.; Kang, H.-J.; Park, K.-H.; Park, H.-D. Direct interspecies electron transfer via conductive materials: A perspective for anaerobic digestion applications. *Bioresour. Technol.* **2018**, *254*, 300–311. [CrossRef]
23. Shao, L.; Li, S.; Cai, J.; He, P.; Lü, F. Ability of biochar to facilitate anaerobic digestion is restricted to stressed surroundings. *J. Clean. Prod.* **2019**, *238*, 117959. [CrossRef]
24. Pan, J.; Ma, J.; Zhai, L.; Luo, T.; Mei, Z.; Liu, H. Achievements of biochar application for enhanced anaerobic digestion: A review. *Bioresour. Technol.* **2019**, *292*, 122058. [CrossRef] [PubMed]
25. Bin Khalid, Z.; Siddique, N.I.; Nayeem, A.; Adyel, T.M.; Bin Ismail, S.; Ibrahim, M.Z. Biochar application as sustainable precursors for enhanced anaerobic digestion: A systematic review. *J. Environ. Chem. Eng.* **2021**, *9*, 105489. [CrossRef]
26. Xiang, L.; Harindintwali, J.D.; Wang, F.; Redmile-Gordon, M.; Chang, S.X.; Fu, Y.; He, C.; Muhoza, B.; Brahushi, F.; Bolan, N.; et al. Integrating Biochar, Bacteria, and Plants for Sustainable Remediation of Soils Contaminated with Organic Pollutants. *Environ. Sci. Technol.* **2022**, *56*, 16546–16566. [CrossRef]
27. Wang, M.; Yu, X.; Weng, X.; Zeng, X.; Li, M.; Sui, X. Meta-Analysis of the Effects of Biochar Application on the Diversity of Soil Bacteria and Fungi. *Microorganisms* **2023**, *11*, 641. [CrossRef]
28. Chiappero, M.; Demichelis, F.; Norouzi, O.; Berruti, F.; Hu, M.; Mašek, O.; Maria, F.D.; Fiore, S. Review of Biochar Application in Anaerobic Digestion Processes. In Proceedings of the Bio-Char II: Production, Characterization and Applications 2019, Cetraro, Italy, 15–20 September 2019.
29. Dutta, S.; He, M.; Xiong, X.; Tsang, D.C. Sustainable management and recycling of food waste anaerobic digestate: A review. *Bioresour. Technol.* **2021**, *341*, 125915. [CrossRef] [PubMed]
30. Tang, S.; Wang, Z.; Liu, Z.; Zhang, Y.; Si, B. The Role of Biochar to Enhance Anaerobic Digestion: A Review. *J. Renew. Mater.* **2020**, *8*, 1033–1052. [CrossRef]
31. Ma, J.; Chen, F.; Xue, S.; Pan, J.; Khoshnevisan, B.; Yang, Y.; Liu, H.; Qiu, L. Improving anaerobic digestion of chicken manure under optimized biochar supplementation strategies. *Bioresour. Technol.* **2021**, *325*, 124697. [CrossRef]
32. Zhao, W.; Yang, H.; He, S.; Zhao, Q.; Wei, L. A review of biochar in anaerobic digestion to improve biogas production: Performances, mechanisms and economic assessments. *Bioresour. Technol.* **2021**, *341*, 125797. [CrossRef]
33. Tomczyk, A.; Sokołowska, Z.; Boguta, P. Biochar physicochemical properties: Pyrolysis temperature and feedstock kind effects. *Rev. Environ. Sci. Biotechnol.* **2020**, *19*, 191–215. [CrossRef]
34. Mézes, L.; Biró, G.; Sulyok, E.; Petis, M.; Borbely, J.; Tamas, J. Novel Approach of the Basis of FOS/TAC Method. In Proceedings of the International Symposium "Risk Factors for Environment and Food Safety" & "Natural Resources and Sustainable Development" & "50 Years of Agriculture Research in Oradea", Oradea, Romania, 4–5 November 2011.
35. Luo, C.; Lü, F.; Shao, L.; He, P. Application of eco-compatible biochar in anaerobic digestion to relieve acid stress and promote the selective colonization of functional microbes. *Water Res.* **2015**, *68*, 710–718. [CrossRef]
36. Leng, R.A.; Inthapanya, S.; Preston, T.R. Biochar Lowers Net Methane Production from Rumen Fluid in Vitro. *Livest. Res. Rural Dev.* **2012**, *24*, 1–13.
37. Pant, A.; Rai, J.P.N. Application of Biochar on methane production through organic solid waste and ammonia inhibition. *Environ. Chall.* **2021**, *5*, 100262. [CrossRef]
38. Pandey, D.; Daverey, A.; Arunachalam, K. Biochar: Production, properties and emerging role as a support for enzyme immobilization. *J. Clean. Prod.* **2020**, *255*, 120267. [CrossRef]
39. Sriphirom, P.; Towprayoon, S.; Yagi, K.; Rossopa, B.; Chidthaisong, A. Changes in methane production and oxidation in rice paddy soils induced by biochar addition. *Appl. Soil Ecol.* **2022**, *179*, 104585. [CrossRef]
40. Baek, G.; Kim, J.; Lee, C. A review of the effects of iron compounds on methanogenesis in anaerobic environments. *Renew. Sustain. Energy Rev.* **2019**, *113*, 109282. [CrossRef]
41. Ugwu, S.N.; Biscoff, R.K.; Enweremadu, C.C. A meta-analysis of iron-based additives on enhancements of biogas yields during anaerobic digestion of organic wastes. *J. Clean. Prod.* **2020**, *269*, 122449. [CrossRef]
42. Wu, F.; Xie, J.; Xin, X.; He, J. Effect of activated carbon/graphite on enhancing anaerobic digestion of waste activated sludge. *Front. Microbiol.* **2022**, *13*, 999647. [CrossRef]
43. François, M.; Lin, K.-S.; Rachmadona, N.; Khoo, K.S. Advancement of biochar-aided with iron chloride for contaminants removal from wastewater and biogas production: A review. *Sci. Total Environ.* **2023**, *874*, 162437. [CrossRef]

Disclaimer/Publisher's Note: The statements, opinions and data contained in all publications are solely those of the individual author(s) and contributor(s) and not of MDPI and/or the editor(s). MDPI and/or the editor(s) disclaim responsibility for any injury to people or property resulting from any ideas, methods, instructions or products referred to in the content.

Article

Modelling the Effect of Water Removal by Reverse Osmosis on the Distillation of Mixtures of Short-Chain Organic Acids from Anaerobic Fermentation

Serena Simonetti and Davide Dionisi *

Materials and Chemical Engineering Group, School of Engineering, University of Aberdeen, Aberdeen AB24 3UE, UK; serena.simonetti23@gmail.com
* Correspondence: davidedionisi@abdn.ac.uk; Tel.: +44-(0)-1224-272814

Abstract: Anaerobic fermentation (AF) to produce sustainable short-chain organic acids (SCOAs) has found no commercial application so far. This is due to several limitations, including the high energy consumption of the SCOAs' separation from water by distillation. This study used AspenPlus simulations to investigate the benefits of reverse osmosis (RO) to remove water and concentrate the SCOAs from AF before their separation by distillation. The effect of RO on distillation reflux ratio, heat energy requirements, column diameter and equipment costs was simulated for the processing of model SCOA-containing streams, representing AF effluents. A total of 90 simulations were carried out, investigating three different SCOA compositions, corresponding to different ratios of lactic, acetic and propionic acids, three different concentrations of the total SCOAs (10, 50, 100 g/kg in the stream entering RO) and different extents of water removal by RO. RO brought a reduction in the distillation reboilers' duty of up to more than 90%, with a reduction of column diameter of up to more than 70%. The total energy consumption, equipment cost and NPV (net present value) of the RO plus distillation process were in all cases more favourable than for the process without membranes.

Keywords: anaerobic fermentation; reverse osmosis; distillation; short-chain organic acids

1. Introduction

Anaerobic fermentation (AF) has been proposed as a process to produce short-chain organic acids (SCOAs), e.g., acetic, butyric, propionic, lactic acid [1,2]. SCOAs are produced in millions of tonnes per year globally for a variety of uses in the food and in the chemical industries [3–5]. Current production processes for SCOAs mainly use fossil resources as feedstocks and are mainly based on high-temperature chemical processes with metal catalysts [6], causing concerns about their sustainability. On the other hand, AF can produce SCOAs from organic waste using open mixed microbial cultures. AF is the same process as the well-known and widely used anaerobic digestion (AD) process but with the operating conditions controlled to avoid the conversion of the SCOAs to methane, the final digestion product. Compared with current processes for SCOA production from fossil resources, SCOA production with AF has the advantages of using biomass or organic waste, which are renewable resources, of using temperature close to ambient values and of not requiring external addition of metal catalysts which are too a non-renewable resource [6].

Despite the advantages of AF for the production of SCOAs, no commercial plant currently uses this process to produce SCOAs. Indeed, production of SCOAs via AF also brings several disadvantages that have so far prevented its full-scale commercialization. The reaction rate of biological processes is slower than that of chemical processes, and therefore AF requires large reactor volumes. AF produces mixtures of SCOAs rather than the pure substances from chemical processes, therefore requiring a higher extent of separation and purification. Furthermore, the mixtures of SCOA from AF are diluted in water that accounts for most of the mass of AF effluents. SCOAs are present in AF effluents in a wide range of concentrations, from a few g/L to over 100 g/L [7]. The separation and purification of SCOAs from AF effluents is one of the main challenges towards the development of AF processes at commercial scale.

Many processes have been proposed for the separation and purification of mixtures of SCOAs in water [8,9], e.g., precipitation, chromatography, liquid-liquid extraction. Although these processes have found application in some cases, they are not considered suitable for the diluted mixtures of SCOAs in water produced by AF.

Distillation and membrane filtration are the separation and purification processes considered in this study. Distillation can be used to separate SCOA mixtures; however, its application is limited by the presence of azeotropes, by the thermal instability of some SCOAs (e.g., lactic acid) and by the diluted nature of AF effluents with consequent high energy costs due to the need to vaporize large volumes of water [10]. Membrane processes have also been investigated for the separation and purification of SCOAs from AF: nanofiltration (NF) membranes were used successfully to concentrate diluted solutions of acetic and butyric acid in water [11]; the concentration of diluted solutions of acetic acid with various types of membranes, including NF and reverse osmosis (RO), was reviewed showing several examples of successful application [5]; NF and RO were successfully used to concentrate solutions of SCOAs from AF showing, under the optimum conditions, only very little losses of SCOAs in the permeate [12,13]; RO was also used successfully to concentrate mixtures of acetic acid and sugars, showing that retention of acetic acid is very dependent on the RO operating conditions [14].

This study investigated, by means of process simulations, the combination of RO and distillation to remove water and purify the SCOAs from AF. To the best of our knowledge, there is no investigation in the literature about the combination of RO and distillation for the separation of these types of mixtures. In the process concept considered in this study, RO is used on the AF effluents, after removal of the suspended solids, to remove water and concentrate the SCOAs, prior to removal of the remaining water and separation of the acids by distillation. The investigated process is expected to have several benefits. The water removal and concentration of the SCOAs in the RO process is expected to reduce the energy consumption and equipment size of the distillation process. In addition, RO only uses electricity as energy input while distillation typically uses natural gas as energy source and steam as energy vector in reboilers. Since electricity is more easily obtainable than steam from renewable resources, the investigated process would contribute to improving the sustainability of SCOA production from AF.

This study used simulations to calculate the benefits of water removal by RO on energy use, equipment size and economic feasibility of the combined RO-distillation process. It is important to observe that most of the process conditions simulated in this study have not been experimentally investigated yet. Indeed, the experimental study of RO of SCOA mixtures is limited to the studies cited above and to the preliminary investigation carried out in our group with diluted SCOA mixtures (Supplementary Materials, Figure S1, [15]). Similarly, the study of distillation for the separation of SCOA mixtures has been limited by the high energy costs required for the removal of large volumes of water, as discussed above.

The value and novelty of this study is to provide quantitative results on which process configurations are expected to be more beneficial and more sustainable for the separation and purification of SCOAs. It is then expected that the most promising configurations will be investigated at lab and pilot scale to verify the model predictions and to develop the process further towards commercialization. This study uses a simple distillation model at atmospheric pressure which does not include azeotropes or thermal degradation effects. These effects can be important and should be accounted for in further model development and in the experimental trials of this process.

2. Methodology

2.1. Streams and Process Scheme

The simulations were based on the process scheme in Figure 1. The anaerobic fermenter coverts biomass or organic waste into a mixture of SCOAs. After removal of the suspended solids, the liquid stream is sent to RO membranes for water removal and SCOA concentration. The SCOA-rich concentrate is sent to distillation for the removal of the residual water and the separation and purification of the acids. It was assumed that the SCOAs are completely retained by RO with the permeate composed of pure water. The simulations considered only RO and distillation (dashed block in Figure 1).

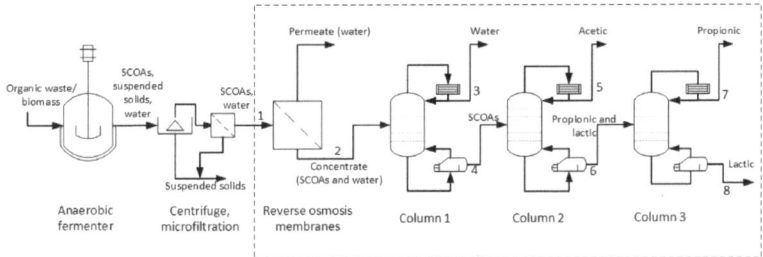

Figure 1. Process scheme considered in this study. The model simulations refer to the dashed block only (RO plus distillation).

In our simulations, the stream entering the membrane RO process (stream 1 in Figure 1) was assumed in all cases to have a total mass flow rate of 1.0×10^6 kg/d (1000 t/d). This represents the output of a large fermenter or of multiple fermenters. The size of anaerobic digesters can vary in a wide range, from a few hundred up to several thousands m^3 [16]. We have chosen to simulate the output of a large fermenter or of multiple joint fermenters because the production of SCOAs is expected to benefit from economies of scale and larger production volumes. Since this study was aimed to simulate the process of RO and distillation for a range of AF effluents, three compositions and three concentrations were assumed and simulated in this study (Table 1). For modelling purposes, the components of stream 1 were assumed to be water (boiling point 100 °C at atmospheric pressure), acetic (118 °C), propionic (141 °C) and lactic acid (217 °C) in different proportions. A large number of SCOAs are present in AF effluents, in this study acetic and lactic acid were chosen because they are often the most abundant under different fermentation conditions, and propionic acid was chosen as representative of acids of intermediate chain length and boiling point. Butyric acid is also often an important component of SCOAs from AD; however, we noted that the inclusion of this acid led to incorrect vapour-liquid equilibrium results with the thermodynamic model and the software (Aspen Plus v.12.1) used in this study. In addition, the inclusion of butyric acid would not have changed the main results of this study significantly. Therefore, we did not include butyric acid among the model SCOA components. In composition 1, lactic acid is the most abundant SCOA, with minor amounts of acetic and propionic. This composition represents effluents of AF carried out at low pH, where lactic acid is often the main product [17]. In composition 2, lactic acid is still the main product but there is a higher fraction of acetic and propionic. This composition still represents effluents from acidic AF, but with a more balanced SCOA composition. In composition 3, acetic acid is the main component and there is no lactic acid. This composition represents effluents of AF carried out at approximately neutral or slightly acidic pH, for example, from dark fermentation processes with hydrogen production [18]. As far as the concentration of stream 1 is concerned, for each composition, the three total

SCOA concentrations of 10, 50 and 100 were modeled. These three concentrations were chosen based on the wide range of SCOA concentrations from AF processes [7].

Table 1. Composition and flow rates of SCOAs and water entering the RO process (stream 1 in Figure 1).

SCOAs		SCOA Composition (% w/w of Total SCOAs)	Mass Flow Rate (kg/d) of Each Component for Total SCOA Concentration of		
			10 g/kg	50 g/kg	100 g/kg
Composition 1	Acetic	10	1.00×10^3	5.00×10^3	1.00×10^4
	Lactic	80	8.00×10^3	4.00×10^4	8.00×10^4
	Propionic	10	1.00×10^3	5.00×10^3	1.00×10^4
	Water		9.90×10^5	9.50×10^5	9.00×10^5
Composition 2	Acetic	40	4.00×10^3	2.00×10^4	4.00×10^4
	Lactic	40	4.00×10^3	2.00×10^4	4.00×10^4
	Propionic	20	2.00×10^3	1.00×10^4	2.00×10^4
	Water		9.90×10^5	9.50×10^5	9.00×10^5
Composition 3	Acetic	60	6.00×10^3	3.00×10^4	6.00×10^4
	Lactic	0	0	0	0
	Propionic	40	4.00×10^3	2.00×10^4	4.00×10^4
	Water		9.90×10^5	9.50×10^5	9.00×10^5

2.2. Distillation Simulations

Distillation simulations were carried out with the software Aspen Plus v12.1. Each of the three distillation columns in Figure 1 was set up with 30 theoretical stages, the condenser being stage 1 and the kettle reboiler being stage 30, with feed entering at the middle stage. The choice of 30 theoretical stages was done after preliminary simulations indicated that this number of stages was enough to obtain the desired purity of the acids with, in most cases, a relatively low reflux ratio. In this study the primary aim was to minimise energy consumption rather than capital costs, therefore a relatively large number of stages was chosen. The simulations were performed in all cases at atmospheric pressure.

The specifications were set as follows:

- In each column, the distillate flow rate was set equal to the mass flow rate entering the distillation process of the component to be purified as distillate, i.e., water in column 1, acetic acid in column 2 and propionic acid in column 3.
- The purity of each of the acids was set as 99.00 (% w/w) or higher.
- The reflux ratio in each column was varied manually to find the minimum value that ensured the required purity of all acids.

The NRTL-HOC (Non-Random Two Liquids with Hayden O'Connell correlation) model was used for the vapour–liquid equilibrium (VLE) in all cases. This model was used in a number of studies simulating the VLE of SCOAs, e.g., [19,20].

For each of the three compositions and for each of the three concentrations in Table 1, 10 distillation simulations were performed for 10 values of the water removed by the RO process (0–900 t/d with intervals of 100 t/d). Therefore, a total of 90 distillation simulations was performed.

2.3. Equipment Sizing

The column diameter was obtained from the AspenPlus simulations, assuming sieve trays and 80% approach to flooding. Each column was split into two sections of different diameter, above and below the feed stage. The column total height was the same in all cases and was equal to 17.07 m, obtained assuming a tray spacing of 0.6096 m for 28 trays (30 stages minus the condenser and reboiler).

The shell mass of the distillation columns was calculated from the column diameter and column height assuming cylindrical shape:

$$\text{Shell mass } (kg) = \pi D H t \rho \tag{1}$$

where D (m) = column diameter, calculated in each case from AspenPlus simulations; H (m) = column height; t (m) = thickness of the vessel walls, assumed to be 0.03 m in all cases; r = density of stainless steel, assumed to be 800 kg/m^3.

Since the columns were split into two sections of different diameter, Equation (1) was applied to each section and then the total mass was calculated as the sum.

The reboiler heat transfer area (A) was calculated from the reboiler duty obtained from the AspenPlus simulations, according to Equation (2):

$$A = \frac{Q}{U \cdot \Delta T} \tag{2}$$

where Q (W) = reboiler duty; U (W m^{-2} °C^{-1}) = heat transfer coefficient in the reboiler, assumed in all cases to be 2270 W m^{-2} °C^{-1} [21]; DT = temperature difference between the steam and the boiling fluid, assumed in all cases to be 5 °C.

The membrane area required (A_{memb}, m^2) was calculated from Equation (3):

$$A_{memb} = \frac{Q_{memb}}{Flux} \tag{3}$$

where Q_{memb} (m^3/d) = water flow rate of the permeate across the RO membranes, which was calculated from the mass flow rate assuming a water density of 1000 kg/m^3; Flux (m^3 m^{-2} d^{-1}) = trans membrane flux, assumed to be 0.24 m^3 m^{-2} d^{-1} on the basis of our preliminary experiments in Supplementary Materials, Figure S1.

2.4. Economic Calculations

The equipment cost of distillation columns and reboilers was estimated according to the Equation (4), from [22] (reference [22] was also used for the numerical values in this equation):

$$C = a + b \cdot S^n \tag{4}$$

For the distillation columns, S was the shell mass (in kg) and the factors were a = 15,000, b = 0.68, n = 0.85. For the reboilers, S was the heat transfer area (in m^2) and the factors were a = 25,000, b = 340, n = 0.90. For the reboilers, since Equation (4) is limited to heat transfer areas of up to 500 m^2, multiple reboilers in parallel were assumed if the total heat transfer area from Equation (2) was higher than 500 m^2. The cost C was obtained in 2013 USD and was converted into 2023 GBP by multiplying by the factor 1.147, obtained from online sources.

The equipment cost of membranes was calculated by multiplying the required membrane area from Equation (3) by the factor GBP 49.53/m^2 calculated from [21].

The NPV (net present value, GBP) was calculated according to the formula:

$$NPV = \sum_{t=0}^{n} \frac{R_t}{(1+i)^t} \tag{5}$$

where R_t was the net cash flow for year t, i was the interest rate (assumed to be 10%) and n was the life span of the plant assumed to be 25 years.

R_t was calculated as follows for every operating year, every term being in GBP:

$$R_t = M_{SCOAs} - C_{cap,dist} - C_{cap,memb} - C_{heat,reb} - C_{util,dist} - C_{pump,memb} - C_{util,memb} - C_{replac,memb} - C_{fixed\ costs\ and\ labor}$$

where each term was defined and calculated as follows, the numerical values refer to the base case with some values being changed in the sensitivity analysis described at the end of this section:

M_{SCOAs} = total market revenue of the SCOAs, calculated as the sum of the products of market value of each acid times their annual production rate with the process. The market values were assumed to be (GBP/kg): 0.729 for lactic, 1.00 for acetic and 2.74 for propionic, calculated by the authors from data in [23].

$C_{cap,dist}$ = total capital cost of the distillation plant, calculated as twice the sum of the equipment costs of the distillation columns and of the reboilers. The factor of 2 between the distillation equipment cost and the cost of distillation columns and reboilers was assumed after preliminary cost analysis with Aspen Process Economic Analyser (APEA).

$C_{cap,memb}$ = total capital cost of the membrane plant, calculated by multiplying the membrane area from Equation (3) by the factor 939.9 GBP/m^2, calculated by the authors from data in [24]. Note that the total capital cost of the membrane plant is higher than the equipment cost of membranes calculated earlier, as the former includes any capital costs associated with the membrane plants, e.g., building, land, ancillary equipment.

$C_{heat,reb}$ = cost of reboiler heat energy, calculated as the reboiler energy requirement from AspenPlus simulations multiplied by heat energy cost, which was assumed to be 7.03 p/kWh (average price of natural gas for industrial uses, UK first quarter 2023 [25]).

$C_{util,dist}$ = utility cost of the distillation plant other than the reboiler costs, assumed to be equal to 10% of $C_{heat,reb}$.

$C_{pump,memb}$ = cost of pumping energy for the RO plant, calculated from the pumping energy consumption (assumed to be 5 kWh/m^3, within the range given in [26]) times the permeate flow rate, assuming an electricity cost of GBP 0.2151/kWh [25].

$C_{util,memb}$ = membrane utility costs other than pumping, assumed to be equal to 10% of $C_{pump,memb}$.

$C_{repl,memb}$ = membrane replacement costs. It was assumed that membranes are replaced every 5 years at a cost of GBP 15.86/m^2 [21]

$C_{fixedcost\ and\ labour}$ = other fixed costs, e.g., maintenance and labour, assumed to be 10% of the total capital costs $C_{cap,dist} + C_{cap,memb}$.

Due to the uncertainties in the estimation of many numerical values for the cost analysis, a sensitivity analysis on the NPV has been carried out varying several cost parameters. The cost parameters that were varied in the sensitivity analysis were interest rate; total capital costs (distillation plus membranes); unit steam cost; unit electricity cost; other costs (sum of utility cost for distillation, utility cost for membranes, fixed and labour costs, membrane replacement costs). Each of the cost parameters was varied at 50, 200 and 400% the value of the same parameter in the base case (100% of the parameter value).

3. Results and Discussion

The simulation results of distillation without membrane concentration are presented in Section 3.1, the results of distillation with previous membrane concentration are presented in Section 3.2. Detailed simulation results (reflux ratios, temperature and composition of all streams) are reported in Table S1 in the Supplementary Materials. The general discussion is presented in Section 3.3.

3.1. Distillation without Membrane Concentration

Figure 2 shows the model results for the case where distillation is performed directly on the AF effluents (after removal of the suspended solids) without any water removal with membranes. Figure 2a shows, for the various compositions and concentrations of the SCOAs, the minimum reflux ratio which was required in column 1 to satisfy the specification of the purity of the SCOAs. For a given feed concentration and composition, the reflux ratio is the key parameter that determines the equipment size and reboiler duty in distillation columns. Column 1 is considered in Figure 2a because it is expected to be the largest and the one with the highest energy demand due to the need to remove large volumes of water in this column. The reflux ratios required in columns 2 and 3 are less critical in terms of energy demand and equipment size due to the smaller volumes to be treated in these columns. The minimum reflux ratio required in column 1 is in the range

0.4–0.6 for compositions 1 and 2 and approximately equal to 1 for composition 3. The reason for the higher reflux ratio for composition 3 and also for the slightly higher reflux ratio for composition 2 than for composition 1 is the higher content of acetic acid. The main task of column 1 is the separation of water from acetic acid and feeds richer in acetic acid make this separation more difficult, requiring a higher reflux ratio. From Figure 2a it can also be observed that for compositions 1 and 2 the minimum reflux ratio in column 1 slightly decreases for more concentrated feeds. This is due to the fact that, as the total mass flow rate of SCOAs in the feed increases, it becomes slightly easier to satisfy the requirement of 99% recovery of each acid and slightly higher concentrations of acids in the water distillate of column 1 become acceptable, requiring lower reflux ratios.

Figure 2b shows the reboiler duty. In all cases, column 1 gives by far the largest contribution to the total reboiler duty, as discussed above. The reboiler duty is higher for composition 3 than for compositions 1 and 2 due to the higher reflux ratio required. For compositions 1 and 2 the reboiler duty decreases as the feed concentration increases due to the lower reflux ratio. Figure 2c shows the reboiler duty per unit mass of products, which as expected decreases by a large factor as the feed concentration increases. For a given concentration of the feed, the reboiler duty per unit mass of products is the highest for composition 3 due to the higher reflux ratio. Figure 2d, which shows the cost of the reboiler energy, follows the same trend as Figure 2c and confirms the benefits of having the highest possible SCOA concentration in the feed, i.e., the highest possible SCOA concentration in the AF effluents. Clearly, one of the requirements for an economically viable process is that the energy costs are considerably lower than the market value of the products. Therefore, Figure 2e shows the ratio between the reboiler energy costs and the market values of the products. For the lowest feed concentration of 10 g/kg, the reboiler energy costs are for all compositions much higher than the market values of the products, and therefore a separation process without membrane concentration is not in this case economically viable. For the intermediate feed concentration of 50 g/kg, the reboiler energy costs are slightly higher or slightly lower than the market value of the products and therefore the process without membranes is also in this case economically unfeasible. For the highest feed concentration of 100 g/kg, the reboiler energy costs are in the range 45–55% of the market value of the products and, although this represents a high energy cost, the process may be economically viable without membranes. Figure 2f shows the diameter of each distillation column. It is confirmed that column 1 is by far the largest of the three columns, due to the water removal, with a diameter in the range 5.5–7.1 m depending on the feed composition and concentration. For column 1, composition 3 requires the largest diameter due to the higher reflux ratio, while the diameter of column 1 decreases as the feed concentration increases due to the lower reflux ratio and the lower flow rate of water to be removed. The diameter of columns 2 and 3 increase as the feed concentration increases, due to the larger volumes of SCOAs to be separated, reaching a maximum value of 1.65 m for column 2 with composition 3 100 g/kg. The total shell cost (Figure 2f) is estimated to be in the range GBP 1.0–1.5 M and slightly increases with the feed concentration due to the higher diameter required for columns 2 and 3.

Overall, the reboiler energy consumption for distillation in the process without membrane concentration is very high in all cases. To the best of our knowledge, there are no publicly available quantitative data on the energy consumption of conventional processes for organic acids' production. For other biotechnology-based processes, the distillation energy consumption of bioethanol purification has been calculated as approximately 0.25 MWh/t for extractive distillation [27], much lower than the values shown in Figure 2 (although the market value of SCOAs is higher than of bioethanol), which indicates the need for reducing the energy consumption, as presented in Section 3.2.

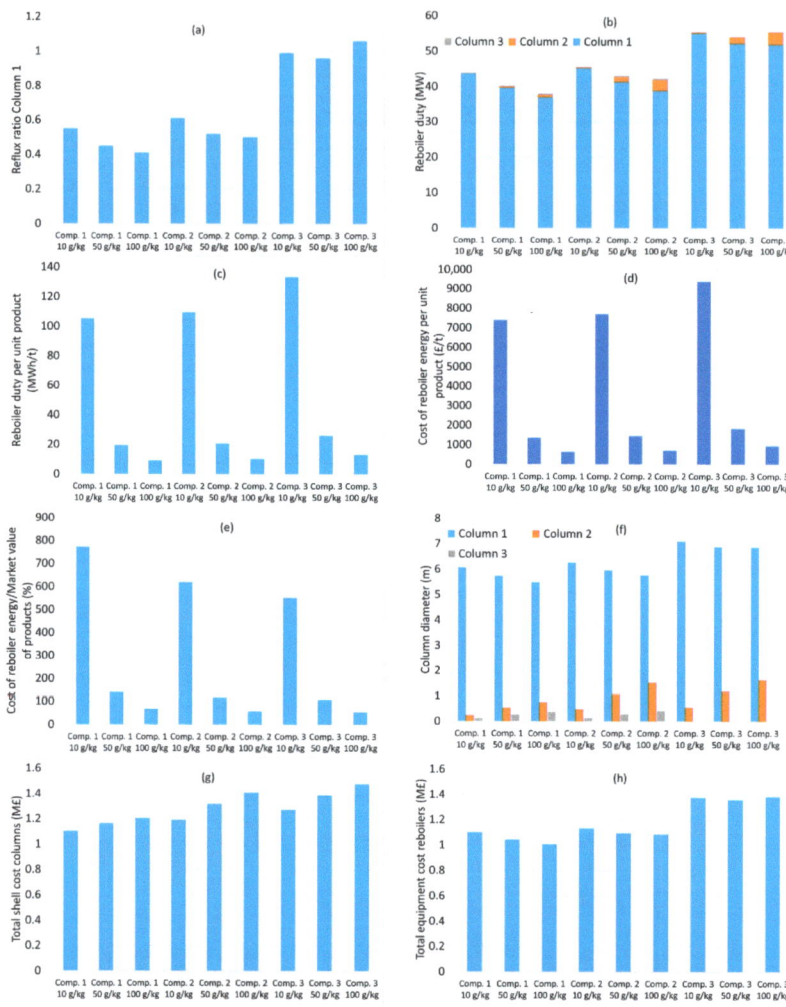

Figure 2. Main simulation results for distillation without previous membrane concentration. (**a**) Minimum required reflux ration for column 1. (**b**) Reboiler duty for columns 1, 2, 3. (**c**) Reboiler duty per unit of total SCOA products. (**d**) Cost of reboiler energy per unit of total SCOA products. (**e**) Ratio between the cost of the reboiler energy and the total market value of the SCOA products. (**f**) Column diameter for columns 1, 2 and 3. (**g**) Equipment cost (shell cost) for columns 1, 2, 3. (**h**) Total equipment cost for the reboilers of columns 1, 2, 3.

3.2. Distillation after Water Removal with Membranes

The aim of the RO membrane process is to reduce the water entering the distillation process, aiming to reduce the distillation energy consumption and costs. Figure 3a shows how the water entering the distillation process reduces as the water removed as permeate in the membrane process increases. For a given permeate flow rate, the water entering the distillation process is lower for the more concentrated feeds, due to their lower water content as they left the AF process. Figure 3b–d show the effect of the water removal in the membrane process on the minimum reflux ratio required in column 1 to satisfy the purity specification of the acids. The reflux ratio in column 1 is a key parameter in determining the energy and capital costs of the distillation process. As the water removed as permeate by the membranes increases, two competing effects influence the minimum reflux ratio. On the one hand, more concentrated feeds tend to require a higher reflux ratio to achieve the same purity of the produced acids. On the other hand, more concentrated feeds allow for the water in the distillate to contain a slightly higher concentration of acids than more diluted feeds while still achieving the specified purity and recovery of the acids. This latter effect allows for the use of a lower reflux ratio in column 1. As a result of these competing effects, for composition 1 the reflux ratio tends to decrease as the water removal by the membranes increases, while for compositions 2 and 3 the reflux ratio increases or decreases depending on the initial concentration in the feed. While the reduction in the water entering the distillation process, shown in Figure 3a, is expected to have a major effect on the reduction of distillation costs, the reflux ratio also plays an important role and the significant increase in the reflux ratio observed (Figure 3d) for composition 3 at 50 and 100 g/kg will reduce the benefits brought by the lower water flow rate entering the distillation. On the other hand, for composition 1, where the minimum reflux ratio decreases as the water removal by the membranes increases (Figure 3b), the benefits of lower water entering distillation and lower reflux ratio will add up.

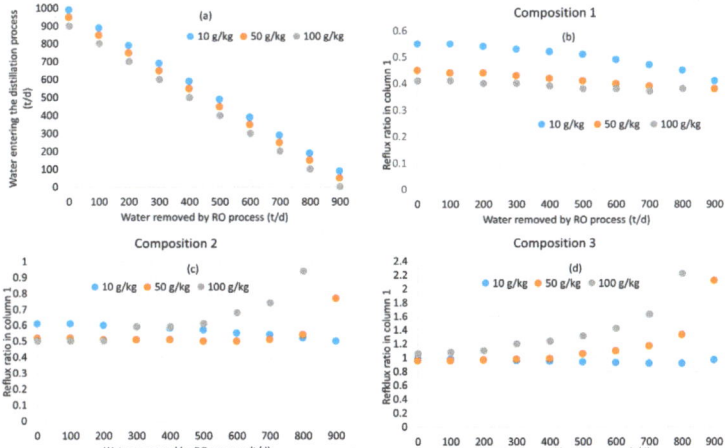

Figure 3. Distillation with previous membrane concentration. Results presented as a function of the water removed in the RO process. (**a**) Water entering the distillation process. (**b**) Minimum reflux ratio required in column 1 for composition 1, for each total SCOA concentration in stream 1. (**c**) Minimum reflux ratio required in column 1 for composition 2, for each total SCOA concentration in stream 1. (**d**) Minimum reflux ratio required in column 1 for composition 3, for each total SCOA concentration in stream 1.

Figure 4a–c show how the water removal by the membranes reduces the reboiler duty in the distillation columns. The reboiler duty decreases from the values of 38–56 MW in the absence of membranes to less than 5 MW for the highest water removal considered here, 900 t/d. This reduction in reboiler duty is very considerable and shows the main benefit of the membrane process. The reboiler duty per unit mass of products (Figure 5a–c) shows the same trend observed in Figure 4, with the values being much lower for the more concentrated feeds than for the more diluted feeds, as expected. The ratio between the reboiler energy costs and the market value of the products becomes much more favorable as the water removed by the membranes increases (Figure 6). For the most diluted feed of 10 g/kg, this ratio becomes lower than 100% for the highest water removals of 800–900 t/d. For the most concentrated feed of 100 g/kg, this ratio reduces from 47–55% in the absence of membranes to 1–2% for the highest water removal of 900 t/d. In all cases, Figure 6 shows the very significant benefits of the membrane process in reducing the reboiler duty.

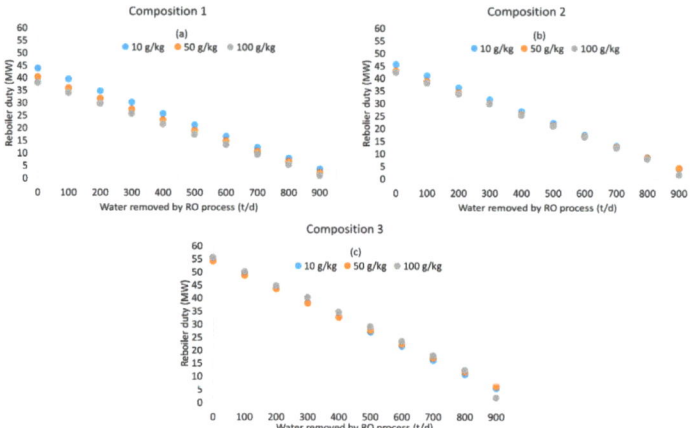

Figure 4. Distillation with previous membrane concentration. Total reboiler duty in columns 1, 2 and 3 reported as a function of the water removed in the RO process, for each value of the total SCOA concentration in stream 1. (**a**) Composition 1. (**b**) Composition 2. (**c**) Composition 3.

Figure 7 shows the effect of membranes on the size of the capital equipment. The area of the membranes is linearly proportional to the permeate flow rate (Figure 7a). Membranes bring a large reduction in the diameter of column 1 (Figure 7b), which is by far the largest of the three columns. The diameter of column 1 reduces from 6–7 m without membranes to 1–2 m. The largest diameters are in most cases obtained for the most diluted feed, 10 g/kg, due to the combined effect of the volume of water entering distillation and of the reflux ratios (Figure 3). Figure 8 shows the effect of membranes on equipment costs. The equipment cost of membranes is estimated to increase linearly (Figure 8a) with the permeate flow rate, due to the assumption of constant membrane flux for all simulations. The total shell cost of the three distillation columns decreases very significantly as the water removed by the membranes increases due to the reduction in the water to be treated by distillation. Compared to the base case without membranes, the reduction in the shell cost is higher than 50% for the highest considered permeate rate of 900 t/d. Generally, the shell cost is slightly higher for the more concentrated feed of 100 g/kg due to the higher contribution of columns 2 and 3, which have a higher role for the most concentrated feed (Figure 2f,g). Considering the combined equipment cost of membranes plus distillation columns (Figure 9), the addition of membranes brings a clear reduction. Indeed, with the assumptions of this study, the equipment cost of membranes is significantly lower than the cost of distillation columns and the cost reductions brought by membranes on distillation columns outweigh by a large factor the equipment cost of membrane systems.

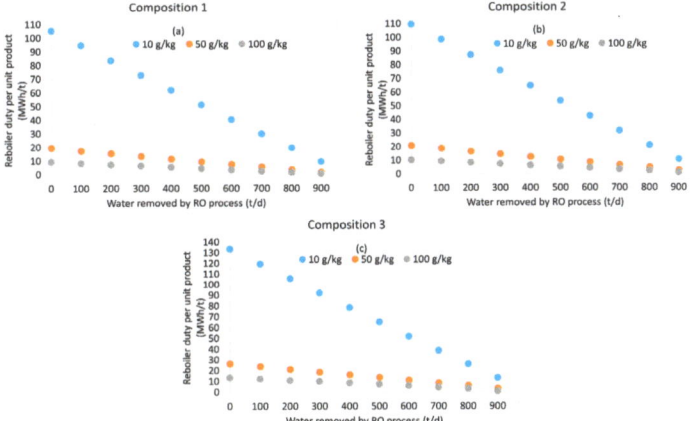

Figure 5. Distillation with previous membrane concentration. Total reboiler duty in columns 1, 2 and 3 per unit of total SCOA products reported as a function of the water removed in the RO process, for each value of the total SCOA concentration in stream 1. (**a**) Composition 1. (**b**) Composition 2. (**c**) Composition 3.

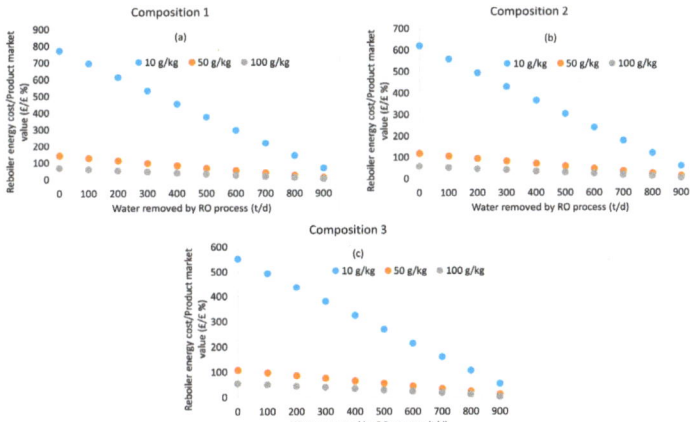

Figure 6. Distillation with previous membrane concentration. Ratio between the total reboiler energy cost and the total market value of the SCOA products, for each value of the total SCOA concentration in stream 1. (**a**) Composition 1. (**b**) Composition 2. (**c**) Composition 3.

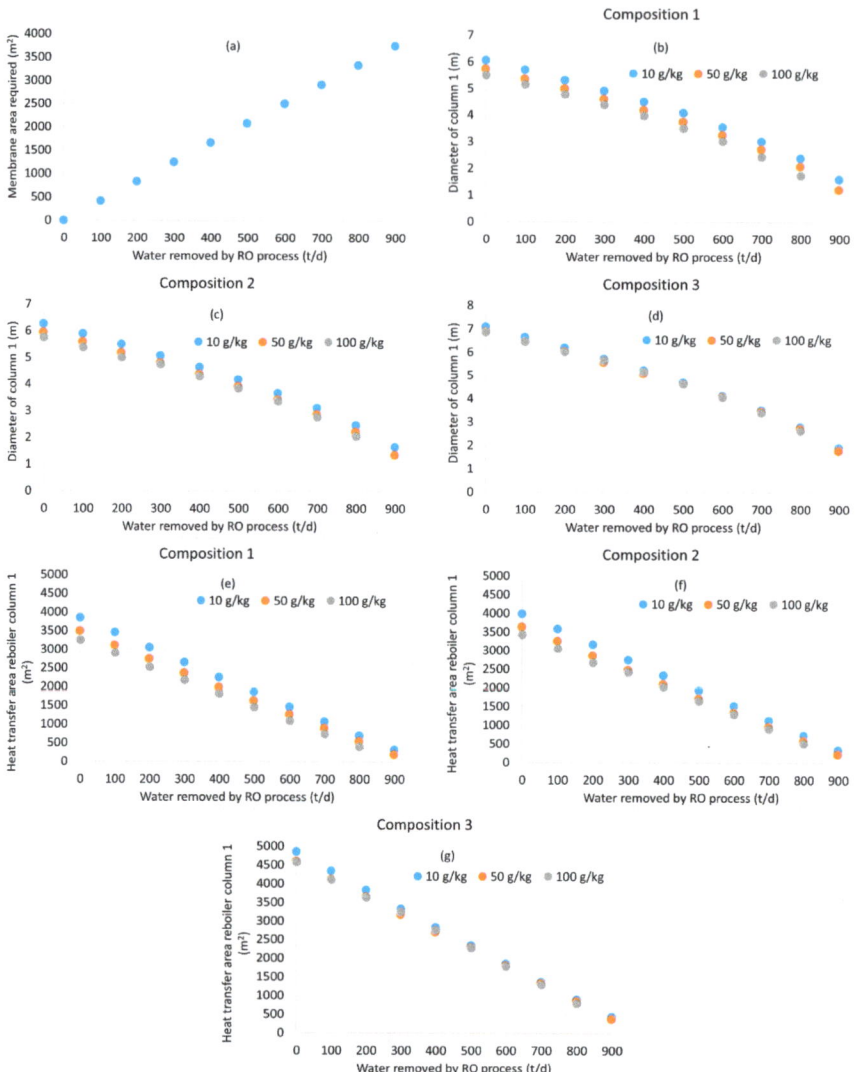

Figure 7. Distillation with previous membrane concentration. Equipment sizing as a function of the water removed in the membrane process, for each value of the total SCOA concentration in stream 1. (**a**) Membrane area. (**b–d**) Diameter for column 1 (largest of the diameters of the two sections) for compositions 1–3. (**e–g**) Required reboiler heat transfer area for compositions 1–3.

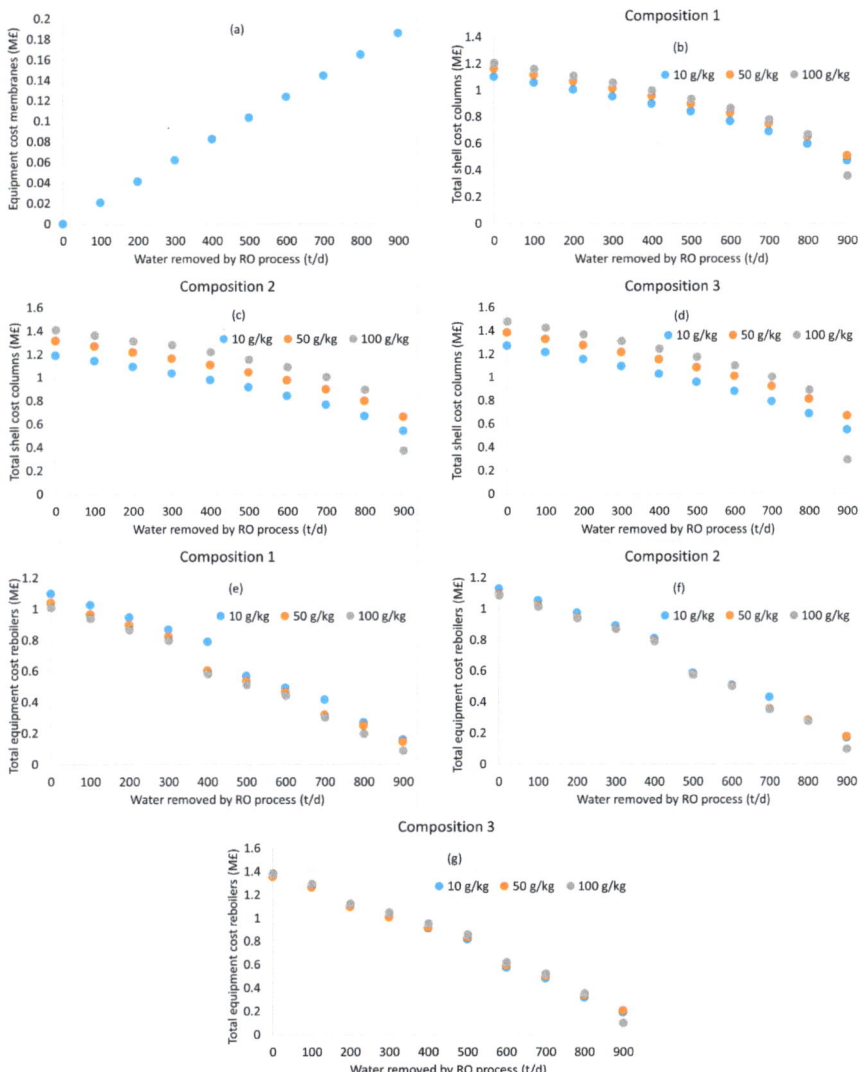

Figure 8. Distillation with previous membrane concentration. Equipment costs as a function of the water removed in the membrane process, for each value of the total SCOA concentration in stream 1. (**a**) Membranes. (**b**–**d**) Total shell cost for columns 1, 2, and 3 for compositions 1–3. (**e**–**g**) Total reboiler cost for columns 1, 2, and 3 for compositions 1–3.

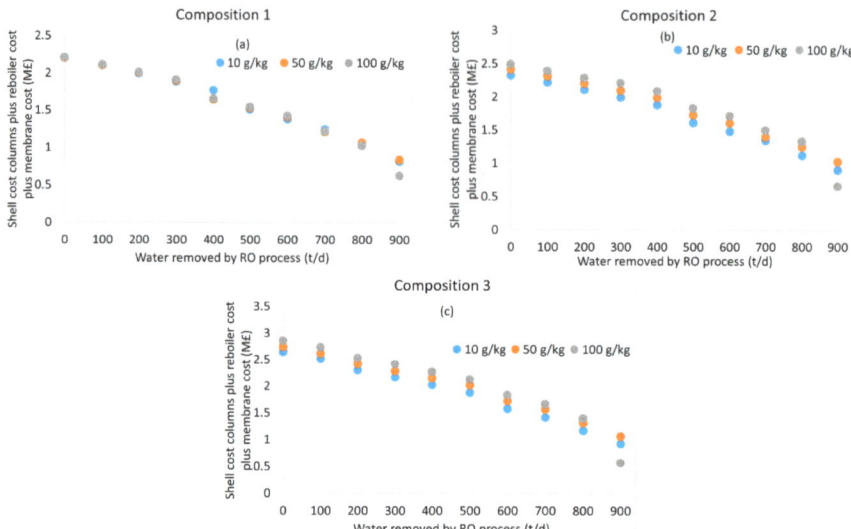

Figure 9. Distillation with previous membrane concentration. Sum of the equipment cost of distillation (columns and reboilers) and of membranes, for each value of the total SCOA concentration in stream 1. (**a**) Composition 1. (**b**) Composition 2. (**c**) Composition 3.

Combining the capital and operating costs together, Figure 10 simulates the effect of the permeate flow rate on the NPV. In all cases the NPV increases with the addition of membranes and with the increase of the water removed by the membranes. This indicates that the RO process prior to distillation has in all cases a positive economic effect. For the most diluted feeds of 10 g/kg, the NPV is negative in almost all cases, turning slightly positive only for the highest value of the water removed by RO of 900 t/d. This indicates that diluted effluents from AF cannot in practice be made profitable with the processes considered in this study. For the intermediate concentration of 50 g/kg, the NPV turns positive for relatively low values of the water removed, while for the highest feed concentration of 100 g/kg, the NPV is positive in all cases. These considerations confirm the importance of producing SCOA effluents from AF at the highest possible concentration. Considering the unavoidable uncertainty in the cost parameters and therefore in the NPV, Figure 11 shows the sensitivity of the NPV to variations in the cost parameters. The sensitivity analysis is shown for the intermediate case of concentration 50 g/kg, composition 1. The largest effect on the NPV is the unit cost of steam, Figure 11c. This is understandable considering the high energy consumption of the distillation process, especially for low water removal by RO. Higher steam costs make the NPV significantly more negative; however, it is important to observe that with high water removal by RO the NPV becomes positive even for an increase in steam costs of 400% compared to current values. This confirms the importance of SCOA concentration by RO in reducing the energy requirements by the process. The variations in the other cost parameters also have an effect on the NPV. Increases in the interest rate (Figure 11a) and in the other costs (Figure 11e) make the NPV less positive but in all cases the NPV is positive for large values of the water removal by RO. Variations in the capital costs have a relatively little impact on the NPV, which is understandable considering that the major role in the NPV is played by the steam costs and by the market value of the

SCOAs. Changes in the unit electricity costs (Figure 11d) give almost no effect on the NPV, which is due to the fact that in the considered process heat energy consumptions in the reboiler is much larger than the electricity consumption in the membrane unit.

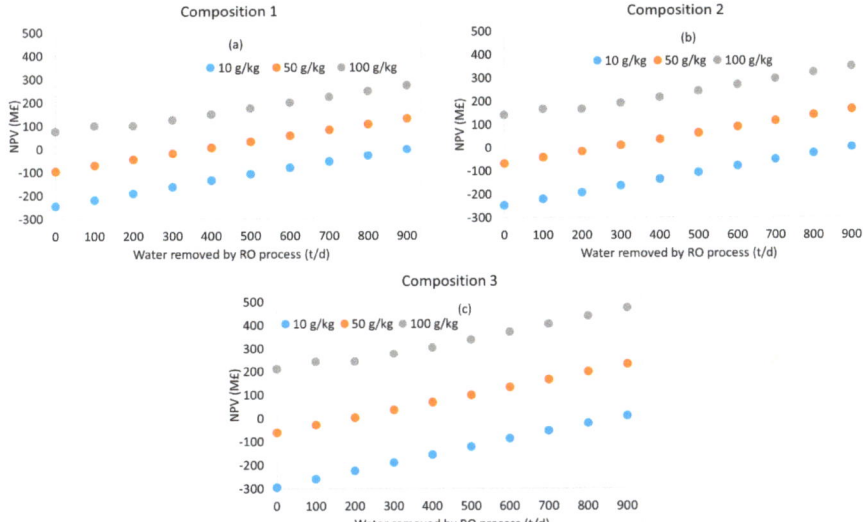

Figure 10. Distillation with previous membrane concentration. NPV as a function of the water removed in the membrane process, for each value of the total SCOA concentration in stream 1. (**a**) Composition 1. (**b**) Composition 2. (**c**) Composition 3.

Overall, addition of SCOA concentration with RO has been shown to significantly reduce the energy consumption of the distillation process. For the best conditions calculated in this study, i.e., SCOA concentration of 100 g/kg in the AF effluents and the highest water removal by RO (900 t/d), the total reboiler duty in the distillation is in the range 0.30–0.50 MWh/t, depending on the SCOA composition. These values make the considered SCOA recovery process more attractive and bring the estimated energy consumption by distillation in the same range of bioethanol distillation [28] or of an innovative proposed sustainable process for acetic acid production from methanol carboxylation with an estimated energy consumption of 0.2–0.6 MWh/t [28]. It is important to observe that the low energy consumption reported by [28] was obtained with energy integration and heat recovery schemes that have not been considered for the process considered in this study, although they are also applicable to it.

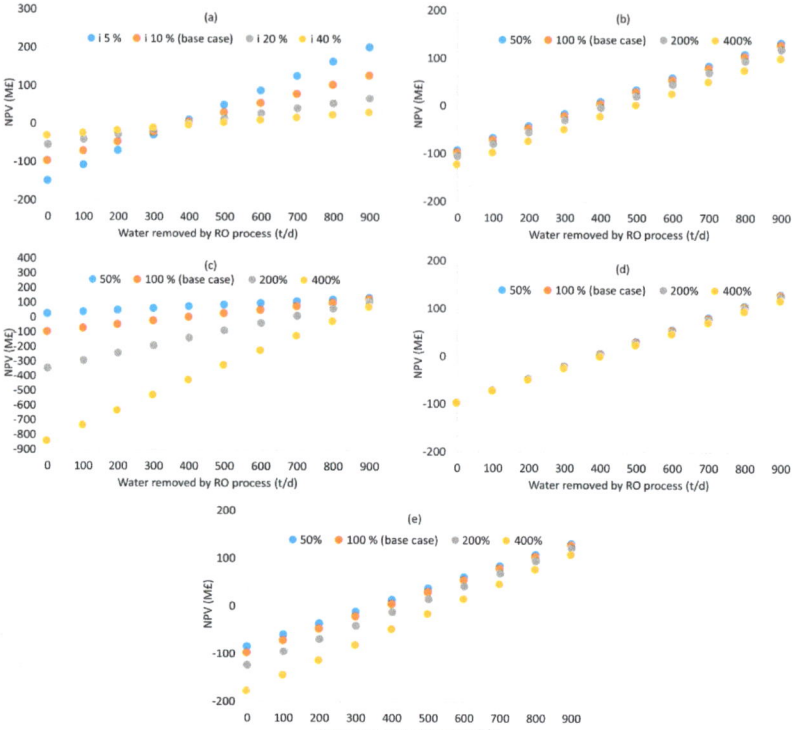

Figure 11. Distillation with previous membrane concentration. Sensitivity analysis on the NPV for composition 1, 50 g/kg. The values of 50, 100, 200 and 400% refer to the deviation from the base case (100%). (**a**) Effect of the interest rate. (**b**) Effect of the total capital costs (distillation plus membranes). (**c**) Effect of the unit cost of steam. (**d**) Effect of the unit cost of electricity. (**e**) Effect of the other costs (sum of utility costs of distillation and membranes, fixed costs and membrane replacement costs).

3.3. General Discussion and Model Limitations

The simulations in this study indicate that using RO to remove water from AF effluents can bring an important reduction, of up to more than 90%, in the energy consumption for the distillation of SCOA mixtures. The benefits in the reduction of energy consumption are even more evident if we consider that the pumping energy for RO is provided by electricity, while the reboiler energy is usually provided by natural gas, and it is easier to produce electricity than heat from renewable resources, e.g., wind and sun. In addition to the benefits in energy reduction, water removal by RO brings a reduction in equipment size and capital costs of the distillation process, which have been quantified in this study and bring additional benefits to the economics and to the sustainability of SCOA production from organic waste via AF.

This study, which to the best of our knowledge was the first to quantitatively investigate the coupling of RO and distillation for this type of effluents, was based on an ideal simplified model. Therefore, like for all models, all the simulations done in this study need to be verified experimentally to quantify the effect of RO on SCOA distillation with real life examples and to develop more accurate models. There are several aspects where experimental simulation is needed:

Efficiency of RO for concentration of water based SCOA mixtures in a wide range of SCOA concentrations. Although there are promising early experimental findings, only a limited range of SCOA concentrations has been investigated experimentally. Depending on the operating conditions of pH, type of membrane and applied pressure, successful retention of SCOAs with RO membranes was obtained with acetic-butyric mixtures at 1–2 g/L [11], with mixtures of various SCOAs at 20–30 g/L [12], with acetic, propionic, butyric acids at total concentration of up to 5 g/L [13] and with acetic acid at up to 10 g/L in solution with sugars [14]. In the preliminary experiments in our group reported in Supplementary Materials (Figure S1), the feed concentration of SCOAs was 7.4 g/L. Since the SCOA concentration in AF effluents can be higher than 100 g/L [7], and only high concentrations are likely to be economically viable, there is need to investigate RO retention of SCOAs at higher concentrations than has been reported so far.

Distillation of SCOA mixtures typical of AF effluents. While distillation is performed at commercial scale for the purification of organic acids from conventional processes based on fossil resources [29], the characteristics of AF effluents are significantly different. The model used in this study is a simple model and does not take into account several effects that may happen in the distillation of water based SCOA mixtures: acetic acid may present an azeotrope at high water concentrations, which may need the use of azeotropic distillation rather than direct distillation [5]; lactic acid degrades at high concentrations in water and at high temperatures because of which lactic acid purification by distillation may need to be carried out under vacuum [30]. However, these findings relate to solutions of single organic acids in water, rather than to mixtures of SCOAs as for AF effluents.

Based on the considerations above, the process simulated in this study needs to be investigated experimentally to test the validity of the model and to identify the actual operating conditions of RO and distillation that will lead to the predicted savings in energy requirements for the separation and purification of the SCOAs in AF effluents. It is hoped that the model developed in this study will foster further studies on this topic, helping to move SCOA production via AF closer to commercial realization.

4. Conclusions

Considering SCOA-rich effluents from AF, we have shown and quantified the benefits of the combination of RO and distillation for water removal and for the separation and purification of the SCOAs. With the process and model considered in this study, water removal by RO can bring down the reboiler energy consumption in the distillation process by more than 90% with additional benefits in terms of reduction of distillation columns' size, mass and cost. The energy consumption by RO is small compared to the energy savings in reboiler heat. Furthermore, the energy required for RO is mainly electricity, which can be generated more easily from renewable resources (e.g., wind or sun) than the heat required by distillation. Overall, the combined RO-distillation process is expected to significantly increase the NPV and the economic feasibility of SCOA separation and purification. It is hoped that this study will stimulate experimental investigations on the combination of RO and distillation to bring the production of SCOAs from organic waste and biomass via AF closer to commercialisation.

Supplementary Materials: The following supporting information can be downloaded at: https://www.mdpi.com/article/10.3390/pr11082362/s1, Figure S1: Process flux in preliminary experiments with AF effluents and RO membranes; Table S1: Simulation results for steams 1-8 in the process scheme).

Author Contributions: Conceptualisation, D.D. and S.S.; methodology, D.D.; investigation, data curation and writing—original draft preparation, S.S. and D.D.; writing—review and editing, D.D.; visualisation, supervision and funding acquisition, D.D. All authors have read and agreed to the published version of the manuscript.

Funding: This study was funded by LEVERHULME TRUST. Serena Simonetti, a Leverhulme Trust Doctoral Scholar, is part of the 15 PhD scholarships of the "Leverhulme Centre for Doctoral Training in Sustainable Production of Chemicals and Materials" at University of Aberdeen (Scotland, UK).

Data Availability Statement: Data is contained within this article and in the Supplementary Materials.

Acknowledgments: The authors wish to thank the company Membranology (Membranology LTD, C/O Azets, Ty Caer Wyr Charter Court, Phoenix Way, Enterprise Park, Swansea, United Kingdom, SA7 9FS, www.membranology.com) and in particular Richard Phillips for carrying out the RO membrane filtration study reported in Supplementary Materials, Figure S1.

Conflicts of Interest: The authors declare no conflict of interest.

References

1. Kleerebezem, R.; Joosse, B.; Rozendal, R.; Van Loosdrecht, M.C. Anaerobic digestion without biogas? *Rev. Environ. Sci. Biotechnol.* **2015**, *14*, 787–801. [CrossRef]
2. Strazzera, G.; Battista, F.; Garcia, N.H.; Frison, N.; Bolzonella, D. Volatile fatty acids production from food wastes for biorefinery platforms: A review. *J. Environ. Manag.* **2018**, *226*, 278–288. [CrossRef] [PubMed]
3. Singh, V.; Ormeci, B.; Radadiya, P.; Dhar, B.R.; Sangal, A.; Hussain, A. Leach bed reactors for production of short-chain fatty acids: A review of critical operating parameters, current limitations and challenges, and prospects. *Chem. Eng. J.* **2023**, *456*, 141044. [CrossRef]
4. Gonzalez-Garcia, R.A.; McCubbin, T.; Navone, L.; Stowers, C.; Nielsen, L.K.; Marcellin, E. Microbial propionic acid production. *Fermentation* **2017**, *3*, 21. [CrossRef]
5. Pal, P.; Nayak, J. Acetic Acid Production and Purification: Critical Review Towards Process Intensification. *Sep. Purif. Rev.* **2017**, *46*, 44–61. [CrossRef]
6. Dionisi, D.; Silva, I.M.O. Production of ethanol, organic acids and hydrogen: An opportunity for mixed culture biotechnology? *Rev. Environ. Sci. Biotechnol.* **2016**, *15*, 213–242. [CrossRef]
7. Simonetti, S.; Saptoro, A.; Fernández Martín, C.; Dionisi, D. Product concentration, yield and productivity in anaerobic digestion to produce short chain organic acids: A critical analysis of literature data. *Processes* **2020**, *8*, 1538. [CrossRef]
8. Li, Q.Z.; Jiang, X.L.; Feng, X.J.; Wang, J.M.; Sun, C.; Zhang, H.B.; Xian, M.; Liu, H.Z. Recovery Processes of Organic Acids from Fermentation Broths in the Biomass-Based Industry. *J. Microbiol. Biotechnol.* **2016**, *26*, 1–8. [CrossRef]
9. Murali, N.; Srinivas, K.; Ahring, B.K. Biochemical production and separation of carboxylic acids for biorefinery applications. *Fermentation* **2017**, *3*, 22. [CrossRef]
10. Kiss, A.A.; Lange, J.P.; Schuur, B.; Brilman, D.W.F.; van der Ham, A.G.; Kersten, S.R. Separation technology–Making a difference in biorefineries. *Biomass Bioenergy* **2016**, *95*, 296–309. [CrossRef]
11. Zacharof, M.P.; Lovitt, R.W. Recovery of volatile fatty acids (VFA) from complex waste effluents using membranes. *Water Sci. Technol.* **2014**, *69*, 495–503. [CrossRef]
12. Domingos, J.M.; Martinez, G.A.; Morselli, E.; Bandini, S.; Bertin, L. Reverse osmosis and nanofiltration opportunities to concentrate multicomponent mixtures of volatile fatty acids. *Sep. Purif. Technol.* **2022**, *290*, 120840. [CrossRef]
13. Bóna, Á.; Bakonyi, P.; Galambos, I.; Bélafi-Bakó, K.; Nemestóthy, N. Separation of volatile fatty acids from model anaerobic effluents using various membrane technologies. *Membranes* **2020**, *10*, 252. [CrossRef]
14. Zhou, F.; Wang, C.; Wei, J. Simultaneous acetic acid separation and monosaccharide concentration by reverse osmosis. *Biores. Technol.* **2013**, *131*, 349–356. [CrossRef]
15. Simonetti, S. Anaerobic Fermentation of Food Waste for the Production of Chemicals. Chapter 7. Concentration of Fermentation Products via Reverse Osmosis Membrane Filtration. Ph.D. Thesis, University of Aberdeen, Aberdeen, UK, 2022.
16. Holm-Nielsen, J.B.; Al Seadi, T.; Oleskowicz-Popiel, P. The future of anaerobic digestion and biogas utilization. *Bioresour. Technol.* **2009**, *100*, 5478–5484. [CrossRef] [PubMed]
17. Simonetti, S.; Martin, C.F.; Dionisi, D. Anaerobic fermentation for the production of short chain organic acids: Product concentration, yield and productivity in batch experiments at high feed concentration. *J. Environ. Chem. Eng.* **2021**, *9*, 106311. [CrossRef]
18. Pandey, A.K.; Pilli, S.; Bhunia, P.; Tyagi, R.D.; Surampalli, R.Y.; Zhang, T.C.; Kim, S.-H. Ashok Pandey. Dark fermentation: Production and utilization of volatile fatty acid from different wastes-A review. *Chemosphere* **2022**, *288*, 132444. [CrossRef] [PubMed]
19. Hsieh, C.T.; Lee, M.J.; Lin, H.M. Multiphase equilibria for mixtures containing acetic acid, water, propylene glycol monomethyl ether, and propylene glycol methyl ether acetate. *Ind. Eng. Chem. Res.* **2006**, *45*, 2123–2130. [CrossRef]
20. Komesu, A.; Oliveira, J.D.; Maciel, M.R.W.; Maciel Filho, R. Simulation of molecular distillation process for lactic acid. *J. Chem. Chem. Eng.* **2016**, *10*, 230–234.
21. Kanchanalai, P.; Lively, R.P.; Realff, M.J.; Kawajiri, Y. Cost and energy savings using an optimal design of reverse osmosis membrane pretreatment for dilute bioethanol purification. *Ind. Eng. Chem. Res.* **2013**, *52*, 11132–11141. [CrossRef]

22. Sinnott, R.; Towler, G. *Chemical Engineering Design*, 5th ed.; Coulson and Richardson's Chemical Engineering Series; IChemE: Rugby, UK, 2013.
23. Available online: www.statista.com (accessed on 8 June 2023).
24. Caldera, U.; Breyer, C. Learning curve for seawater reverse osmosis desalination plants: Capital cost trend of the past, present, and future. *Water Resour. Res.* **2017**, *53*, 10523–10538. [CrossRef]
25. UK Government. Statistical Data Set. Gas and Electricity Prices in the Non-Domestic Sector. Available online: https://www.gov.uk/government/statistical-data-sets/gas-and-electricity-prices-in-the-non-domestic-sector (accessed on 8 July 2023).
26. Kim, J.; Park, K.; Yang, D.R.; Hong, S. A comprehensive review of energy consumption of seawater reverse osmosis desalination plants. *Appl. Energy* **2019**, *254*, 113652. [CrossRef]
27. Hernandez, S. Analysis of energy-efficient complex distillation options to purify bioethanol. *Chem. Eng. Technol. Ind. Chem.-Plant Equip.-Process Eng.-Biotechnol.* **2008**, *31*, 597–603. [CrossRef]
28. Dimian, A.C.; Kiss, A.A. Novel energy efficient process for acetic acid production by methanol carbonylation. *Chem. Eng. Res. Des.* **2020**, *159*, 1–12. [CrossRef]
29. Yoneda, N.; Kusano, S.; Yasui, M.; Pujado, P.; Wilcher, S. Recent advances in processes and catalysts for the production of acetic acid. *Appl. Catal. A Gen.* **2001**, *221*, 253–265. [CrossRef]
30. Komesu, A.; Wolf Maciel, M.R.; Rocha de Oliveira, J.A.; da Silva Martins, L.H.; Maciel Filho, R. Purification of lactic acid produced by fermentation: Focus on non-traditional distillation processes. *Sep. Purif. Rev.* **2017**, *46*, 241–254. [CrossRef]

Disclaimer/Publisher's Note: The statements, opinions and data contained in all publications are solely those of the individual author(s) and contributor(s) and not of MDPI and/or the editor(s). MDPI and/or the editor(s) disclaim responsibility for any injury to people or property resulting from any ideas, methods, instructions or products referred to in the content.

Article

A Comparative Study on the Bioavailability and Soil-to-Plant Transfer Factors of Potentially Toxic Element Contamination in Agricultural Soils and Their Impacts: A Case Study of Dense Farmland in the Western Region of Saudi Arabia

Basma G. Alhogbi *, Shroog A. Al-Ansari and Mohammed S. El-Shahawi

Department of Chemistry, Faculty of Science, King Abdulaziz University, Jeddah 21589, Saudi Arabia; shroog.alansari@gmail.com (S.A.A.-A.); malsaeed@kau.edu.sa or mohammad_el_shahawi@yahoo.co.uk (M.S.E.-S.)
* Correspondence: balhogbi@kau.edu.sa or alhogbib@gmail.com

Abstract: Soil and aquatic pollution by heavy metal (Pb, Cr, Cu, Fe, Zn, and Ni) ions has become one of the prime problems worldwide. Thus, the purpose of the current study is to conduct hydrogeological research and quantify the main trace metals in the edible vegetables, soil, irrigation water, pesticides, and fertilizers in the farmland near Jeddah city, Saudi Arabia. Samples of soil, water, and plants such as coriander (*Coriandrum sativum*), dill (*Anethum graveolens*), parsley (*Petroselinum crispum*), and arugula (*Eruca sativa*) were collected, acid-digested, and analyzed using an inductively coupled plasma–optical emission spectrometer (ICP–OES). The levels of the elements in soil were determined in the order of Fe > Zn > Cu > Cr > Ni > Pb, whereas the sequence in plants was Fe > Cr > Zn > Pb > Ni > Cu, and in water, the order was Pb > Fe > Cu > Zn> Ni = Cr. In soil, the levels of Fe, Cr, and Pb were higher than the recommended values set by the World Health Organization (WHO) and the Food Administration Organization (FAO). In soil, Pb and Zn uptake increased with an increase in the availability of both elements, whereas in plants, Zn and Pb uptake occurs primarily through the plant roots, and some specific proteins facilitate metal transport and movement across the membrane. In soil, the root cell walls first bind to metal ions, which are taken up across the plasma membrane. The levels of the investigated elements in water and vegetables samples were below the permissible limits set by the FAO and within the allowable limits in the available pesticides and fertilizers. The transfer factor (TF) of metal absorption from soil to plant (TF$_{soil-plant}$) and from irrigated water to plant (TF$_{water-plant}$) in the study area was determined, followed by correlation and statistical treatment according to the date. The TF values were used to assess the metal levels in collected plant, soil, and water samples. The computed values of TF implied that plant leaves and soil were safe from the risk of heavy metals. Water irrigation causes heavy metal accumulation in soil and vegetables, with varying concentrations. The results of this study revealed no abnormal metal accumulation due to irrigation and no health risks to consumers.

Keywords: agricultural soil; pollution assessment; toxic elements; edible vegetables; soil-to-plant transfer factors

Citation: Alhogbi, B.G.; Al-Ansari, S.A.; El-Shahawi, M.S. A Comparative Study on the Bioavailability and Soil-to-Plant Transfer Factors of Potentially Toxic Element Contamination in Agricultural Soils and Their Impacts: A Case Study of Dense Farmland in the Western Region of Saudi Arabia. *Processes* **2023**, *11*, 2515. https://doi.org/10.3390/pr11092515

Academic Editors: Antoni Sánchez and Carlos Sierra Fernández

Received: 27 May 2023
Revised: 26 July 2023
Accepted: 1 August 2023
Published: 22 August 2023

Copyright: © 2023 by the authors. Licensee MDPI, Basel, Switzerland. This article is an open access article distributed under the terms and conditions of the Creative Commons Attribution (CC BY) license (https://creativecommons.org/licenses/by/4.0/).

1. Introduction

Safe plant-based foodstuff has played an important role in human life [1,2]. Edible plants, e.g., raw vegetables, are consumed prior to processing and represent the first link in the food chain [3]. Macro- and micrometals can be transferred directly from raw vegetables into the body, causing toxic effects if they exceed the allowable limits set by the World Health Organization (WHO) and the Food Administration Organization (FAO) [4]. Trace elements including heavy metals such as Pb, Cd, etc., and trace micronutrients such as Cu, Zn, Fe, Mn, Mo, and B (required for plant growth) are highly variable and influenced by both physiological and environmental factors. They are essential to the normal growth and health of plants, animals, and human beings at certain allowable levels [5,6]. Elements such as Cu, Zn, Pb, and Cd have been reported to cause contamination of soil, water, and plants [1,2].

In the modern era, trace elements, e.g., Ni, Zn, Cd, Cu, and Pb, have been reported as soil contaminants via agricultural fertilizers and pesticides, municipal waste, traffic, mining, and industrial emissions [7]. In both urban and agricultural areas, soil is a medium and a drain for the release of metals into the atmosphere. Some of these trace elements are permanent due to their immobile existence, whereas other metals are more mobile [8,9]. In soil, the heavy metal concentration plays an important role in controlling uptake of metal bioavailability in plants, as well as root uptake and the eventual transition to the food chain, causing a prospective hazard to human health [10]. A subset of plants known as hyperaccumulators can accumulate high levels of elements, e.g., Cu, As, and Cd, through multiple pathways [11]. The impact on the transfer of trace elements between plants and soil depends on the redox state and chemical form of the heavy elements, soil clay matter, iron and manganese oxide concentration, and climatic circumstances, as reported in [12]. The availability and mobility of elements are also considerably impacted by several factors, e.g., plant species, transpiration rate, soil pH, cation exchange capacity, organic matter, microorganisms, and other coexisting elements [13,14]. The occurrence of elements in surface and groundwater may be attributed to the dissolution of minerals in soil and aquifer materials [15] and/or to human activities and unsuitable disposal of industrial waste [16,17]. Consumption of contaminated food leads to uptake of toxic elements, which can disrupt mental development and disturb the function of organs such as the kidneys, lungs, and liver [15,18].

Saudi Arabia has experienced rapid agricultural development, resulting in an increase in organic and inorganic pollutants in agricultural soils. In North America and Europe, studies have shown that herbivores contain high concentrations of minerals due to their consumption of vegetation with a high concentration of minerals [19]. The toxic effects of trace elements have been studied in humans, animals, and plants [3,20]. The average concentrations of Zn, Cu, Fe, and Pb in well water in the Al-Bahah region in Saudi Arabia were found to be higher than the mean mineral concentration in irrigation water [21]. Edaphic factors and the distribution of diverse vegetation groups in Wadi Fatimah, Saudi Arabia, were found to be significantly correlated [22]. In central and western Saudi Arabia, significant increases in the levels of toxic elements were reported, which were attributed to agricultural activities, including the use of chemical and organic fertilizers and pesticides [23,24]. In the local market of Jeddah city, KSA, herbal plants were found to contain high levels of hazardous trace toxic elements, exceeding the maximum allowable levels set by the World Health Organization (WHO) [25,26] and indicating a need for precise monitoring of the levels of these toxic elements in agricultural areas that are vulnerable to the heavy use of agrochemicals. Total elemental concentrations in plants, soil, water, fertilizers, and pesticides can be precisely assessed by inductively coupled plasma–optical emission spectrometry (ICP–OES), as this technique provides good sensitivity, does not require large samples for measurements, and is an easy and rapid approach for conducting multiple automated core elemental analyses [6,26–29]. Hence, the assessment of Pb, Cr, Cu, Fe, Zn, and Ni uptake by plants is important to draw attention to the monitoring of the levels of these elements in agricultural areas that are vulnerable to the heavy use of agrochemicals.

The accumulation of potentially harmful elements (PHEs) in lettuce (*Lactuca sativa* L.) and coriander (*Coriandrum sativum* L.) irrigated with wastewater, as well as health risk assessment, was reported in a probabilistic meta-analysis of selected Ethiopian spices [30,31]. Trace determination of heavy metals in edible vegetables, soil-to-plant transfer factors, and toxic metal content in parsley (*Petroselinum crispum*), as well as associated health risks in vegetables, were reported for samples obtained from local farms in the Baz Kia Gorab region of western Iran [32–36].

Thus, the aims of this study were to (i) assess the levels of contamination with Pb, Cr, Cu, Fe, Zn, and Ni elements in cultivated soil, irrigation water, fertilizers, pesticides, and different tissues of selected plants coriander (*Coriandrum sativum*), dill (*Anethum graveolens*), parsley (*Petroselinum crispum*), and arugula (*Eruca sativa*), (ii) calculate the TF to assess the concentrations of metals in plants and soil; and, finally, (iii) explore the relationships and combined impacts of these parameters in plants, soil, water, fertilizers, and pesticides in order to properly address environmental risk in the study area through statistical treatment. Overall, this study provides decision-makers with an appropriate solution the level of heavy metals in plants representing the most important food crops in the world. The proposed solution can be helpful in reducing the risk of food chain contamination. The findings of this study can also help the government sector to formulate more stringent management procedures for the discharge of the elements and industrial activities.

2. Materials and Methods

2.1. Study Area and Sampling

The agriculture study area is located in a valley with a low rainfall regime approximately 100 km east of Jeddah city (Huda AL sham) in the Hijaz Mountains. The study area extends for about 70 km across the territory of the western coastal plains (Tihamah) and is surrounded by mountains with heights in the range of 0.0 to 500 m above the mean sea level [29]. The basin covers an area of approximately 4.860 km^2 at a longitude of 39°40'5'' E and a latitude of 21°33'0'' N, as demonstrated in Electronic Supplementary Information Figure S1.

Irrigated and wastewater samples were collected from the farm under study in pre-cleaned low-density polyethylene (LDPE) bottles with nitric acid (1% v/v). The water samples were immediately stored at 4 °C until analysis. The water pH, electrical conductivity (EC), and heavy metal concentrations were measured by ICP–OES as reported in [37].

Fertilizer and pesticide samples were taken from commercial products: urea (carbonic diamide 46% N) and NPK (complesal fluid, 8 + 8 + 6 + TE from Germany) fertilizers, as well as runner (methoxyfenozide 24%) and tiller (glyphosate IPA 48%) pesticides, used on the selected farm. Then, the samples were transported to the laboratory of King Abdulaziz University (KAU), Jeddah, Saudi Arabia, for processing and metal analysis.

Cultivated soil samples were collected from planting fields at a depth of 0.0 to 15 cm with the help of a garden shovel pre-cleaned with concentrated HNO_3. The soil samples were collected in plastic containers that had all been cleaned with detergent and tap water. The soil samples were air-dried, crushed, and passed through a sieve with a particle size of 0.40 mm. Then, soil samples were homogenized, transferred to clean polyethylene bags, and stored at room temperature for laboratory analysis. The pH, electrical conductivity (EC), and organic matter (OM) were measured according to soil analysis methods [4].

Coriander (*Coriandrum sativum*), parsley (*Petroselinum crispum*), arugula (*Eruca vesicaria*), and dill (*Anethum graveolens*) are the most widely grown vegetables in the study area. An approximate mass of 500 ± 0.1 g of each plant was collected from the farm at harvest ($n = 40$). In the lab, each individual vegetable sample was separated into roots, shoots, and leaves. The leaves of the subsamples were washed well with deionized water, dried, and ground to a fine powder using a stainless grinder. The samples were placed in labeled polyethylene bags and stored in a desiccator.

2.2. Recommended Wet Acid Digestion Procedures

2.2.1. Wet Digestion of Vegetable Samples

A total of $n = 40$ plant samples were irrigated with well water and collected at harvest. An accurate mass (0.500 ± 0.001 g) of each part of plant sample was digested in a 50 mL beaker containing 8 mL HNO_3 (69%, CDH). The beaker was covered with a watch glass and left overnight at room temperature, followed by the addition of 2 mL of H_2O_2 (30%, Sigma-Aldrich, Gillingham, England), and heated on a hot plate to 90–120 °C until the light-brown-colored fume disappeared. The digest solutions were filtered through Whatman No. 50 Ashley filter paper and diluted to 50 mL using HNO_3 (0.1 M). The USEPA SW-846 (method 3050) vegetable digestion methodology was followed [38]. Then, the metal concentration was evaluated by inductively coupled plasma–optical emission spectrometry (ICP–OES).

2.2.2. Wet Digestion of Soil, Fertilizer, and Pesticide Samples and Total Organic Carbon (TOC) Content

The soil samples were collected from the farm fields (n = 8), and fertilizer samples (n = 2) (0.500 ± 0.001 g) were placed into beakers (50 mL) containing 10 mL of aqua regia (65% HNO_3 and 37% HCl in a 3:1 ratio CDH). Pesticides (n = 2) were digested by adding 10 mL of 1:4 H_2SO_4 (95% m/v)/HNO_3 (69% m/v) mixtures. In the soil samples, the TOC content was determined as follows. Soil samples were first dried in an oven to remove the excess moisture and obtain the accurate mass (5 ± 0.01 g) of each soil sample. The samples were then placed into a crucible, and the weight of the soil crucible was recorded. The soil samples were heated in a muffle furnace (VULCAN, A-550) up to 300 °C for 5 h then cooled in a desiccator, and the TOC was calculated by employing Equation (1) [39]:

$$\text{TOC \%} = \frac{\text{pre-ignition wight (g)} - \text{post-ignition wight (g)}}{\text{pre} - \text{ignition wight (g)}} \times 100. \quad (1)$$

2.2.3. Digestion of Water Samples

Wet digestion of the water samples (n = 3) was performed as follows. An accurate volume (100 mL) of water sample was digested by adding 5 mL of concentrated HNO_3 (69%, CDH), followed by heating of the solution mixture to 90–120 °C until the solution became transparent. The solutions were then filtered and diluted to 50 mL with deionized water and analyzed as reported in [40]. The overall recommended procedures for preparation and ICP–OES analysis are demonstrated in Scheme 1.

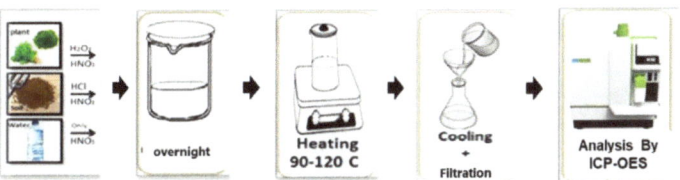

Scheme 1. Preparation of the studied samples and their ICP–OES elemental analysis.

2.3. Recommended Sample Preparation and ICP–OES Measurements

The Pb, Ni, Zn, Fe, Cr, and Cu elements in the sample filtrates were measured using an inductively coupled plasma–optical emission spectroscope (ICP–OES, Optima 8300–PerkinElmer) according to the optimal parameters of each element. The parameters of ICP–OES were a wet plasma aerosol type of axial view, nebulizer startup instant condition, a flow rate (Ar) of 15 L/min, auxiliary flow (Ar) of 0.2 L/min, nebulizer flow (Ar) of 0.8 L/min, sample uptake rate of 1.5 mL/min, and sample flush time of 5 s. The wavelengths used for the observed elements were 217 nm for Pb, 231.6 nm for Ni, 206.2 for Zn, 259.94 nm for Fe, 283.56 nm for Cr, and 324.75 nm for Cu. Based on the IUPAC [41], the values of LOD and LOQ were calculated by employing the following Equations (2) and (3):

$$\text{LOD} = 3\sigma/b \quad (2)$$

$$\text{LOQ} = 10\sigma/b \quad (3)$$

where σ is the standard deviation of five replicate determination values of the blank under the optimized experimental conditions and b is the sensitivity factor, i.e., the slope of the linear calibration plot of the analyte. The percentage of relative standard deviation (%RSD) lies within the range 2.70 and 32.76%.

Digestion was performed on replicates on a routine basis to determine precision. A series of more diluted solutions was prepared from the stock of the standard solution (1000 mg/L, Appli Chem Panreac-ITW Companies) containing Pb, Cr, Cu, Fe, Zn, and Ni to afford working standard solutions of 1.0, 5.0, 10.0, 20.0, 50.0, 100.0, 200.0, and 300.0 mg/L for each metal, the absorbances of which were determined using ICP–OES to construct the calibration curve. The repeatability, expressed as relative standard deviation (RSD), ranged from 1.77% to 3.57% for replicate analyses of the calibration standard for all detected metals. To determine each metal's detection limit, data from replicate measurements of low-concentration samples were used. The detection limit was then derived from the metals' standard deviations. Metal standards were employed to calibrate the instrument for each element being analyzed. The maximum limit of Pb, Cr, Cu, Fe, Zn and Ni) in the samples was adopted as reported by the WHO [4].

2.4. Data Analysis

2.4.1. Estimation of the Soil and Water Transfer Factor to the Plant (TF)

The transfer factor is defined as the ratio of the metal concentration in plant tissue above the ground divided by the total metal concentration in the soil ($TF_{soil\text{-}plant}$) or water $TF_{water\text{-}plant}$ samples. The values of $TF_{soil\text{-}plant}$ and $TF_{water\text{-}plant}$ can be estimated for each element using Equations (4) and (5) [42]:

$$TF_{soil-plant} = C_p \text{ (mg kg--1 dry wt)}/C_s \text{ (mg kg--1 dry wt)}; \quad (4)$$

$$TF_{water-plant} = C_p \text{ (mg kg--1 dry wt)}/C_w \text{ (mg kg--1 dry wt)}, \quad (5)$$

where C_p, C_w, and C_s are the elemental concentrations in plant, water, and soil samples, respectively.

2.4.2. Statistical Analysis

The mean, minimum, maximum, and standard deviation ($\pm$SD) of the analytical results were calculated using Microsoft Excel. The transfer factor (TF) of trace metals from soil to plants was computed using Equation (2). Data collected for all variables were first subjected to statistical analysis. Data on heavy metal concentrations in soil, water, fertilizers, and plants are presented as the means ($\pm$SD) for each sampling. Three-way analysis of variance (ANOVA) was performed on levels of trace element variations in the various water samples (well water, irrigated water, and wastewater) (block 1), fertilizers (urea and NPK) (block 2), and pesticides (tiller and runner) (block 3). The elemental uptake in the leaves of the four plants (coriander, parsley, arugula, and dill) was also critically determined as demonstrated in Figure S2. Three-way ANOVA interactions between the factors were considered significant at $p < 0.05$.

3. Results and Discussion

3.1. Physicochemical Characteristics of Water and Soil Samples

A preliminary study of the uptake of the tested trace elements in the various tissues of the four plants revealed dependence on water, soil pH, and conductivity [43]. Therefore, the physical characteristics (pH and conductivity) of the studied water and soil samples were a primary concern. In well water, irrigated water, and wastewater samples, the pH ranged between 6.53 and 7.73, which is within the permissible limit set by the FAO (pH 6–8.5) [44]. The conductivity of the well water and irrigated water samples was around 2860 µS/cm, which is within the recommended range reported by the FAO/WHO [4] (3100 µS/cm), whereas in the wastewater samples, high conductivity (4980 µS/cm) was noted, with higher concentrations of the labile (free) ions of the elements and fewer complexed metal ions and impurities.

The pH of soil samples Is a criti"al p'rameter of metal content. In normal agricultural soils with low pH (pH 5.0 to 7.0), the solubility of trace elements is generally high, as reported in [45]. Thus, low pH values measured in the soils in the current study account for the elemental transfer from soil to plants. The electrical conductivity (EC) of the soil is an important characteristic that can be used to determine nutrient availability and the presence of soluble salt in the soil. The EC values ranged from 410 to 1480 μS/cm; thus, the level of soluble salt increased, making it more difficult for plants to extract water from soil and resulting in water stress in plants [46]. Total organic carbon (TOC) is an important property of agricultural soil. The soil organic carbon content ranged from 6.30 to 10.60% in the agricultural soil samples, with organic matter affecting both the chemical and physical characters of the soil [46].

3.2. Levels of Trace Elements in the Studied Samples

The analyzed metals (Pb, Cr, Cu, Fe, Zn, and Ni) in the studied water samples were determined and compared according to the guidelines prescribed by the FAO/WHO [4] for water value. The average levels of metals in water samples in the study area are shown in Figure 1. The recorded values of Ni, Zn, and Cr metals were below the methodological detection limit in all water samples. The Pb concentration in well water was 1.171 mg/L, and the levels of Pb concentration in irrigation and wastewater samples were 0.01 mg/L, which is lower than the recommended levels set by international standard guidelines for irrigation water of the FAO (5.00 mg/L) [4]. The Fe levels in water samples ranged from 0.21 to 0.30 mg/L, which is two times greater than the recommended value (0.1 mg/L) set by FAO standards. The farm location may also contribute to the Fe level naturally occurring in the atmosphere and in soil that enters water bodies through natural processes and as a result of human activities. In Al-Kharj region, Saudi Arabia, and the Nangodi region of northern Ghana, the level of Fe in well water was found to be high compared to that determined in the present study area [47–49]. The concentration of Cu varied between 0.003 and 0.21 mg/L. The concentration of Cu was below the permissible limit according to the international standard guideline for irrigation water of FAO (0.02 mg/L) [4]. Furthermore, Cu content was found to be slightly higher in well water (0.2 mg/L) compared to the other water samples, in agreement with the data reported by Brar et al. [48].

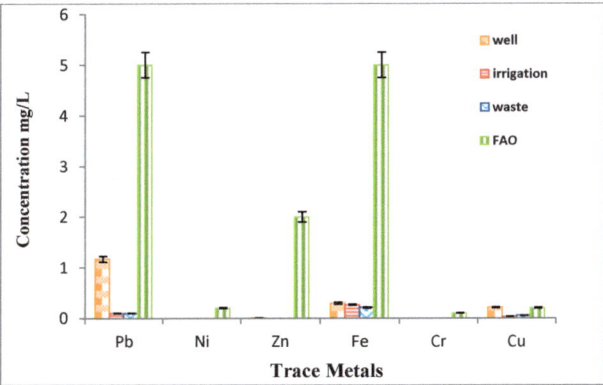

Figure 1. Distribution pattern of trace elements (Pb, Ni, Zn, Fe, Cr, and Cu) in the tested water samples.

In the modern era, soil pollution by trace toxic elements most likely arises from the constant use of element-enriched chemicals, fertilizers, and pesticide, as well as organic alterations, e.g., sewage sludge, wastewater, and other industrial activities [50]. Thus, the average levels ($n = 3$) of the toxic elements were critically studied in tiller and runner pesticides, the results of which are shown in Figure 2. The average concentrations of Pb, Ni, Cu, and Zn in tiller and runner were found to be in the ranges of 0.03–0.04, 0.0006–0.01, 0.004–0.02, and 0.20–0.28 mg/kg, respectively. In tiller, the average Fe level was not detected (ND), whereas in runner pesticides, the average Fe level was determined to be 0.77 mg/kg. In tiller, the Cr level was 0.03 mg/kg, whereas in runner, it was not detected. Thus, the average levels of the measured elements were lower than the levels in other pesticides (0.75–14.25 mg/kg) [51].

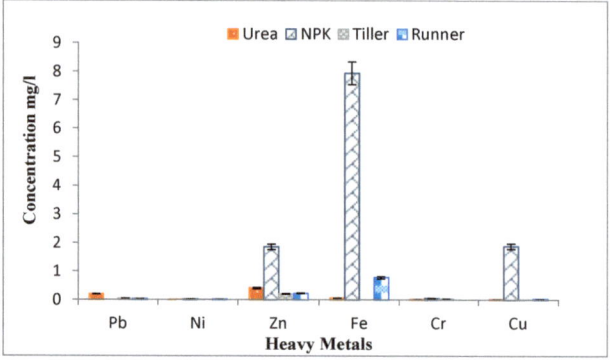

Figure 2. Average concentrations (mg/kg) of trace elements (Pb, Ni, Zn, Fe, Cr, and Cu) in fertilizers and pesticides.

The levels of Zn, Fe, Cu, and Ni in NPK fertilizer were 1.86, 7.39, 1.88, and 0.02 mg/kg, respectively. These values were found to be higher than those measured in urea for Zn (0.41), Fe (0.06), Cu (0.02), and Ni (0.003 mg/kg), whereas the average Ni level in phosphatic fertilizers in Saudi Arabia was in the range of 52.80 to 85.8 mg/kg [52]. The average levels of Pb and Cr contents were below the limit of detection in NPK and urea fertilizers. In urea, the average level of Fe in composite fertilizers was 347.3 mg/kg, revealing that the concentration of trace elements varied considerably depending on the measured element and fertilizer type. In superphosphate fertilizer samples, the average levels of the tested trace elements were substantially higher than those in urea fertilizer. Thus, it can be concluded that the average levels of trace elements in phosphorus fertilizers are above the levels found in other fertilizers. Superphosphate fertilizers resulting from phosphate ores contain a wide range of impurities, including trace elements [23,53]. However, according to Canadian standards, the average levels of trace elements in available urea and superphosphate fertilizers were within the allowable limits [54].

The average levels of trace elements in the agricultural soil in the study area are illustrated in Figure 3. The levels of the measured elements were below the maximum permissible limits set by the WHO/FAO [4]. In soils in which the arugula and dill samples were grown, the average levels of Pb were 33.10 and 37.18 mg/Kg—lower than the permissible limits set by the FAO/WHO [4]. In soils in which the coriander and parsley samples were grown, Pb was not detected, revealing that the Pb originated from other sources, such as leaching during the rainy season, and simplified by soil microbial activities [23]. Natural soil contains Pb, which may be discharged from natural sources, such as the decomposition of plants and animals. The impact of Pb toxicity depends upon its solubility, which is influenced by soil pH and other sources of Pb, including herbicides and insecticides [23]. In the agricultural soils in the current study, the Pb level was lower than the average Pb (1.20 mg/kg) in Al-Taif district, Saudi Arabia [55].

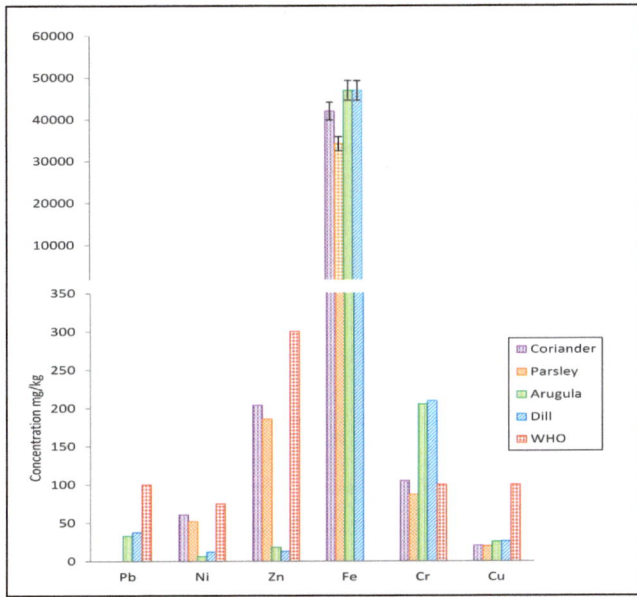

Figure 3. Average concentrations (mg/kg) of trace elements in cultivated soil.

The average Ni level in all locations varied from 6.40 to 60.80 mg/kg, which is less than the maximum permissible standard according to WHO/FAO (75 mg/kg). The average level of Ni in the study area was found to be lower than the Ni level (117.2 to 117.6 mg/kg) in India [48]. Ni levels can be ascribed to the dust and aerosols emitted during plant transportation and the use of organic fertilizers [17,56]. The average Zn level was highest in coriander soil (204.0 mg/kg), followed by parsley (185.90 mg/kg), arugula (18.60 mg/kg), and dill (12.90 mg/kg) soils (Figure 3). These results differ from those reported by Al-Hammad and El-Salam [47] for Zn in soils (38.45 to 174.52 mg/kg). This trend can most likely be attributed to soil conditions and other environmental factors, e.g., high soil acidity may also release the bound Zn pool, resulting in an increase in the level of labile Zn ions in the soil solution [7,23].

The average iron contents in the soil samples are illustrated in Figure 3. The average Fe content was very high (34,196.60 to 46,913.30 mg/kg). In soil samples in which arugula and dill were grown, Fe levels were found to be high, suggesting that the physicochemical conditions of the soil, e.g., redox potential, humidity, morphological conditions, flows, and iron fixation, are affected by different soil components [57]. These data agree with the results reported by Harmanescu et al. (55,489.20 mg/kg and 44,582.45 mg/kg) [17] and Ramteke et al. (18,328 mg/kg to 37,980 mg/kg) [7]. The average Cr level in soil samples is also shown in Figure 3. The average levels of Cr were in the range of 87.20 to 209.50 mg/kg in arugula and dill, which are above the maximum permissible limits set by the WHO/FAO for the Cr ion concentration in soil, with the exception of the soil in which parsley was grown. Additionally, the average Cr levels of soils in the present study were higher than the average level (60.43 mg/kg) in agricultural soil in Al-Kharj region, Saudi Arabia [47]. The Cr content in soil can be attributed to agricultural activities, including the use of chemical and organic fertilizers and pesticides and the high solubility of chromium (VI) species. Cu levels in all soil samples were found to be in the range of 19.90 to 26.30 mg/kg, as shown in Figure 3, which is within the national permissible levels set by the WHO. These values are lower than the Cu levels reported in in Al-Kharj region, Saudi Arabia (68.78 mg/kg), and in India (153 mg/kg) [7,47]. Thus, in the soil in the study area, the potentially toxic trace elements are mainly initiated from anthropogenic activity involving the use of agrochemicals, e.g., fertilizers, pesticides, and organic manure, in the condensed agricultural soils.

The average levels of toxic trace elements in crops are controlled by the contents of trace elements; the pathways of uptake of these elements by plant tissues, such as roots, leaves, and edible parts [58,59]; pH [60]; and the structure of heavy metals [61]. Trace element toxicity directly affects the physiology, structure, and growth of plants, as reported by Jorgensen et al. [62]. Table 1 demonstrates the levels of trace elements in leaves, shoots, and roots of the four vegetables analyzed in the study area. Vegetables can absorb elements from soil, which can be deposited on parts of vegetables exposed to the air in contaminated environments [63]. The average levels of the trace elements in different organs of leafy green plants (coriander, parsley, arugula, and dill) were successfully compared with the permissible levels set by the FAO/WHO [4], as summarized in Table 1. The Pb, Ni, Zn, Fe, Cr, and Cu levels in the leafy green plants were determined in the following order: roots > leaves > shoot. In parsley plants, the levels of Zn, Fe, and Cu were determined in the following order: leaves > roots > shoots. The average Pb levels were determined in the following order: shoots > roots > leaves. The mean experimental results indicate that Cr was not detected in parsley plants. In arugula plants, the Pb, Ni, Zn, and Fe concentrations were determined in the following order: leaves > roots > shoots.

Table 1. Average levels (mg/kg) of trace elements in selected leafy green plants.

Plant Sample	Part of Plant	Pb	Ni	Zn	Fe	Cr	Cu
Coriander	Leaves	3.05 ± 1.36	ND *	29.9 + 3.2	157.80 ± 74.9	1.20 ± 2	9.20 ± 2.1
	Shoots	4.70 ± 0.70	0.23 ± 1.4	14.2 ± 3.7	57.90 ± 17.9	ND	7.40 ± 0.5
	Roots	5.70 ± 0.42	9.70 ± 10.1	38.6 ± 8.6	212.10 ± 45.1	4.40 ± 7.8	11.30 ± 0.7
Parsley	Leaves	5.50 ± 5.23	0.20 ± 0.2	70.9 ± 14.4	101.50 ± 13.2	ND	14.80 ± 1.4
	Shoots	12.50 ± 8.34	0.1 ± 0.1	48 ± 8.5	64.20 ± 10.05	ND	10.50 ± 1.1
	Roots	8.90 ± 4.38	0.03 ± 0.05	58.5 ± 11.8	57.80 ± 17.4	ND	13.40 ± 2
Arugula	Leaves	7.06 ± 1.97	4.40 ± 0.9	37.2 ± 11.3	157.40 ± 30.3	ND	ND
	Shoots	2.75 ± 1.62	2.60 ± 1.0	26.7 ± 5.6	60.06 ± 37.4	0.40 ± 0.7	ND
	Roots	6.85 ± 2.05	2.20 ± 0.2	45.5 ± 4.7	60.10 ± 11.2	ND	ND
Dill	Leaves	7.10 ± 0.14	12.03 ± 14.2	36.8 ± 6.4	158.30 ± 8.6	ND	0.70 ± 1.2
	Shoots	6.35 ± 0.07	3.80 ± 2.2	13.1 ± 0.9	13.90 ± 17.2	3.40 ± 6.1	1.30 ± 2.2
	Roots	4.75 ± 11.68	3.06 ± 0.2	26.9 ± 3.1	327.40 ± 24.5	ND	ND
WHO/FAO		0.3	67.9	99.4	425	0.5	73

* ND = not detected; average concentrations ± standard deviation.

In leaf tissues, Pb levels were higher for all leafy green plants, and the overall Pb uptake was determined in the following sequence: dill > arugula > coriander. Parsley recorded higher levels of Pb in the shoots than in the leaves. The Pb concentration ranged between 2.75 mg/kg in the shoots of arugula to 12.5 mg/kg in the shoots of parsley. It is well known that the leaf tissues of plants are capable of Pb uptake, mainly through the plant roots via passive absorption, and some specific proteins facilitate metal transport through movement across the membrane [60]. The leaf tissue root cell walls first bind metal ions from the soil; then, the metal ions are taken up across the plasma membrane. The difference in the binding sites and the protein structures in the various tissues and organs most likely account for the observed trend. The Pb levels in all the leafy green plants from the farm exceeded the maximum permissible limit set by the FAO/WHO [4] because of the age-dependent accumulation, defense, or tolerance mechanisms of the plants to avoid toxic levels in organs [64]. Muamar et al. [65] reported high Pb levels in leaves of parsley (16.67 mg/kg) in the Skhirat region of Morocco. The Pb level (0.08 mg/kg) reported in roots in the current study is lower than that reported in maize roots (2020 mg/Kg) [23]. Similar levels of Pb (0.54–6.98 mg/kg) in leafy green plant samples grown in industrial and urban cities in Tabouk, Riyadh, Damamm, and Jazan, Saudi Arabia were reported [66]. In leafy vegetables, the average Pb levels in arugula and spinach were found to range from 2.14 to 4.67 and from 1.26 to 4.14 mg/kg, respectively [66].

The average level of Ni in leafy green plant samples is presented in Table 1 (0.03 to 12.03 mg/kg). The highest Ni level was recorded in dill leaves (12.03 mg/kg), followed by coriander roots (9.70 mg/kg), with the lowest level (0.03 mg/kg) in roots of the parsley sample. These values were lower than the recommended limit set by the FAO/WHO [4]. The average level of nickel recorded in the current study was lower than the mean Ni concentrations (28.29 mg/kg) reported in India [67]. In leafy green plants, the Zn level was in the range of 13.1 to 70.9 mg/kg (Table 1), whereas the Zn level in shoot tissue was considerably less than that in leaf tissue and roots. In the leafy green plants, the Zn content was determined in the following order: leaves > roots > shoots. Therefore, we conclude that Zn was highly accumulated in harvestable parts of the plant [8,60]. Zn transport in plants is a complicated physiological process primarily controlled by metal chelators and Zn transporters [68,69]. The leafy green plants exhibited low Zn levels compared to the permissible limit set by the FAO/WHO [4], in agreement with the data reported by Abrham and Gholap [62]. The Zn level (25.86–126.30 mg/kg) in the Aseer region was higher than that in the study area in this work [16].

The average Fe levels in the four leafy green plant species are summarized in Table 1. In all plants, the levels of Fe ranged between 13.90 and 327.40 mg/kg, and the differences between root, shoot, and leaf Fe levels in the tested plants were highest among all elements measured in the present study. Fe levels in the leaves of dill (158.30 mg/kg), coriander (157.80 mg/kg), and arugula (157.40 mg/kg) were higher than those found in the leaves of parsley (101.50 mg/kg). Fe concentrations were higher in root tissue than those in shoot tissue, except in the shoot tissue of parsley. Fe levels did not surpass the maximum permissible limit set by the FAO/WHO in any of the leafy green plants [4]. The Fe level recorded in this study is similar to the significant mean values of Fe (17.01–22.94 mg/L) reported by Malede et al. [54] and Seyyed et al. [28] in landfill leachate, affecting the municipal solid waste composition.

Cr uptake is essential and must lie within a certain range of concentrations (≤ 200 µg/day) for carbohydrate and lipid metabolism in human beings and animals [70]. In arugula shoots, a low level of Cr (0.40 mg/kg) was noticed, whereas the maximum level was recorded in coriander roots (4.40 mg/kg). The Cr levels in coriander leaves and the shoots of dill were 1.20 mg/kg and 3.40 mg/kg, respectively (Table 1), exceeding the allowable Cr limit reported by the FAO/WHO [4]. In parsley plants, Cr was not detected because a variety of contemporary methods are currently being used to remove heavy elements from soil by phytoremediation, phytodetoxification, soil rinsing, and leaching [19]. The Cu content in coriander varied between 7.40 and 11.30 mg/kg, with variation of 10.50 to 14.80 mg/kg in parsley, 0.70 to 1.30 mg/kg in dill, and no Cu detected in arugula (Table 1). In leafy green plant samples, the average Cu content was below the recommended permissible limit (73 mg/kg) set by the FAO/WHO. In this study, the average Cu level was lower than the reported value (32.45 mg/kg) in Gamo, Ethiopia [63]. According to the WHO and FAO, the values of Cu and Cr contents in vegetables should not exceed 30 mg/kg.

3.3. Transfer Factor (TF)

The transfer route and deposition of heavy elements from soil and irrigated water to the edible part of leafy green plants represent the main means of entrance of heavy elements to food chain [20]. Thus, in the current study, considerable attention has been oriented towards heavy element transferability from soil to leafy green plants and from irrigated water to leafy green plants. The transfer factors from soil to plants ($TF_{soil-plant}$) and from irrigated water to plants ($TF_{water-plant}$) were calculated using Equations (4) and (5) [20]. The results are summarized in Tables 2 and 3. As shown in Table 2, the $TF_{soil-plant}$ values, regardless of plant type, were 1.09. 0.27, 0.26, 0.08. 0.005, and 0.002 for Zn, Cu, Ni, Pb, Cr, and Fe, respectively. The mean $TF_{soil-plant}$ of heavy metals in soil–edible plant transfer decreased in the following order: Zn > Cu > Ni > Pb > Cr > Fe. In different leafy green plants, the $TF_{soil-plant}$ of the studied elements varied significantly, with Ni and Zn exhibiting maxima. Arugula and dill revealed higher TF from soil to plants than did the other leafy green plants. In leafy vegetables, the average level of trace element uptake was high compared to that in other vegetables, as leafy vegetables have a high transpiration rate to sustain their growth and the moisture content of the plant [71]. Absorption and accumulation also vary from species to species in the same category of leafy vegetable, e.g., spinach has higher levels of heavy elements (Fe, Zn, Mn, Cu, Pb, Cr, and Co) than lettuce [72]. The total TF decreased in the following order: Barkin Ladi (1.0) mg/kg > Jos South and Jos East (0.7) mg/kg > Bassa and Mangu (0.6) mg/kg [73]. Metal ions play a considerable role in plant growth, moving through various parts of the plant to distribute nutrients for various biological functions (photosynthesis, energy generation, metabolic reactions, and mitochondrial function). Thus, metal chelators such as phytochelatin, metallothionein, nicotianamine, and histidine play a vital role in the metal translocation mechanism, which helps in reducing the toxicity level of heavy elements in plants [74]. In terms of soil–crop transfer, Mingtao et al. reported the synergistic and antagonistic impacts of trace elements following Zn, Pb, and Cr adsorption from soil to crops [75]. Another study revealed that the TF values of Pb^{2+}, Fe^{2+}, and Cu^{2+} were higher than those of Ni^{2+} and Zn^{2+}, leading to the conclusion that Ni^{2+} and Zn^{2+} ions have a restrictive effect on internal transport in crops [69]. The amount of accumulation of Zn, Cu, and Fe in edible vegetables is contingent on the concentration of their water-soluble metal forms in the soil [19]. The $TF_{water-plant}$ summarized in Table 3 indicate that Fe has an effect on plants through transfer from water, which is an essential element found in most living things.

Table 2. Transfer factor (TF) of selected trace elements from soil to plants.

Plant Sample	Part of Plant	Pb	Ni	Zn	Fe	Cr	Cu
Coriander	Leaves	ND *	ND	0.15	0.004	0.01	0.44
	Shoots	ND	0.003	0.06	0.001	ND	0.35
	Roots	ND	0.15	0.18	0.005	0.04	0.54
Parsley	Leaves	ND	0.004	0.39	0.003	ND	0.74
	Shoots	ND	0.001	0.25	0.001	ND	0.52
	Roots	ND	0.0005	0.31	0.001	ND	0.67
Arugula	Leaves	0.22	0.69	2.00	0.003	ND	ND
	Shoots	0.08	0.40	1.43	0.001	0.001	ND
	Roots	0.20	0.34	2.44	0.001	ND	ND
Dill	Leaves	0.18	0.99	2.85	0.003	ND	0.03
	Shoots	0.16	0.31	1.01	0.0002	0.01	0.04
	Roots	0.12	0.25	2.08	0.006	ND	ND

* ND = not detected.

Table 3. Transfer factor (TF$_{water-plant}$) of selected trace elements from irrigation water to plants.

Plant Sample	Part of Plant	Pb	Ni	Zn	Fe	Cr	Cu
Coriander	Leaves	30.5	ND *	ND	584.44	ND	306.66
	Shoots	47	ND	ND	214.44	ND	246.66
	Root	57	ND	ND	785.55	ND	376.66
Parsley	Leaves	55	ND	ND	375.92	ND	493.33
	Shoots	30.5	ND	ND	237.77	ND	350
	Roots	89	ND	ND	214.07	ND	446.66
Arugula	Leaves	70.6	ND	ND	582.96	ND	ND
	Shoots	27.5	ND	ND	222.44	ND	ND
	Roots	68.5	ND	ND	222.59	ND	ND
Dill	Leaves	71	ND	ND	586.29	ND	23.33
	Shoots	63.5	ND	ND	51.48	ND	43.33
	Roots	47.5	ND	ND	1212.59	ND	ND

* ND = not detected.

3.4. Statistical Analysis

The results of our analysis of the correlation between the level of the trace elements based on the combined data of soil and plants (TF$_{soil-plant}$) and some other factors affecting metal uptake (three blocks (water, fertilizer, and pesticide samples), plants, and plant tissues) are summarized in Table S1, with $p < 0.05$ indicating a significant correlation between the element content and the suitability of leafy green plants for human consumption. The Zn, Fe, and Cu levels in the four vegetables in various plant tissues are displayed in Figure 4. Block 1 was found to have a more significant effect on the plant tissues of dill and arugula than blocks 2 and 3. The uptake of Zn was significantly higher in leaves than shoots in block 1 (water samples), as shown in Figure 5. Zn bioaccumulation varies in green leafy plants due to differences in the physiology, morphology, and anatomy of each plant [11]. To determine the probable relationship between Fe content and TF$_{soil-plant}$, correlations with three blocks were calculated. The results reported in Table S1 and Figure 4 reveal a positive correlation between block 1 and coriander plants. The correlation varies widely between the three blocks and the plant tissues. In the plant tissues, the binding sites are totally different from those in soil containing large amounts of humic, fluvic acids, and other phenolic compounds. The highest Fe content was found roots, whereas the lowest Fe content was found in shoots, as shown in Figure 5; however, in some cases, trace elements such as Co, Cr, and Fe were retained in the roots, and only a minor portion reached the shoots [76,77]. In soil and plants, the correlation depends on available forms of elemental ions and the particular conditions of plants. In soil, Fe absorption efficiency depends on the ability of roots to reduce Fe^{3+} to Fe^{2+} to secrete of mugineic acid, which changes the soil conditions and causes reduction [25].

The highest Cu levels of different vegetables are presented in Figure 4. The strong binding of Cu with the available organic matter and other soil colloids and the high mobility of Cu from soil to plants can most likely account for the observed trend. However, the interactive effects of the three blocks used in this study contributed effectively to Cu contents, leading to elevated Cu levels in parsley relative to arugula plants, as shown in Figure 5. The level of Pb was significantly higher in parsley than arugula plants Figure 5. On the other hand, a positive and significant correlation between heavy metal contents was observed, although Ni and Cr were positively but non-significantly correlated (Table S1). Our analysis of the correlation between the level of trace elements based on the combined data of TF and the three factors affecting metal uptake (block, part of plant, and plant) revealed non-significant correlations between element content and blocks 2 and 3, i.e., fertilizer and pesticide samples. The reported data further support the notion of multiple sources from agricultural activities accounting for significant differences.

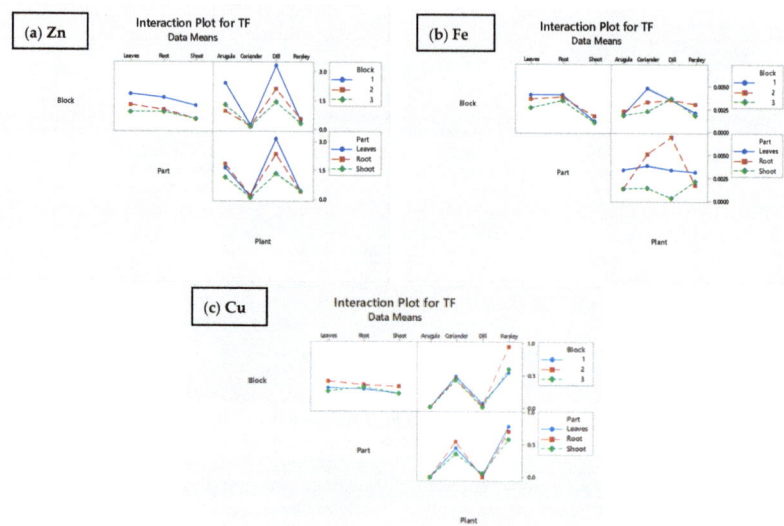

Figure 4. Interaction of trace element uptake (Zn (**a**), Fe (**b**), and Cu (**c**)) in various plant tissues.

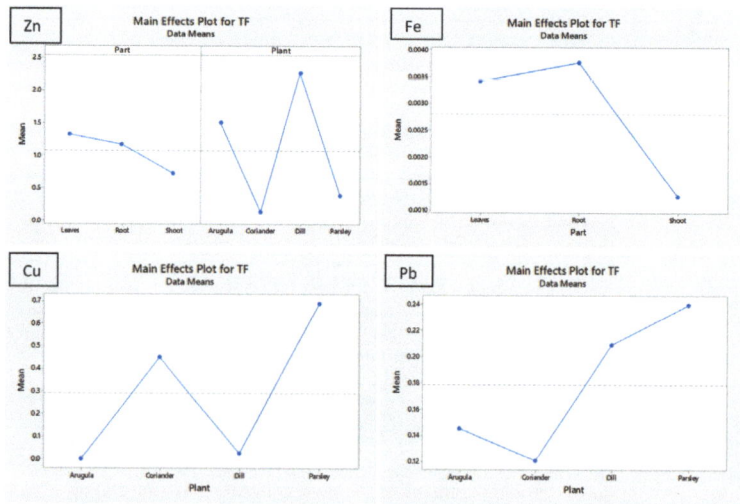

Figure 5. Correlation significance of trace element levels for TF of the plants and various plant tissues.

4. Conclusions and Future Perspectives

In conclusion, the identification and quantification of sources of trace elements in soil and crops, as well as contamination status, are of considerable environmental and scientific importance. The outcomes of this study establish that the water and edible plants in the study area are suitable for public consumption, although regular checking for heavy metals in the study area is recommended. The correlation factors that influence the bioaccumulation of elements in green leafy plants were determined. The concentrations of trace elements in soil, water, pesticides, and fertilizers were found to be within the allowed limits set by the FAO/WHO. The soil and water resources in the study area were not contaminated, whereas certain vegetable species were found to contain trace elements in levels that exceeded the allowed limits. The most significant toxic elements additions constituting soil impurities were Zn, Fe, and Cu. $TF_{soil-plant}$ values were determined in the following order: Zn > Cu > Ni > Pb > Cr > Fe. The mean TF values, irrespective of plant type, were 1.09. 0.27, 0.26, 0.08. 0.005, and 0.002 for Zn, Cu, Ni, Pb, Cr, and Fe, respectively. Hence, Zn was the most bioavailable to plants because it can be transferred from soil to plants more easily than Cu, Ni, Pb, Cr, and Fe. The results reported in this study can provide benefits with respect to improving soil fertility, reducing waste, improving soil health, identifying slow-release sources of nutrients for plant growth, and reducing environmental impacts. Thus, systematic monitoring of the concentrations of potentially toxic trace metals in soil and green vegetables by public environmental agencies is necessary in order to verify operations and to protect the environment from hazardous pollutants. Finally, the study results indicate the need for a more current management program with respect to discharge into agricultural soil. In future work, we will use principal component analysis (PCA) for each of the matrices to be tested.

Supplementary Materials: The following supporting information can be downloaded at: https://www.mdpi.com/article/10.3390/pr11092515/s1, Figure S1. A map describing the study area and sampling sites, Figure S2. An agricultural experiment design for statistical treatment of data, Table S1. Mean element (Pb, Ni, Zn, Fe, Cu and Cr) concentrations based on the combined data of soil and plant.

Author Contributions: B.G.A.: project administration, supervision, writing—original draft, writing—review and editing; S.A.A.-A.: formal analysis, writing—original draft; M.S.E.-S.: validation, data assignment, writing—review and editing. All authors have read and agreed to the published version of the manuscript.

Funding: This project was funded by the Deanship of Scientific Research (DSR), King Abdulaziz University, Jeddah under Grant number G–275-247-38.

Data Availability Statement: Not applicable.

Acknowledgments: The authors would like to thank the Deanship of Scientific Research (DSR) at King Abdulaziz University for their financial support, and many thanks to Mazin Fahad Alahmadi at King Abdulaziz University College of Engineering Industrial Engineering Department for facilitating the statistical analysis.

Conflicts of Interest: The authors declare no conflict of interest.

References

1. Hajeb, P.; Sloth, J.J.; Shakibazadeh, S.; Mahyudin, N.; Afsah-Hejri, L. Toxic elements in food: Occurrence, binding, and reduction approaches. *Compr. Rev. Food Sci. Food Saf.* **2014**, *13*, 457–472. [CrossRef]
2. Gergen, I.; Harmanescu, M. Application of principal component analysis in the pollution assessment with heavy metals of vegetable food chain in the old mining areas. *Chem. Cent. J.* **2012**, *6*, 156. [CrossRef]
3. Karahan, F. Evaluation of Trace Element and Heavy Metal Levels of Some Ethnobotanically Important Medicinal Plants Used as Remedies in Southern Turkey in Terms of Human Health Risk. *Biol. Trace Elem. Res.* **2023**, *201*, 493–513. [CrossRef]
4. FAO/WHO. Joint FAO/WHO Food Standards Programme Codex Alimentarius Commission. Report of the Thirty Three Session of the Codex Committee on Food Additives and Contaminants. Geneva, Switzerland, 2001; ALINORM 01/12A:1289. Available online: http://www.who.int/water_sanitation_health/dwq/GDWQ2004web.pdf (accessed on 10 October 2021).

5. Irshad, M.; Ruqia, B.; Hussain, Z. Phytoaccumulation of heavy metals in natural vegetation at the municipal wastewater site in Abbottabad, Pakistan. *Int. J. Phytoremediation* **2015**, *17*, 1269–1273. [CrossRef]
6. Khan, A.; Khan, S.; Khan, M.A.; Qamar, Z.; Waqas, M. The uptake and bioaccumulation of heavy metals by food plants, their effects on plants nutrients, and associated health risk: A review. *Environ. Sci. Pollut. Res.* **2015**, *22*, 13772–13799. [CrossRef]
7. Ramteke, S.; Sahu, B.L.; Dahariya, N.S.; Patel, K.S.; Blazhev, B.; Matini, L. Heavy metal contamination of vegetables. *J. Environ. Prot.* **2016**, *7*, 996–1004. [CrossRef]
8. Tong, S.; Yang, L.; Gong, H.; Wang, L.; Li, H.; Yu, J.; Li, Y.; Deji, Y.; Nima, C.; Zhao, S.; et al. Bioaccumulation characteristics, transfer model of heavy metals in soil-crop system and health assessment in plateau region, China. *Ecotoxicol. Environ. Saf.* **2022**, *241*, 113733. [CrossRef]
9. Wuana, R.A.; Okieimen, F.E. Heavy metals in contaminated soils: A review of sources, chemistry, risks and best available strategies for remediation. *Isrn Ecol.* **2011**, *2011*, 1–20. [CrossRef]
10. Bhagure, G.R.; Mirgane, S. Heavy metal concentrations in groundwaters and soils of Thane Region of Maharashtra, India. *Environ. Monit. Assess.* **2011**, *173*, 643–652. [CrossRef]
11. Gupta, N.; Yadav, K.K.; Kumar, V.; Kumar, S.; Chadd, R.P.; Kumar, A. Trace elements in soil-vegetables interface: Translocation, bioaccumulation, toxicity and amelioration–a review. *Sci. Total Environ.* **2019**, *651 Pt 2*, 2927–2942. [CrossRef]
12. Wang, J.; Li, H.; Yang, L.; Li, Y.; Wei, B.; Yu, J.; Feng, F. Distribution and translocation of selenium from soil to highland barley in the Tibetan Plateau Kashin-Beck disease area. *Environ. Geochem. Health* **2017**, *39*, 221–229. [CrossRef]
13. Wan, M.; Hu, W.; Wang, H.; Tian, K.; Huang, B. Comprehensive assessment of heavy metal risk in soil-crop systems along the Yangtze River in Nanjing, Southeast China. *Sci. Total Environ.* **2021**, *780*, 146567. [CrossRef]
14. Waseem, A.; Arshad, J.; Iqbal, F.; Sajjad, A.; Mehmood, Z.; Murtaza, G. Pollution status of Pakistan: A retrospective review on heavy metal contamination of water, soil, and vegetables. *BioMed Res. Int.* **2014**, *2014*, 1–29. [CrossRef]
15. Ezez, D.; Belew, M. Analysis of physicochemical attributes, contamination level of trace metals and assessment of health risk in mango fruits from Southern region Ethiopia. *Toxicol. Rep.* **2023**, *10*, 124–132. [CrossRef]
16. Oteef, M.D.; KF Fawy HS Abd-Rabboh, A.M. Idris Levels of zinc, copper, cadmium, and lead in fruits and vegetables grown and consumed in Aseer Region, Saudi Arabia. *Environ. Monit. Assess.* **2015**, *187*, 676–687. [CrossRef]
17. Harmanescu, M.; Alda, L.M.; Bordean, D.M.; Gogoasa, I.; Gergen, I. Heavy metals health risk assessment for population via consumption of vegetables grown in old mining area; a case study: Banat County, Romania. *Chem. Cent. J.* **2011**, *5*, 64–74. [CrossRef]
18. Islam, M.S.; Proshad, R.; Asadul Haque, M.; Hoque, M.F.; Hossin, M.S.; Islam Sarker, M.N. Assessment of heavy metals in foods around the industrial areas: Health hazard inference in Bangladesh. *Geocarto Int.* **2020**, *35*, 280–295. [CrossRef]
19. Kaledin, A.P.; Stepanova, M.V. Bioaccumulation of trace elements in vegetables grown in various anthropogenic conditions. *Foods Raw Mater.* **2023**, *11*, 10–16. [CrossRef]
20. Ashraf, I.; Ahmad, F.; Sharif, A.; Altaf, A.R.; Teng, H. Heavy metals assessment in water, soil, vegetables and their associated health risks via consumption of vegetables, District Kasur, Pakistan. *SN Appl. Sci.* **2021**, *3*, 1–16. [CrossRef]
21. Kirmani, M.Z. Determination of some toxic and essential trace metals in some medicinal and edible plants of Karachi city. *J. Basic Appl. Sci.* **2011**, *7*, 89–95. [CrossRef]
22. Helali, S.; Bohli, N.; Mostafa, H.A.; Zina, H.B.; Al-Hartomy, O.A.; Abdelghani, A. Electrical impedance spectroscopy using single wall carbon nanotubes carboxlic acid functionalized: Detection of copper in Tabuk-Kingdom of Saudi Arabia Water. *J. Nanomed. Nanotechnol.* **2016**, *7*, 396. [CrossRef]
23. Abedi, A.; Gavanji, S.; Amin Mojiri, A. Lead and Zinc Uptake and Toxicity in Maize and Their Management. *Plants* **2022**, *11*, 1922. [CrossRef]
24. Nazir, R.; Khan, M.; Masab, M.; Rehman, H.U.; Rauf, N.U.; Shahab, S.; Shaheen, Z. Accumulation of heavy metals (Ni, Cu, Cd, Cr, Pb, Zn, Fe) in the soil, water and plants and analysis of physico-chemical parameters of soil and water collected from Tanda Dam Kohat. *J. Pharm. Sci. Res.* **2015**, *7*, 89.
25. Fruzińska, R. Accumulation of iron in the soil-plant system in a metal industry area. *Civ. Environ. Eng. Rep.* **2011**, *7*, 59–68.
26. Alhogbi, B.G. Trace Metal Determination in Herbal Plants by Acid Digestion from Jeddah Market in Saudi Arabia. *Int. J. Chem.* **2018**, *10*, 8–14. [CrossRef]
27. Emamverdian, A.; Ding, Y.; Mokhberdoran, F.; Xie, Y. Heavy metal stress and some mechanisms of plant defense response. *Sci. World J.* **2015**. [CrossRef]
28. Beinabaj, S.M.H.; Heydariyan, H.; Aleii, H.M.; Hosseinzadeh, A. Concentration of heavy metals in leachate, soil, and plants in Tehran's landfill: Investigation of the effect of landfill age on the intensity of pollution. *Heliyon* **2023**, *9*, e13017. [CrossRef]
29. Organgi, R.A. Ecological Studies in Makkah Region. 1. Vegetation Development at Wadi Fatma. *J. Coll. Sci. Univ. Riyadh* **1982**, *13*, 25–51.
30. Atamaleki, A.; Yazdanbakhsh, A.; Fallah, S.; Hesami, M.; Neshat, A.; Fakhri, Y. Accumulation of potentially harmful elements (PHEs) in lettuce (*Lactuca sativa* L.) and coriander (*Coriandrum sativum* L.) irrigated with wastewater: A systematic review and meta-analysis and probabilistic health risk assessment. *Environ. Sci. Pollut. Res.* **2021**, *28*, 13072–13082. [CrossRef]
31. Tefera, M.; Teklewold, A. Health risk assessment of heavy metals in selected Ethiopian spices. *Heliyon* **2021**, *7*, e07048. [CrossRef]
32. Sadee, B.A.; Ali, R.J. Determination of heavy metals in edible vegetables and a human health risk assessment. *Environ. Nanotechnol. Monit. Manag.* **2023**, *19*, 100761. [CrossRef]

33. Jalali, M.; Meyari, A. Heavy metal contents, soil-to-plant transfer factors, and associated health risks in vegetables grown in western Iran. *J. Food Compos. Anal.* **2022**, *106*, 104316. [CrossRef]
34. Sheydaei, M.; Ghiasvandnia, P.; Edraki, M.; Sheidaie, M. Investigation of toxic metals content of parsley (petroselinum crispum) obtained from local farms in Baz Kia Gorab region (Lahijan city, north of Iran). *J. Chem. Lett.* **2022**, *3*, 114–118. [CrossRef]
35. Mehmood, A.; Mirza, M.A.; Choudhary, M.A.; Kim, K.H.; Raza, W.; Raza, N.; Lee, S.S.; Zhang, M.; Lee, J.H.; Sarfraz, M. Spatial distribution of heavy metals in crops in a wastewater irrigated zone and health risk assessment. *Environ. Res.* **2019**, *168*, 382–388. [CrossRef] [PubMed]
36. Eid, E.M.; El-Bebany, A.F.; Taher, M.A.; Alrumman, S.A.; Hussain, A.A.; Galal, T.M.; Shaltout, K.H.; Sewelam, N.A.; Ahmed, M.T.; El-Shaboury, G.A. Influences of sewage sludge-amended soil on heavy metal accumulation, growth and yield of rocket plant (*Eruca sativa*). *Appl. Ecol. Environ. Res.* **2020**, *18*, 3027–3040. [CrossRef]
37. Eaton, A.D.; Franson, M.A.H. *Standard Methods for the Examination of Water and Wastewater*; American Public Health Association, American Water Works Association, Water Environment Federation: Washington, DC, USA; Denver, CO, USA; Alexandria, Egypt, 2005.
38. USEPA. *United States Environmental Protection Agency for (Total Sobbed) Heavy Metals in Soil, Sediments and Sludge (USEPA SW-846, Method 3050)*; USEPA: Washington, DC, USA, 1986.
39. Osakwe, S.A.; Okolie, L.P. Physicochemical characteristics and heavy metals contents in soils and cassava plants from farmlands along a major highway in Delta State, Nigeria. *J. Appl. Sci. Environ. Manag.* **2015**, *19*, 695–704. [CrossRef]
40. *Standard Methods for the Examination of Water and Wastewater*, 24th ed.; American Water Works Association: Denver, CO, USA; American Public Works Association: Kansas City, MO, USA; Water Environment Federation: Alexandria, VA, USA, 2022; ISBN 9780875532998.
41. Miller, J.N.; Miller, J.C. *Statistics and Chemometrics for Analytical Chemistry*; Pearson/Prentice-Hall: Harlow, UK, 2005.
42. Cui, Y.J.; Zhu, Y.G.; Zhai, R.H.; Chen, D.Y.; Huang, Y.Z.; Qiu, Y.; Liang, J.Z. Transfer of metals from soil to vegetables in an area near a smelter in Nanning, China. *Environ. Int.* **2004**, *30*, 785–791. [CrossRef]
43. Sowrabha, J.; Narayana, J. Assessment of ground water quality using for drinking purpose in Shivamogga Town, Karnataka, India. *Int. J. Curr. Microbiol. Appl. Sci.* **2014**, *3*, 381–388.
44. Ishibashi, Y.; Matsuo, H.; Baba, Y.; Nagafuchi, Y.; Imato, T.; Hirata, T. Association of manganese effluent with the application of fertilizer and manure on tea field. *Water Res.* **2004**, *38*, 2821–2826. [CrossRef]
45. Wang, A.S.; Angle, J.S.; Chaney, R.L.; Delorme, T.A.; Reeves, R.D. Soil pH effects on uptake of Cd and Zn by Thlaspi caerulescens. *Plant Soil* **2006**, *281*, 325–337. [CrossRef]
46. Cobbina, S.J.; Duwiejuah, A.B.; Quansah, R.; Obiri, S.; Bakobie, N. Comparative assessment of heavy metals in drinking water sources in two small-scale mining communities in northern Ghana. *Int. J. Environ. Res. Public Health* **2015**, *12*, 10620–10634. [CrossRef] [PubMed]
47. Al-Hammad, B.A.; El-Salam, M.M.A. Evaluation of heavy metal pollution in water wells and soil using common leafy green plant indicators in the Al-Kharj region, Saudi Arabia. *Environ. Monit. Assess.* **2016**, *188*, 324. [CrossRef] [PubMed]
48. Brar, M.; Malhi, S.; Singh, A.; Arora, C.; Gill, K. Sewage water irrigation effects on some potentially toxic trace elements in soil and potato plants in northwestern India. *Can. J. Soil Sci.* **2000**, *80*, 465–471. [CrossRef]
49. Benson, N.U.; Anake, W.U.; Etesin, U.M. Trace metals levels in inorganic fertilizers commercially available in Nigeria. *J. Sci. Res. Rep.* **2014**, *3*, 610–620. [CrossRef]
50. Naz, S.; Fazio, F.; Habib, S.S.; Nawaz, G.; Attaullah, S.; Ullah, M.; Hayat, A.; Ahmed, I. Incidence of Heavy Metals in the Application of Fertilizers to Crops (Wheat and Rice), a Fish (*Common carp*) Pond and a Human Health Risk Assessment. *Sustainability* **2022**, *14*, 13441. [CrossRef]
51. Modaihsh, A.; AI-Swailem, M.; Mahjoub, M. Heavy metals content of commercial inorganic fertilizers used in the Kingdom of Saudi Arabia. *J. Agric. Mar. Sci.* **2004**, *9*, 21–25. [CrossRef]
52. Hegade, R.R.; Chethanakumara, M.V.; Krishnamurthy, S.V.B. Influence of Soil Organic Carbon, Water Holding Capacity, and Moisture Content on Heavy Metals in Rice Paddy Soils of Western Ghats of India. *Water Air Soil Pollut.* **2023**, *234*, 192. [CrossRef]
53. Alam, M.N.E.; Hosen, M.M.; Ullah, A.K.M.A.; Maksud, M.A.; Khan, S.R.; Lutfa, L.N.; Choudhury, T.R.; Quraishi, S.B. Pollution Characteristics, Source Identification, and Health Risk of Heavy Metals in the Soil-Vegetable System in Two Districts of Bangladesh. *Biol. Trace Elem. Res.* **2023**. [CrossRef]
54. Malede, M.; Tefera, M.; Mehari, B. Trace metals in the leaves of selected plants used to treat hepatitis in Dembia, Ethiopia. *J. Herbs Spices Med. Plants* **2020**, *26*, 101–112. [CrossRef]
55. Mohamed, A.; Rashed, M.; Mofty, A. Assessment of essential and toxic elements in some kinds of vegetables. *Ecotoxicol. Environ. Saf.* **2003**, *55*, 251–260. [CrossRef]
56. Yadav, A.; Yadav, P.K.; Shukla, D. Investigation of heavy metal status in soil and vegetables grown in urban area of Allahabad, Uttar Pradesh, India. *Int. J. Sci. Res. Publ.* **2013**, *3*, 1–7.
57. Abdella, A.; Chandravanshi, B.S.; Yohannes, W. Levels of selected metals in coriander (*Coriandrum sativum* L.) leaves cultivated in four different areas of Ethiopia. *Chem. Int.* **2018**, *4*, 189–197.
58. Hu, B.; Xue, J.; Zhou, Y.; Shao, S.; Fu, Z.; Li, Y.; Chen, S.; Qi, L.; Shi, Z. Modelling bioaccumulation of heavy metals in soil-crop ecosystems and identifying its controlling factors using machine learning. *Environ. Pollut.* **2020**, *262*, 114308. [CrossRef]

59. Wan, D.; Zhang, N.; Chen, W.; Cai, P.; Zheng, L.; Huang, Q. Organic matter facilitates the binding of Pb to iron oxides in subtropical contaminated soil. *Environ. Sci. Pollut. Res.* **2018**, *25*, 32130–32139. [CrossRef]
60. Shen, B.; Wang, X.; Zhang, Y.; Zhang, M.; Wang, K.; Xie, P.; Ji, H. The optimum pH and Eh for simultaneously minimizing bioavailable cadmium and arsenic contents in soils under the organic fertilizer application. *Sci. Total Environ.* **2020**, *711*, 135229. [CrossRef]
61. Liu, Y.; Liu, D.; Zhao, Q.; Zhang, W.; Chen, X.; Xu, S.; Zou, C. Zinc fractions in soils and uptake in winter wheat as affected by repeated applications of zinc fertilizer. *Soil Tillage Res.* **2020**, *200*, 104612. [CrossRef]
62. Jorgensen, N.; Laursen, J.; Viksna, A.; Pind, N.; Holm, P.E. Multi-elemental EDXRF mapping of polluted soil from former horticultural land. *Environ. Inter.* **2005**, *31*, 43–52. [CrossRef]
63. Abrham, F.; Gholap, A. Analysis of heavy metal concentration in some vegetables using atomic absorption spectroscopy. *Pollution* **2021**, *7*, 205–216. [CrossRef]
64. Baldantoni, D.; Morra, L.; Zaccardelli, M.; Alfani, A. Cadmium accumulation in leaves of leafy vegetables. *Ecotoxicol. Environ. Saf.* **2016**, *123*, 89–94. [CrossRef]
65. Muamar, A.; Zouahri, A.; Tijane, M.; El Housni, A.; Mennane, Z.; Yachou, H.; Bouksaim, M. Evaluation of heavy metals pollution in groundwater, soil and some vegetables irrigated with wastewater in the Skhirat region Morocco. *J. Mater. Environ. Sci.* **2014**, *5*, 961–966.
66. Ali, M.H.; Al-Qahtani, K.M. Assessment of some heavy metals in vegetables, cereals and fruits in Saudi Arabian markets. *Egypt. J. Aquat. Res.* **2012**, *38*, 31–37. [CrossRef]
67. Soni, R.; Mishra, P. Assessment of heavy metals in the vegetables grown in the Suburbs of Jodhpur city. *J. Indian Chem. Soc.* **2017**, *94*, 1037–1043.
68. Tudi, M.; Ruan, H.D.; Yu, Y.; Wang, L.; Wei, B.; Tong, S.; Kong, C.; Yang, L.S. Bioaccumulation and translocation of trace elements in soil-irrigation water-wheat in arid agricultural areas of Xin Jiang, China. *Ecotoxicology* **2021**, *30*, 1290–1302. [CrossRef] [PubMed]
69. Aiqing, Z.; Zhang, L.; Ning, P.; Chen, Q.; Wang, B.; Zhang, F.; Yang, X.; Zhang, Y. Zinc in cereal grains: Concentration, distribution, speciation, bioavailability, and barriers to transport from roots to grains in wheat. *Crit. Rev. Food Sci. Nutr.* **2022**, *62*, 7917–7928. [CrossRef] [PubMed]
70. Brigden, K.; Stringer, R.; Santillo, D. *Heavy Metal and Radionuclide Contamination of Fertilizer Products and Phosphogypsum Waste Produced by the Lebanese Chemical Company*; Lebanon, Greenpeace Research Laboratories, Department of Biological Sciences, University of Exeter: Exeter, UK, 2002; Available online: http://www.greenpeace.to/publications/LCC_2002.pdf (accessed on 10 May 2022).
71. Mahmood, A.; Malik, R.N. Human health risk assessment of heavy metals via consumption of contaminated vegetables collected from different irrigation sources in Lahore, Pakistan. *Arab. J. Chem.* **2014**, *7*, 91–99. [CrossRef]
72. Waheed, H.; Ilyas, N.; Iqbal Raja, N.; Mahmood, T.; Ali, Z. Heavy metal phytoaccumulation in leafy vegetables irrigated with municipal wastewater and human health risk repercussions. *Int. J. Phytoremediation* **2019**, *21*, 170–179. [CrossRef]
73. Waida, J.; Ibrahim, U.; Goki, N.G.; Yusuf, S.D.; Rilwan, U. Transfer Factor of Heavy Metals due to Mining Activities in Some Parts of Plateau State, Nigeria (Health Implications on the Inhabitants). *J. Oncol. Res.* **2022**, *4*, 13–18. [CrossRef]
74. Jogawat, A.; Yadav, B.; Chhaya Narayan, O.P. Metal transporters in organelles and their roles in heavy metal transportation and sequestration mechanisms in plants. *Physiol. Plant.* **2021**, *173*, 259–275. [CrossRef]
75. Xiang, M.; Li, Y.; Yang, J.; Lei, K.; Li, Y.; Li, F.; Zheng, D.; Fang, X.; Cao, Y. Heavy metal contamination risk assessment and correlation analysis of heavy metal contents in soil and crops. *Environ. Pollut.* **2021**, *278*, 116911. [CrossRef]
76. Sharma, D.; Bisla, G. Assessment of Heavy Metals in Fruits and Vegetables Collected from Bareilly Local Market, Uttar Pradesh State, India. *Int. J. Res.* **2022**, *10*, 501–509. [CrossRef]
77. Page, V.; Feller, U. Heavy metals in crop plants: Transport and redistribution processes on the whole plant level. *Agronomy* **2015**, *5*, 447–463. [CrossRef]

Disclaimer/Publisher's Note: The statements, opinions and data contained in all publications are solely those of the individual author(s) and contributor(s) and not of MDPI and/or the editor(s). MDPI and/or the editor(s) disclaim responsibility for any injury to people or property resulting from any ideas, methods, instructions or products referred to in the content.

Article

French Fries' Color and Frying Process in Relation to Used Plant Oils

Bojan Antonic [1], Dani Dordevic [1], Hana Buchtova [2], Bohuslava Tremlova [1], Simona Dordevic [1] and Ivan Kushkevych [3,*]

[1] Department of Plant Origin Food Sciences, Faculty of Veterinary Hygiene and Ecology, University of Veterinary Sciences Brno, Palackého 1-3, 612 42 Brno, Czech Republic; h19001@vfu.cz (B.A.); dordevicd@vfu.cz (D.D.); tremlovab@vfu.cz (B.T.); dordevics@vfu.cz (S.D.)

[2] Department of Animal Origin Food and Gastronomic Sciences, Faculty of Veterinary Hygiene and Ecology, University of Veterinary Sciences Brno, Palackého 1-3, 612 42 Brno, Czech Republic; buchtovah@vfu.cz

[3] Department of Experimental Biology, Faculty of Science, Masaryk University, Kamenice 753/5, 625 00 Brno, Czech Republic

* Correspondence: kushkevych@mail.muni.cz; Tel.: +420549495315

Abstract: Fast-food establishments today often sell fried food without proper control over the frying oil, and french fries are a prime example. Neglecting the maintenance of frying oil can lead to decreased taste, health concerns, and operational inefficiencies. The following plant oils were used in the frying process: rapeseed, sunflower, and palm oil. The degree of frying was measured by the total polar meter (TPM), until the achievement of 24%. To accurately assess the color characteristics of the french fry samples, Minolta CM 2600d color measurement instrument was used. Statistically significant differences were observed between some color parameters (L, a, b, C, and h) and TPM values. The following correlations were observed: 0.530 was obtained for TPM and h (hue angle) in french fries fried in palm oil; negative correlation (−0.214) between TPM and L (lightness) was obtained in french fries fried in rapeseed oil. While we have observed certain correlations from our experimental data, it is important to note that the color of french fries may not be the sole determinant of fried oil quality. Other external factors, such as temperature, chemical composition, and potato cultivar, can also significantly influence the color of french fries.

Keywords: processes in rapeseed oil; sunflower oil; palm oil; frying process; total polar material; correlation

Citation: Antonic, B.; Dordevic, D.; Buchtova, H.; Tremlova, B.; Dordevic, S.; Kushkevych, I. French Fries' Color and Frying Process in Relation to Used Plant Oils. *Processes* **2023**, *11*, 2839. https://doi.org/10.3390/pr11102839

Academic Editor: Antoni Sánchez

Received: 10 August 2023
Revised: 18 September 2023
Accepted: 26 September 2023
Published: 27 September 2023

Copyright: © 2023 by the authors. Licensee MDPI, Basel, Switzerland. This article is an open access article distributed under the terms and conditions of the Creative Commons Attribution (CC BY) license (https://creativecommons.org/licenses/by/4.0/).

1. Introduction

One of the most common ways for food preparation today is deep-fat frying. Immersion of food pieces in the hot vegetable oil gives them a nice golden color, crispy texture, and pleasant taste [1]. The main goal during that way of food preparation is to form the crisp crust using the high temperatures (170–190 °C) and to keep the flavors and juices inside [2]. In many nations, the bulk of potato crop production is used in processing channels, making potatoes (*Solanum tuberosum* L.) an essential staple food required to fulfill the needs of a growing worldwide population [3].

French fries can be considered as the main representative among the fried foods today. It is estimated that more than 30% of all processed potatoes go to french fries in the US [4]. The frying process influences the physical, chemical, and sensory properties of fried food [2]. After a final deep-fat frying phase, french fries (also known as chips or fries), either fresh or pre-frozen, are frequently produced industrially. Exposure studies have shown that french fries are a significant dietary source of the probable human carcinogen acrylamide, which is produced during this procedure [5].

Since it is a practice to use the same oil in the repeated process, various undesirable reactions occur in the oil as well [6]. Frying at high temperatures induces the reactions of hydrolysis, thermal degradation, oxidation, and polymerization [7]. The most reliable way for the determination of stability and quality of frying oils during food preparation is the measurement of total polar matter (TPM). Those polar compounds are mainly dimers and polymers of triglycerides formed in oil at high temperatures [8]. The disposal of frying oil is recommended when the level of TPM reaches 24% (for US, Germany, and France) [9]. It should be emphasized that many fast foods do not control the quality, such as TPM level, of used oils [10]. According to the previous literature data, it can be stated that the main sign for determining how fast frying oil is degrading is the growth of TPM [11].

One of the major sensory characteristics of fried french fries that have impact on consumers' acceptance is the color [12]. Formation of color on french fries' surface during frying is caused by a Maillard reaction: interactions between amino acids and reducing sugars. The final color of the fries' surface is influenced by frying temperature and duration and frying medium [1,4].

The measurement and characterization of the french fries' color can be done with ease and accuracy using an instrumental method that employs a colorimeter with L*a*b* colorimetric parameters [13].

By instrumentally obtaining values of parameters L (lightness), a (redness: green to red), b (yellowness: blue to yellow), C (chroma value, saturation), and h (hue angle, color angle), it is possible to objectively track eventual changes in the color of french fries fried in oils in different stages of degradation [14,15].

Literature findings are limited to the measurements of the color of french fries in differently treated fresh oil [2] or measurements after a certain number of frying cycles with no association with TPM% in the oil [16,17]. A significant change of oil color during repeated frying was recorded [18], but there is a lack of data about its effect on fries' color. The objective of the study was to investigate the relationship between the color characteristics of french fries and the quality of frying oil, as measured by the total polar meter (TPM) using different plant oils (rapeseed, sunflower, and palm oil) in the frying process. Potential industrial applications include improving quality control in fast-food establishments, optimizing frying processes, and selecting suitable frying oils to enhance the overall quality and safety of french fries.

2. Materials and Methods

Samples

For the frying purposes, the french fries (Hearty Food Co., Tesco, Czech Republic) were purchased in the local supermarket. Rapeseed, sunflower, and palm oils (the most often used frying oils in the Czech Republic) were chosen for use as frying mediums. The rapeseed and sunflower oils originated from the Czech Republic and the palm oil was packed in Austria.

Frying process

An FR 2035 deep-fat fryer (Concept, Choceň, Czech Republic) was used for the frying experiments. Frying batches consisted of 100 g of frozen french fries that were fried in about 3.3 L of oil at an average temperature of 175 °C. Each cycle consisted of a 5-minute frying sequence, draining in the frying basket for 1 min, and oil stabilization time of 4 min prior to the TPM measurements. TPM values were recorded by a Testo 270 TPM meter (Testo SE & Co. KGaA, Titisee–Neustadt, Germany). Samples of fried fries were taken for the color measurements after 3 cycles of frying and, further, when the TPM reached values of 10, 15, 20, and 24%. Sample batches and their abbreviations are presented in Table 1. The frying vessel was refilled with the necessary amount of oil each time the level of oil in it dropped below the minimum mark.

Color measurement

Color measurements of the french fry samples were carried out using a Minolta CM 2600d and Spectra Magic 3.61 color data software (Konica Minolta, Tokyo, Japan). A total of 50 measurements were performed for each group of samples. The color values were ex-pressed using the CIELab color space as L (lightness), a (redness/greenness), and b (yellowness/blueness). C (chroma) and h (hue) values were internally calculated by the instrument (C = (a2 + b2)1/2 and h = arctan (b/a) [19].

Table 1. Description of french fries' sample abbreviations and corresponding oil TPM% levels (R—rapeseed oil fried samples; S—sunflower oil fried samples; P—palm oil dried samples).

Sample	Abbreviation	Oil TPM Level (%)		
		R	S	P
Sample 1 batch	1R/1S/1P	6.5	9	6.5
Sample 2 batch	2R/2S/2P	10	10	10
Sample 3 batch	3R/3S/3P	15	15	15
Sample 4 batch	4R/4S/4P	20	20	20
Sample 5 batch	5R/5S/5P	24	24	24

Statistics

Obtained results are presented in the tables, including the mean values and standard deviations. The color was measured 50 times for each parameter in each batch. Statistical analysis was done using the one-way ANOVA for the determination of differences with-in the sample group (rapeseed-, sunflower-, and palm-oil-fried fries). Pearson correlation analysis was done for the observation of associations between the TPM% and color values. The interpretation of correlation coefficients was undertaken as follows: 0.00–0.10—negligible correlation; 0.10–0.39—weak correlation; 0.40–0.69—moderate correlation; 0.70–0.89—strong correlation; 0.90–1.00—very strong correlation [20]. For discussion of the results, the square of the correlation coefficient (coefficient of determination) was used as the proportion of variance once that was accounted for by the other. IBM SPSS software was used for conducting statistical analysis.

3. Results and Discussion

The impact of french fry frying cycles and the number on the TPM value of rapeseed, sunflower, and palm oil are presented in Figure 1. The number of frying cycles needed to reach 24% TPM was the lowest in sunflower oil (80 cycles), followed by rapeseed oil (84 cycles) and palm oil with the highest number after 94 cycles. Palm oil stands out as the most stable among the three oils in our experiment, primarily because of its high content of saturated fatty acids, especially palmitic and stearic fatty acids. This composition leads to a significantly slower rate of deterioration when compared to the other oils studied. This stability makes palm oil a favored choice in the food industry, particularly for products requiring extended shelf life, as it helps maintain flavor and texture over time [21].

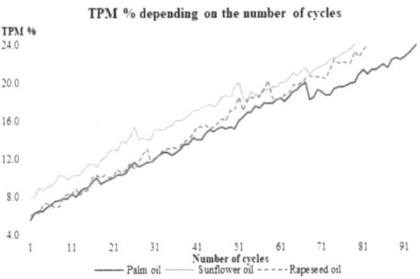

Figure 1. Impact of number of frying cycles on TPM value.

In addition to the price, because of its desirable properties, palm oil has emerged as the most widely utilized frying oil [22]. Furthermore, palm oil imparts a waxy or greasy flavor to the products, particularly in colder climates. The cause is the high melting point of palm oil, which is 38 °C and higher than the average body temperature [23]. Otherwise, in addition to higher saturated fatty acids content (mainly palmitic fatty acid), palm oil has a high smoke point of around 230 °C [24].

On the other hand, rapeseed and sunflower oil contain mainly unsaturated fatty acids, with negligible amounts of polyunsaturated fatty acids (PUFA). Rapeseed oil exhibits a polyunsaturated fatty acid (PUFA) content of around 20%, while sunflower oil PUFA content reaches up to 71% [25,26]. The accelerated degradation rate and attainment of the fastest critical point in sunflower oil, characterized by its high polyunsaturated fatty acid (PUFA) content, specifically reaching up to 24% TPM (total polar materials), can be attributed to the inherent susceptibility of PUFA to rapid degradation at elevated temperatures. The thermally induced oxidative breakdown of PUFA molecules is facilitated by their greater number of double bonds, making them more prone to oxidation compared to other types of fatty acids present in oils [27].

As a result of the substantial abundance of polyunsaturated fatty acids (PUFA) found within sunflower oil, it becomes particularly susceptible to degradation when exposed to elevated temperatures. This heightened vulnerability to deterioration underscores the importance of proper storage and handling practices for this type of cooking oil, especially in circumstances where higher cooking temperatures are employed [27].

In a related study conducted by Enríquez-Fernández and colleagues in 2019, an experiment akin to ours was carried out to assess the stability of palm olein and a blend comprising palm olein and canola oil. In this investigation, the researchers subjected these oils to a rigorous frying experiment involving the preparation of french fries. Over a span of 12.9 h of continuous frying, the researchers observed results in terms of the total polar matter (TPM%) values, which are indicative of oil degradation and deterioration. The findings of this study revealed that palm olein, which is primarily derived from palm oil, exhibited a TPM% value of 12%. Conversely, the palm olein and canola oil blend demonstrated a slightly lower TPM% value of 11.5%. These results suggest that both oils, in isolation and as a blend, have commendable stability during prolonged frying, further highlighting the remarkable resilience of palm-derived oils in high-temperature cooking scenarios [17].

This research by Enríquez-Fernández and colleagues corroborates our own findings regarding the stability of palm oil. It underscores the suitability of palm-based oils for frying applications, particularly when blended with other oils like canola, as it enhances their performance and extends their usability. Such insights are invaluable to the food industry, where the maintenance of oil quality during frying is crucial not only for flavor and texture but also for cost-effectiveness and food safety considerations.

In the context of the current research investigation, it was observed that the duration required to attain a 24% total polar matter (TPM) concentration averaged approximately 16 h. This finding provides valuable insights into the temporal dynamics of TPM accumulation and emphasizes the need for a thorough understanding of these time-dependent processes in order to make informed decisions and optimizations in various relevant fields or applications. Experiments of this kind underscore the intricate and multidimensional nature of the frying processes implicated in the production of french fries. They illuminate the complex interplay of numerous variables, including temperature, oil composition, moisture content, and frying duration, all of which wield a profound influence on the final attributes of this culinary product. The instrumental values for L, a, b, C, and h color parameters are presented in Tables 1–4.

Table 2. Color values of french fries fried in rapeseed oil in different stages of frying (different lowercase letters (a, b, c, and d) indicate statistically significant differences ($p < 0.05$) between rows; the results are presented as the mean values ± standard deviation).

Sample	L	a	b	C	h
1R	67.73 ± 3.41 [a]	0.74 ± 0.93 [a]	28.87 ± 4.74 [a]	28.89 ± 4.76 [a]	88.68 ± 1.63 [a]
2R	56.22 ± 7.58 [b]	6.93 ± 3.60 [b]	33.14 ± 4.99 [b]	34.04 ± 5.00 [b]	78.19 ± 6.08 [b]
3R	61.36 ± 3.88 [c]	5.20 ± 2.78 [b]	33.24 ± 3.96 [b]	33.74 ± 4.07 [b]	81.22 ± 4.46 [c]
4R	58.67 ± 4.86 [bd]	5.53 ± 2.57 [b]	32.96 ± 4.11 [b]	33.51 ± 4.21 [b]	80.54 ± 4.06 [bc]
5R	60.66 ± 8.31 [cd]	3.06 ± 3.00 [c]	29.56 ± 3.80 [a]	29.85 ± 3.93 [a]	84.22 ± 5.39 [d]

Table 3. Color values of french fries fried in sunflower oil in different stages of frying (different lowercase letters (a, b, c, and d) indicate statistically significant differences ($p < 0.05$) within the column; the results are presented as the mean values ± standard deviation).

Sample	L	a	b	C	h
1S	58.80 ± 7.30	2.16 ± 2.32 [ab]	27.03 ± 4.63 [ad]	27.20 ± 4.69 [ad]	85.60 ± 4.98 [ab]
2S	60.20 ± 4.97	2.71 ± 3.06 [a]	29.06 ± 3.88 [ab]	29.32 ± 4.07 [ab]	85.02 ± 5.36 [a]
3S	60.15 ± 7.62	0.92 ± 3.35 [bc]	31.05 ± 4.62 [bc]	31.22 ± 4.69 [bc]	88.61 ± 5.95 [bc]
4S	58.91 ± 5.75	0.29 ± 1.71 [c]	31.80 ± 4.34 [c]	31.85 ± 4.33 [c]	89.49 ± 3.21 [c]
5S	60.03 ± 6.22	0.60 ± 1.45 [c]	26.31 ± 4.27 [d]	26.35 ± 4.28 [d]	88.79 ± 3.18 [c]

Table 4. Color values of french fries fried in palm oil in different stages of frying (different lowercase letters (a, b, c, and d) indicate statistically significant differences ($p < 0.05$) within the column; the results are presented as the mean values ± standard deviation).

Sample	L	a	b	C	h
1P	66.82 ± 4.20 [ab]	3.51 ± 2.67 [a]	29.20 ± 4.29 [a]	29.51 ± 4.44 [a]	83.46 ± 4.70 [a]
2P	67.88 ± 4.84 [a]	3.48 ± 2.77 [a]	33.67 ± 3.57 [b]	33.94 ± 3.73 [b]	84.26 ± 4.19 [a]
3P	64.63 ± 5.13 [bc]	2.63 ± 1.91 [ab]	34.08 ± 4.98 [b]	34.23 ± 5.00 [b]	85.58 ± 3.22 [ab]
4P	64.13 ± 5.82 [b]	1.65 ± 3.07 [b]	34.92 ± 3.70 [b]	35.09 ± 3.68 [b]	87.33 ± 5.10 [b]
5P	67.46 ± 5.64 [ac]	−0.65 ± 1.80 [c]	35.56 ± 4.18 [b]	35.61 ± 4.17 [b]	91.11 ± 2.95 [c]

The coloration of french fries is a multifaceted phenomenon influenced by several key variables. Among these variables, temperature, frying time, and the thickness of the potato slices stand out as crucial determinants of the final visual appeal of this popular food commodity. Temperature plays a pivotal role by initiating the Maillard reaction, which is responsible for browning and flavor development during frying. The precise temperature must be carefully controlled to achieve the desired golden-brown color while avoiding undercooking or over-browning. Frying time is equally important, as it impacts the extent of the Maillard reaction and caramelization, with longer times resulting in deeper coloration. Lastly, the thickness of potato slices affects cooking time, and achieving the right balance is essential for ensuring that french fries boast a uniform, appetizing appearance [28]. The Maillard reaction takes place during frying and involves carbohydrate and aldehyde reactions with amino molecules. When potatoes are fried, the carbon element in them leaches into the oil, giving fried dishes their distinctively black hue. Fat contains unsaturated fatty acids that are subject to heat polymerization and oxidation, which produces nonvolatile breakdown products. Deep frying produces pigments, such as nonvolatile decomposition products and carbonyl compounds, as a byproduct of the oxidation and breakdown of fatty acids, giving the oil its distinctive dark brown hue [29].

The frying of french fries in rapeseed oil resulted in the lowering of the lightness value (L). The mean value for lightness was 67.73 for samples fried in oil that had 6.5% TPM (1R) and 60.66 for samples fried in oil with the highest TPM level (5R). A significant ($p < 0.05$) negative correlation was obtained between TPM% and L parameters, though the correlation can be described as weak: coefficient equals −0.214 (Table 5). The square of the correlation coefficient (coefficient of determination, R^2) was 0.046, meaning that TPM accounted for 4.6% in the variance of the L parameter of rapeseed-oil-fried french fries. On the other hand, no significant ($p > 0.05$) correlation was found between these parameters for fries fried in other two oils (sunflower and palm). The lightness of samples fried in sunflower oil ranged from 58.80 (1S)–60.20 (2S), and no significant difference was found between all samples in the mentioned group.

Table 5. Correlation of TPM% with some measured french fries color values (r—correlation coefficient; R^2—square of correlation coefficient (coefficient of determination); * significant correlation ($p < 0.05$).

Rapeseed-Oil-Fried Fries			Sunflower-Oil-Fried Fries			Palm-Oil-Fried Fries		
Relation	r	R^2	Relation	r	R^2	Relation	r	R^2
TPM%/L	−0.214 *	0.046	TPM%/L	0.012	0.000	TPM%/L	−0.075	0.006
TPM%/a	0.110	0.012	TPM%/a	−0.312 *	0.097	TPM%/a	−0.495 *	0.245
TPM%/b	0.027	0.001	TPM%/b	0.008	0.000	TPM%/b	0.410 *	0.168
TPM%/C	0.028	0.001	TPM%/C	−0.007	0.000	TPM%/C	0.390 *	0.152
TPM%/h	−0.137 *	0.019	TPM%/h	0.317 *	0.100	TPM%/h	0.530 *	0.281

In a prior study, the lowest changes in color were also observed when sunflower oil was employed in the frying process. Sunflower oil, like rapeseed oil, is known for its impact on color stability during frying. This is attributed to its relatively high smoke point and excellent resistance to oxidative degradation, factors that contribute to a more controlled and gradual browning of the food being fried. The phenomenon of minimal color changes when sunflower oil is utilized underscores the importance of oil selection in culinary applications, especially when visual appeal is a key consideration [30].

No significant ($p > 0.05$) difference in L color value was obtained between measurements on the 1P and 5P samples (palm-oil-fried samples). In the investigation conducted by Li et al. (2020), the lightness values of potato strips that underwent frying in different oils were documented. According to their findings, the lightness values recorded for the potato strips fried in rapeseed, sunflower, and palm oil were 66.05, 58.96, and 58.49, respectively. Furthermore, in the study conducted by Enríquez-Fernández and colleagues in 2019, an exploration of the color transformation in french fries was undertaken, particularly in the context of repeated frying cycles. Through the examination of various color parameters, their research provided valuable insights into how multiple rounds of frying affect the visual attributes of french fries [17]. Their results indicate that there was no statistically significant ($p > 0.05$) change in L value in the samples fried in palm olein/canola oil after 40 cycles and after 200 frying cycles. The same experiment with palm olein oil revealed an increase in L value from 58.15 (recorded in fries fried in oil after 40 cycles) to 63.06 (recorded in fries fried in oil after 200 cycles). The a color parameter showed no significant ($p > 0.05$) correlation in respect to change in the TPM% of rapeseed oil. Sample 1R had the lowest mean value (0.74), while the highest mean value (6.93) was recorded in the 2R sample. Oppositely, the color of fries fried in sunflower and palm showed a decrease in the a parameter with an increase in TPM% with correlation coefficients of 0.312 (weak correlation, $R^2 = 0.097$) and 0.495 (moderate correlation, $R^2 = 0.245$), respectively (Table 5). Samples fried in sunflower oil had an a value that ranged from 0.60 to 2.71, and the ones fried in palm oil ranged from −0.65 to 3.51. The measured a value in the work of Enríquez-Fernández et al. (2019) [17] ranged from 1.66–2.48 for french fries fried in palm olein/canola blend and from −0.55–2.91 for fries fried in palm olein oil.

Among all used oils, only frying in palm oil caused a significant change of the b color parameter of fries with the increase in the TPM% parameter. A positive correlation coefficient of 0.410 (moderate correlation, $R^2 = 0.168$) was obtained between these two parameters, and the b value ranged from 29.20 to 35.56. The b value in the work of Enríquez-Fernández et al. (2019) [17] ranged from 20.91 to 31.97.

C (chroma) and h (hue angle) are the parameters that can be obtained from the a and b color values. Chroma ranged from 28.89 to 34.04 in rapeseed oil, from 26.35 to 31.85 in sunflower, and from 29.51 to 35.61 in palm-oil-fried samples. In the work of Kirmaci and

Singh (2018) [31], the mean chroma value for fried potato strips was 36.7. The hue angle (h) values for french fries fried in rapeseed oil ranged from 88.68 for the 1R sample as the maximum value to 78.19 for the 2R sample as the minimum value. A small but statistically significant ($p < 0.05$) negative correlation coefficient of -0.137 was obtained between the TPM% and C values (Table 5). Oppositely, positive correlation coefficients of 0.317 and 0.530 were obtained for those parameters in sunflower and palm oil, respectively. The h values ranged from 85.02 (2S) to 89.49 (4S) in sunflower-oil-fried fries and from 83.46 (1P) to 91.11 (5P) in palm-oil-fried fries.

In the research carried out by Kirmaci and Singh in 2018, a significant revelation emerged from their analysis of the mean hue value (h), which yielded an approximate value of 83. This particular value closely mirrored the 1P value observed in our own experimental study. This similarity between their findings and ours suggests a potential correlation between the hue characteristics identified in their work and the hue parameter identified in our investigation [31]. It suggests a potential correlation between the hue characteristics identified in their work and the hue parameter identified in our own investigation. Furthermore, this correlation emphasizes the importance of replicating and cross-referencing findings across different research endeavors. This highlights the importance of expanding upon established knowledge in order to acquire more profound insights into the complex realm of color analysis in both culinary and scientific research.

4. Conclusions

The study conducted revealed a noteworthy trend: oils containing fewer polyunsaturated and unsaturated fatty acids exhibited greater stability over the course of frying. This observation underscores the crucial role of fatty acid composition in determining oil stability during repeated frying cycles. Interestingly, the color analysis of the french fries did not unequivocally indicate the extent of oil deterioration that occurred after numerous frying cycles. This suggests that relying solely on visual cues, such as color changes, may not provide a complete assessment of frying oil quality. Of particular significance were the statistically significant ($p < 0.05$) correlations observed between TPM% and various color parameters (a, b, C, and h) in french fries fried in palm oil. These correlations highlighted the potential for color analysis to serve as a valuable indicator of frying oil degradation. Conversely, the minimal changes in the lightness parameter seen in sunflower oil samples suggest that this oil type exhibited the least impact from repeated frying cycles. While this study focused primarily on the color characteristics of french fries and their correlation with total polar matter (TPM) values, it is important to acknowledge that comprehensive assessments of frying oil quality may necessitate additional instrumental and chemical analyses. These supplementary methods can provide clearer and more comprehensive insights into the frying process and oil quality. The findings underscore the critical importance of monitoring frying oil quality, as the degree of total polar matter in oil may not be easily discernible by consumers or even producers based solely on visual cues like color changes. It is worth noting that this study, while shedding light on specific color-related aspects of frying oil quality, may not encompass all the factors that impact the overall quality of fried food. As such, further research and comprehensive assessments are necessary to gain a fuller understanding of the multifaceted nature of frying oil quality and its implications for fried food products.

Author Contributions: Conceptualization, B.A. and D.D.; methodology, B.A., D.D., H.B., B.T. and S.D.; software, B.A. and D.D.; validation, B.A., D.D., H.B., B.T., S.D. and I.K.; formal analysis, D.D. and I.K.; investigation, B.A., D.D., H.B., B.T. and S.D.; resources, B.A., D.D., H.B., B.T. and S.D.; data curation, D.D.; writing—original draft preparation, B.A., D.D., H.B., B.T., S.D. and I.K.; writing—review and editing, D.D. and I.K.; visualization, D.D. and I.K.; supervision, D.D.; project administration, B.T.; funding acquisition, D.D. and B.T. All authors have read and agreed to the published version of the manuscript.

Funding: This research was funded by the project 2023ITA23.

Data Availability Statement: The data that support the findings of this study are available from the corresponding author upon reasonable request.

Conflicts of Interest: The authors declare no conflict of interest.

References

1. Li, P.; Wu, G.; Yang, D.; Zhang, H.; Qi, X.; Jin, Q.; Wang, X. Applying Sensory and Instrumental Techniques to Evaluate the Texture of French Fries from Fast Food Restaurant. *J. Texture Stud.* **2020**, *51*, 521–531. [CrossRef] [PubMed]
2. Moyano, P.C.; Ríoseco, V.K.; González, P.A. Kinetics of Crust Color Changes during Deep-Fat Frying of Impregnated French Fries. *J. Food Eng.* **2002**, *54*, 249–255. [CrossRef]
3. Sadeghi, R.; Lin, Y.; Price, W.J.; Thornton, M.K.; Hui-Mei Lin, A. Instrumental Indicators of Desirable Texture Attributes of French Fries. *LWT* **2021**, *142*, 110968. [CrossRef]
4. Li, P.; Wu, G.; Yang, D.; Zhang, H.; Qi, X.; Jin, Q.; Wang, X. Analysis of Quality and Microstructure of Freshly Potato Strips Fried with Different Oils. *LWT* **2020**, *133*, 110038. [CrossRef]
5. Vinci, R.M.; Mestdagh, F.; De Muer, N.; Van Peteghem, C.; De Meulenaer, B. Effective Quality Control of Incoming Potatoes as an Acrylamide Mitigation Strategy for the French Fries Industry. *Food Addit. Contam. Part. A* **2010**, *27*, 417–425. [CrossRef]
6. Bansal, G.; Zhou, W.; Barlow, P.J.; Lo, H.-L.; Neo, F.-L. Performance of Palm Olein in Repeated Deep Frying and Controlled Heating Processes. *Food Chem.* **2010**, *121*, 338–347. [CrossRef]
7. Panadare, D.C.; Rathod, V.K. Applications of Waste Cooking Oil Other Than Biodiesel: A Review. *Iran. J. Chem. Eng.* **2015**, *2015*, 55–76.
8. Fetter, L.F.; Filoda, P.F.; Tischer, B.; de Cassia de Souza Schneider, R.; Teichmann, A.; Santos, R.O.; Helfer, G.A.; da Costa, A.B. At-line Monitoring of Industrial Frying Processes Using ATR-FTIR-PLS Method. *J. Food Process Eng.* **2018**, *2018*, e12891. [CrossRef]
9. Song, J.; Kim, M.-J.; Kim, Y.-J.; Lee, J. Monitoring Changes in Acid Value, Total Polar Material, and Antioxidant Capacity of Oils Used for Frying Chicken. *Food Chem.* **2017**, *220*, 306–312. [CrossRef]
10. Esfarjani, F.; Khoshtinat, K.; Zargaraan, A.; Mohammadi-Nasrabadi, F.; Salmani, Y.; Saghafi, Z.; Hosseini, H.; Bahmaei, M. Evaluating the Rancidity and Quality of Discarded Oils in Fast Food Restaurants. *Food Sci. Nutr.* **2019**, *7*, 2302–2311. [CrossRef]
11. Haider, S.; Akhtar, A.; Khalid, N. Quality Assessment of Fried Oils from Different Street Food Vendors and Restaurants in Different Areas of Gilgit, Pakistan: Cooking Oil Quality in Northern Areas of Pakistan. *PPASB* **2023**, *60*. [CrossRef]
12. del Rocio Teruel, M.; Gordon, M.; Linares, M.B.; Garrido, M.D.; Ahromrit, A.; Niranjan, K. A Comparative Study of the Characteristics of French Fries Produced by Deep Fat Frying and Air Frying: Air Frying Compared with Deep Fat Frying. *J. Food Sci.* **2015**, *80*, E349–E358. [CrossRef] [PubMed]
13. Sberveglieri, V.; Bhandari, M.P.; Carmona, E.N.; Betto, G.; Soprani, M.; Malla, R.; Sberveglieri, G. Spectrocolorimetry and Nanowire Gas Sensor Device S3 for the Analysis of Parmigiano Reggiano Cheese Ripening. In Proceedings of the 2017 ISOCS/IEEE International Symposium on Olfaction and Electronic Nose (ISOEN), Montreal, QC, Canada, 28–31 May 2017; pp. 1–3.
14. Gerald, M.S.; Bernstein, J.; Hinkson, R.; Fosbury, R.A.E. Formal Method for Objective Assessment of Primate Color. *Am. J. Primatol.* **2001**, *53*, 79–85. [CrossRef] [PubMed]
15. Manamohana, K.; Bijur, G.; Malarout, N.; Singla, B.; Pavithra, S.; Naik, N. Applications of Colour Models in the Food Processing Industry: A Systematic Review. *PalArch's J. Archaeol. Egypt Egyptol.* **2020**, *2020*, 3496–3512.
16. Ahmad Tarmizi, A.H. Effect of Frying on the Palm Oil Quality Attributes—A Review. *JOPR* **2016**, *28*, 143–153. [CrossRef]
17. Enríquez-Fernández, B.E.; Álvarez de la Cadena y Yañez, L.; Sosa-Morales, M.E. Comparison of the Stability of Palm Olein and a Palm Olein/Canola Oil Blend during Deep-Fat Frying of Chicken Nuggets and French Fries: Comparison of the Stability of Palm Olein and a Palm Olein/Canola Oil Blend. *Int. J. Food Sci. Technol.* **2011**, *46*, 1231–1237. [CrossRef]
18. Maskan, M. Change in Colour and Rheological Behaviour of Sunflower Seed Oil during Frying and after Adsorbent Treatment of Used Oil. *Eur. Food Res. Technol.* **2003**, *218*, 20–25. [CrossRef]
19. Giusti, A.; Colombaro, I.; Garra, R.; Garrappa, R.; Polito, F.; Popolizio, M.; Mainardi, F. A Practical Guide to Prabhakar Fractional Calculus. *Fract. Calc. Appl. Anal.* **2020**, *23*, 9–54. [CrossRef]
20. Schober, P.; Boer, C.; Schwarte, L.A. Correlation Coefficients: Appropriate Use and Interpretation. *Anesth. Analg.* **2018**, *126*, 1763–1768. [CrossRef]
21. Stavila, E.; Yuliati, F.; Adharis, A.; Laksmono, J.A.; Iqbal, M. Recent Advances in Synthesis of Polymers Based on Palm Oil and Its Fatty Acids. *RSC Adv.* **2023**, *13*, 14747–14775. [CrossRef]
22. Oboh, G.; Falade, A.O.; Ademiluyi, A.O. Effect of Thermal Oxidation on the Physico–Chemical Properties, Malondialdehyde and Carotenoid Contents of Palm Oil. *Riv. Ital. Delle Sostanze Grasse* **2014**, *2014*, 59–65.
23. Matthäus, B. Use of Palm Oil for Frying in Comparison with Other High-stability Oils. *Eur. J. Lipid Sci. Technol.* **2007**, *109*, 400–409. [CrossRef]
24. Mba, O.I.; Dumont, M.-J.; Ngadi, M. Palm Oil: Processing, Characterization and Utilization in the Food Industry—A Review. *Food Biosci.* **2015**, *10*, 26–41. [CrossRef]
25. Matthaus, B.; Özcan, M.M.; Al Juhaimi, F. Some Rape/Canola Seed Oils: Fatty Acid Composition and Tocopherols. *Z. Für Naturforschung C* **2016**, *71*, 73–77. [CrossRef]

26. Aydinkaptan, E.; Mazi, B.G.; Barutçu Mazi, I. Microwave Heating of Sunflower Oil at Frying Temperatures: Effect of Power Levels on Physicochemical Properties: Repetitive microwave heating of oil at frying temperatures. *J. Food Process Eng.* **2017**, *40*, e12402. [CrossRef]
27. Molina-Garcia, L.; Santos, C.S.P.; Cunha, S.C.; Casal, S.; Fernandes, J.O. Comparative Fingerprint Changes of Toxic Volatiles in Low PUFA Vegetable Oils Under Deep-Frying. *J. Am. Oil Chem. Soc.* **2017**, *94*, 271–284. [CrossRef]
28. Krokida, M.K.; Oreopoulou, V.; Maroulis, Z.B.; Marinos-Kouris, D. Colour Changes during Deep Fat Frying. *J. Food Eng.* **2001**, *48*, 219–225. [CrossRef]
29. Ujong, A.E.; Emelike, N.J.T.; Owuno, F.; Okiyi, P.N. Effect of Frying Cycles on the Physical, Chemical and Antioxidant Properties of Selected Plant Oils during Deep-Fat Frying of Potato Chips. *Food Chem. Adv.* **2023**, *3*, 100338. [CrossRef]
30. Yılmaz, B.; Şahin, T.Ö.; Ağagündüz, D. Oxidative Changes in Ten Vegetable Oils Caused by the Deep-Frying Process of Potato. *J. Food Biochem.* **2023**, *2023*, 6598528. [CrossRef]
31. Kirmaci, B.; Singh, R.K. Process Severity Affects Texture and Color of Potato Strips Baked in Pilot-Scale Infrared Radiant Wall Oven. *LWT* **2018**, *97*, 261–268. [CrossRef]

Disclaimer/Publisher's Note: The statements, opinions and data contained in all publications are solely those of the individual author(s) and contributor(s) and not of MDPI and/or the editor(s). MDPI and/or the editor(s) disclaim responsibility for any injury to people or property resulting from any ideas, methods, instructions or products referred to in the content.

Article

Production of High-Porosity Biochar from Rice Husk by the Microwave Pyrolysis Process

Li-An Kuo [1], Wen-Tien Tsai [2,*], Ru-Yuan Yang [3] and Jen-Hsiung Tsai [1]

[1] Department of Environmental Science and Engineering, National Pingtung University of Science and Technology, Pingtung 912, Taiwan; sanck112204@gmail.com (L.-A.K.); tsaijh@mail.npust.edu.tw (J.-H.T.)
[2] Graduate Institute of Bioresources, National Pingtung University of Science and Technology, Pingtung 912, Taiwan
[3] Department of Materials Engineering, National Pingtung University of Science and Technology, Pingtung 912, Taiwan
* Correspondence: wttsai@mail.npust.edu.tw; Tel.: +886-8-7703202

Abstract: This study focused on the highly efficient pyrolysis of rice husk (RH) for producing high-porosity biochar at above 450 °C under various microwave output powers (300–1000 W) and residence times (5–15 min). The findings showed that the maximal calorific value (i.e., 19.89 MJ/kg) can be obtained at the mildest microwave conditions of 300 W when holding for 5 min, giving a moderate enhancement factor (117.4%, or the ratio of 19.89 MJ/kg to 16.94 MJ/kg). However, the physical properties (i.e., surface area, pore volume, and pore size distribution) of the RH-based biochar products significantly increased as the microwave output power increased from 300 to 1000 W, but they declined at longer residence times of 5 min to 15 min when applying a microwave output power of 1000 W. In this work, it was concluded that the optimal microwave pyrolysis conditions for producing high-porosity biochar should be operated at 1000 W, holding for 5 min. The maximal pore properties (i.e., BET surface area of 172.04 m^2/g and total pore volume of 0.1229 cm^3/g) can be achieved in the resulting biochar products with both the microporous and the mesoporous features. On the other hand, the chemical characteristics of the RH-based biochar products were analyzed by using Fourier-transform infrared spectroscopy (FTIR) and energy-dispersive X-ray spectroscopy (EDS), displaying some functional complexes containing carbon–oxygen (C–O), carbon–hydrogen (C–H), and silicon–oxygen (Si–O) bonds on the surface of the RH-based biochar.

Keywords: rice husk; microwave pyrolysis; biochar; texture characteristics; calorific value; surface complex

1. Introduction

As a cereal grain, rice may be the most widely consumed staple food in Asia and Africa, providing human nutrition and calorific intake by its richness in starch (one of the carbohydrates) and other components such as protein and fiber. However, rice husk, the most significant by-product, will be generated when rough rice (or paddy rice) is husked in a milling plant. In general, each kg of milled white rice results in approximately 0.28 kg of rice husk as a by-product during milling [1]. This hard biomass material is mainly composed of silica and lignocelluloses to protect the rice seed during the growing season [2–4]. Due to its rich contents of lignocellulosic constituents (about 80 wt%, dry basis), the rice husk is mostly used as a biomass fuel for energy production by combustion [5–8] and gasification [9–12]. In Taiwan, the energy utilization of rice husk has indicated an increasing trend [13]. In 2022, about 123 thousand metric tons was reused as an auxiliary fuel, as compared to about 78 thousand metric tons used in 2018. To increase the energy density and combustion performance, rice husk briquettes and/or pellets can be produced using densification [14,15]. It should be noted that we still cannot change the heating values of these biomass fuel products (or their calorific values). In this regard, carbonized rice husk has been extensively studied under a limited supply of oxygen (O_2) and at moderate pyrolysis temperatures to enhance its calorific value, carbon content, and pore properties in recent years [16–23]. The biochar produced from rice husk can be used as soil amendment, liquid-phase adsorbent, or as a precursor for activated carbon [24–27].

Concerning the novel production of biochar from agricultural biomass or organic waste, the microwave-assisted pyrolysis (MAP) process has been widely adopted and reviewed in recent years [28–33]. As compared to the conventional pyrolysis process (i.e., heat flow from the outside to the inside due to the power from electricity or fuel combustion), MAP can reduce the energy consumption because the heat is generated inside of the biomass feedstock by molecular vibration from microwave stimulation, thus causing rapid heating within the material and high energy efficiency [34,35]. It was concluded that the microwave system shows a rapid, targeted, and energy-efficient heating process compared to the conventional electrical oven and combustion furnace processes. However, only a few studies have been reported that used MAP for producing biochar from rice husk alone [22,36–38]. Sahoo and Remya investigated the effect of heating time and microwave power on biochar yield from rice husk [22], resulting in a high-quality biochar with a significant increase in calorific value (Max. 25.46 MJ/kg) and specific surface area (Max. 190 m^2/g), which could be used as a potential source of energy, nutrient captive media, and soil amendment. Zhang et al. studied the yields and properties of the products obtained from microwave pyrolysis (set at 700 W and held for 20 min, reaching the pyrolysis temperature of about 550 °C) of rice husk samples after undergoing different pretreatment processes (including water washing, torrefaction, and a combination of the two) [36], showing that the resulting biochar products had a high surface area (S_{BET} 157.81–267.84 m^2/g), which could be potentially used as soil amendments. Shukla et al. produced rice husk biochar at the operating conditions of a microwave power of 900 W, a holding time of 15 min, and a pyrolysis temperature of about 600 °C, which was further used as an adsorbent for the removal of nutrients (nitrate and phosphate) from the aqueous solution, due to its high BET surface area of 190 m^2/g [37]. Halim et al. prepared rice husk biochar at 500 and 800 °C with a microwave power of 1000 W applied for approximately 9 and 15 min (i.e., heating rate of about 55 °C/min), concluding that the resulting biochar products had high calorific values (i.e., 19.42 and 19.71 MJ/kg, with an increase rate of about 23.5%) [38]. Obviously, the resulting rice husk biochar from the microwave pyrolysis can be used as bio-coal fuel, or soil amendments, due to its high porosity and/or calorific value.

In previous studies [39,40], the torrefied products from rice husk and its pretreatment by soda leaching (0.25 M NaOH) were produced at 240–360 °C with holding times of 0–90 min by the conventional method (electricity-resistance heating) in order to enhance its fuel properties. Torrefaction operated at the proper conditions would be optimal to produce torrefied products with significantly higher calorific values of 19.71 MJ/kg (raw rice husk without pretreatment) and 28.97 MJ/kg (rice husk with NaOH pretreatment), as compared to that of rice husk (i.e., 13.96 MJ/kg). In this work, the production of biochar products from rice husk was performed in a modified microwave oven as a function of output power (300–1000 W) for a holding time of 0–20 min. The calorific values and the textural and chemical characteristics of the resulting biochar products were analyzed by using adiabatic calorimetry, scanning electron microscopy (SEM), energy-dispersive X-ray spectroscopy (EDS), and Fourier-transform infrared spectroscopy (FTIR). These analytical results were further discussed and correlated with the microwave pyrolysis conditions.

2. Materials and Methods

2.1. Materials

In this study, the starting biomass material (i.e., rice husk) for producing biochar products was collected from a local rice-milling factory, which is located in Puzi Township (Chiayi County, Taiwan). Prior to the determinations of the thermochemical properties and the microwave pyrolysis experiments, the feedstock was dried at about 100 °C for 24 h in an air-circulation oven to obtain a stable weight within 0.5% of water loss. Thereafter, the sample was stored in a desiccator or air-circulation oven for subsequent use.

2.2. Thermochemical Properties of RH

Based on the test methods of the American Society for Testing and Materials (ASTM), a proximate analysis (i.e., moisture content, ash content, volatile matter content, and fixed carbon content) of the as-received rice husk was performed in triplicate. The fixed carbon (FC) content was calculated by the difference. According to a previous study [41], the primary inorganic elements in the RH ash were silicon (Si) and potassium (K), accounting for 4.987 wt% and 0.582 wt%, respectively. Its calorific value was measured by using an adiabatic calorimeter (CALORIMETER ASSY 6200; Parr Instrument Co., Moline, IL, USA). There were three replicates for the determination of the calorific value, where about 0.3 g of the dried sample was used for each analysis. On the other hand, a thermogravimetric analyzer (TGA) instrument (TGA-51; Shimadzu Co., Tokyo, Japan), under a nitrogen (N_2) flow rate (50 cm^3/min), was used to examine the thermal decomposition behavior of the dried rice husk in a temperature range of 25 to 1000 °C under four heating rates of 5, 10, 15, and 20 °C/min. When observing the microscopic structures on the surface of the rice husk and resulting biochar products by scanning electron microscopy (SEM), their elemental compositions were also characterized by energy-dispersive X-ray spectroscopy (EDS).

2.3. Microwave Pyrolysis Experiments

Using rice husk as a starting material, the resulting biochar products (noted as BC-RH) were obtained by using a modified microwave oven (Mei Lin Energy Technology Co., Ltd., Kaohsiung, Taiwan), which can be operated at an oscillation frequency of 2450 MHz and an electric power consumption of 1350 W (Figure 1). The oven was equipped with a K-type thermocouple for monitoring the temperature profile of the quartz tube (length of 30 cm by inner diameter of 2 cm), which served as a pyrolysis reactor, where about 5.0 g of dried rice husk was placed for each microwave pyrolysis experiment. Prior to the microwave pyrolysis process, the nitrogen (N_2) flow (about 500 cm^3/min) was purged for 5 min to an ensure oxygen-free environment. Subsequently, the pyrolysis experiments were performed with a series of sets by the combination of the microwave output power (300–1000 W) and holding time (5–15 min). After the completion of microwave pyrolysis for each experiment, the resulting biochar was collected and weighted for calculating its mass yield compared to the initial loading weight (i.e., ca. 5 g). To code the resulting biochar products easily, they were indicated by the notation of the BC-RH power time. As an example, the biochar product BC-RH-800W-20M referred to the RH-based biochar product that was pyrolyzed by applying 800 W and holding for 20 min in the microwave system.

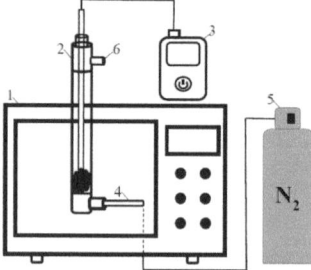

Figure 1. Schematic diagram of the microwave pyrolysis system. The system's components are denoted as numbers in parentheses, which are the microwave oven (1), quartz tube reactor (2), temperature monitor with K-type thermocouple (3), nitrogen gas inlet tube (4), nitrogen (N_2) gas cylinder (5), and the outlet (to hood) (6).

2.4. Determinations of Calorific Values and Textural Characteristics of RH-Based Biochar Products

As mentioned in Section 2.2, the calorific values of the RH-based biochar products were determined with a bomb calorimeter. In order to characterize the textural characteristics of the resulting biochar, the accelerated surface area and porosimetry system (ASAP 2020; Micromeritics Co., Norcross, GA, USA) were used to determine the pore properties (i.e., surface area pore volume and pore size distribution), which were based on the nitrogen adsorption–desorption isotherms at 77 K (i.e., −196 °C). Prior to this property analysis, the biochar samples (about 0.25 g, dried at 100 °C)) were degassed using a vacuum setpoint (≤10 μmHg or 1.33 Pa) at 200 °C for about 10 h. The data on the specific surface area were based on the Brunauer–Emmett–Teller (BET) model [42,43], using a relative pressure (P/P_0) range of 0.05 to 0.30. The total pore volume was given by the ratio of the volume of liquid adsorbate (N_2) at saturation (usually at a relative pressure of 0.995) per gram to the liquid nitrogen density at 77 K (i.e., 0.8064 g/cm^3). The micropore surface area and micropore volume were calculated using the *t*-method, which is based on the Harkins and Jura equation [43]. Concerning the dual (slit-cylinder) pore size distribution, the Barrett–Joyner–Halenda (BJH) equation (i.e., a modified Kelvin equation) was adopted to calculate the mesopore (pore width in a range between 2 nm and 50 nm) size distribution of the resulting biochar by using its isotherm data in the desorption branch [43]. Furthermore, the Horvath–Kawazoe (HK) method was used to determine the micropore size distribution (pore width or diameter of less than 2 nm) under the relative pressure range of 0 to 0.00115, which was assumed to be the slit-pore geometry [43].

The microscopic structure and elemental compositions on the surface of the resulting biochar were analyzed with a scanning electron microscope (S-3000N; Hitachi Co., Chiyoda, Tokyo) and an energy-dispersive X-ray spectroscope (7021-H; HORIBA Co., Kyoto, Japan), applying a 15 kV acceleration potential. Prior to the SEM–EDS analysis, the dried samples (including the feedstock rice husk and biochar products) were ground into powders, which were deposited with a gold (Au) film using an ion sputter (E1010; Hitachi Co) to provide the conductive samples. The analysis of the functional groups on the surface of the potassium bromide (KBr)-containing samples (made into discs with a diameter of 1.2 cm) was conducted by using an FTIR instrument (FT/IR-4600; JASCO Co., Easton, MD, USA), where the reflectance spectra were recorded by using a range of 4000 to 400 cm^{-1} with a scanning resolution of 4 cm^{-1}.

3. Results and Discussion

3.1. Thermochemical Characteristics of RH

Table 1 lists the proximate analysis and calorific values of the as-received feedstock RH, which were determined in triplicate. As indicated in the review reports [2–4], this biomass featured a high ash content of 13.93 wt%, thus resulting in a lower calorific value (16.94 MJ/kg, dry basis), as compared to those of the woody biomass. Therefore, ash melting (or slagging) may cause severe problems in biomass-derived fuel combustion systems [41,44–46], especially for rice residues and their resulting biochar products. Figure 2 shows the thermogravimetric analysis (TGA) and derivative thermogravimetry (DTG) curves of the feedstock RH, which were obtained at four heating rates (i.e., 5, 10, 15, and 20 °C/min) under the nitrogen (N_2) flow (i.e., 50 cm^3/min). In the initial stage, the slight weight loss started at about 100 °C, which should be indicative of the thermal desorption of the moisture adsorbed/attached to the samples. Obviously, these curves similarly revealed the significant thermal decomposition behaviors in the pyrolysis temperature range of 250–450 °C. This was caused by the near-devolatilization of the lignocellulosic components (i.e., hemicellulose, cellulose, and lignin) at above 450 °C; however, the weight loss occurred at higher temperatures. In the microwave pyrolysis system (Figure 1), the process temperature profile was monitored to show the temperature above 450 °C. In this regard, the resulting biochar products from the microwave pyrolysis experiments should be fully carbonized and charred in this work.

Table 1. Proximate analysis and calorific value of rice husk (RH).

Property	Value
Proximate analysis [a,b]	
Moisture (wt%)	7.14 ± 0.78
Ash (wt%)	13.93 ± 0.09
Volatile matter (wt%)	70.60 ± 1.51
Fixed carbon [c] (wt%)	8.34
Calorific value (MJ/kg) [a,d]	16.94 ± 0.21

[a] Mean ± standard deviation for three determinations; [b] the values were determined by an as-received sample; [c] by difference; and [d] the values were determined by a dry sample.

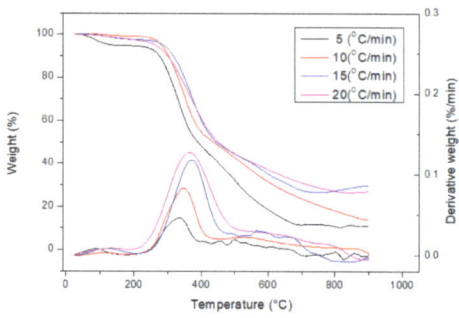

Figure 2. Thermogravimetric analysis/derivative thermogravimetry (TGA/DTG) curves of dried RH samples at the heating rates of 5, 10, 15, and 20 °C/min.

3.2. Mass Yield and Calorific Value of RH-Based Biochar Products

In this work, there were several microwave pyrolysis experiments as a function of the output power (i.e., 300–1000 W) and residence time (i.e., 5–15 min). Obviously, the mass yields indicated a declining trend, due to more serious pyrolysis reactions occurring at larger output powers when holding for 5 to 10 min. Taking an example at a residence time of 5 min, the mass yields were 36.62% (300 W), 32.08% (440 W), 27.46% (800 W), and 25.60% (1000 W). The maximal variations of the mass yields of the RH-based biochar products seemed to occur in the range of 300 W to 440 W at a short holding time (5 min). As compared to a previous study [39], the time scale for the microwave pyrolysis of RH was significantly lower than that of conventional conductive heating, thus ensuring a high heat transfer rate. In addition, the calorific values of the RH-based biochar products showed a slight variation in correlating with the process parameters of the microwave pyrolysis. It was found that the maximal calorific value (i.e., 19.89 MJ/kg) was produced under the mildest microwave conditions of 300 W with a holding time of 5 min in the present study, having a slight increase by 17.4% in comparison with 16.94 MJ/kg (seen in Table 1). This result was due to the enhancement of the carbon content and the reduction in the oxygen content in the RH-based biochar product produced from the microwave pyrolysis system, which will be further verified by the elemental compositions in the EDS analysis (seen in Section 3.4).

3.3. Pore Properties of RH-Based Biochar Products

Table 2 summarizes the data of the main pore properties (i.e., BET surface area, total pore volume, micropore surface area, and micropore volume) of the RH-based biochar products produced by the microwave pyrolysis process. Figure 3 shows their N_2 adsorption–desorption isotherms (i.e., −196 °C). Figures 4 and 5 show their pore size distributions based on the Barrett–Joyner–Halenda (BJH) method and the Horvath–Kawazoe (HK) method, respectively. Using the results in Table 1 and Figures 3–5, the main findings were addressed as follows:

1. The pore properties of the RH-based biochar products significantly increased as the microwave output power increased from 300 to 1000 W, with a holding time of 5 min, giving more pore formation and the increments of the surface area and pore volume. The maximal pore properties (i.e., BET surface area of 172.04 m^2/g and total pore volume of 0.1229 cm^3/g) were obtained at a microwave output power of 1000 W at a holding time of 5 min. Obviously, the pore formation was more developed as the pyrolysis reaction increased at a higher microwave output power, leading to larger pore properties;
2. As shown in Table 1, the residence time also played a determining role in the pore properties of the RH-based biochar products in the microwave pyrolysis process. For example, the values of the BET surface area decreased with an extending residence time from 5 min to 15 min at a microwave output power of 1000 W, showing a BET surface area of 172.04 m^2/g (BC-RH-1000W-5M) to 154.04 m^2/g (BC-RH-1000W-10M) and 63.43 m^2/g (BC-RH-1000W-15M). This result may be attributable to the collapse or destruction of the formed pores by severe microwave pyrolysis at longer reaction times. Therefore, the optimal microwave pyrolysis conditions for producing high porosity should be performed at a microwave power of 1000 W and a holding time of 5 min. The maximal BET surface area (i.e., 172.04 m^2/g) and total pore volume (i.e., 0.1229 cm^3/g) listed in Table 1 were slightly lower than those shown in similar studies [22,36,37];
3. As shown in Figure 3, the resulting biochar products are characteristic of microporous and mesoporous features, thus displaying Type I and Type VI isotherms [42,43]. It can be seen that the slight hysteresis loops (Type VI isotherms) start from approximately 0.15 of relative pressure in the N$_2$ desorption isotherms. According to the classification by the International Union of Pure and Applied Chemistry (IUPAC) [43], the hysteresis loops should be associated with Type H4 loops, indicating narrow slit pores. In this work, the mesopore size distributions obtained by the BJH method using the N$_2$ desorption isotherm data are depicted in Figure 4. It shows the peak at about 3.8 nm, displaying the mesopores (pore width in the range between 2 nm and 50 nm) in the resulting biochar products;
4. Figure 5 further depicts the micropore size distribution of the optimal biochar product (i.e., BC-RH-1000W-5M), using the HK equation for a more accurate description of its micropores [43]. Obviously, the resulting biochar is a microporous material, which showed significant micropores at about 0.6 nm.

Table 2. Pore properties of RH-based biochar products.

Biochar Product [a]	S_{BET} [b] (m^2/g)	S_{micro} [c] (m^2/g)	V_t [d] (cm^3/g)	V_{micro} [c] (cm^3/g)
BC-RH-300W-5M [d]	1.36	0.92	0.0030	0.000
BC-RH-440W-5M	8.64	6.67	0.0141	0.003
BC-RH-600W-10M	63.97	51.87	0.0476	0.027
BC-RH-800W-5M	75.34	49.47	0.0594	0.025
BC-RH-800W-10M	58.65	35.77	0.018	0.000
BC-RH-1000W-5M	172.04	120.48	0.1229	0.063
BC-RH-1000W-10M	154.04	116.36	0.1138	0.059
BC-RH-1000W-15M	63.43	47.87	0.0523	0.025

[a] Sample notation indicates the resulting RH-based produced by applying a microwave power of 300 W, holding for 5 min, using 5 g RH. [b] BET surface area (S_{BET}) based on a relative pressure range of 0.05–0.30 (15 points). [c] Micropore surface area (S_{micro}) and micropore volume (V_{micro}) were obtained by using the t-plot method. [d] Total pore volume (V_t) was obtained at a relative pressure of about 0.995.

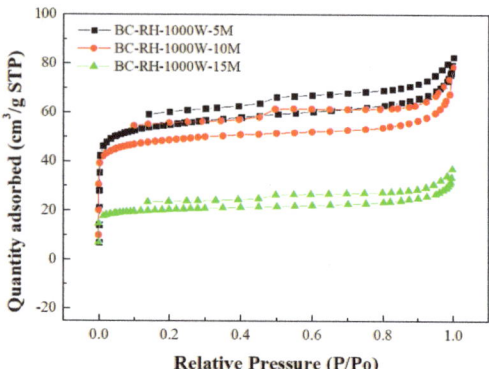

Figure 3. N$_2$ adsorption–desorption isotherms of some RH-based biochar products.

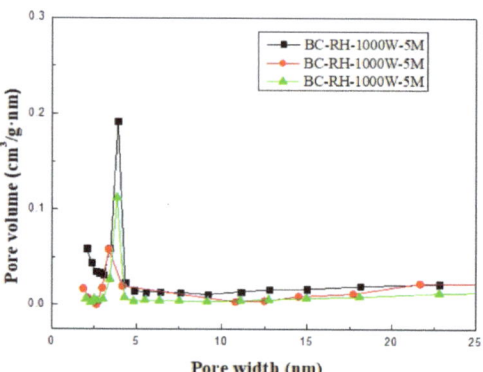

Figure 4. Mesopore size distributions of some RH-based biochar products.

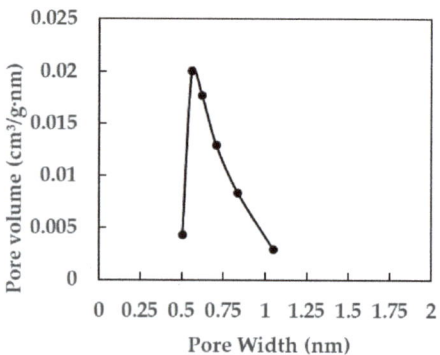

Figure 5. Micropore size distribution of the optimal biochar product (i.e., BC-RH-1000W-5M).

3.4. Textural and Chemical Characteristics of RH-Based Biochar Products

In order to provide the microstructural and chemical characteristics of the RH-based biochar products, their textural changes were observed by using a scanning electron microscope (SEM) equipped with an energy-dispersive X-ray spectroscope (EDS). Figure 6 reveals the SEM images of the RH and BC-RH-1000W-5M at different magnifications (×500 and ×1000), showing similarly shaped surfaces [41]. However, the surface of the RH-based biochar has become more corrugated after the microwave pyrolysis, which can be seen in Figure 6b. As a consequence, the resulting biochar had higher pore properties. This could be attributed to the thermal deformation and structural decomposition of the outer layer, composed of lignocellulosic components and minerals (e.g., silica), under microwave pyrolysis.

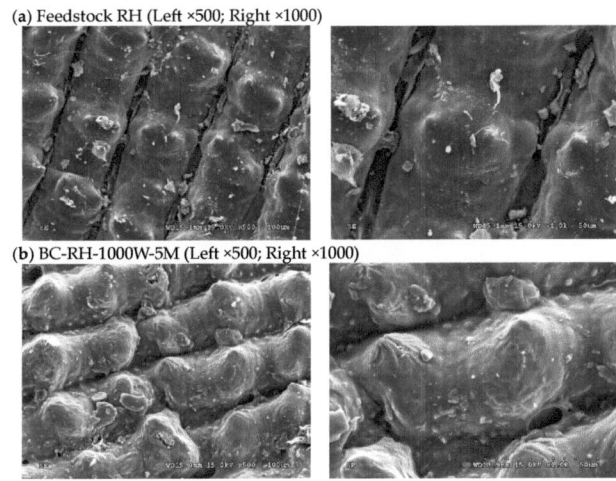

Figure 6. SEM/EDS analyses of (**a**) feedstock RH and (**b**) the optimal biochar product (i.e., BC-RH-1000W-5M).

On the other hand, energy-dispersive X-ray spectroscopy (EDS) was adopted to preliminarily determine the elemental compositions of the resulting biochar products. As indicated in Figure 7, the EDS spectrum of the optimal biochar BC-RH-1000W-5M contained significant amounts of carbon (C, 41.16 wt%), oxygen (O, 29.56 wt%), silicon (Si, 27.99 wt%), and potassium (K, 0.85 wt%) on the outer surface. As compared to the EDS spectrum of the feedstock RH (seen in Figure 6a), these observations were attributed to the devolatilization of the lignocellulosic constituents by releases of oxygen-containing gases (e.g., H_2O, CO, and CO_2) during the microwave pyrolysis process, thus causing the carbon content to increase and the oxygen content to reduce. Furthermore, Figure 8 displays the FTIR spectra of the feedstock RH and some of the biochar products (BC-RH-1000W-5M and BC-RH-1000W-10M). Based on the functional groups of the carbon materials [47–50], the peak at around 3500 cm^{-1} corresponds to the hydroxyl (O-H) functional group of the water molecule (H_2O) by stretching vibration, suggesting that there are more hydrophilic features in the feedstock RH. Comparing the other FTIR peaks of the feedstock RH with those of the RH-based biochar products, it can also be observed that the peaks of the latter were slightly dissipated, as elucidated above. The peaks at about 2960 and 2360 cm^{-1} could be due to the C–H and C–C bonds from the aromatic/aliphatic structures. The peak at 1385 cm^{-1} may be attributed to the oxygen-containing functional groups like the phenolic

C–O bond or the C–C stretching vibrations in the aromatic ring. The peak at 1107 cm^{-1} could correspond to the C–O groups in the polysaccharides or the Si–O bonds associated with silica in the RH-based biochar (also seen in Figure 7).

(a)

Element	Weight%
C	20.90
O	44.70
Si	33.68
K	0.73
Total	100.00

(b)

Element	Weight%
C	41.61
O	29.56
Si	27.99
K	0.85
Total	100.00

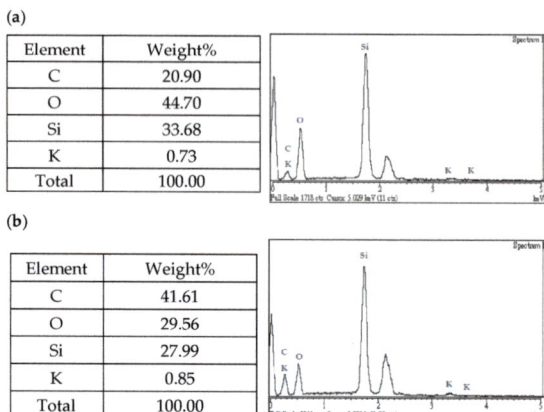

Figure 7. Elemental compositions of feedstock RH and the optimal biochar product (i.e., BC-RH-1000W-5M) by EDS analysis. (**a**) Feedstock RH and (**b**) BC-RH-1000W-5M.

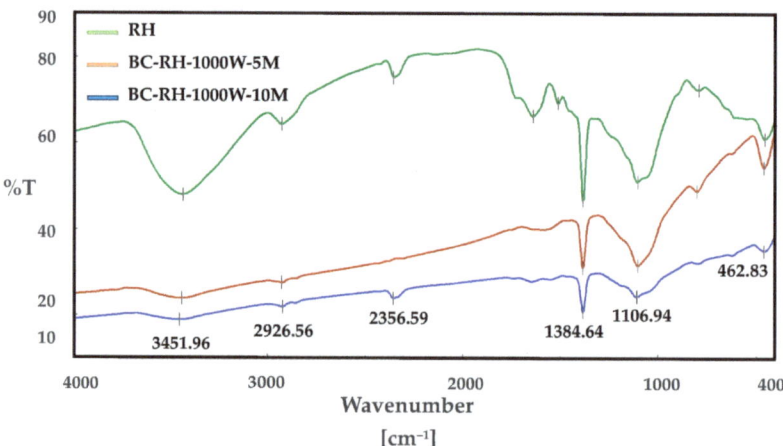

Figure 8. FTIR spectra of feedstock RH and some biochar products (i.e., BC-RH-1000W-5M and BC-RH-1000W-10M).

4. Conclusions

In this work, crop residue rice husk (RH) was used as a starting precursor for producing porous biochar via the microwave pyrolysis process. The results have indicated that the process parameters, including the microwave output power and the residence time, played determining roles in the calorific value and pore properties (i.e., the BET surface area and the total pore volume) of the resulting RH-based biochar. When compared to the calorific value of the feedstock RH (i.e., 16.94 MJ/kg, dry basis), the findings showed that the maximal calorific value (i.e., 19.89 MJ/kg) can be obtained at the mildest microwave conditions of output power of 300 W and a holding time of 5 min. However, the high contents of silicon (Si) and the lower amounts of potassium (K) were still present, thus leading to a slight potential for slagging and fouling when using the RH-based biochar as an auxiliary fuel. In contrast, the pore properties of the RH-based biochar products significantly increased as the microwave output power increased from 300 to 1000 W, but they declined at longer residence times. In this work, it was concluded that the optimal microwave pyrolysis conditions used in the production of high-porosity RH-based biochar should be performed at a microwave output power of 1000 W and at a holding time of 5 min, where the maximal pore properties (i.e., a BET surface area of 172.04 m^2/g and a total pore volume of 0.1229 cm^3/g) can be achieved. Therefore, the resulting RH-based biochar products had the potential to be used as a soil amendment in agricultural applications or as a liquid-phase adsorbent in water purification and wastewater treatment.

Author Contributions: Conceptualization, W.-T.T. and R.-Y.Y.; methodology, L.-A.K.; formal analysis, L.-A.K.; data curation, L.-A.K.; writing—original draft preparation, W.-T.T.; writing—review and editing, W.-T.T.; visualization, L.-A.K. and W.-T.T.; supervision, R.-Y.Y. and J.-H.T. All authors have read and agreed to the published version of the manuscript.

Funding: This study was supported by funding from the Ministry of Science and Technology, Taiwan, (MOST 111-2622-E-020-001) and Sun Carbon Technology Co., Ltd (Kaohsiung, Taiwan).

Data Availability Statement: Data are contained within the article.

Acknowledgments: Sincere appreciation is expressed to acknowledge the National Pingtung University of Science and Technology for their assistance in the scanning electron microscopy (SEM) and the energy-dispersive X-ray spectroscopy (EDS) analyses. The authors also thank Tai-Ju Shih (Department of Materials Engineering, National Pingtung University of Science and Technology) and Tasi-Jung Jiang (Graduate Institute of Bioresources, National Pingtung University of Science and Technology) for their assistance in the microwave pyrolysis setup and the Fourier-transform infrared spectroscopy (FTIR) analysis, respectively.

Conflicts of Interest: The authors declare no conflict of interest.

References

1. Rice Knowledge Bank (International Rice Research Institute). Available online: http://www.knowledgebank.irri.org/ (accessed on 30 September 2023).
2. Vassilev, S.V.; Vassileva, C.G.; Vassilev, V.S. Advantages and disadvantages of composition and properties of biomass in comparison with coal: An overview. *Fuel* **2015**, *158*, 330–350. [CrossRef]
3. Cai, J.; He, Y.; Yu, X.; Banks, S.W.; Yang, Y.; Zhang, X.; Yu, Y.; Liu, R.; Bridgwater, A.V. Review of physicochemical properties and analytical characterization of lignocellulosic biomass. *Renew. Sustain. Energy Rev.* **2017**, *76*, 309–322. [CrossRef]
4. Yan, J.; Oyedeji, O.; Leal, J.H.; Donohoe, B.S.; Semelsberger, T.A.; Li, C.; Hoover, A.N.; Webb, E.; Bose, E.A.; Zeng, Y.; et al. Characterizing variability in lignocellulosic biomass: A review. *ACS Sustain. Chem. Eng.* **2020**, *8*, 8059–8085. [CrossRef]
5. Fernandes, I.J.; Calheiro, D.; Kieling, A.G.; Moraes, C.A.M.; Rocha, T.L.A.C.; Brehm, F.A.; Modolo, R.C.E. Characterization of rice husk ash produced using different biomass combustion techniques for energy. *Fuel* **2016**, *165*, 351–359. [CrossRef]
6. Blissett, R.; Sommerville, R.; Rowson, N.; Jones, J.; Laughlin, B. Valorisation of rice husks using a TORBED® combustion process. *Fuel Process. Technol.* **2017**, *159*, 247–255. [CrossRef]
7. Baetge, S.; Kaltschmitt, M. Rice straw and rice husks as energy sources-comparison of direct combustion and biogas production. *Biomass Conv. Bioref.* **2018**, *8*, 719–737. [CrossRef]
8. Steven, S.; Restiawaty, E.; Bindar, Y. Routes for energy and bio-silica production from rice husk: A comprehensive review and emerging prospect. *Renew. Sustain. Energy Rev.* **2021**, *149*, 111329. [CrossRef]
9. Yoon, S.J.; Son, Y.I.; Kim, Y.K.; Lee, J.G. Gasification and power generation characteristics of rice husk and rice husk pellet using a downdraft fixed-bed gasifier. *Renew. Energy* **2012**, *42*, 163–167. [CrossRef]
10. Vaskalis, I.; Skoulou, V.; Stavropoulos, G.; Zabaniotou, A. Towards circular economy solutions for the management of rice processing residues to bioenergy via gasification. *Sustainability* **2019**, *11*, 6433. [CrossRef]
11. Nyakuma, B.B.; Wong, S.; Mong, G.R.; Utume, L.N.; Oladokun, O.; Wong, K.Y.; Ivase, T.J.P.; Abdullah, T.A.T. Bibliometric analysis of the research landscape on rice husks gasification (1995–2019). *Environ. Sci. Pollut. Res.* **2021**, *28*, 49467–49490. [CrossRef]

12. Dafiqurrohman, H.; Safitri, K.A.; Setyawan, M.I.B.; Surjosatyo, A.; Aziz, M. Gasification of rice wastes toward green and sustainable energy production: A review. *J. Clean. Prod.* **2022**, *366*, 132926. [CrossRef]
13. Ministry of Agriculture, Taiwan. Green National Income Account—Agricultural Solid Waste. Available online: https://agrstat.moa.gov.tw/sdweb/public/common/Download.aspx (accessed on 30 September 2023).
14. Saeed, A.A.H.; Yub Harun, N.; Bilad, M.R.; Afzal, M.T.; Parvez, A.M.; Roslan, F.A.S.; Abdul Rahim, S.; Vinayagam, V.D.; Afolabi, H.K. Moisture content impact on properties of briquette produced from rice husk waste. *Sustainability* **2021**, *13*, 3069. [CrossRef]
15. Kipngetich, P.; Kiplimo, R.; Tanui, J.K.; Chisale, P. Effects of carbonization on the combustion of rice husks briquettes in a fixed bed. *Clean. Eng. Technol.* **2023**, *13*, 100608. [CrossRef]
16. Claoston, N.; Samsuri, A.; Ahmad Husni, M.; Mohd Amran, M. Effects of pyrolysis temperature on the physicochemical properties of empty fruit bunch and rice husk biochars. *Waste Manag. Res.* **2014**, *32*, 331–339. [CrossRef]
17. Phuong, H.T.; Uddin, M.A.; Kato, Y. Characterization of biochar from pyrolysis of rice husk and rice straw. *J. Biobased Mater. Bioenergy* **2015**, *9*, 439–446. [CrossRef]
18. Menya, E.; Olupot, P.W.; Storz, H.; Lubwama, M.; Kiros, Y.; John, M.J. Optimization of pyrolysis conditions for char production from rice husks and its characterization as a precursor for production of activated carbon. *Biomass Conv. Bioref.* **2020**, *10*, 57–72. [CrossRef]
19. Singh, S.V.; Chaturvedi, S.; Dhyani, V.C.; Kasivelu, G. Pyrolysis temperature influences the characteristics of rice straw and husk biochar and sorption/desorption behaviour of their biourea composite. *Bioresour. Technol.* **2020**, *314*, 123674.
20. Vieira, F.R.; Luna, C.M.R.; Arce, G.L.A.F.; Ávila, I. Optimization of slow pyrolysis process parameters using a fixed bed reactor for biochar yield from rice husk. *Biomass Bioenergy* **2020**, *132*, 105412. [CrossRef]
21. Yadav, K.; Jagadevan, S. Effect of pyrolysis of rice husk–derived biochar on the fuel characteristics and adsorption of fluoride from aqueous solution. *Bioenerg. Res.* **2021**, *14*, 964–977. [CrossRef]
22. Sahoo, D.; Remya, N. Influence of operating parameters on the microwave pyrolysis of rice husk: Biochar yield, energy yield, and property of biochar. *Biomass Conv. Bioref.* **2022**, *12*, 3447–3456. [CrossRef]
23. Anando, A.I.; Ehsan, M.M.; Karim, M.R.; Bhuiyan, A.A.; Ahiduzzaman, M.; Karim, A. Thermochemical pretreatments to improve the fuel properties of rice husk: A review. *Renew. Energy* **2023**, *215*, 118917. [CrossRef]
24. Bushra, B.; Remya, N. Biochar from pyrolysis of rice husk biomass—Characteristics, modification and environmental application. *Biomass Conv. Bioref.* **2020**. Online ahead of print. [CrossRef]
25. Herrera, K.; Morales, L.F.; Tarazona, N.A.; Aguado, R.; Saldarriaga, J.F. Use of biochar from rice husk pyrolysis: Part a: Recovery as an adsorbent in the removal of emerging compounds. *ACS Omega* **2022**, *7*, 7625–7637. [CrossRef] [PubMed]
26. Kim, H.; Kim, S.; Lee, J.; Kim, M.; Kwon, D.; Jung, S. Pyrolysis of rice husk using CO_2 for enhanced energy production and soil amendment. *Energy Environ.* **2023**, *34*, 873–885. [CrossRef]
27. Li, Z.; Zheng, Z.; Li, H.; Xu, D.; Li, X.; Xiang, L.; Tu, S. Review on rice husk biochar as an adsorbent for soil and water remediation. *Plants* **2023**, *12*, 1524. [CrossRef]
28. Ethaib, S.; Omar, R.; Kamal, S.M.M.; Awang Biak, D.R.; Zubaidi, S.L. Microwave-Assisted Pyrolysis of Biomass Waste: A Mini Review. *Processes* **2020**, *8*, 1190. [CrossRef]
29. Fodah, A.E.M.; Ghosal, M.K.; Behera, D. Microwave-assisted pyrolysis of agricultural residues: Current scenario, challenges, and future direction. *Int. J. Environ. Sci. Technol.* **2022**, *19*, 2195–2220. [CrossRef]
30. Hadiya, V.; Popat, K.; Vyas, S.; Varjani, S.; Vithanage, M.; Gupta, V.K.; Delgado, A.N.; Zhou, Y.; Show, P.L.; Bilal, M.; et al. Biochar production with amelioration of microwave-assisted pyrolysis: Current scenario, drawbacks and perspectives. *Bioresour. Technol.* **2022**, *355*, 127303. [CrossRef]
31. Narde, S.R.; Remya, N. Biochar production from agricultural biomass through microwave-assisted pyrolysis: Predictive modelling and experimental validation of biochar yield. *Environ. Dev. Sustain.* **2022**, *24*, 11089–11102. [CrossRef]
32. Zhang, Y.; Fan, S.; Liu, T.; Fu, W.; Li, B. A review of biochar prepared by microwave-assisted pyrolysis of organic wastes. *Sustain. Energy Technol. Assess.* **2022**, *50*, 101873. [CrossRef]
33. Potnuri, R.; Surya, D.V.; Rao, C.S.; Yadav, A.; Sridevi, V.; Remya, N. A review on analysis of biochar produced from microwave-assisted pyrolysis of agricultural waste biomass. *J. Anal. Appl. Pyrolysis* **2023**, *173*, 106094. [CrossRef]
34. Motasemi, F.; Afzal, M.T. A review on the microwave-assisted pyrolysis technique. *Renew. Sustain. Energy Rev.* **2016**, *28*, 317–330. [CrossRef]
35. Bartoli, M.; Frediani, M.; Briens, C.; Berruti, F.; Rosi, L. An Overview of temperature issues in microwave-assisted pyrolysis. *Processes* **2019**, *7*, 658. [CrossRef]
36. Zhang, S.; Dong, Q.; Zhang, L.; Xiong, Y.; Liu, X.; Zhu, S. Effects of water washing and torrefaction pretreatments on rice husk pyrolysis by microwave heating. *Bioresour. Technol.* **2015**, *193*, 442–448. [CrossRef]
37. Shukla, N.; Sahoo, D.; Remya, N. Biochar from microwave pyrolysis of rice husk for tertiary wastewater treatment and soil nourishment. *J. Clean. Prod.* **2019**, *235*, 1073–1079. [CrossRef]
38. Halim, S.A.; Mohd, N.A.; Razali, A. A comparative assessment of biofuel products from rice husk and oil palm empty fruit bunch obtained from conventional and microwave pyrolysis. *J. Taiwan Inst. Chem. Eng.* **2022**, *134*, 104305. [CrossRef]
39. Tsai, W.T.; Jiang, T.J.; Tang, M.S.; Chang, C.H.; Kuo, T.H. Enhancement of thermochemical properties on rice husk under a wide range of torrefaction conditions. *Biomass Conv. Bioref.* **2021**. Online ahead of print. [CrossRef]

40. Tsai, C.H.; Shen, Y.H.; Tsai, W.T. Effect of alkaline pretreatment on the fuel properties of torrefied biomass from rice husk. *Energies* **2023**, *16*, 679. [CrossRef]
41. Tsai, C.H.; Shen, Y.H.; Tsai, W.T. Thermochemical characterization of rice-derived residues for fuel use and its potential for slagging tendency. *Fire* **2023**, *6*, 230. [CrossRef]
42. Gregg, S.J.; Sing, K.S.W. *Adsorption, Surface Area, and Porosity*; Academic Press: London, UK, 1982.
43. Lowell, S.; Shields, J.E.; Thomas, M.A.; Thommes, M. *Characterization of Porous Solids and Powders: Surface Area, Pore Size and Density*; Springer: Dordrecht, The Netherlands, 2006.
44. Zhu, Y.; Niu, Y.; Tan, H.; Wang, X. Short review on the origin and countermeasure of biomass slagging in grate furnace. *Front. Environ. Res.* **2014**, *2*, 7. [CrossRef]
45. Zhu, C.; Tu, H.; Bai, Y.; Ma, D.; Zhao, Y. Evaluation of slagging and fouling characteristics during Zhundong coal co-firing with a Si/Al dominated low rank coal. *Fuel* **2019**, *254*, 115730. [CrossRef]
46. Lachman, J.; Balas, M.; Lisy, M.; Lisa, H.; Milcak, P.; Elbl, P. An overview of slagging and fouling indicators and their applicability to biomass fuels. *Fuel Process. Technol.* **2021**, *217*, 106804. [CrossRef]
47. Li, L.; Yao, X.; Li, H.; Liu, Z.; Ma, W.; Liang, X. Thermal stability of oxygen-containing functional groups on activated carbon surfaces in a thermal oxidative environment. *J. Chem. Eng. Jpn.* **2004**, *47*, 21–27. [CrossRef]
48. Islam, M.S.; Ang, B.C.; Gharehkhani, S.; Afifi, A.B.M. Adsorption capability of activated carbon synthesized from coconut shell. *Carbon Lett.* **2016**, *20*, 1–9. [CrossRef]
49. Johnston, C.T. Biochar analysis by Fourier-transform infra-red spectroscopy. In *Biochar: A Guide to Analytical Methods*; Singh, B., Camps-Arbestain, M., Lehmann, J., Eds.; CRC Press: Boca Raton, FL, USA, 2017; pp. 199–228.
50. Qiu, C.; Jiang, L.; Gao, Y.; Sheng, L. Effects of oxygen-containing functional groups on carbon materials in supercapacitors: A review. *Mater. Des.* **2023**, *230*, 111952. [CrossRef]

Disclaimer/Publisher's Note: The statements, opinions and data contained in all publications are solely those of the individual author(s) and contributor(s) and not of MDPI and/or the editor(s). MDPI and/or the editor(s) disclaim responsibility for any injury to people or property resulting from any ideas, methods, instructions or products referred to in the content.

Article

Modelling of Drinking Water Recarbonization in Fluidized Bed Reactor

Ján Derco [1,*], Nikola Šoltýsová [1], Tomáš Kurák [1], Anna Vajíčeková [2] and Jozef Dudáš [1]

[1] Institute of Chemical and Environmental Engineering, Faculty of Chemical and Food Technology, Slovak University of Technology in Bratislava, Radlinského 9, 81237 Bratislava, Slovakia; nikola.soltysova@stuba.sk (N.Š.); tomas.kurak@stuba.sk (T.K.); jozef.dudas@stuba.sk (J.D.)
[2] Water Research Institute, Nábrežie arm. gen. L. Svobodu 5, 81249 Bratislava, Slovakia
* Correspondence: jan.derco@stuba.sk

Abstract: Calcium and magnesium are important not only for human health but also for reducing problems related to the corrosive and aggressive effects of soft water on drinking water distribution materials. Experimental and mathematical modeling of the recarbonization process aimed at increasing the content of these biogenic elements in water was carried out using the novelty of continuous laboratory- and pilot-scale fluidized bed reactors. A methodology for scaling-up the modeled system was extended with mathematical modeling. Water remineralization was performed using half-calcined dolomite (HCD) and CO_2. The influence of operating conditions, i.e., $Q(CO_2)$, freshwater inflow, and HCD dose, on quality indicators of treated drinking water ($c(Ca^{2+})$, $c(Mg^{2+})$, $c(Ca^{2+} + Mg^{2+})$ and Ca/Mg) was studied. Results show that the Mg^{2+} concentration is more significantly affected by the amount of HCD in the system and the flow of CO_2, while the effect of freshwater inflow is less significant. At constant CO_2 flow, the Ca^{2+} content decreases and the Mg^{2+} content increases as the tap water inflow increases, which results in a decrease in the Ca/Mg molar ratio. However, the Ca/Mg ratio can be effectively controlled by adding an appropriate amount of HCD at certain time intervals. Overproduction of ions is easily controlled by the CO_2 flow.

Keywords: calcium; drinking water; experimental and mathematical modeling; fluidized bed; HCD; Mg; water quality improvement

Citation: Derco, J.; Šoltýsová, N.; Kurák, T.; Vajíčeková, A.; Dudáš, J. Modelling of Drinking Water Recarbonization in Fluidized Bed Reactor. *Processes* **2023**, *11*, 3209. https://doi.org/10.3390/pr11113209

Academic Editor: Antoni Sánchez

Received: 14 October 2023
Revised: 5 November 2023
Accepted: 8 November 2023
Published: 10 November 2023

Copyright: © 2023 by the authors. Licensee MDPI, Basel, Switzerland. This article is an open access article distributed under the terms and conditions of the Creative Commons Attribution (CC BY) license (https://creativecommons.org/licenses/by/4.0/).

1. Introduction

The content of Mg and Ca in drinking water is very low in many regions of Slovakia, which influences the health of the population. Moreover, low content of these biogenic elements negatively affects the water distribution system due to the aggressive and corrosive effect of water. Increasing the effect of biogenic elements is commonly referred to as recarbonization.

Several recarbonization methods are known and used depending on the drinking water composition and the country of application. Many publications in open literature discuss the content of biogenic elements in drinking water and their effect on public health. Health issues include cardiovascular diseases, oncologic diseases, diabetes mellitus, and diseases of the digestive system and respiratory tract. The strong chronic impact on human health has been investigated especially in connection to magnesium deficiency and it is believed that it is necessary to add magnesium to drinking water if its content is below the endorsed norm [1–5].

Recarbonization is a drinking water treatment to increase water quality parameters such as the calcium and magnesium content in drinking water with low level of mineral content. A large body of scientific evidence has attributed health problems to these biogenic elements. In addition to this, very low concentrations of calcium and magnesium in water have been recognized as the cause of the problems, with corrosive and aggressive impacts. Water with a very low level of minerals is unstable and unbuffered. Various treatment methods can be applied to increase the mineral content of drinking water, each offering several advantages and disadvantages. A fluidized bed reactor offers the potential to increase the interfacial reaction surface and overall reaction rate and appears to be a new approach in water treatment [6,7].

Most authors recommend a content of calcium from 20 to 80 mg/L and that of magnesium in the range of 10–50 mg/L [7–13]. Biogenic elements such as calcium and magnesium are not only essential from a health point of view but they are also of technological importance because soft water, which contains low concentrations of calcium and magnesium, has a corrosive and aggressive effect on distribution pipes [14].

Despite the demonstrable significance of calcium and magnesium in drinking water, there are no precisely defined limits in the world that would legally define their optimal range of concentration in drinking water. The limit of calcium and magnesium in drinking water is stated only as recommended in Slovak legislation [2,10].

To improve the quality of life in Slovakia, the recarbonization process should be applied to places where drinking water is poorly mineralized. There are many recarbonization methods using both alkaline and acidic reagents in an appropriate ratio [15].

One of the simplest and most effective methods of recarbonization is the direct dosing of biogenic elements solutions to water. For instance, calcium chloride is the most frequently added in combination with sodium bicarbonate. The biggest disadvantage of this process is the cost of chemicals. For this reason, this approach has very limited application [15,16]. A more affordable process is carbonization with carbon dioxide. Soft water flows through a fixed bed composed of limestone and magnesium carbonates or limestone and magnesite in the presence of carbon dioxide [17,18]. Suitable candidates for the recarbonization treatment are dolomite and half-calcined dolomite. Disadvantages of a fixed-bed system include the large diameter of the equipment typically used and high probability of nonuniformity of the liquid flow and, thus, local formation of magnesium carbonate which can block water flow, leading to low effectiveness of the process and low utilization of recarbonization material.

The availability of drinking water is a basic human right and recarbonization processes must be simple and cheap so that they are feasible in rural areas. Therefore, a reactor has been proposed with a highly efficient fluidized bed utilizing half-calcined dolomite with a simple operation that is applicable both in small and in large capacities. It is a new approach in drinking water recarbonization processes, introducing carbon dioxide into the bottom of the reactor together with processed water.

According to our knowledge and literature search, a fluidized bed recarbonization reactor (FBRR) has not been used for drinking water remineralization so far. On the other hand, the dissertation of Van Schagen [19] and conference paper of Kramer et al. [20] focused on modeling the management of drinking water treatment plants using a pellet reactor with a fluidized bed to perform the reverse process, i.e., decarbonization of water with high content of total hardness.

Our fundamental research was carried out in a laboratory FBRR, proving the effectivity of the drinking water mineralization process [21]. This reactor provides the potential to increase the interfacial reaction surface and the overall reaction rate and appears to be a new approach in water treatment. The research was focused on comparing different recarbonization materials, the performance of fixed and fluidized beds, and the investigation of hydrodynamic characteristics of FBRRs. HCD was selected as recarbonization material based on the results of laboratory tests on Ca and Mg extraction from rocks [22].

The experimental work was carried out with different fractions of the recarbonization material. The effect of water and carbon dioxide flow on the performance of the process was studied. Changes in the particle size of the material during the process were monitored. The results indicated half-calcined dolomite as the most suitable material. The results of preliminary experiments showed a positive effect of fluid bed hydrodynamics and an increased rate of the recarbonization process due to the presence of CO_2. The concentration of calcium and magnesium ions obtained in a fluidized bed reactor at a liquid flow rate equal to the minimum fluidization velocity of the particles used was almost twice as high as their concentration obtained in a fixed-bed reactor. Continuous feeding of CO_2 to the FBRR resulted in an increased recarbonization rate by about one order of magnitude in comparison to the process without CO_2 introduction. A first-order kinetic model describes the data from the recarbonization process with good accuracy and the Richardson and Zaki expansion model was found to be a very good description of the hydrodynamic characteristics of the fluidized bed [20,23].

Most of the previous experiments were performed in a fluidized bed reactor with external recirculation of processed water. The main idea was to prepare a concentrate of calcium and magnesium ions [21,24].

It is commonly known that batch systems are not suitable for processing large amounts of drinking water; thus, a flow system was chosen for drinking water, CO_2, and HCD located in the reactor, as shown in Figure 1. Processed water was circulated from a reservoir and CO_2 was added below the liquid and gas distributor in the reactor. The size of the HCD was a compromise between small particles (i.e., high reaction rate) and larger particles (pressure drop in the system). From this point of view, it was decided to use a fraction of (2–4 mm) of HCD particles [24].

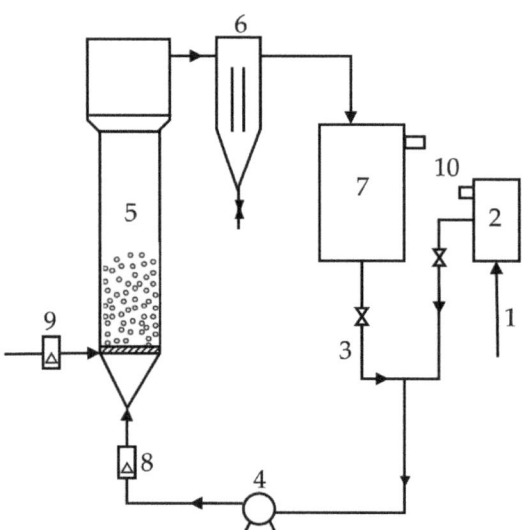

Figure 1. Scheme of the laboratory water recarbonization system, 1—drinking water feed, 2—buffer tank, 3—recirculation valve, 4—pump, 5—fluidization reactor, 6—sedimentation tank, 7—storage/water tank, 8—rotameter, 9—CO_2 feed, 10—storage tank outlet; reactor height: 90 cm and diameter: 4.8 cm.

The aim of the work was to extend the FBRR design and scaling methodology [24] by mathematical modeling. For this purpose, modeling of the process of recarbonization of drinking water was carried out in laboratory and pilot scales. An algorithm for the experimental and mathematical modeling of this process was developed and is included as Figure S1. Experiments in the FBRR laboratory were aimed at obtaining basic hydraulic characteristics and kinetic data of water saturation with calcium and magnesium ions. Experimental measurements in continuous reactors operated on both scales were aimed at determining the influence of operating parameters (flow of water and CO_2, pH, T, conductivity) on the content of calcium and magnesium in treated drinking water. The results of the experimental modeling were processed statistically using multiple regression analysis. Optimal values of operating parameters were determined for the maximum and minimum values of monitored drinking water quality indicators using the grid search optimization method.

2. Materials and Methods

2.1. Fluidized Bed Reactor

A scheme of the testing rig for drinking water recarbonization is shown in Figure 1. Treated water (1) is pumped from the water supply network to buffer tank (2) at a suitable flow rate and through rotameter (8) by pump (4) to a fluidized bed reactor (5) to the storage/water reservoir/water tank (7). Since the one pass system did not satisfy the requirements of water enrichment by biogenic elements, a system with external circulation was used. Carbon dioxide (9) is introduced below the liquid–gas distributor. The concentrate of treated water is accumulated in the water reservoir.

Based on the kinetic and hydrodynamic characteristics of the process, optimal concentration of calcium and magnesium salts for the recarbonization process was determined to provide reasonably high process rate and material consumption.

The recarbonization system is dimensioned so that only about one-tenth of the volume of the storage tank (7) is replaced daily by the supply of tap water (1) and the same amount of concentrate (10), which is discharged into the drinking water distribution system.

Hydraulics of Fluidized Bed Reactor

An important parameter of a fluidized bed is minimum fluidization velocity. This velocity is strongly affected by particles' geometry, density, and porosity. Physical properties of fluids are also important parameters affecting fluidization characteristics (expansion, etc.). The Richardson and Zaki [20,23] correlation is widely used to describe the expansion of fluidized beds:

$$\varepsilon = \sqrt[n]{\frac{U}{U_t}} \tag{1}$$

where ε is fluidized bed voidage, dimensionless, U is superficial velocity, L/T, U_t is particle terminal velocity, L/T, and n is bed expansion parameter, dimensionless.

$$U_t = \left[\frac{4(\rho_s - \rho_l)g d_p}{3 C_d \rho_l}\right]^{0.5} \tag{2}$$

where ρ_s is particle's density, M/L^3, ρ_l is liquid density, M/L^3, g is gravitational acceleration, L^2/T, C_d is drag coefficient, dimensionless, and d_p is particle's diameter, L.

The overall bed voidage is given by

$$\varepsilon = 1 - \frac{h_0}{h} \tag{3}$$

where h_p is the height of compact bed of particles, L^3, A is the bed cross-sectional area, L^2, and h is fluidized bed height, L.

Since particles can change physical properties during the recarbonization process (particle's diameter and porosity) and the hydrodynamic behavior of the fluidized bed's drag coefficient was developed experimentally [24],

$$C_d = a\, Re_t^{-b} \tag{4}$$

$$n = c\, Re_t^{-d} \tag{5}$$

$$Re_t = \frac{d_p\, \rho\, U_t}{\mu} \tag{6}$$

where Re_t is Reynolds number for particle's terminal velocity, dimensionless, ρ_s is solid density, M/L^3, μ is dynamic viscosity of liquid, Pa s, and a, b, c, d are parameters of empirical correlation equations, dimensionless.

Diameter d_p of half-calcined dolomite (HCD) particles was expressed by the geometric mean, L:

$$d_p = \sqrt{d_1 d_2} \tag{7}$$

where d_1 and d_2 are diameters of two mesh of sieve fraction, L.

2.2. Materials Used

Recarbonization experiments were performed using recarbonization materials, half-calcined dolomite (HCD), Magno Dol (Akdolit, Gerolstein, Germany), and Semidol (Brenntag, Pezinok, Slovakia). HCD is prepared from dolomite containing 50% $CaCO_3$ and 50% $MgCO_3$ at 650–800 °C. This treatment causes the decomposition of $MgCO_3$ into MgO, while $CaCO_3$ does not change during calcination.

During the recarbonization process, the following equations proceed:

$$MgO + 2\,CO_2 + H_2O \rightarrow Mg(HCO_3)_2 \tag{8}$$

$$CaCO_3 + CO_2 + H_2O \rightarrow Ca(HCO_3)_2 \tag{9}$$

Conventionally, HCD is mostly used as a granular material in recarbonization filters where water and CO_2 flow downwards. In the HCD layer, the reaction between carbon dioxide and HCD takes place and HCD is gradually consumed, which means that the process has to be stopped, spent material removed, the filter filled with new material, and the process restarted. The recarbonization fixed bed (filter) reactor needs to be washed regularly to prevent sintering of the filter bed [25]. In an FBRR, the material can be added periodically without stopping the process; fine particles formed during the process are entrained from the bed by water flow and trapped in the water reservoir.

2.3. Water Saturation with Calcium and Magnesium

Kinetics of the recarbonization process work by the first order equation:

$$\frac{dC}{dt} = d_c\,(C_{eq} - C) \tag{10}$$

where C is total concentration of dissolved calcium and magnesium ions, mmol/L, for reaction time t, C_{eq} is equilibrium concentration of calcium and/or magnesium, mmol/L, d_c is rate constant of dissolution of Ca^{2+} and/or Mg^{2+} ions [1/min], and t is reaction time, min.

Equilibrium concentration of Ca and Mg ions was determined experimentally. The system depicted in Figure 1 was used without water inlet and outlet forming a batch system, i.e., water was recirculated from the water reservoir through the fluidized bed and the concentration of biogenic elements was monitored. Once the concentration was constant, the water was considered as saturated with Ca and Mg ions and the concentration achieved equilibrium concentration C_{eq}.

Equation (10) can be integrated between the boundary values t = 0 and t = t and C = C_0 and for the case that C_0 = 0, obtaining

$$C_t = C_{eq}\left(1 - e^{-d_c t}\right) \tag{11}$$

2.4. Applied Analytical Methods

Recarbonization was monitored by measuring the solution conductivity and pH and determining the content of calcium and magnesium ions. A WTW Multi 3420 conductometer was used to measure conductivity. A JENWAY 3510 pH meter was used for continuous monitoring. The content of Ca^{2+} and Mg^{2+} was determined by a complexometric method using the indicator Eriochrome Black T. Concentration of Ca^{2+} was measured by a chelatometric method with EDTA using murexide as an indicator. Concentration of Mg^{2+} was calculated from the total content of $Ca^{2+} + Mg^{2+}$ and the determination of the content of Ca^{2+} [23].

2.5. Multiple Regression Analysis

Experimental values of $c(Ca^{2+} + Mg^{2+})$, $c(Mg^{2+})$, $c(Ca^{2+})$, and $c(Ca^{2+})/c(Mg^{2+})$ in treated water (dependent variable Y) at different flow rates of water and carbon dioxide (independent variables Xi, Xj, ...) were processed by multiple regression using a general regression equation in the form:

$$Y = a_0 + \sum(a_j \cdot X_j) + \sum(a_{jj} \cdot X_j \cdot X_j) + \sum(a_{ij} \cdot X_i \cdot X_j) \tag{12}$$

where a_0, a_j, a_{jj}, and a_{ij} are regression coefficients.

2.6. Processing of Experimental Data

Values of used nonlinear hydraulic models (Equations (1), (2), (4), and (5)) were determined by grid search optimization [26]. To determine the values of the parameters of the general regression Equation (12), which corresponds to the minimum value of the objective function, the Nelder–Mead simplex optimization method [27] was used.

The residual sum of squares (S_r^2) between the experimental and predicted values of dependent variables (Equation (13)) given by the models, divided by its number of degrees of freedom, ν, was used as the objective function.

$$S_r^2 = \frac{\sum(y_i^{exp} - y_i^{cal})^2}{n - m} \tag{13}$$

where n is the number of measurements and m is the number of parameters.

Correlation coefficient (Equation (14)) was applied for qualitative description of the relationship between two variables:

$$R_{YX} = 1 - \frac{(n - m)S_r^2}{(n - 1)S_y^2} \tag{14}$$

where S_y^2 is dispersion (Equation (15)):

$$S_y^2 = \frac{n\sum y_i^2 - (\sum y_i)^2}{n(n - 1)} \tag{15}$$

The quality of the description of the recarbonization process using Equation (12) was assessed by the correlation coefficient R_{YX} (Equation (14)). To assess the influence of independent variables on the process, we used the coefficient of determination R_{YX}^2.

Optimum values of independent variables Xi, Xj, ... for the calculated regression coefficient values corresponding to the minimum objective function for the dependent variable Y were also determined by the grid search optimization method [26].

The algorithm for the modelling of drinking water recarbonization is shown in Figure S1.

3. Results

3.1. Lab-Scale FBRR

3.1.1. Hydraulic Characteristics

Hydraulic conditions in FBRRs are affected by particle size, porosity, density, and by properties of the water–CO_2 gas–liquid mixture. The system is complex and therefore the minimum fluidization velocity must be determined experimentally for the relevant system. Optimum gas–liquid flow must respect the process economy, i.e., the cost of water circulation through the bed and the level of water enrichment by biogenic elements. Experimental data show that it is advantageous to work at minimum fluidization velocity.

Figure 2 shows the dependence of pressure drop (ΔP) in FBRRs on superficial fluid velocity (w) [21].

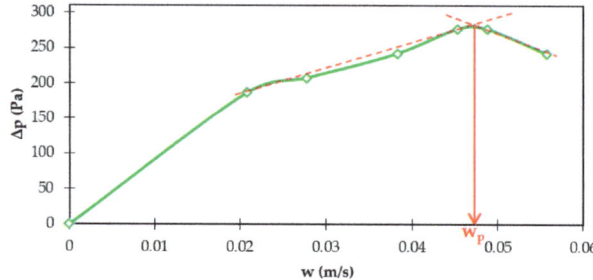

Figure 2. Experimental dependence of pressure drops (ΔP) on superficial water velocity (w) for fraction 2.0–4.0 mm of HCD dolomite Magno Dol (Akdolit) in the presence of CO_2.

These experiments were performed using 360 g of HCD. The minimum fluidization velocity $w_p = 0.0475$ m/s was determined graphically.

The measurements were carried out under the following conditions:
- Particle mass in the bed: $m_c = 0.36$ kg;
- Voidage of fixed bed: $\varepsilon = 0.4217$;
- Volume of fixed bed of solids: $V_s = 0.266 \times 10^{-3}$ m^3;
- Cross-sectional area of the column: $A_p = 1.8 \times 10^{-3}$ m^2.

Experimental data of the dependence of the height of the fluidized bed on the water flow were used to calculate parameter values of the expansion Equations (Equations (4)–(6)) using the grid search optimization method. Values of the parameters and the correlation coefficient are shown in Table 1.

Table 1. Values of parameters of hydraulic equations.

a	b	3c	D	c_d	n	R_{XY}
34.2	0.71	4.97	6.39	0.23	3.18	0.70

3.1.2. Saturation of Treated Water in the Reactor

At the beginning of the experiment, 360 g of fraction 2–4 mm of HCD Magno Dol (Akdolit, Gerolstein, Germany) was added to the fluidization reactor. The fixed bed of solid particles in the reactor reached a height of 14.0 cm. After starting the CO_2 flow at a flow rate of 0.5 L/min and external recirculation of water between the storage tank and the fluidized bed reactor at a flow rate of 6.8 L/min, the height of the fluidized bed of solid particles was 15.1 cm. The saturation phase lasted 64 h, during which parameters such as pH and conductivity were continuously recorded with a digital multimeter and the concentrations of calcium and magnesium in the storage tank were analytically determined. Using conductivity (κ), the increase in the sum of the concentration of Ca^{2+} and Mg^{2+} ions can also be expressed as the solution conductivity increases with the ion concentration. Figure 3 shows time dependences of the measured values in the water reservoir.

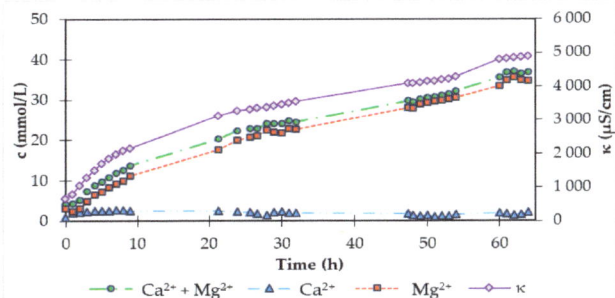

Figure 3. Time dependence of conductivity and Ca^{2+} and Mg^{2+} concentrations during saturation phase in laboratory FBRR.

The production (product of concentration and water flow) of calcium and magnesium ions, Mg^{2+} and Ca^{2+}, was calculated. After the first 9 h of the saturated phase (Figure 4), Mg^{2+} production was in the range of 1.3–2.6 g/h. In the following hours, it fell below 1.0 g/h. Ca^{2+} production was initially 1.3 g/h on average during the first 9 h of saturation and decreased with time to 0.06 g/h, specifically in the 64th hour of saturation. The decrease in produced ions is due to the consumption of HCD components. To sustain the production of required ions during the recarbonization process, HCD needs to be added into the system. The doses of HCD to the fluidization reactor are listed in Table 2.

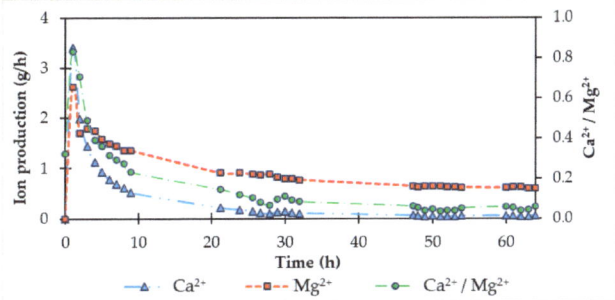

Figure 4. Time dependence of Mg^{2+} and Ca^{2+} production and the ratio of molar concentrations of ions during the recarbonization phase in laboratory FBRR.

Table 2. Doses of HCD Magno Dol (Akdolit) to laboratory FBRR during saturation phase.

HCD Refill Time [h]	HCD Dose [g]	Hight of Fluidized Bed [cm]
0	360.0	-
9	29.1	15.9
53	36.8	14.9

To compare the monitored variables at the beginning and end of saturation, the measured data are given in Table 3.

Table 3. Measured data at the beginning and end of saturation phase in laboratory FBRR.

Time (h)	pH (-)	K (µS/cm)	c(Ca²⁺ + Mg²⁺) (mmol/L)	c_m (Ca²⁺) (mg/L)	c_m (Mg²⁺) (mg/L)
0	7.00	672	4.10	40.08	75.33
64	7.51	4900	36.75	84.17	842.00

According to the measured values of $c(Ca^{2+} + Mg^{2+})$ depending on the reaction time, values of the kinetic parameters of recarbonization Equation (11) were calculated to obtain the sum of squared deviations between the experimental and calculated values. The values of the kinetic parameters and statistical characteristics are given in Table 4. The content of $Ca^{2+} + Mg^{2+}$ experimentally determined and calculated using the kinetic equation is shown in Figure 5.

Table 4. Values of kinetic parameters of recarbonization Equation (11) and statistical characteristics.

c_{max} (mmol/L)	d_C (1/min)	S_y^2	S_r^2	R_{XY}
37.10	$3.95 \cdot 10^{-2}$	118.60	4.77	0.9611

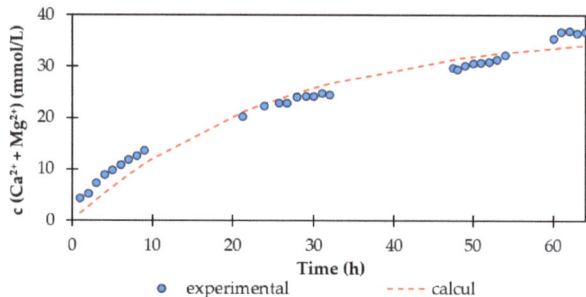

Figure 5. Time dependence of $Ca^{2+} + Mg^{2+}$ content during the saturation phase of laboratory FBRR.

After 64 h of the saturation phase, we started the continuous supply of water from the water supply network to the device and the outflow of treated water, followed by the so-called continuous phase. Water from the supply network contained 40.08 mg/L Ca^{2+}, 75.33 mg/L Mg^{2+}, and the sum of calcium and magnesium was equal to 4.10 mmol/L. The goal was to enrich the water from the distribution network with calcium and magnesium ions. The recarbonization process in continuous mode lasted 508.8 h, and together with the initial saturation, the total recarbonization time was 572.8 h.

The continuous phase was operated at different values of water flow from the distribution network drinking water and carbon dioxide inflow in the ranges as follow

$$Q (CO_2) = 0.24\text{--}0.54 \text{ L/min,}$$

$$Q (H_2O) = 40\text{--}76 \text{ mL/min.}$$

During the saturation phase, we also monitored the conductivity, pH, and content of calcium and magnesium in the continuous phase. Figure 6 shows the time dependence of the conductivity and molar concentration of $Ca^{2+} + Mg^{2+}$ during the continuous recarbonization process.

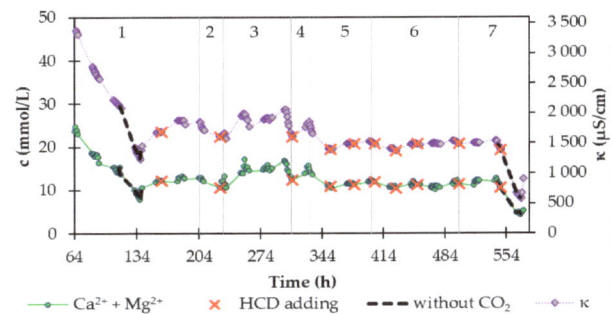

Figure 6. Time dependence of conductivity and molar concentration of $Ca^{2+} + Mg^{2+}$ during the continuous operation of a laboratory FBRR.

The mentioned dependence in Figure 6 was divided into seven areas according to the inflow of water from the distribution network and carbon dioxide. In area 1 (Figure 6), which followed immediately after saturation, we set the continuous water flow to 20 mL/min and the carbon dioxide supply was at the level of 0.5 L/min. After the introduction of a continuous inflow of water, the concentration of calcium and magnesium in the storage tank began to decrease from 26.3 mmol/L to 12.8 mmol/L, which represents a decrease of up to half. At the same time, the determined values in the storage tank were the same as the outflow values of the system. In area one (Figure 6), there was also a section during which CO_2 was not supplied to the system. In the mentioned section, we observed a faster decrease in the concentration of $Ca^{2+} + Mg^{2+}$, while the concentration of $Ca^{2+} + Mg^{2+}$ started to rise again after the subsequent supply of CO_2. The same section is also seen in area seven, where even after the addition of HCD, but without CO_2 access, the concentration of $Ca^{2+} + Mg^{2+}$ dropped significantly, and when the CO_2 supply was re-introduced, the concentration of $Ca^{2+} + Mg^{2+}$ increased. In the mentioned two sections without CO_2 access, we were convinced of the seriousness of the presence of carbon dioxide, which needs to be supplied to the system to increase the solubility of HCD in water.

In area two in Figure 6 at $Q(CO_2)$ = 0.5 L/min, the inflow of water from the distribution network was increased from 20 mL/min to 53 mL/min and we observed a decrease in concentration by only 2 mmol/L. At the end of this area, we dosed the new HCD Magno Dol (Akdolit) into the system to increase the concentration of ions.

We continued to increase the inflow in area three (Figure 6), where the inflow of treated water was 63–68 mL/min. By 277 h, the CO_2 flow was at the level of 0.5 L/min, and after this time, the CO_2 flow increased to 0.52–0.54 L/min with constant water supply from the distribution network. The effect of the change in this flow rate can be observed in area three (Figure 6) as an initial increase in the concentration of $Ca^{2+} + Mg^{2+}$, which then started to decrease, apparently due to the consumption of HCD. That is why we added recarbonization material to the system and reduced the flow of water from the water network to 58 mL/min. The behavior of the system after the addition of HCD Magno Dol (Akdolit) with reduced water flow and maintained CO_2 flow from area three (Figure 6) can be seen in area four (Figure 6), where the concentration of $Ca^{2+} + Mg^{2+}$ started to rise again. After increasing the concentration of $Ca^{2+} + Mg^{2+}$ to a value of 15.6 mmol/L, we suddenly increased the water flow from the distribution network up to 70–76 mL/min, which we reduced to 60 mL/min after twenty hours because we noticed a sharper decrease in $Ca^{2+} + Mg^{2+}$ concentration. After this drop in concentration to 10.8 mmol/L, we dosed another amount of HCD Magno Dol (Akdolit) into the system and gradually reduced the flow of water to 56 mL/min and carbon dioxide to 0.33 L/min, while the concentration of calcium and magnesium in the drinking water was relatively stable.

In area six (Figure 6), we monitored the behavior of the system with small gradual changes in water flow in the range of 60–66 mL/min, with gradual changes in CO_2 flow from 0.23 L/min to 0.35 L/min during more frequent replenishment of the HCD mass. The maximum difference of 2 mmol/L for Ca^{2+} + Mg^{2+} concentration values occurred when the experimental conditions were changed.

We carried out a gradual reduction in the CO_2 flow at water inflows of 50–57 mL/min in area seven (Figure 6), where we exposed the system to the already mentioned zero CO_2 flow.

3.1.3. Regression Analysis of Experimental Results

We used the regression Equation (12) and optimized its parameters to describe the behavior of the continuous recarbonization system at different flows of supplied treated drinking water and flows of carbon dioxide.

Using the mentioned regression model with the Nelder–Mead method for parameter optimization, we determined with 95% probability the values of the parameters of the regression equation, which are listed in Table 5. The correlation coefficient of the model with the specified parameter values is 0.9570; that is, the determined quadratic equation with mutual links of independent variables is suitable for describing the process.

Table 5. Parameter values of the regression model $(Ca^{2+} + Mg^{2+})$ = f $(Q(CO_2), Q(H_2O))$ for laboratory FBRR.

Parameter	Value
P_0	33.994
P_1	2.790
P_2	−0.847
P_{11}	10.000
P_{22}	0.007
P_{12}	−0.021

According to the determined values of the parameters, the regression equation took the form:

$$c\left(Ca^{2+} + Mg^{2+}\right) = 33.994 + 2.790\, Q(CO_2) - 0.847\, Q(H_2O) + 10.0\, (Q(CO_2))^2 + \\ +0.007\, (Q(H_2O))^2 - 0.021 \cdot Q(CO_2) \cdot Q(H_2O) \quad (16)$$

where $c(Ca^{2+} + Mg^{2+})$ is the concentration of calcium and magnesium (mmol/L) and $Q(H_2O)$ and $Q(CO_2)$ are the flow of water and carbon dioxide. Using this equation, we calculated the concentration of Ca^{2+} + Mg^{2+} and in Figure 7 we illustrated in a three-dimensional graph the comparison of calculated values with measured values. It is clear from the above graph that the highest achieved measured and calculated value of the Ca^{2+} + Mg^{2+} concentration is at a CO_2 flow rate of 0.5 L/min and a value of the supplied treated drinking water flow rate of 76 mL/min. However, we can assume that with the mentioned water flow rate of 76 mL/min, the experimental concentration of Ca^{2+} + Mg^{2+} would be even higher with a higher CO_2 flow rate, which is also confirmed by the calculation using Equation (16) optimization; we determined with 95% probability the values of the parameters of the regression Equation (16).

For a more illustrative comparison of the measured values with the calculated values using Equation (16), we constructed a two-dimensional graph in Figure S2 (Supplementary Materials) in which the Ca^{2+} + Mg^{2+} concentration values from different inflows of treated water from the distribution network are shown. From Figure S2, we can also see that the process (without the first saturation phase) is described by the above-mentioned quadratic equation with mutual interconnections of parameters (Equation (16)) which have a convex shape.

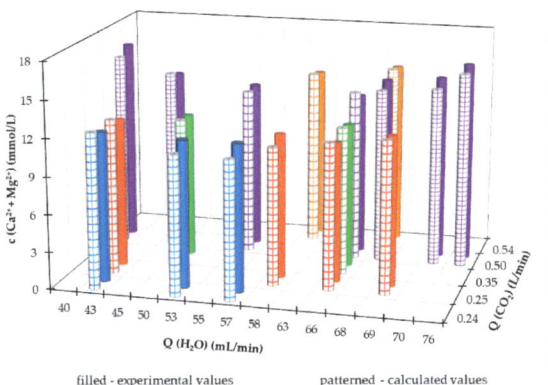

Figure 7. Calculated and measured values of $Ca^{2+} + Mg^{2+}$ concentration during continuous operation of laboratory FBRR.

In the statistical treatment of dependence,

$$c\left(Ca^{2+} + Mg^{2+}\right) = f(Q(CO_2), Q(H_2O)) \tag{17}$$

we also calculated the value of the coefficient of determination, which is 0.919. This value of coefficient of determination (R_2) indicates that 91.9% variability of the total variability in the sum concentration of calcium and magnesium cations was attributed to investigated experimental independent variables. The remaining 8% is the influence of non-included independent variables. Thus, it can be concluded that the developed model (Equation (16)) adequately describes the relationship between studied variables.

We also applied the regression model of the quadratic equation with mutual links of independent variables for the dependence of the ratio of calcium and magnesium on the flow of carbon dioxide and supplied water from the distribution network. The model of the regression equation took the form of (18) and the determined values of the parameters are listed in Table 6.

$$c\left(Ca^{2+}\right)/c\left(Mg^{2+}\right) = P_0 + P_1 Q(CO_2) + P_2 Q(H_2O) + P_{11}(Q(CO_2))^2 + P_{22}(Q(H_2O))^2 + P_{12} Q(CO_2) \cdot Q(H_2O) \tag{18}$$

where P_1 to P_{12} are parameters of the regression equation, $c(Ca^{2+})/c(Mg^{2+})$ is the molar concentration ratio of calcium and magnesium, and $Q(H_2O)$ and $Q(CO_2)$ are the flow of water and carbon dioxide. Using this equation, we calculated the concentration of $Ca^{2+} + Mg^{2+}$.

Table 6. Values of regression coefficients of the model $c(Ca^{2+})/c(Mg^{2+}) = f(Q(CO_2), Q(H_2O))$ for the laboratory FBRR.

Parameter	Value
P_0	−0.1249
P_1	−0.8076
P_2	0.0194
P_{11}	−0.4775
P_{22}	−0.0002
P_{12}	0.0160

We compared the measured values of the ratio of the molar content of calcium and magnesium with the calculated values using the regression Equation (18) in Figure 8. The correlation coefficient between the measured and calculated values is 0.922 and the coefficient of determination is 0.850.

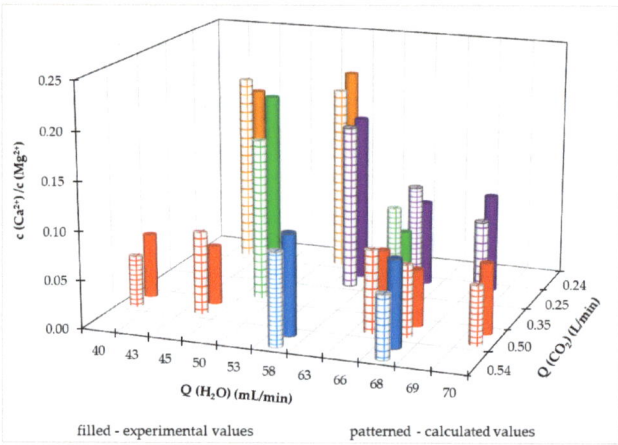

Figure 8. Experimental and calculated $c(Ca^{2+})/c(Mg^{2+})$ during continuous operation of the laboratory FBRR.

3.1.4. Optimizing the Conditions of the Recarbonization Process in Laboratory FBRR

We used the determined values of the parameters of the regression Equations (16) and (18) to determine the optimal conditions of the process, i.e., independent variables, or CO_2 and H_2O flows. Using the grid search of the optimization method, we determined the values of these flows for the maximum and minimum value of the dependent variable in question. The optimal process conditions were determined for the range of values of the independent variables at which the experiments were performed.

For the optimal conditions of the dependent variable $c(Ca^{2+} + Mg^{2+})$, we also calculated the optimal values of the ratio $c(Ca^{2+})/c(Mg^{2+})$. Also, for optimal conditions of maximum and minimum values of the $c(Ca^{2+})/c(Mg^{2+})$ ratio, we calculated optimal values of the sum of $c(Ca^{2+} + Mg^{2+})$ concentrations. The results are presented in Tables 7 and 8.

Table 7. Results of the optimization of recarbonization process conditions for the dependent variable $c(Ca^{2+} + Mg^{2+})$.

Value	$c(Ca^{2+} + Mg^{2+})$ (mmol/L)	$Q(CO_2)$ (L/min)	$Q(H_2O)$ (mL/min)	$c(Ca^{2+})/c(Mg^{2+})$
Maximum	16.20	0.54	76.00	0.01
Minimum	10.90	0.24	57.20	0.18

Table 8. Results of the optimization of recarbonization process conditions for the dependent variable $c(Ca^{2+})/c(Mg^{2+})$.

Value	$c(Ca^{2+})/c(Mg^{2+})$	$Q(CO_2)$ (L/min)	$Q(H_2O)$ (mL/min)	$c(Ca^{2+} + Mg^{2+})$
Maximum	0.20	0.24	47.10	11.60
Minimum	0.05	0.54	70.00	14.80

From the results of process optimization in the laboratory FBRR within the investigated range of values of independent variables, i.e., the flow of carbon dioxide 0.24–0.54 L/min and water from the distribution network 40–76 mL/min, it follows that the minimum value of the sum of calcium and magnesium ions was 10.9 mmol/L and the maximum value of the sum of these ions was 16.2 mmol/L. Both values comply with the recommended values according to Annex no. 1 to the decree of the Ministry of Health of the Slovak Republic no. 247/2017 Coll.

From the optimization calculations for the maximum and minimum values of the molar ratio of calcium and magnesium in drinking water, it follows that the values of the ratios do not correspond to the requirements according to the above-mentioned decree of the Ministry of Health of the Slovak republic. The maximum calculated value of the molar ratio of calcium and magnesium for experimental conditions is 0.20, while the minimum recommended value according to the recommended content of individual ions in drinking water is 0.6 [28].

3.2. Pilot Reactor

We operated the pilot FBRR in flow mode with continuous inflow and outflow of treated drinking water without an initial saturation phase. The initial concentration of the sum of calcium and magnesium ions in the treated water was 4.3 mmol/L. At the beginning of the experiment, we dosed 20.6 kg of HCD Magno Dol (Akdolit) into the fluidized bed reactor. Considering that the pilot FBRR is a larger device and the stabilization of the process when the conditions change takes longer than in the laboratory FBRR, we varied the conditions of the recarbonization process ($Q(CO_2)$, $Q(H_2O)$) in smaller ranges:

$$Q(CO_2) = 0.4–0.7 \text{ L/min},$$

$$Q(H_2O) = 118.0–132.8 \text{ L/h}.$$

The time dependence of conductivity and the concentration of calcium and magnesium ions in drinking water are shown in Figure 9.

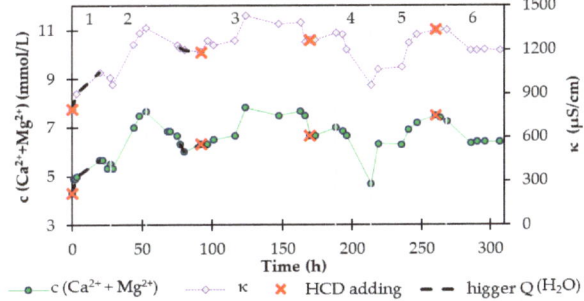

Figure 9. Time dependencies of conductivity and molar concentration of $Ca^{2+} + Mg^{2+}$ during operation of pilot FBRR.

The evaluation of monitored quantities in Figure 9 is divided according to the flow of carbon dioxide into seven areas. The CO_2 flow rate for individual areas is shown in Table 9.

During the first 27 h (Figure 9, area one) we operated the reactor at $Q(CO_2) = 0.4$ L/min and the flow of treated drinking water from the distribution network was initially 132.8 L/h, while later we stabilized it at a value of 120 L/h. The concentration of $Ca^{2+} + Mg^{2+}$ after 27 h of operation was increased by approximately 1 mmol/L.

Table 9. Flows of carbon dioxide for individual areas shown in Figures 9 and 10.

Area	Q(CO$_2$) (L/min)
1	0.4
2	0.7
3	0.5
4	0.3
5	0.5
6	0.4

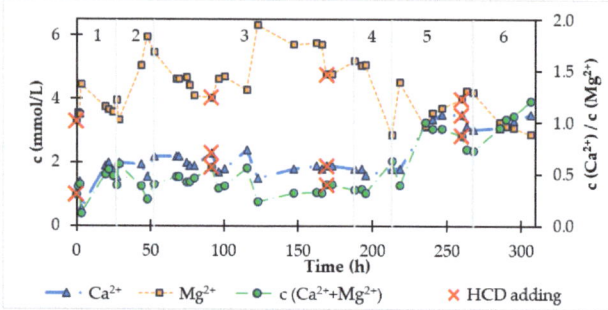

Figure 10. Time dependencies of the molar concentrations of Ca^{2+} and Mg^{2+} and the ratio of the molar concentrations of Ca^{2+} and Mg^{2+} during the operation of pilot FBRR.

In area two (Figure 9), after 27 h, to achieve a higher concentration of calcium and magnesium ions with a constant inflow of treated water, we increased the flow of carbon dioxide to the level of 0.7 L/min. With an increased flow of carbon dioxide, the content of calcium and magnesium in the drinking water was significantly increased up to 7.7 mmol/L. At this concentration, which we considered sufficiently high, we reduced the carbon dioxide flow to a value of 0.5 L/min in order to stabilize the outflow concentration and prevent its further increase.

The course of the process at a constant CO$_2$ flow rate of 0.5 L/min is shown in area three in Figure 9. The concentration of calcium and magnesium in the drinking water after 15 h decreased more than expected, by approximately 1.5 mmol/L. This decrease could also have occurred because of a slight increase in the inflow of treated water from 120 L/h to 132.8 L/h and wear of the HCD in the reactor. We dosed HCD Magno Dol (Akdolit), weighing 3.4 kg into the reactor, and adjusted the water inflow from the distribution network to 120 L/h. The concentration of Ca^{2+} + Mg^{2+} started to rise again and stabilized at approximately 7.5 mmol/L. At the next observed decrease in concentration, we again dosed another amount of HCD.

We can assume that for a steady effluent concentration of calcium and magnesium in drinking water at a carbon dioxide flow rate of 0.5 L/min and a water inflow from the water network of 120 L/h, it is necessary to dose approximately 3.5 kg of new HCD Magno Dol (Akdolit) every 75 h into the pilot FBRR.

After 188 h of operation, the equipment reduced the CO$_2$ flow to 0.3 L/min for 24 h. The concentration of calcium and magnesium ions in the water dropped significantly from 7.0 mmol/L to 4.7 mmol/L. When the CO$_2$ flow rate was again increased to 0.5 L/min at a constant Q(H$_2$O) = 120 L/h in area five (Figure 9), we observed a further increase in the content of Ca^{2+} + Mg^{2+} ions by 1.5 mmol/L. Based on this observation, we can state that if there is a brief loss of carbon dioxide supply to the system during operation in practice, after re-introduction of CO$_2$ the system can be returned to steady state in approximately less than 4 days, according to the flow of reintroduced carbon dioxide.

Before the end of area five (Figure 9), we added the new recarbonization material, HCD Magno Dol (Akdolit), and during the first 8 h after dosing we recorded a steady concentration of calcium and magnesium in the drinking water of approximately $c(Ca^{2+} + Mg^{2+}) = 7.3$ mmol/L. After this stabilization, we again reduced the CO_2 flow in the system to a level of 0.4 L/min in area six, shown in Figure 9, where we observed a significant effect of a lower CO_2 flow, where even with sufficient recarbonization mass, there was a decrease in $c(Ca^{2+} + Mg^{2+})$, which was stabilized at a value of 6.4 mmol/L within five hours.

In addition to the total content of calcium and magnesium in water, their ratio, i.e., the content of individual ions, is also important. The calculated value of the ratio of calcium and magnesium according to the recommended content of individual elements in drinking water [28] should be in the range of 0.6 to 1.0. The temporal evolution of the concentrations of individual ions is illustrated in Figure 10. Increasing the carbon dioxide flux (areas two and five in Figure 10) resulted in a much higher release of magnesium ions into the water than calcium ions. When dissolving HCD in water, a high flow of carbon dioxide stimulates the dissolution of the magnesium component of HCD.

After each dosing of a new amount of HCD, the value of the ratio of calcium to magnesium content is lower. This is probably due to the higher solubility of the magnesium component of the HCD, while the surface and porosity of the recarbonization material also changes during dissolution and the ions inside the pores become more accessible. It is known that the used HCD Magno Dol (Akdolit) has a higher content of calcium components; therefore, after exhausting the mass, the magnesium component from the mass, we expected a gradual increase in the concentration ratio of calcium and magnesium ions.

After 213 h of operation of the pilot FBRR at a reduced flow of carbon dioxide (Figure 10, area four) the Ca^{2+}/Mg^{2+} ratio changed periodically in the range of 0.2–0.6. After its increase (Figure 10, area five,) the increase in $c(Ca^{2+})/c(Mg^{2+})$ up to a value equal to 1.0 was observed. We can assume that if the experiment were to continue in area six (Figure 10) after further dosing of HCD, we would keep the ratio of calcium and magnesium at a value close to 1.0 at a constant flow of treated drinking water 120 L/h and CO_2 flow 0.4 L/min.

3.2.1. Statistical Processing of Experimental Results

For the mathematical description of the process of enriching drinking water with calcium and magnesium, we used a quadratic equation model with interrelationships between independent variables, i.e., the flow of carbon dioxide $Q(CO_2)$ and the flow of treated drinking water from the distribution network $Q(H_2O)$.

We applied the regression Equation (12) for four different dependent variables:

- $c(Ca^{2+} + Mg^{2+})$,
- $c(Ca^{2+})/c(Mg^{2+})$,
- $c(Mg^{2+})$,
- $c(Ca^{2+})$.

Through statistical processing, we obtained four regression models of the quadratic equation with mutual interferences, $Q(CO_2)$ and $Q(H_2O)$, and determined the values of the regression coefficients of these models with 95% probability (Table 10). We assessed the quality of the description of the recarbonization process using Equation (12) with determined parameter values by the R_{XY} correlation coefficient, which acquires relatively high values for the individual dependencies of the variable depending on $Q(CO_2)$ and $Q(H_2O)$. Based on the values of the correlation coefficients, we can conclude a good agreement between the measured and calculated values of the dependent variables.

Table 10. Parameter values of Equation (12) and statistical characteristics for individual dependent variables Y.

Parameter	Dependent Variables Y			
	$c(Ca^{2+} + Mg^{2+})$	$c(Ca^{2+})/c(Mg^{2+})$	$c(Mg^{2+})$	$c(Ca^{2+})$
P_0	90.785	238.760	29.965	288.433
P_1	−118.575	−67.015	−75.558	−86.230
P_2	−0.788	−3.546	−0.123	−4.160
P_{11}	16.279	2.524	16.645	−3.577
P_{22}	1.09×10^{-3}	1.31×10^{-2}	-5.17×10^{-4}	1.49×10^{-2}
P_{12}	0.834	0.526	0.500	0.724
R_{XY}	0.9635	0.9929	0.9796	0.9357
R_{XY}^2	0.9597	0.8755	0.9858	0.9283

To assess the influence of independent variables on the process, we used the coefficient of determination R_{XY}^2. In Table 10, the values of the individual coefficients of determination are listed, which range from 0.8755 to 0.9858. We can say that the recarbonization process in a pilot FBRR is 88% to 99% influenced by the flow of carbon dioxide and water from the water network.

Experimental data and calculated values using a multiple regression equation at different $Q(CO_2)$ and $Q(H_2O)$ for individual dependent variables are illustrated in Figures 11–14. Because the pilot FBRR is a larger reaction system and stabilization of the process when conditions change takes longer than in the laboratory, we approached the change of independent variables during the experiment with caution and changed them gradually.

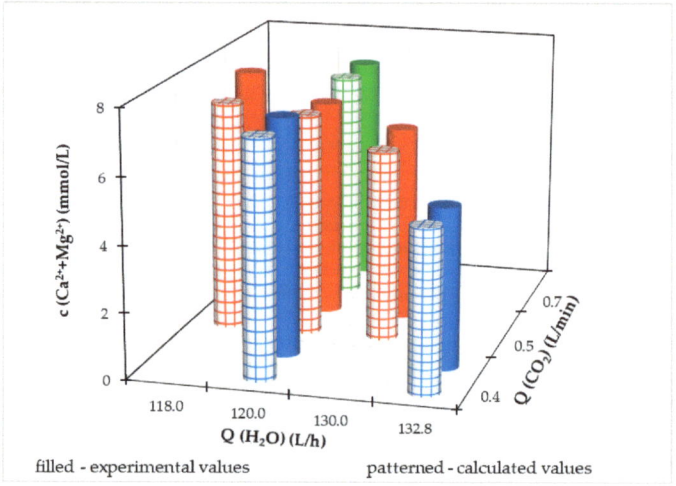

Figure 11. Experimental and calculated values of molar concentration of $Ca^{2+} + Mg^{2+}$.

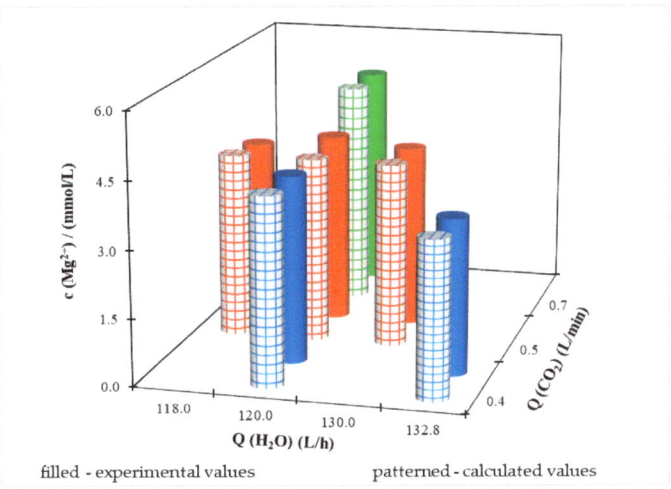

Figure 12. Experimental and calculated values of molar concentration of Mg^{2+}.

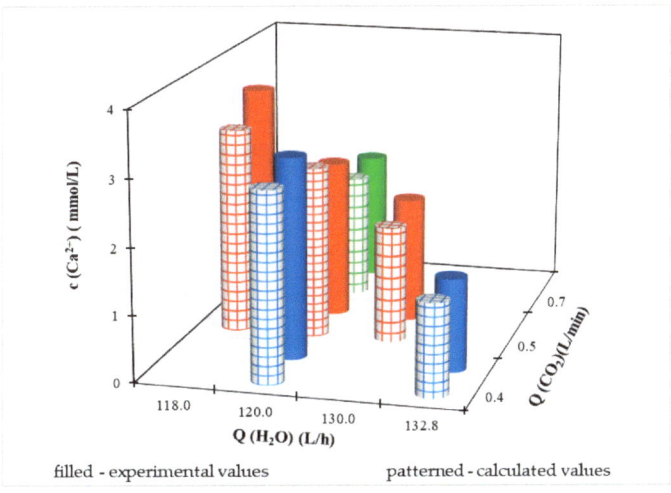

Figure 13. Experimental and calculated values of molar concentration of Ca^{2+}.

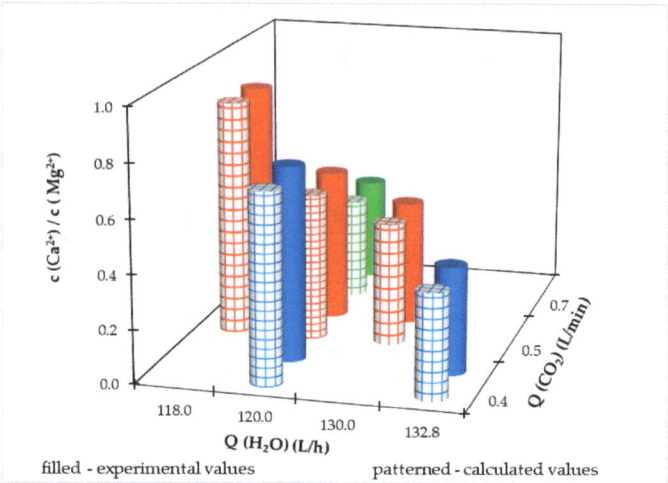

Figure 14. Experimental and calculated values of molar concentration of Ca^{2+} a Mg^{2+}.

For a clearer comparison of the values of the dependent variable, in Figures S3–S6 (Supplementary Materials) the achieved measured and calculated values at different flow rates of treated drinking water from the distribution network at a constant flow rate $Q(CO_2)$ = 0.5 L/min are shown. Based on the illustrated graphs, we can claim that with a constant flow of carbon dioxide, as the flow of water from the water supply network increases (up to a maximum of 132.8 L/h), it

1. Reduces the sum of the molar concentration of calcium and magnesium ions in drinking water,
2. Reduces the molar concentration of calcium ions in drinking water,
3. Reduces the ratio of the molar content of calcium and magnesium in drinking water.

Regarding the magnesium content, we cannot say such a conclusion unequivocally due to the dependence of the concave shape for experimental values, seen in Figure S4, where the molar concentration of Mg^{2+} is shown. At the minimum and maximum water flow from the distribution network, the experimental concentration of magnesium ions is lower than at the mean value of $Q(H_2O)$. With the calculated values of $c(Mg^{2+})$, the difference in magnesium ion concentration is in the order of hundredths, based on which we can conclude that the value is quasi-steady.

A comparison of the measured and calculated values of the dependent variable at a constant water flow from the water supply network of 120 L/h and different CO_2 flows is shown in Figures S6 and S7.

If we evaluate the process with a constant flow of water from the distribution network and different flows of CO_2 supplied to the system, we can conclude that

1. As the CO_2 flow increases, the ratio of the molar content of Ca^{2+} and Mg^{2+} decreases,
2. With increasing CO_2 flow, the molar concentration of Mg^{2+} in drinking water also increases,
3. At the same time as the CO_2 flow increases, the molar concentration of Ca^{2+} in drinking water decreases.

As the Mg^{2+} content increases and the Ca^{2+} content decreases with increasing CO_2 flow, the sum of concentrations does not have a clear decreasing/increasing trend with increasing CO_2 flow.

3.2.2. Optimization of the Process in the Pilot FBRR

Using the Solver program in MS Excel using the non-linear algorithm solution method, we calculated the optimal values of the independent variables ($Q(CO_2)$, $Q(H_2O)$) in the pilot FBRR for the maximum and minimum value depending on the regression equations with determined parameter values (Table 11). We performed optimization calculations within the range of experimental conditions:

- $Q(CO_2)$ = 0.4–0.7 L/min,
- $Q(H_2O)$ = 118.0–132.8 L/h.

Table 11. Optimization of the conditions of the process in the pilot FBRR for the maximum values of the dependent variables.

Dependent Variables	Value	$Q(CO_2)$ (L/min)	$Q(H_2O)$ (L/h)
$c(Ca^{2+} + Mg^{2+})$	7.59 mmol/L	0.40	118.00
$c(Mg^{2+})$	4.30 mmol/L	0.40	118.00
$c(Ca^{2+})$	3.53 mmol/L	0.40	118.00
$c(Ca^{2+})/c(Mg^{2+})$	1.14	0.40	118.00

Using the determined values of the parameters of the regression equations for the maximum values of the dependent variables, from Table 11 we can notice the same conditions for all four dependent variables.

The maximum concentration of the sum of calcium and magnesium in drinking water, which can be achieved under the conditions $Q(CO_2)$ = 0.4 L/min and $Q(H_2O)$ = 118.0 L/h, is 7.59 mmol/L. At the same time, under these process conditions, a content of calcium ions of 3.53 mmol/L is reached, i.e., 141.5 mg/L and magnesium ions 4.3 mmol/L, which represents 104.5 mg/L. The value of the molar ratio of calcium and magnesium in drinking water can reach a maximum of 1.14 under the above-mentioned process conditions.

Under the stated conditions of the process in Table 11, drinking water is prepared, which is very hard [29], and is satisfactory from a health point of view.

In Table 12, the determined process conditions for the minimum values of the dependent variable are listed. We can see that during the recarbonization process in the pilot FBRR, it is possible to achieve minimum concentrations of Ca^{2+} and ($Ca^{2+} + Mg^{2+}$) ions that correspond to the recommended range according to Annex no. 1 to the Decree of the Ministry of Health of the Slovak Republic no. 247/2017 Coll [28]; even the specified minimum magnesium content in drinking water is higher than the recommended range. At the same time, under process conditions that correspond to the minimum value of the dependent variable, it is not possible to achieve the required molar ratio of 0.6–1.0 of calcium and magnesium contents in drinking water.

Table 12. Optimization of the conditions of the process in the pilot FBRR for the minimum values of the dependent variables.

Dependent Variables	Value	$Q(CO_2)$ (L/min)	$Q(H_2O)$ (L/h)
$c(Ca^{2+} + Mg^{2+})$	4.93 mmol/L	0.40	132.80
$c(Mg^{2+})$	3.52 mmol/L	0.40	132.80
$c(Ca^{2+})$	1.30 mmol/L	0.40	130.24
$c(Ca^{2+})/c(Mg^{2+})$	6.93×10^{-4}	0.40	127.35

3.2.3. Comparison of the Used Two Recarbonization Materials

We also operated the pilot FBRR with the 2.5–4.5 mm HCD Semidol recarbonizing material. During operation with this material, we maintained a constant flow of carbon dioxide, $Q(CO_2)$ = 0.4 L/min, and inflow of treated drinking water from the distribution network, $Q(H_2O) \approx$ 120 L/h.

Both HCDs Semidol and Magno Dol (Akdolit) have approximately the same chemical composition, volume density, and carbon dioxide consumption per unit weight of the material prescribed by the supplier. HCD Semidol is a more fragile material compared to HCD Magno Dol (Akdolit) and when dosing HCD Semidol into the device, we noticed a lot of HCD dust particles.

When operating a pilot FBRR using HCD Semidol, we can achieve higher average concentrations and outflow values of magnesium ions (Table 13). However, the conditions of the recarbonization process with Magno Dol (Akdolit) were not constant during the entire operation as in the operation with HCD Semidol; therefore, a comparison of the average effluent concentrations during the process is not relevant.

Table 13. Average values achieved when using different HCDs.

	Magno Dol (Akdolit)	Semidol
Average inflow of freshwater (L/h)	121.8	119.7
Average $c(Mg^{2+})$ (mg/L)	105.3	146.2
Average $c(Ca^{2+})$ (mg/L)	86.5	70.5
Average outflow Mg^{2+} (g/h)	12.8	16.6
Average outflow Ca^{2+} (g/h)	10.5	8.5

When operating a pilot FBRR using HCD Semidol, we can achieve higher average concentrations and outflow values of magnesium ions (Table 12). However, the conditions of the recarbonization process with Magno Dol (Akdolit) were not constant during the entire operation as in the operation with HCD Semidol; therefore, a comparison of the average effluent concentrations during the process is not relevant.

For a more accurate comparison of the used recarbonization materials we used the balance values, which we related to the HCD weight unit. These values are shown in Table 14.

Table 14. Values of reaction time and balance values when using two different recarbonization materials.

	Magno Dol (Akdolit)	Semidol
Reaction time (h)	306.6	167.0
Total added HCD (kg)	31.2	23.1
Reacted amount of HCD (kg)	15.9	18.4
Reacted HCD to added HCD (%)	51.0	79.9
Total consumption of CO_2 (kg)	35.3	18.2
Total production of Mg^{2+} (kg)	3.9	2.8
Total production of Ca^{2+} (kg)	3.2	1.4
Average production of Mg^{2+} per added HCD (g/kg)	125.8	119.8
Average production of Ca^{2+} per added HCD (g/kg)	103.2	61.2
Average production of Mg^{2+} per reacted HCD (g/kg)	246.8	149.9
Average production of Ca^{2+} per reacted HCD (g/kg)	202.5	76.5
CO_2 consumption per added HCD (kg/kg)	1.1	0.8
CO_2 consumption per reacted HCD (kg/kg)	2.2	1.0

In the process with HCD Magno Dol (Akdolit), a smaller amount of the added HCD reacted (51.0%) than in the operation with HCD Semidol (79.9%). Even though a smaller amount of HCD Magno Dol (Akdolit) reacted during the process, the production of magnesium and calcium ions per kilogram of the reacted amount of HCD was higher than with HCD Semidol. The same applied to the kilogram of added mass.

Since it is necessary to supply carbon dioxide to the system, when comparing the balance values of carbon dioxide, its consumption of 1.14 kg per 1 kg of added HCD Magno Dol (Akdolit) is close to the value stated by the manufacturer (1.2–1.3 kg). For HCD Semidol, the consumption is approximately 30% lower, i.e., 0.79 kg CO_2/kg HCD. The stated consumption of carbon dioxide per kilogram of added Semidol material is also lower than stated by the manufacturer (1.2–1.3 kg). The reason for the lower consumption may be the fragility of the material and the occurrence of particles smaller than 2.5–4.5 mm.

To compare the used recarbonization materials in practice, we performed balance calculations for the conditions of a real water treatment plant, where the introduction of a tested pilot FBRR into operation is being considered. The goal is to treat water with an annual water flow of 11,000 m^3 with a required increase in magnesium ion content of 10 mg/L. It means that the annual increase in magnesium ions is 110 kg.

The annual consumption of carbon dioxide and compared materials under the same process conditions is shown in Table 15.

Table 15. Consumption of CO_2 and recarbonization materials in a pilot FBRR with an annual increase of 110 kg Mg^{2+}.

	Magno Dol (Akdolit)	Semidol
HCD consumption (kg/year)	874.7	917.9
CO_2 consumption (kg/year)	989.6	721.2

Based on the above-mentioned balance calculations for a potential water treatment plant using HCD Magno Dol (Akdolit), the annual consumption of HCD is 874.7 kg, which corresponds to the consumption of 989.6 kg of CO_2 per year. When using HCD Semidol, the annual material consumption is only 43.3 kg higher, but the carbon dioxide consumption is more than 200 kg lower.

In addition to enriching the water with magnesium ions, calcium ions are also released from the recarbonization materials. The amounts of Ca^{2+} released during the production of 110 kg of Mg^{2+} per year are shown in Table 16.

Table 16. Amounts of Ca^{2+} released and increased concentrations of Ca^{2+} using different recarbonization materials in a pilot FBRR, corresponding to an annual increase of 110 kg Mg^{2+} in treated water.

	Magno Dol (Akdolit)	Semidol
Released Ca^{2+} (kg/year)	90.3	56.2
Increases $c(Ca^{2+})$ (mg/L)	8.2	5.1

The production of calcium during long-term operation of the FBRR can be considered significant in view of the current requirements placed on the quality of drinking water [28]. Annually, 38% more calcium ions are released from the Magno Dol material (Akdolit) compared to the Semidol material. When drinking water is enriched with magnesium of 10 mg/L using HCD Magno Dol (Akdolit), this represents an increase in calcium content by 8.2 mg/L. While, when using HCD Semidol, the content of calcium ions increases by 5.1 mg/L. The operator's decision on the choice of material can also be influenced by the current selling price of materials.

The aim of this chapter was to compare the operation using these different recarbonization materials in the treatment of drinking water with an annual volume flow of 11,000 m^3 with an increase in magnesium ions by 10 mg/L. When using HCD Semidol, the annual consumption of material is higher by approx. 5% and, at the same time, the annual consumption of carbon dioxide is lower by approx. 27% compared to the operation of the equipment with HCD Magno Dol (Akdolit). In addition to magnesium, calcium is also released from the mass. The increase in the concentration of calcium ions is higher by 38% when using the recarbonization material Magno Dol (Akdolit) compared to HCD Semidol.

The resulting choice of recarbonization material is up to the operator, who can decide based on the price ratios of the materials used or from the point of view of the added value of the production of calcium ions in drinking water.

4. Discussion

Recarbonization of drinking water is aimed at increasing the quality of water with a very low content of magnesium and calcium minerals. These biogenic elements are important not only for human health but also for reducing the problems related to the corrosive and aggressive effects of soft water on the materials of the drinking water distribution system. Water with very low total hardness is unstable and unbuffered.

Considering the demonstrable positive relationship between the content of Ca^{2+}, Mg^{2+}, and human health, the application of the recarbonization process appears to be a beneficial perspective for improving the quality of life in areas where the source of drinking water is poor in these biogenic elements. The use of a fluidized bed recarbonization reactor (FBRR) offers the possibility of treating large volumes of drinking water in a relatively short time and in smaller facilities.

The process of enhancing drinking water with biogenic and water-stabilizing calcium and magnesium ions has been investigated. The chemistry of the process is based on half-calcined dolomite in combination with carbon dioxide. The high interface reaction surface, homogenization of reaction conditions, and intensifying the potential of the fluidized bed reactor represent novel approaches to investigating recarbonization processes and reactor techniques in the drinking water industry.

This process is characterized using renewable sources of raw materials with a minimal amount of produced waste, which is environmentally acceptable. The proposed drinking water recarbonization technology using a fluidized bed recarbonization reactor for the preparation of concentrate in a side stream arrangement with respect to the drinking water distribution in main streams minimizes the energy requirements, which are only related to water recirculation near the threshold velocity. In addition, the supply of carbon dioxide under the liquid distributor in the reactor also contributes to the reduction in the required supplied energy.

It is known from published experimental results that it is advantageous to use half-calcined dolomite (HCD) in combination with CO_2 when enriching drinking water with calcium and magnesium. Half-calcinated dolomite is commercially available from several companies, and for this reason we also focused on testing two HCDs, Magno Dol (Akdolit) and Semidol, with similar fractions. The results showed that even though they are chemically the same materials, they are of different quality. In general, with the same amount of magnesium ions released, a different amount of calcium ions is released and the consumption of recarbonization materials is different. From a practical point of view, it is advisable to conduct experiments that would deal with the influence of operating parameters on the recarbonization process when using Semidol and compare the results with the operation of MagnoDol (Akdolit).

Experimental and mathematical modelling of the recarbonization process aimed at increasing the content of these biogenic elements in water was carried out in the continuous laboratory- and pilot-scale fluidized bed reactors. Water remineralization using half-calcined dolomite (HCD) and carbon dioxide in a fluidized bed reactor is a novelty in water treatment. Although the chemistry of the process is known and used, the specific conditions in this type of reactor can significantly affect the efficiency of the process. In the presented work, we deal with the possibility of the recarbonization process in a fluidized bed reactor.

The influence of operating conditions ($Q(CO_2)$, freshwater inflow, and dose of HCD on some quality indicators of treated drinking water ($c(Ca^{2+})$, $c(Mg^{2+})$, amount of $Ca^{2+} + Mg^{2+}$, Ca/Mg) was investigated. Subsequently, the operating conditions were optimized for the minimum and maximum value of the mentioned qualitative indicators. The results show that the Mg^{2+} concentration is more significantly affected by the amount of HCD in the system and the CO_2 flow. The influence of the freshwater inflow on the Mg^{2+} content is to a lesser extent. At a constant CO_2 flow, as the inflow of tap water increases the Ca^{2+} content decreases and the Mg^{2+} content increases, resulting in a decrease in the Ca/Mg molar ratio.

However, the Ca/Mg ratio can be effectively controlled by adding an appropriate amount of HCD at certain time intervals. The overproduction of ions can be easily controlled by the flow of CO_2. When using HCD Semidol, the annual consumption of recarbonization material is higher by approx. 5% and, at the same time, the annual consumption of carbon dioxide is lower by approx. 27% compared to the operation of the device with HCD Magno Dol (Akdolit). With an increase in Mg^{2+} by 10 mg/L, the increase in the concentration of calcium ions is higher by 38% when using the recarbonization mass Magno Dol (Akdolit) compared to HCD Semidol.

The results of the experimental measurements were processed by regression analysis and optimization methods. Statistical models were developed to describe the dependence between the above water quality indicators and operating parameters. Using the grid search optimization method, the optimal values of operating parameters were determined for the maximum and minimum values of the monitored drinking water's quality indicators. Each source of drinking water has a different quality so it is important to investigate the effect of basic operating conditions on the recarbonization process. Knowing the influence of operating conditions facilitates the design of such a device in practice, and the recarbonization process can be optimized so that the treated drinking water meets the required quality.

The laboratory and pilot FBRRs were designed, built, and verified for soft water treatment. The results of the measured hydraulic characteristics of the fluidized bed and the values of the optimal conditions of the recarbonization process make it possible to make the operation of the recarbonization system more efficient and facilitate its further expansion to full operation.

5. Conclusions

The use of the recarbonization process in a fluidized bed reactor using carbon dioxide and recarbonization materials based on half-calcined dolomite is a novel technology for enriching drinking water with calcium and magnesium. Among the main advantages of using a fluidized bed is a relatively large contact area between the solid particles and the liquid, which minimizes the residence time of the liquid phase in the reactor. With this advantage, it is possible to adjust large volumes of drinking water in a short time. The aim of this work was experimental and mathematical modelling of the operation of a laboratory and pilot FBRR using CO_2 and selected recarbonization materials.

From the results of the work in the investigated range of recarbonization operating parameters, it follows that the Ca/Mg ratio can be effectively regulated by adding a suitable amount of PVD at certain intervals. An overproduction of Mg^{2+} ions can be easily controlled by CO_2 flow. In the tested laboratory and semi-operational equipment, it is possible to increase the concentration of Mg^{2+} by 10 mg/L, which was the requirement for the recarbonization process in the case study in question. At the same time, the concentrations of Mg^{2+} and Ca^{2+} are maintained in both modeled systems, which are in accordance with the recommended values of Slovak standards for drinking water. When applying HCD Magno-Dol to maintain a stable Ca/Mg ratio at a freshwater inflow of 120 L/h and a CO_2 flow of 0.5 L/min, it is advisable to dose approximately 3.5 kg of new PVD Magno-Dol into the system every 75 h.

The key values of our results include the development and verification of a sustainable remineralization system for enriching drinking water with the specific biogenic elements calcium and magnesium. Based on our results, a methodology for scaling-up the modeled system was extended with mathematical modelling and an industrial recarbonization system was designed. This system is put into operation in a locality with a deficient content of these elements in the drinking water and related health problems of the inhabitants.

Supplementary Materials: The following supporting information can be downloaded at: https://www.mdpi.com/article/10.3390/pr11113209/s1. Figure S1. Algorithm of Modelling of Drinking Water Recarbonization. Figure S2. Calculated and measured concentrations of $Ca^{2+} + Mg^{2+}$ at different flows of treated water and CO_2 flow at the level of 0.5 L/min during operation of the laboratory FBRR. Figure S3. The total concentration of the sum of Ca^{2+} and Mg^{2+} ions in drinking water at $Q(CO_2)$ = 0.5 L/min. Figure S4. Molar concentration of Mg^{2+} in drinking water at $Q(CO_2)$ = 0.5 L/min. Figure S5. Molar concentration of Ca2+ in drinking water at $Q(CO_2)$ = 0.5 L/min. Figure S6. Molar concentration ration of Ca^{2+} and Mg^{2+} in drinking water at $Q(CO_2)$ = 0.5 L/min. Figure S7. Molar concentration of the sum of Ca^{2+} and Mg^{2+} in drinking water at $Q(H_2O)$ = 120 L/h. Figure S8. Molar concentration of the sum of Mg^{2+} in drinking water at $Q(H_2O)$ = 120 L/h. Figure S9. Molar concentration of the sum of Ca^{2+} in drinking water at $Q(H_2O)$ = 120 L/h. Figure S10. Molar ratio of Ca^{2+} and Mg^{2+} concentration in drinking water at $Q(H_2O)$ = 120 L/h.

Author Contributions: Conceptualization, J.D. (Ján Derco) and J.D. (Jozef Dudáš); methodology, J.D. (Ján Derco); software, T.K.; validation, N.Š. and J.D. (Ján Derco); formal analysis, N.Š.; investigation, T.K., N.Š. and A.V.; resources, all authors.; data curation, J.D. (Ján Derco); writing—original draft preparation, J.D. (Ján Derco); writing—review and editing, J.D. (Ján Derco); visualization, N.Š.; supervision, A.V.; project administration, N.Š. and A.V. All authors have read and agreed to the published version of the manuscript.

Funding: This research was funded by "Improvement of health status of population of the Slovak Republic through drinking water re-carbonization" LIFE-Water and Health LIFE17 ENV/SK/000036.

Data Availability Statement: Data are contained within the article and Supplementary Materials.

Conflicts of Interest: The authors declare no conflict of interest.

References

1. Rylander, R.; Bonevik, H.; Rubenowitz, E. Magnesium and Calcium in Drinking Water and Cardiovascular Mortality. *Scand. J. Work. Environ. Health* **1991**, *17*, 91–94. [CrossRef] [PubMed]
2. Yang, C.-Y. Calcium and Magnesium in Drinking Water and Risk of Death from Cerebrovascular Disease. *Stroke* **1998**, *29*, 411–414. [CrossRef] [PubMed]
3. Rosanoff, A. The High Heart Health Value of Drinking-Water Magnesium. *Med. Hypotheses* **2013**, *81*, 1063–1065. [CrossRef] [PubMed]
4. Kaluza, J.; Orsini, N.; Levitan, E.B.; Brzozowska, A.; Roszkowski, W.; Wolk, A. Dietary Calcium and Magnesium Intake and Mortality: A Prospective Study of Men. *Am. J. Epidemiol.* **2010**, *171*, 801–807. [CrossRef] [PubMed]
5. Cotruvo, J. *Drinking Water Quality and Contaminants Guidebook*; Chapman and Hall/CRC: Milton, MA, USA, 2018; ISBN 9781351110464.
6. Rubenowitz, E.; Axelsson, G.; Rylander, R. Magnesium in Drinking Water and Death from Acute Myocardial Infarction. *Am. J. Epidemiol.* **1996**, *143*, 456–462. [CrossRef] [PubMed]
7. Rosborg, I. *Drinking Water Minerals and Mineral Balance*; Springer: Berlin/Heidelberg, Germany, 2014.
8. WHO. *Guidelines for Drinking-Water Quality*, 4th ed.; World Health Organization: Geneva, Switzerland, 2011; p. 531.
9. Jiang, L.; He, P.; Chen, J.; Liu, Y.; Liu, D.; Qin, G.; Tan, N. Magnesium Levels in Drinking Water and Coronary Heart Disease Mortality Risk: A Meta-Analysis. *Nutrients* **2016**, *8*, 5. [CrossRef] [PubMed]
10. Barloková, D.; Ilavský, J.; Kapusta, O.; Šimko, V. Importance of Calcium and Magnesium in Water—Water Hardening. *IOP Conf. Ser. Earth Environ. Sci.* **2017**, *92*, 012002. [CrossRef]
11. Rapant, S.; Letkovičová, A.; Jurkovičová, D.; Kosmovský, V.; Kožíšek, F.; Jurkovič, Ľ. Differences in Health Status of Slovak Municipalities Supplied with Drinking Water of Different Hardness Values. *Environ. Geochem. Health* **2021**, *43*, 2665–2677. [CrossRef]
12. Whelton, A.J.; Dietrich, A.M.; Burlingame, G.A.; Schechs, M.; Duncan, S.E. Minerals in Drinking Water: Impacts on Taste and Importance to Consumer Health. *Water Sci. Technol.* **2007**, *55*, 283–291. [CrossRef] [PubMed]
13. Nelson, N.; De Luca, A. Remineralization and Stabilization of Desalinated Water. In *Pathways and Challenges for Efficient Desalination*; IntechOpen: London, UK, 2022.
14. Birnhack, L.; Shlesinger, N.; Lahav, O. A Cost-Effective Method for Improving the Quality of Inland Desalinated Brackish Water Destined for Agricultural Irrigation. *Desalination* **2010**, *262*, 152–160. [CrossRef]
15. Bang, D.P. Upflow Limestone Contactor for Soft and Desalinated Water. Master's Thesis, Delft University of Technology, Delft, The Netherlands, 2012.
16. Lehmann, O.; Birnhack, L.; Lahav, O. Design Aspects of Calcite-Dissolution Reactors Applied for Post Treatment of Desalinated Water. *Desalination* **2013**, *314*, 1–9. [CrossRef]

17. Van Schagen, K.M. Model-Based Control of Drinking-Water Treatment Plants. Ph.D. Thesis, Technical University of Delft, Delft, The Netherlands, 2009.
18. Kramer, O.; Jobse, M.A.; Baars, E.T.; van der Helm, A.W.C.; Colin, M.G.; Kors, L.J.; van Vugt, W.H. Model-Based Prediction of Fluid Bed State in Full-Scale Drinking Water Pellet Softening Reactors. In Proceedings of the 2nd IWA New Developments in IT & Water Conference, Amsterdam, The Netherlands, 8–10 February 2015; pp. 8–10.
19. Derco, J.; Dudáš, J.; Luptáková, A.; Vrabeľ, M. Method of Increasing the Content of Mineral Substances in Water and Equipment for Performing This Method. (Industrial Property Office of the Slovak Republic—WebRegisters PP 50035-2018). Available online: https://wbr.indprop.gov.sk/WebRegistre/Patent/Detail/50035-2018 (accessed on 6 November 2023).
20. Ca and Mg Extraction from Rocks: Laboratory Tests. Available online: https://fns.uniba.sk/fileadmin/prif/envi/kge/LifeWater/PDF/Sum_of_Laboratory_tests_of_water_recarbonation_Ca_Mg.pdf (accessed on 3 November 2023).
21. Richardson, J.F.; Zaki, W.N. Sedimentation and Fluidisation: Part I. *Trans. Instn. Chem. Eng.* **1954**, *32*, 35–53. [CrossRef]
22. Dudáš, J.; Derco, J.; Kurák, T.; Šoltýsová, N.; Jelemenský, Ľ.; Vrabeľ, M. Design, Scale-Up, and Construction of Drinking Water Recarbonization Fluidized Bed Reactor System. *Processes* **2022**, *10*, 2068. [CrossRef]
23. Rice, E.W.; Baird, R.B.; Eaton, A.D.; Clesceri, L.S.; American Public Health Association; American Water Works Association. *Water Environment Federation Standard Methods for Examination of Water and Wastewater 2012*; American Public Health Association: Washington, DC, USA, 2012.
24. Mulcahy, L.T.; Shieh, W.K.; Lamotta, E.J. Simplified Mathematical Models for a Fludized Bed Biofilm Reactors. *Am. Inst. Chem. Eng.* **1981**, *209*, 273–285.
25. Olejko, Š. Study of Drinking Water Treatability and Environmental Aspects of Water Flows. In *Sub-Task 02: Treatment of Drinking Water Mineralization*; Final Report of the Task 1999; VÚVH: Bratislava, Slovakia, 1999.
26. Dang, J.S.; Harvey, D.M.; Jobbagy, A.; Grady, C.P.L. Evaluation of Biodegradation Kinetics with Respirometric Data. *Res. J. Water Pollut. Control Fed.* **1989**, *61*, 1711–1721.
27. Nelder, J.A.; Mead, R. A Simplex Method for Function Minimization. *Comput. J.* **1965**, *7*, 308–313. [CrossRef]
28. Ministry of Health of the Slovak Republic. Decree No. 247/2017 Coll. Slovak Standard Values for Drinking Water. 2017. Available online: https://www.slov-lex.sk/pravne-predpisy/SK/ZZ/2017/247/20171015 (accessed on 6 November 2023).
29. Pitter, P. *Hydrochemistry*, 5th ed.; University of Chemistry and Technology: Prague, Czech Republic, 2015; p. 792.

Disclaimer/Publisher's Note: The statements, opinions and data contained in all publications are solely those of the individual author(s) and contributor(s) and not of MDPI and/or the editor(s). MDPI and/or the editor(s) disclaim responsibility for any injury to people or property resulting from any ideas, methods, instructions or products referred to in the content.

Article

Preparation of PVA/SA-FMB Microspheres and Their Adsorption of Cr(VI) in Aqueous Solution

Jinlong Zuo [1], Jin Ren [1], Liming Jiang [1], Chong Tan [1], Junsheng Li [1], Zhi Xia [1,*] and Wei Wang [2,*]

[1] School of Food Science and Engineering, Harbin University of Commerce, Harbin 150028, China; 101760@hrbcu.edu.cn (J.Z.); 15103558302@163.com (J.R.); 101716@hrbcu.edu.cn (L.J.); 102776@hrbcu.edu.cn (C.T.); 101719@hrbcu.edu.cn (J.L.)
[2] State Key Laboratory of Urban Water Resource and Environment, School of Environment, Harbin Institute of Technology, Harbin 150090, China
* Correspondence: 102820@hrbcu.edu.cn (Z.X.); wangweirs@hit.edu.cn (W.W.)

Abstract: Biochar, a carbon-dense material known for its substantial specific surface area, remarkable porosity, diversity of functional groups, and cost-effective production, has garnered widespread acclaim as a premier adsorbent for the elimination of heavy metal ions and organic contaminants. Nevertheless, the application of powdered biochar is hindered by the challenges associated with its separation from aqueous solutions, and without appropriate management, it risks becoming hazardous waste. To facilitate its use as an immobilization medium, biochar necessitates modification. In this investigation, sodium alginate, celebrated for its superior gelation capabilities, was amalgamated with polyvinyl alcohol to bolster mechanical robustness, thereby embedding biochar to formulate sodium alginate biochar microspheres (PVA/SA-FMB). A meticulously designed response surface methodology experiment was employed to ascertain the optimal synthesis conditions for PVA/SA-FMB. Characterization outcomes unveiled a highly developed surface abundant in functional groups and confirmed the successful incorporation of iron ions. Adsorption trials revealed that at a temperature of 25 °C and a pH of 2, the adsorption capacity of PVA/SA-FMB for Cr(VI) was 13.7 mg/g within the initial 30 min, reaching an equilibrium capacity of 26.03 mg/g after 1440 min. Notably, the material sustained a Cr(VI) removal efficiency exceeding 90% across five cycles, underscoring its rapid and effective Cr(VI) eradication performance. Kinetic and isothermal adsorption analyses suggested that the adsorption of Cr(VI) adheres to a pseudo-second-order kinetic model and the Freundlich isotherm, indicative of monolayer adsorption dominated by reaction mechanisms. X-ray photoelectron spectroscopy (XPS) analysis inferred that the adsorption mechanism predominantly encompasses electrostatic attraction, redox processes, and complex formation.

Keywords: biochar; sodium alginate microspheres; adsorption; Cr(VI)

1. Introduction

The adsorption technique emerges as a notably efficient and convenient strategy for the removal of metal ions, consistent with established theories encompassing adsorption thermodynamics, kinetics, and isotherms. This method integrates chemisorption, involving complexation reactions, with physisorption, characterized by electrostatic interactions between heavy metal ions and adsorbents [1]. The critical challenge lies in identifying adsorbents that exhibit both high capacity and selectivity for metal ion removal. Presently, the array of adsorbents spans activated carbon, biomass, graphene oxide, various carbon-based materials, nanoparticles, and synthetic polymers [2]. Despite their utility, traditional adsorbents like biochar suffer from limitations such as limited adsorption capacity and slow kinetic rates. Recent advancements have focused on enhancing the activity of adsorbents using methods like chemical structure modification, crosslinking, and grafting.

Sodium alginate (SA), a naturally occurring, water-soluble polysaccharide extracted from kelp or brown algae, stands out as an environmentally friendly option due to its cost-effectiveness, non-toxicity, biodegradability, and biocompatibility [3,4]. It is composed of β-D mannuronic acid (ManA) and α-L guluronic acid (GulA) in variable proportions and sequences, offering exceptional gelling properties. However, its application in heavy metal adsorption is often hindered by limited porosity, mechanical strength, stability, and thermal resistance, necessitating modifications to improve its performance characteristics. The chemical structure of SA, depicted in Figure 1, illustrates its potential for modification and enhancement in adsorption applications.

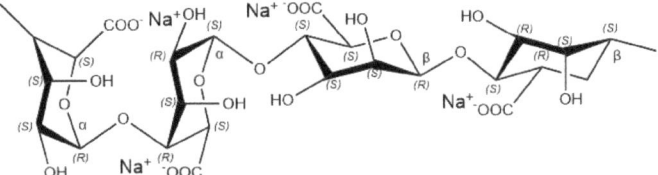

Figure 1. Chemical structure formula of sodium alginate.

Crosslinking significantly transforms the solubility characteristics of sodium alginate (SA) and augments the mechanical robustness of the adsorbent by fostering a three-dimensional (3D) network [5]. This advancement in crosslinking technology has bolstered the SA matrix, creating a durable 3D framework that plays a crucial role in the more efficacious entrapment of heavy metal ions. The deliberate integration of biochar not only amplifies the composite's structural resilience but also elevates its environmental compatibility, positioning it as a potent candidate in the heavy metal ion adsorption arena. This enhancement process is facilitated by crosslinking agents, which foster the linkage of macromolecular entities to SA via diverse mechanisms, including ion exchange, polyelectrolyte crosslinking, hydrogen bonding, hydrophobic interactions, condensation polymerization, chemical grafting polymerization, and free radical polymerization. These methodologies ingeniously modify SA's inherent solubility and bolster its mechanical attributes [6,7]. Prominent crosslinking agents encompass calcium chloride, glutaraldehyde, epichlorohydrin, formaldehyde, and concentrated sulfuric acid.

In ion crosslinking, the guluronic acid (GulA) units in SA predominantly serve as the binding locales. The carboxylate groups on these units are adept at chelating with divalent or polyvalent metal ions, which supplant the sodium ions (Na+) in various SA molecular strands, thereby interlinking them and crafting a hydrogel network [8]. Calcium chloride is particularly esteemed as a crosslinking agent due to the optimal size of the Ca(II) ions for interacting with the -OH and -COOH groups on the polysaccharide chains. This synergy, coupled with the surface charge density of Ca(II), culminates in the creation of a formidable physical crosslinking lattice [9]. The ratio of mannuronic acid (ManA) to guluronic acid (GulA) monomers in SA critically influences the characteristics of the resultant hydrogels, with an elevated GulA content generally leading to enhanced mechanical properties.

Covalent crosslinking capitalizes on the -OH and -COOH groups on the SA molecular chain as anchorage points. Crosslinking agents such as glutaraldehyde and polyethylene glycol (PEG-200) are deployed, resulting in the genesis of hydrogels. This technique further refines the structural and functional efficacy of SA across various domains [10].

Embedding modification entails the judicious selection of appropriate filler materials for integration into SA, aiming to surmount challenges associated with fine material loss and recovery, while simultaneously boosting adsorption efficiency and environmental adaptability. The overall performance of the resultant composite material is intimately linked to the type, amount, and concentration of the incorporated substances. Filler materials commonly employed include activated carbon, biochar, graphene, and carbon nanotubes [11,12]. When embedded into SA, these substances significantly enhance the composite's structural and functional traits, rendering it more apt for diverse applications, especially those necessitating efficient adsorption properties.

The profusion of hydroxyl and carboxyl groups in SA endows it with a pronounced affinity for adsorbing heavy metal ions. By amalgamating biochar, renowned for its porous architecture and extensive surface area, with SA, a composite has been developed that transcends the limitations of conventional adsorbents, such as inferior capacity and sluggish kinetics, while showcasing superior adsorption capabilities. This study delves into the composite's morphology, structure, elemental composition, and functional groups, alongside scrutinizing its adsorption dynamics under varying conditions to unravel the mechanisms underlying Cr(VI) adsorption.

2. Materials and Methods

2.1. Experimental Reagents

Corn straw biomass was collected from the experimental field (from Harbin University of Commerce); Ferric chloride(FeCl$_3$, AR) from Tianjin Beilian Fine Chemicals Development Co., Ltd. (Tianjin, China); Sodium alginate(SA, AR) from Qingdao Mingyue Seaweed Group Co., Ltd. (Qingdao, China); Polyvinyl alcohol(PVA, AR) from Shanxi Sanwei Group Co., Ltd. (Linfen, China); Calcium carbonate(CaCO$_3$, AR) from Xilong Science Co., Ltd. (Shantou, China); Hydrochloric acid(HCl, AR) from Nanjing Chemical Reagent Co., Ltd. (Nanjing, China); Sodium hydroxide(NaOH, AR) from Tianjin Continental Chemical Reagent Factory (Tianjin, China).

2.2. Preparation of PVA/SA-FMB Microsphere

2.2.1. Preparation of the FMB

A measured quantity of 10 g of corn stover biomass was measured and placed in a 100 mL beaker, and then immersed in 100 mL of 2 mol/L FeCl$_3$ solution, maintaining a solid-to-liquid ratio of 1:10 (g/mL). This mixture underwent magnetic stirring for 30 min, followed by a 30 min water bath at 80 °C. Afterward, the biomass was separated from the solution, dried, and then pyrolyzed at a temperature of 500 °C in a nitrogen (N$_2$) atmosphere. Once cooled to room temperature, the biomass was washed repeatedly with deionized (DI) water to remove chloride ions and then dried at 80 °C. This process yielded FeCl$_3$-modified corn stover biochar, referred to as FeCl$_3$-modified biochar (FMB), which was subsequently sealed and stored for future use.

2.2.2. Preparation of PVA/SA Solution

Polyvinyl alcohol (PVA) was dissolved in boiling water until it formed a clear solution, which was then cooled to room temperature. A total of 0.6% of SA was then added to this PVA solution and water-bathed at 60 °C for 90 min to obtain the PVA/SA solution.

2.2.3. Preparation of PVA/SA-FMB Microspheres

Biochar was ultrasonically dispersed in a PVA/SA-FMB solution, to which 0.6 g of CaCO$_3$ was added and magnetically stirred for an hour. This solution was then dripped into a FeCl$_3$ solution to form ionic crosslinked gel balls, which were hardened for 24 h. The gel balls were washed with distilled water to remove surface Fe^{3+} ions, treated in HCl solution for 2 h to create porous PVA/SA-FMB microspheres, and finally dried and stored at 40 °C.

2.3. Optimization of Parameters for the Preparation of PVA/SA-FMB Microspheres

The study optimized crucial parameters for preparing PVA/SA-FMB microspheres, focusing on SA concentration, the SA-to-PVA ratio, CaCO$_3$ concentration, crosslinking solution concentration, and pickling time. Using response surface methodology (RSM), we examined how these factors influenced Cr(VI) adsorption using PVA/SA-FMB microspheres to determine the optimal preparation conditions.

2.4. Characterization and Principle of Materials

- Element composition analysis: An element analyzer was utilized to quantitatively assess the elemental composition of biochar, focusing primarily on carbon (C) and oxygen (O).
- X-ray diffraction (XRD) analysis: The phase structure of the materials was studied using a EVASTAR Y2 X-ray diffractometer from Suzhou Ivan Zhitong (Suzhou, China), covering a test range of $2\theta = 10–90°$.
- Surface area and pore size analysis (BET): The pore structures of different biochars have their own characteristics. The specific surface area, total pore volume, and average pore diameter of the test samples were analyzed using the ChemStation-001 type nitrogen adsorption–desorption instrument from mainland China (Zhejiang, China) to examine the types of adsorption–desorption curves.
- Scanning electron microscope (SEM): In this experiment, the morphology of the samples was observed using a Supra55 scanning electron microscope from the German company Zeiss (Jena, Germany), with an EHT of 15 KV. Before testing, the samples were thoroughly dried and sputter-coated with gold.
- X-ray photoelectron spectroscopy (XPS): In this experiment, the elemental composition and valence state information of the samples were characterized using the ESCALAB 250 X-ray photoelectron spectrometer(Thermo Fisher Scientific Company, Waltham, MA, USA). The Al Kα radiation was 1486.6 eV, with a vacuum level better than 5×10^{-10} mbar.
- Fourier transform infrared spectroscopy (FTIR): The structure of the samples was characterized using the VERTEX 80 Infrared-Raman spectrometer from the German company Bruker (Berlin, Germany), with a spectral range of 4000–400 cm^{-1} and a resolution of 0.07 cm^{-1}.

2.5. Evaluation of Adsorption Properties

Single factor adsorption experiment: Different quantities of adsorbent were added to 50 mL solutions of varying concentrations of Cr(VI). The pH of the Cr(VI) solution was adjusted, and the mixture was subjected to a constant temperature water bath oscillation at 25 °C and 140 r/min for 24 h. Post-experiment, the solutions were filtered through a 0.22 μm membrane, the Cr(VI) concentration in each sample was measured by UV-Vis spectrophotometry, and the removal rate and amount were calculated.

Adsorption kinetics experiment: A total of 0.1 g of adsorbent was mixed with 50 mL of 50 mg/L Cr(VI) solution and oscillated in a 25 °C, followed by 140 r/min constant temperature water bath at various intervals (0, 10, 30, 60, 90, 120, 180, 360, 540, 720, and 1440 min). The absorbance of residual Cr(VI) was measured to determine the removal rate and adsorption capacity.

Isothermal adsorption experiment: Cr(VI) solutions of pH 2 and concentrations ranging from 10 mg/L to 100 mg/L were prepared, with 0.1 g of adsorbent added to each. These were oscillated in a 25 °C, followed by 140 r/min constant temperature water bath for 24 h and then filtered through a 0.22 μm membrane to evaluate the removal rate and adsorption capacity.

Adsorption cycle regeneration experiment: A total of 0.1 g of adsorbent was added to a 50 mL, 50 mg/L Cr(VI) solution (pH 2) and oscillated under the same conditions as above for 24 h. After reaching adsorption saturation, the adsorbent was placed in a 50 mL eluent (0.1 mol/L NaOH) and oscillated again to release Cr(VI). The regenerated adsorbent's efficiency in removing Cr(VI) was then assessed.

3. Results and Discussion

3.1. Optimization of Preparation Parameters for PVA/SA-FMB Microspheres

3.1.1. Analysis of Single Factor Test Results

1. The effect of SA concentration on the preparation of PVA/SA-FMB microspheres

Figure 2 underscores the paramount importance of SA concentration in the morphogenesis of PVA/SA-FMB microspheres, delineating a concentration-dependent impact on their structural integrity and formation efficacy. At suboptimal concentrations below 0.6% (w/v), the resultant low viscosity of the solution is detrimental to effective microsphere formation, culminating in the development of flocculent structures and microspheres with compromised durability, prone to disintegration during adsorption processes. This phenomenon is attributed to an inadequate SA quantity, insufficient to counteract PVA agglomeration [13,14]. In contrast, concentrations surpassing 0.6% (w/v) induce an excessive viscosity, obstructing the syringe extrusion process and leading to the formation of microspheres with irregular shapes and the potential for syringe nozzle obstructions.

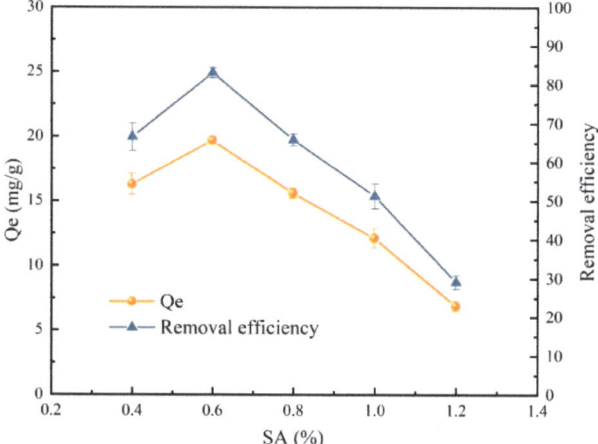

Figure 2. Influence of SA concentration on adsorption of Cr(VI) by PVA/SA-FMB microspheres (C_0 = 50 mg/L, V = 50 mL, pH = 2.0, T = 25 °C).

The optimal formation of microspheres, marked by uniformity and spherical morphology, is realized at an SA concentration of 0.6% (w/v). This observation highlights the criticality of precise SA concentration in achieving the desired physical properties of PVA/SA-FMB microspheres, balancing between solution viscosity and syringe extrudability. It establishes a threshold concentration for SA that ensures the production of structurally robust and morphologically consistent microspheres, essential for their application in environmental remediation, particularly for the adsorption of heavy metal ions.

2. Effect of PVA concentration on the preparation of PVA/SA-FMB microspheres

In the synthesis of PVA/SA-FMB microspheres, PVA is instrumental in augmenting the mechanical resilience of the microspheres. An insufficiency of PVA compromises their structural fortitude, rendering them incapable of withstanding the rigors of the adsorption process. Conversely, a PVA concentration exceeding 3% enhances mechanical properties but concurrently impairs the adsorption efficiency for Cr(VI), likely due to the resultant denser microsphere structure which impedes mass transfer [15]. Figure 3 illustrates that a PVA concentration of 2.4% (w/v) strikes an optimal equilibrium between mechanical robustness and adsorptive capacity, facilitating the most effective Cr(VI) removal in PVA/SA-FMB microspheres. This concentration allows for a substantial adsorption capacity of 22 mg/g for Cr(VI) following a 24 h oscillatory adsorption procedure, underscoring the microspheres' proficiency under these conditions.

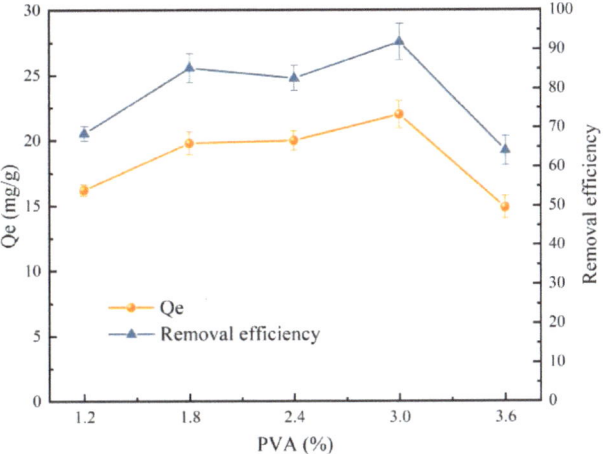

Figure 3. Influence of PVA concentration on adsorption of Cr(VI) by PVA/SA-FMB microspheres (C_0 = 50 mg/L, V = 50 mL, pH = 2.0, T = 25 °C).

3. Influence of FMB mass on the preparation of PVA/SA-FMB microspheres

Figure 4 delineates a discernible pattern in the adsorptive dynamics of PVA/SA-FMB microspheres. Initially, an increase in FMB mass correlates positively with enhanced Cr(VI) adsorption capacity, highlighting FMB's pivotal contribution to the adsorption mechanism amidst constituents such as SA, PVA, and calcium carbonate ($CaCO_3$). Nevertheless, this upward trajectory in adsorption capacity plateaus and subsequently diminishes upon exceeding an FMB mass of 0.3 g. This downturn is attributed to the complications in achieving uniform FMB dispersion within the solution at higher concentrations. Excess FMB not only poses challenges like syringe clogging during microsphere fabrication but also compromises microsphere integrity. Optimal adsorption efficiency, therefore, necessitates a judicious balance in FMB content, ensuring both effective Cr(VI) adsorption and the structural cohesiveness of the microspheres.

4. Influence of $CaCO_3$ mass on the preparation of PVA/SA-FMB microspheres

Investigating the impact of varied $CaCO_3$ masses on Cr(VI) adsorption using PVA)/SA- FMB microspheres and experiments with $CaCO_3$ masses of 0.3 g, 0.6 g, 0.9 g, 1.2 g, and 1.5 g were conducted. Figure 5 illustrates an initial enhancement in the microspheres' adsorptive performance with increasing $CaCO_3$ mass, attributable to the intensified interactions between Ca(II) ions and the guluronic (G) units of SA. However, a notable stabilization in the adsorption rate at approximately 20 mg/g is observed beyond a $CaCO_3$ mass of 0.6 g. This leveling effect is linked to the achievement of an equilibrium state between dehydration and water reabsorption processes, facilitating stable gel formation [16]. Furthermore, under consistent hydrochloric acid (HCl) concentration and exposure duration, the internal microporosity of the PVA/SA-FMB microspheres remains unchanged beyond the threshold CaCO$_3$ mass required for optimal chemical interaction with HCl.

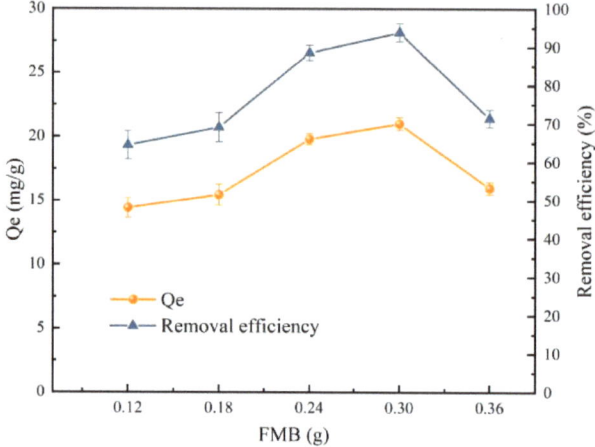

Figure 4. Influence of FMB mass on adsorption of Cr(VI) by PVA/SA-FMB microspheres (C$_0$ = 50 mg/L, V = 50 mL, pH = 2.0, T = 25 °C).

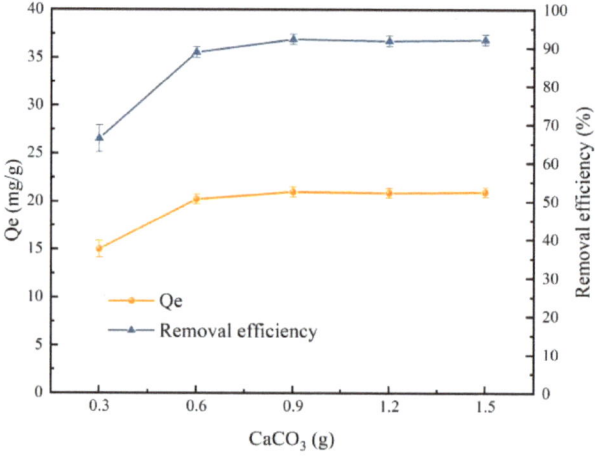

Figure 5. Influence of CaCO$_3$ mass on adsorption of Cr(VI) by PVA/SA-FMB microspheres (C$_0$ = 50 mg/L, m = 0.1 g, V = 50 mL, pH = 2.0, T = 25 °C).

3.1.2. Establishment and Analysis of the RSM Model

1. Design of RSM test

Employing the Box–Behnken response surface design [17], the study delineated four critical determinants in the synthesis of PVA)/SA-FMB microspheres: SA concentration (A),

PVA concentration (B), FMB mass (C), and CaCO$_3$ mass (D), targeting adsorption capacity as the response variable. A structured four-factor, three-level response surface analysis was executed, as encapsulated in Table 1, to establish the paramount preparation conditions.

Table 1. Factors and levels of response surface test.

Variables	Code	Horizontal Coding		
		−1	0	1
SA/%	A	0.4	0.6	0.8
PVA/%	B	2.4	3	3.6
CaCO$_3$/g	C	0.3	0.6	0.9
FMB/g	D	0.24	0.3	0.36

2. Establishment and analysis of the regression model

Adhering to the Box–Behnken design framework, this study scrutinized the Cr(VI) adsorption efficacy of PVA/SA-FMB microspheres under diverse composite conditions. Data accrued from these evaluations were meticulously analyzed to pinpoint the optimal parameters for microsphere synthesis, with outcomes tabulated in Table 2. This analysis confirmed that the interplay among the four scrutinized parameters adheres to a quadratic model. Consequently, the adsorption capacity (Qe) of the PVA/SA-FMB microspheres is quantitatively delineated by an equation comprising coded variables, as specified in Equation (1). Within this equation, a positive coefficient before a term delineates a synergistic influence, while a negative coefficient signifies an antagonistic impact.

$$Y = 25.32 + 0.46 \times A - B + 0.42 \times C - 0.45 \times D - 0.27 \times A \times B + 0.36 \times A \times C - 1.43 \times A \times D + 0.18 \times B \times C + 0.69 \times B \times D - 0.67 C \times D - 4.27 \times A^2 - 1.20 \times B^2 - 5.34 \times C^2 - 0.57 \times D^2 \quad (1)$$

Table 2. Design and results of response surface test.

No.	A	B	C	D	Adsorption Amount of Cr(VI)/mg/g		No.	A	B	C	D	Adsorption Amount of Cr(VI)/mg/g	
					Test Value	Predicted Value						Test Value	Predicted Value
1	−1	−1	0	0	18.95	19.41	16	0	1	1	0	19.05	19.08
2	1	−1	0	0	20.71	20.86	17	−1	0	−1	0	15.59	15.2
3	−1	1	0	0	18.86	19.36	18	1	0	−1	0	15.64	15.38
4	1	1	0	0	19.53	19.74	19	−1	0	1	0	15.81	15.31
5	0	0	−1	−1	18.9	18.77	20	1	0	1	0	17.31	16.95
6	0	0	1	−1	20.63	20.95	21	0	−1	0	−1	25.12	24.98
7	0	0	−1	1	18.87	19.22	22	0	1	0	−1	23.52	23.01
8	0	0	1	1	17.92	18.71	23	0	−1	0	1	22.96	22.71
9	−1	0	0	−1	18.89	19.04	24	0	1	0	1	24.1	23.49
10	1	0	0	−1	22.5	22.82	25	0	0	0	0	24.96	25.32
11	−1	0	0	1	21.23	21.01	26	0	0	0	0	24.88	25.32
12	1	0	0	1	19.12	19.06	27	0	0	0	0	26.14	25.32
13	0	−1	−1	0	18.76	18.83	28	0	0	0	0	25.47	25.32
14	0	1	−1	0	17.51	17.88	29	0	0	0	0	25.15	25.32
15	0	−1	1	0	19.59	19.31							

The precision of the model was quantified using the correlation coefficient R^2, with values closer to 1 indicating a tighter concordance between model predictions and empirical observations. For this model, an R^2 of 0.9855 was reported, signifying a notably high accuracy in its predictive capability. The disparity between predicted outcomes and actual data was observed to be less than 0.2, affirming the model's reliability. A detailed juxtaposition of actual measured values against the predictions derived from the model's equation is presented in Table 2.

3. Response regression analysis

The model's validity was established through F-value and p-value analysis, as detailed in Table 3, highlighting the significance of SA concentration, ferric oxide-modified biochar quality, and PVA concentration as impactful model terms. ANOVA results underscored a coefficient of determination (R^2) at 0.9855 and an adjusted R^2 (R^2adj) of 0.9711, elucidating that the model accounts for 97.11% of the response variability. The model's precision, quantified at 25.804, far exceeds the benchmark of 4, reinforcing its appropriateness. With a Coefficient of Variation (CV) at 2.65%, markedly below the 10% threshold, the model's reliability and accuracy are affirmed. These analytical outcomes collectively confirm the regression equation's robustness and its capacity to accurately predict experimental results, validating the model's applicability for determining the optimal synthesis parameters for PVA/SA-FMB microspheres.

Table 3. Results of response surface regression analysis.

Items	Sum of Squares	Degrees of Freedom	Mean Square	F-Value	p-Value	Significance
Model	221.27	14	15.8	85.33	<0.0001	**
A	3.5	1	3.5	18.88	0.0117	*
B	0.12	1	0.12	0.67	0.0836	
C	3.03	1	3.03	16.34	0.0187	**
D	2.67	1	2.67	14.43	0.0131	*
AB	1.54	1	1.54	8.29	0.3395	
AC	0.53	1	0.53	2.84	0.2048	
AD	7.08	1	7.08	38.22	0.0001	*
BC	0.13	1	0.13	0.69	0.5227	
BD	0.86	1	0.86	4.62	0.0245	*
CD	0.71	1	0.71	3.82	0.0276	*
A^2	92.01	1	92.01	496.79	<0.0001	**
B^2	6.98	1	6.98	37.7	<0.0001	**
C^2	136.42	1	136.42	736.54	<0.0001	**
D^2	0.41	1	0.41	2.2	0.0191	*
Residual	2.59	14	0.19			
Missing fitting item	1.54	10	0.15	0.58	0.4732	
Absolute error	1.05	4	0.26			
Total	223.86	28				

Note: $p < 0.01$, extremely significant "**"; $p < 0.05$, significant "*".

4. Optimized model response surface analysis

The three-dimensional (3D) response surface diagrams are instrumental in delineating the regression equation, offering a visual exposition of how each variable's response value correlates with its test value. Figures 6–8 display the response surface models for variables such as SA concentration, ferric oxide-modified biochar mass, $CaCO_3$ mass, and PVA concentration, illustrating their respective impacts on Cr(VI) adsorption rates. Notably, the contour shapes within these figures underscore the interactions between variable pairs [18].

Figure 6 elucidates the relationship between $CaCO_3$ mass and SA concentration with respect to Cr(VI) adsorption capacity. An increase in SA concentration from 0.4 wt% to 0.8 wt% leads to a peak in Cr(VI) adsorption rates at an SA concentration of 0.6 wt%, with an elliptical contour shape and a p-value of AD below 0.05 (0.0001) signifying a significant interaction between $CaCO_3$ mass and SA concentration on Cr(VI) adsorption.

Figure 7 showcases the impact of $CaCO_3$ mass and PVA concentration on Cr(VI) adsorption rates through response surface and contour lines. It reveals that increasing PVA concentration from 1.8 wt% to 3 wt%, with a constant $CaCO_3$ mass, leads to a decrease in Cr(VI) adsorption, underscoring the influence of PVA concentration. The elliptical contours and a p-value of 0.0245 (below 0.05) indicate a significant interaction between $CaCO_3$ mass and PVA concentration, emphasizing their critical role in modulating Cr(VI) adsorption rates.

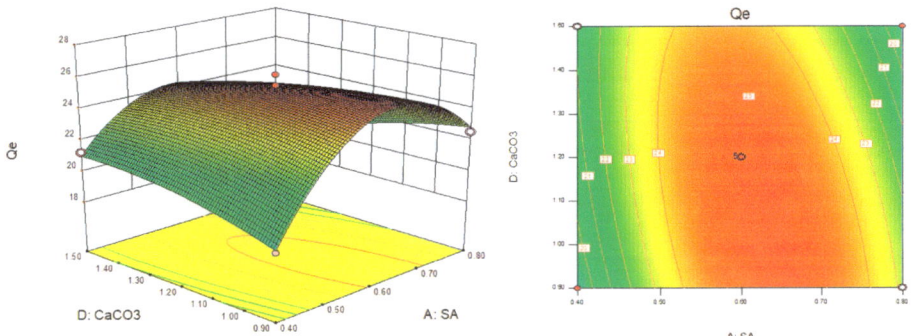

Figure 6. Response surfaces and contours of SA and PVA concentrations on Cr(VI) adsorption capacity.

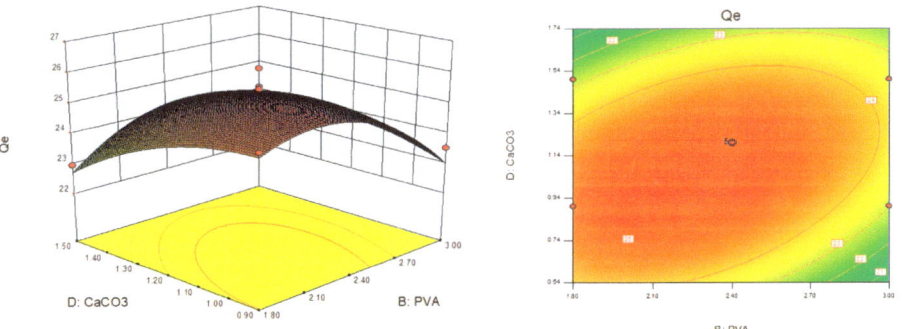

Figure 7. Response surfaces and contours of $CaCO_3$ mass and PVA concentration on Cr(VI) adsorption capacity.

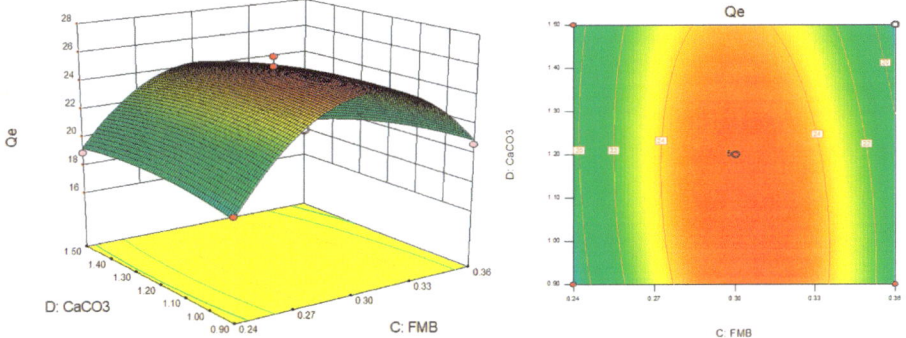

Figure 8. Response surfaces and contours of $CaCO_3$ mass and FMB mass on Cr(VI) adsorption capacity.

Figure 8 displays the response surface and contour lines representing the influence of $CaCO_3$ mass and FMB mass on the Qe for Cr(VI). According to the figure, the optimal adsorption rate of Cr(VI) occurs when the FMB mass is at 0.3 g. The elliptical shape of the contour lines and a p-value for the interaction (AD) of 0.0276, which is less than 0.05, indicate a significant interaction between the masses of $CaCO_3$ and FMB in affecting Cr(VI) adsorption. Furthermore, the analysis suggests that the interaction between SA concentration and PVA concentration does not significantly influence the efficiency of Cr(VI) removal.

The three-dimensional analysis provided a deeper insight into the interactions among different variables and their influence on achieving optimal conditions. The relative importance of the four response parameters affecting the Qe of Cr(VI) was established in the following order: $CaCO_3$ content, SA concentration, FMB quality, and PVA concentration. Using Design Expert 8.0 software for analysis, the optimal preparation conditions for PVA/SA-FMB microspheres to attain the highest Cr(VI) adsorption performance were determined. The ideal concentrations and amounts were found to be an SA concentration of 0.73 t%, a PVA concentration of 3 wt%, an FMB mass of 0.31 g, and a $CaCO_3$ concentration of 1 g. Under these conditions, the microspheres are expected to exhibit maximum efficiency in adsorbing Cr(VI) from solutions.

3.2. Characterization and Principle of the Materials

3.2.1. Analysis of Element Composition

The elemental composition analysis of PVA/SA-MB and PVA/SA-FMB is shown in Table 4. Based on the ratios of O/C and (O + N)/C, it was found that PVA/SA-FMB possesses higher polarity and hydrophilicity compared to PVA/SA-MB, further proving that the polarity and hydrophilicity of adsorptive materials are closely related to their adsorption performance.

Table 4. Elemental composition of biochar.

Samples	C	O	N	O/C	(O + N)/C
PVA/SA-MB	68.85	30.09	1.06	0.4370	0.4524
PVA/SA-FMB	24.07	73.89	2.04	3.0698	3.1545

3.2.2. X-ray Diffraction (XRD) Determination

X-ray diffraction (XRD) analysis on PVA/SA, PVA/SA-MB, and PVA/SA-FMB revealed significant structural alterations attributable to the embedding modification process (Figure 9). Pure SA displayed characteristic diffraction peaks at 2θ values of 13.5° and 21.5°, absent in both PVA/SA-MB and PVA/SA-FMB, indicating modifications in SA's structure post-embedding. PVA/SA-MB retained broad biochar-associated diffraction peaks around 2θ = 16–22°, suggesting the preservation of biochar's amorphous cellulose and hemicellulose structures. Conversely, PVA/SA-FMB exhibited distinct peaks at 2θ = 20.197°, 21.440°, and 29.649°, which aligned with Fe_2O_3 and FeO standards (PDF#21-0920 and PDF#74-1886) [19], denoting the incorporation of both divalent and trivalent iron forms, indicative of complex interactions enhancing adsorption capabilities.

3.2.3. Specific Surface Area (BET) and Pore Size Analysis

The nitrogen (N_2) adsorption–desorption isotherms of PVA/SA, PVA/SA-MB, and PVA/SA-FMB, as shown in Figures 10–12, are categorized as type IV according to the International Union of Pure and Applied Chemistry (IUPAC), suggesting mesoporous or macroporous structures within the microspheres. The initial sharp increase in adsorption at low pressures indicates monolayer adsorption, affirming the microporous nature of the microspheres. The emergence of a closed hysteresis loop in the mid- to high-pressure ranges, classified as H3 type, signifies the presence of slit-like pores due to particle layering.

Pore size analysis via Non-Local Density Functional Theory (NLDFT) revealed that microspheres incorporating biochar exhibited a pronounced micro and mesopore structure within the 0–10 nm range, enhancing the overall pore architecture of PVA/SA. Conversely, the shift from larger pores in the 10–100 nm range to biochar's smaller pores during embedding improves adsorption efficacy. The specific surface area, an essential parameter for adsorbent evaluation, underscores the adsorptive capacity and delineates the intrinsic properties of the adsorbent materials, reflecting both their advantages and limitations in adsorption applications. (See Table 5).

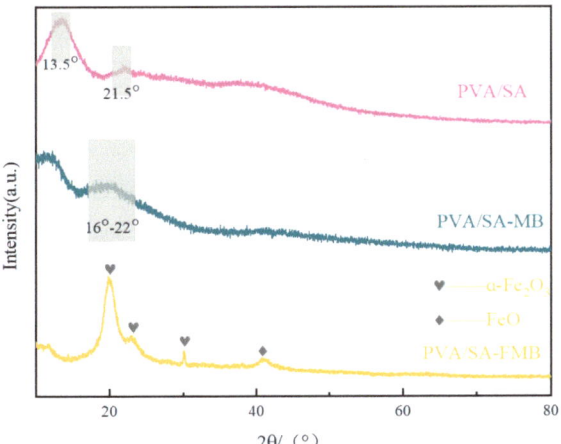

Figure 9. X-ray diffraction pattern of biochar.

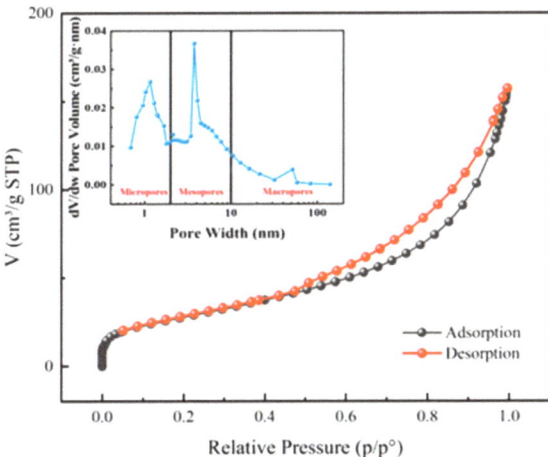

Figure 10. N_2 adsorption and desorption isotherm and pore size distribution of PVA/SA.

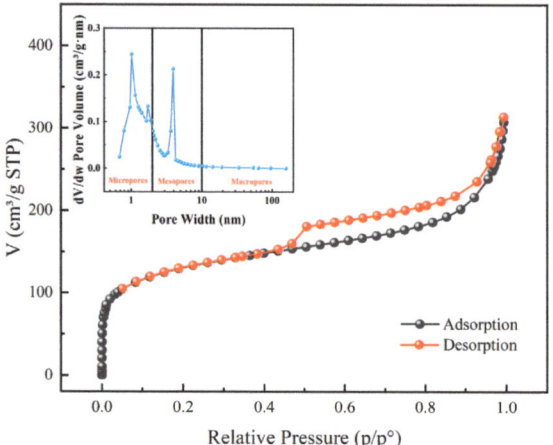

Figure 11. N_2 adsorption–desorption isotherm and pore size distribution of PVA/SA-MB.

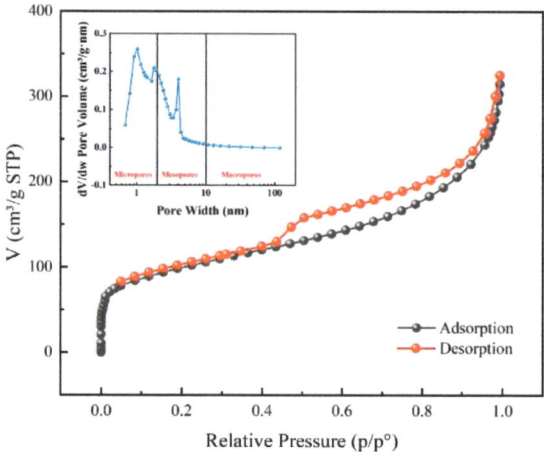

Figure 12. N_2 adsorption–desorption isotherm and pore size distribution of PVA/SA-FMB.

Table 5. Characterization parameters of specific surface area and pore structure of microspheres.

Sample	BET Surface Area/($m^2 \cdot g^{-1}$)	V/<1.1 nm ($cm^3 \cdot g^{-1}$)	V/<1.1 nm ($cm^3 \cdot g^{-1}$)	Average Pore Diameter/(nm)
PVA/SA	100.6120	0.00289	0.228412	9.21610
PVA/SA-MB	441.7465	0.09947	0.4146567	4.05464
PVA/SA-FMB	344.2612	0.16795	0.451204	5.32073

3.2.4. Scanning Electron Microscope (SEM) Determination

SEM was employed to analyze the morphology of modified microspheres, showcasing their unique advantages. Figure 13 displays the SEM images of MB, PVA/SA, PVA/SA-MB, and PVA/SA-FMB microspheres.

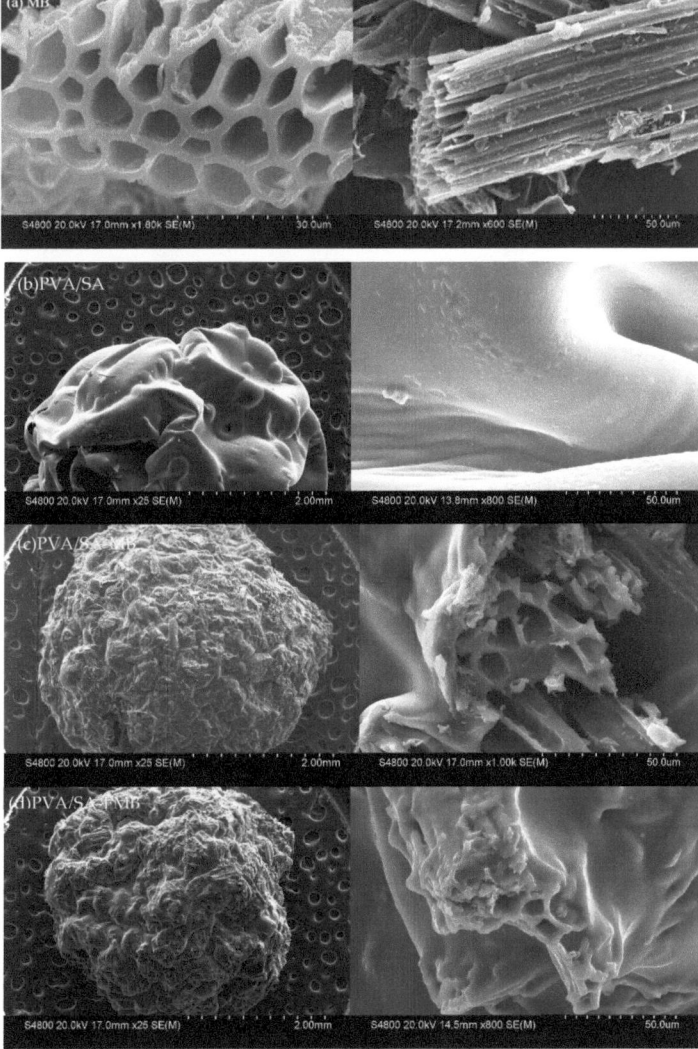

Figure 13. SEM of microspheres (**a**) MB; (**b**) PVA/SA; (**c**) PVA/SA-MB; (**d**) PVA/SA-FMB.

For PVA/SA microspheres, a smooth surface with irregular folds and limited porosity is observed, attributed to the cohesive nature of PVA. The integration of biochar, however, markedly transforms the microspheres' surface and internal architecture, introducing a rougher texture and a proliferation of pores, including distinctive honeycomb-like structures. This transformation results from biochar interfering with the original hydrogen bonds of PVA while establishing new interactions with its hydroxyl groups, thereby diminishing PVA's adhesive effect. Such alterations suggest that biochar-enhanced microspheres feature an expanded specific surface area and a more intricate pore network, augmenting their adsorptive capacity. Biochar serves as an efficient medium, augmenting the adsorption sites on PVA/SA, which in turn amplifies the microspheres' overall adsorptive performance. Specifically, PVA/SA-FMB microspheres display more pronounced and complex pore configurations than PVA/SA-MB, corroborating with the BET surface area and pore size distribution findings.

3.2.5. X-ray Photoelectron Spectroscopy (XPS) Determination

Figure 14b elucidates the C1s peak fitting in the XPS spectra of PVA/SA-MB and PVA/SA-FMB microspheres, diverging from pure biochar. This peak encompasses a spectrum of carbon bonds, notably C-C/C-H, C-O, and C=O/O-C=O, with significant absorptions at C-O and C=O, signaling the presence of carbon–oxygen compounds.

Furthermore, Figure 14c delineates the Fe 2p spectral peak in PVA/SA-FMB microspheres' XPS spectrum, demonstrating a broader and distorted peak. This feature suggests the oxidation state of iron, affirming the effective amalgamation of SA with iron. Before the adsorption of Cr(VI) by PVA/SA-FMB, five absorption peaks appeared in Figure 14c. binding energies at 710.87 eV and 724.25 eV denote divalent iron, whereas 714.76 eV and 727.56 eV correspond to trivalent iron, alongside a satellite peak at 716.9 eV linked to the Fe(II) Fe 2p3/2 orbital, indicating complex iron valence states within the microspheres.

3.2.6. Fourier Transform Infrared Spectroscopy (FTIR) Determination

Figure 15 showcases the FTIR spectra for SA and its composite microspheres (PVA/SA, PVA/SA-MB, and PVA/SA-FMB), covering the 400–4000 cm^{-1} wavelength range. SA's spectrum, displaying characteristic peaks at specified wavelengths, confirms its structural attributes [20]. The composite microspheres exhibit functional group structures akin to SA, indicating the retention of SA's chemical properties through the compounding process.

Notable across all materials is the peak at 3300 cm^{-1}, signifying -OH stretching vibrations from hydroxyl groups. The 2800–3000 cm^{-1} range highlights C-H stretching vibrations, while the 1600 cm^{-1} peak suggests C=O stretching in ketones and acids. Peaks at 1024 cm^{-1} and 818 cm^{-1} are attributed to C-H bending vibrations, with the 1420 cm^{-1} peak indicating carboxyl group stretching.

Differential features in the composite microspheres include enhanced absorption peaks at 1680 cm^{-1} and 473 cm^{-1}, indicative of a rise in oxygen-containing functional groups. The 1680 cm^{-1} peak, more prominent in PVA/SA-MB and PVA/SA-FMB, is linked to C=C stretching, suggesting biochar's role in augmenting the aromatic structure. The 473 cm^{-1} peak, associated with Fe-O bonds, underscores the successful integration of $FeCl_3$ and biochar FMB, particularly evidenced in PVA/SA-FMB, marking the effective crosslinking of Fe-containing groups in the microsphere synthesis.

3.3. Evaluation of Adsorption Properties

3.3.1. Adsorption Single Factor Experiment

1. Initial concentration

Figure 16 illustrates the impact of initial Cr(VI) concentration on the adsorption capacity of adsorbents, revealing an increase in adsorption capacity with rising Cr(VI) concentration at a stable temperature, alongside a reduction in removal rate. This pattern is ascribed to an augmented driving force necessary to counteract the mass transfer resistance of Cr(VI) across the aqueous–solid interface at elevated concentrations [21]. Notably,

PVA/SA-FMB demonstrates a pronounced adsorption capacity for Cr(VI), even at lower concentrations (10 mg/L), achieving up to 4.1 mg/g. This highlights PVA/SA-FMB's strong affinity for Cr(VI), underscoring its potential for effective Cr(VI) removal from aqueous solutions at minimal concentrations.

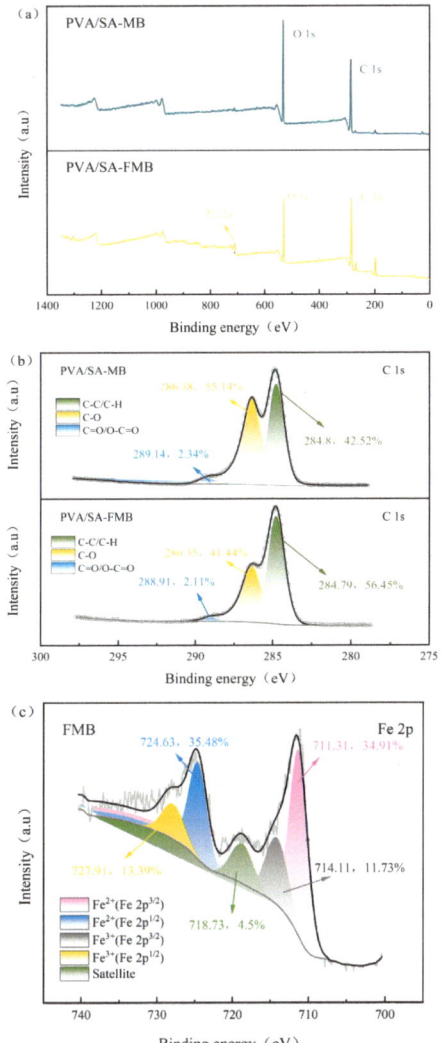

Figure 14. XPS spectrum of the microsphere. (**a**) Total spectrum; (**b**) C 1s; (**c**) Fe 2p.

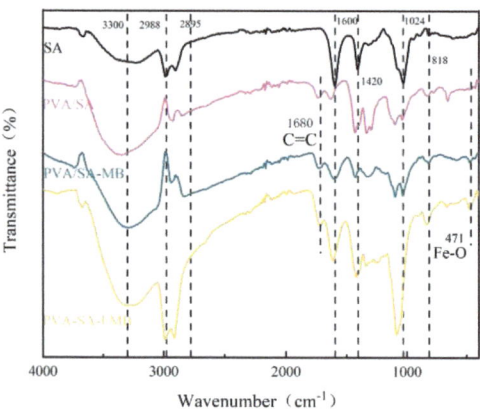

Figure 15. Infrared spectrum of microspheres.

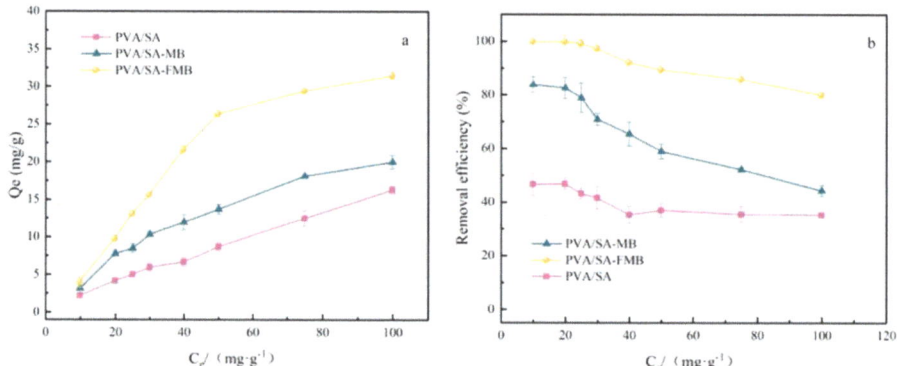

Figure 16. Effect of initial concentration on the adsorption of Cr(VI) by microspheres. (**a**) Qe; (**b**) removal efficiency.

2. Dosage

An experiment was conducted to evaluate the influence of adsorbent dosage on Cr(VI) removal efficiency using 50 mL of simulated wastewater with an initial Cr(VI) concentration of 50 mg/L and a pH of 2. Various dosages of adsorbents (0.05, 0.1, 0.15, 0.2, and 0.25 g) including PVA/SA, PVA/SA-MB, and PVA/SA-FMB, were introduced into conical flasks, which were then agitated in a constant temperature water bath at 25 °C and 140 r/min for 24 h. Following equilibrium, the residual Cr(VI) concentration was determined to assess the adsorbent dosage effect on adsorption capacity, with findings depicted in Figure 17.

The experiment revealed a distinct trend in Cr(VI) removal efficiency relative to adsorbent dosage. With increasing doses of PVA/SA, PVA/SA-MB, and PVA/SA-FMB, a notable decline in adsorption capacity per unit mass was observed, recording reductions of 2.21, 8.3, and 23.36 mg/g, respectively. Despite this, the overall adsorption efficiency for each adsorbent significantly improved by 51.9%, 63.7%, and 44.19%, respectively. This phenomenon is attributed to the presence of unsaturated adsorption sites at lower doses.

As the adsorbent dosage increased, more adsorption sites became available, enhancing the total removal efficiency. A marked increase in Cr(VI) removal efficiency was noted at an adsorbent dose of 3.0 g/L, eventually plateauing at higher doses. This plateau indicates an equilibrium state between Cr(VI) ions and the adsorbent, suggesting that further increases in adsorbent dosage beyond this point do not significantly impact Cr(VI) removal, thereby identifying an optimal adsorption capacity within the tested conditions.

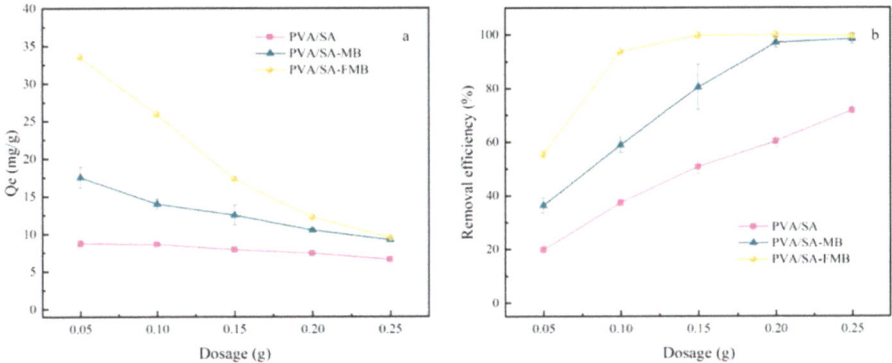

Figure 17. Effect of dosage on adsorption of Cr(VI) by biochar. (**a**) Qe; (**b**) removal efficiency.

3. pH

The response of various adsorbents to the adsorption of Cr(VI) ions is significantly influenced by the pH of the solution. To assess this effect, experiments were conducted across a pH range of 1–10, using an initial Cr(VI) ion concentration of 50.0 mg/L, an adsorbent dosage of 2 g/L, and at a temperature of 25 °C. Figure 18 illustrates the impact of pH on the removal efficiency of Cr(VI) ions by three different adsorbents.

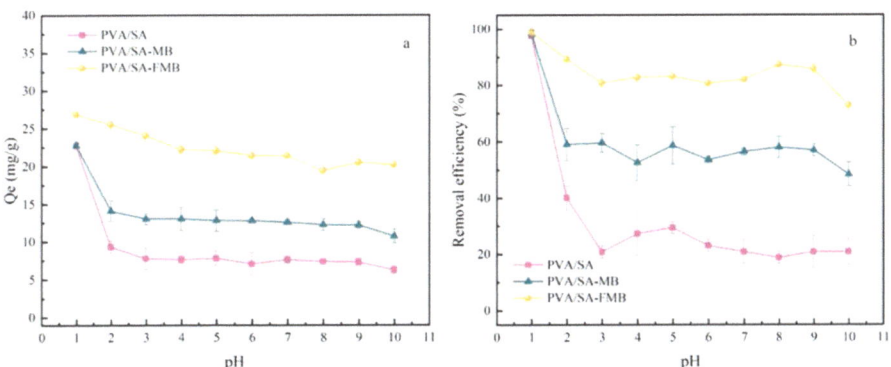

Figure 18. Effect of pH biochar on Cr(VI) adsorption. (**a**) Qe; (**b**) removal efficiency.

The analysis of Cr(VI) adsorption using different adsorbents reveals a consistent trend across the pH spectrum. All adsorbents show enhanced performance under acidic conditions compared to alkaline and neutral environments, with the highest adsorption capacity occurring at a pH of 1. As the pH increases, the efficiency of Cr(VI) adsorption declines significantly before stabilizing. The reasons for this trend are as follows: (1) At low pH, the adsorbent's positively charged functional groups interact more effectively with the negatively charged dichromate ions, thereby facilitating adsorption. (2) The hydroxyl (-OH) groups on the adsorbent act as electron donors. Under acidic conditions, these groups consume protons (H^+) from the solution, partially reducing Cr(VI) to Cr(III). As the solution becomes less acidic, the availability of H^+ diminishes, adversely affecting the adsorbent's performance [22]. (3) With increasing pH, the concentration of -OH groups increases, leading to competition between the -OH radicals and Cr(VI) ions for adsorption sites on the adsorbent's surface. These observations suggest that electrostatic interactions play a significant role in the adsorption mechanism of Cr(VI) by the microspheres, particularly under acidic conditions.

At a pH of 1, for FMB and PVA/SA-FMB, the capacities are 23.76 mg/g and 26.96 mg/g, respectively. In contrast, for MB and PVA/SA-FMB, the capacities are 22.48 mg/g and 22.81 mg/g, respectively. These values indicate that the addition of PVA/SA positively influences the adsorption capacity, likely due to PVA/SA providing an abundance of H^+ ions in the solution. At the same pH, PVA/SA-FMB always maintains the highest Cr(VI) removal rate and adsorption capacity, and is almost unaffected by the pH value of the solution. This stability is attributed to the presence of a Fe^{3+} and -OH composition buffer pair in PVA/SA-FMB, which effectively counteracts pH fluctuations, ensuring efficient adsorption performance over a wide pH range. Given that the pH of industrial wastewater containing Cr(VI) typically ranges from 2 to 3, the adsorption performance of adsorbents at pH 2 is particularly relevant and noteworthy [23].

3.3.2. Adsorption Kinetics Experiment

To further understand the mechanism of Cr(VI) removal by PVA/SA, PVA/SA-MB, and PVA/SA-FMB, as well as to identify the rate-limiting steps in the adsorption process, this study applied both quasi-first-order and quasi-second-order kinetic models to the kinetic data. Figure 19 displays the time-dependent adsorption curves for Cr(VI) using these adsorbents, with the relevant fitting parameters detailed in Table 6. For PVA/SA, the fit with the quasi-first-order model (correlation coefficient of 0.93918) was more precise than with the quasi-second-order model (0.91584), indicating that the adsorption process of PVA/SA might be primarily influenced by the rate of adsorption and the availability of free sites on the adsorbent surface. In contrast, for PVA/SA-MB and PVA/SA-FMB, the quasi-second-order kinetic model provided a better fit, with model parameters closely matching the observed equilibrium adsorption capacities, suggesting that the adsorption processes for these adsorbents might be related to the number of free sites on the adsorbent surface and the potential forces or chemical bonds formed.

Table 6. The quasi-primary and quasi-secondary kinetic fitting parameters of Cr(VI) adsorption by microspheres.

Microspheres	Q_e/(mg·g^{-1})	Quasi-First-Order Kinetics			Quasi-Second-Order Kinetics		
		Q_t/(mg·g^{-1})	k_1/min^{-1}	R^2	Q_t/(mg·g^{-1})	k_1/(g·mg^{-1}·min^{-1})	R^2
PVA/SA	9.34	9.28	0.0053	0.94	11.04	5.29×10^{-4}	0.92
PVA/SA-MB	14.07	13.36	0.0105	0.92	14.52	0.0011	0.95
PVA/SA-FMB	26.03	22.61	0.0277	0.95	24.99	0.0016	0.99

A notable finding is that PVA/SA-FMB exhibited a maximum adsorption capacity of 26.03 mg/g for Cr(VI). Remarkably, within the first 30 min, it achieved an adsorption capacity of 13.7 mg/g, accounting for 52.6% of its total capacity. This capacity increased to 76.2% (20.5 mg/g) in the following two hours. These results demonstrate the high number of active sites on PVA/SA-FMB, enabling rapid interaction with Cr(VI) and showcasing its exceptional efficiency in swiftly removing Cr(VI).

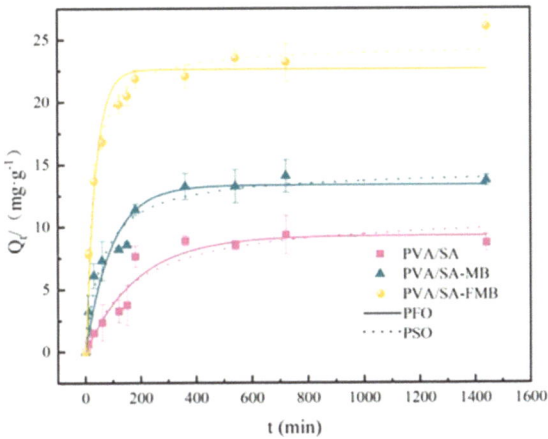

Figure 19. Fitting curve of adsorption kinetics of Cr(VI) by microspheres.

Applying the Weber–Morris intraparticle diffusion model to evaluate Cr(VI) adsorption by PVA/SA, PVA/SA-MB, and PVA/SA-FMB, the relevant fitting parameters detailed in Table 7. Figure 20 illustrates that the model's fitted lines do not intersect the origin. This observation signifies that intraparticle diffusion alone does not constitute the sole rate-limiting step [24]. The adsorption mechanism encompasses two distinct phases: boundary diffusion and intraparticle diffusion, with the initial boundary diffusion phase exhibiting more pronounced slopes and correlation coefficients. This indicates that boundary diffusion acts as the primary rate-limiting step in Cr(VI) removal by these adsorbents.

Table 7. Fitting parameters of adsorption particle diffusion for Cr(VI) by microspheres.

Microspheres	R_{d1}^2	$k_{id1}/$ $(mg·g^{-1}·h^{-0.5})$	C'_1 $(mg·g^{-1})$	R_{d2}^2	$k_{id2}/$ $(mg·g^{-1}·h^{-0.5})$	C'_2 $(mg·g^{-1})$
PVA/SA	0.76865	0.53247	1.51448	0.0366	0.01627	8.83264
PVA/SA-MB	0.89788	0.63434	1.86151	0.38649	0.01919	12.99951
PVA/SA-FMB	0.94667	1.26448	5.58574	0.94309	0.19211	18.76642

3.3.3. Isothermal Adsorption Experiment

Analyzing the adsorption capacity of PVA/SA, PVA/SA-MB, and PVA/SA-FMB for Cr(VI) using Langmuir and Freundlich models (Figure 21) reveals nuanced insights into their adsorption mechanisms. The model parameters are listed in Table 8. The Langmuir model slightly favored PVA/SA, indicating adsorption involves both monolayer and multilayer processes. In contrast, the Freundlich model better suited PVA/SA-MB and PVA/SA-FMB, suggesting a preference for multilayer adsorption. Freundlich isotherm calculations positioned PVA/SA-FMB with the highest adsorption capacity at around 60 mg/g, outperforming PVA/SA-MB. The Freundlich constant 1/n values for all adsorbents were below 1, denoting favorable Cr(VI) adsorption, with PVA/SA-FMB showing the lowest 1/n value, indicating a more homogeneous adsorption site distribution [25]. This underscores PVA/SA-FMB microbeads' enhanced efficacy for Cr(VI) removal.

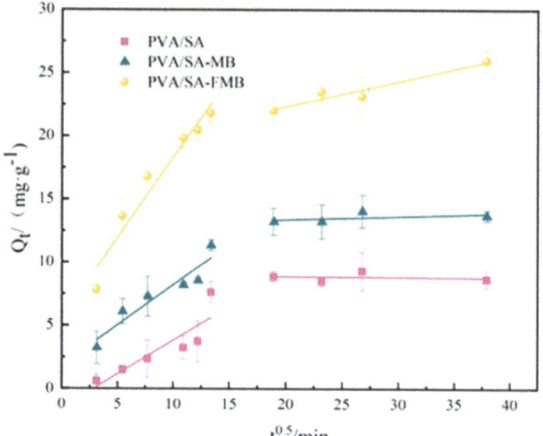

Figure 20. Particle diffusion fitting curve of microspheres for Cr(VI).

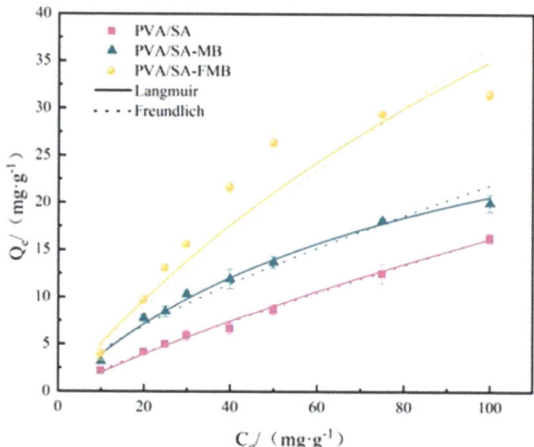

Figure 21. Isothermal adsorption fitting curve of Cr(VI) by microspheres.

Table 8. Isotherm model parameters of Cr(VI) adsorption by microspheres.

Microspheres	Langmuir				Freundlich		
	Q_m/(mg·g^{-1})	K_L/(L·mg^{-1})	n	R^2	K_F/(L·mg^{-1})	n	R^2
PVA/SA	46.81	0.0052	1.51–1.05	0.97	0.38	1.23	0.96
PVA/SA-MB	48.86	0.0079	1.79–1.08	0.99	0.57	1.25	0.98
PVA/SA-FMB	59.93	0.0107	2.08–1.11	0.99	1.44	1.47	0.98

3.3.4. Adsorption Cycle Regeneration Experiment

Figure 22 depicts the adsorption efficiency of PVA/SA, PVA/SA-MB, and PVA/SA-FMB microbeads across five adsorption–desorption cycles, revealing a 5% decrease in removal rates after the initial cycle for each microsphere type. This decline is linked to the release of non-crosslinked Fe^{3+} ions into the desorption solution, reducing the adsorption site density on the microspheres. Subsequent cycles showed stabilization in adsorption capacity, with a slight efficiency decrease attributed to diminished availability of hydroxyl groups crucial for Cr(VI) reduction [26]. Remarkably, PVA/SA-FMB maintained a Cr(VI) removal rate above 90%, outperforming conventional biological carbon. This performance highlights PVA/SA-FMB's efficacy and potential as a superior adsorbent for Cr(VI) remediation in water.

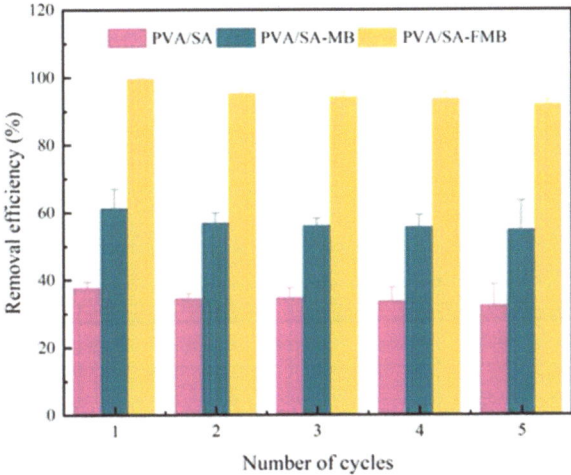

Figure 22. Performance of Cr(VI) adsorption by recycling microspheres.

3.4. Exploration of Adsorption Mechanism

3.4.1. Electrostatic Adsorption

Under acidic conditions, the surface functional groups of the microspheres, primarily hydroxyl (-OH) and carboxyl (-COOH), interact with hydrogen ions (H^+), leading to an increased polarization of these groups. The -OH groups can attract H^+ to form more polarized hydroxyl groups, enhancing their positive character, and -COOH groups can release H^+ to the solution, slightly increasing the surface positive charge by exposing the positively charged hydrogen of the carboxyl group. These modifications enhance the electrostatic attraction between the microsphere and negatively charged Cr(VI) species. This electrostatic interaction facilitates the adsorption of Cr(VI) onto the microsphere surface and may contribute to its reduction to the less toxic Cr(III) species [27].

$$4CrO_4^{2-} + 20H^+ + 3C^+ \rightarrow 3CO_2 + 4Cr^{3+} + 10H_2O \tag{2}$$

3.4.2. FTIR Analysis after Cr(VI) Adsorption

Fourier transform infrared spectroscopy analysis of PVA/SA-FMB microspheres, as illustrated in Figure 23, demonstrates consistent absorption peaks within the 400–4000 cm^{-1} range before and after adsorption, indicating the enhanced stability of SA-embedded adsorbents over traditional biochar. Crucial functional groups, including -OH, C=O, -COOH,

C=C, and C-H, are pivotal in Cr(VI) adsorption and reduction. The -OH group's stretching vibration peak at 3300 cm^{-1} diminishes post-adsorption, suggesting complexation or ion exchange with Cr(VI). Changes at the 1600 cm^{-1} peak reflect the C=O interactions with Cr(VI), indicative of redox activities [28,29]. Additionally, shifts at 1680 and 1420 cm^{-1} point to redox reactions involving C=C or carboxyl groups, while a weakened C-H peak implies the role of polycyclic aromatic hydrocarbons (PAHs) as proton donors in Cr(VI) reduction [30,31].

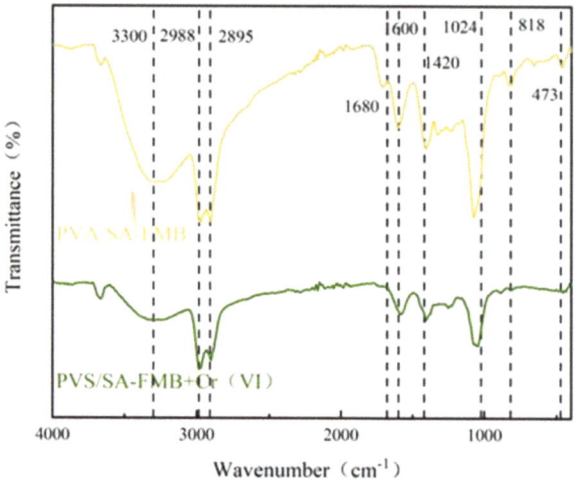

Figure 23. Infrared spectra of Cr(VI) adsorbed by PCA/SA-FMB.

3.4.3. XPS Analysis after Cr(VI) Adsorption

Figure 24a presents the XPS spectrum of Cr(VI) adsorbed by microspheres, illustrating a distinct Cr absorption peak and confirming successful Cr adsorption. In Figure 24b, the Cr 2p spectrum post-adsorption reveals four peaks at binding energies of 577.31 eV, 584.47 eV, 580.15 eV, and 589.31 eV for Cr(III) and Cr(VI) states, with a Cr(III) to Cr(VI) ratio of 79.19% to 20.81%, signifying a partial reduction of Cr(VI) to Cr(III). Conversely, PVA/SA-FMB's Cr 2p XPS spectrum is dominated by Cr(III) peaks, highlighting the composite's superior reduction capability, attributed to surface Fe(III) enhancing Cr(VI) reduction and facilitating electron transfer with modified biochar.

Figure 24c examines C 1s post-adsorption, showing shifts in C-O and C=O/O-C=O functional groups, indicating their role in Cr(VI) adsorption through hydrogen bonding and complexation. These observations underscore the significance of these functional groups in heavy metal complexation on the surfaces of PVA/SA-MB and PVA/SA-FMB microspheres, aligning with infrared analysis findings. The specific reaction process is as follows:

$$\text{C-OFe}^{2+} \text{HCrO}_4^- \rightarrow \text{C-OFeHCrO}_4^+ \qquad (3)$$

$$\text{C-COOH} + \text{HCrO}_4^- + \text{H}^+ \rightarrow \text{C-COOH}_2\text{HCrO}_4 \qquad (4)$$

$$\text{C-OH} + \text{HCrO}_4 + \text{H}^+ \rightarrow \text{C-OH}_2\text{HCrO}_4 \qquad (5)$$

$$\text{C-COOH} + \text{Cr(OH)}^{2+} \rightarrow \text{C-COOr(OH)}^{2+} + \text{H}^+ \tag{6}$$

$$\text{C-OH} + \text{Cr(OH)}^{2+} \rightarrow \text{C-OCr(OH)}^{2+} + \text{H}^+ \tag{7}$$

Figure 24d illustrates a shift in the Fe(II) and Fe(III) content following Cr(VI) adsorption by PVA/SA-FMB, with Fe(II) absorption peaks decreasing from 80.62% to 68.78% and Fe(III) peaks increasing from 19.64% to 31.22%. This variation is due to Fe(II) donating electrons to reduce Cr(VI) to Cr(III), while some Fe(II) is oxidized to Fe(III), which is then adsorbed onto the PVA/SA-FMB surface. The increase in the Fe(III) content highlights its role as an electron shuttle, facilitating further Cr(VI) removal. This change emphasizes the crucial involvement of redox reactions in the adsorption mechanism of Cr(VI) onto PVA/SA-FMB.

$$\text{CrO}_7^{2-} + 6\text{Fe}^{2+} + 7\text{H}_2\text{O} \rightarrow 2\text{Cr}^{3+} + 14\text{OH}^- + 6\text{Fe}^{3+} \tag{8}$$

$$3\text{Fe}^{2+} + \text{HCrO}_4^- + 7\text{H}^+ \rightarrow 3\text{Fe}^{3+} + 4\text{H}_2\text{O} + \text{Cr}^{3+} \tag{9}$$

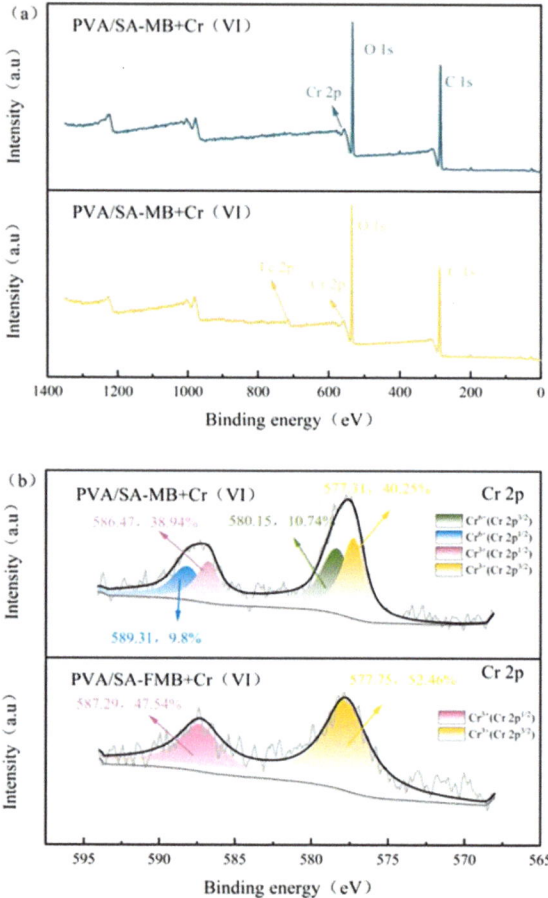

Figure 24. *Cont.*

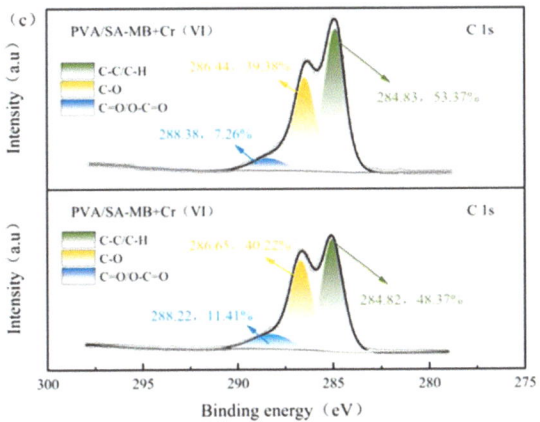

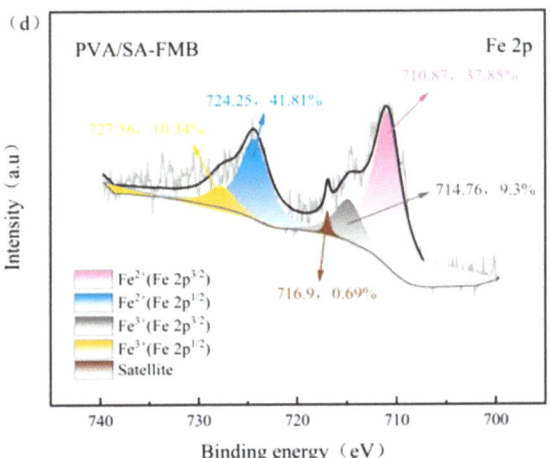

Figure 24. XPS spectrum after Cr(VI) adsorption using microspheres. (**a**) Total spectrum; (**b**) Cr 2p; (**c**) C 1s; (**d**) Fe 2p.

4. Conclusions

The optimal preparation conditions for the PVA/SA-FMB composite were established with a SA concentration of 0.73 wt%, PVA concentration of 3 wt%, FMB mass of 0.31 g, and a $CaCO_3$ mass of 1 g, ensuring the effective incorporation of FMB into the polymeric matrix. Adsorption experiments conducted at 25 °C and a pH of 2 revealed that while Cr(VI) adsorption onto PVA/SA adhered to the quasi-first-order kinetic and Langmuir isothermal model, indicative of physical multilayer adsorption, the adsorption onto PVA/SA-MB and PVA/SA-FMB followed the quasi-second-order kinetic model and Freundlich isotherm model, suggesting a more complex, multilayer chemisorption process. SEM analysis showed that PVA/SA microspheres presented a smooth surface, in contrast to PVA/SA-MB and PVA/SA-FMB, which exhibited numerous bundle structures typical of biochar, with PVA/SA-FMB displaying a notably rougher and more porous surface than its PVA/SA-MB counterpart. Further analyses, including FTIR, XPS, and XRD, identified various functional groups on the microsphere surfaces and highlighted the inclusion of Fe_2O_3 and FeO in different valence states within the FMB. BET analysis confirmed the presence of micropores and mesopores across all microsphere types, supporting their potential for enhanced adsorption capacities. Collectively, these findings underscore the multilayer adsorption character of Cr(VI) by PVA/SA-MB and PVA/SA-FMB, driven by a synergy of electrostatic interactions, redox reactions, and complexation, marking a significant advancement in the development of efficient adsorption materials for heavy metal removal from aqueous solutions.

Author Contributions: Conceptualization, J.Z.; software, Z.X.; formal analysis, L.J.; investigation, Z.X.; data curation, L.J.; methodology and writing—original draft preparation, J.R.; writing—review and editing, C.T.; supervision, J.L.; resources, validation, W.W.; project administration, and funding acquisition, J.Z. All authors have read and agreed to the published version of the manuscript.

Funding: This research was funded by the 2023 Heilongjiang Natural Science Foundation Joint Guidance Project (LH2023E029).

Data Availability Statement: Data are contained within the article.

Conflicts of Interest: The funders had no role in the design of the study; in the collection, analyses, or interpretation of data; in the writing of the manuscript; or in the decision to publish the results.

References

1. Rashid, R.; Shafiq, I.; Akhter, P.; Iqbal, M.J.; Hussain, M. A state-of-the-art review on wastewater treatment techniques: The effectiveness of adsorption method. *Environ. Sci. Pollut. Res.* **2021**, *28*, 9050–9066. [CrossRef]
2. Pakade, V.E.; Tavengwa, N.T.; Madikizela, L.M. Recent advances in hexavalent chromium removal from aqueous solutions by adsorptive methods. *RSC Adv.* **2019**, *9*, 26142–26164. [CrossRef] [PubMed]
3. King, A.H. Brown Seaweed Extracts (Alginates). In *Food Hydrocolloids*; CRC Press: Boca Raton, FL, USA, 2019; pp. 115–188.
4. Rhim, J.W. Physical and mechanical properties of water resistant sodium alginate films. *LWT-Food Sci. Technol.* **2004**, *37*, 323–330. [CrossRef]
5. Gao, X.; Guo, C.; Hao, J.; Zhao, Z.; Long, H.; Li, M. Adsorption of heavy metal ions by sodium alginate based adsorbent-a review and new perspectives. *Int. J. Biol. Macromol.* **2020**, *164*, 4423–4434. [CrossRef] [PubMed]
6. Wróblewska-Krepsztul, J.; Rydzkowski, T.; Michalska-Pożoga, I.; Thakur, V.K. Biopolymers for Biomedical and Pharmaceutical Applications: Recent Advances and Overview of Alginate Electrospinning. *Nanomaterials* **2019**, *9*, 404. [CrossRef] [PubMed]
7. Thakur, S.; Sharma, B.; Verma, A.; Chaudhary, J.; Tamulevicius, S.; Thakur, V.K. Recent progress in sodium alginate based sustainable hydrogels for environmental applications. *J. Clean. Prod.* **2018**, *198*, 143–159. [CrossRef]
8. Zhang, H.; Han, X.; Liu, J.; Wang, M.; Zhao, T.; Kang, L.; Zhong, S.; Cui, X. Fabrication of modified alginate-based biocomposite hydrogel microspheres for efficient removal of heavy metal ions from water. *Colloids Surf. A Physicochem. Eng. Asp.* **2022**, *651*, 129736. [CrossRef]
9. Kaklamani, G.; Cheneler, D.; Grover, L.M.; Adams, M.J.; Bowen, J. Mechanical properties of alginate hydrogels manufactured using external gelation. *J. Mech. Behav. Biomed. Mater.* **2014**, *36*, 135–142. [CrossRef] [PubMed]
10. Mahou, R.; Borcard, F.; Crivelli, V.; Montanari, E.; Passemard, S.; Noverraz, F.; Gerber-Lemaire, S.; Bühler, L.; Wandrey, C. Tuning the properties of hydrogel microspheres by adding chemical cross-linking functionality to sodium alginate. *Chem. Mater.* **2015**, *27*, 4380–4389. [CrossRef]
11. Alshehari, A.M.; Salim, E.; Oraby, A.H. Structural, optical, morphological and mechanical studies of polyethylene oxide/sodium alginate blend containing multi-walled carbon nanotubes. *J. Mater. Res. Technol.* **2021**, *15*, 5615–5622. [CrossRef]
12. Xiang, X.; Yi, X.; Zheng, W.; Li, Y.; Zhang, C.; Wang, X.; Chen, Z.; Huang, M.; Ying, G.G. Enhanced biodegradation of thiamethoxam with a novel polyvinyl alcohol (PVA)/sodium alginate (SA)/biochar immobilized Chryseobacterium sp H5. *J. Hazard. Mater.* **2023**, *443*, 130247. [CrossRef]
13. Zain, N.; Suhaimi, M.S.; Idris, A. Development and modification of PVA–alginate as a suitable immobilization matrix. *Process Biochem.* **2011**, *46*, 2122–2129. [CrossRef]
14. Idris, A.; Zain NA, M.; Suhaimi, M.S. Immobilization of Baker's yeast invertase in PVA–alginate matrix using innovative immobilization technique. *Process Biochem.* **2008**, *43*, 331–338. [CrossRef]
15. Lv, X.; Jiang, G.; Xue, X.; Wu, D.; Sheng, T.; Sun, C.; Xu, X. Fe_0-Fe_3O_4 nanocomposites embedded polyvinyl alcohol/sodium alginate beads for chromium (VI) removal. *J. Hazard. Mater.* **2013**, *262*, 748–758. [CrossRef]
16. Ramdhan, T.; Ching, S.H.; Prakash, S.; Bhandari, B. Time dependent gelling properties of cuboid alginate gels made by external gelation method: Effects of alginate-$CaCl_2$ solution ratios and pH. *Food Hydrocoll.* **2019**, *90*, 232–240. [CrossRef]

17. Hameed, B.H.; Din, A.M.; Ahmad, A.L. Adsorption of methylene blue onto bamboo-based activated carbon: Kinetics and equilibrium studies. *J. Hazard. Mater.* **2007**, *141*, 819–825. [CrossRef] [PubMed]
18. Crini, G.; Badot, P.M. Application of chitosan, a natural aminopolysaccharide, for dye removal from aqueous solutions by adsorption processes using batch studies: A review of recent literature. *Prog. Polym. Sci.* **2008**, *33*, 399–447. [CrossRef]
19. Kumar, L.; Kumar, P.; Narayan, A.; Kar, M. Rietveld analysis of XRD patterns of different sizes of nanocrystalline cobalt ferrite. *Int. NanoLett.* **2013**, *3*, 8. [CrossRef]
20. Fei, Y.; Yong, L.; Sheng, H.; Ma, J. Adsorptive removal of ciprofloxacin by sodium alginate/graphene oxide composite beads from aqueous solution. *J. Colloid Interface Sci.* **2016**, *484*, 196–204. [CrossRef] [PubMed]
21. Fan, H.; Ma, X.; Zhou, S.; Huang, J.; Liu, Y.; Liu, Y. Highly efficient removal of heavy metal ions by carboxymethyl cellulose-immobilized Fe3O4 nanoparticles prepared via high-gravity technology. *Carbohydr. Polym.* **2019**, *213*, 39–49. [CrossRef] [PubMed]
22. Yan, L.; Dong, F.-X.; Li, Y.; Guo, P.-R.; Kong, L.-J.; Chu, W.; Diao, Z.-H. Synchronous removal of Cr(VI) and phosphates by a novel crayfish shell biochar-Fe composite from aqueous solution: Reactivity and mechanism. *J. Environ. Chem. Eng.* **2022**, *10*, 107396. [CrossRef]
23. Chen, J.H.; Xing, H.T.; Guo, H.X.; Weng, W.; Hu, S.R.; Li, S.X.; Huang, Y.H.; Sun, X.; Su, Z.B. Investigation on the adsorption properties of Cr (VI) ions on a novel graphene oxide (GO) based composite adsorbent. *J. Mater. Chem. A* **2014**, *2*, 12561–12570. [CrossRef]
24. Srivastava, S.; Tyagi, R.; Pant, N. Pant, Adsorption of heavy metal ions on carbonaceous material developed from the waste slurry generated in local fertilizer plants. *Water Res.* **1989**, *23*, 1161–1165. [CrossRef]
25. Zhang, W.; Zhang, S.; Wang, J.; Wang, M.; He, Q.; Song, J.; Wang, H.; Zhou, J. Hybrid functionalized chitosan-Al_2O_3@SiO_2 composite for enhanced Cr(VI) adsorption. *Chemosphere* **2018**, *203*, 188. [CrossRef] [PubMed]
26. Song, L.; Liu, F.; Zhu, C.; Li, A. Facile one-step fabrication of carboxymethyl cellulose based hydrogel for highly efficient removal of Cr(VI) under mild acidic condition. *Chem. Eng. J.* **2019**, *369*, 641–651. [CrossRef]
27. Park, D.; Yun, Y.-S.; Park, J.M. The past, present, and future trends of biosorption. *Biotechnol. Bioprocess Eng.* **2005**, *10*, 86–102. [CrossRef]
28. Zhang, S.; Lyu, H.; Tang, J.; Song, B.; Zhen, M.; Liu, X. A novel biochar supported CMC stabilized nano zero-valent iron composite for hexavalent chromium removal from water. *Chemosphere* **2019**, *217*, 686–694. [CrossRef]
29. Wan, Z.; Cho, D.-W.; Tsang, D.C.; Li, M.; Sun, T.; Verpoort, F. Concurrent adsorption and micro-electrolysis of Cr(VI) by nanoscale zerovalent iron/biochar/Ca-alginate composite. *Environ. Pollut.* **2019**, *247*, 410–420. [CrossRef]
30. Yu, Y.; An, Q.; Jin, L.; Luo, N.; Li, Z.; Jiang, J. Unraveling sorption of Cr (VI) from aqueous solution by $FeCl_3$ and $ZnCl_2$-modified corn stalks biochar: Implicit mechanism and application. *Bioresour. Technol.* **2020**, *297*, 122466. [CrossRef]
31. Yusuff, A.S.; Lala, M.A.; Thompson-Yusuff, K.A.; Babatunde, E.O. $ZnCl_2$-modified eucalyptus bark biochar as adsorbent: Preparation, characterization and its application in adsorption of Cr (VI) from aqueous solutions. *S. Afr. J. Chem. Eng.* **2022**, *42*, 138–145. [CrossRef]

Disclaimer/Publisher's Note: The statements, opinions and data contained in all publications are solely those of the individual author(s) and contributor(s) and not of MDPI and/or the editor(s). MDPI and/or the editor(s) disclaim responsibility for any injury to people or property resulting from any ideas, methods, instructions or products referred to in the content.

MDPI AG
Grosspeteranlage 5
4052 Basel
Switzerland
Tel.: +41 61 683 77 34

Processes Editorial Office
E-mail: processes@mdpi.com
www.mdpi.com/journal/processes

Disclaimer/Publisher's Note: The title and front matter of this reprint are at the discretion of the Guest Editor. The publisher is not responsible for their content or any associated concerns. The statements, opinions and data contained in all individual articles are solely those of the individual Editor and contributors and not of MDPI. MDPI disclaims responsibility for any injury to people or property resulting from any ideas, methods, instructions or products referred to in the content.

www.ingramcontent.com/pod-product-compliance
Lightning Source LLC
LaVergne TN
LVHW072251110526
838202LV00106B/2292